MEGAPROJECTS

MEGAPROJECTS

Challenges and Recommended Practices

EDITED BY **DAVID J. HATEM**, PC, AND **DAVID H. CORKUM**, ESQ.

AMERICAN COUNCIL OF ENGINEERING COMPANIES

AMERICAN COUNCIL OF ENGINEERING COMPANIES

American Council of Engineering Companies
1015 15th Street, NW, 8th Floor
Washington, DC 20005-2605
(202) 347-7474
(202) 898-0068
www.acec.org

Design by Michael Brady Design

Contents

About the Authors

All of the authors donated their time to this project. Book royalties will be donated to ACEC for engineering education and advocacy purposes. The authors and editors gratefully acknowledge the proficiency and talents of ACEC's Mary Jaffe and Donovan Hatem LLP's Marketing Director Lisa Zagami in shepherding this project from concept to completion.

Eldon L. Abbott, P.E., is a vice-president and principal project manager with Parsons Brinckerhoff and has managed the design of numerous complex transit, marine, parking, tunnel, and highway projects in the U.S. and abroad, including the Port of Miami underwater tunnel and a large-diameter highway tunnel as part of the replacement of the aging Alaskan Way Viaduct in Seattle.

Walter Armstrong was a senior vice-president at CDM and has worked on major water projects in Cincinnati, Hartford, Connecticut, Onondaga County, N.Y., and New York City. He worked on the Boston Harbor Cleanup, serving as the Massachusetts Water Resources Authority's Director of Program Management from 1992–1999.

Richard Bayer is president of The ReAlignment Group and is a lawyer, mediator, arbitrator, and facilitator. He has practiced construction law for 35 years and has been an AAA arbitrator since the mid-1980s and a credentialed mediator since 1993. He is a member of the United States Institute for Environmental Conflict Resolution and has served on the boards of the National Conflict Resolution Center, the California Independent Petroleum Association, ADR–San Diego, and the California Dispute Resolution Council.

Chris D. Breeds, P.E., has been the engineer of record, consulting engineer, or advisor for numerous large-diameter tunnels, including the Metro Goldline West in Los Angeles and the Brightwater tunnel near Seattle, and has worked on the planning of a project to route up to 4 billion gallons of water per day from the Mediterranean Sea to the Dead Sea through a 70-km tunnel and 1,600 MW underground powerhouse. He contributed to ASCE's *Recommended Contract Practices for Underground Construction* and *Guidelines for Geotechnical Baseline Report* and wrote *Guide for Specifying Underground Shotcrete.*

Stephen D. Butler has more than 35 years of experience in claims, litigation, and dispute resolution on engineering and construction matters in both the public and private sectors. He was general counsel of Parsons Brinckerhoff and before that special counsel for Bechtel Corporation, representing them on the Central Artery/Tunnel Project. He worked on the Eurotunnel, Hong Kong Airport, and similar megaprojects. He served with the Center for Public Resources in New York, the Disputes Avoidance and Resolution Task Force, and the Stanford University Center on Conflict and Negotiation.

Charles Button, P.E., is the chief engineer for the Massachusetts Water Resources Authority and has more than 35 years of experience in design, construction, and operations of water, wastewater, and drainage systems. Working for local and national consulting firms, he has vast experience in design and construction of water, wastewater and drainage systems in many locations of the United States and internationally. He is a life member of NSPE, MSPE, ASCE, and BSCES and past president of BSCES. He is a member and has been involved on technical committees of WEF and NEWEA, APWA, and NE/APWA and a past member of the Board of Directors of NE/APWA.

David Caiden, principal, Arup, New York, has worked on major infrastructure projects, including road, rail, and utility tunnel schemes, in Europe, Asia, and Australia. He is currently a deputy project manager working on the Second Avenue Subway. He is a fellow of the Institution of Civil Engineers, serving Council as representative for the Americas. He is also a fellow of the American Society of Civil Engineers, Engineers Australia, and the Hong Kong Institution of Engineers.

Peter Chamley is a UK-based director of Arup with over 30 years of experience. He has a background in geotechnics and foundation engineering and has managed the delivery of tunnels, wastewater projects, railways, deep excavations, casting basins, major earthworks, and ground treatment projects, including London's Crossrail, New York's Second Avenue Subway, and the Hull Flow Transfer Tunnels in the UK. He has worked as designer and project manager in the U.S., Europe, Asia, and Australia. He had joint responsibility for Arup's Leeds, UK office with a staff of over 150 and was responsible for the technical and financial control of projects and their successful delivery.

David H. Corkum, Esq., is an attorney specializing in the planning, design, and construction of heavy civil and underground projects, particularly in the defense of architects, engineers and construction managers. He also advises clients on risk management practices and procedures on large construction projects. Prior to joining Donovan Hatem in 2001, he spent 23 years as a geologist and construction manager on large-scale projects (Seabrook nuclear power plant, the Alaskan Natural Gas Pipeline, a high-level nuclear waste storage facility in West Texas, the Red Line Tunnel Extension for MBTA, and the Deer Island Waste Water Treatment Facilities).

Raymond Crawford is a certified quality manager and an accredited ISO 9001 lead auditor and trainer. He is the Director of Quality for both Parsons Brinckerhoff Construction Services Company and PB Design Infrastructure Company, responsible for developing and implementing the quality program and maintaining ISO 9001 certification for all U.S.-based PB companies, including design and construction companies. PB developed an Environmental Management System and Mr. Crawford assisted in the plan for implementation and certification to ISO 14001 standard.

Joseph Dennis is general counsel and an officer of Arup for its Americas Region, responsible for overseeing contracts, disputes, corporate affairs, and risk management. Prior to joining Arup, Mr. Dennis served as general counsel and corporate secretary to Syska Hennessy Group, which specializes in consulting, engineering, technology, and construction. Before that, he worked in private practice, representing design professionals, owners, developers, general contractors, and subcontractors. Since 2007, he has served as general counsel to the Council on Tall Buildings and Urban Habitat. He is a board member on the NYC AIA/ACEC Contracts and Risk Management committees.

Kurt Dettman, Esq., is the director of east coast operations for the ReAlignment Group, Ltd., and owns Constructive Dispute Resolutions. Previously, he was the associate project director for claims resolution and chief counsel of Boston's CA/T Project, advising in the areas of construction and design claims and disputes, alternative dispute resolution, owner-controlled insurance programs, intergovernmental agreements, and federal and state procurement practices and regulations. He was formerly a commercial litigator with Palmer & Dodge and then Hutchins & Wheeler, in Boston.

Ted Devens is Corporate Safety Director for Parsons Brinckerhoff, Inc. Previously, he was an insurance consultant and safety director on large OCIPs, including a $944 million light rail project with over 300 contractors, the Nike World Campus expansion, Portland International Airport, and the Bureau of Environmental Services. He has consulted in the development of OCIPs or wrap-ups on both construction management and safety management aspects. He has worked for an engineering design company and as a contractor and construction manager. He is a member of the American Society of Safety Engineers and the Construction Management Association of America.

Peter Dewes, P.E., has worked on many of the major rail projects in the New York area in the past 20 years. He is an expert on rail operations, restoration of service on existing lines, modernization of service, and design of new rail connections. He managed planning and design of the Secaucus Transfer project, which connected eight of NJ TRANSIT's rail lines. He worked on the East Side Access project to build a rail tunnel between Long Island and Midtown Manhattan, and is currently working on the Access to the Region's Core project, which includes a new rail tunnel under the Hudson River.

Peter F. Donahue, P.E., is a vice-president, senior professional associate, and principal project manager with Parsons Brinckerhoff. He holds a B.S. and M.B.A. degree and is licensed as a professional engineer in multiple states. His career ranges from transportation projects to heavy industrial facilities and commercial operations. He was the design manager and deputy program manager on Boston's Central Artery/Tunnel Project. Currently, he is a consultant on the Alaskan Way Viaduct Replacement Project in Seattle and is the deputy project manager for the Port of Miami Tunnel Project.

William W. Edgerton, P.E., is currently president of Jacobs Associates, a consulting engineering company in San Francisco, in charge of strategic planning, business development, and administration. He has advised owners and contractors of water and transit tunnels under both design-build and design-bid-build contracts. He has extensive experience in project management, cost estimating, and dispute resolution on civil, highway, transit, dam, bridge, marine, process, and power plant projects. He served as chair of the steering committee of the Underground Construction Association of the Society for Mining, Metallurgy, and Exploration and is an ASCE program evaluator for the Accreditation Board for Engineering and Technology.

Tom Farina is the lead in-house legal counsel for Parsons Brinckerhoff Americas' Northeast Region, providing advice and counsel to the regional project staff by assisting with the identification and resolution of legal and contractual risk issues. He has a total of 30 years of experience, beginning his career as an engineer and continuing in his current capacity as an attorney. Megaprojects within PB's Northeast Region include several underground in the greater New York area, specifically the Trans-Hudson Tunnel project, East Side Access, the No. 7 Subway Line Extension, and the Second Avenue Subway line.

Dan Fauchier is vice-president of The ReAlignment Group, Ltd., an experienced facilitator for their Lean Partnering method, a construction dispute resolutionist, forensics consultant, design manager, construction project manager, college teacher, mediator, arbitrator, and construction management expert. He has more than 30 years of experience in development, design, and construction management, including alignment partnering and facilitation on the world's largest dam raise, a major canal relining, and fast-track prototype design of seven prison hospitals. He has trained over 4,000 construction professionals in construction management and forensics seminars and workshops.

Geoffrey A. Fosbrook, P.E., FASCE, is a senior vice-president with AECOM and has more than 45 years of design and CM experience. He was a U.S. Army combat engineer and later taught engineering at the U.S. Military Academy at West Point. He has managed design and construction of major rail projects throughout the U.S., including the Second Avenue Subway in New York, San Francisco Airport Extension, the Tren Urbano in San Juan, Puerto Rico, and the JFK and LaGuardia Airport Access Program for PANY&NJ.

Richard Fox has served as president of CDM since 2001. He has 33 years of experience in program management, environmental engineering, and labor relations. He has served as director of the Boston Harbor Cleanup Project, program manager of the multifaceted upgrade to 225-million-gallon-per-day (mgd) wastewater facilities system serving Minneapolis–St. Paul, Minnesota, and senior program management advisor to the Hong Kong Drainage Services Department on the $900 million effort to clean up Victoria Harbor with a new 410-mgd wastewater treatment works.

Patricia B. Gary, Esq., is a trial and appellate lawyer with 20 years of experience. She was a judicial clerk for the chief justice of the New Hampshire Supreme Court and later was a business litigation and appellate attorney in the appellate department of a large Boston law firm. Prior to joining Donovan Hatem in 2005, she worked for 5 years at a smaller Boston law firm specializing in all types of insurance policies and insurance coverage matters in every American jurisdiction and foreign countries. At Donovan Hatem, she works in the defense of architects and engineers and in insurance coverage and appeals.

Robert J. F. Goodfellow, P.E., holds a B.Eng. and M.Sc. from Imperial College, London. He has led planning, design, and construction management for many underground infrastructure megaprojects. He is currently an associate vice-president of Black & Veatch and director of their Tunnel Business Line. He worked on Boston's Central Artery/Tunnel, the Washington Metro, New York City water tunnels, and the Jubilee Line Extension in London and was a contributing author to the *Better Contracting Practices Manual* (2008). He sits on the Transportation Research Board subcommittee on risk management and is currently a member of the executive committee of the UCA of SME.

David J. Hatem, PC, is a founding partner of the multi-practice law firm, Donovan Hatem LLP. He is an expert in law related to the design and construction industry and leads the firm's Professional Practices Group, which represents engineers, architects, and construction management professionals. He frequently lectures on issues of professional liability for design and construction management professionals, risk management and design-build procurement issues, and has authored numerous related articles. He edited *Subsurface Conditions: Risk Management for Design and Construction Management Professionals and Design-Build Subsurface Projects* (2d edition, July 2010). Mr. Hatem has served as ACEC/Massachusetts Counsel since 1988 and was the recipient of the 2008 American Council of Engineering Companies of Massachusetts Distinguished Service Award. He currently teaches Legal Aspects of Engineering at Tufts University.

Donna M. Hunt, Esq., AIA, is the director of claims services for the Architects & Engineers Claims Unit of Lexington Insurance Company. Previously, she practiced law at Donovan Hatem LLP, specializing in contract review and preparation, and provided risk management services to insurance policy holders and firm clients. She is a licensed architect who practiced for 15 years at firms in New York and Boston. She is a member of the Boston Society of Architects and the American Institute of Architects.

Michael J. Landry, P.E., is a senior claims consultant at DH Consulting Group and has over 18 years of experience in claims analysis and in construction management, with an emphasis on cost and scheduling engineering. He worked as a claims analyst on the Deer Island Wastewater Treatment Plant as part of the Boston Harbor Cleanup Project and on the Walnut Hill Water Treatment Plant, analyzing complex claims and preparing comprehensive recommendations. He received his B.S. in Civil Engineering, University of New Hampshire and a J.D. from Massachusetts School of Law. He is admitted to practice in New Hampshire and Massachusetts and is also a registered patent attorney.

Colin Lawrence, C.Eng., Eur.Ing., MICE, is a senior vice-president of Hatch Mott MacDonald. He has worked on some of the world's most challenging tunnel projects, including several megaprojects, as both owner and consultant. He has experience in the planning, design, program management, and construction supervision for megaprojects, including the Channel Tunnel between England and France, Great Belt Rail Tunnel in Denmark, the Bangkok Metro in Thailand, the Strategic Sewage Disposal Scheme in Hong Kong, the East Side Access Project in New York, and WASA CSO in Washington, D.C.

James McKelvey is an associate vice-president with Black & Veatch. A civil engineer with 33 years of experience, he has been project director, project manager, construction manager, and designer on more than 100 miles of tunnels, including the Lesotho Highlands Water Project, Charleston Water System's sewer tunnel replacement program, the WSSC Bi-County Main (Montgomery and Prince George's counties, Maryland), City of Charleston Spring-Fishburne Drainage Improvements, and the Fall Creek/White River Tunnel System in Indianapolis. He is past president of South African National Committee on Tunnels and past member of the ITA Executive Council.

Thomas Peyton, P.E., is a vice-president at Parsons Brinckerhoff. He was a contractor on City Tunnel #3 and the 63rd St. Subway in New York, the Washington, D.C., and Boston subways, and the early stages of the Boston Harbor cleanup. After that, he was a construction manager on the MetroWest Tunnel in Boston and the Second Avenue Subway in New York. He is a past president of both the Underground Construction Association of the Society for Mining, Metallurgy, and Exploration and the American

Underground Construction Association, and is a member of the board of directors of SME.

Donald Phillips, P.E., is a principal and board member of Arup Americas, responsible for PPP, design-build, transit, high-speed rail projects, and for complex multidiscipline and underground structures. He has over 30 years of experience primarily on megaprojects and major multidisciplinary projects, currently including the Lake Mead Intake #3, two California high-speed rail projects, the A30 Highway in Montreal, Vaughan Corporate Centre in Toronto, Spadina Stations York University, UK, and the Alaskan Way Tunnel in Seattle. He has worked on projects in New York, London, Hong Kong, and Sydney.

John Reilly provides consulting on strategic management, organization, risk and cost mitigation, partnering, and innovative project delivery services for four agencies, contractors, and engineers working with large, complex infrastructure programs.

Robert Rogers is assistant vice-president for Architects & Engineers Professional Liability for Lexington Insurance Company. In this role, he is responsible for the underwriting and marketing of annual practice- and project-specific policies to Lexington design clients worldwide. He has held this position since 2005. Mr. Rogers joined Lexington Insurance Company in 1999, having worked for 7 years at another division of AIG. Prior to his current position he managed Professional Liability and Construction underwriters in Lexington's National Branch handling business countrywide.

Stephen P. Warhoe, PE, CCE, CCM, has 28 years of experience in project and construction management, including nuclear power plant construction, green field airports, public schools, and transportation programs. He is a licensed civil engineer and graduate of the University of Colorado-Denver, and is currently completing his doctoral dissertation, which studies how changed work in construction affects the outcome of projects. He is an adjunct professor at SKEMA Business School in Paris, lecturing on project management and project controls. He has been a member AACE International for over 20 years and served as its president for 2008–2009.

Steve Wojtasinski, Esq., has over 25 years of experience in contracts and procurement management, construction law, contract dispute resolution, and public- and private-sector development management His areas of expertise include administration of complex claims resolution organizations, federal and state procurement regulations, and facilities operation and construction contracts. On Boston's Central Artery/Tunnel Project, he was responsible for management and administration of contracts, changes, and construction claims. He managed the claims and changes program for the MBWT's Deer Island–Boston Harbor Cleanup Project. He helped develop an integrated management system for administering multiprime contract project claims.

Sue E. Yoakum, Esq., AIA, of counsel at Donovan Hatem LLP, is an attorney and licensed architect with over 25 years of experience in design and construction. She has focused on large projects, initially designing sports facilities and later as an attorney assisting design professionals involved in megaprojects. Her U.S. projects include stadiums for the Indianapolis Colts, Washington Nationals, Arizona Cardinals, and St. Louis Cardinals, as well as the New Meadowlands stadium, the Great American Ballpark in Cincinnati, and the Indianapolis Convention Center. Internationally, she has worked on sports construction in England, Portugal, and Australia.

PART I

Context, Practices, and Major Issues on Megaprojects

Preceding page:
Construction of
the 57 kilometer
(35 mile) Gotthard
Base Tunnel in the
Swiss Alps, showing
the Wye junction in
the western tube
at Multi-Function
Station Faido in
Switzerland. The
right tunnel is the
main western bore,
the left tunnel is a
connection into the
main eastern bore.
Once completed
the 2 km-long MFS
Faido will be a multi-
purpose station
2,000 meters
below the surface
for maintenance
and emergency
evacuation
purposes. The
entrance of the
access tunnel is
near the village of
Faido, © 2006 by
Cooper.ch.

CHAPTER 1

Historical Perspective

David J. Hatem, PC, Donovan Hatem LLP
David H. Corkum, Esq., Donovan Hatem LLP

The objective of this book is to explore a range of issues associated with the planning, management, design, and construction of major public infrastructure projects — megaprojects — and to provide the reader with specific recommendations for the realization and successful accomplishment of such projects. The ranges of issues addressed involve a number of different areas of expertise and experience, and the authors of the various chapters have been selected based on those considerations.

Many public owners have occasion to plan and execute megaprojects, but very few have the opportunity (never mind the experience) to do so on a frequent or repetitive basis or within short intervals of time (probably, within a decade). Each of these public owners has different experiences in megaprojects — some are not able to "get the first shovel in the ground" due to political, environmental, funding, or other threshold or stakeholder impediments; others experience severely disappointed expectations (e.g., significant cost overruns and schedule delays); and others achieve a successful result despite a painful process of "getting there."

Despite the history of megaprojects in the United States, how does the experience — plus and minus — get captured and communicated so that future public owners contemplating megaprojects may benefit from the "lessons learned"? There may be no particular internal or institutional reason why any specific project owner may wish to record these "lessons learned," as such an owner may never plan or experience a megaproject anytime in the next decade or probably more. Yet, it is unquestionably true that each project owner's megaproject experience is important and needs to be assessed and understood — to the benefit of other project owners contemplating and planning a megaproject. This book seeks to achieve the objective of transmitting the megaproject "lessons learned" experiences to public owners, consulting engineers, and other stakeholders involved in megaprojects.

The decades ahead present substantial opportunities for megaprojects and for the successful achievement of those projects. Those decades also present the prospect of repetitive failures on megaprojects if we do not learn from the experiences of the past. The reality and perception (if there be a meaningful distinction in the context of major

Gavin Hamilton Jack's panoramic view of the Panama Canal, showing part of the Culebra Cut and Stevens Town on far bank, c. 1906. The Culebra Cut was an artificial valley excavated through the Continental Divide that extended almost 8 miles from Lake Gatún on the Atlantic side to the Pedro Miguel Locks on the Pacific side. The name was officially changed in 1915 to the Galliard Cut to honor Major David du Bose Galliard, who was the engineer in charge of the central section of the canal. Photograph from the Library of Congress.

3

public infrastructure projects), however, is that many of these projects have been the subject of substantial political controversy — at their inception and throughout their execution — and significant disappointed cost, schedule, and quality expectations due to deficient planning, management, design, and construction. While these megaprojects present tremendous promise for the benefit of the public and other stakeholders, unless the confidence of the public and those stakeholders is restored and improved, the very conception and materialization of megaprojects will be imperiled.

In many respects, now is the time — while many more megaprojects are being contemplated and in early stages of planning — for a book like this to be published. The objective of this book is to promote the realization and successful achievement of megaprojects by capturing and communicating "lessons learned" and by recommending best practices for megaprojects.

We can all look back at some of mankind's monumental accomplishments and undertakings and easily compile a list of generally recognized megaprojects. These projects either fundamentally altered the civilized world or represented monuments to the sovereign or deity that controlled the treasury and human resources of that society. Our interest in historical megaprojects will not focus on undertakings such as the Great Pyramids of Giza, the Taj Mahal, the Great Wall of China, or the cathedrals of Europe. While they were "mega" in scope, duration, and costs, and their accomplishments as feats of civil engineering were epic for their time, they were mostly tokens to the egos of the society's ruling elite. Of far greater pragmatic value are the aqueducts, roads, railroads, and canals that changed the face of the earth and the development of civilization. Many of these more modern megaprojects had been envisioned and dreamed of for a considerable time prior to being executed during the maturing of the Industrial Revolution. Indeed, it was the development of power sources beyond that of mere muscle that allowed humans to recognize the possibilities and realize the dreams of the more modern megaprojects.

It is fair to say that a search for modern megaprojects need look no further back than the middle of the 1800s. By 1850 steam was being used to power ocean-going vessels and land-based locomotives. Steam also began to power the factories of the Second Industrial Revolution that was driving the economies of Europe and North America. Trade and commerce beyond the borders of a country's own domestic markets became the key to that country's wealth and security. As these international interlinked commercial ties solidified and commodity volume increased, efficient transportation became commensurately more important. The Suez Canal, linking the Mediterranean with the Red Sea and thus providing a sea-level canal between the Mediterranean Sea and the Indian Ocean, eliminated the need to send maritime shipments from Europe to Asia by sail or steam around the Cape of Good Hope. The canal's ten-year construction effort finished in 1869, leaving an excavation approximately 120 miles in length that was wide enough

and deep enough to accommodate traffic in one direction. Widened anchorage areas placed strategically along its length allowed approaching convoys to pass each other. Over the years the canal has been further widened and deepened to accommodate larger vessels and greater volumes of traffic.

While the modern canal was the brainchild of a French entrepreneur, Ferdinand de Lesseps, during Napoleon Bonaparte's reign, similar canals had been constructed by the Egyptian pharaohs nearly 3,000 years earlier. The French construction plan for the canal was similar to that of the pharaohs in de Lesseps' reliance on using forced labor, with estimates of over 30,000 individuals being compelled to

A section near Ismailia of the partially completed Suez Canal, c. 1855–1860. Photograph by Francis Firth, from the Library of Congress.

work on the project through threats of death, displacement, or destitution. Financing for the project may well have been the first public-private partnership, when the French obtained a concession from the Egyptian viceroy for a land lease of the real estate and permission for the French company to operate the canal for profit.

With the successful completion of the Suez Canal, promoter and businessman de Lesseps turned his attention, talents, and enthusiasm to a long-dreamed-of canal between the Pacific and Atlantic oceans through the Isthmus of Panama. The potential of this project had been envisioned by many of the earliest conquistadors and explorers. The Roman Catholic Church, seeking to strengthen its ties with and influence in Peru and Ecuador, actively sought a canal route 300 years before de Lesseps dared to undertake the project. De Lesseps promoted the project and by 1880 had raised the money to form a company that began construction of what was meant to be a sea-level canal similar to his Suez project. The company severely underestimated the engineering challenges of the terrain, but more importantly the venture was unprepared for the disease and devastation of malaria and yellow fever carried by mosquitoes throughout this tropical rainforest. Stymied by the lack of solutions to the technical challenges and unable to keep its labor force and supervision alive long enough to become experienced and efficient, construction ground to a halt. Ultimately, after an estimated 20,000 deaths, de Lesseps' company declared bankruptcy and suspended all but caretaker efforts on the project as it sought to recoup something for its equipment and work in place. The French company, its concession, and its work-in-progress were sold to the United States

at the turn of the century. National defense interest in the era of gun-boat diplomacy and the strategic advantage of being able to shuttle warships quickly from one coast to the other undoubtedly factored into the United States' decision to fund the project.

By this time the link between mosquito-borne parasites and tropical diseases was fully understood. The United States put the project under the control of the Army Corps of Engineers, who recognized the immediate need to stabilize and improve conditions for the workforce. The Corps assigned William Gorgas as chief sanitation officer, whose first decisive action was to undertake an aggressive campaign of draining and filling swamps and eliminating other mosquito-breeding, stagnant water areas. This effort combined with fumigation and screened windows virtually eliminated mosquito-borne diseases that had doomed the French effort. At the same time, the company was developing the infrastructure needed to support the massive construction effort. This included reasonable housing for workers and an upgrading of the railroad system purchased from the French company, which would be the main mechanism for earth removal. At the peak of construction more than 40,000 workers were engaged in building the canal, its lock system, dams, and infrastructure. The excavation itself required more than 268 million cubic yards of material to be removed at a total construction cost of $375 million (in 1914 dollars). The workhorse of the excavation was a fleet of Bucyrus B-50 steam shovels, which loaded spoils onto continuously cycling muck trains that transported the soil and rocks to fill locations for dams and dikes. The excavation cycle was a model of efficiency. It has been estimated that even if the work were to be done today, it would likely not have been accomplished any quicker because the critical path ran through spoil removal, which was about optimal. Construction of the canal was completed in October 1913 and opened to commercial traffic by the summer of 1914—just in time to be eclipsed by the outbreak of hostilities in Europe that would soon engulf nearly the entire developed world. While it was the most expensive construction project ever attempted up until that time, no one has ever questioned whether it was worth the financial investment. Its presence and operation over the next 50 years dramatically changed trade and strategic alliances throughout the world.

Both the Suez and Panama canals are still in use today, and it is hard to imagine our modern world existing without these transportation links in place. Indeed, both facilities have been improved and enlarged over the years, and the Panama Canal is currently undergoing a $5 billion upgrade to increase its capacity to handle ever-larger vessels.

At the same time the Suez Canal was being constructed, the westward expansion in the United States was in full swing. The Gold Rush of 1849 drew thousands of pioneers to California. An extensive rail network had developed to connect the major cities and commercial centers of the eastern United States. By 1856, a railroad bridge had been constructed across the Mississippi at Rock Island, Illinois, and the dream of a Transcontinental Railroad inched a step closer to reality. Like all megaprojects, the Transconti-

nental Railroad project had its visionaries and supporters who lobbied Congress and garnered public support for the project. Steven Ambrose's book, *Nothing Like It in the World*, is a compelling story of the courage and tenacity of these proponents and the foresight of leaders like President Lincoln, who recognized the enormous positive impact such a project would have on the young country. While a number of private consortiums and investors began to coalesce and position themselves in anticipation of the project, it was not until President Lincoln signed the Pacific Railway Act of 1862 that work began in earnest. The act authorized the construction of a railroad from Omaha, Nebraska, to Sacramento, California. It pitted two com-

The Golden Spike, linking the Union Pacific and Central Pacific railroads, March 10, 1869. Photograph by Andrew. J. Russell. National Archives and Records Administration.

panies against each other in a race for progress and rewarded that progress with riches that epitomized robber barons of the Gilded Age. The Union Pacific Railway Company was to begin its construction in Omaha and head west. The Central Pacific Railroad was to begin at the same time in Sacramento and head east. The contest was to lay as much track as possible as quickly as possible in order to recoup payments ranging from $16,000 to $48,000 per mile, more in the mountains and less in the plains. In addition to the cost of construction, the companies were granted the rights-of-way and large sections of adjacent land for private development. The frugal Congress, unwilling to turn over complete control of the project's purse strings, required periodic reauthorization of the act.

In addition to the technical accomplishment, the Transcontinental Railroad was notable for the level of rampant corruption that seemed to seep through every aspect of the project. For example, the Crédit Mobilier scandal, brought to light in 1872, revealed that the primary construction contractor, Crédit Mobilier, was owned by the major stockholders of Union Pacific, which, while feigning open competition, had awarded themselves sweetheart construction contracts. Union Pacific had also given an ownership stake in Crédit Mobilier to a number of congressmen who were responsible for overseeing construction and approving subsidies for that construction. This fox-guarding-the-chicken-coop arrangement resulted in the construction contractor and its investors realizing obscene profits while the railroad company itself begged for more governmental support and more lucrative renegotiations of the act while it appeared to be on the brink of bankruptcy.

Despite the scandals, the completed railroad had a huge positive effect on life in America. Whereas before the railroad, coast-to-coast travel by stagecoach took five to six months at a cost of more than a $1,000.00, after the railroad, the trip took only five days at a cost of $150.00. The main construction effort, occurring at the end of the Civil War, provided much-needed employment for both Union and Confederate veterans, as well as for immigrants from China and Ireland. It also gave the nation reason to be optimistic as it struggled with the dark days of Reconstruction. The project provided a symbolic East-West linking of the country that paralleled the attempts to reconcile North and South. The completion of the project demonstrated that with enough money and determination anything was possible. It also provided the model for the efficient organization of a construction company in military-like fashion with strict management of supply chains and logistics. This model was to be copied by many successful construction contractors for years to come.

Immediately after the completion of the Panama Canal, the world turned its attention to fighting the war in Europe. Resources and talents that could have been devoted to great projects were instead expended on destruction and defense. Following World War I, the United States embarked on a program of constructing large dam megaprojects throughout the western part of the country. These dams, envisioned and funded by the Bureau of Reclamation, contributed to flood control, created reservoirs for irrigation water, and produced power for the expanding growth of the country. The Hoover Dam, constructed between 1931 and 1935, is a perfect example of a government-sponsored megaproject. Originally envisioned in the early 1920s, construction did not begin until 1931 and was completed four years later. At the time of its construction, this concrete arch-gravity dam was the world's largest, requiring the development of new construction means and methods for placing and curing vast quantities of concrete. With its construction period coinciding with the Great Depression, the project provided employment, a paycheck, and dignity to tens of thousands of workers. Indeed, the project schedules were actually accelerated in order to increase the number of workers who could be employed on the project. Nevertheless, even in those hard times labor unrest was common. Six Companies, Inc., a joint venture of six construction companies, resorted to using thugs to break strikes and keep the labor force in line and working. Such repressive actions were not uncommon in this period of the country's development, as labor and management faced off over working conditions and safety provisions that we take for granted today. The construction of the Hoover Dam took the lives of more than 100 workers. The strife and conflict between labor and management contributed to the passage of the National Labor Relations Act in 1935, which protected workers' right to unionize, strike, and participate in collective bargaining with their employer.

Shortly after work commenced on the Hoover Dam, the Bureau of Reclamation began construction on the Grand Coulee Dam on the Columbia River in Washington State.

A simpler gravity design, Coulee eclipsed Hoover Dam in size, quantity of concrete, and power produced. Likewise the workforce eclipsed Hoover's, as this became the largest single construction project in history. But aside from the engineering feat, the Grand Coulee Dam project is perhaps most notable for the impact it had on the environment and the indigenous people of the valley flooded by the impounded 125-square-mile Franklin Delano Roosevelt Lake. Not until 42 years after the project was completed did the Bureau of Reclamation prepare an environmental impact statement. Not surprisingly, the project decimated the Indian society that had been living in the valley. The lack of fish ladders resulted in

Grand Coulee Dam looking south, showing Columbia River bridge, residential area, and buildings on eastern side. Library of Congress, Historic American Engineering Record.

the elimination of salmon spawning in the upstream tributaries. The project's main beneficiary was the booming economy of the Pacific Northwest. Unfortunately, this trend of disregarding the rights of the powerless in deference to the desires of the powerful in the name of progress, and blatant ignorance of the environmental consequences of large dams, was an approach that would later be adopted and exported throughout the world as the World Bank financed similar hydroelectric projects in developing countries. The Grand Coulee project also saw an innovation in public relations as the government sought to bolster the project's popularity. In 1941 it hired singer Woody Guthrie to write and perform songs promoting and praising the project as the "mightiest thing ever built by a man" on the "wild and wasted" Columbia River Plateau.

By 1939, the world had once again turned its attention to war both in Europe and in the Pacific. From 1939 until 1945, the industrial might and engineering talent of many nations were again forced to focus on weapons and defensive facilities. In the United States, the Manhattan Project stands out as one of the true megaprojects, employing more than 130,000 people and costing more than $2 billion (in 1946 dollars). The project to develop an atomic bomb was spread across three huge, specially built and developed research centers in Hanford, Washington, Oak Ridge, Tennessee, and Los Alamos, New Mexico. Additional facilities were located throughout the United States and Canada. While the Manhattan Project was above all a weapons program initiated and justified by a unique cost-benefit analysis, the civil engineering aspects of supporting that program were monumental. The military and civilian managers of this project pushed

the boundaries of project management in their attempts to coordinate the required pure research and development, delivery of components, and supply-chain control required to deliver the project.

The devastation of the war in Europe left shattered economies and infrastructure. The Marshall Plan, established by the Truman administration in 1947, recognized the need to assist in the revival of Europe. The grandiose plan was to evaluate the needs and then provide the funding and expertise to rebuild the roads, bridges, railroads, and factories destroyed during the war. The participating nations negotiated the priorities and distribution of funding, the result of which was to shape the post-war economies of Western Europe. This international reconstruction effort required unprecedented cooperation and collaboration by the participating nations. The plan was considered essential not only so that European nations could take their place in the work economy again but also to preempt the dissent, dissatisfaction, and deep recession that had been experienced after World War I, when similar destruction had arguably contributed to the rise of the German Nazi Party. Unfortunately, Eastern Europe and the Soviet Union refused to participate and failed to realize the same level of economic recovery experience under the Marshall Plan.

In the United States after World War II, euphoria and self-satisfaction with the industrial might of the nation that was largely untouched by the war led to an ever-expanding economy and growing influence in the world. This expanding economy required power plants and transmission lines. It also demanded better and better transportation networks. This need for better transportation and the growing reliance on trucks and automobiles led to the federal government's decision to fund the Interstate Highway System. This network of high-quality, high-speed roads promoted by the Eisenhower administration was originally envisioned as a national defense initiative that would allow for the rapid distribution of troops and supplies throughout the country. In 2008, the cost in dollars of the original system has been estimated at approximately $500 billion. A number of studies have attempted to quantify the economic benefits that the highway system has had on the United States. No matter what the return on investment, no one questions whether that investment was well worth it in terms of mobility or that the new-found mobility allowed for the nation's growth. This federally funded highway system represented something of a unique cooperation between federal and state agencies of government. The alignment of the original 37,000-mile system was the result of negotiations between the various state transportation agencies and the Public Roads Administration, the predecessor to the Federal Highway Administration (FHWA). The Public Roads Administration also developed and set the design standards for this Interstate system. The actual design and construction was left to the states, with a promise of federal funding of the major portion of the construction in exchange for adopting the federal standards. The initial funding mechanisms envisioned municipal bonds retired over a 30-year period by revenues raised from a tax on gasoline. In that manner the system would be paid for by its users or potential users. Since the inauguration of the Interstate system, the need for continued maintenance, repair, and upgrades has been recognized, but we still struggle with how to fund these costs. Because the federal government typically funds 90 percent of the construction costs, the FHWA is in a position to influence which projects are built and which are dropped.

Indeed, securing financing for an FHWA-sponsored project has become a very complicated and seemingly opaque endeavor. The federal funding component for highway transportation projects is realized through multiyear bills, such as the Intermodal Surface Transportation Efficiency Act (ISTEA) or the more recent Transportation Equity Act for the 21st Century (TEA-21), each of which covers a six-year span. Modern megaprojects that fall under the auspices of FHWA generally cover a much longer time period to accomplish the planning, design, and construction, and thus the funding must continue in place from one act to its successor. This bridging between acts or continuation of a project is often accomplished with a specific legislative appropriations act authorizing the expenditure of funds. All funding acts—and thus all proposed projects—are first independently reviewed in the House Ways and Means Committee (and more focused subcommittees) and in a corresponding Senate Finance Committee (and subcommittees). If the project survives this review, and if each chamber votes to approve it, and if the Senate and the House bills can be reconciled into a single bill, then that bill can be submitted to the President for execution.

The FHWA has spearheaded many engineering and construction innovations in highway construction. In addition to its leadership role with respect to the bricks-and-mortar aspects of construction, it also plays a significant role in the the management of highway projects. Most importantly, FHWA has recognized that megaprojects are different from typical highway construction projects. This difference was brought home to FHWA during the execution of the much-maligned Central Artery/Tunnel Project (CA/T Project) in Boston. This project has been described as the largest, most complex, and most technically challenging highway project ever attempted in the U.S. The CA/T Project was also the longest-running construction project in the nation's history. The technical challenges encountered and successfully overcome, as well as the design and construction innovations and the commitment to community mitigation, were all unfortunately eclipsed when public opinion turned against the project. Funding was secured on the basis of the initial cost-benefit analysis and cost estimates, which were based on pre-conceptual design and scope documents, devised and submitted to FHWA in accordance with the applicable guidelines at the time. These estimates proved to be woefully inadequate to reflect the project scope by the time construction was underway and for the project that was actually going to be built. Danish researcher Bent Flyvbjerg euphemistically referred to the process of advocating and supporting a project for fund-

ing as a "strategic misrepresentation," where the proponents overestimate the benefits and underestimate the costs. This observation certainly seems to fit the CA/T Project. It is unlikely that the CA/T Project would have received funding rather than the other projects competing for funds if its ultimate scope and more realistic cost estimates were disclosed by the project owner at the outset. The politics of the time, however, demanded that the project owner's "strategic misrepresentation" be propagated. During both design and construction, scope growth initiated by the project owner was rampant, and in an environment where cost and schedule validation were secondary to securing funding and "getting the first shovel in the ground," the budget spiraled out of control.

It is beyond question that more and more of the world's future heavy-civil construction projects will qualify for the label "megaprojects." Recent history suggests that many of these will be transportation related or infrastructure projects. As such, the projects will be overseen by public owners resulting in a broad, diverse interest in the planning, financing, and execution of the projects. Many will also occur in densely populated urban areas, assuring a significant impact on the daily lives of the population during the construction. The objective of this book is to learn from the past such that future megaprojects can take advantage of the lessons learned from predecessor projects. The authors of the following chapters have all participated in significant roles in a variety of megaprojects. They bring with them the wisdom of what worked and what did not work so well. They analyze the issues that challenges they experienced on these projects and provide recommended best practices for future engineers and project owners on their own projects.

CHAPTER 2
Owner Project Planning

Geoffrey A. Fosbrook, P.E., AECOM
Colin Lawrence, C.Eng., Eur.Ing., Hatch Mott MacDonald

"The Easy Bits!"

"If you don't know where you are going, you will wind up somewhere else."

— *Yogi Berra*

Begin with the end in mind! In planning for a megaproject, a well-developed and thoroughly thought-out concept is the strongest possible foundation for success.

This chapter outlines the sequence and approach commonly adopted in the planning of a megaproject from the original idea through to the establishing of a concept, schedule, and funding program. Complete and comprehensive early planning is essential to achieve a successful project outcome. This chapter explores the various elements and criteria that serve to stimulate and then facilitate the development of the megaproject.

Megaprojects are not a modern phenomenon; there are as many examples of megaprojects from the ancient world as there are from modern history. The Great Pyramids of Giza in Egypt, Stonehenge in England, and the Great Wall of China are some of the most famous examples of megaprojects built in the ancient world still existing and visible today, whereas the Panama Canal, the Golden Gate Bridge, the Channel Tunnel, and the Empire State Building are some of the most famous modern-day examples. All megaprojects require extensive planning in order to turn the idea or vision into a reality. To this end the ancient megaprojects were no different from those of the modern era, although inevitably there are many different reasons why such projects are considered successful.

There are many drivers that justify the need or the beginnings of a megaproject; however, the merits by which the project will be gauged a success or not—by either the owner, the end users, or the wider society—can differ considerably from one project to another.

Given the usual intricacy of the components of a megaproject, the process can take over the project in an uncontrolled manner if it is not managed with care and attention, starting at the planning stage.

There are many factors to consider in planning for a megaproject, all requiring early consideration and development to meet the specific project needs. Rather than focusing

Vasco da Gama Bridge, the longest in Europe, connecting Sacavém, north of Lisbon, Portugal (left), with Alcochete. View from the southwest. (The panoramic effect of the photograph counteracts the curving path of the viaduct and seems to straighten it.) Photo © 2001 by Jos van Leeuwen.

on a particular facet of planning that is of most interest to the planner, successful projects tend to optimize the focus across a broad range of all of the relevant parts of the project from the beginning through to completion.

Such aspects can include:

- Defining the project objectives
- Functional and operational criteria
- Laying out the full process including project organization
- Implementation, operations, and maintenance
- Identifying all of the major challenges from a technical, political, and social perspective
- Determining the appropriate level of community and industry outreach

Megaprojects can be deemed failures for many reasons. There are examples of megaprojects that never succeeded at the planning stage or that were designed but then left on the shelf and never constructed. Some would say that the most perfect design was the project that was never built. Some projects also failed during construction, demonstrating that critical risks can occur throughout the project's life.

For those involved at any stage in the creation of a megaproject, the goal is always to make the project a reality. However, there are many potential pitfalls along the way that have the ability to either totally or partially derail the project. Understanding what these pitfalls are is the best way to keep the megaproject alive during transitions to subsequent phases of the megaproject.

There are a number of risk categories that require careful consideration, including technical, construction, economic, political, social, and environmental risks. Megaprojects certainly will have many risks; success in overcoming these challenges will be a direct function of early identification and mitigation of these risks to a manageable level. All risks, if not sufficiently addressed, can be project killers at each stage of the process up to and including construction.

Large projects can sometimes go through periods of controversy and temporary loss of public confidence, often caused by political shifts, community disruption, changes in the scope of the project, cost overruns, schedule delays, and other external forces. Thus, it is vital for the project to follow a well-defined development process.

The early steps in the development of a megaproject typically include:

- Developing a statement of the mission (purpose and need) to be achieved by the project
- Evaluating potential concepts and subjecting them to alternatives analysis, including early risk evaluation
- Defining the stakeholders and their objectives

- Subjecting the alternatives to evaluation by stakeholders
- Developing detailed cost estimates for the alternatives
- Developing preliminary schedules for the alternatives
- Confirming that the mission statement is met by all alternatives
- Undertaking the environmental evaluation and permitting process
- Developing funding mechanisms to satisfy the budget for the selected alternative
- Seeking formal support in the form of grants from state or federal agencies to assist in project funding
- Establishing the project management structure for design and construction (to be discussed in following chapters)
- Providing the necessary enabling project framework to permit commencement of the final design phase

Some of the many important components of a typical megaproject are discussed in detail below. While some of the definitions may vary by project or by country, the essence of a megaproject's contents remain largely similar.

Project Sponsor

The project sponsor is a person or entity that initiates or assumes the role of champion, promoter, or leader of the project above all organizations engaged at all stages from project inception through to project implementation.

Many megaprojects are developed to satisfy an outstanding need, while some are made to benefit a non-existent requirement or to create a legacy (pet project).

The project sponsor needs to possess the leadership and vision necessary to create the foundations for project implementation and delivery. The sponsor's leadership must fundamentally include: defining how the project will be managed from beginning to end; engaging the right team(s) to perform the work; laying out the complete process to be followed from inception through to project completion and operations; scoping the limits of the project; being satisfied that the demand for the project has been correctly and realistically captured; and most importantly, identifying the cash flow and funding stream required to complete the project.

Project Genesis

"If we could first know where we are and whither we are tending, we could better judge what to do and how to do it."
                                                                 —*Abraham Lincoln*

The original sponsor must have strategic thinking that creates an embryo for subsequent development into a megaproject. Regardless of who the individuals or entities are, every megaproject begins with an idea or need being addressed with a proposed solution. Actually, very few individuals engaged in engineering of megaprojects are fortunate enough or get the opportunity to be the originator of the project, either drawing the first pencil line on the map or sketching out the function or form of the structure. Most individuals are engaged in the project at a later stage, after the genesis of the project.

Those who are lucky enough to be sowing the seeds of a megaproject should be mindful that the first lines, sketches, or ideas do not always represent the best solution or final design for the project. The initial ideas should generate a process with sufficient flexibility to produce the best possible solution. The first lines should not become so rigid that ultimately they lead to adopting a sub-optimal solution.

Maximum flexibility in accepting subsequent improvements to the original ideas is recommended; however, care should be taken so that ownership or protection of ideas does not skew the desired outcome of the project.

Another dynamic involves entertaining too many ideas, which can cause confusion and delay in reaching the ultimate solution. For this reason, an evaluation process should be developed with appropriately weighted criteria representing discriminators between various options or alternative components within options, as described below.

Large projects occasionally suffer from both internal and external pressures to improve the project but which potentially threaten its successful implementation. Keeping it simple is sometimes the right course of action!

Other dynamics are also an important consideration at the project genesis stage. "Project pile-on," whereby adjacent pet projects or non-essential add-ons become implanted in the project scope but are not essential for successful implementation of the project, should be avoided. If sufficient funding exists to cover such "wish-list" items, then this is clearly not an issue. However, such "extra" items can become a potential conflict when scope, budget, and schedule are adversely impacted.

Finally, megaprojects do not always emerge from the concept of a large project. They can begin as small simple ideas that develop into megaprojects as the scale of the solution is realized. Both small and large acorns can grow into large oak trees!

Project Drivers

"It takes as much energy to wish as it does to plan."   — *Eleanor Roosevelt*

Some megaprojects are driven by a functional or quality-of-life need, whereas others may be commercially or financially driven. For instance, new highways, tunnels or bridges, transit systems, major wastewater or water treatment facilities, and airports satisfy quality-of-life needs and improvements that perhaps did not exist previously in the community.

Alternatively, there are also schemes that address deficiencies to the existing infrastructure (such as regional or coastal flooding, wastewater, water or power deficiencies) or that are a major rehabilitation of existing transportation infrastructure (such as rail stations, rail lines, or highway improvements), which result in quality-of-life improvements.

Projects such as major building structures, new sports stadia, and commercial and retail developments may be undertaken to achieve a desired financial return on investment. A project being implemented under a public-private partnership can fall into this category, inasmuch as all require a financial return on the project outlay over an identified period in order to make the project viable.

At the concept phase, multiple ways of satisfying a stated need should be identified.

Functional Compliance and Acceptance

There are several different mechanisms that can stimulate a megaproject. Some large owners are driven by a need for continuous improvements and enhancements to the infrastructure within its jurisdiction or ownership. By continually assessing and ranking priorities, sponsors can maintain an ongoing program of capital works, which often results in megaprojects.

This is a somewhat idealistic description of the process, where the funding stream is consistent with the priorities of the capital program. More often than not, there is a disparity between the needs of the owner and the funding available.

In 2009, the American Society of Civil Engineers estimated that the United States would need to spend $2.2 trillion to restore the nation's infrastructure (highways, railways, waterways, airports, power plants, etc.) to a state of good repair. The ratings by category of existing facilities were:

• Aviation	D		• Schools	D
• Dams	D		• Transit	D
• Drinking water	D–		• Wastewater	D–
• Roads	D–			

(A grade of "D" on a scale of A to F was a poor rating.)

Such a regular appraisal of the nation's infrastructure at a general level of assessment provides a good mechanism to highlight where the immediate needs for improvements exist. By looking at trends each year from this independent assessment, further analysis on incremental improvement or deterioration can be made.

A national assessment such as this helps to impose pressure on the federal, state, and local governments to make improvements to components in these various categories. At this scale, the solution often results in a megaproject to resolve the problem.

Project Process

> *"By failing to prepare, you are preparing to fail."*
> — *Benjamin Franklin*

Achieving the core objectives of any megaproject usually begins with the early establishment and scrutiny of the trinity of quality, time, and cost. These are always of major consideration, but along with them are many other facets that need to be considered at the very early stages.

Most large municipal, state, and federal agencies have organizations with functions that operate at the stage through which a project is progressing, such as planning, design, procurement, construction, construction oversight, and operation and maintenance. All stakeholders throughout the organization and in any affected external agencies should have input into the development of the project.

The project process consists of a number of essential elements, including funding, sequence and timing, the environmental process, scoping, compliance with any consent decrees, and early identification of any real estate and easement requirements.

For a megaproject, the sponsoring organization typically includes a program management entity, design teams for each stage of the design (split into different disciplines, where appropriate), construction management and inspection specialists, contractors, and commissioning and operational entities.

In order to optimize the efficiencies in collaboration, cooperation, and communication, some owners mandate that all entities be integrated within a project office with the sponsor agency or owner, program management, design and construction staff all co-located during the development, design, and construction phases of the project.

Environmental Permitting

Based upon the definition of a megaproject, usually there will be a need for some form of an environmental evaluation process.

In the United States, if the construction project will be seeking some form of federal funding, it must satisfy the requirements of the National Environmental Policy Act (NEPA [42 U.S.C. 4321 et seq.]). It was signed into law on January 1, 1970, and established national environmental policy and goals for the protection, maintenance, and enhancement of the environment and provided a process for implementing these goals within the federal agencies which, in this case, might be acting as the federal sponsor of the megaproject.

An important aspect of any environmental assessment or impact statement is to perform adequate public outreach in order to gain community support. Any evaluation of the project should be sensitive to the needs of the local and regional community.

A recent trend within the industry is to identify the sustainability aspects and possibilities provided by the project. The scale of megaprojects is such that many opportunities may exist to provide sustainable measures that have a far-reaching environmental benefit without necessarily increasing costs. Such carefully developed sustainable measures can prove very attractive in gaining public acceptance of the project.

Alternatives Evaluation Process

Most megaprojects begin with a number of alternative options or configurations, each of which may produce a solution as a functional project; however, some options prove to be of greater benefit than others.

The goal in this early stage is to identify the option that offers the best solution in terms of all the criteria. Consequently, the selection criteria need to be carefully tailored to only those that provide discriminators between the various options.

For example, safety is usually the most important issue in planning for a project. However, if all options are considered to be safe, then there is little to discriminate between each option for a criterion of safety.

This does not diminish the importance of safety on the project in any way. Rather, because a high standard of safety should be required by all options to begin with, safety would not be a variable aspect of the project that would help the owner discriminate between options.

Typical environmental permitting and alternatives analysis might include such subjects as:

- Project purpose
- Project alternatives
- Project benefits
- Project phasing
- Construction methods
- Environmental design
- Public outreach and review process
- Social and economic conditions
- Construction impacts
- Operational impacts
- Displacement and relocation
- Short-term disruption
- Long-term or permanent displacement
- Historic and archaeological resources
- Operational impacts
- Air quality
- Noise and vibration
- Infrastructure and energy
- Safety
- Environmental justice
- Indirect and cumulative effects
- Construction impacts
- Operational impacts
- Summary of mitigation measures

For each project the evaluation criteria will vary as the regional, functional, and socio-economic constraints vary. Each evaluation should be customized to fit the requirements of the particular project.

In order to produce the appropriate selection, the identified criteria should also be weighted in proportion to the importance applied to each criterion by the project stakeholders. This is usually performed through periodic facilitated workshops involving all stakeholders. As with many aspects in life involving a large group, full concurrence on every facet is not usually achieved, so a consensus position is normally derived.

Each option is then evaluated with an achievement score for each of the established criteria. A total ranking for each option is then calculated, based on the weighted values associated with each criterion.

At this stage as a further check on selection and for the benefit of those who did not concur with some of the applied weighting, a sensitivity analysis can be performed, running the assessment numbers once again with adjustments to the weighting. This is performed in order to gauge whether the final selection was influenced or not by the weighting bias applied to the more critical criteria. This sensitivity analysis helps generate further consensus from stakeholders who may have doubted the final selection.

Federal Funding Application Process

By definition, megaprojects will involve significant program costs. Funding these projects is a challenge for local or state agencies, and therefore many megaprojects will be seeking funds from the federal government to enable the project to be undertaken. Various federal agencies have a certain amount of funds specifically allocated by Congress to enable them to participate.

In order to use the funds wisely and for the highest public purpose, funding agencies have certain evaluation procedures, some of which are established by law, that enable them to commit the limited funds to those projects that best serve the public need.

For instance, in determining which transit projects will receive funding, the Federal Transit Administration (FTA) has published "New Starts Criteria," which specify how projects seeking federal funding will be evaluated and then ranked. The law for New Starts funding categorizes the evaluation criteria into three broad areas:

- Alternatives Analysis and Preliminary Engineering
- Project Justification
- Local Financial Commitment

The *Alternatives Analysis and Preliminary Engineering* process begins with the establishment of the need and justification and may include the development of the Draft Environmental Impact Statement. To specifically qualify for New Starts funding (49 USC § 5309), candidate projects must have resulted from an alternatives analysis study (also known as major investment study or multimodal corridor analysis) which evaluates appropriate modal and alignment options for addressing mobility needs in a given corridor. Alternatives analysis can be viewed as a bridge between systems planning

(which identifies regional travel patterns and transportation corridors in need of improvements) and project development (where a project's design is refined sufficiently to complete the NEPA environmental process).

The alternatives analysis study is intended to provide information to local officials on the benefits, costs, and impacts of alternative transportation investments developed to address the purpose and need for an improvement in the corridor. Potential local funding sources for implementing and operating the alternatives should be identified and studied, and New Starts criteria should be developed. Involvement of a wide range of stakeholders — including the general public — in the alternative analysis study process is strongly encouraged.

The *Project Justification* section involves specific criteria and the prescribed measurement of them. It includes measures of benefits and impacts that would exist if the project were to be undertaken.

While the criteria and measures are subject to change over time, they might include:

Criterion	Measure(s)
Mobility improvements	Normalized travel time savings (transportation system user benefits per project passenger mile) The number of transit-dependent riders using the proposed New Starts project Transit-dependent user benefits per passenger mile on the project The share of user benefits received by transit dependents compared to the share of transit dependents in the region
Environmental benefits	EPA air quality designation
Cost effectiveness	Incremental cost per hour of transportation system user benefit Incremental cost per new rider (for informational purposes only)
Transit supportive land use and future patterns	Existing land use Transit supportive plans and policies Performance and impacts of policies
Other factors	Economic development Making the case for the project Congestion pricing Optional considerations

The purpose of including the FTA's table above is merely to provide an example of the types of evaluation to which a project might be subjected if it were to compete for federal funding.

The FTA's three measures for the *Local Financial Commitment* include:

Criterion	Measure(s)
Local financial commitment	Stability and reliability of capital financing plan Stability and reliability of operating financing plan Local share of project costs

The Federal Transit Administration will not make a firm commitment in funding until the requesting agency has satisfied the requirements listed above, has proven that the project has satisfied the environmental evaluation process, and has shown that a thorough risk evaluation has been completed. Among other factors being evaluated, the risk evaluation must include a determination that an adequate level of cost contingency and schedule float has been included in the project planning.

Risk and the Planning Phase

All too often the early planning of a project is prone to an overly optimistic projection of the benefits, underestimation of the costs, and insufficient schedule durations being planned. While optimistic projections of project benefits have implications for the cost and schedule, there are also implications in terms of future patronage once the project is commissioned. Overestimating benefits has a consequential risk of creating the feared "white elephant" legacy where the benefit is never achieved.

Underestimating costs and having insufficient schedule are sometimes symptomatic of either deliberate or unintentional strategies, adopted at the planning stage, to enable the project to pass the various stages of the approval process. As a consequence, reality is not appreciated until much later in the process when sufficient momentum has been achieved to take the project into or through implementation.

Another approach is to attempt to identify a realistic schedule with adequate float, with all costs fully escalated, and having sufficient contingency. This could represent the opposite extreme to the former strategy, as there is a real risk that the cost and duration will become extremely high at concept stage, thereby inhibiting further development of the project.

The above consideration of strategies could lead one to consider that there is no panacea strategy to adopt when planning for a megaproject. However, there is a middle way that aims to optimize the fundamentals of project benefit, cost, and schedule.

By using a risk management–based approach for a megaproject early in the planning

stage and continuing to address risk throughout the design and construction of the project, significant risks to cost, schedule, and health and safety can be reasonably identified and addressed at the earliest opportunity. (Risk management for megaprojects is described below in chapter 10.) Typical risk identification might include such areas as schedule, cost escalation, permits, labor availability, funding, loss of political support, loss of community support, adverse weather, real estate availability, market conditions years out, tunneling risk issues, and the list goes on.

This risk-based approach has the benefit of mitigating or reducing major risks, thus providing greater confidence in the conceptual or preliminary design and requiring a reduced contingency allocation for both cost and schedule. The net result is to establish a project budget and schedule that is not prohibitive in terms of procurement but does provide sufficient contingency for finalization of the design and timely implementation of the project.

One cautionary note is that some risks may be considered small or insignificant at the commencement of a project and can therefore be overlooked or ignored during concept development. Such small risks can have major impacts or consequences to cost and schedule if left unaddressed. For this reason, the scope of early risk assessment should be sufficiently unrestricted in terms of risk identification and capture, even if the immediate action at the time is to defer addressing the mitigation measures, if any, to a later date. At the very least, identifying such risks enables the risk to be captured for ongoing consideration throughout the life of the project development.

Risk assessment and mitigation may take many different forms through the life of a project. Tren Urbano is a $2 billion new-start heavy-rail transit system in the metropolitan area of San Juan, Puerto Rico. At the time the system was being planned by the Puerto Rico Highway and Transportation Authority (PRHTA), there was not a lot of existing local knowledge in the design and construction of subways and transit systems.

The PRHTA recognized the risk that this posed and considered various ways of mitigating it. By developing a coalition of both local and international technical talent, the PRHTA achieved its goal of transferring technical knowledge about transit planning, design, and construction. Additionally, through the design and implementation of a conscientious program by which Tren Urbano staff participated in structured mentorship programs and attended monthly seminars by project experts, the local pool was expanded and strengthened.

A professional development program with M.I.T. and the University of Puerto Rico was implemented and coordinated by the agency to open career pathways for local students interested in pursuing transportation-related design and engineering professions. This local knowledge was then available for future on-island transit programs.

The PRHTA also recognized the lack of local knowledge in the operation and maintenance of rail transit systems. To overcome this deficiency the agency developed a contracting strategy that required the vehicle, systems, and maintenance facility construction contractors to operate the system for the initial five-year period and to train a local workforce to undertake this activity in the future.

Another risk faced by the PRHTA on the Tren Urbano project was the need to provide service to the historic area of Rio Piedras and the centuries-old cathedral in the center of that town, without impacting the cathedral or diminishing the historic significance of the square and the University of Puerto Rico's nearby Rio Piedras campus.

This risk of having the project delayed or otherwise impacted by adverse public reaction was mitigated by having the alignment through this area placed underground in a subway system. Construction of the subway system in the area posed an additional risk that underground construction might have an adverse impact on the historic structures around the square. This was overcome by including specific building monitoring and protective construction practices, which resulted in no adverse impacts.

James S. Simpson, former Federal Transit Administrator, in a February 13, 2008, speech to the National Transit Forum in Ontario, Canada, paraphrased noted transportation analyst Bent Flyvbjerg in saying, "We must find ways of institutionally embedding risk and accountability in the decision-making process for megaprojects."

Simpson then continued: "We take this very seriously at the FTA. First, we look to see whether the project sponsors have the right mix of management, technical, and financial capacity to handle a megaproject—and see it through the years. Have they done this type of project before? Do they know how to structure the best type of contract for the project? Is their local funding secure and stable?" What Simpson points out is precisely what a project sponsor should be considering when planning to undertake a megaproject. Early risk management, commencing during the planning phase and involving all major stakeholders of the project, is imperative in striving for successful project implementation.

Public Support

Megaprojects by their nature provide a legacy to the community in which they are built. To be successful, most megaprojects must gain public trust and support. Public concerns must be addressed early so that solutions can be developed before design and construction progresses to a point where changes are certainly more costly.

By enjoying public trust and support, if it becomes clear that it is not possible to totally mitigate a concern, the owners will at least have an opportunity to explain why the issue cannot be eliminated or rectified—there is time for explanation and negotiation.

To create a platform for success, a collaborative and good-neighbor approach is necessary, and it should include positive early media coverage and sincere and meaningful public and agency outreach programs.

Media Support

Early engagement of the media, with full disclosure of project particulars — such as needs, benefits, limitations, funding, and schedule — is necessary to avoid adverse coverage that would serve to damage the megaproject's image in public.

A proactive working relationship with the media is recommended. This could include popular national, regional, and local press, and television and radio networks. Holding regular press briefings about the project (including benefits and planned and current activities), hosting a Website with regularly updated project news and information, and highlighting project challenges and solutions are several proven ways of building public support.

The last point — talking about difficulties — is an area that is commonly avoided by megaproject owners for fear of divulging a developing contractual position or weakening one party's hand towards another party. However, engaging the media early with positive intentions can often avoid incorrect or inaccurate rumors from developing into an adverse public reaction to the project. Set up a public relations arm of the project organization to provide a communications focal point to the media throughout the life of the project.

Planning for Construction

There are several important elements to consider in planning for the construction of a megaproject.

It is essential that the sponsor establish itself as a "preferred owner," with contract terms that are not one-sided, and where there is a sincere effort at achieving "risk sharing" between the owner and the contractor, with the risks being assigned to the entity best able to manage and mitigate them.

Early outreach to the construction parties is often overlooked or taken for granted. For megaprojects, this is a vital component for owners, given the scale and large costs involved.

Often bidding for large-value work is limited to very few contractors or contractor consortia bidding for the work, which in turn leads to unexpected project cost escalation.

Early attention to construction contractor outreach, appropriate contract packaging from the outset of the project, and fair apportionment of risk leads to a more competitive bidding climate. This approach serves to control project costs from the beginning through to completion. If the owner establishes a good relationship with the construction community at the planning phase, contractors are then in a position to track and gauge the viability of making a bid.

Some owners may suffer from a reputation of past one-sided risk allocation practices that were rightly (or wrongly) considered to be adversarial or unfair, in the opinion of contractors. In a strong construction market, such owners may be open to a more even apportionment of construction risk, with the aim of achieving a more attractive bidding climate resulting in a competitive price for construction.

In order to achieve this, a greater level of outreach to the contractors may be necessary to continually demonstrate the risk allocation and sharing measures that will be implemented. Provided at the concept development stage, such measures can be broadcast to the industry early and often in order to generate maximum interest by the time of the bid for each contract within the project.

Obtaining a competitive bid is important to the project, but having sufficient budget to cover construction costs is paramount. Project economics should be continually evaluated, including industry inflationary trends, factors influencing escalation, using the "right" indices, establishing a realistic cash-flow strategy for financial commitment and budgetary purposes, and consideration of the full extent of life-cycle costs applied to the megaproject.

Where a megaproject requires multiple construction contract packages within the overall program, a separation of packages should be established prior to commencement of the project design. It is common to complete the preliminary designs for the various major construction packages at the same time. Decisions can then be made about whether to use a just-in-time completion of the final design for each separate contract package, or if time permits, to complete the final design for each package at the same time.

Analysis and Discussion

> *"Reduce your plan to writing. The moment you complete this, you will have definitely given concrete form to the intangible desire."*
> —*Napoleon Hill*

In planning for megaprojects, there are many lessons to be learned from past projects, both ancient and modern, from around the world. A common desire for all owners is to achieve a successful project. An important consideration in planning a megaproject is how to gauge this success.

Most projects, both large and small, are monitored against the three factors of quality, schedule, and cost. The fundamentals of project management are established to achieve this goal. Early estimates of project cost and schedule must include realistic projections of project benefits and sufficient allocation of cost contingency and schedule float.

For megaprojects, given the scale of the undertaking, there are additional criteria,

some of which carry greater significance than quality, schedule, or cost in terms of successful achievement.

Establishing the criteria of success against which the project will be gauged is an important aspect that can help the public, the media, and government appreciate the scale of accomplishment of the undertaking through project implementation.

The Channel Tunnel project between England and France has become world famous for going over budget and for overrunning the schedule. On closer examination of the project details, however, there is perhaps another story to consider that gives valuable insights into the achievements that were made and the lessons that were learned for subsequent megaprojects.

The project began construction in 1987 and finished by 1993, some four months late out of a schedule of six years. Interestingly, the tunneling was completed either ahead of schedule or on schedule, depending on whose viewpoint was considered: the tunneling was on time, in the opinion of TML (the contractor), or it was late, according to Eurotunnel (the project sponsor). Either way, tunneling was a considerable achievement with respect to schedule.

The Channel Tunnel's problems in meeting the scheduled opening date were twofold: delays in delivery of the trains, which were to be designed and manufactured as part of the project, and delays with the implementation of the terminals and fixed equipment, including state-of-the-art smart signaling and the ventilation and cooling systems.

The greatest contributors to cost escalation on the project were the shuttle trains, followed by the terminals and fixed equipment, with the tunnel construction contributing a marginal increased difference. Interestingly, different procurement methods were used for these project elements.

A surprising outcome was that, for a project of this complexity and risk, one would intuitively expect that the risk to the schedule and cost would more likely occur with tunneling operations (from unexpected ground conditions) rather than the supposedly more identifiable risks associated with rolling stock and fixed equipment.

The invaluable lesson for megaprojects is that the greatest impact to the success of the project may not always come from the most obvious major risks, but rather from less obvious but high-severity risks.

There are a number of other achievements of the Channel Tunnel project, in terms of scale of achievement:

- It is the only fixed link connecting the United Kingdom with France and mainland Europe.
- This was the first successful attempt at creating a link in 190 years.
- Construction was at the limits of available technology of the day.

- Innovation was required for state-of-the-art trains, underground operations, and smart fixed equipment.
- The tunnel is the longest undersea crossing in the world.
- The tunnel required excavating the largest undersea cavern in the world to facilitate a rail crossover.
- It was a pioneer for subsequent projects, such as the Channel Tunnel Rail Link itself, which enables a Europe-wide connection for long term high-speed network objectives.
- It provided invaluable lessons for tunnel megaprojects that followed.
- It was the first of many subsequent undersea transportation tunnel projects.

In planning for megaprojects, every effort should be made to establish an appropriate framework upon which to build success. It is important to research and understand the causes of past successes and failures of megaprojects and to establish the criteria against which project achievements can be gauged.

Many dynamics can conspire to make it difficult to achieve these goals. Attention should be continually given to the "must-have" ideas and measures versus the non-essential wish lists that continually arise throughout the course of the project process.

Proactive planning should be adopted as much as possible in preference to reacting to adverse trends, which, if left unabated, will develop. That said, there will of course always be a need to react to unforeseen project dynamics that could potentially derail the project.

Undertaking early risk assessments, value engineering, and constructability reviews are all worthy mechanisms for controlling costs and staying on schedule.

While there are no panaceas or guarantees for achieving a successful megaproject, it is the combination of lessons learned on past megaprojects together with timely and appropriate application of a risk-based approach that will produce a solid platform for success as the project proceeds from planning to the subsequent design and construction phases.

Reference Sources

Hunt, Donald. (1994). *The Tunnel: The Story of the Channel Tunnel, 1802 to 1994*. Upton-upon-Severn, England: Images Publishing.

Flyvbjerg, B., Bruzelius, N., and Rothengatter, W. (2003). *Megaprojects and Risk: An Anatomy of Ambition*. Cambridge: Cambridge University Press.

CHAPTER 3

Owner Project Management

Richard Fox, CDM
Charles Button, P.E.
Walter Armstrong

Boston Harbor's iconic historical significance is undeniably based on the actions of the American colonists who boarded a merchant ship at Griffin's Wharf in 1773 and dumped its cargo of tea in the harbor to protest British taxation without representation. Tea washed up on the shores of Boston for weeks.

By the 1980s, however, Boston Harbor was known more infamously for being one of the most polluted harbors in the United States. A court-ordered cleanup and facilities upgrade—deemed the largest wastewater project in U.S. history—reversed that reputation, providing effective wastewater treatment to 43 surrounding communities and meeting the ambitious goal of restoring water quality in the harbor. This megaproject, under an aggressive consent decree timetable, daunting logistical challenges, and intense public scrutiny, delivered a massive wastewater treatment system at a cost of $3.8 billion, far below the initial estimate of $4.3 billion. This chapter—prepared by three representatives of the project owner—outlines the issues and critical success factors that most contributed to these exceptional results.

Background

Disposal of sewage and other waste into Boston Harbor had markedly reduced water quality, deteriorated habitats, polluted beaches, and compromised the quality of life for residents along its 180-mile shoreline. By 1968, all dry-weather sewage flows were receiving primary treatment at two facilities in the harbor, with effluent and sludge discharged, after some digestion and chlorination, through short outfalls near the harbor entrance. The Clean Water Act of 1972 mandated that by 1977 all publicly owned treatment plants achieve secondary treatment prior to discharge to a water body. By 1978, however, the U.S. Environmental Protection Agency (EPA) provided guidelines for waivers of the secondary treatment requirements for facilities discharging to coastal waters. Boston engaged in an iterative waiver application process that began in 1979. Ultimately, by 1985, that waiver was denied. An intervening action in 1983, in which the city of Quincy sued the Metropolitan District Commission for polluting its beaches, resulted in

Panoramic view of San Francisco looking west from Treasure Island. Part of the San Francisco–Oakland Bay Bridge is visible on the left. Picture continues on next spread, showing the Presidio and the Golden Gate Bridge. Photo © 2009 by Leonard G.

a Massachusetts Supreme Court order for a strict timetable of remediation (though it did not specify secondary treatment) and creation of a new state agency with the power to issue bonds outside the control of the state legislature. By the end of 1984, the legislature created the Massachusetts Water Resources Authority (MWRA) and gave it bonding and rate-setting authority. In January 1985, the EPA sued the newly formed authority in U.S. district court for polluting the harbor. A 1986 federal court order required the MWRA to implement a planning and construction schedule to meet EPA's secondary treatment requirement by the end of 1999.

The major components of the Boston Harbor Project (BHP) included:

- Upgraded primary treatment facilities on Deer Island, to treat peak wet-weather flows of 1.27 billion gallons per day
- New secondary treatment plant on Deer Island capable of treating up to 780 mgd
- A remote headworks facility on Nut Island, screening 400 mgd of wastewater from the southern communities
- Inter-island conveyance system, including a 4.8-mile rock tunnel that transports flows from the Nut Island facility to the Deer Island treatment plant
- A 9.5-mile rock effluent outfall tunnel, which discharges effluent through a series of 55 diffusers into deep waters of Massachusetts Bay
- On-island residuals processing facilities, including 12 egg-shaped digesters
- Sludge processing and pelletizing plant at Fore River in Quincy

The sheer scale of these facilities would constitute a megaproject. Add to that the complexity of building the primary and secondary treatment facilities on peninsulas, posing extreme logistical challenges. The design and construction of the project involved execution of 32 design contracts and 133 construction and support services contracts.

The measures of success for this megaproject were:

- The facilities met or surpassed the discharge limits.
- Court-ordered schedule milestones were met.
- Total costs were about 15 percent ($580 million) under budget.
- Benchmarks were met for the costs of management, design, and construction services.
- Dolphins, seals, and other aquatic life have returned to Boston Harbor.
- The project contributed significantly to the economic development of the waterfront.

The Best-Laid Plans Can Drive Success

Issue

By definition, megaprojects are very complex, extend over time, and affect dozens of major stakeholders. Because of these characteristics, major changes can and must be anticipated over the life of the project. Is it reasonable to expect that a definitive, implementable plan is possible prior to initiating major elements of design and construction? The BHP was indeed driven by an exceptionally well-conceived, phased facility plan that guided the successful execution of this megaproject.

Discussion

Every megaproject must follow an extensive and thorough assessment of the design and construction requirements, as well as technical, regulatory, financial, and communal effects. Completed in 1988 and further refined seven years later, the BHP's facilities plan provided a reliable, innovative, and visionary guide for one of the most complex wastewater treatment projects ever accomplished. The plan:

- Detailed an effective management structure;
- Established the technical components for secondary treatment of wastewater;
- Outlined measures to manage costs and other institutional factors;
- Provided for an extensive public information program to gain public support; and
- Required minimal changes, thereby keeping the massive design and construction project focused and on schedule.

The major issues at play at the outset of the planning process included:

- How much flow should be treated, to what level, and by what process?
- Where should the facilities be located?
- Who should share in the costs, and how?
- What is the appropriate mitigation for the "hosting" communities?
- What will be the governance and oversight of the program?
- How can the stakeholders and public be involved to build buy-in for the plan?
- How should the project be programmed over time — physical sequencing, political consensus, cash flow?

The stage for the plan was set by 37 prior planning studies completed following the passage of the Clean Water Act in 1972 — with no consensus or resolution emerging.

Clearly, the plan needed to be informed by some of these prior studies, but it had to greatly surpass them by providing firm recommendations and a detailed road map for execution. The facilities plan provided resolution of these major issues, forging a course for the cleanup.

Development of the facilities plan involved hundreds of meetings and difficult decisions about siting the large and complex facilities, environmental protection and mitigation, and the logistics of construction in a densely populated urban environment. Eight volumes, supported by 20 detailed technical appendices, comprised the plan:

- Executive Summary
- Facilities Planning Background
- Treatment Plant
- Inter-Island Conveyance System
- Effluent Outfall
- Early Site Preparation
- Institutional Considerations
- Public Participation and Responsiveness Summary

Three key aspects contributing to the plan's success are outlined below.

Broad criteria for evaluation. The plan's scope, which encompassed an unusually broad range of technical, regulatory, financial, and public and community concerns, ensured that the project would secure and sustain the acceptance and support of the diverse community, government, and business interests that it would affect. The process of developing the plan was not merely an engineering exercise to produce a technical document, but an intense and dynamic program that produced a valuable guide for the 13-year design, construction, and start-up process.

In making major decisions to select an appropriate treatment process, size and locate all facilities, and plan the initial site preparation for construction, the planning team was guided by the following broad criteria:

- Environmental criteria (air, noise, traffic, and marine resources) and the measurement of potential impacts to each;
- Technical criteria, focusing on engineering issues such as reliability, flexibility, constructability, operational complexity, space and staging requirements, and power needs;
- Cost criteria, defining the financial investment necessary to build and operate the alternatives; and
- Institutional criteria, which assessed the differences among alternatives according

to the time required for construction and the coordination among the many public and private entities.

Aerial view of the distinctive egg-shaped water-treatment vessels of the new facilities on Deer Island, a principal part of the Boston Harbor Project. Photo courtesy Massachusetts Water Resources Authority.

Every major aspect of the project had to address all of these criteria to produce an integrated plan that was technically feasible, cost-effective, compliant with environmental goals, constructible within the aggressive schedule, and acceptable to the political and regulatory stakeholders and the public. The consideration and interplay of these criteria ensured that all bases were covered and synergies could be fostered.

Stakeholder involvement. To succeed, the plan needed a foundation of extensive public participation and consensus-building to help secure the support by a large, diverse community of public and private stakeholders. This broad community involvement proved critical as the project moved forward. The planners aptly noted, "The planning process was based not on technical strength alone, but also on the continual reconciliation of political, legal, environmental, economic, and community interests."

The public's interests were multidimensional. While they were concerned with the restoration and protection of Boston Harbor, they were also troubled by the tremendous cost burden that they would have to shoulder, especially at a time when federal funding had ceased and stalled regional growth had limited state assistance. And, of course, they were concerned about the location and neighborhood impacts of the facilities themselves. New England's fishing industries were concerned with potential ecological impacts of the deep water discharge and the possible effect on employment and the economy.

More than 300 public meetings were held, many of them resulting in agreements and formal memoranda of understanding that addressed the concerns of community groups and municipal governments. The results of these meetings formed the basis for the mitigation of construction impacts, odor control, aesthetic features, as well as fostering public understanding of the need, benefits, and costs of this major undertaking.

Recognizing the importance of building and maintaining trust over the course of the program, the plan committed to an unusually aggressive completion of the primary facilities, partly so that the public and regulators would witness tangible progress toward remediating the harbor as early as possible. In addition, the plan demonstrated other significant early water quality improvements through the cessation of scum and sludge discharges to the harbor by the end of 1989. These visible improvements were apparent

33

at a time when water and sewer rates were rising, allowing the public to make a positive connection between higher rates and a cleaner harbor.

The MWRA's water quality monitoring program also provided the public with a window into the benefits of their investment. A harbor studies group convened in 1987 was charged with developing baseline water quality data and tracking water quality improvements directly resulting from the project. Data from the monitoring program allowed the MWRA to identify sources of contaminants and prioritize spending. For the public, however, the monitoring program gave the cleanup program scientific credibility and provided the much-needed assurance that the harbor was improving.

Building flexibility for a "living plan." The aggressive court-ordered schedule necessitated that the plan be completed in early 1988, with preliminary construction work beginning that same year. Accommodating this compressed schedule, the plan had been necessarily conservative in estimating capacity and treatment requirements. With this in mind, the planners also anticipated the need to collect more specific data on influent flow and quality to guide the detailed design. During the ensuing years, the MWRA built a substantial database of influent flows and loads and constructed a pilot plant on Deer Island to obtain operating information specific to the plant wastewater.

The facilities plan established sufficient flexibility in the design and construction schedule to allow an opportunity to reassess capacity of the second half of the proposed secondary treatment and residuals handling facilities, even while construction was underway. In 1993, after all the facilities proposed for primary treatment and the initial portions of the secondary treatment were either under construction or had been designed, the planning team critically examined flows and loads, generated performance goals and design criteria to meet water quality requirements, reviewed innovative and emerging technologies, validated design criteria using the pilot plant, conducted detailed mathematical modeling of effluent blending scenarios, and recommended cost-effective enhancements to the facilities plan that could meet discharge permit requirements even during storm flows. As a result, the secondary treatment facilities were able to be downsized from 1,080-mgd capacity to 780 mgd. These studies determined that one of the four originally proposed secondary treatment batteries and 25 percent of the residuals digesters were not required, saving $160 million in capital costs.

Recommended Practices

- Recognize that planning must embrace the entire spectrum of major issues needed for implementation. Going beyond the technical and even quantifiable parameters is essential.

- Anticipate that many of the major issues will require political and stakeholder resolution, and constantly focus on the forums that can inform and assist in this process.

- Build trust with the public through extensive participation; reinforce that trust through early, clearly visible improvements; and steadfastly honor all commitments made.

- Leverage program requirements, such as environmental reviews, by thoughtfully structuring them to provide a public forum for understanding and resolution.

- Build flexibility into the project planning and execution phases, especially if further justification for the facilities needed or costs seems warranted.

Mitigation Can Remove Barriers

Issue

Megaprojects have "mega-impacts," and mitigating these can be essential for project execution. Mitigation also comes with substantial financial commitments. Critical barriers to implementation and potential tradeoffs must be identified early, with the mitigating actions ratified at the outset.

Discussion

Areas of contention had the potential to obstruct the BHP, but the court-ordered schedule did not allow for delays. Issues related to the level of treatment, siting of facilities, and construction impacts had to be resolved early to build support and keep the project on track. Early resolution also avoided changes in either the design or construction contracting, minimizing change orders and delays that frequently plague large public projects.

Level of treatment. Although the federal court order mandated secondary treatment, agreement on the level of treatment was not unanimous. Some of the scientific community advocated that primary treatment with a long outfall would be more than enough to restore and protect the harbor. Shore communities argued for secondary treatment with a long outfall as far from their communities as possible. Environmentalists preferred the most stringent approach of tertiary treatment with a long outfall. Regulators maintained that secondary treatment was the minimum acceptable option.

Resolving these competing views was a priority for the planning process. The compromise reached was secondary treatment with a long outfall (9.5 miles), with the discharge centrally located from all shore communities. As mentioned earlier, the facilities plan also allowed for revisiting the exact components of secondary treatment following the collection and analysis of flow and load data and evaluation of treatment through pilot testing. To satisfy the demands for tertiary treatment, sufficient space for such facilities was reserved in case post-operations testing suggested that additional levels of treatment were required.

Facilities siting. The "not in my backyard" mindset was certainly in play as the sites of one of the largest wastewater treatment facilities were being evaluated. The MWRA evaluated eight sites, considering implementability, reliability, impacts on neighbors, equitable distribution of regional impacts, harbor enhancement, cultural and natural resources, cost, and non-environmental mitigation. Deer Island was selected as the most suitable site, a decision that had a political majority, but by no means a consensus. Concomitant with this decision, the MWRA committed to short- and long-term mitigation measures to reduce impacts on the communities where the facilities were to be constructed. These included limits on noise (1 decibel above ambient conditions at the boundary), odor (zero odor at the plant boundary), underwater high-voltage power supply, natural physical barriers to screen the site, and foot traffic access to the site perimeter for recreational use.

Water transportation system. Perhaps the most innovative mitigation measure, however, was the commitment to the barging of construction materials and ferrying or busing of workers to minimize negative impacts on local traffic patterns. With the only road access to Deer Island via the narrow residential streets of Winthrop, MWRA had to devise and execute a complicated transportation scheme. All materials were transported to the site by barge from a mainland staging area in Quincy. Workers arrived by bus or boat — no individual vehicles were allowed.

One of the first contracts awarded was for the construction of a network of transportation facilities. In a bold move, the MWRA actually purchased an abandoned shipyard in Quincy (5 miles across the harbor) to facilitate the substantial and complex logistical maneuvers, dedicating a portion for the massive staging and transport operations and the remainder of the site for sludge processing facilities. Piers were constructed at the staging area in Quincy and on Deer Island to handle the barge loads of construction equipment, flatbeds, trailers, and service vehicles. Likewise, piers were built in Squantum to facilitate the transport of construction workers to and from the site. A fuel depot and concrete batch plant were also set up on Deer Island to preclude the congestion that might be caused by each contractor providing these essential services.

These transportation mitigation measures did not come cheaply. MWRA's commitment to transport workers and equipment to the site by ferry, bus, and barge added approximately $250 million to the cost of the project. Included in this figure was the $50 million purchase of the Fore River Shipyard in Quincy for the barge transportation site. The benefits of minimizing neighborhood impacts and facilitating complex and concurrent activities on a remote site far outweighed this capital outlay.

The transport of workers by bus and ferry also extended the commute time to the job site. To compensate for this, workers received a daily travel allowance equal to one hour of pay, as the travel time to Deer Island was 30 minutes each way. This standard travel

allowance was incorporated into the project labor agreement, ensuring a uniform allowance for all workers, rather than abiding by the varying travel policies of the individual trade unions, which ranged from no allowance to $10 or $25 per day, to starting the workday from the transportation site (a policy that added both benefits and premium time to the hour of travel). In negotiating the project labor agreement, the MWRA standardized the travel allowance for all workers to one hour's pay per day with no add-on for benefits and travel premium time. According to MWRA's estimates, the cost of the uniform travel allowance approximated the cost of the existing policies in the individual labor agreements.

This unorthodox transportation scheme and remote site posed concerns for another constituency — the construction firms and vendors who would be responsible for meeting the strict deadlines and expectations of safety and quality. The project labor agreement and aggressive outreach to potential constructors and vendors allayed fears regarding water transportation, work rules, and site considerations. This crucial outreach demonstrated the value of extending the mitigation philosophy to the supply chain as well as the neighbors.

Recommended Practices

- Mitigation and planning of megaprojects must be managed as a single effort, with mitigation measures contemplated for the life of the project. Often, mitigation issues are deferred to late in the planning process because they are the most difficult to resolve. Resolution of constituency concerns, such as siting, must be made early in the planning process so that they can be considered and integrated into the scheduling, cost, and logistical deliberations.

- Mitigation measures demand planner creativity. Be willing to consider unorthodox alternatives. Find the opportunities and spend the money to save time and money and satisfy key constituencies.

- The tools of environmental review are useful for directing some mitigation resolution, particularly those relating to air, noise, and water quality impacts. Use established review pathways and methodologies to build understanding and resolution.

Structuring a Public–Private Management Team

Issue

How does a public agency retain and organize the necessary in-house and private-sector resources to execute a megaproject with the effective oversight and controls required when expending public funds?

Discussion

Concerned about the newly formed MWRA's ability to execute such a rigorous schedule and large-scale facilities planning, design, and construction project, Federal District Judge A. David Mazzone, who issued the court order, requested that MWRA "investigate and evaluate construction management approaches for the facilities construction program in order to provide a basis for determining its efficacy and cost for use in the program."

The demanding schedule, physical scale, and complexity of the facilities, logistical challenges, intense public scrutiny, and pressure for cost control dictated the need for an effective management structure capable of taking the project from facilities planning to design, construction, and startup. The MWRA devised a management structure based on a combination of in-house staff and private-sector consultants. This public-private program management approach provided a substantial level of resources temporarily needed by the public agency for a "once in a lifetime" project.

The program management approach relied on three major entities:

An in-house MWRA group dedicated solely to the project, known as the Program Management Division (PMD). In forming this group, the MWRA identified and recruited talent with program management skills from within and outside the agency. The PMD was responsible for the executive direction, management, and coordination of the project, including monitoring the performance of the consultants and contractors. The PMD issued bids, selected consultants, authorized change orders and progress payments, and issued completion certificates. The PMD's role was overall management, seeking the best value for the ratepayer's investments, while the consultant resources provided technical support.

In recruiting the PMD, the MWRA board made the strategic decision that the complexities of the Boston Harbor Project necessitated paying private-sector salaries to recruit qualified and experienced senior staff. To lead the PMD, the MWRA recruited a senior vice-president from one of the nation's leading environmental firms and paid him, as the media enjoyed noting, a salary that exceeded the governor's salary. The top 12 senior managers in PMD brought extensive private-sector experience and were very capable of managing, directing, and negotiating with their senior management counterparts at the numerous consulting and contracting firms involved in the project.

The assignment of the project to a newly recruited management team that was paid higher salaries than most other MWRA staff did lead to some resentment. That resentment diminished as MWRA staff observed that the new management team was committed to constructing quality facilities and doing so at the least cost to the ratepayers, though it was never fully extinguished throughout the life of the project. Still, the competence and dedication of this strong, steady leadership team was a critical success factor for the overall management of the consultants and the project.

A private-sector team serving as the construction manager (CM). The day-to-day program management responsibilities resided with the CM, with oversight and direction from the PMD. Scheduling, cost estimating, cost control, public information, permitting, water transportation, value engineering, equipment prepurchase, facility testing, startup, and training were within its purview. It also provided technical support for MWRA decisions regarding contractor selection, change orders, progress payments, and final acceptance. The CM was created to be the "owner's representative" and had no responsibility in design except for value engineering and constructability reviews. This allowed it to provide resident engineering and inspection and oversee startup without a vested interest in the performance of the design, equipment, or construction. The CM was also responsible for an extraordinarily aggressive safety program, which achieved a commendable safety record of total lost-time incidents 40 percent lower than the industry average for heavy construction.

A second consultant team serving as the lead design engineer (LDE). The LDE had primary responsibility for directing the design of the major project components. They developed project-wide design standards, prepared conceptual-level (10–15 percent completion) plans and specifications, prepared final designs for facilities requiring early completion, and directed the work of all the project design engineers preparing detailed designs for the remaining facilities. The MWRA separately contracted with individual design firms to develop the detailed designs of the various project components and provide engineering services during construction. Design of the new facilities was broken down into 30 detailed design packages. Designs were required to adhere to the project-wide design standards, and to use a single, designated computer-aided design and drafting (CADD) system, also provided by the MWRA. These standards and CADD system ensured consistency and quality control while using multiple designers and created the basis of an information system for the ongoing management and maintenance of the completed facilities.

The MWRA's construction management model was distinguished by the following key features:

- *Selection of the CM prior to selection of the LDE.* Selection of the CM began immediately after the core in-house program management team was assembled. Because the CM was charged with day-to-day management of the project, its selection had to precede selection of the design team. The CM was responsible for planning and sequencing construction, which guided the design schedule, and for constructability and operability input in the design.

- *Separate procurement of the CM and LDE.* To ensure that the MWRA was able to procure the most qualified CM and LDE, these firms were selected in independent procurements, rather than considering a teaming of design and construction management firms under a single proposal.

- *LDE had ultimate responsibility for coordinating all design work.* In its design role, the LDE reported directly to the MWRA's Program Management Division.
- *Use of multiple design firms.* The MWRA separately contracted with individual design firms to develop the detailed designs of the project components and to provide engineering services during construction.
- *Value engineering and constructability and operability reviews by CM.* This approach enhanced quality control in the design and applied construction and operations knowledge at key points in the design process.
- *CM management of overall program schedule and budget.* All design consultants and construction contractors submitted their schedule and cost information to the CM for monitoring and analysis.
- *CM served as the "owner's representative."* With the exception of providing independent value engineering and constructability reviews, the CM had no responsibility for design. This allowed the CM to provide resident engineering and inspection and to oversee startup of the new facilities without a vested interest in the performance of the design, equipment, or construction.

Five key goals guided the program management approach and united the team in project execution:

- Meet or beat the court-ordered schedule.
- Begin actual construction as quickly as possible.
- Reduce costs.
- Develop a good business reputation.
- Make the completed project work.

Through a program management approach that integrated the leadership and clearly defined the responsibilities of the PMD, CM, and LDE, all the expertise and performance of the designers, constructors, and vendors was harnessed to successfully meet these goals.

Recommended Practices

- Create a "special unit" — a dedicated in-house management team with a clear, finite, all-consuming mission — to help attract a talented and experienced group with a singular commitment to successful project execution. A clear exit plan for this unit can greatly enhance the public's perception of the mission focus of this team.
- Leverage private-sector resources to deliver the necessary expertise on demand while retaining in-house vision, direction, and control of the program.

- Integrate constructability and operability into the design process through the value engineering efforts of an "independent" construction manager.

- Designate a single entity with the sole responsibility for managing day-to-day activities to achieve adherence to schedule and cost control.

- Create a standard design manual and a project-wide conceptual design, executed on a common program-wide CADD system, to focus the efforts of the design engineers, ensure consistency across many mega-design efforts, and create an information system to guide ongoing facilities management.

Controlling the Mega-Costs

Issue

The cost of a megaproject places a substantial financial burden on the public. Project success and public acceptance are determined, in a large part, by the ability to control costs.

Discussion

The MWRA took a progressive approach to cost control that yielded exceptional results. Overall, the program was delivered on schedule and under budget, an extraordinary feat for such a massive public works project.

Inflation-adjusted cost estimate. The MWRA made the strategic decision to inform the taxpayers of the fully inflated cost of the project. Learning from the experience of other regional megaprojects (such as the Seabrook Station Nuclear Power Plant in New Hampshire) and not bound by federal guidelines restricting estimates to current dollars (such as Boston's Central Artery/Tunnel with the Federal Highway Administration), MWRA factored into the estimate the inflationary increases that could be expected over the life of the 15-year project. To be even more conservative, the MWRA used the inflation rate incurred over the 3-year period prior to the release of the estimate, a period in the mid 1980s when the local economy was booming and construction costs had increased significantly.

The decision to issue a fully inflation-adjusted conservative number versus a base-year cost without inflation is a strategic decision faced by all megaproject owners. Some owners who are anxious to gain the public's acceptance often choose the non-inflated cost because it seems more palatable to their constituency. The trade-off is to gain greater public acceptance in getting the project started, but it often translates into severe public resentment as the costs escalate over time. And, of course, the costs will grow dramatically as the price of megaprojects (given their long duration) at least doubles due to inflation — even if the base costs and scope of the project do not change at all.

41

The MWRA was under a federal court order to undertake the Boston Harbor Project. As such, the project's costs did not determine whether or not it would proceed. Of equal importance, the MWRA placed an enormous value on dealing with the public in a transparent manner. Consequently, the MWRA chose to disclose the fully inflated costs at the outset of the project.

MWRA's strategic choice in issuing the inflation-adjusted number had two consequences—one unpleasant and the other quite positive. Initially, the cost of the project led to a tremendous and constant public outcry that was raised in the media on what seemed to be a daily basis. The positive outcome was that the state legislature, in reaction to the public outcry, provided financial aid to the project (and to other similar Clean Water Act projects in Massachusetts). The state aid plus special federal assistance obtained by the state's congressional delegation meant that 40 percent of the project's costs were paid by the federal and state governments, with the remaining 60 percent paid by the ratepayers. In marked contrast, the initial cost estimates had assumed that ratepayers would pay 90 percent of the costs.

Design management. Construction cost control was facilitated, in part, through the design standardization and oversight provided by the LDE, the application of a program-wide CADD system, and independent value engineering, constructability, and operability reviews. The LDE's standard design manual and project-wide conceptual design facilitated a common understanding among the project design engineers, and they were given a limited period to generate suggested improvements in the conceptual design before the basis for the detailed design was "locked in," to the extent feasible, so that design could be expedited.

Managing to cost targets. One of the initial project goals was to limit design costs to between 5 and 7 percent of total construction costs, a goal that was met with design costs at 5.2 percent of construction. Likewise, the target for engineering services during construction (including review of contractor submittals, shop drawings, and support during check-out and testing) was set at 4 to 6 percent of construction, with these costs coming in at 4 percent. Overall, engineering services on the entire project represented 9.2 percent of construction costs, well within the program target of 9 to 13 percent.

Expedited regulatory review. The ability to obtain permits in a timely manner was critical to maintaining the schedule and controlling costs. The MWRA and the CM assisted the regulatory agencies in expediting permitting reviews by (1) incorporating the permitting schedule into the overall program schedule, (2) consolidating permit applications into logical packages, and (3) coordinating all permitting activities through the CM team. Very early in the project, the MWRA and CM team worked with the regulatory agencies to establish the time requirements for permit processing and incorporated these into the overall program schedule. The CM had single-source accountability for coordinating with the regulatory agencies. Design firms provided the technical support in preparing the permit applications, but the CM provided the overall quality control and consistency in dealing with the regulatory agencies.

Labor agreement. At the outset, a project labor agreement was negotiated with the Building and Construction Trades Council of the Metropolitan District to ensure that labor disputes would not interrupt the project. The CM felt this was critical because delays could jeopardize the ability to meet the schedule and increase the cost of the project. This concept was challenged in district court, but upheld by the U.S. Supreme Court, a decision that also extended the right to negotiate similar agreements to other public agencies across the country. In over a decade of construction, there was not one strike, and all disputes were resolved expeditiously without any work stoppage.

Construction packaging. With the project on a court-ordered schedule and the potential of substantial financial penalties for delays, keeping the project advancing according to schedule was in itself a critical cost control factor. The potential cost of delay was estimated at $2 million per week. To maintain and meet the accelerated schedule, the MWRA could not wait until the entire facility was designed before beginning to advertise for construction.

The mammoth construction effort was divided into discrete, logically sequenced packages to allow work to begin in sequence once designs were completed. This innovative packaging approach also created maximum price competition and provided opportunities for small local firms to bid on project work. The project was subdivided into 133 construction and construction-support packages, ranging in value from $10 million to over $200 million. The CM held regular contractors' forums during the first two years of the project and published a newsletter, *The Hardhat News*, to keep the contracting industry informed and to further encourage local, small-firm participation. The combination of effective packaging, timely bidding, and a regional economic downturn from late 1990 to early 1992 resulted in construction bids that averaged 10.4 percent below the engineers' estimates and yielded savings of $225 million.

Construction contract packaging was also key to sequencing construction to coordinate the logistics of the extensive work. A site utilization plan defined every phase of the construction, and specifications tailored to each contract set out precise dates for starting and completing the work, assigned laydown and storage areas, and described how each construction contract fit with dozens of others taking place concurrently. These detailed logistics facilitated coordination, cost control, and adherence to schedule.

The MWRA also provided an incentive for proposing innovative construction methods and techniques. If a contractor conceived of a more cost-effective construction approach that was approved by the MWRA and its design engineer, the MWRA and the contractor could negotiate a sharing of the associated cost savings.

Effective change order procedures. The CM and MWRA developed effective change order and claims procedures that included checks and balances across three organizations — MWRA's PMD, the CM, and MWRA's procurement department — to safeguard the expenditure of public funds. The procedures required an initial analysis to determine legitimacy and magnitude of the proposed change order and a detailed analysis that included preparation of independent fair-cost estimates and schedule analyses. The initial validity determination involved a recommendation from the CM staff, verification from PMD that it was technically feasible, and an opinion from the procurement department that it was legally valid. The involvement of the MWRA's procurement department was dictated by the executive director at the outset of the Boston Harbor Project. The procurement department was staffed predominantly by attorneys whose focus was to ensure that a proposed change was legal and the associated cost estimate was reasonable and auditable.

All change orders were processed initially by a dedicated CM contract administration staff that was located on-site and interacted regularly with the resident engineers and cost and schedule analysts. Ultimate authority for change order settlement rested with the MWRA. On the average, change orders were settled for 37 percent less than the contractor's proposal.

The MWRA set a target of keeping the cost of change orders and claims on plant construction (excluding the two major tunnel projects) to within 10 percent of the awarded value of construction contracts. The actual change order percentage was approximately 12 percent, exceeding the target primarily due to the large volume of change order activity associated with two problematic construction packages (pump station rehabilitation and on-site thermal/power plant).

Although the multiple checks and balances extended the change order process, the loss of some efficiency was justifiable to provide the integrity and transparency necessary in spending $3.8 billion of public funds.

Independent reviews. The CM's independent review teams helped to control design costs. They conducted value engineering reviews on the conceptual design prepared by the LDE and on the 50-percent design submittals prepared by the detailed design engineers. Constructability and operability reviews were conducted at the 30-, 60-, and 90-percent intervals. These reviews brought valuable insights to the design process and helped preclude potentially expensive construction and start-up problems. The $2 million spent on value engineering produced savings of $200 million, as documented by an independent review of the program. This was an exceptional return on investment.

Quality assurance/quality control (QA/QC). Although the contractor had the responsibility for quality control, the CM routinely monitored contractor compliance with the contractor's QC program. The CM prepared checklists that defined the requirements of the contractor's QC program, developed a list of critical equipment for which the contractor was required to provide off-site inspection, conducted QC audits, tracked audit findings and responses, and analyzed audit trends to determine if modifications were needed to improve quality. Out of the CM's 185 quality audits (involving approximately

36,000 individual observations), fewer than 9 percent of the audits identified unsatisfactory work or materials that required contractor correction. By minimizing the required amount of rework while ensuring quality construction according to design specifications, the CM's QA/QC program proved to be an effective cost management tool.

Planning for construction support services. The CM planned for site-wide construction support services contracts to provide centralized services, such as water transportation for equipment and materials, bus and ferry transport of workers, hazardous waste remediation, security, concrete supply, road maintenance, trash disposal, fuel supply, rodent control, snow removal, and other on-demand needs. Through this extensive preconstruction planning effort, the difficulties of working on an island site were minimized and the transportation and support systems functioned efficiently.

Stabilizing construction support costs. The MWRA negotiated long-term contracts to stabilize costs for several of the key construction support services. As noted previously, a dedicated transportation system was critical for ensuring that equipment, materials, and workers could reliably reach the site with minimum road access to mitigate construction impacts on the neighboring community. To stabilize the cost of the transportation system, three separate contracts (barge, personnel ferry, and bus) were each bid for a 5½-year term. This allowed the MWRA to lock in the cost, except for a fuel escalation clause, for an extended period.

Similarly, the MWRA controlled the cost of concrete for the project. A concrete batch plant on Deer Island became the single source of concrete for the project. Because the supplier was essentially being given a monopoly, bidders were asked to incorporate MWRA-set fixed unit prices for various types of concrete for the duration of construction. Inflationary escalation in the supplier's cost over the project's duration was offset by quarterly escalation payments made directly by the MWRA according to a formula based on the construction cost index provided by *Engineering News Record*.

MWRA also made innovative arrangements for the electric power supply. Standard practice would have required an up-front payment in full from MWRA before construction of any substantial new facilities required solely for service to them. Instead, MWRA negotiated an agreement with the local utility to supply power to Deer Island by financing, through a new subsidiary, the construction of a submarine transmission cable from the mainland to substation facilities on Deer Island. This arrangement provided savings to the authority because it avoided the substantial tax liability that an up-front payment in full would have created for the utility. Under Massachusetts Department of Public Utility regulations, the utility would have required MWRA to reimburse it for this liability. The contract provided a guaranteed cost ceiling for the submarine cable, thereby avoiding the risk of construction cost increases, and spread payment over a 25-year period. Finally, the contract secured power for the MWRA at very favorable rates compared to those charged to other large customers.

Recommended Practices

- Plan and provide design standards that facilitate a common understanding and "language" across the program and among all design engineers. These include a design manual, a common CADD platform, and a time-limited process for establishing the detailed basis of design.

- Centralize support services and stabilize their costs through long-term contracts with pre-set, built-in escalation or inflation formulas. Consider innovative financing approaches for large-scale services that require significant capital improvements, such as power.

- Recognize the influence of timely permit approvals on the critical path. To expedite the process, consolidate permit applications into logical packages and provide a single-source authority for coordinating regulatory reviews.

- Divide construction into logically sequenced construction packages that will allow work to begin in progression once designs are completed. This innovative packaging approach can also stimulate price competition and provide opportunities for small local firms to bid on project work.

- Negotiate a project labor agreement that will provide a standard approach across all labor unions (applicable primarily to traditional union sites).

- Leverage the CM to provide independent reviews for value engineering, constructability, and operability, and to monitor compliance with health and safety plans and QA/QC plans.

- Set program-wide targets (e.g., design costs, change orders, safety performance), monitor performance to target, and institute corrective actions when necessary to stay within the expected "performance zone."

Risk Management

Issue

By virtue of their size and complexity, megaprojects carry mega-risks. How do you manage worker safety with multiple concurrent construction contracts, in limited space on an island site, to which workers are ferried each day? What steps can you take to facilitate accountability and contract performance of the consultants and contractors? How do you minimize the unforeseen conditions that can cause delays and escalate costs?

Discussion

Consider the conditions of the Boston Harbor Project: a newly created public agency as owner, working as a program management partner with a private-sector construction manager and a lead design engineer, executing a massive project with 32 design engineers, 133 contractors, vigorous labor representation, immovable deadlines, and high-risk construction (tunneling and maritime operations). These conditions demanded early and thoughtful attention to define a risk management strategy that pushed the limits of traditional public-sector risk management. The risk management strategy for the BHP provided the foundation for an aggressive approach to health and safety, competitive pricing, risk sharing among public and private parties, and well-defined contract documents.

Inventory the risks. The risk management approach began with the acknowledgement that traditional philosophy was not acceptable. MWRA retained a firm specializing in risk inventory, quantification, and management. They were able to document a risk register supported by credible actuarial databases. The inventory identified the most significant risks (marine transport operations, tunneling), as well as more modest risks that could have significant schedule impacts, such as commissioning on a site where many adjacent contractors could significantly affect startup.

This risk inventory:

- Provided a foundation for assessing owner-furnished wrap-up insurance (limited to builders' risk);
- Quickly identified levels and types of contractor-furnished insurance;
- Demonstrated the need for an aggressive approach to worker safety, including a rigorous substance-abuse testing program; and
- Identified a clear, single-source responsibility on the very congested and active site.

The inventory had to provide a clear understanding of the risks that had to be recognized and managed within the first 12 to 18 months because the designer scopes, construction documents, owner-furnished insurance, drug and alcohol programs, and safety responsibility all had to be defined in program contract documents prior to design completion and the finalization of the very first contract documents.

Risk management plan. With the understanding provided by the risk inventory, the MWRA was able to devise a risk management plan that guided all work on the project. Early decisions on insurance were possible with external advisors because the basis for coverage and costs were quickly known. The CM was given extraordinary authority over all contractors, including the authority to issue "stop work" orders, direct substance-abuse testing, and manage labor relations. This single point of authority promoted greater clarity on risk management and work-site safety. The CM was reimbursed for special insurance to cover these extraordinary duties, and their contract included incentive and penalty clauses for worker safety.

While the individual contractors had the primary responsibility to establish, implement, and actively maintain effective safety programs, the CM developed a project-wide safety program with which all individual project-specific safety programs had to comply. This project-wide program included a safety orientation for all new workers, follow-up instruction during the first 6 months to promote safety consciousness, and regular safety inspections by the CM. Every construction contract required the contractor to develop and implement a project-specific safety plan, which the CM reviewed to ensure consistency with the contract requirements, and to have a full-time safety officer on-site. The CM also monitored contractor compliance with these plans.

The CM also negotiated a comprehensive substance-abuse agreement with the Building and Construction Trades Council of the Metropolitan District, representing more than 15 international and 25 local unions. The agreement required that all new hires pass a pre-employment drug test and stipulated that a substance-abuse test would be administered upon reasonable suspicion that a worker may have been under the influence on the job or after any accidents on a project. Throughout the history of the program, fewer than 5 percent of those tested failed a substance-abuse test. Through a well-defined health and safety plan and diligent oversight of the CM, the project posted safety results that surpassed industry norms.

Also as part of the risk management plan, risks that the engineering and construction contractors traditionally did not manage (maritime operations, hazardous waste holding, concrete batch plant) were transferred to pre-placed specialty contractors to ensure safety, protect change order negotiations, and avoid schedule delays. The daily bus and ferry transport of workers, as well as the barging of equipment and materials, posed risks not usually encountered on a facilities project.

Often, public owners will attempt to require construction contractors to bear risks associated with variation in subsurface conditions, resulting in the contractors including substantial contingency funds in their bid prices. From the outset, the tunneling projects were recognized as higher-risk projects because of the demanding environment and unpredictable subsurface conditions. An aggressive risk-sharing philosophy and greater risk allocations were executed for these projects. The MWRA invested $20 million to conduct extensive geotechnical investigations along the prospective tunnel routes—making the core and boring data available to all prospective bidders on the tunnel projects—and adopted risk-sharing practices recommended by the Underground Technology Research Council. Although significant change orders were encountered on these projects due to unforeseen conditions, these cost increases did not increase the total program budget.

Audit performance. The risk management plan and performance were audited annually by the same independent firm that had prepared the initial risk register. The audits were required to be thorough and produce actionable results for corrective measures. In the initial 1 to 2 years, the audits were severe and challenging, and these drove the management team to place special focus on areas that might otherwise have been given lower priority. Any changes made in the risk transfer philosophy were communicated clearly and frequently to the bidder community to maintain bidder understanding and comfort.

Recommended Practices

- Conduct an early and thorough identification of risks to best inform a comprehensive risk management philosophy and plan. Use an independent, credible specialty firm to prepare the risk register and to audit performance annually.

- Clearly communicate the risk philosophy and expectations to bidders.

- Transfer some risk components to specialty contractors to ensure a consistent approach and control across all contracts.

- Provide clear direction, expectations, and responsibility for safety to all contractors. Monitor their performance and maintain the authority to stop work for any unsafe conditions.

Conclusion

The Boston Harbor Project was a success that delivered major and sustained benefits for the public, environment, marine resources, and waterfront economic development. As a well-managed megaproject, it demonstrated approaches that can be applied to help public agencies complete complex public works projects on time and on budget, with the participation and trust of the public.

CHAPTER 4

Design Management

Peter Dewes, P.E., STV Inc.
Donald Phillips, P.E., Arup

Introduction

What is a megaproject?

First, *mega*. What is "mega"? In the context of the design and construction industry this term is usually applied to a project that is complex, that takes many years to develop and construct, operates for many years, and costs billions of dollars.

Second, *project*. What is a "project"? When one looks at, say, a railway line, one sees trains, stations, tunnels, bridges, embankments, cuttings, yards, shops, many staff operating and maintaining the system, tracks, signaling and control systems, electrical systems, communications systems, access paths and roads, parking facilities, bus stops, taxi drop-offs, and, last but not least, passengers or freight. If any element of the line is missing, then the railway may not work! If it is made too small, it may be illegal. If it cannot cope with passenger increases over a period of 50 years, then it may become unsafe. It should probably be functional for more than 100 years, and some projects are even older than that. A megaproject is all of these very visible things and the various tools and techniques required to plan, design, construct, operate, and maintain them.

Who participates in a megaproject?

First, the owner, who owns, usually operates, and maintains the project; second, the stakeholders, who are the various neighbors living near the project or others who can be influenced by it; third, the designers, who plan and design the project; fourth, the contractors, who construct the project; fifth, the operator and maintainer, who performs the daily operations and maintenance of the project; and finally, the customers, who use the project or obtain a service from it. Each of these participants eventually becomes involved in the design of the project. For a megaproject, that number can reach into the hundreds of thousands! Who are they? Consider a subway in Manhattan running along the East Side from Harlem to Wall Street. It will affect most of the inhabitants of Manhattan, the rest of New York City, many people in the state of New York, and, if funding and material procurement is considered, many inhabitants of the United States.

The Millau Viaduct, at left, crosses the Tarn River Valley near the town of Millau in south central France. Designed by Norman Foster and Partners and built by the Compagnie Eiffage consortium (Eiffage, Eiffel, and Enerpac), the bridge is 8,000 feet long, has 7 pylons, and is 886 feet above the ground at its highest clearance. It was opened to the public in December 2004. Photo 2006 by Vincent.

51

Design is a fundamental part of all megaprojects. Design takes the initial idea or concept of a megaproject and, through many iterative steps, delivers drawings, specifications, and construction sequences that individually shape the result. Design turns ideas into reality. Design is a key communicator of the project's intent and as such must interact carefully with all the project participants and work with the existing infrastructure that will contain the project. Approval and acceptance of the project by the various stakeholders is also achieved by the owners and designers through the design process.

Design is not a simple mechanistic process. Rather, it is iterative and holistic, and, to achieve good results, it must incorporate all the requirements of the project and work with all of the various teams in the process. Ove Arup once noted, "Engineering problems are under-defined; there are many solutions, good, bad and indifferent. The art is to arrive at a good solution. This is a creative activity, involving imagination, intuition and deliberate choice."

We have but one chance to complete the design of a megaproject. Then it is with us for all of our lives and our children's — sometimes longer — be it "good, bad or indifferent." Whatever we do will be our legacy. As Winston Churchill said, "We shape our buildings; thereafter, they shape us."

This chapter will take the reader through the design process for a megaproject.

Design Phases

The design for a megaproject should proceed in an iterative manner to allow sufficient information to be made available sequentially, to obtain key approvals and funding, and to accomplish other key objectives. It is not possible to complete the design in one single phase, as a number of associated tasks must be accomplished to give certainty to the project. Each design phase has a key objective, and as time passes and the project becomes more clearly understood, it can be defined more accurately. Typically, the phases of a megaproject are:

- Feasibility study
- Project definition
- Environmental impact statement
- Preliminary design
- Final design
- Contract document preparation
- Construction and commissioning
- As-built/operation and maintenance manuals
- Operation and maintenance of the megaproject

As with any process, risks and opportunities exist at each phase until the project is com-

plete and successfully operational. As the project advances, it is critical that these risks and opportunities be recorded and then sequentially and proactively managed and mitigated.

The project's design will continue to advance and develop throughout each phase, which will call for appropriate contingencies for cost, time, investigations, and the need to reassess and amend the design. Project functionality may also vary during the design process as the actual cost and implications of certain project aspects become better defined.

Design and engineering are not exact sciences, so that a good deal of understanding and some latitude in application is necessary to achieve an acceptable outcome. Addressing the British Institution of Structural Engineers in 1976, A. R. Dykes observed, "Engineering is the art of modeling materials we do not wholly understand, into shapes we cannot precisely analyze, so as to withstand forces we cannot properly assess, in such a way that the public has no reason to suspect the extent of our ignorance."

Feasibility Study

This phase establishes the technical feasibility of a project, defines the likely cost and time scales, and gives a reasonable indication of the project's form, alignment, and key elements, which allow its interaction with the adjacent land and usage to be comprehended. It is possible that at the end of this phase, several solutions to the project may exist, so that additional phases might be needed to narrow the options under consideration.

At the end of this phase, the feasibility of the project should be determined, with costs and time ranges calculated and accepted as reasonable.

Project Definition

Megaprojects are so complex that the mere definition of one may take several inches of paper to properly summarize. During this phase, the project will be described in sufficient detail to allow the operational performance of the project to be defined, understood, and approved. This is also the phase when the owner will be able to determine whether the project will render the requisite performance for the investment required to construct the megaproject. (That is, will the performance, income, and other benefits from the project exceed its costs?)

Project definition and design should proceed in parallel in order to describe the project properly. Before the final design commences, the project should be defined in terms of:

- Project objectives
- Service requirements
- Functional requirements

- Fire safety strategies
- Previously approved design report
- Environmental impact statement and stakeholder requirements
- Land requirements
- Impacts upon existing infrastructure and solutions that allow the project to be implemented
- Property development interface reports
- Project schedule
- Project cost estimate and finance plan
- Design criteria, including national and local codes and standards
- Standard spatial requirements
- Standard specifications
- Standard details
- Standard schedules
- Guidance notes
- Drawing and CADD manual
- General system assurance requirements

The owner's specific requirements for the operations, maintainability, system safety, reliability, and testing and commissioning should be included in the various project definition documents. Similarly, stakeholders' requirements that will impact the project should also be included.

The project definition phase may become part of the feasibility phase or the EIS phase, which comes later. But because it is so important, it is noted here separately to emphasize the function of this phase.

Environmental Impact Statement (EIS)

In the United States, projects seeking federal government funding are usually required to complete an environmental impact statement (EIS). In many other parts of the world similar assessment processes are required to obtain governmental approval and support for megaprojects

Typically, the EIS is divided into "Draft" and "Final" subsections and creates a project definition that conforms to federal, state, and city government planning processes. The larger the scope of the project, the larger the planning process becomes and the more extensive the interaction with stakeholders, which increases the detailed investigation into the project. By the nature of the EIS process, many good ideas surface to form alternative options, which can relate to potentially all aspects of the project. Although these alternate ideas will not be designed in detail, they will be studied sufficiently to assess

them. They can cover the range of environmental topics, such as impacts to wetlands, flood plains, surface water, benthos, noise, air quality, traffic disruption, utility demand, habitat, etc. The EIS process also examines the contamination of the impact corridor, the impact on the contaminated sites by the project, and the impact on the project by the contaminated sites. The alternates are evaluated for their ability to achieve the project's objectives and for their cost and time requirements.

Each alternate is evaluated against a set of criteria and ranked from the best to the least attractive. The best alternate is usually taken forward to the next phase for further development.

Since the process is ongoing and many stakeholders have input into it, the project definition will be continuously revised throughout the EIS phase and modified to negate or mitigate the impacts determined to be of concern. This has been the typical routine through many different projects of the "mega" class. For highway and railway projects, defining each alternate usually takes the form of an alignment change, though these changes often include many other subtle and distinct differences that may significantly impact each alternate's cost, time, and functional performance. Such changes occur for many reasons, from improvements to the roadbed alignment and increased speed, to reduced curvature and a more comfortable ride or a reduction in land acquisition, lessened impact upon adjacent structures, lowered cost, and shortened time to complete the project.

Preliminary Design (PD)

The preliminary design (PD) phase is the first phase of designing the project, as defined in the original concept. By the completion of the EIS phase, many risks and opportunities will have been identified that will need to be reviewed and assessed. Also at this time, when the preferred modifications are chosen, it will be necessary to commence site investigations and surveys to define or confirm the various assumptions that may have been made in the earlier project phases.

Based on various site and other data, the PD will usually include peer reviews, value engineering recommendations, or constructability reviews of the schemes to minimize the risks and maximize the opportunities previously identified.

As the EIS process comes to a close, the preliminary design phase begins. The start of the PD phase and the end of the EIS phase usually overlap. For the project, this is good, but for those performing either the EIS or preliminary design, it is a mixed blessing. Why? The EIS team members have usually been working on the project for many months — in some cases, years — developing what they believe is the perfect project. They have identified and assessed, and then tweaked, all the possibilities and, through a long and arduous process, they have finally produced a project definition that meets all criteria and is agreeable to the myriad of stakeholders. And now . . . a new group of

designers is invited to join them. At this point in its life, the project trades planners for engineers. (There will be one more hand-off with the same trepidation, when the project exchanges engineers for construction teams.)

The engineers are usually obliged, as their first task during the PD phase, to verify the existing design and the cost estimate. This is a moment when the direction of the project can be changed. The first step is to develop the project definition documents. These criteria increase exponentially from EIS to PD to FD (final design) phases of the project as more detailed design assessments are able to be undertaken. Whatever happened to the EIS design criteria? Most of the time, these criteria become the higher-level criteria, service requirements, and functional requirements. In the PD phase, more detailed criteria are developed, which more precisely define the project and result in greater certainty in the design. PD phase criteria and designs may not continue into the FD. And if the EIS phase used the details of the PD phase, the EIS process would never be completed and the costs of the EIS phase could grow beyond reason.

At first, the PD task of verifying the design and cost may seem to ignore the environmental requirements, with alignments being examined in detail, additional site investigations being undertaken to define topographic conditions and restraints, and subsequently designs and costs being re-examined using the new data. The consequences, for example, could result in a roadway alignment that might change the route of the project to a slightly different zone, which would affect slightly different properties with slightly different environmental impacts. The rock elevation may be found in the PD phase to be lower than in the EIS phase, so tunnels would be moved deeper and surface projects would require deeper foundations. And then, through the constructability review process, additional cost impacts might be uncovered, which then require value engineering and revisions to the design to bring costs back in line with the project budgets.

By the end of the PD process, the project would have changed and a revised project definition would have been created. Because the EIS and PD processes are developed concurrently, the EIS would then adopt the new project definition. Impacts would be weighed against it and refined criteria developed during the public process. On occasion, the EIS team might be able to accept the revised project definition, but generally, only some of the proposals will be accepted, so another project definition would be developed.

At this point in the project timeline, three or four project definitions will have been established, not counting the alternatives that never saw the light of day. And we are not finished with the potential for yet more revised definitions. Each time an amended project definition is accepted, it is published in a public document so stakeholders can be aware of it and consider its impact upon their facility or structure. In our experience on three other megaprojects, no two went through the same process and changes.

Final Design (FD)

The final design (FD) phase continues to develop the PD scheme so that the construction documentation can be prepared and the cost estimates carefully and critically reviewed and finalized, together with detailed construction schedules and contract procurement packaging. During this phase, further site investigation and advanced utility investigations will be undertaken, if required.

Of course, the PD scheme will require more changes to incorporate all the requirements of the EIS and project definition and to satisfy the new and likely changed data submitted from the various detailed investigations.

Further, as the design is developed and finalized, it may be determined that some areas of the project require further amendment, which will have an impact on the scheme, its cost, and potentially its functionality.

All aspects of the PD scheme may change, and the owner needs to be informed of required changes. The means of procuring the contract (i.e., in terms of contracting strategies, contract packages, and size and scope of each contract) should be decided upon with sufficient lead time to prepare proper documents and to avoid any incorrect definition of the various contract packages, particularly the critical interfaces between these contracts.

Under the design-bid-build means of procurement, the owner engages a designer to complete the design, and once that is done, the owner seeks bids from contractors who then construct the works. Under this procurement approach some elements of the design are completed by the contractor, such as reinforcement details, steelwork connections details, and temporary works. There are other means of design and construction procurement, such as design-build, design-build-operate, and design-build operate-finance. Each of these procurement types subtly adjusts the requirements of the design, design phasing, and schedule.

Contract Document Preparation

To prepare the contract documents, details of the contract size, type, work sites, construction means, electrical power requirements for construction, road and railway diversions, utility diversions, and structure repairs and removal must be specified to accurately define the construction works. As these details become known, the design may need to change. Adequate time and flexibility will be required to complete the work.

Construction

Not all projects require the design to be complete before construction contracts are let, but if this approach is followed, then the FD documents must include adequate in-

formation to obtain competent bids and, of course, include adequate contingencies to allow some design development to occur.

The contractor's means and methods and temporary works themselves will often require significant further design, and in some cases they will impact the permanent works, thus necessitating adjustments to the project's otherwise complete final designs.

Projects that include vehicle procurement and other complex equipment may require sophisticated testing and commissioning to provide systems that achieve the required levels of performance, safety, reliability, and maintainability. If a system safety assurance scheme is required, this will call for significant efforts to develop the appropriate framework, contract obligations, and collation of the specified documentation.

As-Built Drawings, Operation Documents, and Maintenance Manuals

As the construction proceeds, as-built drawings need to be produced which either confirm that the works have been constructed in accordance with the original design documents or show where deviations from them have occurred. The designer will then need to assess these deviations and confirm or make changes to the design.

All the operation and maintenance manuals are produced at this time, using technical data from the actual equipment that is used in the works.

Design Process

Approvals

The approval process for a megaproject is long and one that continuously impacts the design. Achieving project approval requires the concurrence of many stakeholders, professionals, and the general public, the people who will use the project when it is finally completed and operating. The design professionals may believe they have the right answer, but that depends on whether the project is used once it is operating. For all the great ideas and design that created it, a megaproject (*mega* not only because of the costs, but also because of the size of the population touched by the project) must be *used* by the mega-population, which accounts for the large number of parties involved in the approval process. The project's design is guided by these parties outside the design professionals.

Generally, for rail transit projects in the United States, the Federal Transit Administration (FTA) approval process remains open during the preliminary design phase. As the PD advances, modifications continue to be made to the design, which in turn require modifications to be made part of the FTA approval process. The project schedule may be shortened by the concurrent advancement of both the FTA approval process and PD, which will cause the coordination between the two phases of project development to be increased.

After the FTA approval process, the more arduous process of federal, state, and local permits begins. A significant proportion of megaproject approvals involves environmental and code compliance. The environmental approval process involves the U.S. Environmental Protection Agency, the Army Corps of Engineers, and state environmental departments, agencies, and commissions, which have jurisdiction over construction within regulated environs. In the New York metropolitan area, for example, megaprojects can be located in flood plains, wetlands, riparian lands, tidal areas, or brownfield sites, all of which require permits and public review processes before approvals can be secured.

In addition to the environmental approvals, building code compliance is also required. Although some of the agencies sponsoring megaprojects are self-certifying, not all are, and approvals from the "authority having jurisdiction" (AHJ) is required. Depending on the type of construction (e.g., stations, tunnels, underground occupied space, high-rise development, foundations, and utility services), the code review process is varied and can be extensive. Since the code review process comes at the end of design, coordination with the AHJ during the development of the megaproject is recommended. Although early coordination can prove beneficial to the approval process and ultimately the schedule, many owner agencies are reluctant to schedule early coordination meetings with the AHJ because it gives the AHJ too many opportunities to impact the design, which usually has an effect on the budget or schedule. However, last-minute requirements by the AHJ can have a greater impact on the schedule due to redesigns. Redesigns at the end of the process are not usually met with the same enthusiasm as during the design development phase because the changes must be made quickly, without the luxury of time for integration due to the impending need to bid the construction packages.

A well-planned schedule, with contingencies for the agency approval process and schedule impacts, can reduce delays caused by an extended approval process or design modifications to comply with the approving agency's requirements.

Stakeholders

Stakeholders are people having a vested interest in the outcome of the project. They may not be professionals in the design field, but they can be users of the project. The quip, "I may not know what art is, but I know what I like," applies to the design and development of megaprojects. Through public meetings, comments, and hearings, the designers learn what the public want. On transportation projects, where the people want to go and how they want to get there is all-important. Although the public are usually quite visibly involved in the EIS phase of the project — with its many informational presentations and websites describing current details about the developments — their reactions are measured throughout the entire design life. This almost inevitably leads to more opportunities to change or expand the project definition.

Environmental Groups

Public input is required before the approvals can be issued, especially when they involve the EPA, the Army Corps of Engineers, and state environmental departments and commissions. This includes written and oral comments presented or submitted during the process. Environmental groups — with either a national or local membership — are usually in attendance at these public meetings. Their positions on the megaproject, whether negative or positive, can have an impact on the project definition, for example, requests to provide amenities such as river walks, recreational facilities, intersection traffic improvements, roadway improvements, or utility improvements. Such requests often occur late in the development phase of the project when budgets and schedules are at their limits and the ability to modify the project definition is limited.

Land Acquisition

The acquisition of property for the project is a major component of the project definition, impacts design solutions, and may constrain possible construction techniques. Because the cost of property, the political nature of property acquisition, and the process to acquire property all have major impacts on megaprojects, at some point during the design process property acquisition must be reduced or ended. If the owners have been unable to obtain a certain parcel of land, the project definition must be revised either by repositioning alignments or facilities, reducing facility sizes, or erecting walls to limit construction.

Owner

From the start of the preliminary design to the start of construction, the definition of the project will be revised many times. One party who contributes to that change is the owner. The owner is typically not an individual but a large organization, with many separate departments, with objectives that initially may not be aligned, but as the project evolves apparent differences may be negotiated toward a single integrated solution, so that changes to the project may well be necessary. For example, operating departments may develop standards and requirements, some of which may not have been considered in the EIS phase. The project definition often includes expanding the infrastructure to accommodate redundancy or for ease of maintenance. Requests for an increase in the number of substations for electric railroads are frequent project definition revision. Train storage yards often need more utility service points, working power outlets, wider paved aisleways between storage tracks, and weather-protected work areas.

Revisions to the project definition add to the costs, increase the design effort, and extend the design or construction schedule, all of which result in a more costly project due to the increased cost of money.

Regulatory Agencies

Decisions by regulatory agencies during the permitting process often have the effect of revising the project definition. Although the project will already have been defined in the EIS phase, mitigation requirements that arise later during the design process when permit applications are filed will be more specific and will probably expand. For example, mitigation requirements for filling wetlands may increase during the approval process, or expected contributions to wetland banks may become more costly, thus requiring a larger share of the project budget. Whatever the results, the imposed permit conditions become a revision to the project definition.

Collectively, all of these entities contribute to revisions to the project definition, usually at an increase to the project cost and schedule. To maintain the base project is almost impossible in the present day. During the preliminary design phase, the project definition must be reviewed on a regular basis with current budgets to identify potential project deletions. Components may have to be reduced or eliminated—trading substations for storage tracks or station amenities may be necessary to maintain the budget.

Designer's Tools

Configuration Management Plan (CMP)

The configuration management plan (CMP) is a process through which the designers are able to define, control, and proactively manage the scope and cost of a project. As stated before, the period spanning the EIS phase and preliminary design is an opportune time for scope growth. Likewise, towards the end of preliminary design and the early stages of final design is another opportunity for scope growth. Sometimes the designer proposes ideas to improve project performance, and sometimes the owner wants to improve the project with various modifications during the design phases. If designers and owners do not resist these temptations, the megaproject will increase in scope and cost and additional time will be required to complete the project. To control such scope growth, an explicit procedure to examine the proposed changes and related costs by a group of persons with controlling budget authority and outside the detailed design process is needed. Although this evaluation procedure would be subject to political forces, at least there would be an opportunity to make a conscious decision about proposed changes and to document the process.

The CMP method has been used to varying degrees on many megaprojects. From the

61

least-involved process, with just documenting the decision-making process and the decisions by the owner and the design team, to formal meetings and detailed analysis by senior management, with presentations by the proposers that fully describe the proposals, CPM has proved itself capable of controlling megaproject budgets. The authors have also seen examples of successful control of change, for example, when an integrated project control group made up of senior members of the owner's key departments and designers worked together to comprehend each proposed change and its impact upon the function, cost, and time to complete the project, then agreed to changes only after careful consideration and evaluation.

Work Breakdown Structure

The work breakdown structure (WBS) is the work task that can be assigned a budget and a duration of time that can then be placed into the design CMP schedule. The compilation of the WBS elements of the project becomes the project schedule. The more WBS items that can be developed, the better the schedule and budget can be tracked. But the more WBS elements that are developed, the more manpower it takes to track the budget and schedule. A balance will need to be struck between the number of WBS elements and number of staff to track them, depending on the complexity of the project. For megaprojects, the number of WBS elements can be in the thousands. A team of project control personnel is usually required to manage the schedule and budgets. The key is to be able to use "roll-up" WBS tasks so that they can be easily measured, seen, and appreciated by many project team members, thus easing the identification of changing trends.

The upkeep of the WBS elements falls to the discipline managers, as they are responsible for the schedule and budget. The managers should also develop the WBS elements for the project because the execution of the work plan, including any interruptions, is critical to meeting the scope requirements.

The details of the scope of work usually have sufficient latitude to allow the discipline managers freedom to develop WBS elements based on their own experience. However, all the managers involved in the project will have input to the WBS. The managers' contributions to the WBS depend on what is important to them to be tracked in the schedule and budget. Some may want the WBS elements to be of short durations so their progress is reported more often. Others may prefer to have WBS elements set by the scope activities, regardless of duration. Elements designated as "Begin Survey" or "Continue Survey" have no meaning and lack any capability to be tracked. A WBS survey by areas of the project will be more beneficial to tracking schedule and completeness, but usually it is too detailed, creating too many elements to track or be subject to revisions, which in turn cause the survey requirements to be adjusted. Striking a balance between the number of WBS elements and the project's needs is the true test of project management.

Status Reports

Monthly or weekly status reports are a way to manage the progress of the design. They have been used to different degrees on different megaprojects. Monthly status reports have been used in conjunction with monthly status meetings. Typically, they describe the work started, currently underway, and completed during the month. For each task, the report estimates the percentage completed, which can be compared to its proportion in the final budget. The overall cost incurred during the period covered by the report would be presented in another section, which would list the amount spent for the reporting period and calculate it as a percentage of the budget expended.

A status report would also include the date of project submissions and review periods. It helps keep the design schedule in the forefront of the participants' consciousness and gives everyone current information to discuss at the status meetings.

The report may also contain a log of all the decisions made during the preceding month and the documents where those decisions were recorded (which are usually minutes of meetings, telephone conversation memorandums, and letters or e-mails). The decisions are logged by discipline and numbered and dated for easy sorting in a database.

Recording project details keeps them fresh in people's memories and tends to keep the design on budget and on schedule.

Design Costs Reports

Besides describing the size or magnitude of these projects, the word *mega* also describes their costs. With multibillion dollar budgets, a change of even a fraction of a percentage point represents many millions of dollars. Containing the costs of megaprojects is a full-time job.

Designers must be vigilant in reining in "scope creep," as there always seem to be bigger and better improvements to the design during its development. Attitudes range from "What's a few million in the scope of the project cost?" to "Additional spare conduits are required for future expansion of the system." Two miles of a 4-inch conduit may not seem like much until all the junction boxes and project multipliers are included, and then it adds up to millions of dollars. The cost escalation becomes far more dramatic if each discipline and each designer add "small" amounts to the project hard costs — but the resulting total would not become apparent until the final roll-up of the project cost.

How then are the project costs controlled in the design phase of the project? A tool that has proved to be useful is a monthly "design cost control report." Such a report has taken different shapes on different projects, but the result is the same. The report divides the design costs into the work breakdown structure (WBS) for each design aspect, contract, discipline, or design unit, so that the costs become small enough to be man-

ageable and recognizable. Too many times the big picture creates a false impression that there is ample capacity in the budget to complete the project. In actuality, there are so many parts to the project that if each discipline requires more budget allocation, it gets to the point that the sum of the allocations exceeds the whole budget. With monthly reporting by WBS, the percentage of the budget spent each month can make apparent how large the total budget will need to be. The monthly reporting of budget consumption will require each WBS manager to estimate the percentage complete. (In practice, the estimate of percentage complete should be made before the information on the percentage spent is made available in order to obtain an unbiased analysis.) The WBS method can effectively describe the design budget condition and flag aspects of the project that require more attention or decision-making.

Buildability Workshops

Buildability workshops at specific phases of the project are very important for megaprojects because the larger a project becomes, the more involved the construction becomes. Buildability workshops are usually convened with individuals familiar with the construction aspects of the project. For example, on previous projects, buildability workshops included meetings with individual contractors to discuss such topics as: particular construction requirements to determine whether the best possible field condition is being presented, or how can it be made easier for the contractor; issues of piles versus caissons in underwater sites; and the ability to access each site and dispose of the spoils in an efficient manner that minimizes costs. Responses varied depending on the contractor, their equipment, and their experience with the different types of construction. And some owners are not comfortable with the concept of holding a workshop with contractors who may one day bid for the work.

Conducting workshops with members of the construction management industry will probably result in altogether different responses to the same conditions, and the same can be said if the workshop is comprised of designers. Each group brings its own biases to the workshop. The designer has to collate the information obtained in the workshops and determine the direction to proceed in, because there can be more than one right response.

The goal of the buildability workshops is to *not pick the wrong response*. The design has to be buildable. Each contractor will choose the method that works best for the experience and equipment they bring to the project.

Buildability workshops have proven most beneficial during the preliminary design phase, before the design really progresses, at a point when the results can help develop a foundation for the design decisions before it is too late to redesign. They are also helpful during the final design phase as a way to define the details.

Value Engineering

Value engineering is a useful tool in the design process. Although the design team's impression of the value engineering team may be that they are only charged with reducing the cost of the project, the real goal of value engineering is to achieve the same function of the project at a lower cost. Projects seem to grow in scope the longer the design phase takes, and megaprojects take the longest, so on megaprojects there are more opportunities to grow. Growth is generated by either the owner or the design team. The owner grows the scope of the project when its operating departments think of more items to make the system operate easier, to improve reliability or redundancy, and to provide for future needs. The designer can grow the scope by upgrading finishes and enhancements in public areas to add a degree of elegance to the project.

The value engineering team studies the functions of the project and its components, whether the same function can be accomplished at a lower cost, and what can be eliminated or postponed from the project and still achieve the desired result. By the end of the value engineering process, at least some of their proposals will be accepted and included in the project — causing a redesign.

Design Deliverables

A megaproject will require thousands of documents to define the project and record various facts and data. It is important to specify each of these documents and, where possible, the format, style, and other relevant characteristics. These documents include:

- Drawings
- Construction sequences
- Specifications
- Terms and conditions
- Site investigation data reports
- Geotechnical data reports
- Geotechnical interpretative reports
- Geotechnical baseline reports
- Calculations
- Design reports
- Geographical Information System (GIS) to hold these documents and allow the owner to use them following the completion of the project

It is important that a suitable electronic control and issuing system be used to store and manage the issue data, circulation, and purposes of the project documents. With

such a large quantity of documents, some issued a number of times, there will be many thousands of pages. Managing document storage and retrieval contributes to the overall success of the design effort as well as the construction effort. The ability to recall the design information is important to the final transfer of documents from the designer to the contractor. The designer must inform the contractor of the information discovered and produced during the design phase so the contractor is aware of decisions and becomes as knowledgeable as the designer.

Conclusion

It is beyond question that high-quality, cost-effective design services will contribute to the success and owner's and users' satisfaction with a megaproject. Similarly, and perhaps more importantly, the owner's greatest opportunity to influence the final project costs occurs during the design phase. Accordingly the megaproject owner must insist on rigorous management of the design process and demand accountability by its consultants and by its own oversight staff. Avoiding "surprises" during the design phase and demonstrating to the general public a methodical approach to identifying and dealing with the particular project's challenges and issues will go a long way to bolstering support for the project.

CHAPTER 5

Cost and Schedule Control

John Reilly, John Reilly Associates International, Ltd.
William W. Edgerton, P.E., Jacobs Associates
Chris D. Breeds, P.E., SubTerra
Stephen P. Warhoe, P.E., Independent Consultant

Introduction

Arguably the most important factor in determining whether a complex infrastructure megaproject will receive political approval to move forward is an accurate prediction of its ultimate cost. This occurs because there are usually a number of projects competing for a finite supply of funding, and the primary method for comparing them, using a common measurement scale, is the initial estimate of total project cost.

This chapter will address cost, cost estimating, use of cost estimates, scheduling, and the importance of these capabilities in the planning, design, and construction of megaprojects. It will address project phases, including planning and preliminary design, final design, bidding (tendering), and construction. It will also address recent processes that are expected to improve the quality and completeness of the estimates regarding probable cost and risk.

Megaprojects

Megaprojects Are Different

There are many factors that contribute to cost and schedule growth on megaprojects. Megaprojects are inherently complex, normally involving major work in dense urban environments. Because of their size, complexity, and substantial impacts on the fabric of cities, they involve many stakeholders and take many years to plan, design, and construct. In addition, megaprojects are usually the subject of significant public attention, which can result in special interest groups seeking changes and benefits due to alleged impacts from, and specific needs of, the project.

Because of the long time frame, many changes due to unknowns and new circumstances are possible. These contribute to major uncertainties in scope, schedule, and character early in the project's life, and these uncertainties can cause difficulty in accurately and sufficiently characterizing the project—in scope, complexity, time frame, impacts, and circumstances. These factors contribute to significant difficulty in develop-

View looking south of the new (left towers, with square braces) and old (right, with X-braces) spans of the Chesapeake Bay Bridge near Annapolis, Maryland. When first opened in 1952, the bridge was the longest over-water steel structure and third-longest bridge in the world. The second bridge, built to ease congestion, opened in 1973. Photo © Mike DelGaudio.

67

ing accurate, reliable cost and schedule estimates, especially in the early phases of the megaproject.

Public Expectations

Since megaprojects require a relatively large proportion of public funds and resources and have a very significant effect on local economies, their impact is usually very high profile and thus their successful delivery is critical. When the public looks to the success of megaprojects, there are three elements that they generally focus on — cost, schedule, and whether they perform as planned or promised.

Therefore, early in the planning process it is essential to demonstrate clarity and capability in:

1. Reliably estimating the probable cost and schedule of complex megaprojects;
2. Communicating this clearly to the public and political decision-makers, including the conditions, assumptions, and key issues that could, if they occur, affect the final cost and schedule outcome;
3. Demonstrating that megaprojects can be managed within approved budgets and schedules; and
4. Articulating what such management will require, recognizing that significant uncertainties will need to be anticipated and provided for.

Historical Concerns Regarding Cost and Schedule Performance

Well-publicized failures of some high-profile megaprojects to be delivered at or under budget and on schedule have created problems for agencies in maintaining necessary credibility in order to raise funding for projects through public taxation and other initiatives. The number of high-visibility projects where it appears (to the public) that costs are "running away" or "out of control" is significant, and the cost increases involved have been very large. Several examples demonstrate the extent and seriousness of the problem. These include the Jubilee Line Transit Project in London — two years late and £1.4 billion (67 percent)[1] over budget; the Channel Tunnel — £3.7 billion (80 percent) over budget; Denmark's Great Belt Link — 54 percent over budget; and Boston's Central Artery/Tunnel — many billions over the initially published budget.[2]

Several studies (Reilly, 2001; Flyvbjerg et al., 2002; Salvucci, 2003; Flyvbjerg, 2003) have indicated the seriousness and pervasiveness of the problem. Flyvbjerg paints a poor picture of the reliability of cost estimating on 258 major infrastructure projects spanning 70 years, of which 90 percent were over budget. During this time, the process by which the estimates for these projects were made was not sufficiently capable of correcting the chronic underestimation of the final (outturn) costs of complex infrastructure projects. If it had had this capability, we would expect that there would have been as many results over budget as under budget. Flyvbjerg notes that the problem is not only an inability to estimate accurately, but also a bias to estimate on the optimistic side, plus what he calls "strategic misrepresentation" by public officials.

There is also an indication that there is a lack of consistent, objective, and reliable cost performance data available to understand why such problems have occurred. This means that conclusions that have been drawn regarding the cost performance of, or problems with, megaprojects, while in general seeming reasonable, may be flawed or limited in their application to management of future megaprojects.

Discussion Regarding Cost and Schedule Performance

Early in 2001, the American Underground Construction Association convened a regional conference in Seattle, Washington,[3] that focused on managing the costs of complex underground and infrastructure megaprojects. In this case, the conference was held to assist local governments with planning for anticipated megaprojects in the Puget Sound region, including the Sound Transit Light Rail program, Washington State Department of Transportation highway megaprojects, the King County wastewater program, and the Sea-Tac third runway project.

Boston Central Artery/Tunnel project under construction. View looking northeast. Photo © 2006 by Philip Greenspun.

Examples were presented of several mega- and other projects that had substantially exceeded their initial budgets. The conference did not discuss or address deficiencies in the means and methods typically applied to cost and schedule estimating. Rather, the major cost overruns were, for the most part, attributed to: inadequate strategic planning (e.g., unclear project scoping); an "optimistic bias" on the part of politicians, agencies, engineers, and managers; problems with the expertise and management policies of owners; specifics of procurement (contracting) methods; lack of project management capability; and lack of suitable risk identification, management, and mitigation procedures.

Several approaches to improving cost and schedule estimating methods for megaprojects were also discussed at this conference including methods of quantifying uncertainty and risk and the need to address life-cycle costs in order to make better long-term cost decisions.

The collective opinion of the conference participants was that a sound and professionally prepared engineer's estimate, with a full appraisal of the accompanying risk factors, would be the best way of forecasting, accounting for, and managing project costs. The question of optimistic bias and specific cost-estimating methods was beyond the scope of the conference.

Subsequent Actions Regarding Megaprojects–Risk and Uncertainty

After the Seattle AUCA conference, with the concern that several high-profile programs were experiencing significant cost increase trends,[4] a more detailed examination of possible changes to management, cost estimating, and consideration of risk and uncertainty was raised and considered by owner agencies such as Federal Transit Administration, Federal Highway Administration, and Washington State Department of Transportation. Several of these initiatives are outlined below (FTA 2004, FHWA 2006, WSDOT 2009).

Considerations Regarding Risk and Uncertainty

Risk and uncertainty have a large influence on the ultimate cost and schedule of a project. They are major factors in the ability to reasonably forecast the cost and schedule of complex megaprojects. Two basic approaches have been taken to address this:

1. Removing or dramatically reducing the optimistic bias commonly found in the thinking of project proponents; and
2. Addressing uncertainty[5] and risk[6] through a structured verification and risk identification process.

Obviously, reducing as much as possible the uncertainty associated with cost and schedule estimates is important. It is also important to communicate probable ranges of cost and schedule reasonably and clearly to the public and political decision-makers. By reporting ranges of cost and schedule, results can be presented with an indication of the uncertainty associated with those results, which can help to avoid the perception that, if the results are reported as single (deterministic) numbers, they will seem to be more precise than can be justified in the early developmental stages. This was the method followed by the Washington State Department of Transportation (WSDOT) when they reported initial probable ranges of cost and schedule for several megaprojects in June of 2002, using the newly developed probabilistic Cost Estimate Validation Process (CEVP®) (Reilly et al. 2004).

Addressing Uncertainty

Uncertainty must be sufficiently accounted for at each stage of design, requiring that estimated costs and schedule be adjusted in parallel with design development. Cost estimating tools that incorporate an explicit and quantitative understanding of uncertainty must be used in order for sufficiently informed decisions to be made during design. Additionally, communicating how uncertainty is presented regarding probable outcomes, including cost and schedule estimates, is important.

Risk is a consequence of the uncertainty in outcomes and is quantified by the combination of:

1. The probability of a risk event occurring, and
2. The consequences (either positive or negative) if the event occurs.

By quantifying risk in this way, the high cost or schedule risks can be determined and, from this, explicit risk management and mitigation plans can be developed. These plans mitigate risk by reducing the probability of a risk event occurring and/or minimizing the consequences if it does.

See "Probabilistic Risk-Based Estimating" (below, p. 82), which describes WSDOT's Cost Estimate Validation Process. In general, the CEVP® approach is to:

1. Validate the base cost and schedule of the project (base cost is defined as the result or outcome that would occur "if all goes as planned");
2. Characterize and quantify risks that lead to increases in cost and schedule;
3. Produce a "range of probable cost and schedule" from the combination of base cost and risk, using a Monte Carlo simulation or other range-based approach; and
4. Develop risk mitigation plans to manage risk and enhance opportunity.

The results are presented as "ranges of probable cost and schedule," not as a single (deterministic) number.

Optimistic Bias Is Common for Complex Megaprojects

Bent Flyvbjerg believes that it is fundamentally impossible to remove the generally optimistic bias of the project team, including the owner, designer, and proponents, and, therefore, some external method is necessary to sufficiently remove bias (Flyvbjerg, 2002, 2003, 2004, 2007, 2009). As a result, he advocates using historical, statistically valid data to apply an "uplift factor" to the initial cost estimates (see Flyvbjerg & COWI 2004 and the "Reference-Class Estimating" section below, p. 84). The reference-class estimating process quantifies the uplift factor depending on the type of project, stage of development, and historical underestimation for that type of project at that stage of development.

It is clear that the "optimistic bias," normally apparent in the early stages of a mega-project, must be accounted for in order to make a reasonable cost estimate.

Methods to Address Bias

The CEVP® approach, range estimating, and reference class estimating using uplift factors, includes methods of dealing with uncertainty and bias. For a successful analysis using these approaches, one should

1. Adequately address the level of contingency,[7] which is a part of every estimate;
2. Be explicit about the estimator's policy regarding quantification of contingency; and
3. Be explicit about the estimator's policy regarding treatment of "optimistic bias."

Flyvbjerg's critique of the CEVP® process is that it is impossible to completely remove human bias and that an external reference class of projects must be used to adjust cost estimates by use of uplift factors.

Cost Management

For most projects, management of cost is generally the most important success factor for the owner. For megaprojects, where the financial stakes and scope complexity are very high, it is important that the owner's team have an established cost management system (not just accounting) in place and the skilled and experienced staff to run it.

Managing project costs must begin in the earliest stages when public expectations are formed. On most construction projects, owner budgets are typically developed prior to the start of project planning and design. However, for megaprojects, the final budget is often the result of an iterative process of several developmental steps as part of planning and early design development. Costs are an important consideration in making decisions during this development period, and therefore appropriate types and levels of estimates should be made and updated during this period.

The purpose of these cost estimates is to get the most realistic forecast of the final cost of the project. It is necessary to recognize that estimates, at this time, may have large variations depending on the methods used, data available, and skill of the estimators. Typically such estimates are made by one or more estimators, engineers, or project managers. Usually, these professionals develop the estimates based on many years of experience, as well as data from several sources, such as commercial or custom databases plus contractor and supplier sourced information. As a result, if sufficient data and skill are used, a reasonable estimate can be developed for those scope items that are defined at that time.

Managing project costs is a requirement of every project manager responsible for overseeing a budget. For megaprojects, it is essential that good and sufficient cost management practices be used, specifically a cost-control system of sufficient capability to be able to adequately integrate the three primary elements of project management and control — scope, cost, and schedule, such as an earned value management (EVM) system (see "Using Earned Value Management to Control and Forecast Costs," below, p. 94).

Cost Estimating

Cost Estimates

Cost estimating seeks to define the final cost of a project by quantifying base costs,[8] allowances,[9] and the probable cost of risk (generally referred to as contingency). It is a quantitative assessment of the likely costs, resources, level of effort, productivity and durations (i.e., costs and/or schedules) for a specific project. Estimates are made at different stages of a project (which are usually preceded by a modifier, e.g., "preliminary," "conceptual," "order-of-magnitude," etc.). The final "engineer's estimate" is produced to quantify the anticipated value of the work to be bid by a contractor, based on the information (drawings, specifications, special conditions) provided to the contractors by the owner for bidding. The final engineer's estimate is used to evaluate the reasonableness of the contractor's bids.

Work of the cost estimator. A cost estimator should be able to plan and schedule the work, anticipate appropriate crews and equipment and materials to do the work, estimate reasonable productivity rates for that work, and add the appropriate margins for overhead, market conditions, profit, and cost escalation.

Methods of preparing cost estimates. There are many references regarding cost estimating procedures and best practices — see References below, particularly chapter 7, "Project Cost Management," in PMI's *Project Management Body of Knowledge*, and WSDOT's *Cost Estimating Manual for WSDOT Projects*.

Types of Cost Estimate

There are several different ways of preparing a cost estimate, depending on the purpose, level of planning or design, and project type, size, complexity, circumstances, schedule, and location. Initial planning or early design estimates may utilize historic cost databases or rely on historic unit price data (e.g., dollars per linear foot or per unit quantity, etc.). As the project advances, contractor-type estimating (based on detailed quantities, prices, labor rates, and other "bottom-up" specifics) may be used. The types of estimates typically used at each of the various project stages are summarized below, and the related "Estimate

Class Level" is given in Table 1 (p. 76), which relates the estimate class level to the level of project definition, end use of the estimate, expected accuracy, and contingency range.

Parametric estimates. Parametric estimates are normally used for projects in the planning or early design stage. They use historical data to estimate the cost of project elements based on such components as cost per square foot, cost per linear foot, cost per unit (if similar), and cost per project in total (if comparable). Typically the data used to develop the estimate comes from similar projects.

Historical bid-based estimates. These are appropriate when the project definition is such that quantification of work units is possible and comparable historical price data is available. Unit costs are applied to the work units to determine a total cost for the project, adding contingency and price escalation factors.

Cost-based estimates. Cost-based estimates quantify a typical contractor's cost for labor, equipment, materials, and specialty subcontractor effort needed to complete the work, adding contractor's overhead and profit. This method is preferable where project, geographical influences, market factors, and volatility of material prices mean that use of historical data is not adequate. This method is generally used by contractors in preparing bid or tender estimates. Cost-based estimates require significant time, data research, and an experienced estimator and are appropriate for complex megaprojects.

Risk-based estimates. Risk-based estimating involves use of probabilistic methods, requiring an understanding of uncertainty. These processes can vary from a simple range-based estimate in which the line items, quantities, or prices are not single valued (deterministic) but are expressed as ranges, usually around a mean or average value, to more complex probabilistic applications involving use or probabilistic techniques such as Monte Carlo simulation (WSDOT 2007).

Basis of Estimate

A basis of estimate (WSDOT 2009b) should be prepared, documented, and agreed before cost estimating is started. The basis of estimate is a way to consistently understand and assess the estimate, independent of other supporting documentation. The basis of estimate defines the purpose of the estimate, the project scope, pricing basis, allowances, assumptions, exclusions, and how risks, opportunities, and special conditions are to be included.

Role of Independent Estimators

Cost estimates prepared by the design team may be influenced by explicit or, more frequently, implicit pressure to keep costs below a certain maximum number ("optimism bias"). Therefore, they may not have the independent perspective of a hard-money contractor who is required to objectively estimate construction costs, for the design defined by the plans and specifications and the methods required to construct the facility. To address this concern, some owners require that an independent outside estimator, or estimators, review the estimate at each stage of design development. This is particularly appropriate for complex infrastructure megaprojects.

Levels of Estimate, Definition, Use, Accuracy and Contingency Ranges

The Cost Estimate Classification Table (see Table 1, next page), which draws from Association for the Advancement of Cost Engineering International (AACEI), relates the estimate class level to the project stage, level of project definition, end use of the estimate, expected accuracy and gross contingency ranges that may be required. It should be noted that the expected accuracy and contingency ranges are important measures of uncertainty and need to be considered carefully with respect to the usual optimistic bias in initial cost estimates and discussions.

Project Phases and Elements Related to Cost Estimating

The following phases describe the level of project definition available and the corresponding cost elements.

Planning Phase

During the planning phase, cost estimates are frequently used to evaluate alternatives, for example, in determining the most feasible project type, configuration, construction methods, and location. Although a number of other factors, such as public benefit and impact, are also considered in these initial siting studies, typically the merits of different alternatives are compared by using benefits and probable cost as common factors, enabling project proponents to reach decisions related to best value.

In most instances, these siting studies are done before significant preliminary design work is completed and, in this case, are based on information developed from similar previous projects, adjusted for location, time, and scope. Some agencies and many architectural or engineering firms have large databases of unit costs for making such preliminary cost studies. These unit cost studies are sufficient for projects where the cost is primarily a function of the scope, but they are less accurate for projects where a significant part of the cost is site-specific. Examples would be underground construction projects, where the cost can vary significantly depending upon the ground conditions, or projects constructed in remote locations where availability of labor and materials is a key factor. In such cases, owners are encouraged to obtain advice from specialists before making decisions based upon cost.

75

Table 1. **Cost Estimate Classification Table: Levels Usage, Accuracy, and Contingency**

Estimate Class	Project Stage	Project definition (% of final)	End Usage	Description	Expected Accuracy Range (%)[a]	Contingency Range (%)[b]
5	Very preliminary, conceptual	0–2	Feasibility, comparison of initial alternatives, concept screening	Parametric models, judgment, analogy, historical comparisons. Information from outline plan	L: −20 to −50 H: +30 to +100	30–75
4	Schematic design feasibility	1–15	Narrowing of alternatives, selection of preferred alternative	Parametric models, rough quantities and prices, historical comparisons, large allowance for unknowns/ design development	L −15 to −30 H: +20 to +50	20–50
3	Design development	10–50	Established probable costs of project for budget and funding determination	Quantities and prices with allowances, some historical comparisons, consideration of level of uncertainty	L: −10 to −20 H: +10 to +30	10–25
2	Pre-final construction documents	50–90	Refine the probable cost of the project with most design uncertainty eliminated	Fully developed cost takeoff using quantities and prices, reduced allowances, design well established	L: −5 to −15 H: +5 to +20	5–10
1	Bid documents final definition	100	Solicit bids for construction	Completely defined design, known terms and conditions	L: −3 to −10 H: +3 to +15	0–5

a. The values in the "Expected Accuracy Range" do not represent + or − percentages but instead represent an index value relative to a best range index value of 1. For example, for a particular type of project or category, a Class 1 estimate has an accuracy range of +15/−10%, then a Class 5 estimate for that application may have an accuracy range of +100/−50%.

b. The contingency outlined is in addition to provision for allowances and escalation and is sensitive to type of project, local conditions, political drivers, human error.

Based on "Figure 1–Generic Cost Estimate Classification Matrix," p. 2, in AACE, "Cost Estimate Classification System." *AACE International Recommended Practice No. 17R-97*, 2003.

Preliminary Design Phase

During the preliminary design phase, cost is frequently a factor in deciding between various design alternatives, e.g., a tunnel vs. pipeline, an earthfill vs. rockfill dam, an elevated highway or tunnel vs. at-grade highway. When making such decisions related to alternative methods of construction, it is important to consider not only site-specific factors that might affect one method more than another but also market conditions, particularly the availability of skilled labor and qualified contractors, which can affect the amount of economic competition. In addition, this is the time to evaluate life-cycle costs, which may vary depending upon the alternatives, especially if there are significant differences in design life, maintenance, or operations costs.

Establishing the Budget

At the completion of the preliminary design phase, when the alternative locations and methods have been identified and evaluated and the environmental documentation is either complete or well underway, this is an appropriate time to determine and agree upon a project budget. The budget should include not only the construction cost expected to be represented in the contractor's bid prices, but also factors such as escalation, owner contingencies (reserves), taxes, insurance, design engineering, construction management, startup (prior to operations), and owner's administration costs.

Other costs that must be included in the overall budget include purchase of real estate, permit fees, mitigation costs resulting from community or environmental agreements, utility relocations, and, in some jurisdictions, an allowance for public art. Some owners or agencies handle these costs in a number of different ways, but the following are common processes for identifying costs and associated factors (more sophisticated processes are described later in this chapter).

Construction cost: At the preliminary design phase, this can usually be estimated within a significantly large range (perhaps from 20 to 40 percent) depending upon the type of work and the completeness of the preliminary design documents (see Table 1). Unit prices are sufficient for some types of construction, such as buildings, but other types of work, such as underground and heavy civil construction, usually must be estimated using a work-up of crew sizes, equipment, anticipated production rates, and other factors.

Inclusion of escalation: Many owners prepare construction cost estimates in year-of-expenditure (YOE) dollars, but others prepare cost estimates in current dollars and include a separate line item for escalation. If the construction timeline is relatively certain, the first method (YOE) is recommended, because it can be more easily reconciled with contractor bid prices as they are received. On the other hand, the second method (current dollars) is more appropriate when the timing of construction is uncertain (for

example, if funding sources are undetermined), and it allows a separate adjustment of escalation assumptions based on economic models.

Owner contingencies: At the preliminary design phase, the cost estimate should include an allowance for design details that are not yet shown on the preliminary plans but will eventually be added, plus a contingency for unknowns. In addition to design allowances, the budget should include provision for construction cost changes, which can be based on the agency's historical outturn cost, adjusted for the type of construction. Many estimators and owners use a percentage-based system to quantify allowances and contingencies; however, the advent of risk-based statistical systems allows for projecting allowance and contingency amounts based on specific risks. Although probabilistic risk-based methods are not currently prevalent, they have been used to determine contingency amounts on several megaprojects.

As noted above, most estimators include an allowance, appropriate to the level of design completion, for costs due to design details that are not yet fully developed but will be included in the final plans and specifications. These design allowances can range from 30 percent at the conceptual level, to 5 percent at the 90 percent level, ending with zero design allowance at 100 percent design (bid documents).

Taxes: In most cases, taxes (such as payroll taxes and sales taxes) on purchased materials are included in the contractor's bid price. However, in some jurisdictions the owner pays a sales tax on the value of the contractor's monthly progress payment. The budget must include an allowance for these taxes.

Insurance: As is the case for taxes, it is common for the construction cost estimate to include insurance that the contractor pays, including workers' compensation, various types of liability, and builder's risk, which are for the most part based on a percentage of either the total cost or the labor cost. For many megaprojects, the owner may find it beneficial to purchase an owner-controlled insurance program (OCIP), for which the owner pays the premiums. In such a case, the owner must include a separate allowance for insurance, but in these instances, to avoid double-counting, the construction cost should exclude the insurance premiums.

Agency/owner administration: The owner's staff assigned to the project should be included in the budget. This can usually be estimated based upon the number of staff employees, functions required, and the project schedule.

Design engineering: Initially, estimates for the cost of design engineering can usually be based on a percentage of construction cost, recognizing that the percentage will vary by type of work, complexity, and size of total project. As the project is more defined, estimates can be made by level of effort required for specific activities, consistent with need, size of project, and complexity.

Construction management: The cost for construction management services is directly related to the project schedule. It can usually be estimated as a percentage of construction cost, although, as is the case for the design fees, the percentage varies significantly by type of work and size of total project.

Start-up: Many projects require an extensive start-up program to verify that the new facilities will function as expected, can be constructed and operated safely, and can be operated without a negative impact to the existing facilities. Examples include equipment and chemicals for water/wastewater systems and signal and communication testing for rail systems. To the extent that the owner's operations and maintenance staff are required for this start-up before the facilities are delivered, those administrative costs should be budgeted as well.

Real estate: An allowance for real estate acquisition, whether temporary or permanent easements, should be included in the budget. An allowance should also be made for the cost associated with property surveys, title search, and legal services.

Permit fees: All projects require a number of different permits. Some of these are best obtained by the owner, particularly if they require a long lead time and could affect the design. Fees for such permits should be included in the budget in an allowance item. Other permits that are required based upon the contractor's means and methods are best obtained by the contractor, and the cost for these permits should be included in the construction cost estimate.

Mitigation costs: It is not unusual for large projects to enter into agreements with communities, businesses, or environmental groups in which the owner agrees to specific constraints on construction or to fund improvements in infrastructure, relocations, or environmental projects in exchange for the group's agreement to support, or at least not to oppose, construction. To the extent that these agreements stipulate constraints on construction methods or hours of work, it is appropriate for these costs to be included in the construction base-cost estimate. On the other hand, the cost of infrastructure improvements that are not related to the specific project objectives may be appropriately included in an item labeled "mitigation costs." Such a separate allowance item is particularly appropriate for public owners because it provides for transparency in the use of taxpayer funds.

Utility relocations: In many jurisdictions, some utility relocations must be done by the utility owner, not necessarily the project construction contractor. The costs related to the design and construction of these utility relocations should be included as a line item in the budget.

Art allowance: Many public agencies are obligated by statute to include a certain percentage of the total project cost for public art. The amount allocated for art should be included in the total budget.

Final Design Phase

During the completion of the final design phase, details are completed and construction plans and specifications are prepared. In order to maintain control of the cost, it is necessary that a method be used to update the cost estimates that takes into account the impact of changes.

Update cost estimates at each design milestone, e.g., when the project is 30 percent, 60 percent, 90 percent, and 100 percent complete. This is a normal approach but it may have two disadvantages:

1. It can be a long time — several months to a year — between these deliverable dates, and this frequency may not offer sufficient control; and
2. Each estimate requires a significant work effort, which increases the design cost and time of performance. (On the other hand, this method enables the owner to engage a cost-estimating team that is independent of the designer, presumably producing estimates that are not influenced by the design team.)

Develop a "trend system," by which the designer identifies changes to the work as the design progresses and the estimating staff calculates the cost and time impact of those changes (not of the entire project). The trend system consists of an ongoing tally that keeps track of the total project cost by adjusting the cost as the design changes and improvements are made. The estimating effort is significantly reduced, and the resulting cost impacts of design decisions are available to the management team much sooner. One benefit of using this method is that, with the exception of the design changes specifically authorized by the client and included in the trend estimate, the design team is held accountable for designing the project to the established budget, thus placing the cost responsibility on the designer.

Value engineering. Many large projects include a process known as value engineering, which consists of an evaluation of the project concept by a panel of experts who are charged with reducing the cost while maintaining or improving functionality. Such value engineering efforts are commonly done at the end of preliminary design — before the final design — so that new ideas that add value can be implemented without adverse impact on the ongoing design or schedule. If done when the project design is significantly advanced, such value engineering studies frequently encounter resistance from the owner and design team and the results, which may require significant changes, are frequently not accepted.

Provisions for escalation. During final design, contract provisions can be included in the bidding documents to manage total cost during construction. Such provisions can include allowances for escalation on key materials and an allocation of risk for differing conditions. Escalation provisions are particularly useful on projects of long duration

(4 or more years) because the owner's willingness to pay full or partial cost escalation for labor or materials means that the bidders do not have to include bid items for conditions over which they have no control, and the owners benefit by paying for that escalation only if it occurs.

Differing site conditions. There is a similar logic for the incorporation of a differing site condition clause, where, by stipulating the expected conditions that should be in the bid price, the owner agrees to pay for conditions more adverse than those baseline conditions only if they occur. In addition to the inherent benefits of such risk allocation provisions, bidders are more likely to compete for projects where risk is reasonably and equitably shared. Thus there is increased economic competition, which lowers bid prices.

Engineer's estimate. At the completion of the final design, an "engineer's estimate" is commonly prepared. This estimate is intended to represent what a reasonable contractor would bid for the work, considering the established contract risk allocation, associated bid factors, provision for uncompensated construction costs, and including reasonable overhead and profit. The engineer's estimate can be compared to the construction cost carried in the established budget for a check on adherence to budget goals, but the primary purpose of the engineer's estimate is

1. In a competitively bid procurement, to confirm the reasonableness of the low bidder's price; or
2. In a negotiated procurement, to serve as a major element of the owner's negotiating plan.

The engineer's estimate must consider not only the scope and schedule requirements included in the bidding documents, but also the contract terms and conditions, the legal environment, and market conditions that can have a significant effect on the total project cost.

During award and construction. Upon the awarding of the contract, many owners adjust the budget to take into account the agreed contract price. When making such adjustments, a certain contingency amount is kept to cover changes in construction. Although some owners may have standard policies with respect to the level of contingency that should be kept in the budget (e.g., 5 percent of the contract award), the recommended approach is to determine the contract risks that have been allocated to the owner in the bid documents on a job-specific basis and to establish a reasonable amount of contingency for such risks. For instance, long duration projects that include an escalation clause and underground projects where there is a finite risk of encountering a differing site condition may need a higher construction contingency for changes than would a shorter duration building project or one with sufficiently known site conditions.

In order to proactively manage cash flow, the owner should ask for a detailed cash flow projection from the contractor as one of the early submittals. This cash flow can be

correlated to the contractor's proposed schedule and thus provide the owner with the best estimate on the size and timing of progress payments.

Probabilistic Risk-Based Estimating

Range Estimating

Estimating ranges of cost and schedule and their importance was discussed above. A relatively simple method to quantify ranges is to develop deterministic (single value) estimates and then to consider if elements of the estimate — either units, quantities, prices, or line items — might be lower or higher than the deterministic value. The upper and lower values will then give an indication of the range of the cost or schedule. This can be a relatively simple procedure that is easily understood by managers. Its accuracy, as for any estimate, depends on the skill and knowledge of the persons making the judgments required.

WSDOT's Cost Estimate Validation Process (CEVP®)

In 2001, the Washington State Department of Transportation was looking at a large highway construction program with several megaprojects, on the order of $30 billion in total. The cost estimating and communication problems, cited earlier, led the state Secretary of Transportation to ask for:

1. A critical review of the problem and its extent; and
2. Development of a better cost estimating methodology to deal with the major uncertainties implicit in megaprojects with long implementation time frames.

The review reached the following conclusions:

1. There was a general failure to adequately recognize that an estimate of a future cost or schedule involves substantial uncertainty (risk).
2. The uncertainty must be included in the cost estimating process.
3. Costs, especially construction costs, must be validated by qualified professionals, including experienced construction personnel who understand "real-world" bidding and construction.
4. Large projects often experience large scope and schedule changes that affect the final cost. Provision for this must be made in the cost estimates, and management must deal competently with these changes.

WSDOT decided to address these findings by

1. Using an improved cost estimating methodology;
2. Incorporating the cost validation and quantification of risk in the estimate; and

3. Communicating "ranges of probable cost" to the public, media, and key political decision-makers.

Essential elements of the new process included:

1. An external review by independent professionals, including validation of base cost, schedule, and assumptions;
2. Replacing contingencies (provision for unknowns) with explicit, quantified cost and schedule risks;
3. Treating opportunities on a probabilistic basis; and
4. Reporting results in terms of ranges, not single value numbers.

As a result of this study, WSDOT developed its Cost Estimate Validation Process (CEVP®), which considers the current cost estimate and uses a cost validation process to comprehensively and consistently define base costs (the cost if all goes as planned). This is done through a peer-level review, or "due diligence" analysis, of the scope, schedule, and cost estimate for the project. A specific objective of this method is to evaluate the quality and completeness of the base cost together with quantifying the inherent uncertainty in the estimate.

In parallel, risk is identified, examined, and quantified in terms of probability and consequence. Risk is considered to include negative and positive (opportunity) results. The base costs, together with the risk and opportunity costs, are combined in a simulation model to produce a range of probable costs and schedule.

The results of the assessment are expressed as a probable distribution of cost and schedule values for the project (see Figures 1, 2, and 3 on pp. 84–85). In summary, the CEVP® process

1. Critically examines the project estimate to validate cost and quantity components, including allowances for known elements, using independent external professionals;
2. Removes all contingency for unknowns;
3. Replaces contingency with individually identified and explicitly quantified uncertainty events (risks and opportunities);
4. Builds a model of the project (normally in spreadsheet form) from a flowchart of key planning, design, permitting, and construction activities;
5. Assigns the quantified uncertainty events to flowchart activities with associated probabilities and impacts, correlated and/or interdependent, as appropriate, in the model;
6. Runs a simulation to produce the projected "range of probable cost and schedule"; and
7. Reports the results (Figures 2 and 3).

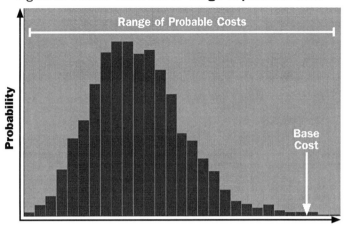

Figure 1. **Future costs are a "range of probable cost"**

- In the beginning, there is a large potential range for "ultimate cost."
- The "ultimate cost" will depend on the outcome of many factors.
- We can't predict exactly, but we can develop probable ranges of cost that include all relevant risk and opportunity events we can identify.
- The cost of risk events, plus the savings from opportunity events, are added to the "base costs" to develop the "range of probable costs."

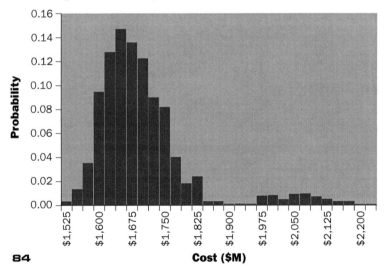

Figure 2. **CEVP® probable cost output**

Specifics of the process can be found in referenced papers (Reilly et al. 2004, 2006; Roberds & McGrath, 2005).

CEVP® is iterative in nature. For many project applications, it is appropriate to conduct a reassessment of the project from time to time to update project changes, cost, and schedule estimates. The example, Figure 3, which compares the 2003 results to the 2002 results for a complex highway project, shows a reduction in both probable cost and uncertainty (i.e., a reduced range).

Reference-Class Estimating

Reference-class estimating was developed by Flyvbjerg and COWI to create megaproject cost estimating guidelines for the U.K. Department for Transport (Flyvbjerg & COWI, 2004). The reason for this process is to objectively and externally reduce the opportunity for optimistic bias to negatively affect results.

The method creates a list of projects similar to the one being proposed (a "reference class"), looks at past performance of projects in that class, and creates a forecast of the probability of outcomes from the best to worst case. The output results in an "uplift factor" that is applied to the "normal" cost estimate.

Subsequent to the introduction of the reference-class method into estimates for U.K. transport infrastructure projects, individual government departments commissioned their own research to develop department-specific optimism bias uplifts. The method is described in Flyvbjerg and COWI report to the U.K. Department for Transport (cited above). The Department for Transport has made reference-class forecasting mandatory policy for infrastructure projects larger than £5 million and the U.K. Treasury has adopted a similar policy for all transportation projects larger than £40 million.

Schedules and Scheduling

Why Are Project Schedules Important?

The old adage, "Plan the work and work the plan," may seem simplistic and trite, but this approach is necessary in order to significantly improve the probability that a project will be completed on time—and this is especially true for complex megaprojects. Schedule management is a key tool for defining, communicating, and managing the integration of all activities, including sequencing, time requirements for work elements, and resource usage.

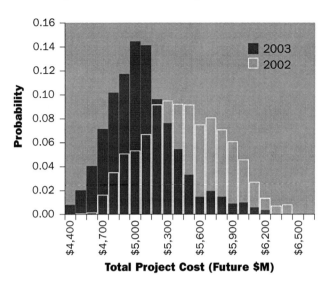

Figure 3. **Improvement in probable cost (mean and distribution)**

Appropriate scheduling and schedule control is important since the owner must normally coordinate the staging, cash flow, interface management, and completion dates of multiple prime contractors. The owner's project master schedule incorporates input from various governmental agencies, stakeholders, planners, designers, construction contractors, and commissioning agents.

It is important that the schedule be consistent with the size and complexity of the project in terms of scope, deliverables, milestones, and constraints, as well as the elements that will impact the successful completion of the project, such as:

- Project complexity
- Needs of key stakeholders
- Extraordinary time constraints
- Financing strategy
- Delivery or contracting method

- Labor market
- State of the economy
- Political pressures
- Previous relationships with designers and contractors

Each of these elements influences the overall schedule, including relationships between activities, assumed logic constraints, durations, critical path,[10] and overall duration. They also present potential financial, time-related, or other risks to the project. Some of these risks can be managed and controlled by the owner (or contractor) and some cannot. Those risks that cannot be entirely mitigated by the owner should be acknowledged and provision made for them in the schedule.

Master Schedules

Master schedules include all project development elements, not just construction elements. Owners should plan and develop project schedules from the early planning stages through design development, final design, bidding, construction, testing, integrated testing, and start-up of operations. The owner, or its construction management consultant, must initiate, manage, update, and integrate the overall schedule, of which the contractors' schedules are just one element. For a megaproject there will be multiple contractors, subcontractors, vendors, and suppliers whose individual schedules will affect the final outcome and who therefore need to be actively managed.

The master schedule is the only tool that the owner has available to plan the project and to track overall performance from design concept to final commissioning. In the event that work elements or phases of the project have problems, the master schedule is the basis for planning remedial action.

Project Phases

The phases of a megaproject generally include the following. These phases may occur sequentially or concurrently, depending on the needs of the project and its stakeholders.

1. Concept development, planning studies, and alternatives
2. Environmental process, documentation, and review
3. Approval by funding agencies or internal finance departments
4. Permitting and environmental "record of decision"
5. Real estate acquisition
6. Preliminary and final design
7. Procurement and construction
8. Testing and commissioning
9. Owner occupancy and operation

Depending on the project being constructed, the list and sequencing of phases can vary significantly.

Importance of Realistic Schedules

As the owner develops an integrated plan for design and construction, an appropriate project master schedule is developed that best reflects that plan. The owner's master schedule will include all phases of the project from initial concept, preliminary design, financing, site selection, and environmental approvals through construction, commissioning, and operations. The schedule thus represents the project implementation plan scaled across time, including interrelationships between each of the plan's elements.

Project planning includes an evaluation of schedule requirements and interrelationships including important milestones, deadlines, critical activities, internal and external contractual or logistical constraints, and other factors that may affect project completion. Evaluation of these factors must be objective and realistic, in order to produce a schedule that reflects a sufficiently accurate and reliable result.

In its first iteration the master schedule might be little more than a series of logical activities, considering milestones, relationships, and constraints, with a rough timeline. As planning and preliminary design advances, definitions and logical relationships between activities and milestones become more specific. As the specifics become more detailed, the feasibility of completing the project on the projected completion date can be better assessed.

Schedule Complexity, Critical Path Method (CPM)

Soon after the initial rough schedules are developed, frequently using simple bar charts (sometimes called Gantt charts[11]), a more detailed definition consistent with the stage of project planning and development will be needed. At this point, most owners will require a critical path method (CPM) schedule to be developed, and such practice is now routine. The CPM schedule is required earlier in the initial development phases for megaprojects due to the higher level of complexity and long time frames of these projects.

Essentially, the cause-and-effect relationships between the many tasks in a megaproject become too difficult to accurately represent using just Gantt charts. The complexity of the schedule grows as the project moves from the planning to design phase, and it increases again as the project moves into construction.

Schedule updates

Updates to the project master schedule should be carried out at regular intervals or when it is most appropriate to do so in terms of phases, milestones, management need, payment and cash-flow determination, and public process information. Typically updates to the program schedule will take place on a monthly basis, with significant review and changes perhaps on a quarterly basis or in preparation for public and funding decisions.

Milestones, Deliverables, Liquidated Damages

The owner's requirement to achieve key milestones and deliverables at specific dates is often contractually managed by the inclusion of such dates in the contract for which an unexcused delay triggers assessment of liquidated damages or other action. Contractors are contractually required to incorporate the specified milestone dates into their

construction schedules and to manage their work and levels of effort to meet those milestones. Setting these dates reasonably, consistent with the accuracy of the scheduling process, is the responsibility of the owner.

Constraints

Constraints can be represented in many ways. Although constraints are often thought of as milestone dates (where the contractor is expected to complete a specific portion of the project either no later than, or start no earlier than, a specific date), they are also created by limitations related to resource availability, or usage, funding and cash-flow limitations, environmental limitations, site availability, and many other potential factors.

Importance of the Planning Stage

It is important to note that the construction phase, while a major focus, is just a portion of the entire project even though the costs associated with this phase are large. It is in the early planning and design phases that many critical decisions regarding the overall schedule are made. The importance of key rules and guidelines for schedule development in this early stage should be emphasized because they influence critical planning, logistical, funding, and political decisions, as well as stakeholder expectations.

Influence of Contracting Methods

For a megaproject, with many elements and activities, the method of contracting and subcontracting is important, and the schedule interrelationships thus required can be complex. For example, if the project will be constructed using a number of prime contractors, i.e., a multiprime approach, the owner's master schedule must be created in such a manner that it recognizes the scope of each prime contractor, their key milestones and critical activities, and the relationships of these to other prime contractors. It is the owner's responsibility to recognize, plan, and manage (normally assisted by construction management firms) the linkages among the multiprime contractors, along with any external actions that are required by the owner or third parties.

Schedule Management

Where milestones must be determined for one contractor that will affect the performance of another (e.g., release of an area for use by a second contractor after substantial completion by a prior contractor), the master schedule logic plus that of the subschedules of the individual contractors must be consistent and related. The owner should be prepared to anticipate potential slippage of the first contractor and its effect on the second and to adjust the affected dates accordingly.

Management of Multiple Contractor Schedules

In order to facilitate the integration of multiple contractor schedules into the master schedule, it is important that the basic scheduling architecture and nomenclature be defined in advance. This is typically accomplished through a scheduling specification, developed by the owner and included in the construction contracts, which defines how each contractor must schedule their work.

Content of the Owner's Master Schedule

There are various actions taken by the owner and other parties, beginning early in the planning, design, funding, and approval phases, leading up to the beginning of construction, over which the contractor has no control. Schedule management during these phases is exercised through the owner's master schedule.

This schedule must include sufficient activities, durations, and logical requirements (constraints, interrelationship of activities) to adequately represent the schedule requirements of the owner. There is currently no recommended industry practice that defines how many activities or logic ties there should be relative to the size and complexity of the project. Certainly, the requirements of complex megaprojects must be recognized at a higher level than for smaller, more traditional projects and therefore the level of detail and effort that is required for the master schedule must be appropriate to the application.

In this respect, there are recommended attributes for the schedule to ensure that it is technically sound and appropriate in terms of identifying critical issues and to provide data needed to address the risk of schedule-related problems in the future. The following steps can be used to gauge the appropriate level of data and complexity that should be included in the master schedule and in order to define specifics for inclusion in construction contract documents:

1. Development of a well-thought-out scheduling specification, at the appropriate level, for the planning, design, and construction phases;
2. Assurance that activities and milestones are included in the schedule for every party and stakeholder whose work or deliverables are necessary for successful project completion;
3. Assurance that the durations of all activities are reasonable and can be managed by the responsible party; and
4. Assurance that the progress and projected completion of all activities can be measured and reported.

Schedules and Cost Estimates Should Be Developed Together and Linked

The interrelationship between schedule and cost, especially for megaprojects, is critical and it needs to be carefully considered in terms of commitments and public announcements, as well as cost, schedule, and risk management (see sections above on cost, especially WSDOT's CEVP® process, and related references).

Previously, some owners used separate departments to develop the cost estimates and schedules for the same project. Sometimes the two departments acted independently of one another and as a result might disagree on key results important to the success of the project. Accordingly, a process for integrating cost, schedule, and risk is increasingly recognized by megaproject owners as an essential business practice.

Successful integration of cost and schedule requires the scheduler and estimator to cooperate in developing an understanding of the contractor's means and methods, activity durations, activity sequencing, logical relationships, work processes, workforce assumptions and productivity rates, resource availability, and imposed time constraints.

The link between the estimate and the schedule is generally made by the project's work breakdown structure (WBS). The WBS is a hierarchical means of organizing the project's scope of work, in which each element of the work is identified with a unique label, often by using a numbering system in which each work element of the cost estimate is identified and tied to a schedule activity.

During the early planning and design phases, there are many uncertainties in the project definition—for example, asking the question, "What can we build for the money we have, in the time we need it, that will accomplish our objectives?" will result in a range of possibilities, which must be understood and managed to achieve the desired result. Decisions relating to those possibilities are frequently done in an iterative manner, evaluating alternatives on the basis of cost, schedule, environmental, and community impact, in order to reach an agreed-upon planning, design, or construction solution.

Advantages of Cost-loaded Schedules

Cost-loaded schedules are those where the budgeted cost for each activity in the CPM schedule is quantitatively linked to that activity. Almost all of the scheduling software applications today have the capability for cost-loading schedules at the activity level, where the scope of each activity is verified to be in alignment with the associated cost line item in the budget or cost estimate.

A prime advantage of cost loading a schedule is that it integrates the project's estimated costs with the time-based activities to perform the associated scope, thereby allowing for time-based analyses of project costs, including forecasting. From this, analysis of cash flow and productivity is possible.

It is often very difficult for project participants to agree to a productivity analysis or to measure a disruption to productivity (e.g., in a dispute or claim) if they have little relevant and consistent data on which to base their judgment or decision. An approved contractor's cost-loaded schedule can therefore facilitate getting an agreement regarding productivity or productivity disruptions.

A second advantage for cost loading the schedule is that it allows the contractor and owner to better understand and manage resource usage and cash flow. At any point in a project it is possible to see which activities should be underway or already complete and to evaluate the actual cash flow associated with those activities, compared to what was planned. This comparison helps the owner to recognize whether the contractor's cash burn rate or productivity is in alignment with what was planned for that period of time. One of the biggest cost-saving advantages to using planning schedules that are cost-loaded is the improved opportunity to avoid problems later with respect to productivity, productivity disruption disputes, and claims.

Processes and Factors of Schedule Management

Business and Project Management Processes

Competent management of megaprojects is one of the most important keys to successful delivery and fulfilling of expectations. Developing and implementing "best project management practices," defined as the project starts, is a necessary condition (but not the only condition) for success. Examples of business practices that should be put in place by the owner's management include, but are not limited to:

1. Most appropriate management approach, consistent with the needs of the project (for megaprojects this is not necessarily the same as normal agency practice);
2. Care in the selection and procurement of consultants, contractors, materials, and supplies;
3. Project controls for cost, schedule, and earned value;
4. Configuration control, change management, document control;
5. Invoice processing and fair and timely compensation;
6. Risk management;
7. Design quality assurance and review;
8. Construction quality assurance, oversight, and management;
9. Real estate acquisition (strategy); and
10. Disputes and claims management.

There are no universally accepted standard processes for all of these elements; however, there are many existing templates or models that have been successful.

Available Cost and Schedule Tools

Having the best and most advanced tools available generally will make work more efficient and effective, allowing management to better accomplish key goals in a productive and timely manner. The field of project management is no exception, including the areas of schedule and cost management. The primary tools to adequately develop and implement sufficient cost and schedule systems consist of the best available software systems and engineers with the appropriate skills, knowledge, and experience to effectively apply these systems.

Management, Leadership, and Technical Proficiency

Management of schedule, cost, scope, and quality requires that the management team use the most appropriate processes and tools available and that personnel are trained and skilled in their use. This means that the project manager must understand the technical aspects of the project and effectively lead and coordinate a diverse project team, with multiple inputs and stakeholder requirements, in a changing and sometimes politically intense environment.

Schedule Specification

The purpose of a schedule specification, in terms of project management, is to clearly communicate the owner's schedule measurement, compliance process, and deliverable requirements to the contractor. Schedule specifications should define the schedule development, measures and metrics, and reporting and maintenance processes.

Writing a specification calls for an author who clearly understands the technical aspects required by the owner, and who can balance performance and prescriptive requirements to the benefit of the owner, consistent with the ability of the contractor. The specification writer must understand and address schedule risk allocation consistent with the risk management policy of the owner. Risk allocation is important because if the owner allocates too much schedule risk to the contractor through the schedule specification (or other contractor documents), it will be reflected either in a higher bid price or in an increased number of change order requests during construction.

An important consideration for the owner is the willingness and ability to enforce the schedule specification and requirements in a complex project environment. This requires construction management staff with the appropriate skills, knowledge, and understanding to determine contractor compliance.

Scheduling Processes

Examples of processes and tools typically described in a schedule specification include:

- Specific scheduling software to be used, if required;
- Qualifications of the contractor's scheduling personnel;
- Preliminary schedule submittal prior to baseline schedule submittal;
- Schedule development: the project baseline;
- Schedule development: look-ahead schedules;
- Updating of schedules, including formatting and submittal frequency;
- Change management, including the schedule revision process;
- Schedule resource loading and management;
- Schedule review meetings; and
- The use of earned value management and other cost control methods, if required.

Specifications may be more prescriptive or more performance-based and may address these processes in greater or lesser detail.

Performance Measures

Being able to measure, to identify, and, if necessary, to react to poor schedule performance on a project is a basic construction management requirement. The two main questions are:

1. Whether the project will be completed on time or not, and
2. Which activities are most at risk and, if delayed, would impact the project completion date.

Both of these questions are addressed by continually reviewing and evaluating the schedule's critical path and threats to activities on or near the critical path. The critical path typically identifies those activities which, in sequence, define the earliest possible completion of the project. Therefore, the forecasted completion date for the latest-finishing activity determines the completion date of the project.

"Total float" is an indicator of which activities are on the critical path, which are near the critical path, or which have less risk of impacting the project's completion date. A project delay does not occur unless the activity that is being delayed is critical. Reviewing the project schedule at a more detailed level allows the performance of individual activities or a series of related activities (known as "fragnets") to be evaluated in terms of risk to the overall completion schedule.

Other performance measures can be used with a CPM schedule, if activities are loaded with resources such as labor hours and money. In a resource-loaded schedule, metrics such as cash-flow and labor productivity can be reviewed. Use of resources can be measured in total or by individual activities.

Managing Inflation and Cost Escalation

Inflation is commonly understood as a rise in the general level of prices of goods and services over time. Similarly, cost escalation can be defined as the rise in the level of prices for specific goods and services in a given economy over time (Hollmann & Dysert, 2007). Put differently, cost escalation can represent the rate at which market conditions change for a specific commodity or service in a geographic area.

Inflation and cost escalation are two of the most unpredictable and uncontrollable factors affecting the overall cost of a project. This is particularly important for megaprojects, which evolve over a long period. Inflation and cost escalation are one of the primary reasons that projects run over budget and schedule. Accounting for the effects of inflation and cost escalation is therefore a critical activity, requiring the following:

1. Care in not being optimistic regarding projected inflation and cost escalation;
2. Procedures to address "optimistic bias";
3. Use of respected methods to quantify inflation and cost escalation; and
4. Consideration of variability in the projection of inflation and cost escalation (see "Cost Estimating," pp. 73ff.).

Using Earned Value Management to Control and Forecast Costs

Earned Value Management (EVM) is a well-defined process that integrates a project's financial, schedule, and scope status to determine its current condition or to forecast its status at any future point through completion.

The concept of EVM has been in use for many years, developed by industrial engineers to track productivity in manufacturing plants. The U.S. government adopted and formalized the process several decades ago. Even today in many cases, federal agencies such as the Departments of Energy and Defense require their contractors to use certified Earned Value Management Systems (EVMS).

Because EVM integrates the current status of scope, schedule, and budget, the interplay between them is monitored and, when any one of them changes, it is possible to evaluate where the productivity slowdown (and resulting budget overrun) is occurring. For instance, if the project is behind schedule, the project manager may choose either to accelerate current productivity or to cut scope, and the EVM system can not only capture the relevant changes but also forecast the final cost of the project. Through the use of EVM, the project manager can also forecast the necessary productivity increase to put the project back on a pace to finish on budget and on schedule.

By using an EVM system regularly, the owner can review previously incurred costs, currently estimated costs of each piece of incomplete work and, optionally, the historical, current, or anticipated productivity rates. The EVM method offers an advantage over other cost management techniques that forecast final costs based on previous productivity rates or estimated costs-to-complete that can be subjective.

The EVM model relies on a well-developed cost estimate and CPM baseline schedule. Together, the baseline schedule and approved budget estimate represent the project's as-planned data. Significant discrepancies in the budget estimate or the baseline schedule will affect the reliability of the EVM model and its results. One such discrepancy is a misalignment between the cost estimate and the baseline schedule, for example, on a project where assumed productivity rates in the cost estimate do not correlate with the duration of the related schedule activity. Therefore, it is important that

1. The project's budget estimate and baseline schedule be consistent with the associated scope, and
2. The cost estimator and scheduler collaborate in the development of their respective products.

EVM, like all cost and schedule management tools, requires that the costs and schedule be updated periodically to represent the contractors' construction work and planning. In a complex megaproject, as work progresses, it is often necessary for contractors to change their work plan and sequence of activities due to resource availability, site access, work sequence required by external factors, and other circumstances.

As an objective tool for resolving labor disruption disputes, EVM is a good method for complex megaprojects. Although there are other techniques that are more accepted in the legal and academic realms to determine productivity loss, they have significant limitations on when they can be used. For complex megaprojects, EVM can be an effective way to identify and manage productivity, including the identification of points when productivity loss takes place. Through a group of predefined and easy to read report formats, EVM allows a complex project's cost and schedule data to be considered in a small set of understandable reports. These reports allow for transparent reviews of the project's financial and schedule status, and thus enhance effective project management.

Reference Sources

AACEI. (2003). "Cost Estimate Classification System." *AACE International Recommended Practice No. 17R-97*. Retrieved March 10, 2010, from http://www.aacei.org/technical/rps/17r-97.pdf.

Anderson, S., Molenaar, K., & Schexnayder, C. (2007). *Guidance for Cost Estimation and Management for Highway Projects During Planning, Programming and Preconstruction*, NCHRP Report 574. Washington: Transportation Research Board.

Department of the Environment, Transport and Regions, Great Britain, & Ove Arup Partnership. (July 2000). *The Jubilee Line Extension, End-of-Commission Report*. London: Author.

Einstein, H. H., & Vick, S. G. (1974). "Geological Model for a Tunnel Cost Model." *Proceedings of the Rapid Excavation and Tunneling Conference*, 2d, II:1701–1720.

Federal Highway Administration. (October 2006). *Guide to Risk Assessment and Allocation for Highway Construction Management*. Report FHWA-PL-06-032. Washington, DC: Author.

Federal Transit Administration. (November 10, 2003). "Risk Assessment Procedures, Requirements and Report Formats for PMO Contractor Deliverables and Services." Operating Guidance Memorandum No. 22. Washington, DC: U.S. Department of Transportation.

Federal Transit Administration. (May 2004). "Risk Assessment Methodologies and Procedures," Project No. DC-03-5649, Work Order No. 6.

Flyvbjerg, B. (2007). "Can removing human bias deliver more realistic project forecasts?" [Interview]. *www.lttonline.co.uk* [magazine], May 10–23, 2007, pp. 10–13.

Flyvbjerg, B. (Winter 2009). "Delusion and Deception in Large Infrastructure Projects: Two Models for Explaining and Preventing Executive Disaster," *California Management Review*, Vol. 51, No. 2.

Flyvbjerg, B., Bruzelius, N., & Rothengatter, W. (2003). *Megaprojects and Risk: An Anatomy of Ambition*. Cambridge: Cambridge University Press.

Flyvbjerg, B., & COWI. (June 2004). U.K. Department for Transport, "Procedures for Dealing with Optimism Bias in Transport Planning," Guidance Document.

Flyvbjerg, B., Holm, M. S., & Buhl, S. (2002). "Underestimating Costs in Public Works Projects: Error or Lie?" *Journal of the American Planning Association*, Summer 2002. 68:3, pp. 279–295.

Grasso, P., Mahtab, M., Kalamaras, G., & Einstein, H. (March 7, 2002). "On the Development of a Risk Management Plan for Tunnelling." In *Proceedings of AITES-ITA Downunder*, 2002 World Tunnel Congress, Sydney.

Hollmann, J. K., & Dysert, L. R. (2007). "Escalation Estimation: Working With Economics Consultants," *AACE International Transactions*. Morgantown, WV: AACE International.

Isaksson, T. (2002). *Model for Estimation of Time and Cost, Based on Risk Evaluation Applied to Tunnel Projects*. Doctoral dissertation. Stockholm: Royal Institute of Technology, Division of Soil and Rock Mechanics.

Lockhart, C., & Roberds, W. (April 1996). "Worth the Risk?" *Civil Engineering,* 66:4, 62–64.

Project Management Institute. (2008). *Project Management Body of Knowledge (PMBOK Guide),* 4th ed., Chapter 7, "Project Cost Management." Newton Square, PA: Author.

Reilly, J. J. (March 2001). "Managing the Costs of Complex, Underground and Infrastructure Projects." Paper presented at the American Underground Construction Conference, Regional Conference, Seattle.

Reilly, J. J. (May 2005). "Cost Estimating and Risk Management for Underground Projects." In *Proceedings of the International Tunneling Conference,* Istanbul: A. A. Balkema.

Reilly, J. J. (April 2006). "Risk Identification, Risk Mitigation and Cost Estimation," *Tunnelling & Trenchless Construction,* 20, 43–44.

Reilly, J. J. (June 2006). "Cost Estimating: Probable Cost, Risk Identification and Risk Management for Infrastructure/Rail Projects," *Proceedings of the APTA Rail Conference,* New York.

Reilly, J. J. (June 2008). "Probable Cost Estimating and Risk Management," *Proceedings of the North American Tunneling Conference 2008,* San Francisco.

Reilly, J. J. (May 2009). "Probable Cost Estimating and Risk Management, Part 2," *Proceedings of the International Tunneling Association,* World Tunnel Conference, Budapest.

Reilly, J. J., & Brown, J. (May 2004). "Management and Control of Cost and Risk for Tunneling and Infrastructure Projects." In *Proceedings of the World Tunneling Conference,* International Tunneling Association, Singapore.

Reilly, J. J., McBride, M., Sangrey, D., MacDonald, D., & Brown, J. (Fall/Winter 2004)."The development of CEVP®—WSDOT's Cost-Risk Estimating Process," *Proceedings of the Boston Society of Civil Engineers.*

Roberds, W., & McGrath, T. (October 2005). "Quantitative Cost and Schedule Risk Assessment and Risk Management for Large Infrastructure Projects," *Proceedings of the Project Management Institute.*

Salvucci, F. P. (April 2003). "The 'Big Dig' of Boston, Massachusetts: Lessons to Learn." In *Proceedings of the International Tunnelling Association Conference,* Amsterdam, pp. 37–42.

Schexnayder, C., Fiori, C., & Weber, S. (July 2003). *Project Cost Estimating: A Synthesis of Highway Practice.* Report submitted to AASHTO; prepared as part of NCHRP Project 20-7, Task 152. National Cooperative Highway Research Program, Transportation Research Board.

WSDOT. (2007). *Guidelines for CEVP® and Cost Risk Assessment,* October 31, 2005, updated 2007. Retrieved April 6, 2010, from http://www.wsdot.wa.gov/projects/projectmgmt/riskassessment.

WSDOT. (January 2009). *Glossary for Cost Risk Estimating Management.* Retrieved April 6, 2010, from http://www.wsdot.wa.gov/publications/fulltext/CEVP/Glossary.pdf.

WSDOT (2009). "Basis of Estimate Form [Template]." Available online at http://www.wsdot.wa.gov/Projects/ProjectMgmt/RiskAssessment/Information.htm.

WSDOT (July 2009). *Cost Estimating Manual for WSDOT Projects, M3034.02*. Retrieved April 6, 2010, from http://www.wsdot.wa.gov/publications/manuals/fulltext/M3034/Estimating Guidelines.pdf.

Notes

1. The over/under budget numbers (and percentages) are based on the cost initially published for the project or reported at the time of decision to proceed. This is consistent with Flyvbjerg's assertion of "systematic deception" (Flyvbjerg et al., "Underestimating Costs in Public Works Projects: Error or Lie?").

2. The initially published "number," less than $3 billion, was not a budget estimate; however, the public and press have focused on that number, causing embarrassment to the industry as the project cost rose to over $15 billion. For an overview of the Central Artery initial budget disclosure, compared to the Boston Harbor Project (which was completed close to the announced budget), see Reilly et al., "The development of CEVP — WSDOT's Cost-Risk Estimating Process."

3. AUCA, Regional Northwest Conference, Seattle, Washington, March 19, 2001.

4. It was about this time (2000–2002) that major concerns were raised regarding cost increases for the Boston Central Artery/Tunnel project, notably reported in the *Boston Globe* "Spotlight" series of that time.

5. Uncertainty is defined as a lack of knowledge of the outcome for a particular element or value.

6. Risk is defined as the combination of the probability of an uncertain event and the consequences (either positive or negative) if it occurs.

7. "Contingency" is an added amount normally applied to account for substantial uncertainties in quantities, unit costs, and the possibility of unforeseen events related to quantities, work elements, or other project requirements.

8. "Base cost" is the cost (and schedule) that would eventuate if all goes as planned and assumed.

9. "Allowances" are additional costs included in an estimate to cover the cost of known but unquantified elements for an activity or work item.

10. The critical path in a schedule is that sequence of activities that determines the minimum time for completion, considering activity durations, interrelationships, constraints, and predecessor-successor requirements (*see* Project Management Institute, *PMBOK Guide*).

11. A Gantt chart is a type of bar chart that illustrates a project schedule. Gantt charts illustrate the start and finish dates of the elements of a project.

CHAPTER 6

Logistical Considerations

Robert J. F. Goodfellow, P.E., Black & Veatch
James McKelvey, Black & Veatch

"The line between disorder and order lies in logistics . . ."   – Sun Tzu

"My logisticians are a humorless lot . . . They know if my campaign fails, they are the first ones I will slay."   – Alexander

It is interesting to note, and some would say entirely appropriate in the "war" of underground construction, that notable quotes on logistics abound in military history.

Introduction

The essential difference between a $100 million project and a megaproject is the logistical demands of execution at a scale that challenges the imagination. The issues of logistics cover every aspect of the megaproject, from the grand vision of its inception, through the morass of stakeholders, permits, and even treaties that are considered during planning and design, to the mobilization and maintenance of labor equipment and material resources to feed the construction phase.

Logistics has been defined as "the science of planning and carrying out the movement and maintenance of forces."[1] The purpose of logistics in a construction megaproject is simply to arrange all aspects, resources, and impacts of the project in an orderly and predictable way to allow the project to continue along the expected course in accordance with predicted cost and schedule profiles.

All parties make decisions based on the cost and time associated with logistics. In one sense, logistics is a funding plan devised by the owner that sets the overall cash flow and hence the timetable and schedule for procurement, design, and construction of the project. Logistics is also the design schedule, which is most often constrained by geotechnical investigation, drilling, and laboratory testing at the beginning of the design period and determined by permits and right-of-way acquisitions at the later stages of design. Finally and most visibly to the general public, logistics is key in mobilizing the contractor, labor, equipment, and materials to the job site, including such articles as explosives, large tun-

Panoramic view taken in 1938 of construction of the Grand Coulee Dam on the Columbia River in eastern Washington state. View shows the town of Mason City (now known as the city of Coulee Dam), built to house the workforce. Library of Congress, from the Historic American Engineering Record collection.

nel boring machines, and many hundreds of concrete supply and spoil removal trucks.

This chapter considers issues at all these stages of a megaproject. Our discussion centers on cost and schedule and the impact of a project and its associated activities on the environment, both built and natural. When prosecuting a megaproject, it is critical to properly assess the different impacts it has, such as the disruption of daily activities in cities, because without due regard for logistics, political will can falter, funding streams dry up, and the projects will fail.

Logistics in Planning

The Channel Tunnel is the classic example of a megaproject long thought of but not built. It was initially conceived by Albert Mathieu-Favier and begun by the engineers of Napoleon in 1802. But the tunnel was only realized once the logistics of financial, environmental, design, and construction were reliably presented to the national governments of the United Kingdom and France. Detailed plans for spoil removal and equipment mobilization and demobilization (including the burying of one of the tunnel boring machines) were essential and enabled the owners to convince decision-makers that the logistics of the project were feasible. Knowing the purpose and impact of project logistics was central to the framing of the discussion.

The sheer size of a megaproject frequently results in impacts that extend beyond any single city, county, state, and even country. The Channel Tunnel and the Lesotho Highlands Water Project, which diverts south-flowing rivers in Lesotho northward to the thirsty industrial heartland of South Africa, are just two examples of completed megaprojects that involve two countries. They exemplify the need both for a champion of the cause and also for legislative enactments to allow negotiations when more than one party (i.e., country) is involved, an agreement that clearly defines the roles, responsibilities, and benefits for all stakeholders. Inevitably the parties will have conflicting aims and aspirations about some details, even if there is broad agreement of the project need in principle.

For the Channel Tunnel and the Lesotho Project, the agreements took the form of international treaties. However, the principle is the same for any megaproject. As soon as possible, a formal agreement signed by all relevant parties should be ratified to maximize alignment of all stakeholders and thus the chance of a successful project.

The Channel Tunnel

Sir Nicholas Henderson and A. F. Gueterbock describe a number of supporters that kept the vision of a channel tunnel alive since Napoleon's time. For example, French engineer Thomé de Gamond spent 40 years in the mid-nineteenth century attempting to

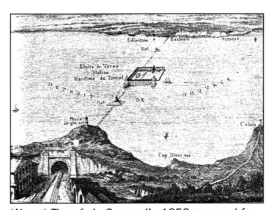

(Above) Thomé de Gamond's 1856 proposal for a Channel tunnel across the Straits of Dover. It included building an artificial island on the Verne sandbank for ventilation shafts to the tunnel.
(Right) The rail entrance to the Channel Tunnel at Beussingues, near Coquelles, in France. Photo © 2001 by Nicholas Hodder.

find a practical solution, including the first systematic geological survey of the seabed, during which Gamond himself made death-defying dives in 100 feet of water with the most primitive equipment, weights on his feet, pig bladder floats, and ears stuffed with fat (and complained about being attacked by "malevolent fish").

Connecting England to France had long been opposed by the English because they feared a fixed link would aid a military invasion.[2] There is no record of anything but support for a tunnel from the French. The turning point came in 1955, when the British Minister of Defense Harold Macmillan announced that a tunnel would not constitute a threat to national security. This ultimately led to Prime Minister Margaret Thatcher enthusiastically supporting the Channel Tunnel in a joint announcement of the project with an equally enthusiastic French President François Mitterand on November 30, 1984. With their public support, the British and French cabinets drew up guidelines and requested proposals from private enterprises for a scheme that did not require any government financial support. Even after the Channel Tunnel Group/France Manche proposal had been formally accepted on January 20, 1986, it was necessary for both governments to conclude a concession agreement with these companies and to enact legislative powers to sign a treaty through bills in Parliament and the French National Assembly, which finally culminated in the signing of the negotiated Treaty of Canterbury on February 12, 1986. This treaty "dealt with the grant of a concession, the political guarantee and compensation between Governments, jurisdiction and legal matters, finance, inter-governmental machinery and disputes."[3]

The concrete arch Katse Dam on the Malibamatso River, part of the Lesotho Highlands Water Project, is 185 meters high and 710 meters in length. It was completed in 1997 and fully filled by 1998. Photo © 2005 by Christian Wörtz.

The Lesotho Highlands Water Project

In the case of the Lesotho Highlands Water Project, the real benefits to both countries were tempered by the significant differences in economic status between South Africa and Lesotho, as well as seemingly insurmountable political differences. South Africa is the powerhouse of southern Africa. Lesotho, on the other hand, is a poor, largely undeveloped, land-locked country completely surrounded by South Africa, with almost no natural resources other than abundant clean water. For 40 years prior to 1994, South Africa enforced strict apartheid laws. It is understandable that their policies, which ensured domination by a minority of whites,

did not find favor in the overwhelmingly black population of Lesotho. This may in part explain why it took so long for the project to be realized. In the 1950s, the governments of the Basutoland Protectorate and the Union of South Africa began studying diversion of the headwaters of the Orange River (called the Senqu River in Lesotho) to the upper reaches of the Vaal River in South Africa.[4]

Perhaps the most celebrated champion of the cause was the late Ninham Shand, an engineer from South Africa. During the 1950s, he proposed a limited diversion of 5 m³/s (114 million gallons per day, mgd). Ultimately, the accepted scheme would provide a flow of 70 m³/s (1,598 mgd) in four phases. Phase I, completed in early 2004, produced a firm yield of 29.6 m³/s (676 mgd), with any future phases requiring the agreement of both governments before implementation.

It was clear that, in addition to what one would normally expect, the treaty had to address issues specific to the circumstances of both countries at the time of signing. Examples of items considered in the treaty include: overall project schedule, prevention of pollution of delivered water, in-stream flow requirements, and community mitigation measures. In addition, the treaty included clauses addressing the economic disparity between the countries, the sovereignty of Lesotho, and security of diverted water supplies without the possibility of either party disrupting this flow, among many other issues. The "Treaty on the Lesotho Highlands Water Project between the Government of the Kingdom of Lesotho and the Government of the Republic of South Africa" was signed into law in Lesotho by the foreign ministers of both countries on October 24, 1986.[5]

Gestation periods of megaprojects are measured in decades, as exemplified in the descriptions above of the Channel Tunnel and the Lesotho Highlands Water Project. In democratic countries, this extended duration can be problematic when decision-making politicians have short horizons driven by reelection concerns. It is a good policy to make sure that schedules during planning and implementation account for agreements, regulatory liaison, permitting, public relations, informing of stakeholders, and soliciting input from directly affected members of the public to be incorporated or mitigated, as appropriate.

Funding

Financing infrastructure, with price tags running into billions of U.S. dollars, is obviously a challenging logistical problem when it comes to megaprojects. In poorer countries, this can amount to a discernible part of their GNP. According to World Bank country classification statistics,[6] from a total of 210 national economies that were considered, 98 are classified as "low income" or "lower-middle-income" economies, i.e., those countries having a gross national income (GNI) of less than $3,855 per capita, based on 2008 data. Even wealthy countries experience difficulties arranging megaproject revenue streams and maintaining these for the duration of construction, which typically lasts several years. Establishing the necessary revenue streams may take several forms, including government guarantees, private bank backing, public-private partnerships (PPP), or other means of shared capital funding procurement.

As if this in and of itself were not complex enough, there are several other economic factors that should be considered before, during, and after megaprojects are planned and executed. While a substantial cash injection into the local economy may seem like a good idea at the time, it behooves planners to remember that megaprojects are built within a finite duration and do not sustain long-term employment that even comes close to the manpower requirements at the height of construction. This boom-and-bust economic cycle needs careful planning to maximize the positive effects while minimizing the downside.

Although each megaproject is unique, the resettlement and rehabilitation program for the 1,500 megawatt Nathpa Jhakri Hydroelectric Power Plant in India presents examples of positive benefits that can accrue. The plant's owner, Satluj Jal Vidyut Nigam Ltd., factors in rehabilitation expenditures that include, among other measures, a mobile health van, income-generating activities, training, merit scholarship schemes, and restoration of water sources.[7] While none of this comes free, the reported expenditure of about $30 million has resulted in real long-term improvements to the standard of living for the affected residents (as audited by the Agro Economic Research Centre, Himachal Pradesh University, Shimla).

What is not as well documented are some of the less desirable local impacts of mega-projects. The writer has personal experience on the Lesotho Highlands Water Project. After building safe access to previously remote areas in the country and introducing a migratory workforce of overwhelmingly single men with surplus cash to spend relative to the local population, an unprecedented growth of squatter camps occurred. Increased crime and prostitution disturbed the tranquility of what was a subsistence-farming-based rural life. Single megaprojects can have a significant impact on regional and national economies, and if multiple megaprojects occur in close proximity, their impact is magnified. This situation exists currently in New York City, with major construction on up to four transit megaprojects and at least one water supply megaproject planned to be designed and constructed simultaneously. The strain on labor would ordinarily be extreme, and the strain will be further exacerbated by the closed labor market and strong unions in New York City. Freely importing skilled labor from elsewhere in the U.S. or internationally is not easy. This issue has the obvious corollary that at the end of this surge of projects, the labor union (the internationally famous Local 147, or "Sand Hogs") will have several hundred members who will eventually have no tunnel work.

Scheduling of contracts is discussed in detail in chapter 5 of this book, and changes in schedule priorities can produce serious logistical consequences to a project's cash flow. "Affordability" is a word heard frequently in municipal wastewater planning, particularly with reference to combined sewer overflow (CSO) megaprojects in the United States. These are publicly funded and may well exceed $1 billion for larger cities, which is often paid for with substantial year-to-year rate increases for the residents of the city in question. This becomes a logistical consideration in scheduling cash-flow expenditures to match payment receipts, resulting in multiyear, phased programs. By contrast, privately funded entities constructing a revenue-generating facility, such as a massive hotel and casino construction in Las Vegas, find the rate of expenditure is not as large a consideration as compressing the overall schedule so as to hasten the start of revenue income. On such projects, it is not unusual to see multiple contractors working next to each other, with round-the-clock work and with cost issues secondary to schedule. Each of these examples has a schedule objective that is very different, and the result is a correspondingly different logistical challenge for successful project completion.

Anticipated Impacts

In planning megaprojects, one focus of project risk management is mitigation of adverse impacts to the natural and social environment. Most often, everyone on the project team works to minimize the effect of construction on the cost and schedule. This often runs into direct conflict with the ultimate desire of most stakeholders and the public, which is for construction to have a minimal impact on daily life and the environment.

Of course, constructing underground infrastructure has the most positive impact on the natural and built environment, providing water, wastewater, or transportation links that remain essentially invisible to the public. However, the need to control impacts throughout construction can lead to decision-making for the most efficient project completion that is not immediately self-evident. Spoil removal is a primary focus of mitigating impacts on the natural environment from an underground megaproject. Together, public outreach and media management are examples of a *counterintuitive* social impact that was frequently overlooked in the past, but which, through a series of adverse events on many projects, has become one of the first departments set up by the owners at the start of a megaproject.

The Three Gorges Dam on the Yangtze River is the world's largest electricity-generating plant of any kind. Photo © 2009 by Le Grand Portage.

Just one example of severe social and cultural objections to a megaproject over a number of years during construction is encapsulated in a series of news articles about the $3 billion multipurpose Tehri Dam in India (which have been compiled on the Uttarakhand website[8]). Opposition to this dam ranged from social and environmental concerns in 1997, when activists accused the government of turning a blind eye toward "dam safety, quality of Ganga water after impoundment, impact on health of people, security of life and property of the people in the densely populated Indo-Gangetic belt, [and] the economic viability of the project," to unsatisfactory compensation of residents who had to be relocated[9] and religious objections because the dam would flood a famous and ancient Satyeshwar temple of Lord Shiva situated in the heart of Tehri, as well as diluting waters that were self-purified in the holy Gangajal River.[10] This protest sought immediate cessation of work even though some 75 percent of the project cost had been spent.

The mighty Three Gorges Dam in China, while a great technical success, has attracted the unwelcome reputation of being an environmental catastrophe. Even China, with a strongly centralized and powerful government that normally brooks no internal opposition, has not been immune to both internal and worldwide criticism for riding roughshod over environmental considerations during construction. The 460 km (398 mile) reservoir has caused relocation of more than one million people from 13 cities, 140 towns, and 1,350 villages and significant loss of arable land. Valuable archeological sites have been flooded, and during filling, earth tremors (normal for large dams) caused

concern. Of more concern is the increased erosion and landslides of reservoir banks, which has worsened water quality and increased algae blooms in tributaries as they are flooded. Ironically, Three Gorges Dam was designed to provide clean, sustainable power to replace dirty coal-fired power stations.[11]

Logistics in Design

Moving on from concept and planning, we find that the design of megaprojects requires the application of significant resources. The opportunity to work on these prestigious projects attracts the best designers in the world. There are many aspects during design that are characteristic of megaprojects, and the logistics involved with changing contractual formats, the conditions of the contracts, the creation of standard specifications, and appropriate insurance and surety provisions are significant. We believe it is important to use megaprojects — which are indeed flagship projects — to research technological improvements in construction to further develop and enhance the whole industry. Advances in technology and the ability of designers and owners to carry out a research and development process in a controlled manner — one that does not allow costs to spiral — can be impressive examples of logistics during design. Beyond that, research is not limited to the design and construction aspects. For example, Isshiki and Wiczalek (1997) have reported on the safe and effective use of regenerative braking on both passenger and freight trains in the 54 km (33.5 mile) Seikan tunnel connecting the islands of Honshu and Hokkaido in Japan.

A major decision to be made early on in the project is whether the project owner will assemble its own internal engineering team or rely on paid consultants for both planning and construction management of the project, such as the Washington (D.C.) Metropolitan Area Transit Authority (WMATA) (begun in 1967 with Bechtel, but later its employees were absorbed into new client organization) and Boston's Central Artery/Tunnel (which handled everything through external consultants). A primary factor in this decision is the overall schedule and size of the project. For the design of the Washington Metro system, the city hired an external consultant to manage the design and geotechnical programs and used individual section designers. Construction began with the creation of the WMATA, which conducted the construction management essentially in-house after the transfer of a core of employees from Bechtel, the original program management company. WMATA expanded to operate as a semiautonomous agency of the District government, and in 2008, 35 years after its creation, it is now the second-largest mass transit authority in the United States, with 2008 average daily ridership around 1 million and 106.3 route miles.[12] Only the New York City subway boasts greater ridership of 4.7 million passengers average per day in 2008 on 229 miles of heavy rail rapid transit infrastructure.[13] Many

employees of WMATA have enjoyed long careers in all types of underground construction of one of the great megaprojects of the twentieth century.

The corollary to this is an organization like the New York City Department of Environmental Protection (NYCDEP), which historically has designed and provided construction management in-house for the New York City water tunnels. Only recently has the city requested outside construction management services for their tunnels.

Logistics in Construction

Once planned and designed, the earth must be turned and the project actually constructed to realize the benefits envisioned so many years beforehand. All construction processes begin with the procurement of the contractor. Megaprojects are almost always built using multiple contracts, whether several similar-sized contracts, like the Jubilee Line Extension in London, or one very large contract consortium with other enabling and finishing works, like the Channel Tunnel. The importance of managing the contractual interfaces and risks associated with these interfaces cannot be overemphasized.

Delivery of a program is purely a logistical challenge revolving around the procurement method, chosen technique, and structure of delivery. Methods of procurement affect important aspects of delivery (such as the elapsed schedule up to the start of construction by selection of procurement method), cash flow (from payment of simultaneous construction and/or design contracts), and risk allocation among parties.

Procurement is considered in more detail in chapter 3 of this book. For a thorough discussion of alternative delivery methods in underground construction, see Brierley and Hatem (2002). It should be noted that considerations associated with selection of methods of procurement and delivery, particularly the use of design-build procurement can include nontechnical logistics, such as the desire by political figures to participate in ceremonies for early construction activities within their finite term in office.

Risk allocation in contracts is covered in detail in Part II of this book. This discussion identifies all logistics issues that must be contemplated completely before allocating risk in contracts. One example is truck traffic associated with spoil removal. The consequences of failure in this activity include stakeholder protest, adverse press coverage, fines from regulatory agencies, delays to the schedule, and claims associated with additional work "not foreseen" in the contractor's bid. These are hardly what you would call contractor problems. Indeed, the owner will bear the majority of the costs and reputation damage from these consequences. Spoil removal, however, is frequently allocated to the contractor for mitigation.

A thorough risk assessment and risk management program can clarify for all concerned the consequences of certain actions, so that appropriate risk allocation for those

actions can be made. A specific section on, or specific consideration of, logistics is an important part of the risk management program.

Risk and Opportunity

With megaprojects come "mega-risks" and "mega-opportunities." Early implementation of a structured risk program, including a risk register, helps to identify both logistical hazards and opportunities, so that political will, funding, the macroeconomic value of the project, environmental impact of construction on the immediate area, and any other issues can be discussed in an orderly and structured fashion at an early stage. These discussions will enable a risk-based approach to project logistics, carried out along the lines of established risk management codes of practice (e.g., "A Code of Practice for Risk Management of Tunnel Works," ITIG, 2006), to provide guidance during conceptual planning and in assessing the feasibility and desirability of the project design and construction. It is a truism to say that at this stage and throughout the many years of the project's execution, many of the major decisions and actions are based on whether the logistics for the proposed solution or action are feasible and tolerable to the project stakeholders.

Even before construction of the project itself commences, site preparation and the infrastructure associated with it often calls for a major undertaking all of its own. Urban projects may require special parking areas of significant size in places where there is no such space. Remote projects require temporary accommodations and infrastructure, including roads and services that can take several years to construct before work on the actual project can begin. According to William Joe Simonds in his essay entitled "The Boulder Canyon Project: Hoover Dam,"[14] in September 1930, some six months before the notice to proceed for construction of Hoover Dam was signed between the federal government and Six Companies, Union Pacific Railroad began construction on a 22.7-mile-long rail link from Las Vegas to Boulder City. There were a number of additional major infrastructure elements that had to be provided during this period before dam construction could start:

- Boulder City itself, planned to house upwards of 5,000 workers. It was not completed before workers began arriving in numbers, which led to the establishment of desperate squatter camps (Ragtown).
- A 10-mile continuation of the railroad from Boulder City to the dam site.
- A 24-mile highway constructed by the state of Nevada, to link Las Vegas and Boulder City.
- A road from Boulder City to the Boulder Canyon rim at Hoover Dam.
- Government-supplied construction power, provided via a 222-mile transmission line from San Bernardino, California.

- A 150-ton permanent cableway for transporting equipment and material into the canyon.

This expenditure was significant, some $4 million in 1930 dollars (approximately $57 million in 2008 terms), amounting to around 10 percent of the value of the contract to construct the dam itself.

Even in urban areas, the enabling work that involves clearing the site of utilities and buildings, and building the preparatory underpinning for underground structures, can be significant undertakings. For example, the Massachusetts Bay Transportation Authority notes that 29 miles of gas, electric, telephone, sewer, water, and other utilities maintained by 31 separate companies had to be relocated for the Big Dig.[15]

Logistics of Labor

During construction itself, supplying trained labor, equipment, and construction materials in a timely manner to the correct location presents major logistical challenges. Assembling the labor resources in one place for a megaproject is a significant task during both design and construction. This problem is compounded on underground megaprojects by the specialized nature of the work. While modern electronic communications allow remote groups of designers to be actively involved in production, which can mitigate this issue somewhat during design, stretching local resources is probably inevitable during construction. Two contrasting examples illustrate this point.

New York

While there is a long-standing and well-trained labor force in New York City, the many simultaneous construction projects placed a significant strain on local union labor capacity during the recent surge of tunnel work in the city. The unions, the construction community, and owner agencies within New York City have recognized the potential labor problem and have taken several pragmatic and well-coordinated steps to mitigate impact on the current and upcoming project work, including:

- Union recruitment programs were set up in locations with recently completed major tunnel work, such as Boston, Atlanta, and Chicago, to bolster the ranks of trained tunnel labor.
- Skilled activities not previously considered in New York City, such as waterproofing membrane installation, were introduced by waivers on the initial contracts for skilled labor in exchange for training programs, so that subsequent projects can be staffed from within local union ranks.

These steps have fostered a spirit of cooperation with contractors and owners and at the same time have kept the unions at the center of discussions on how to achieve project objectives that are critical to New York City.

Iceland

On the Kárahnjúkar hydroelectric megaproject in Iceland, the question of labor demands during construction at a remote location was important enough to be included in the European Free Trade Association Surveillance Authority Decision of March 14, 2003.[16] This decision addressed vital legal and economic issues that would determine the project's feasibility. In addition to taxes (as noted in the title), the EFTA described agreements on other matters such as the period of the concession with Alcoa, Inc., real estate needs, and costs, etc. According to this decision, executives from the construction companies anticipated 2,300 person-years for project implementation between 2003 and 2007. Because the total population of the East Region, where the project is located, was only about 12,000, the parties agreed that the expected source of construction labor would be:

- Local residents – 10%
- Workers from outside the East Region who would temporarily relocate with their families for the project duration – 15%
- Foreign construction workers – 30%
- Icelandic workers housed in construction camps but returning home during time off work – 45%

Clearly, this megaproject demanded that resources be mobilized from around the world to provide adequate numbers of trained labor.

Logistics of the Location

Supplying materials and equipment is arguably the single most critical logistical issue on any project, and it is only magnified when the size of the project increases to "mega" proportions. The issues of supply depend on the location and conditions surrounding the project. A rural or remote location is challenging because of the difficulties of supplying resources to the project. An urban site can have similar issues (at the time of this writing, delivery time for a large crane in New York City was up to one year) but urban construction is usually constrained more by the allowable level of disruption of the surrounding residents and by the requirements of permitting agencies. Other conditions—such as noise limitations, work hour limitations, or target percentages for non-road removal of spoil—produce severe logistical demands over and above the regular issues faced on the project.

The stakeholders' requirements in a megaproject can be the most difficult and all-

encompassing challenge to logistical efforts during planning, design, and construction. Some stakeholders may seek to impose constraints on working areas or hours or insist that additional facilities be left in place after construction, and they frequently assume that the large proposed budget will bear these demands without change. These expectations are clearly unfounded, and the challenge facing the project participants is to predict the regulatory constraints and cost them appropriately so that future changes do not appear as increases to the overall budget.

Outreach and Public Relations

Megaprojects naturally attract attention from stakeholders—supportive and otherwise—and attention takes many forms, including treaties, legislation, ordinances, construction permits, and quick-take, compulsory purchase, or some other forced condemnation of property. These issues and the problems they can create can largely be mitigated by the use of a comprehensive public outreach program. Programs of this size do have some advantages of scale. Megaprojects often generate so much demand for local permitting decisions that a separate department is set up or priority is given to this project. In order to facilitate the regulating and permitting matters involved, it is advisable to initiate informal discussions about the project's development early and update the results often with all affected regulators and with interested politicians who may influence regulators. It is also advisable to work with regulators to establish the parameters they require to expedite approvals and develop reports that address each regulator's parameters.

It is clear that, even with the best will in the world, it is simply not possible to build megaprojects without directly impacting people in the area of the project, and possibly on a much wider scale financially. Large-scale construction, frequently continuing 24 hours per day, will increase activity, traffic, noise, vibration, dust, and lighting pollution. There are real and perceived reasons why nobody wants this in their backyard. As soon as the project's definition allows answers to the specific questions, inform stakeholders of the current state of the project. At these sessions, it is vital that stakeholders be encouraged to raise all their concerns. Project champions should *not* assume they know what the stakeholder issues will be; it is important to listen at this stage. It is equally important that ongoing communications with the stakeholders be maintained, and that it is clear to them how all their concerns will be addressed, what mitigation measures will be put in place, how long-term planning issues will be described, etc. Stakeholder interaction is important throughout the construction and commissioning phases. Feedback on issues that were not foreseen and that result in stakeholder concerns must be addressed as they arise. Stakeholder programs are as necessary in first-world geographical locations as they are in third-world settings.

The New York City Water Tunnel Number 3 has several shaft locations in wealthy

Manhattan neighborhoods that required a delicate balance between the need to tie in the deep supply tunnel with fixed access points within the city, to maintain reasonable construction progress to actually finish the project, and to cushion the impact of the construction blasting and other noise, dust, and vibration issues on the nearby residents and businesses. These were issues with far-reaching logistical consequences that had to be managed from the original shaft-siting study through, planning, design, public involvement, and comment periods, as well as the construction itself. At the time of writing, the project had been constructed successfully, with only the surface connection and commissioning work remaining to be completed.

Although by comparison, rural communities affected by the Lesotho Highlands Water Project are poor and underdeveloped, it would be unwise to assume that they are unsophisticated. Since 1998, the Lesotho Highlands Development Authority has conducted an Annual Stakeholder Conference in Maseru, the capital of Lesotho. Attendees include communities affected by the Lesotho Highlands Water Project, nongovernmental organizations, government ministries, parastatals, students and lecturers from the National University of Lesotho Sociology Department, the World Bank Panel of Experts (international), the Development Bank of Southern Africa, the European Investment Bank, and the South African Department of Water Affairs. The Lesotho Highlands Development Authority (LHDA) at the October 2006 Stakeholders Meeting reported the World Bank description of the project as world class with minimal community impacts.[17] The issues raised by affected communities were addressed by crafting specific recommendations:

- Audit cooperatives on time and expedite cooperatives at Mohale.
- Consider incorporating local governments within LHDA programs.
- Encourage further training on income generation ventures for affected communities.
- Make compensation payments on time.
- Respond to complaints on time.
- Rehabilitate some LHDA lands and return them to the people.
- Eradicate corruption by all means.
- Supply diving equipment to Lesotho Defense Force and use them for diving work.
- Repair snow removal equipment.
- Increase honoraria for citizen's advisory committees.
- Schedule regular visits by managers to local communities.
- Implement zoning plan to encourage tourism.
- Decrease the rents for LHDA houses to accommodate low-income government staff.

One should anticipate extensive interest from the general public and various groups, not only the affected communities, each with its own agenda and priorities. There are

likely to be as many people against the project as those who support it. For example, in 2001, the Georgia Chapter of the Sierra Club strongly advocated a complete sewer separation as the only acceptable remedy to Atlanta's combined sewer overflow problems. On September 8, 2001, they arranged a protest against the proposed plan for tunnels, storage, retention, and ultimately treatment of combined sewer overflows (CSOs). In addition to correctly pointing out that this solution would not eliminate all CSOs, they claimed that the costs of complete sewer separation and additional detention ponds had been overestimated, while consolidated storage, relocation, and treatment has been underestimated. They called the project "risky tunnels" and "a billion dollar Band-Aid" that would not meet the legislated consent decree requirements.

Perhaps the most obvious reason for negative public attitudes towards megaprojects is the seemingly inevitable and sometimes dramatic cost increases that seem to plague construction in general and megaprojects in particular. For the Boston Central Artery/ Tunnel, colloquially known as the "Big Dig," cost increases have been paraded in public in a multitude of press reports that are familiar to anyone in the industry. In a 2003 *Boston Globe* article, Sean P. Murphy and Raphael Lewis wrote, "The project's budget had ballooned by $1.4 billion despite public assertions to the contrary."[18] Three years later in the *Boston Globe*, Rick Klein reported that "costs skyrocketed from $1 billion to more than $14 billion."[19] He went on to say the repercussions for this expenditure had generated far-reaching political impacts, all the way to the House and Senate in Washington, D.C. It matters not that such comparisons are unfair and that apples are being compared to oranges: this clearly demonstrates a perception that requires careful management. It is vital that early cost estimates provided to the public err on the conservative side. Scope creep is one of the enemies of megaprojects that needs to be confronted early and often.

A good approach to help ensure balanced reporting of the issues is to appoint a dedicated public relations team. They can get information from engineers and contractors in order to develop comprehensive documentation that does several things: sets out project needs and benefits (some of which, like reintroducing fish into previously heavily polluted waterways, may only be realized years after the project's completion), describes consequences of not proceeding with the project, and identifies mitigating actions. This material can be disseminated to both press and stakeholders under the control of the PR team, and their operation will typically continue throughout the project and probably until well after completion.

In a similar vein, it is wise to try to limit the development of public misconceptions by assigning an individual to control all formal press interaction. The duties of this position would include setting up press briefings, receiving questions and getting answers to those questions from the appropriate project member, and responding to the press. The position would also track all press reports, postings, and blogs about the project and cor-

rect mistakes, misconceptions, and inaccurate reports. Press relations may be included as part of the construction contract while the major infrastructure is being built. However, it is our opinion that the owner is best placed to ensure proactive press relations.

Contractors and engineers alike should be cautioned about the dangers of providing any unauthorized information to the press. The public press has an undeniable interest in reporting possibly controversial stories. Reporters, particularly those active in the daily news business, face unforgiving deadlines that militate against exhaustive research and confirmation of facts. Seemingly innocent commentary from construction staff can be damaging to a project's image, such as the affable "informal discussion" with a construction superintendant in Baltimore during subway construction about aspects of the construction process that led to several days of less than flattering news coverage about the project (sourced from anecdotal personal discussions).

A project historian can give the owners an opportunity to discuss the historic context of the project and can lead to the publishing of a number of books and other materials related to the planning, design, and construction, seen from an impartial observer's vantage point. Professional writers and recorders know what is required to produce electronic and hard copy and how to use suitable materials for public, technical, and archival publications. This type of project documentation is something that is common in many parts of the world and provides a great tool for future reference. Some recent megaprojects that have attractive coffee-table-type publications include:

The Big Dig, by Dan McNichol, with photographs by Andy Ryan. New York: Silver Lining, 2000.

Exploring the Mystery of Matter: The ATLAS Experiment, by Kerry-Lane Lowery, photography by Claudia Marcelloni, edited by Kenway Smith. London: Papadakis, 2008. ("ATLAS" is an acronym for "A Toroidal LHC ApparatuS," part of the Large Hadron Collider at the CERN facilities in Geneva.)

The Official Channel Tunnel Factfile, by Philip Clark. London: Boxtree, Ltd., 1994.

Westerschelde Tunnel: Approaching Limits, by J. Heijboer. Lisse, The Netherlands: A. A. Balkema Publishers, 2004. (About a vehicular tunnel under the Westerschelde River in Zeeland, the Netherlands.)

The Seikan Railroad Tunnel: World's Longest Tunnel, by Mark Thomas. New York: Rosen Publishing, 2002. (A children's book.)

Conquering Gotham: A Gilded Age Epic: The Construction of Penn Station and Its Tunnels, by Jill Jonnes. New York: Viking Adult, 2007.

The Jubilee Line Extension: A Celebration, by Kenneth Powell. London: Laurence King Publishing, 2001. (About the largest extension of the London Underground.)

Waterworks: A Photographic Journey Through New York's Hidden Water System, by Stanley Greenberg. New York: Princeton Architectural Press, 2003.

Water-Works: The Architecture and Engineering of the New York City Water Supply, by Kevin Bone, Gina Pollara, and Gerald Koeppel. New York: The Monacelli Press, 2006.

Logistics is an important consideration throughout any construction project, and this importance is increased in a megaproject. Every stage of a megaproject, from concept and planning, through design and construction to public relations, contains significant logistical decisions, and cost, schedule, and environmental and social impacts are the consequences of these decisions. This chapter has described the major logistical considerations with project examples in an attempt to promote successful megaproject campaigns, thus allowing more teams to win the "logistical war" that these megaprojects require us to fight.

List of Megaprojects Mentioned in This Chapter

URLs verified on March 20, 2010.

Atlanta CSO
http://cleanwateratlanta.org,
Boston Big Dig
http://www.massdot.state.ma.us/Highway/bigdig/bigdigmain.aspx
Channel Tunnel
http://www.theotherside.co.uk/tm-heritage/background/tunnel.htm
The Hoover (Boulder Canyon) Dam
http://www.usbr.gov/lc/hooverdam/
Jubilee Line Extension, London
http://www.tfl.gov.uk/tfl/corporate/modesoftransport/tube/
linefacts/?line=jubilee
Lesotho Highlands Water Project (LHWP)
http://www.lhwp.org.ls/overview/default.htm
Nathpa Jhakri Hydroelectric Power Plant
http://www.power-technology.com/projects/nathpa
New York Water Tunnels
http://www.nyc.gov/html/dep/pdf/wsstat01b.pdf
Seikan Rail Tunnel
http://www.absoluteastronomy.com/topics/Seikan_Tunnel
Tehri Dam
http://www.euttaranchal.com/uttaranchal/highlight/tehri_dam.php

Three Gorges Dam
http://www.travelchinaguide.com/attraction/hubei/yichang/three-gorges-dam-project.htm

Washington Metropolitan Area Transit Authority (WMATA)
http://www.wmata.com/about_metro

Reference Sources

Brierley, G. S., and Hatem, D. J. (2002). *Design-Build Subsurface Projects.* Scottsdale, AZ: Zeni House Books.

Gueterbock, A. F. (1992). "Concepts, reality and expectations." In *Proceedings of the Institution of Civil Engineers: The Channel Tunnel, Part 1: Tunnels.* (Supplement to Civil Engineering), 2–5.

Heijboer, J., Hoonaard, J.v.d., and Linde, F. W. J.v.d. (2004). *The Westerschelde Tunnel: Approaching Limits.* Lisse, The Netherlands: A. A. Balkema Publishers.

Henderson, N. (1989). "Channel Tunnel — The early stages." Paper delivered at the Channel Tunnel Conference, Paris, September 20–22, 1989.

Isshiki, S., and Wiczalek, F. A. (1997). "Seikan Tunnel Electric Train Propulsion Regenerative Energy Management." In *Proceedings of the 32nd Intersociety Energy Conversion Engineering Conference*, Honolulu, Hawaii. Volume 3, 1997. Retrieved on January 23, 2009, from http://ieeexplore.ieee.org/xpl/freeabs_all.jsp?arnumber=656671.

Jonnes, J. (2007). *Conquering Gotham: A Gilded Age Epic: The Construction of Penn Station and Its Tunnels.* New York: Viking.

Lowery, K.-L., and Marcelloni, C. (2008). *Exploring the Mystery of Matter: The ATLAS Experiment.* London: Papadakis.

McNichol, D., and Ryan, A. (2000). *The Big Dig.* New York: Silver Lining Books, Inc.

Nthako, S., & Griffiths, A. L. (1997). "Lesotho Highlands Water Project: Project Management." In *Proceedings of the Institution of Civil Engineers — Civil Engineering*, Lesotho Highlands Water Project, Supplement to Civil Engineering Vol. 120. Special Issue 1997, pp. 3–14.

Powell, K. (2000). *The Jubilee Line Extension: A Celebration.* London: Laurence King.

Thomas, M. (2002). *The Seikan Railroad Tunnel: World's Longest Tunnel.* New York: PowerKids Press.

Yang, L. (October 12, 2007). "China's Three Gorges Dam Under Fire," *Time Magazine.* Retrieved on January 23, 2009, from http://www.time.com/time/world/article/0,8599,1671000,00.html.

Yardley, J. (November 19, 2007). "Chinese Dam Projects Criticized for Their Human Cost." *New York Times.* Retrieved on January 23, 2009, http://internationalrivers.org/en/node/2758.

Notes

1. "Logistics." *Department of Defense Dictionary of Military and Associated Terms*, Joint Publication 1-02 (April 12, 2001), p. 319.

2. Henderson, N. (1989). "Channel Tunnel — The early stages." Paper delivered at the Channel Tunnel Conference, Paris, September 20–22, 1989.

3. Henderson, N. "Channel Tunnel — The early stages."

4. Nthako, S., & Griffiths, A. L. (1997). "Lesotho Highlands Water Project: Project Management." In *Proceedings of the Institution of Civil Engineers — Civil Engineering*, Lesotho Highlands Water Project, Supplement to Civil Engineering Vol. 120. Special Issue 1997, pp. 3–14.

5. The interested reader who desires to see just how intricate this can become may download a free version of the 45-page treaty, excluding annexes and protocols, at http://www.fao.org/docrep/w7414b/w7414bow.htm.

6. World Bank, "Data and Statistics" (Web pages). Retrieved March 9, 2010, from http://go.worldbank.org/D7SN0B8YU0.

7. See the project's website at http://sjvn.nic.in/projects/projects_nathpa_se_rr.asp.

8. See http://uttarakhand.prayaga.org/archive/tehri.html.

9. *The Times of India* News Service, June 17, 1999.

10. *The Times of India* News Service, August 9, 1999, and July 14, 2000.

11. Yang, L.. "China's Three Gorges Dam Under Fire," *Time Magazine* (October 12, 2007); and Yardley, J. "Chinese Dam Projects Criticized for Their Human Cost," *New York Times* (November 19, 2007).

12. See http://www.wmata.com/about/metrofacts.pdf.

13. See http://www.urbanrail.net/am/nyrk/new-york.htm.

14. Retrieved March 9, 2010, from http://www.usbr.gov/history/hoover.html.

15. See http://www.massdot.state.ma.us/Highway/bigdig/facts_figures.aspx.

16. "Proposed Financing and Tax Measures Concerning the Construction of an Aluminium Plant in the Township of Fjarðabyggð, Iceland." Retrieved March 9, 2010, from www.eftasurv.int/?1=1&showLinkID=3982&1=1.

17. See http://www.lhwp.org.ls/downloads/default.htm.

18. Murphy, S. P., & Lewis, R. (May 28, 2003). "Author Criticizes Big Dig Accounting," *The Boston Globe*.

19. Klein, R. (August 6, 2006). "Big Dig Failures Threaten Federal Funding, Future Projects May Be Shortchanged," *The Boston Globe*.

CHAPTER 7

Utility and Third-Party Considerations

Eldon L. Abbott, P.E., Parsons Brinckerhoff
Peter F. Donahue, P.E., Parsons Brinckerhoff

Megaprojects are large, complex construction projects that generally involve multiple construction contractors and multiple design teams. Management of all of these entities requires coordination provided by either the owner or a program manager retained by the owner. It is important that the program manager be responsible for project-wide functions that cross design and construction contract boundaries or that come into play at project interface points. The management team should be in a position to anticipate and manage utilities and third-party issues in a timely manner, serve as a single point of responsibility and single point of contact, and present a single, unified message to local third-party groups. (A "third party" is anyone who is not under contract to the contractor, owner, construction management, or the design team.)

Construction of megaprojects is by its very nature linear in progression, because they will have various portions under design, construction, and planning simultaneously. It is not unusual for the scope elements of a megaproject to change during the course of the work due to the length of time it takes to fully execute the project. Thus, any unforeseen impacts to specific planned work on any portion of a megaproject can have significant impacts on other portions of the work. Two areas where these kinds of impacts occur are utilities and third-party coordination.

While not as glamorous or as much in the public eye as the high-profile components of a megaproject, utilities and third-party interfaces run throughout all megaprojects, and problems that arise in them can adversely impact any aspect of the project. Dealing with these two issues can prove to be very challenging and difficult. Any risk assessment of a megaproject, particularly ones in urban areas, should include them, and the planning to deal with utility and third-party interface issues should begin as early as practical to minimize the impact they may have on the project. The impacts of encountering an unexpected third-party interface or discovering an unknown utility during the construction stage of a megaproject can be quite disruptive, including significant schedule delay, increased unanticipated costs, and delay claims. The good news is that these impacts can be mitigated if approached early and in the proper manner.

The Thames Barrier, a flood-control mechanism east of London, consists of eight steel barrier walls that rotate into place to prevent storm- and tide-driven flood waters to inundate London. It was built between 1972 and 1982 and officially opened in 1984. Photo © 2008 by Bill Bertram.

In the following sections of this chapter, methods to plan for and prevent adverse impacts due to utilities and third parties will be discussed.

Utilities and Megaprojects
Issue

Subsurface risk embraces more than just geologic and groundwater conditions and includes utility infrastructure, either known or unknown, within and adjacent to the construction project area. In the early stages of planning for a megaproject, the owner should allow ample time for subsurface investigations and research of utilities.

In today's economic climate of consolidation, utilities are being combined, taken over, changing names, and changing services, all of which can impede information-gathering efforts. Often, utility owners do not have complete or accurate records of their installations. Moreover, in this post–9/11 era, some utilities are reluctant to divulge information on their infrastructure for security reasons.

What is needed is a logical, systematic approach that will result in the development of a database of sufficient detail and robustness to identify utilities in and around the megaproject and allow for the proper planning of execution and mitigation efforts necessary for the successful completion of the megaproject with minimal impact on the functionality of the various utility systems.

By definition, the time for execution of a megaproject is years long, and during that time, the area in which the megaproject takes place must remain active. Businesses must remain open, residences must be lived in, amenities such as passive and active recreation areas, historical attractions, museums, schools, and everything else that make up the community must remain usable. All of these elements of the community depend on reliable utility services, and they cannot be interrupted without adverse consequences for the community as well as the project.

The owners and designers of a megaproject must take this into consideration when planning and designing it. Time and effort spent at the beginning on understanding the utility infrastructure and the project's impact on it is time well spent, because this is the only thing that will ensure that both the community and the megaproject can coexist using the utility infrastructure that both depend on.

Analysis and Discussion

Once a megaproject is under way, any issues that arise unexpectedly can and will cause disruption. The key to success is to identify and mitigate these issues as early in the process as possible. Any unknown that can impact a contractor's cost or schedule is a risk that has to be covered by either adding contingency budget to a bid or including

a contractual relief clause to provide relief in the event the unknown becomes a reality. Identifying the utilities early in the process is a necessity in order to understand the costs of — and therefore the budget needed for — the megaproject.

Most megaprojects are built in urban areas, and utilities are the life blood of an urban area, whether it is a professional services district, a manufacturing district, an entertainment district, a warehousing and delivery district, or a residential district. Utilities are also necessary for the prosecution of the megaproject, and the need for them cannot be neglected in the planning process. During the course of a megaproject, life must go on in and around the project, and uninterrupted service for all utilities allows for this coexistence to occur.

Because of the importance of this issue to the community and to the success of the project itself, once the preferred alignment or conceptual design is complete, the process of developing an accurate and complete utility database should commence. Besides the actual identification of the utility infrastructure, it is equally important to ascertain the legal instrument or authority by which a utility is allowed to occupy its space in the ground. Certain questions need to be answered: (1) On private property, is the utility in an easement or is it there simply by permission or permit? (2) Where is the interface juncture between the utility ownership and private ownership? (3) On public property, is it in the right-of-way by means of a formal grant of location with inherent rights, or is it there by permission only? Answers to these questions are necessary to fully understand the entire utility issue, to identify the point of contact with the utility, to understand the utility standards that apply, and to know what approvals are required, because relocation of a utility service may involve more than simply digging a new trench.

Planning must also include understanding the utilities themselves. Which utilities will not allow outside contractors to work on their infrastructure, thus requiring the establishment of force accounts and creating a schedule dependency? Which utilities have specialized infrastructure requiring consideration of lead times for ordering pieces and parts? Which have specialized or standardized specifications and procedures that must be followed? Is the decision-making authority local or not? Which utilities are planning major upgrades or expansion projects that may need to be taken into consideration?

Understanding the internal working processes of the various utilities is needed as well. What is the approval process for changes to a system and how long does it take? Is there a different process or criteria for interim or temporary work versus permanent work? Are there techniques or special design procedures that must be followed? The more that is known about the internal workings of the utilities, the higher the likelihood that misunderstandings will not develop during the utility investigation and design periods and will not disrupt the processes.

Many megaprojects have benefited from the establishment of a standing utility committee made up of representatives from the project and the public and private utilities.

The purpose of this committee is to facilitate the development of a full and detailed understanding of the existing conditions in and adjacent to the megaproject, to develop an understanding of the utilities' planned work in the area, to develop an understanding of the interim or temporary needs of the megaproject and what impact those needs may have on the ability of the utility to service its customers, to help the identification and prosecution of any requisite force account work, to maintain the utility database throughout the course of the megaproject, and to deal with planned and unplanned utility outages and the discovery of unknown utilities during the course of the work.

Even with the most extensive research and field investigations, the likelihood of encountering an undocumented utility or, worse, hitting a utility during construction is a risk that must be dealt with. Establishing a training program and initiating work protocols have proven to be effective measures to mitigate such occurrences. Training programs using video presentations with handout booklets are inexpensive but very effective methods to raise contractor awareness of the issue. They can be conducted at the beginning of a contract and at various times during the construction work to maintain a heightened awareness. Submittal requirements for utility exploration and detailed excavation plans can give a full picture of the contractor's approach to subsurface work and allow an opportunity for the owner or engineer to give input to ensure that proper precautions are taken. Including an allowance for subsurface utility exploration (SUE) is another tool that can be used to mitigate the consequences of encountering an undocumented utility, and it may also reduce the contingency that a contractor includes in its bid to cover the cost of encountering an unexpected utility. SUE has been most effective in older urbanized areas, where recorded information is lacking and utilities are very congested. It can result in the best, most accurate information available to aid in reducing risk exposure and making effective risk allocations. Unless an owner performs a sufficiently rigorous investigation to permit baselining the utilities (and thereby takes on the risk of encountering an undocumented utility during the performance of the project), most construction contracts require the contractor to verify the utilities in the area of its work, usually via a field survey and test pits (potholing), which thus passes the risk on to the contractor. In this instance, the more accurate and complete the utility information provided by the owner, the lower the contingency the contractor will include in its bid.

Encountering an undocumented utility will raise a number of questions. The project team must determine which utility it is (and at times this is not readily apparent), whether it is in service or abandoned, how it fits into the utilities' overall working systems, and finally, how best to deal with the unexpected utility. All of these decisions must be made before work in the area can proceed safely, and they can be time-consuming. It is therefore paramount that the project team, working in concert with the utility agencies and companies, establish a protocol ahead of time on how to deal with

each of these. The contractor's crews also need to be well versed in the protocol and its implementation in order to resolve issues quickly and in a workable manner for both the megaproject and the utility involved.

One aspect of subsurface utility work that is often overlooked is consideration of the materials used. Some utility companies in the past used materials that are now considered hazardous or contaminated, and their removal must be handled according to established regulatory procedures. Asbestos is one material that comes readily to mind. It was used in water and sewer lines, electrical conduit, and insulation. Likewise, oil-filled high voltage cables are still in use. Sediment in manholes, catch basins, and pipelines needs to be characterized prior to disposal. Beyond the hazardous/contaminated material itself, the soil surrounding the installation may have been contaminated, exacerbating the removal problem. This applies to planned utility work as well as unplanned work, such as encountering an undocumented utility. One method of dealing with hazardous/contaminated materials is to engage the services of an environmental engineering firm as part of the initial subsurface exploration program and to include in its scope of work not only the traditional identification of hazardous/contaminated materials in soil and groundwater, but also the characterization of utilities or the contents of utilities for the purposes of disposal. This aspect should be performed early (along with other subsurface investigations), as it may reveal areas that the project team may consider designing around rather than through to avoid extensive hazardous/contaminated material remediation or having to work through a maze of fragile, congested utilities.

Recommended Practices

How can building around subsurface utilities be handled so that adverse impacts to the megaproject and its community are minimized? The first step is to develop a database of existing utility infrastructure in and adjacent to the project area.

Hire a local civil engineering firm with experience in dealing with the local utility infrastructure to conduct the investigative effort. Such a firm will (or should) already have established contacts within the utility companies and agencies and be familiar with their internal processes, will understand how the utilities establish themselves in certain areas, and may already have information on the utilities in office files. Identify all of the utility companies and agencies and each of their systems. For instance, in Boston the Water and Sewer Commission runs three separate water systems at different pressure levels. When identifying the utility companies and agencies, include those that may no longer be in existence but which may have infrastructure still in place. This may seem to be an unnecessary step; however, if a piece of infrastructure is uncovered that is not accounted for, the ensuing delay to the work while it is identified can be lengthy, especially if it is not part of the owned infrastructure of an existing utility agency or company.

The research should start with the record drawings, field books, installation sketches, etc., of each utility. The area researched should extend outside of the boundaries of construction far enough to understand the impact to a system by any work done within the construction area. The research may reveal apparent conflicts in which two different utilities seemingly occupy the same space. In this case, research and field work must proceed carefully, with no preconceived notions as to what is correct. There are instances where what appears to be a conflict is in fact reality. In one example, the research conducted for an underground parking garage indicated an abandoned steam line in the same location as a telephone service. Further investigation showed that the steam line was still in place, but was being used as a conduit for the telephone service. In another instance, utility research for an urban renewal project in a very congested area showed a gas line making a bend around a catch basin where there didn't appear to be sufficient space for both to exist. Additional research revealed that the gas line did not bend around the structure, but went through it. In this case, both utilities occupied the same space, creating a dangerous situation. When something like this is discovered, the utilities involved need to be contacted immediately to rectify the situation.

The project team must develop a method of recording the research information and setting up the database to make it a usable and updatable document, including such data as the number of utility agencies or companies in the area, the number of systems in the area, the types of systems, how the attributes of the systems will be catalogued, and how the database will be managed. All of this information will be useful in determining the size and robustness of the database, the degree of flexibility required, and the most efficient structure for the database.

The database should be set up in a layered format for ease of use. One format that has been used successfully is a four-layer system, where each layer is dedicated to one type of service, such as:

A – Gravity (sanitary sewers and storm drainage)
B – Pressure (water systems, gas, steam, etc.)
C – Power (electrical distribution), and
D – Communications (telephone, cable, fire alarm and security systems).

It is important that entire systems are shown together in one layer, although sometimes portions of a utility overlap two layers (e.g., a sanitary sewer system or a storm drainage system is pressurized). Putting whole systems only on one layer also allows the inclusion of combined sewers, which are still prevalent in urban areas. Water tunnels and sewer/combined sewer overflow tunnels will be shown on these systems as well. The communications layer includes more than actual communication systems and includes any electrical system other than power. This arrangement works in another way as well: in a street cross-section, generally the gravity systems are the deepest, with the next

deepest being the pressure systems, followed by the power systems, and the shallowest are usually the communications and signal systems.

At a minimum, the database should be developed in two dimensions showing the actual size of pipes, conduit duct banks, manholes, and structures. This is especially important in congested urban areas where underground space can be at a premium. Infrastructure elements, such as jacketed pipelines and utility vaults, can occupy more underground space than anticipated and hinder the relocation of other utilities in the area. There are systems today that allow the database to be developed in three or even four dimensions, with time or schedule being the fourth dimension. The appropriateness of the database type and its intricacies will depend on a number of factors, such as the scope of work of the megaproject, the number of utility systems, the impacts to the systems, the duration of the work, etc. While it may seem out of the ordinary to be discussing a three- or four-dimension database for subsurface infrastructure, this is truly a case where the more information that can be provided, the more risk is mitigated and the less likely a delay will be incurred. Also, as megaprojects are executed over a period of years, providing a snapshot of what various utility systems will look like at various times in the future is a useful planning tool both for packaging and managing the work and for coordination with the utility agencies and companies.

Once the initial research has been done and loaded into the database, the results can be analyzed to identify areas of heavy congestion that may warrant further field investigation and areas that appear to lack information. As this analysis is underway, field surveys should be commenced to locate visible appurtenances such as manholes, catch basins, hand holes, gate boxes, and the like to confirm as much as possible of the record information obtained. Manholes and catch basins should be opened and their size, elevation, and number of connections confirmed.

Today, there are many ways to collect further information on subsurface infrastructure, and all of them should be reviewed for feasibility and appropriateness. Certainly, the traditional test-pit method still has its place, along with newer methods, such as vacuum excavation, pipe and cable locators, and ground-penetrating radar, and each will ascertain different types of information. Hence the need to analyze the record information and understand the type of additional information needed prior to instituting a field investigation program. For example, on a local combined sewer overflow tunneling project, the tunnel bore was driven very successfully directly beneath a number of existing outfalls, one of which crossed through the supporting piles within a foot of the outfall. This was accomplished because the designer and owner decided not to rely solely on the existing outfall as-built plans, circa 1900, but to conduct further investigation by having divers swim into the outfalls and survey the invert and crown and take cores of the wall at specific locations to determine their as-built thickness.

It is important that the information shown in the database be defined to its level

of accuracy or quality. Is it just record information or has it been verified in the field? Has the vertical location been confirmed through excavation? *Standard Guideline for the Collection and Depiction of Existing Subsurface Utility Data* (ASCE Publication 38-02) describes a system for accuracy or quality level of information in the database. Each object in the database, whether it is a pipe, ductbank, or structure, should have a number of attributes attached to it. The type of materials and whether or not they are defined as hazardous/contaminated (requiring special handling), the condition (if known), the age (if known), and the size are all examples of the kind of information that is needed to really understand the subsurface infrastructure and how it can be modified to accommodate the megaproject.

Share the database with the utility agencies and companies for review and comment, as it is being built up, to develop an understanding of which items may be inactive or abandoned in place. Also, hold meetings with the utility agencies and companies to understand how the various systems function under different scenarios, to review any expansion or upgrade programs that may be planned, to discuss which parts of the systems will be affected by the megaproject, and to identify any special aspects of the systems that need to be considered in prosecuting the work.

In addition, information should be obtained from the utility companies about standard materials, specifications, and details that must be used on their systems. Discussions regarding any planned expansion or upgrade programs that could be designed into the utility work should be held in order to avoid digging up the same utility several times, as well as to avoid multiple contractors occupying the same area, with the inherent coordination issues.

Once the database has been established, it will be utilized by a number of entities working with the project. The owner will use it to understand the extent of utility work on the project, the program manager will use it to develop the preliminary designs and utility agreements, the final designers will use it to develop construction contract packages, and the contractor will use it to plan and execute its work. This means that it is important that the information in the database is as current and as accurate as possible.

Because this database will be used by a wide range of entities over the course of the project, it is recommended that a utility engineer (or engineers, depending on the number of utilities, extent of geographic area covered by the megaproject, and size of the database) be specifically assigned the responsibility for its upkeep and issuing of the information. This is particularly important because the database is not a static document, but one that will continually evolve over the course of the project.

In the development of the preliminary project design, the database is an essential tool in understanding the impact on a utility system of a change necessitated by the project work. During all of the planned utility work, the utility system must remain functional both during and after the proposed work on the system, and the database can provide a

system overview for this purpose. Since the database is meant to represent what is actually in the ground, it is recommended that during the planning of proposed utility work another database be spun off from it as a separate file to be used in preliminary design development, while the actual database itself remains intact and uncontaminated.

As the work on the megaproject progresses from preliminary design to final design, the database should be issued to the designers as a snapshot of the subsurface infrastructure at a specific point in time, representing the conditions that pre-exist their design. Likewise with contractors, as the construction contracts that make up the megaproject are awarded, the database should be issued as a representation of what to expect under the ground surface. The database should be issued in a standard format each time, with hard copies and CADD files — one for each layer, i.e., for the gravity systems, the pressure systems, the power systems, and the communications systems, and one for the entire database.

After construction commences, keeping the database current is critical to fully understanding the conditions of the utility systems during the course of the megaproject. The database updates must be accurate and timely. The dedicated utility engineer needs to maintain open communication with the resident engineer's office at each construction contract and obtain as quickly as possible any new information related to the utilities, including: missing utilities (ones thought to be in existence but not appearing in the excavation); unexpected utilities (ones where no documentation is available that were discovered while excavating); utilities abandoned, removed, or relocated in the course of the work; and new utilities installed, as well as temporary connections installed for the benefit of the contractor or as interim measures between the abandoning of an existing system and the installation of a new one.

All of this information must be collected and verified and then input into the database appropriately, so that the updated database provides a new snapshot of the existing infrastructure as of a specific date. Once completed and back-checked, the updated database should be issued to all designers and contractors involved with the project, noting that this issue supersedes the previous issue. This updating process should occur at regular intervals throughout the course of the megaproject. If this is done properly, it can dramatically reduce the risk exposure for a utility disruption during the project.

Another measure for the timely updating of the database is to include an allowance in all construction and final design contracts for subsurface utility exploration. Under such an approach, the final designers will be encouraged to collect additional information in areas of concern that develop as the design progresses; likewise, construction contractors will be encouraged to investigate areas of concern prior to commencing heavy construction activities in those areas. This can be a very efficient and cost-effective method of mitigating risk. It is essential that all information garnered though SUE programs be added to the database so that all parties in the megaproject benefit to the maximum extent possible.

Beyond the accurate development and the timely updating and distribution of a utility database, there are other measures that can be taken to mitigate the risk of a utility issue during construction. One way is to develop plans and procedures for utility issues and have them available for immediate implementation. This means that not only are the plans developed, but the proper individuals on the project are aware of them and are trained in the implementation of the plans. This group includes contractor personnel as well as project personnel.

These plans should include a procedure for dealing with the discovery of an unidentified utility and a procedure for what happens when a utility is damaged that causes interrupted service. These plans should specify points of contact at the various utilities and contacts within the project organization (usually the dedicated utility engineer or the utility subcommittee, as well as appropriate individuals in the management structure) and directions for actions to be taken by the resident engineer and contractor. There should be a set procedure to be followed in the investigation of the unknown utility. For a utility hit and interrupted service, the plan may include a list of materials to have on standby for such occurrences and protocols for working with the various utilities to reestablish the utility service. The plan for a utility hit should also have an investigatory aspect to identify the reason for the hit or services interruption so that steps can be taken to avoid future reoccurrences.

Requiring a contractor's workforce to undergo training that outlines proper work practices and reviews established plans to deal with the unexpected utilities and service disruption is another measure to deal with utilities and to keep hits and disruptions to a minimum. This training would be required prior to the start of any utility work and can be conducted as refresher courses during the prosecution of the work, as needed. It is an inexpensive but effective method to implement.

Another strategy used on projects is to let early utility relocation contracts. This method was used very successfully on the Big Dig in Boston. The Big Dig required tunneling through the heart of Boston's financial district, a historic area, and residential areas of the city. Underground, the utility infrastructure was a haphazard growth of public and private entities consisting of sanitary sewers, combined sewers, storm drainage, three levels of water service, steam distribution, three levels of power distribution, telephone systems, cable systems, fire alarm, Western Union system, and street lighting, among others. This array of pipes and conduits wrapped around catch basins and manholes in a spaghetti-like manner with no rhyme or reason to positioning. To implement a heavy civil tunneling contract worth hundreds of millions of dollars among this confusing tangle, considering the age and materials of some of them, was fraught with risk. To mitigate the risk, early utility relocation contracts were used. This approach allowed the project to investigate the utilities for location, hazardous materials, and methods of relocation that would not disrupt the service and would mesh with expan-

sion or upgrade plans of the utilities. The utilities were relocated into dedicated utility corridors that tunnel designers were aware of and designed into their contracts. This allowed the heavy civil contractor to hit the ground running without having to be concerned with the removal of utilities prior to the start of its tunneling work. During the course of this work, the other measures mentioned above, such as the timely issuance of the updated utility database and training in dealing with unexpected utilities, were instituted as well. Overall, these measures resulted in a way to deal with the myriad of utilities installed haphazardly over more than 100 years beneath the city streets, which minimized utility disruption and kept the city active and functioning throughout the project period.

As mentioned previously, the primary factor in any subsurface utility program is open communication and cooperation with the utility agencies and companies. Establishing contact early in the process and continuing that contact through the design and construction is essential. Beyond the technical issues, there are commercial issues that need to be addressed. If a utility wants to upgrade its infrastructure in lieu of an in-kind replacement, how will that be handled? If a utility requires a new easement for its relocation, how will that be handled? As the utility will be getting a brand-new system, replacing one that may be many years old, should it contribute to the cost of the replacement or relocation since it will realize a benefit from the new installation? All of these issues need to be addressed as part of the subsurface utility work, and agreement should be obtained prior to the start of major design and construction work.

Subsurface utilities represent an unknown risk to the owner of a megaproject that can, if not dealt with properly, cause excessive delay, cause cost overruns, create third-party issues, and create difficult relations with the community. The measures discussed here can mitigate this risk and allow the megaproject to progress smoothly.

Third Parties and Megaprojects

Apart from the obvious permitting agencies (i.e., city and state agencies having approval jurisdiction over the project) and neighborhood groups, third parties can sometimes be difficult to identify and can often be overlooked until work begins in the field. One example of this is a project designed for a local transit agency that required the contractor to demolish an opening in the roof of the subway tunnel for a new emergency fan structure to upgrade the life safety system on the subway. Because the contractor had to demolish the roof of the tunnel, the transit agency owner required the contractor to perform the work at night after the transit line had stopped service for the day (after midnight). The work site was in the middle of a heavily trafficked urban street, but what was not realized was that on one corner of a nearby intersection there was a newly renovated condominium building whose occupants did not care about the traffic in the

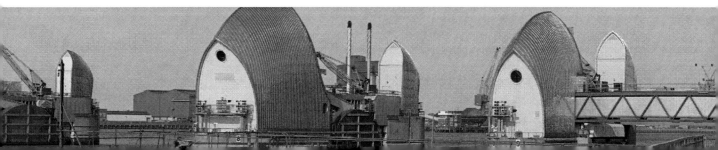

street or the possible disruption to train service if the demolition work was done during operating hours for the system. The nighttime demolition work was keeping them awake at night, they had not been consulted about the work hours, and, being a condo association, they were already well organized. It only took them a couple of nights to form their opposition to the nighttime demolition work and create an issue that had to be dealt with, which did result in schedule and budget impacts.

So how does one go about identifying third parties to a project, especially those who have the potential to negatively impact the project? One answer is that anyone who is not under contract to the contractor, owner, or design consultant is a potential third party. Once the project team understands that almost anyone can become a third party to the work, it then becomes everyone's responsibility to maintain good relations with all public groups that surround the work and that have to travel through or by the work site.

With such a large number of potential third parties, it quickly becomes obvious that the risk of a third party negatively impacting a project is one that needs to be managed by the project team. What makes managing all of the possible third-party activists so difficult is that they have nothing invested in the project and, if they become dissatisfied with the way the project impacts their quality of life, then they have nothing holding them back from delaying the work by seeking relief from the courts or otherwise making their displeasure about the project known.

Step One: Identification of Third Parties

Larger third-party groups are generally known to the megaproject participants. Permitting agencies, approval committees such as the planning boards, building departments, environmental groups, the U.S. Environmental Protection Agency (EPA), the U.S. Army Corps of Engineers (US ACOE), local conservation committees, and so on are well known to anyone used to working in an urban area. Sometimes, when working along the waterfront or on or near an airport, federal agencies such as the Federal Aviation Administration, the EPA, and the US ACOE will be considered third parties to the project. However, smaller third-party groups, such as a site-specific condominium association or a local business, may not be recognized until they make themselves known to the project. One third-party issue that can have a great influence on large projects is the need for right-of-way (ROW) takings by a public agency. If a property owner is not willing to give the ROW or is not satisfied with the amount offered for the ROW, this property owner may become a disgruntled third party who can affect the entire community outreach efforts that the project has spent much time and energy in getting under way.

It is recommended that a formal system of tracking interested third parties and their hot buttons on issues be implemented, particularly on large projects, so that a contact

list can be generated and notices of meetings and special events can get wide distribution, thus fostering good communications, which is a key aspect of managing third-party risks. On large projects, it is also recommended that the project owner or sponsor retain a community liaison person familiar with local neighborhoods to assist in identifying issues and concerns. This community liaison person can also be very helpful in identifying the real underlying issues or concerns of the neighborhood and how best to mitigate their concerns in a manner consistent with the project's schedule and budget.

However, remember that there is a difference between a public relations outreach and a community outreach. Community outreach is identifying the groups and their concerns and then helping to mitigate their concerns in a manner compatible with the project's goals. One example of this is a project that had an "artist community" adjacent to an underground portion of the project. The artist community's concerns were noise, vibration, and dust impacts on their ability to work in their lofts. Project mitigation included full-height insulated sound walls around the construction area and replacement of single-pane windows with thermo-pane windows in the lofts, as well as monitoring of the contractors' adherence to noise and vibration limits.

Public relations outreach is the effort to continually present the project in a favorable view to the public. One example of this type of outreach is the use of community betterment opportunities (CBO), in which the project would have a budget set aside that can be used to fund an identified community opportunity that would better the quality of their lives, such as a small park or recreation area that could be constructed with funds provided by the project.

Step Two: Be a Good Neighbor During Construction

A good relationship between the community and the construction team is important to completing a project on time and within budget. In fact, a third-party issue can be created by a contractor's failure to consider the project's impact on a party's interest, issues, and lives. It is recommended that the project take a proactive approach that reaches out to the community, meeting with groups and individuals to identify and address issues of concern, rather than sitting back and waiting for issues to be raised by interested parties. Websites, leaflets for small groups in the immediate vicinity of the planned construction, newsletters, and weekly meetings are all tools to communicate with third-party groups, and they can be effective as long as the information is accurate and up to date with the planned construction means and methods.

A potential danger in this approach is the "big project open checkbook" scenario, where third parties get the impression that this is a big project with a lot of money so they want to get a piece of it. With a proactive approach, it would be easy to fall into this mistake, and so the outreach program has to be conducted fairly and transparently with

131

open books and accountability to prevent this "open checkbook" feeling from developing in the community.

Step Three: Keep Community Outreach Going Through All Phases of the Project

Community outreach should be conducted during all phases of the megaproject, from planning to design and all the way through construction. The outreach program should give current information on the design approach and construction means and methods, and as things change, community constituencies need to be informed, new issues identified, and mitigation measures implemented.

Finally, do not overlook the impacts on third parties that the operations phase of the megaproject may produce. For instance, the operation of a sewer tunnel may generate objectionable odors during rapid filling, which can upset neighborhood groups and significantly impact a project's acceptance by the community. Care must be taken to prevent this situation from becoming a major issue, which will likely require numerous meetings with the neighborhood residents to explain beforehand how this situation will be mitigated to ensure that it will not become an unpleasant problem for them. It is recommended that the community outreach program be continued into the operations phase of the project so that the community feels that they have a place to go and be heard if operational issues arise, and where they can get action as they feel it is needed. Setting up a call-in center/public information office can be an effective way to provide this follow-up service to the community.

Public Versus Private Parties

With third parties, a good general rule of thumb is that no one size fits all. It is very likely that a good community outreach program will use different approaches for different constituencies. For instance, reaching out to individual homeowners may require a door-to-door approach, spending time meeting people to get to know them and understand what their most significant concerns are for the project. Conversely, a public agency or permitting agency will probably need a formal scoping meeting or several meetings to explain the project and to identify the agencies' concerns and issues that need to be addressed before mitigation measures can be determined.

Other Third-Party Impacts Imposed by City or State Departments

Occasionally, a project will encounter situations that are not of their making but that have serious schedule or financial implications to the project, such as encountering contaminated ground or groundwater, which requires cleanup and supervision by state

agencies, or stringent city requirements to reconstruct all disability access ramps and sidewalks to ADA Accessibility Guideline requirements in an intersection whenever construction occurs within 10 feet of that intersection. While these may result in additional project costs, the work is necessary, and the earlier that the issues can be identified to the project sponsor, the easier it will be to incorporate the needed improvements into the project budget while at the same time providing an additional benefit to the community.

Sometimes a third-party issue may arise only after the project's completion and its being placed into service. Bright lights from a major interchange where before there were none or exhaust fans running all night long for tunnel ventilation during the summer may create issues with nearby residents. A project team needs to consider the potential impact of operational issues on abutters and adopt measures to mitigate such things as noise and lighting impacts to enhance the prospects of a final acceptance of the project.

Recommended Practices

The risk of a third party negatively impacting a project is one that needs to be proactively managed by the project team throughout the project, from conceptual design through completion and placing into service. The larger the project, the more third parties the team will have to deal with, and the more conflicting and complicated the interests of each third party may become in attempting to mitigate their concerns. Some recommended practices to consider in managing third-party issues on a large project are:

1. Identification of potential third parties that may have an interest in the project is a key first step that must become an ongoing process managed and implemented throughout the life of the project.

2. Smaller third-party groups or individuals are more difficult to identify but can have important consequences for a project. Be proactive and take the time to become aware of what is going on in the neighborhood of the project to help in identifying third parties and their issues. Avoid being surprised, if at all possible.

3. Start the project by setting up a database system to aid in identifying each interested third party and record in the database for each party, their interest in the project, and their concerns that may need to be addressed as time goes on.

4. Appoint a community liaison person for each neighborhood in the project's vicinity to keep up with the concerns and issues of the neighborhoods surrounding the project. (Depending on the project's size and the diversity of the neighborhoods, a single liaison person may be appropriate in lieu of multiple liaisons for each neighborhood.)

5. Managing third-party expectations should be an ongoing effort through all phases of a megaproject. As such, make sure that those personnel who work with third par-

ties are current and informed about the design approach and construction means and methods as things change. Third parties need to be given accurate up-to-date information in order for the liaison to maintain credibility and to obtain their cooperation in identifying issues and new mitigation measures, as the need arises.

6. Involve the general contractor in maintaining good relations with the local community around the project. Avoid creating a third-party issue by a contractor's failure to consider the project's neighbors during construction.

7. Some third-party constituencies may be more directly or severely impacted by the project's completion and going into service, such as additional noise from the opening of a new highway ramp close to a residence. The project team should be aware of the operational impact of their project on project abutters. Again, be proactive, set up a call-in-center/public information service to help get information out to interested parties and to provide a place for third parties to tell their concerns and issues that need to be addressed. In the instance described above, it may become necessary to add a noise wall to mitigate the noise the new highway ramp may bring to nearby residences. For a large project, having a contingency budget for such post-construction issues can greatly assist in the public acceptance of the project.

Third-party issues, like subsurface utility risks, need to be proactively addressed by the owner to avoid surprises and unnecessary delays. Because third parties present an unknown risk to contractors bidding on megaproject contracts as well, the owner of a megaproject should make contract provisions to mitigate third-party impacts, to the greatest extent possible. As outlined in this chapter, a proactive approach to both subsurface utility and third-party issues is recommended to provide the owner with the best possible opportunity to complete the project on time and within budget.

Conclusions

As discussed, utility and third-party issues can and do represent credible risks to the successful execution of a megaproject. The discovery of an undocumented utility or a utility hit that disrupts service can not only inhibit the progression of the work, but also damage the public image of the megaproject. Third-party expectations can override the technical excellence of a project with respect to whether a project is considered a success or a failure. These risks can result in schedule delay, cost increases, claims, and issues with the public image of the project if not properly identified, managed, and resolved.

Fortunately there are processes and procedures that, when implemented early in the project, can effectively mitigate these risks. The methods described in this chapter, if undertaken early and managed proactively, can lessen the risk exposure due to these issues on a megaproject.

CHAPTER 8
Labor Relations

Joseph Dennis, Esq., Arup
Tom Farina, Parsons Brinckerhoff
David H. Corkum, Esq., Donovan Hatem LLP

Introduction

From a purely cost standpoint, labor is the single largest component of any major civil construction project, including most, if not all, megaprojects. We refer here, of course, not to the design professionals, planners, politicians, regulatory agencies, and other individuals whose efforts also represent a portion of the project costs, but rather to the construction labor that directly contributes to the "brick and mortar" components of the project. A typical rule-of-thumb estimate holds that one-third of a construction contract's price to an owner is the cost of craft labor. Obviously then, efficiency and productivity considerations of that labor should be of paramount concern to all participants. Construction contractors will also freely acknowledge that their single greatest risk to cost overruns on a project revolves, around labor productivity.

Objective measurements of construction labor productivity are notoriously difficult to quantify, making comparisons difficult. This is partly a result of the fact that each project is unique, and while a class of laborers may perform the same task on numerous projects year after year, no project is designed or built exactly the same as the previous one. Likewise, and probably more importantly, no two projects are sequenced and managed exactly alike. Therefore, any attempt to assess labor productivity is often an assessment of construction management efficiency. Notwithstanding the influence of management and leadership on labor productivity, there is no substitute for an intelligent, cooperative, and flexible workforce. Accordingly, it is in the financial interests of an owner to take steps that promote those positive attributes in the workforce.

Despite the difficulties of objectively measuring productivity, the general perception of the industry is that labor productivity has fallen, or at best has remained flat, over the last 30 years, compared to a generally increasing trend in other sectors of the economy.[1] Many of these same studies show that a typical craftsman's actual productive time over the course of a construction project amounts to no more than 3½ hours out of a typical 8-hour day involved in direct labor. The balance, almost 60 percent, of the craftsman's time is consumed by unproductive tasks, such as administrative delays, inefficient work

The Göltzsch Valley Bridge (Göltzschtalbrücke) in Saxony, Germany, is the largest brick bridge in the world. A railway bridge built between 1846 and 1851 (and still in use), it contains more than 26 million bricks and is 574 meters long and 77 meters at its highest clearance above the valley. Photo © 2009 by André Karwath.

135

methods, labor jurisdiction disputes, and other work restrictions. Accordingly, it would appear the greatest potential for increase in labor productivity is not with the worker but with the management of that worker's environment, scheduling, materials delivery, etc.

A project's design can either intentionally or inadvertently require a greater or lesser amount of labor to accomplish a particular task. Consider for example the use of a precast segmental tunnel lining compared to a cast-in-place lining. Similarly, one design may favor one craft over another, such as in the case of a post-tensioned segmental concrete bridge versus a steel bridge. Some construction techniques may be impossible or completely impracticable to implement, given the available labor force. Attempting a New Austrian Tunneling Method (NATM) tunnel, for example, without an experienced and trained crew, each member of which knowing instinctively how to react to situations in the field, could prove to be a disaster. If the local labor force objects to importing such a proven crew, then the owner should consider rejecting the proposed technique. Owner decisions about contract packaging strategies will also have an impact on the labor force size and makeup. A number of smaller contract packages will likely result in a higher total workforce, as the efficiencies of scale are not realized when using multiple employers. A strategy that promotes numerous smaller packages may also favor local small businesses and contractors and their existing labor force.

Labor considerations are not just about money and the cost of a project. An owner, particularly a public owner about to embark on a megaproject, wields a powerful sociological stick. Within limits, the owner can dictate labor force preferences, such as a preference for local citizens, disadvantaged citizens, or workers of specific gender and ethnic backgrounds. It can dictate community outreach and training programs. The Helmets-to-Hard-Hats program, which seeks to engage veterans in the construction trades, has gained in popularity across the nation. The megaproject owner also has a significant political trump card, which it can choose to hold or trade for future favors.

Not only are labor considerations important to the bottom line cost of the megaproject and the political/social aspirations of the megaproject owner, but they can also have a significant impact on the community in general. A depressed area with a high unemployment rate will be hostile to a project that it perceives as benefitting residents of other, "outside" areas. Similarly, a megaproject requiring thousands of workers may upset the balance of the existing economy in an area if contractors begin to offer higher-paying jobs than the local market currently supports.

Background

In considering the available labor force for a project, there are two broad categories, union or nonunion, that serve as proxies to define the roles and expectations of the employer and employee. It is the employer, the construction contractor, that decides in the first instance whether it will operate as a nonunion (or open-shop) contractor, or else bind the company to collective bargaining agreements that are the hallmark of a union shop. Each type of operation has its proponents and detractors, and the validity of their arguments varies from region to region within the country.

In an open-shop arrangement, a construction contractor hires and fires its labor force as it sees fit and pays at a rate that the market will bear, including fringe benefits, which are also a function of market forces. The contractor has no set expectation as to the skill level, training, and experience of its hired workers and can tailor its compensation and benefit package accordingly.

A variation on a pure open-shop arrangement is referred to as merit-shop, which is more typical for the larger nonunion construction contractors with a national book of business. These merit-shop contractors adhere to policies and procedures of contractor associations, such as the Associated Builders and Contractors, Inc. The merit-shop worker has the ability to move from project to project and from contractor to contractor throughout the affiliated merit-shop organization, and his portfolio of past project performances will be recognized among the contractors within that organization.

An open-shop — and particularly a merit-shop — labor force probably has a closer affiliation with the management of the construction company, and both benefit from successful completion of projects. The open-shop/merit-shop contractor enjoys a degree of flexibility and freedom in deploying its labor force and is unrestricted by jurisdictional rules that require certain crafts to perform certain types of activity. The construction contractor is fully responsible for training and developing the skill level of the workers, and its motivation to develop such skills is justified by the greater efficiency and productivity of that individual worker.

Union-shop construction contractors agree to be bound by collective-bargaining agreements with one or more of the labor unions for the construction trades. These collective-bargaining agreements are typically negotiated between the labor union and a representative group of construction contractors operating in the region. The agreements set the hourly rates, working conditions, hiring protocol, training programs, and benefits associated with each worker in each category within the craft, i.e., journeymen and apprentice. Most importantly, the construction contractors agree to hire workers directly from the union rather than seeking employees on their own. In this way, the union controls the referral of workers to the contractor organizations. Each local union is, of course, organized to support a particular craft. The workers within each local are skilled in that craft or, if an apprentice, have some base level of skill and are in the process of being trained to be full-fledged journeymen. Partly because of the referral system in an industry that generally does not retain workers 12 months out of the year, union laborers tend to align their loyalties with the union rather than the construction contractor. Laborers recognize that their future employment depends on that referral from the union

and that such referrals will be lacking if they fail to adhere to recognized union rules.

The local unions are typically affiliated with an international union in some form of association. These international associations have the power to issue or revoke the local union charter but typically do not involve themselves with the day-to-day operations of the union or the collective bargaining of that local. With a large number of construction trade unions currently in existence, it is unavoidable that there are disputes among unions as to who "owns" a particular type or category of work. The contractors, particularly out-of-town contractors not used to working with the union, may end up assigning a particular type of work to one union that is claimed to be under the jurisdiction of another union. Such an assignment, no matter how innocently made, can result in labor unrest and declining productivity, work slow-downs, or strikes as the two disputing unions focus on the issue and old wounds, to the exclusion of all else. Resolving the dispute can be expensive and time-consuming, and it is rare that all sides are fully satisfied with the resolution. The efficient and effective utilization of labor on any constructed project requires diligent project management in order to integrate the labor with the availability of material and equipment in the planned-for sequence. Labor disputes will challenge management to reach beyond the nuts and bolts of construction skills and demonstrate an expertise in counseling and psychological analysis.

Issue

An adequate supply of skilled labor, ready and willing to fill the construction job openings, is critical to the success of a project. For a megaproject, the demand could easily outpace the supply, which would result in slower progress or lower quality of workmanship. An owner and its consultants must take stock of the available workforce and attempt to shape and manage the project so that it is feasible within the constraints of that workforce.

Analysis and Discussion

Simply put, a megaproject owner has too much at stake to dismiss labor availability, quality, and cooperative disposition as being only a contractor issue. Bad habits and unsafe practices developed on one project with one contractor can infect the entire project and haunt the owner in the form of low productivity, poor quality, and a high accident rate for the duration of that project.

The owner needs to understand how its project and the anticipated pay, benefits, and prestige fit into the pecking order of the labor market. During the 1848–1849 California Gold Rush, sailing ships piled up and rotted in San Francisco as the sailors deserted to hunt for gold. A pulp and paper company in Maine refused to develop and exploit economical mineral deposits because of fear that the higher-paying mining jobs would decimate its efforts to harvest timber. In a tight market, the owner needs to promote its project and offer the incentives to attract the desired labor. The owner also needs to foresee what the impact of its project will be on the community so that support for the project is not undermined. A large number of transient workers, for example, may strain relations with the local community. Similarly, the project may drain workers from local businesses, causing distress to the status quo.

For a publicly funded project where there are many stakeholders, the owner may find itself under pressure to engage in unsupportable levels of social engineering, by mandates to hire disadvantaged persons. These goals or mandates are often negotiated early in the life of the project and should be carefully considered before being accepted.

Throughout history, immigrant labor has been a factor for many megaprojects. In much of the world even today, and particularly in the Middle East, immigrant labor makes up the construction labor force of large projects. In North America, the number of young people choosing construction as a career continues to decline, and if current trends continue, construction projects may need to begin importing its labor force. Indeed, immigrant labor makes up a large percentage of the generally open-shop housing construction labor force. This sector of the labor force is usually considered low-skill and low-pay and not suitable for a contractor's demands on a modern megaproject. If an owner is going to rely on this sector of the market, then it will likely need to establish aggressive training programs targeting the requisite skills very early in the life of the project.

The owner's team also needs to evaluate whether it is possible and/or desirable to prefabricate large components or modules off-site and then transport and erect them on-site. Such practice is most feasible where barge access to the site is possible and would facilitate large portions of the project being completed in another labor market, perhaps another country. This practice can take advantage of cheaper labor but may introduce strife and discontent if that cheaper labor displaces underutilized local labor. A cost savings for one contractor may result in strikes, slowdowns, or stoppages for others.

Recommended Practices

- Survey the existing labor force either through direct outreach to unions and labor organizations or through discussions with construction contractors operating in the area. Develop an understanding of whether there is a clear preponderance of union versus non-union labor that will likely contribute to the project, but be aware that the sources of information on the union/non-union preponderance are likely skewed toward the correspondent's bias.

- Survey other owners, both public and private, to determine which projects will be competing with your project for the available labor force. Recognize the "pull" of

desirable projects in other geographic areas that could deplete the workforce you are counting on.

- Evaluate the need for arrangements to import labor with special skills, e.g., divers or NATM miners, and their ability to work harmoniously with local labor. If that is not feasible, mandate designs that can be accomplished with the existing labor force.
- Consider the scheduling and sequencing of the project in a manner that is supportable by the available labor force.
- Promote and support training and skills development of the existing labor force if that level is unacceptably low. Absolutely promote and demand that contractors provide safety training.

Regulatory Framework

In 1935, Franklin D. Roosevelt signed the National Labor Relations Act (NLRA) protecting the rights of workers in the private sector to organize labor unions and to engage in collective bargaining. The act specifically allowed workers and unions to initiate and take part in strikes or other work-related activities to further their negotiating positions or enforce agreements. The act was amended in 1959 to validate and protect master collective-bargaining agreements that would bind all contractors and subcontractors upon a construction project. The 1959 amendment recognized the special arrangement and needs of the construction industry to coordinate a variety of skilled labor crafts and promote harmonious interaction among the crafts and with management throughout the life of a project. These master agreements, or project labor agreements, were particularly important for large and long-duration projects over which a number of specific collective-bargaining agreements with individual unions would expire and be renegotiated. The problem, of course, was that each renegotiation was an opportunity for a strike and picket by the union, which could impact or stop the work of a number of other crafts and contractors.

The NLRA's recognition of the construction industry's need for unique considerations derives from that industry's differences from other typical labor-management arrangements. In the construction industry, employment tends to be for shorter periods of time. Workers often move from employer to employer as that contractor wins, executes, and completes projects. For union workers, long-term relationships with their union halls are stronger than the employer-employee bond considered important for non-union construction companies. Moreover, post-hire bargaining is not practicable between a contractor and its labor force. Rather, the practice of pre-hire collective bargaining is the norm, where contractors bidding for work know the cost of labor in advance of retaining that labor force.

The construction industry is also unique in that a number of different crafts and subcontractor employers are compelled to work in close proximity and often in interdependent manner. NLRA sections (a), (e), and (f) specifically recognize this unique arrangement and allow for project labor agreements.

Project Labor Agreement

Project labor agreements (PLA) are multiparty agreements that establish the parameters of the relationships between ownership, management, and labor for the duration of a particular project. The agreement is negotiated between the project owner or its agent and the representatives of the local labor force, typically the unions whose charter grants them jurisdiction over the geographic area and type of work involved in the project. This PLA sets the ground rules for all labor relations on the project. The owner may require, as a condition precedent to awarding a contract, that all contractors submitting bids agree to become signatory to the terms and conditions of the PLA. The contractor and the labor unions are thus bound by that agreement for the duration of the project. That agreement has absolutely no effect on other contracts or projects that are not defined within the scope of the PLA.

During the course of project construction, the parties to the PLA generally include the project owner, the general contractor(s), all levels of construction subcontractors, and the labor trade unions. In essence, the project stakeholders establish the basic terms and conditions which describe how labor issues will be addressed through the course of the work. They establish these terms prior to commencing the work.

While sometimes characterized as a form of prehire collective-bargaining agreement (CBA), project labor agreements differ from CBAs in several important respects. First, although either may be used in the context of a construction project, PLAs are site-specific, while CBAs generally are not. PLAs include all labor crafts as parties to the agreement, while CBAs are generally executed with the crafts individually. In addition, the term of a PLA is generally for the duration of a project, while CBAs are generally effective for a defined period of years.

When utilized on complex construction projects, which are characteristically multi-year, multitrade, multimillion dollar investments, whether public or private, PLAs can bring a degree of certainty to the parties with respect to some of the inevitable labor-related risks associated with such work.

Project Owners' Perspective

PLAs have been utilized on complex construction projects in the United States for decades. This country's first PLA is generally thought to have been executed for the Grand Coulee Dam in Washington State. Shortly thereafter, a similar agreement was drafted for the Shasta Dam in California. These two Bureau of Reclamation megaprojects helped

pull the western states out of the Great Depression and provided enormous flood control, irrigation, and power production benefits for the region. The government relied on PLAs for a number of domestic Department of War installations during World War II. More recently, the Kennedy Space Center at Cape Canaveral, Florida, was constructed under a PLA. Privately funded megaprojects such as the Trans-Alaskan pipeline, Florida's Disneyland, and a number of the large nuclear plants and other power installations constructed in the 1960s and 1970s routinely utilized project labor agreements

Whether a public or private entity, the interests of an owner of a complex construction project are primarily focused on efficient delivery as defined in terms of cost, schedule, safety, and quality of the work. Each of these important measurements of project performance may be optimized by including the requirement of a project labor agreement in the bid specification. A PLA will typically be used to establish wage rates and benefits for the duration of the project. Unexpected wage demands or disputes, which have a tendency to arise during the course of a long-term project, are effectively eliminated by such agreements.

No matter how well-meaning the parties may be, complex long-term construction projects inevitably give rise to labor-related problems or disputes. Schedule risks resulting from job actions, in the form of work slowdowns or stoppages caused by labor disputes, are minimized through PLA provisions that deal with the swift resolution of disputes and by the inclusion of no-strike, no-slowdown clauses. By minimizing disruptions and enhancing the likelihood that the project will be delivered on time, the owner may also realize lower finance costs and other benefits from getting the project in commercial operation as quickly as possible.

Enhanced quality and safety are generally a reflection of a stable and well-trained workforce. PLAs foster the establishment of such stability, which may also be reflected in reduced rework and insurance costs for the project.

These benefits are balanced against the increased cost of labor of a unionized labor force as opposed to open-shops. Opponents of PLAs argue that they have the practical effect of eliminating competition from merit-shop contractors and that the decrease in the number of bidders increases the costs of projects. Contractors argue that their companies would be discouraged from bidding on projects resulting from a PLA's effect of discriminating against their employees. The view from this group is that PLAs increase the cost of construction by mandating inefficient and archaic union work rules and limit the pool of potential quality bidders, without any increased economy or efficiency to procurement. A Beacon Hill Institute study, released in 2009, analyzed Massachusetts school construction during a period (2001–2008) when government-mandated PLAs were prohibited. The study controversially concluded that PLAs *increased* federal project construction costs and their absence showed no material instances of labor disruption or significant project delays.[2]

Contractors' and Subcontractors' Perspectives

Contractors and subcontractors share some of the same interests as the owner of a construction project, particularly with respect to cost, schedule, safety, and quality of the work. To further those interests, PLAs offer the same potential benefits to all levels of contractors as they do to owners.

In the context of the owner's source selection process, contractors and subcontractors are typically required to submit their bids and await the owner's decision regarding contract award before they begin the process of hiring their workforce. As a prehire agreement, the PLA is often negotiated among the owner, the contractor, and the labor unions as representatives of the employees prior to the employees being hired. The PLA permits construction subcontractors at any tier to establish what their costs will be for specific labor classifications. The PLA provides the basis for their bids. Upon award, construction subcontractors execute letters of assent, whereby they agree to be bound by the terms of the PLA.

In most construction projects, subcontractors providing differing labor trades work side by side on the job site. For example, employees of a plumbing subcontractor may be present with the employees of a specialty welder. Carpenters may work alongside electricians, masons, or plasterers. The job may call for the installation of underground and above-ground piping. Absent a single agreement that includes all of the project participants, such an environment has the potential for giving rise to many issues. In projects where the different trades have individual labor agreements, the probability is greater for disputes to arise between the trades about issues such as jurisdiction over the work. The implementation of project labor agreements minimizes the likelihood of such disputes by establishing the jurisdictional parameters of each trade for the project. In the event disputes do arise, the PLA defines an agreed-upon resolution process with minimal disruption of the work.

PLAs and the Workforce

Project labor agreements typically create a labor policy that will apply uniformly to all construction workers involved in a specific project. Proponents claim that PLAs create and enhance a stable environment for the workforce by establishing a systematic treatment of wages and benefits, including overtime, starting time, holidays, health benefits, and overall working conditions for the duration of the project. In addition, PLAs provide for the peaceful settlement of disputes between labor and management, through the use of an agreed-upon dispute resolution process, which minimizes the potential for disruption of the work by specifying that there will be no strikes or lockouts.

The terms of each PLA are unique to each project, and some do require the use of

union labor. Under the National Labor Relations Act, construction contractors and their employees may choose whether or not to unionize. While there are certainly so-called "union-only" PLAs — those which exclude merit- or open-shops — PLAs need not limit their participation to unionized labor. While a PLA may require all employees to be hired through a union hiring hall, the hiring hall may not discriminate between union and non-union workers. It is not a necessary element for a PLA to require workers to join the local union in order to be referred for work, nor is it a general requirement that non-union workers must pay union dues, as they would with a collective-bargaining arrangement.

Effect on the Community

The execution of megaprojects requires the mobilization of a workforce that may contain many different job classifications with a wide array of skill levels. While the community is not a party to a PLA, such agreements arguably benefit the community in the vicinity of the project by turning the need to fill those positions into employment opportunities for local residents. PLAs may include provisions that require the project workforce to have a composition of certain percentages of local hires. They may also require that local residents receive priority over non-residents in hiring for specific job classifications. In addition, PLAs may require the establishment of a certain number of apprentice-level positions and the sponsorship of training or mentoring programs to encourage the long-term development of the skills of the local labor pool. They may also establish subcontracting goals based on contract dollar values or percentages of project capital cost for the participation of specific levels of minority, women-owned, and small disadvantaged business enterprises.

The proportion of union to non-union labor in the United States construction industry peaked in the mid to late 1970s. Since that time the number, and perhaps more importantly, the political influence of merit-shop construction contractors has increased. With a continuing rise in numbers and influence, merit-shop contractors began to question the legality of project labor agreements on public projects. These non-union contractors objected to being precluded from competing on these publicly funded projects and challenged them through the courts.

Legality of PLAs

The legality of a public owner choosing to enact such an agreement was fairly well settled by the Supreme Court in the Associated Builders and Contractors challenge to Massachusetts Water Resources Authority's project labor agreement for the Boston Harbor Project.[3] Since that decision, three states — Montana, Utah, and Missouri — have enacted legislation that prohibits project labor agreements on state-procured projects.

Minnesota and Arkansas are states where PLAs are prohibited through executive order of the governor. Illinois, New York, and New Jersey, on the other hand, are states where the legislature has taken steps to encourage PLAs on state and municipal construction projects. Notwithstanding the politics of a state's or its governor's apparent predisposition for or against using a PLA in situations where a project labor agreement has been successfully challenged, the opponents of a PLA are usually able to demonstrate that the public owner failed to demonstrate "more than a rational basis" for implementing it.

Not satisfied to allow the legality of project labor agreements to be decided in the court system, nor to allow the advisability of employing such agreements to be left to the construction project administrators, four presidents have weighed in on the use of project labor agreements for publicly funded construction projects. In 1992, President George H. W. Bush issued an executive order forbidding project labor agreements on any federally funded projects. Within a month of taking office in 1993, President Bill Clinton rescinded the executive order of his predecessor and, over the course of his administration, supported and promoted project labor agreements for federal construction projects. Indeed, the Clinton administration attempted to enact legislation that would require all of his administrative agencies to utilize project labor agreements. President George W. Bush demonstrated that turnabout is fair play by cancelling Clinton's order within one month of becoming president. His February 17, 2001, executive order stated in part:

> Section 1: To the extent permitted by law, any executive agency awarding any construction contract after the date of this order, or obligating funds pursuant to such a contract, shall ensure that neither the awarding government authority nor any construction manager acting on behalf of the government shall, in its bid specifications, project agreements, or other controlling documents:
>
> > (a) Require or prohibit bidders, offerors, contractors, or subcontractors to enter into or adhere to agreements with one or more labor organization on the same or other related construction project(s); or
> >
> > (b) Otherwise discriminate against bidders, offerors, contractors, or subcontractors for becoming or refusing to become or remain signatories or otherwise to adhere to agreements with one or more labor organizations on the same or other related construction project(s).
> >
> > (c) Nothing in this agreement shall prohibit contractors or subcontractors from voluntarily entering into agreements described in subsection (a).
>
> . . .
>
> Section 3: To the extent permitted by law and executive agency issuing grants, providing financial assistance, or entering into cooperative agreements for construction projects shall ensure that neither the bid specifications, project agreements, nor other controlling documents for construction contracts awarded after the date of this order by

recipients of grants or financial assistance or by parties to cooperative agreements nor those of any construction manager acting on their behalf, shall contain any of the requirement prohibitions set forth in sections 1(a) or (b) of this order.

And on February 8, 2009, less than three weeks after his inauguration President Obama signed Executive Order 13502, entitled "Use of Project Labor Agreements for Federal Construction Projects." This new and latest order revokes President George W. Bush's Executive Order 13208 and announces a policy that encourages executive agencies to consider using project labor agreements in connection with large-scale construction projects in order to promote economy and efficiency in federal procurement. Obama's executive order only encourages the use of PLAs in such large-scale projects, it does not mandate them: "Executive agencies may, on a project-by-project basis, require the use of a project labor agreement by a contractor where use of such an agreement will . . . advance the Federal Government's interest in achieving economy and efficiency in Federal procurement." Under the order, the government cannot compel a contractor to enter into an agreement with any particular labor organization, and it does not explicitly exclude non-union contractors from competition.

Key Attributes of Project Labor Agreements

The modern project labor agreement has taken on a fairly familiar form with a generally expected set of terms and conditions. The key attribute from management's perspective is the so-called "no-strike" and "no-walkout" provision. This provision requires that trade work continue in the face of disputes, removing the risk of delay and disruption that might otherwise be experienced. Subsidiary to this "no-strike," "no-walkout" provision is a mechanism for resolving disputes, both those between labor and management and also the more common jurisdictional disputes between various trade unions. Using binding arbitration or designated third-party neutrals, preselected to hear and resolve disputes, accomplishes this element of the agreement on an expedited basis.

From labor's perspective, the "must-have" attribute is the requirement that all contractor hiring on the project be accomplished through the applicable local union's hiring hall. This is not a requirement that union-only labor be utilized, which would be patently illegal for a publicly procured project, but rather that the hiring hall, and its protocol for referring workers to various construction projects, be the clearinghouse for all labor assigned to the project. Non-union workers can register at the hiring hall alongside of union workers, and the hiring halls cannot discriminate between union and non-union workers when making referrals to contractors. Approximately half of the states in the United States are so-called "right-to-work" states, which prohibit the excluding of workers based on their non-affiliation with a particular union. PLAs in those states will re-

inforce this point of law, as well. Federal and state laws also prohibit discrimination on the basis of race, gender, age, etc., and these nondiscriminatory statutes are typically reinforced in a project labor agreement. Contractors signatory to a PLA are required to recognize the local unions as the representative of all workers on the project.

The PLA also generally provides that management's rights to manage are not usurped by the agreement. Contractors are entitled to establish and enforce reasonable work rules and to introduce labor-saving techniques, processes, equipment, and materials without objection from the labor force or its union representation. Similarly, non-union contractors awarded contracts on the project are allowed to import, engage, and employ their own key employees for the project. The size of this core group of employees differs from agreement to agreement. The purpose, however, is to allow a non-union contractor to execute its construction tasks with first-line supervision and key laborers in the manner in which it is used to working.

The final key element of nearly all project labor agreements permits the standardization of shift starting and ending times, rules for overtime, holidays, breaks, show-up times, and travel time, etc. Wages and benefits are also set at union scale and, for publicly procured projects, at no less than the minimum prevailing wage rates for the state. Similarly, classes of worker, the rate structure for apprentices versus journeyman, and the proportion of each within a crew can be negotiated in the PLA. For all practical purposes, an owner has very little hope of negotiating more favorable labor rates because it is about to become a very large procurer of labor. Certain project labor agreements have included prescribed rate increases over the life of the project, eliminating one source of uncertainty. An owner may be in a position to eliminate some of the arcane workforce requirements, work rules, or overtime policies of some local unions that seem to be most abhorrent to proponents of open-shop/merit-shop contractors. Yet, it is these same hard-won benefits that the unions are notoriously stubborn to concede.

The owner should strive to anticipate the needs of its contractors over the entire life of the project and address these needs in the agreement. For example, there may be a need for a contractor to resort to a 24-hour-a-day, 7-day-a-week operation for an extended period of time. A shift-crew schedule of rolling four–10s, or four–12-hour days plus three–12-hour days, or other nonstandard arrangement may be impossible or prohibitively expensive to implement after the PLA has been signed.

Issue

Whether or not an owner chooses to enter into a PLA for a megaproject will undoubtedly spark an emotional debate within the community. The main protagonists in that debate with the loudest and most influential sway over public opinion usually prove to be extremely self-interested in wanting their positions to prevail. The sides generally align

behind the union proponents and the non-union opponents. Each side will support their arguments with biased studies and slippery-slope public policy predictions. The owner responsible for the decision will be forced to cut through the rhetoric, objectively weigh the evidence, and carefully consider the political ramifications in order to make a sound decision. As with all major decisions, the owner will likely rely on its planning and project management consultants to assist in this decision. Many owners also turn to public policy consultants for recommendations concerning the impact of enacting such an agreement.

Analysis and Discussion

Unlike some of the earliest PLAs for public construction projects, union-only agreements are no longer legal in the United States. While a privately funded project's owner is free to contract in any manner it desires, if state or federal funding is used in the project, then both union and non-union contractors must be allowed to bid on contracts being executed under a project labor agreement. Those bidders will be instructed that as a condition precedent to awarding a contract, that winning bidder must sign on and agree to the terms and conditions of the previously negotiated PLA. In the early 1990s, in the face of anticipated challenges to the legality of its project labor agreement, the Massachusetts Water Resources Authority's precedent condition stated only that the responsible low bidder had to demonstrate that it was able to promote and maintain labor harmony on the project, and that one way of demonstrating such harmony was to execute the project labor agreement. All contractors executed the PLA.

In those states where they are not prohibited from doing so, public owners and (at least for the pendency of the current administration) federal agencies are free to consider whether a PLA makes sense for their project. Notwithstanding the legislative or administrative preferences, restrictions, or guidance on them, PLAs have also been repeatedly challenged by private court actions. In those situations where a project labor agreement has been successfully challenged, the opponents of the agreement were usually able to demonstrate that the public owner's inclusion of a PLA represented a violation of the public bidding laws. In a case brought by non-union subcontractors in New York and often cited by PLA opponents, the court found that the owner had failed to demonstrate "more than a rational basis" for implementing the PLA.[4] For a public owner to show that a PLA is necessary or desirable for its particular project, it will likely be required to demonstrate that the PLA would somehow fulfill its governmental objectives of achieving the best constructed project for the lowest price without running afoul of the public procurement laws. The standard of review is that there must be more than a rational basis for that owner believing that a PLA is in the best interest of the public. In order to satisfy this standard, articulated in the *New York State Thruway Authority* case, the court stated:

The standard of more than a rational basis cannot be based on loose projections, un-verifiable calculations, or a project which lacks unique history or complexity such that otherwise applicable provisions of the General Municipal Laws should be ignored. Here, the legislature based its decision on unverifiable dollars, lack of history of labor unrest, and a lack of showing of any type of unique complexity to this project. These omissions make it impossible for the County to establish that their action was even reasonable let alone more than rational.

PLAs have been upheld in all cases except those in which the public owner failed to properly document that it carefully considered the decision to adopt a PLA and perform the due diligence necessary to demonstrate the economic benefit of the agreement to the public. The legality of PLAs, in the absence of specific state legislation to prohibit them, has seemingly been settled. Executive orders of presidents and governors come and go. The real debate over whether or not a PLA makes sense for a project seems to re-volve around public policy issues. That debate typically focuses on the following issues: (1) Is it fair to require contractors to agree to the terms of a PLA? (2) Will the PLA de-crease the competition from the contractors in discouraging the non-union contractors from bidding on the work? (3) Will the PLA actually drive up the cost of construction? (4) Does a PLA amount to discrimination against non-union construction workers?

Recommended Practices

- First and foremost, the owner's decision whether or not to enter into a project labor agreement will be a function of the location and timing of the project. Mega-projects in the heavily unionized Northeast during an active construction market are more likely to benefit from a PLA than those in Southern or Midwestern states during a slow construction market.
- Second, the attributes of the particular megaproject, how geographically diverse it is, and whether the various contracts are piled one on top of the other or are spread out over time and space affect labor relations. The more congested the site and the tighter the schedule, the greater the risk of labor unrest affecting the proj-ect and the more attractive a PLA's no-strike clause will be to an owner. On the other hand, if the disgruntled craft or labor force can be isolated from the rest of the project, the no-strike provision is of less value to the owner because the strike is of less consequence.
- Consider the entire spectrum of pros and cons, not just the immediate unit cost of labor. Consider the collateral impact that adopting a PLA will have on the commu-nity, i.e., whether it will bolster or detract support for the project.
- Negotiate the most positive terms possible. Union representatives will be hard

pressed to give up any of their hard-won work rules, but other provisions, such as mandatory drug and alcohol testing at the point of hiring and dismissal "for cause" or suspicion during the execution of a project, will promote project safety. Requiring certification of safety training, such as an OSHA 10-hour course, is a reasonable expectation of a labor force on a megaproject. If unions are to be the brokers and labor referral agents for the project, these two safety precautions should be doctrinally noncontroversial. Push for a reasonable number of key contractor travelers to be assigned to the project without being held up in the generally accepted referral protocol. If there is a need for specialized labor forces, such as NATM miners for a portion of the project, carve out the ability to specially and specifically assign workers with unique skills for that particular project. Anticipate the needs of contractors over the life of the project and address their labor needs as best you can.

- If the owner decides to adopt a PLA, then it must do so in a manner that is unassailable by opponents. Retaining a third-party consultant to study and determine that the PLA is in the best interest of the public and consistent with procurement laws, rather than a rush to sign an agreement, will eliminate the expensive and embarrassing court challenge that, if the opponents prevail, could severely disrupt the project.

Notes

1.   Haas, C., Borcherding, J., Allmon, E., & Goodrum, P. (1999). *U.S. Construction Labor Productivity Trends, 1970–1998*. Center for Construction Industry Studies Report No. 7. Austin: The University of Texas.

2.   Tuerck, D., Glassman, S., & Bachman, P. (August 2009). *Project Labor Agreements on Federal Construction Projects: A Costly Solution in Search of a Problem*. Boston: Beacon Hill Institute, Suffolk University. Retrieved on March 14, 2010, from http://www.beaconhill.org/BHIStudies/PLA2009/PLAFinal090923.pdf.

3.   *Building & Construction Trades Council of the Metropolitan District v. Associated Builders & Contractors of Mass./R.I.* (91-261), 507 U.S. 218 (1993).

4.   *New York State Thruway Auth.*, 207 A.D. 2d 26 (3d Dept. 1996).

CHAPTER 9

Construction Management, Safety, and Quality Assurance

Thomas Peyton, P.E., Parsons Brinckerhoff
Ted Devens, Parsons Brinckerhoff
Raymond Crawford, Parsons Brinckerhoff

In prior chapters the reader has learned about the incredible amount of time and effort that goes into the conception, planning, and championing of a megaproject to bring it to the actual construction phase. Megaprojects are complex and consume enormous resources; you could say they are more than the sum of their parts. They involve a number of contract packages in order to lessen the risk to any one company, increase competition, and stay within current bonding limits. In addition to the actual construction, there are many other parts of a megaproject. In each contract (and some megaprojects can have up to 20 contract packages), there will be provisions for multiple construction schedules, environmental monitoring, community outreach, site inspection, etc. To guarantee comprehensive and accurate oversight, one entity should be responsible for the activities of the many. In other words, a professional construction management (CM) approach must be employed that will strive to ensure smooth interface between the various contracts.

This chapter will discuss the construction management approach, why it is important, and how it should be used. This chapter will also discuss the importance of safety and quality assurance, which can help lessen risk to the owner agency and the contractor.

Megaprojects require enormous resources to manage such complex undertakings. Skilled people are needed to manage each part of a typical construction project. What sets megaprojects apart is the number of people who are needed, working as an integrated team, using consistent procedures, maintaining consistent records to keep the project on course and under control. Risk is associated with all construction, and especially underground construction. Megaprojects by their sheer size are extremely risky. In order to successfully manage these megaprojects, the construction manager must manage the project's risk.

Starting in 2000, the New York City region experienced unprecedented growth in new infrastructure. This growth spawned numerous megaprojects, all happening at once, all competing for resources to successfully manage and control these historic projects. Table 1 (next page) is a partial list of megaprojects that are currently under construction or in design in the New York region, totaling $20.5 billion in construction costs. They all employ a specialist construction manager.

The New York region has two distinct challenges associated with managing megaproj-

Panoramic view of Sydney Harbor, with the Harbor Bridge, designed by John Bradfield in 1916 (but not completed until 1932 because construction was delayed by World War I). It is the widest steel arch bridge and the fifth longest in the world. To the left of it is the Sydney Opera House, designed by Jørn Ultzon and built under the engineering supervision of Ove Arup and Partners. After a long period of construction difficulties, it opened in 1973. Photo © 2006 by Peggyapl.

151

Table 1. **New York Region Megaprojects (Winter 2009)**

Project	Owner	Schedule	Cost
East Side Access	Metropolitan Transportation Authority	2001–2015	$7.2 billion
No. 7 Line Subway	Metropolitan Transportation Authority	2007–	$2.2 billion
Second Ave. Subway	Metropolitan Transportation Authority	2007–2015	$4.4 billion
Trans-Hudson Express Tunnel	New Jersey Transit	2009–2015	$4.5 billion
World Trade Center Transportation Hub	Port Authority of New York and New Jersey	2005–2011	$2.2 billion

ects. The first is that these special projects require great numbers of skilled, highly trained and highly coordinated managers, technical specialists, and inspectors; and the second is that each of these megaprojects is competing with the others for these scarce resources.

According to the Construction Management Association of America, "Construction Management evolved as a professional practice distinct from design and construction in the early 1960s in response to increasing complexities in the construction industry."[1] In the 1960s and 1970s, projects increasingly suffered from contract disputes, budget overruns, poor quality, design deficiencies, and production shortfalls. A new approach to managing construction projects effectively had to be found in order to deal with these problems. Professional construction management developed in response to these needs. This new advancement in managing projects has been refined and fine-tuned so that the CM approach has become a highly effective tool for managing megaprojects.

Megaprojects compounded these problems and needs. The projects are bigger, more complex, and suffer from trends to exaggerate the benefits and understate the costs just to get them approved and started. Megaprojects have exceedingly poor records on cost overruns and project benefits and, because of these, they lack public support. This is certainly a poor point from which to start construction projects that usually have adverse public impacts of noise, dust, vibration, traffic disruption, and degradation of quality of life for those around the project.

CM Organization Size

The construction of a megaproject usually involves many contract packages. Each one is a unique management challenge. The CM must be organized to manage the project correspondence so that it is routed and acted upon by the correct party in a timely fash-

ion. There are project records to keep, and they must be detailed and accurate so that there is no arguing about the facts of any given situation. The payments to the contractor must be efficiently processed, to verify the quantity of work accomplished and that the work conformed to the requirements of the contract documents.

When disputes arise between the contractor and the owner, they must be addressed quickly and fairly to maintain the momentum of the project and avoid delays. Change orders and claims must be dealt with quickly and efficiently, again to keep the project moving forward. The CM must monitor the performance of the contractor against the baseline schedule and budget and help mitigate any slippage of these elements.

What size of CM organization is needed to effectively manage a megaproject that contains many contracts, some of which occur simultaneously?

Analysis and Discussion

We have worked on numerous projects, both mega and sub-mega, and find that there are several elements they have in common. Both require knowledgeable, experienced individuals at all levels of the organization to make the project a success. Both usually involve multiple contracts happening simultaneously, each with its unique requirements and challenges.

We find that it is useful to organize a project into a project-wide core group of individuals who are responsible for the overall management of the project, management of the CM's contract with the owner agency, and management of the budget, schedule, change orders, and claims. In addition, this core group is responsible for establishing the procedures that are used to gather and store project information, developing consistent inspector's reporting formats, establishing the overall risk approach used on the project, and capturing and disseminating the lessons learned as the project goes forward.

This core group is paired with contract package staff consisting of a resident engineer, office engineer, document control personnel, and inspection staff. This "package" staff would use the standard procedures developed by the core staff to ensure consistency of management approach and data collection.

Megaprojects just require more of these individuals. On a past project that involved the construction of 18 miles of water supply tunnels, 8 contracts, and a budget of approximately $738 million, the total CM staff peaked at about 45 full-time equivalents when 4 contracts were under construction simultaneously. On a recent megaproject with a budget of $4.4 billion, 12 construction contracts, and up to 8 simultaneous contracts, the CM team reached 100 full-time equivalents. As projects get larger and have more and more simultaneous contracts, the size of the CM staff also rises. There is also a minimum staffing level that is needed to manage major infrastructure projects. Finding all these trained and experienced people is one of the biggest challenges facing professional CM providers.

Recommended Practices

The CM organization should be structured to manage these projects efficiently; to control the scope, schedule, budget, and changes to the work; and to manage the risk to the owner, the CM, and the contractor, in order to be successful. A structure that contains a core staff and contract staffs working under one set of procedures is the best way to accomplish this task. The main challenge is to attract the right talent in the right numbers. CM organizations must recruit and retain these individuals if they are to successfully secure the work. The owner organization should recognize that the CM staff should be the best, and it should be willing to pay for these high-level people. The success of the project will depend to a great extent on the experience of the people inspecting the work and managing the process.

Managing Risk

Risk management is simply managing surprises on a project! It involves the evaluation of alternatives and the assessment of the hazards of each of the alternatives. Managing risk is making choices among the alternatives, understanding the consequences of those choices, and planning to make the hazards as harmless as possible.

On any project, risks arise from many different sources, and a great deal of the CM's time is spent in dealing with these risks. The CM must understand where risks come from, what impacts they have or can have on the project's cost and schedule, how they can be eliminated or mitigated, and how the residual risks can be assigned to the contracting party best able to deal with them.

Analysis and Discussion

Risk management on megaprojects should start during the early stages of the project, continue through the preliminary and final design, and be handed off to the CM during the construction phase. We recommend that the CM be brought into the project team early enough in the planning and design phase to allow the CM's construction experience and lessons learned from other projects to be incorporated on the megaproject. Figure 1 shows that the effectiveness of managing project risks is greatest when the CM is brought in early but diminishes the later the CM is brought into the process.

Risk management should be a formal process that involves the entire project team sitting down to talk about and capture all possible risks the project may encounter. Once identified, the risks can then be analyzed. What is the probability that the event will occur? If the event occurs, what are the consequences to the project's cost and schedule? The team should reach a consensus on all the risk events and record these in a risk reg-

ister so that the details and conclusions will not be lost and so that future risk tracking can occur. Once the risks are identified, the team must then discuss how they can be mitigated or eliminated. Who is responsible for the risks and their mitigation, and what are the impacts and costs associated with the mitigation? After the mitigation or elimination of as many risk events as possible, what is to be done with the residual risks? Who is now responsible for these residual risks? The best result is for the residual risks to be allocated to the project participant best able to deal with them. This could be the owner agency, as in most geological or site condition risks; or it could be the contractor, as in most performance risks (labor, equipment, means, and methods); or the residual risks could be transferred to an outside party like an insurance company.

Risk management is just as important on megaprojects, but the sheer size and complexity of these projects complicates the undertaking. The risk process very well might require that the project be broken down into smaller pieces and each piece analyzed by a separate team to make sure that details are not overlooked. Once this is completed, the overall risks of the project can be addressed so that both the micro and macro elements are captured, analyzed, and accounted for. The risk register for megaprojects can then be an exceedingly useful tool, recording the risk process, the mitigation efforts, responsible parties, and frequency of risk management efforts.

As a result of going through this risk process, the project team will be able to compare the risk-adjusted impacts among dissimilar risks to provide a common definition of risk exposure, to prioritize the risks, and to quantify the cost and schedule impacts of the risk events. A properly conducted and documented risk process can allow the project team to estimate the contingencies that the project should carry in both cost and schedule so that the project budget and schedule reflect a truer picture of what is likely to occur.

Figure 1. **Timing and Effectiveness of Construction Management**

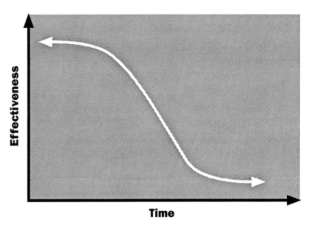

Construction Management can help review the project and make recommendations on risk management, contract types, and contractor selection. The earlier CM is used, the better.

From: Parsons Brinckerhoff and Colorado School of Mines.

Recommended Practices

The objective of a risk management program is to provide the senior management with a systematic process of identifying, evaluating, managing, and documenting risks that impact the project's cost, schedule, quality, project perception, and safety.

The first recommended practice is to establish early in the planning phase a formal

risk management process and to use a risk register to capture and document the risk-related efforts on the project. Due to the complex nature of megaprojects, the risk assessment should be broken down into smaller segments so that no detail is lost. This should be followed by a project overall risk evaluation to identify the macro- and micro-risks and their associated impacts.

Next, the risk efforts must become a living part of the overall project structure. Risk reviews must be conducted during preliminary and final design efforts and at any time the project is taken in a new direction. The risk efforts should then be passed on into the construction phase, managed by the CM (which may even include the participation of the contractor).

The risk process should be used to establish the cost and schedule contingencies for the project. It can also provide a realistic appraisal of the uncertainty associated with the construction and a knowledge basis for these numbers.

Definitions

Risk assessment: The systematic process of evaluating both the likelihood of an identified outcome occurring and the magnitude of its consequence.

Likelihood: An assigned probability that an identified outcome will occur. Suggested likelihood ratings are shown in Table 2.

Consequence rating: The magnitude, expressed either qualitatively or quantitatively, of the outcome of a project decision, activity, or other event. Suggested consequence ratings are shown in Table 3.

Risk rating: The severity of the risk, established by computing the product of the assigned likelihood (probability) of the outcome happening and the magnitude of the impact (consequence).

Background

Understanding the environment in which the megaproject is to be designed and constructed is critical to defining the context in which project decisions, activities, and events are developed and in which the identified outcomes attain their respective risk levels.

The project may have to function in a very dynamic environment where the activism of labor, the level of community organization and their expectations, the large set of stakeholders, each with agendas, and an unequaled and ever-changing set of political players demand a very difficult balancing act to achieve success.

The environments on some megaprojcts may consist predominantly of third-party interfaces. To be successful, the risk management program would be structured to interact extensively with the third parties. A plan would be developed to facilitate this interac-

Table 2. **Likelihood and Risk Level**

Likelihood	Description of Frequency of Event	Probability	Scale Value
Frequent	Event occurs many times during period of project	>70%	5
Probable	Event occurs several times during period of project	40–70%	4
Occasional	Event could occur during period of project	20–40%	3
Remote	Event is unlikely to occur, but it is possible during period of project	10–20%	2
Improbable	Event is so unlikely that it can be assumed not to occur during period of project.	0–10%	1

Table 3. **Consequence and Risk Level**

Consequence	Description of Effect of Event				Scale Value
	Cost	Schedule	Safety	Project Perception/ Political Fallout	
Catastrophic	Adds up to $250 million	Adds 12 months	Multiple public casualties	Public perception very poor. Project seriously jeopardized. Serious political fallout to client.	5
Critical	Adds up to $100 million	Adds 6 months	Single public casualty and multiple workforce casualties	Project jeopardized. Requires considerable effort to regroup public/political support.	4
Serious	Adds up to $50 million	Adds 4 months	Single public casualty or multiple workforce casualties	Some concern for project viability. Some political fallout experienced by client. Moderate effort required to re-establish viability.	3
Moderate	Adds up to $25 million	Adds 1 month	Single workforce casualty	Minor concern for project and effect on client politically.	2
Marginal	Adds up to $10 million	Adds 1 week	Little possibility of casualty	Little or no concern for project and effect on client politically.	1

tion, with an aim to reach a consensus on risk perception between the project and the third parties that will ultimately permit more effective risk management.

The framework of the risk management program should fully take into account the environment in which the project is being built. The risk program should meet the owner's objective of delivering a quality megaproject system with exceptional value by focusing on avoidance of adverse project impacts in the following areas: (1) cost increase, (2) schedule delays, (3) degradation of anticipated quality, (4) unfavorable political fallout, and (5) unfulfilled community expectations.

The risk management program is structured to identify and manage decisions, activities, and events that emanate from labor, community boards, stakeholders, and politicians, and that have a probability of resulting in an adverse impact to the project.

Policy

The megaproject's senior management will define and implement a risk management program, consistent with the project's objective of building a safe, quality megaproject that provides exceptional value to client and users.

The risk management program will identify key risks and mitigation plans and prioritize actions. These items will be documented in a risk register. The risk register will be continuously reviewed with management and used as the basis of reporting.

The senior project management must be fully committed to the risk management program, recognize it to be an integral part of the project's good management practices, and ensure that this plan is understood, implemented, and maintained throughout the project organization.

Risk Identification

The risk manager facilitates the effective identification of risks through risk workshops/brainstorming sessions and risk reviews with key personnel. Risks can also be raised by anyone at anytime for consideration and potential addition to the register.

Risk workshops take place at key stages in the project. Generally, these are at the outset of each new phase (e.g., concept design, scheme design, detailed design, or after a set time has elapsed from the previous workshop).

The following risk workshops, with key invitees noted, would be typical:

- Senior project team risk workshops (senior managers from the various project departments, external interface, client, relevant third parties or agencies)
- Design/construction risk workshops (design managers, construction managers)
- Project management workshop (contract, procurement, scheduling, cost)

Figure 2. **Risk Categorization**

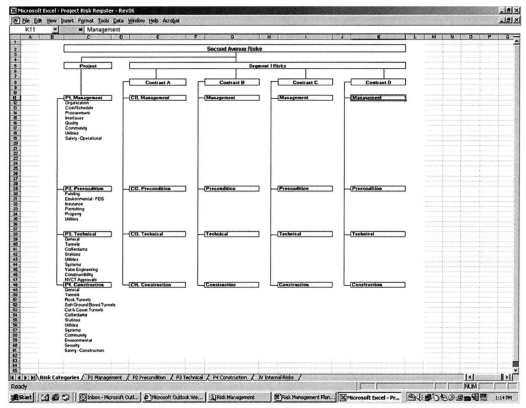

Risk categories as shown in the project risk register.

Risk Categorization

Risks are categorized as follows (see Figure 2):

Management: These are risks that result from project planning, strategies, and work processes that are used to manage and direct the project, the procurement and contracting process, and the environmental process. Examples: establishing the project organization structure and reporting requirements, approach to quality, decisions regarding the hardware and software to be used, identification and management of internal and third-party interfaces, approach to community issues, procurement strategies, contract delivery methods and terms, etc.

Precondition items: These are items that must be completed or available to support the project schedule. They almost always become risks when they are not available or completed as scheduled. Examples: project funding and financing plans, final environ-

mental impact statement, permitting, property acquisition and easements, and utility design and agreements to the extent planned, etc.

Technical: Risks in this category originate in a design activity/specification requirement, or lack of an appropriate requirement, and manifest themselves in a construction product or as a result of the means and methods used to achieve the product. Examples: settlement of building foundations adjacent to an excavation due to deficient design or means and methods, excess water infiltration into a structure, etc.

Construction: Risks in this category result from the planning and execution of the construction work or from contractor work practices. Examples: labor availability and restrictions, productivity, safety plan, compliance with regulatory requirements, encountering differing site conditions, encountering hazardous materials or archeological items, contractor work practices that adversely impact communities such as lane closures, and dirty work areas adjacent to the community, etc.

Risk (and Opportunities?) Register

The notes from the risk workshops will be formalized and entered into a risk register. Through an initial iterative risk assessment process, the risk manager will record the following information in the risk register (roughly corresponding to the headings from left to right in Figure 3):

Risk category
Refined risk descriptions
Risk owners
Risk status (e.g., being worked, transferred, incorporated in design, insured against, avoided)
Mitigation plan
Actions required
Dates for action completion
Party responsible for actions
Likelihood, consequence, and risk rating

The risk register is a "live" document and should be updated regularly to reflect changing mitigation plans and actions. It forms the basis for reports and reviews.

Risk Assessment

The objective of risk assessment is to establish a rating for each risk by assigning two values to the risk:

Likelihood of occurrence, and
Magnitude of the consequence.

Figure 3. **Risk Register**

				L	Likelihood
				C	Consequence
				R	Risk Rating

Category	Number	Risk	Risk Owner			Risk Owner	Status	Last Reviewed	Mitigation Plan	Action	Action Date	Action By Whom	Reference	Unmitigated			Mitigated		
			Client	Des	Cont									L	C	R	L	C	R

The product of these two values establishes the risk rating. Suggested thresholds are included in Table 3 (see page 157).

The risk manager convenes a group of experienced individuals to develop these values. The values may be assigned by consensus or, if deemed necessary by the risk manager, an analysis may be conducted, performance records evaluated, or other appropriate methods used. Initially these values may be qualitative, but eventually, project requirements will necessitate using quantitative values.

Risk Evaluation

The objective of risk evaluation is to use the risk ratings determined in the risk assessment process to prioritize the risk list and to exclude from further consideration risks that are below a predetermined threshold level. In this way the program can focus on the higher-level risks in a systematic manner.

Senior project management provides guidance on establishing the threshold risk level.

Risk Mitigation

After a set of risks has been identified, analyzed, and evaluated, the risk manager will convene a group of experienced personnel to identify individual risk mitigation and the party responsible for the mitigation.

Mitigation of risks can include avoidance, transfer, or inclusion in design. Reducing the likelihood or the magnitude of the consequence or taking out insurance where appropriate can also mitigate risks.

Proposed decisions about risk mitigation are reviewed and approved by senior management.

Review and Reporting

On a regular basis the risk register is reviewed and risks that have materialized as the project develops are added, risk levels are updated, and mitigation measures are assessed.

The risk manager provides senior management with program status and updates on a periodic basis.

The client and senior management should agree early in the project on the format and content for reporting of activity and status of items in the risk register. At a minimum, risk management should be reported at regular project progress meetings at different levels of the project organization and in regular project progress reports.

Quantitative Risk Analysis

Risk analysis techniques can be used to formalize the link between risk and its impact on schedule and cost. The following software packages are recommended for schedule and cost risk analyses, respectively:

> Schedule risk analysis — Primavera Risk Analysis, by Oracle
> Cost risk analysis — @RISK, by Palisade (an add-on to Microsoft Excel)

Both of the above analyses are based on a similar Monte Carlo simulation methodology. The schedule risks generate a range of durations for various activities, while the cost risks have cost ranges. In addition, the statistical results from the schedule risk model are incorporated into the cost model to reflect the cost impact of delays.

In general, the cost model is used to set initial contingency with regular reforecasting, which gives an indication of the likely final completion cost of the project and how this compares with the available project budget.

The schedule model highlights activities that need mitigation based on the input of risk

and logic links. The results from the analyses are presented in a statistical format that shows varying levels of confidence in completion dates and forecast final completion costs.

Both models can also be used to investigate scenario analyses.

Design for Construction Safety Initiative

There is a construction safety initiative that appears to be gaining traction within certain segments of the design and construction industry, commonly called "Design for Construction Safety," or alternatively, "Prevention through Design." The initiative arises from a working group consisting of members associated with the Occupational Safety and Health Administration's (OSHA) Alliance Program and the National Institute of Occupational Safety and Health (NIOSH). In 1995, the United Kingdom promulgated legislation for designers to consider the safety of design from design conception to maintenance and protection. Other European nations and Australia have adopted similar rules. Planning prevention into the design of a project has been used in design-build contracts and adopted by some owners. The concept of "Prevention through Design," as indicated by NIOSH, can be defined as:

> Addressing occupational safety and health needs in the design process to prevent or minimize the work-related hazards and risks associated with the construction, manufacture, use, maintenance, and disposal of facilities, materials and equipment.[2]

While the concept is noble, the potential liability implications for design professionals and the consequences to the industry are far-reaching and require a full hearing by designers, contractors, owners, and insurance carriers before adoption.

Every decision by a design professional requires the balancing of trade-offs among costs, aesthetics, operational and maintainability considerations, and construction safety. The industry's current state of the practice is that the construction contractor bears complete responsibility for its workers' safety during project construction. This is consistent with the commonly understood risk management maxim that a risk should be allocated to the party in the best position to control that risk. *The Design for Construction Safety initiative, whether intended or not, will reallocate a portion of that risk to the design professional.*

We urge design professionals to stay involved with their local and national professional associations as this safety initiative evolves by actively participating in discussions and roundtables regarding the initiative. The potential consequence of the industry's adoption of a Design for Construction Safety initiative is that the standard of care for design professionals could include a heightened burden on the design professional to evaluate construction safety considerations. Certain specialty contractors and material suppliers could face obsolescence if their technique or product is deemed too risky by design professionals who are overly cautious as a result of the safety initiative.

Preface

One chapter does not do justice to the topic of construction safety on a megaproject. That is not the goal here. The goal is to make the reader aware of some best practices involving construction safety on large projects. For more in-depth information, visit the American Society of Safety Engineers website (www.asse.org). A very useful book is *Construction Safety Management and Engineering*, edited by Darryl C. Hill, published by ASSE in 2004.

Influencing Construction Safety Performance

Issue

Project safety should start during the predesign phase. That being said, the message of the old adage that the safety manager is the "last to come and first to go" should be avoided. From a safety perspective, megaprojects are not too different from any other project. The goal of safety is the prevention of incidents and the protection of life, property, and the environment. On a megaproject, the scale or magnitude of the effort will need to be increased.

Project safety can be compared to a three-legged stool. The project is supported by the owner or client, construction manager, and contractor. All three must work in unison to achieve a balanced approach to developing a safety culture on the project. When one of the legs does not hold up, the stool will tilt or fall.

Analysis and Discussion

Client/Owner

The owner plays a distinct role in the safety process. It is the owner who has the ability to establish the safety roles that each party will have. The project contract documents are controlled by the owner and thus can be changed or modified to incorporate specific safety language. The contract should have the means for planning for safety so that it emphasizes being proactive and not reactive. The Business Roundtable issued report A-3 in 1982 (later reprinted in 1995) on "Improving Construction Safety Performance." The report focused on the economic impact of accidents and indicated several areas where an owner can influence safety. The first was in the contractor selection process. The second was on the owner's influence on contractor safety programs. The knowledgeable owner will understand that, as a project stakeholder in the safety process, they will see a benefit economically, receive a higher quality product, and benefit by not being publicly exposed when incidents end up in the news media.

The legal system places undue liability on those attempting to promote safety. For

this reason, many owners find that their legal counsel transfers risk liability for safety onto others through the contract. Contract responsibility for safety should be borne by the entity that is in the position to best control the risk. Assigning safety does not always promote or create a project environment that is conducive to a proactive safety culture. The bottom line is that when an accident occurs, all of the contracted parties will be legally involved in one way or another. How many prevented accidents end up with people being injured or in a court of law?

The issue is, How can safety be influenced prior to the activity? Planning for safety is an attitude that can be instilled on a project through owner involvement. The owner does not need to be intimately involved with the means and methods, but should understand the process and ask how the activity will be performed. This is where quality and safety go hand in hand. The construction manager provides the bridge between the owner and the contractor to help the owner better understand how safety and quality will be attained by the contractor.

Construction Manager

The construction manager (CM) will always have responsibility for the safety of its own employees, but it may or may not have a safety role as it pertains to the contracted work. Worker safety is an aspect of the employer-employee relationship that is the basis for the OSHA construction standards, CFR 1926. The CM must understand construction safety. This process begins at the company level through education and training. Establishing minimum standards for the CM staff, such as the 10-hour OSHA training program, will help to promote a basic understanding of construction safety. When the CM understands the hazards associated with the construction activities, they will be better positioned to help the contractor plan for safety.

The CM must understand the owner's intent for construction project safety. The contracts are the first item to consider. What is the role of the CM in regard to safety on the project? Does the contract agree with what the owner has indicated in negotiations and their project safety intent? Has the CM adequately planned for what is in the contract? Next, the CM should review the contractor's contract to ensure that the CM agreement and the contractor's agreement are consistent with how project safety is supposed to be implemented. Has the responsibility for safety been contracted to the party that is in the best position to control the work site?

General Contractor

The general contractor (GC) has contracted to perform work on a project or multiple projects. There may be more than one GC, when dealing with megaprojects. A single

project might be broken into smaller projects for purposes of creating smaller bidding packages to allow for more bidders. Each contractor will have its own company- and site-specific safety program. The issue becomes, What plan is used and how does the CM attempt to promote safety among so many project participants?

Megaprojects have the added benefit that the contract values are generally high enough to limit the potential bidders. GCs that can bid are usually very large or enter into a joint-venture agreement. The larger GCs understand the importance of employee and project safety and how it can impact the bottom line of the company. Many of the larger companies are self-insured and have a stake in safe performance.

No matter how well a company understands the financial aspect of safety, the human element must also be understood. Project safety lies in the hands of project staff who manage the day-to-day operations of the field activities. Safe performance must start at the top management level and be promoted at all levels. The adage that one must "walk the walk and talk the talk" applies. Actions do speak louder than words. When the project managers perform a safety walk of the project with the sole intent of looking at the overall safety of the project, the human element can be reached. Workers on the site will take notice and recognize that safety is being promoted.

Many general contractors do apply safe performance measures to the project and management staff. Accidents and injury information should be part of the overall measurement of the performance of a project. A project might be on schedule and on budget but have significant losses due to accidents. The accidents can involve workers, equipment, materials, and the general public. These losses can be calculated and applied to the overall performance of the project and the management staff. All too often, we think of the cost of safety only—or mainly—as the price paid for personal protective equipment (PPE), training, and the direct costs of injuries. The cost of shutting down a project as a result of an accident or work stoppage—because safety was not planned or activities occurred when state or federal compliance officers visit a site—is not always captured. We know that the indirect costs of accidents can be anywhere from 4 to 10 times the direct cost.[3] What is the cost benefit of prevention? Immeasurable.

Recommended Practices

Business Roundtable *Report A-3* indicated a series of areas where an owner can influence contractor safety. Influencing safety performance can be attained in a number of ways:

- Provide language in the contract concerning safety that the contractor must follow.

- Require a site-specific safety program, including hazard analysis.
- Require the use of permit systems, especially for hazardous activities that might interfere with existing systems.
- Have site safety assigned to responsible managers. This should be their only job on a megaproject.
- Plan safety into the work. This can be accomplished when reviewing schedules and conducting preinstallation meetings.
- Conduct site safety walks with the owner, CM, and GC management.
- Require the GC to conduct full incident investigations of all incidents.

Qualifying contractors by using a prequalification process can help identify contractors with a history of safe experience. This process usually evaluates historical information using the Experience Modification Rate, OSHA incidence rates, and some questions pertaining to safety management. Many of the large GC companies act more as a broker and not an actual builder. The tendency is to subcontract the work to individual self-performing contractors. The prequalification process should take this into consideration. A large GC can historically look good on paper because they are not performing the majority of the work themselves.

Contract Review—CM, Contractor

The owner has the ability to establish project contract language for a project. A typical contract will generally include compliance with all local and federal laws. The CFR 1926 standards are federal law. In states that have a state-run occupational safety and health plan, both federal and state laws come into play. Going above and beyond the required standards is where the owner can make a difference in project safety. A more site-specific safety approach can be established in the contract. A CM who is given the opportunity to coordinate the contract language prior to sending the RFPs out on the street can help find gaps in contract language, which can then be looked at to determine the best approach to managing safety on the project. This is critical for large construction projects with multiple general contractors.

The CM must ensure that the language that is in the CM contract is consistent with the owner's expectations and the contractor's contract. Safety language and expectations need to be balanced. If the owner has indicated a desire for the CM to manage some aspect of the safety system on the project, the CM needs to make sure that it not only hires a qualified person, but that it has adequately been compensated for the additional liability exposure. On megaprojects, an owner-controlled insurance program (OCIP) or contractor-controlled insurance program (CCIP) is usually put in place

to allow for higher, and in some cases more, insurance coverage at a lower cost to the owner. An OCIP will usually cover a CM in the event there is an accident involving a third-party liability exposure. There are many occasions when the CM is not included in the OCIP, which leaves the CM at a substantial risk for third-party liability exposures. The CM becomes the lone party for those searching for deep pockets. A CM acting as an owner's representative or agent on a construction site will usually not be part of a CCIP. The GC has purchased the insurance for the project and will usually not include the CM as an additional insured.

The GC should review all safety language in the contract documents to ensure that all safety-related requirements that might be above their normal means are included in the bid process. Some contractors may not be familiar with specific safety measures that require additional documentation or may not have adequate staff that might be needed to meet the contract safety requirements. Contract safety language should be passed down into subcontractor agreements. A megaproject might require a specific number of safety managers based on the number of workers or employees on the site. The positions might be required to be fully dedicated to safety. The specific requirement may also include subcontractors. Meetings and the orientation process might be longer than normal. Mandatory PPE requirements, such as 100 percent eye protection and fall protection, might be required in the contract. The issue here is to make sure that all parties understand that there is an up-front cost associated with safety.

Partnering

When done right, partnering is a great opportunity to establish the means for communication and a decision process. Partnering usually starts out as a formal process to obtain consensus on how all of the project partners will work together, in harmony. Partnering allows the management of the project the opportunity to consider safety as a separate yet interwoven aspect of the project. Consider a four-burner stove. The four burners are on at different levels of heat. On one burner there is a change order, on another a request for information, on another the monthly estimate, and on the final one, an estimate that needs to be negotiated for a scope change. The items on the four burners are constantly shifting or moving, due to meetings and demands on one's time. All of a sudden, there is a safety issue — perhaps not imminent danger, but one that could result in loss. The items on the burners are shifted to allow for the safety issue to be resolved. Partnering allows the project participants the opportunity, when it is a safety issue, to choose to move it ahead of all the other things and make a decision on how to proceed. Safety moves to the hot burner and is resolved quickly. Remember that, while people are discussing the safety issue, a worker may be at risk.

Planning for Safety

Safety may be the first item on the agenda, but don't forget to include it throughout the meeting. The weekly look-ahead should include safety. The CM can assist the GC in planning for safety by asking questions and promoting safety. Preinstallation or pre-construction meetings are also a good time to ask about safety. A one-plan approach that includes all elements of the work—workers, equipment, materials, quality, safety, etc.—allows for everyone to be on the same page. A job hazard analysis (JHA) can be used to review specific operations or tasks so that the hazards associated with the work can be identified and means for control established. The same JHA can also be used to plan the work by incorporating manpower, equipment, materials, and subcontractors. How often does one hear a complaint about one contractor or subcontractor working above another or one operation interfering with another due to lack of planning? A combined working schedule can help to eliminate hazards and improve efficiency on the site.

On a megaproject, separate safety meetings that are attended by the project safety staff are needed to help coordinate their efforts to cover all of the work or to let others know what is happening from a safety perspective. When there are several GCs on a project, the safety managers of the individual projects might not communicate on a regular basis. Project safety meetings allow the interaction needed to communicate project needs. This is especially necessary on a vertical construction project. One GC's work might overlap with other GCs' operations. Consider the number of tower cranes on a large building site. If every GC has its own tower crane, there is an obvious need for site coordination. Horizontal projects require end-to-end coordination as well as an opportunity to share and learn from the other GCs about what might be going right or wrong. This level of coordination is usually managed by a project safety manger representing the owner. Project or program safety meetings should be held to promote interaction between the safety managers of the contractors on the site.

The Culture of Safety

The outcome of shaping a safety culture is to produce behavioral change for, or to reinvigorate a belief in, safety self-awareness and a mindset of being "my brother's keeper," so to speak. When you walk onto a project site and look around and talk to the first few people you see, what is your impression and how is it shaped? We all have a set of core values and beliefs. How these beliefs and values are shaped by where we work is a cultural influence. An owner can shape the safety culture of a project by setting the tone for safety in the contract through safety site walks and by talking about

safety in meetings. The CM can take on a role similar to that of the owner. The GC has the ultimate role in establishing the overall culture for the project. How the culture is ultimately shaped can depend greatly on the project staff and culture of the GC involved.

Project safety is an outward reflection on the GC and its project staff. We have all heard the saying, "When going get tough, the tough get going." It is the "get going" part that becomes the issue. There is nothing wrong with getting tough. It is how we get there that can either continue the promotion of safety or cause it to take a back burner. How can we keep safety at the forefront even when financial or schedule implications become involved? The safety culture must continue to override the need to just get the job done. We need to get safety tough when the going gets tough. We need to continue to promote safety, and thus quality and efficiency, among the workforce so that they do not start to behave as if the culture has shifted from safe production to getting the job done. A stronger focus on planning becomes instrumental when a project runs into schedule and financial restraints.

As a team, the owner, CM, and GC can conduct site walks that strictly focus on safety issues. This should be done as a group so that what is seen is seen by all involved and brought to the attention of the appropriate correcting entity on the site. When there is an emphasis on safety by project management that is visible to the project workers, their behavior conforms to what is expected. Dan Peterson said, "What gets measured, gets done."[4] The workers perceive a visual measurement of their safe performance when the management of the project takes a visible and active interest in safety during the site walks. The opposite happens when project management on a site walk appear to condone unsafe acts or approve of methods that have not been adequately planned, or when the site walk appears to be just a walk through the site. When a site walk is being performed, there needs to be an agreement that distractions and other issues will be set aside until the walk is complete.

When a project site becomes large, as on some megaprojects, site walks should be limited to specific areas. Management site walks can focus on specific areas on a weekly basis, so that management continues to show commitment to safety while not taking too much time. Limit distractions and focus on targeted areas, as indicated by the safety staff for the project. Provide feedback to the workers when they perform safely and in instances when there could be a hazard associated with what they are doing. The important purpose is improving worker performance and safe behavior.

Quality Assurance

Success in the provision of construction management services demands a commitment to the highest level of quality in the performance of those services. Maintain-

ing consistently high levels of quality requires review procedures that measure performance levels and provide a mechanism for acknowledging excellence and correcting deficiencies.

Definitions

The terms "quality assurance" (QA) and "quality control" (QC) are much confused and the terms, though distinctly different, are often interchanged and used as if they are the same. The following definitions of quality assurance and quality control are taken from ISO 8402, which is the international standard referencing quality vocabulary. It is also important to define "quality" so that we all understand what quality assurance and quality control are designed to produce.

Quality. The totality of features and characteristics of a product or service that bear on its ability to satisfy stated or implied needs. In a contractual environment, needs are specified. Needs may include aspects of visibility, safety, availability, reliability, maintainability, economics, and environment.

Quality assurance. All those planned and systematic actions necessary to provide adequate confidence that a product or service will satisfy given requirements for quality. For effectiveness, quality assurance usually requires a continuing evaluation of factors that affect the design or specification for intended applications as well as verification and audits of production, installation, and inspection operations. Providing confidence will usually involve producing evidence.

Quality control. The operational techniques and activities that are used to fulfill requirements for quality. Quality control involves operational techniques and activities aimed both at monitoring a process and at eliminating causes of unsatisfactory performance at relevant stages of the quality loop in order to result in economic effectiveness.

In effect, quality control consists of those activities required to meet the specified requirements, while quality assurance consists of those oversight activities that confirm and assure that quality control is in place and is effective.

All QC and QA procedures are, by definition, negative, after-the-fact events. They are a policing process designed to follow up on installation activities to check that quality has been built into the work. Necessary as these procedures are, it is of equal importance to provide a positive role in the QA process by the promotion of quality prior to installation of the work. Quality promotion should be designed to inculcate a positive attitude on the part of all the field forces to provide maximum quality because of pride in their work. The aim must be satisfaction with a job well done rather than the minimum necessary to pass inspection.

The job of the QA/QC team, with client concurrence, is to promote a program of quality before and during the work to ensure no rework is necessary. Total quality manage-

ment is a tool that can be used to promote quality by fostering a desire for excellence in the finished product in the attitudes of the contractor's workforce at all levels. One way this can be achieved is by reviewing the work methods so that, in addition to passing the work as acceptable, the inspector can also give recognition to individuals, crews, subcontractors, and contractors whose work is of a consistently high quality. The resident engineer (RE), in reviewing these reports, should be willing to pass on these commendations to the client, giving recognition where due to the noteworthy individual or crew.

The RE may want to consider offering to the contractor and their staffs occasional tool-box meetings, similar to Safety Tool-box Meetings, which will address quality issues. The quality manager or inspectors, if capable, could give ten-minute presentations on such subjects as concrete finishes, formwork tolerances, masonry ties and reinforcing, and other quality issues.

The quality manager (QM) and field staff should work with contractor's staff to promote a team approach to quality assurance and control, to inspection and testing, everyone working together towards a common goal of quality construction. Everyone should be made aware of the costs of poor quality, of the time and cost of rework and the negative effects on morale of having to tear out work that one has labored hard to install. The inspection/testing program should be seen as only one element in a total quality program designed to assist all participants in achieving superior levels of quality. Too often, the quality field staff are seen as people with a negative, "out-to-get-you" mentality. They should be seen as a positive force that is dedicated to promoting superior quality through teamwork and cooperation.

Responsibilities

It must first be firmly established that the contractor is contractually responsible for the quality of the work, and QA or QC activities performed by other parties in no way invalidate the contractor's responsibility for quality. As such, the contractor must have in place QC activities to ensure that quality requirements are met.

Despite this contractual requirement, many, if not most, owners will provide both QA and QC resources, either through in-house resources, the designer of record, a construction manager, a construction engineering and inspection consultant, a QA/QC consultant, or a combination of the above. The construction manager or CEI (Construction Equipment Institute) consultant for the construction of projects is usually charged with provision of QA or QC or both. Occasionally, the client will provide QA oversight of QC activities.

Some contracts require the contractor to provide QC activities through a specific contractor quality control (CQC) plan. The construction contract documents will specify the level of QC activities required, and the contractor is usually required to submit a formal CQC plan for approval. In these instances, it is usually restricted to QA oversight activi-

ties, although these can be extensive and time-consuming if the contractor is deficient in fulfilling the requirements of the CQC plan.

The client/consultant agreement, when read in conjunction with the construction contract, will stipulate the extent of QA/QC activities for which the CM is responsible. The RE and field staff should be thoroughly conversant with the contract requirements and ensure that adequate facilities and resources are available at the site. Where the client/consultant agreement does not include sufficient resources, the RE shall discuss the matter with the principal in charge (PIC) and determine satisfactory approaches with the client.

Some clients will have very explicit and unique QA/QC requirements and/or a formal QA/QC program. The RE will need to ensure that the quality manager (QM) and field staff study and become familiar with the implementation of that program. In all cases, the QM is required to produce, with support from the PIC, a project quality control plan.

The QA/QC program will usually be under the direction of the QM. The QM will be assisted by trained and experienced inspectors and an office staff capable of documenting the operation and results of the QA/QC program. The QM must have available, either on staff or on call, qualified personnel or subconsultants for sampling and testing, for survey checks of the contractor's work, and for other specialist QA/QC activities.

Contractor Quality Control Plan

If the construction contract specifically requires QC to be performed by the contractor, the contractor will be required to provide a CQC plan. The QM should require submittal of the CQC plan before any construction work is begun. Normally, the contract will forbid commencement of any construction prior to approval of the CQC plan. Where the contract language is not specific, the RE should inform the contractor that no work should be installed prior to approval of the CQC plan and that any work installed without an approved CQC plan will not be approved for payment.

If the construction contract does not specifically assign QC to the contractor, the RE should still require that the contractor submit a QC plan. Preferably at the preconstruction conference, the contractor should be reminded of his contractual responsibilities for the quality of the work and be requested to submit a written quality control plan to indicate the personnel, activities, and resources to be employed to ensure that the work meets the required quality levels.

In the absence of specific contract language requiring submission of such a plan, it may be difficult, in some cases impossible, to get the contractor to comply. However, the contractor should be informed of the advantages to providing such a plan. These will include improved quality resulting in less rework and lower costs, coordination of QC activities with the staff thus avoiding delays for inspection, testing and

173

sign-off activities, and inclusion of all acceptable work in the payment applications.

QC plans should be reviewed by the QM and discussed with the contractor. When satisfactory, they should be copied to the client and designer of record (DOR) for their approval/acceptance. Compliance with the approved plan should be monitored and recorded.

"Contractor construction control requirements" normally requires the contractor to submit construction work plans (CWPs) for each phase of work to be performed. Specific requirements should be identified in the contract documents.

Construction work plans are detailed descriptions of a specific activity, including, at a minimum, the sequence of events, construction methods, responsibilities, and methods for verifying that work meets contract document requirements.

Properly developed and used, CWPs are a useful tool for both the contractor and the project. Preparing CWPs for upcoming construction activities helps the contractor better plan its work and simplify the readiness review process. By alerting the QM and quality control inspectors to upcoming contractor activities, the CWPs enhance the CM's ability to perform its construction management duties by promoting better planning, communication, and understanding.

The contractor may not begin activities covered by a CWP until the applicable plan is accepted by the appropriate reviewing entity. The contractor and RE should agree on work activity CWPs. The contractor should prepare the CWPs and submit them to the QM for acceptance. When requested by the QM, assistance should be provided to the QM for these submittal reviews from other staff support (i.e., quality assurance, quality control, geotechnical, survey, environmental, etc.).

The QM is responsible for reviewing quality system work plans, which should include:

- Supplier control
- Document control
- Control of materials, equipment, parts, components, and services
- Control of special processes
- Test control
- Control of measuring and testing equipment
- Processing of nonconformances
- Records

CWPs are required to be retained as contract records.

Inspection

The key individual in the quality effort is the inspector. Inspectors are expected to be knowledgeable in the work, familiar with the contract plans, specifications, and contract conditions, and experienced in the methods of installation. It is the duty of the chief

inspector (CI) and inspectors to monitor and verify that the project is being constructed in accordance with the plans and specifications and in compliance with the terms of the contract. The inspector has, and should exercise, the authority to reject both unsatisfactory workmanship and materials. Such rejections must be made immediately upon discovery, be made in writing to the contractor, and refer to the appropriate plan or specification requirement. However, the work shall not be directed to stop, except for an emergency situation as described in the section above.

Occasionally, the contractor will not immediately correct unsatisfactory work and will start to cover it with other work. This should not be allowed. In such cases, the RE should confer with the client to gain concurrence for a limited work stoppage until unsatisfactory work is corrected. Documentation, in the form of a nonconformance, must be completed and the contractor be required to correct the deficiencies before continuing the work activity. If necessary, the unsatisfactory work should include photographs of the unsatisfactory condition.

The QM or CI will ensure that inspection of the work is organized so as to support the contractor's schedule and that inspection forces are available and sufficient to meet the schedule. Every effort should be made to cooperate with the contractor so that inspection activities will dovetail with the contractor's work. The inspection staff must be aware of the daily and weekly schedules provided by the contractor and schedule their own work accordingly. The QM or CI QA plan should identify the intervals and size of the samples to be taken to meet the QA requirements of the contract.

The key document the inspector uses to record their quality activities is the daily inspection report. The inspectors will provide daily inspection reports indicating work performed, inspections and tests carried out, nonconformances noted (and subsequently recorded on a nonconformance report), and any other information relative to the quality of the work.

The inspectors must observe any tests performed by the testing consultants or statutory agencies. The inspector shall note the time, place, type and, if available, results of tests, identity of testing agent, and test equipment used. Any test certificates issued must be safeguarded and delivered to the field office for logging, distribution, and filing.

Off-site inspections may be required. These will be authorized by the client and scheduled by the QM with the contractor. Inspectors shall provide detailed travel and expense records, travel time, and time at off-site locations and details of inspections, tests, sampling performed, and conditions observed. Status of progress in fabrication/production and conformance with required schedule(s) should be noted and the RE informed of any potential for delays due to quality or production problems.

The inspection staff is required to inspect all materials delivered to the work site and to confirm that the materials meet the specified requirements. All incoming materials should have required documentation, including certification that materials have been

manufactured/processed in accordance with specified quality standards and passed all required inspections and tests. The inspectors will check all such documentation and forward it to the field office for filing. Storage and protection of all delivered materials shall be checked periodically to ensure that there is no deterioration in the materials prior to incorporation in the work.

Testing

Another key element of quality during construction is testing, both on-site and off-site. The project quality manager should be familiar with all testing requirements of the contract. To aid in becoming familiar and to better track the required testing, before construction begins, the quality manager should develop a testing plan based on the project specifications. The testing plan should indicate the specification section, test required, frequency of testing, and pass/fail criteria. The testing plan should be reviewed with the DOR and the testing subconsultant to verify that all testing requirements are identified.

For on-site testing, the QM is responsible for ensuring that adequate, accurate testing equipment is calibrated and recalibrated in accordance with testing specifications and standards. A log should be maintained on-site to confirm that all testing equipment is calibrated and has been maintained within calibration.

Alternatively, on-site testing may be subcontracted to a qualified testing laboratory that will be responsible for maintenance of test equipment. The testing subconsultant must provide records of the status of qualifications and records of calibration, recalibration, and maintenance of all relevant testing equipment. The quality manager shall perform periodic audits to confirm that testing laboratories are maintaining qualification requirements, including test equipment calibration, and document the results.

The field staff responsible for conducting tests must be fully trained in the conducting of such tests and the checking of test equipment and maintenance of records. The test equipment must be maintained in good order, cleaned regularly, and safeguarded against loss or damage. An inventory of all test equipment must be maintained and must indicate all required calibration or certification status and check dates. Inspector personnel records should indicate training and capabilities for performing tests. Particular certifications, such as operation of nuclear density test equipment, should be kept up to date and maintained on file.

Daily, weekly, and monthly schedules should be reviewed to determine the testing that will be required and a testing program developed to ensure that testing resources will be available and testing performed to support the work schedule. The project staff should schedule the subcontract testing services to ensure that their resources are planned and available. To the fullest extent possible, testing performed by testing laboratories at the site should be observed by an inspector.

Particular attention should be given to testing work or materials that will shortly thereafter be covered up or become otherwise inaccessible. Satisfactory testing results are required in order that follow-on work may proceed. The testing resources should be organized to be available as the work is installed and test results provided as soon as reasonably possible. Every effort should be made to cooperate with the contractor, but in no circumstances should tests be waived or reduced.

Off-site testing may be conducted by client resources, subcontract services, or by the fabricator/producer, depending upon the specification requirements. The quality manager should examine the contract conditions and the client/consultant agreement to determine the extent of their involvement and should provide staff to monitor subcontract services as required. Where the quality manager is responsible for coordinating off-site testing, the quality manager should require the contractor to provide adequate notice for all testing requirements in the form of an off-site testing schedule. This schedule must be reviewed regularly and updated as necessary.

All test results are to be distributed to all required parties upon receipt and all test reports are to be maintained on file at the field office. All test reports must clearly identify the following:

- Project number and description of work;
- Type of test and specification reference;
- Person/company performing the test, location, date, and equipment used;
- Sample source and date secured;
- Narrative description of tests performed;
- Results of tests, given in units required by specifications, and, as appropriate, units of recognized standards;
- Recommendation (as applicable) as to acceptance or rejection;
- Signature of responsible person controlling the testing work;
- A list of observers; and
- Required follow-up action if test results were not in conformance.

Test results for all off-site testing must be received at the site before material/equipment is incorporated in the work. If the contractor elects to use/install material/equipment without test results being available, the contractor shall be notified in writing that it will be entirely at the contractor's risk and responsibility for any consequent costs or delays.

Coordination with Designer of Record (DOR) and Statutory Authorities

The designer of record will have a direct interest in the testing and test results, and the QM should regularly confer with the DOR on testing matters. The DOR should re-

ceive copies of all test results and must be consulted with regard to matters arising out of unsatisfactory test results.

Statutory authorities such as cities, counties, and states and public and private utilities such as water, gas, sewer, power, telephone, and cable TV will have a direct interest in testing and may require observing or performing testing related to their interests. The field staff must be familiar with the specification requirements and any referenced testing standards and specifications of statutory authorities. It is the responsibility of the contractor to include all testing requirements in the scheduling of the work and to coordinate with the statutory agencies where they require observing or performing tests. The QM should ensure receipt of test results and distribution to statutory agencies of the results of testing performed on their behalf.

Quality Audits

The first line of responsibility for quality management lies with the individual project manager/resident engineer, who should perform regular audits of personnel performance and fulfillment of contractual responsibilities. The second line of responsibility lies with the PIC and company management, who should provide oversight and periodic reviews of total project performance. Without these two levels of responsibility, there can be no effective and consistent achievement of the quality levels demanded by the client.

From time to time, all projects will be audited by an outside agency. The procedures for this audit will be as laid down by the agency performing the audit. The auditor will be a member of the staff at the agency and, where necessary, will be accompanied by specific technical experts as are required for a particular project.

Normally, projects will be notified in advance as to when an audit is to be performed. A checklist, which will indicate the matters to be audited, will be forwarded to the PM/RE in advance of the auditor's arrival to perform an audit. The auditor will coordinate visits with the PM/RE to avoid busy periods. The exit interview between the auditor and the project personnel is an important function, at which time project personnel will have an opportunity to review and discuss perceived deficiencies, and methods to remedy deficiencies can be discussed and, in many cases, be adopted.

The audit report will not be a catalog of complaints but a working document to record that contract requirements are being met at or better than the required level of quality and that any deficiencies have been noted and will be addressed and measures taken to correct deficiencies. The audit report will also provide an opportunity for project personnel to advise PICs and other managers of the company of problems, difficulties, and frustrations that affect the quality of their efforts or their ability to fulfill requirements. It can also provide a vehicle to disseminate to other projects information on common problems and solutions to overcome such problems.

If the audits are to achieve their intended purpose, there must be enthusiastic acceptance of the auditor by each PM/RE and staff at the project offices. Furthermore, the auditor cannot be viewed as other than a distinct resource who is available to help achieve and maintain quality levels required by the contractual commitments and the competitive nature of our business.

Where the construction calls for contractor quality control, operated by contractor staff separate from the construction staff, it will be necessary from time to time for the RE to conduct audits of the CQC operation. The audit report should be reviewed with the PIC and project staff before release to the client.

Notes

1. Construction Management Association of America. *An Owner's Guide to Construction Management*. (2002). McLean, VA: Author, p. iii.
2. "NIOSH Safety and Health Topic: Prevention through Design." Retrieved March 14, 2010, from http://www.cdc.gov/niosh/topics/PTD/.
3. Liberty Mutual Research Institute for Safety, "Workplace Safety Index," 2002.
4. Peterson, D. *Safety by Objectives: What Gets Measured and Rewarded Gets Done*, Hoboken, N.J.: John Wiley & Sons, Inc, 1996.

CHAPTER 10

Claims, Changes, and Disputes

Kurt Dettman, Esq., Constructive Dispute Resolutions
Dan Fauchier, The ReAlignment Group, Ltd.
Richard Bayer, The ReAlignment Group, Ltd.
Steve Wojtasinski, Esq., DH Consulting Group LLC
Michael J. Landry, P.E., DH Consulting Group LLC

Introduction

Often parties do not pay adequate attention to the inevitability of disputes and claims arising on megaprojects. The parties' primary focus is on getting the project planned, funded, permitted, designed, and sent out for bid. And the beginning of the project is always the time of hope that the planned megaproject is going to be a success, combined with the early optimism of the project proponents and participants that "we're not going to have disputes and claims." However, one endemic characteristic of megaprojects is that there will be disputes and claims, and they often will be high in number and large in size. So, the prudent megaproject manager should assume that there will be a large volume of disputes and claims and plan accordingly.

The authors propose that addressing potential disputes and claims should be given just as high a priority as planning, permitting, design, and bidding, since disputes and claims can derail a project just as surely as other causes. Likewise, the authors recommend that this be addressed at the beginning of the project when the parties are cooperative—it is much easier to address dispute avoidance and resolution processes when there are no disputes than to leave that issue until a dispute has arisen or a formal claim has been made.

The authors will first address ways to avoid or minimize disputes,[1] since a dispute that is either avoided or resolved before it becomes a claim obviously will save time, money, and resources. The authors then address systems of control to manage the inevitable changes and claims, with the goal that all issues be resolved at the project level and that the project close out without the traditional "litigation tail." The authors finish their review by exploring the use of alternative dispute resolution (ADR) mechanisms that can avoid the morass of lengthy and expensive post-project litigation.

Partnering on Megaprojects

At the most basic level of work, a construction project is accomplished through a complex network of commitments—individual promises from one person to another.

View of the Verrazano Narrows Bridge, which spans the Narrows between the upper bay in New York harbor and the lower bay and connects Staten Island (foreground) with Brooklyn. When it opened in 1964, it was the longest suspension span in the world (it is now the eighth longest). Photo 2008 by Dogma5.

181

These discrete promises include what will be done, by whom, when, at what cost, and to what standard of quality. At this most basic level of work, megaprojects are different principally in the quantity of promises and the complexity of their interrelatedness.

Because the success of the megaproject relies on the fulfillment of these commitments as they are created or changed, the quality of human relationships on a job has a direct and material impact on the execution of the project. Humans engage with each other at several levels, and they telegraph the quality and nature of the relationship through communication. "Communication" can vary from relatively obscure gestures or body language to direct and understandable statements. We communicate conflict by a gesture as simple as a frown of annoyance or a feeling as profound as betrayal. Managing a megaproject requires managing conflict. The best way to manage conflict is through continuous, healthy, focused, direct human communication. The bridge between communication and conflict is often called "politics"; the space between communication and conflict is the "political space."

Not all conflicts can be resolved between project people, even people of extraordinary goodwill acting responsibly. But most can be resolved by effectively isolating positions from interests, with the ultimate interest of the participants being what is best for the project as a whole. For this reason, conflict management starts with the management of human relationships on a project. As projects increase in size and complexity, the impact of individual human relationships becomes magnified, and such impact is often reflected both in the multitude of project inefficiencies (waste) and in the nature of project disputes (additional resources). This is especially the case on a megaproject, where the risks are so much greater and the distances between people can be substantial.

In the 1980s an approach to managing the "political space" on a project called "partnering" began to be used. Partnering became important and respected when the Army Corps of Engineers adopted it as its chosen method of project kickoff. Over the intervening years, partnering has been defined in a variety of ways. In 1991, the Construction Industry Institute published *In Search of Partnering Excellence* to underscore the importance of partnering as a means of reducing adversarial relationships. That study provided the following definition of partnering (Partnering Task Force 1991):

> . . . a long-term commitment between two or more organizations for the purpose of achieving specific business objectives by maximizing the effectiveness of each participant's resources. This requires changing traditional relationships to a shared culture without regard to organizational boundaries. The relationship is based upon trust, dedication to common goals, and an understanding of each other's individual expectations and values. Expected benefits include improved efficiency and cost effectiveness, increased opportunity for innovation, and the continuous improvement of quality products and services.

Robert Cushman defines partnering as an important part of the commitments that are exchanged on projects. According to Cushman, partnering is

. . . a more or less formal commitment by all concerned parties on a project to implement and use a forum that provides opportunities for open communications between the parties on a regular basis to achieve joint resolution of problems. . . . The goal of partnering is to obtain a genuine commitment from each member of the construction team to work toward the resolution of issues when they are identified.[2]

The commitment parties make in partnering is that they will establish and use healthy, resilient lines of communication between all project participants. This is meant to result in robust managerial and interpersonal relationships that can continuously resolve the day-to-day conflicts and disputes that arise. Partnering seeks to develop a "project culture" from the many company cultures that organizations bring to the job. Thoughtfully and responsibly done, partnering may actually avoid claims and litigation, improve morale, and enhance value to the customer — in other words, deliver a quality project on time and on budget.

Expectations of Partnering

When parties partner, they usually engage in social activities aimed at creating a feeling of shared community and shared humanity. This normally happens at the outset of the project and involves all the project participants — sometimes hundreds of people. The parties expect that the enhanced communication developed in a one-day session will lead to greater efficiency on the job. The parties also expect that the newly developed bonds among participants will result in a quicker resolution of conflicts as they arise at all levels of the job. Partnering attempts to foster the growth of relationships among the participants through regular facilitated activities, including conversations between project participants.

Traditional partnering often develops a charter, a list of common understandings and a commitment from job participants that they will value the project first. Partnering facilitators often encourage the parties to develop a mutually agreed upon mechanism for the identification of disputes and a process for clarifying who "owns" the issue and who is responsible for resolving it. Ironically, the concept of a shared responsibility for resolution of issues is thereby dropped in favor of a simplistic resolution mechanism: the creation of a "dispute resolution ladder." The resolution ladder provides a stair-stepped escalation of disputes up the chain of command, ostensibly resulting in no dispute lingering for more than a few days. However, there is no conscious attention given to resolving the dispute at the lowest level; rather, resolutions await elevation to a higher level.

The Problem with Partnering

Although the results sought by partnering are essential to project success, the fact remains that roughly half the time partnering fails to put in place appropriate mecha-

nisms to resolve disputes and prevent claims. When it fails, its failure is primarily related to the fact that partnering is a one-day event; the relationships crafted are not durable. Even with quarterly check-ins, the kinds of team-building events usually employed by partnering facilitators do not deal with the on-the-ground problems encountered on the project. The relationships so necessary to a common understanding of project interests, and thus the shared responsibility in the resolution of the problems, often breaks down in the attempt to allocate all the responsibility for a problem to one party. The parties rarely employ the partnering facilitator's skills in attempting to resolve the matter at the lowest level and in a manner that is best for the project.

By way of example, a June 2000 study of the Texas Department of Transportation's (TxDOT) partnering program, which found that it had generally been effective, also found that follow-on sessions were rarely employed:

- The survey revealed that 70 percent of TxDOT and contractor personnel did not know about follow-up and close-out workshops, did not know they were available, or did not know the purpose of these workshops.

- Only 20 percent of TxDOT and contractor personnel indicated they had attended a follow-up workshop, and only 5 percent indicated they had attended a close-out workshop.

- Of the 20 percent who had experienced follow-up and close-out workshops, all rated these workshops as from "beneficial" to "extremely beneficial."[3]

Another difficulty in making project relationships durable is the fact that project participants remain within their company organizations — within their "organizational silos" on the project. This means that they remain charged with protecting and enforcing their company's interest first, with the project's interests second. Such a scenario is not what the Construction Industry Institute envisioned in terms of partnering "changing traditional relationships to a shared culture without regard to organizational boundaries."[4] In order to make partnering effective as a project management tool, projects need to break down company barriers and develop a "project first" culture that is implemented throughout the life cycle of the project.

Partnering's mixed results have been documented by some of the most dynamic proponents of the process. As pointed out above, Grajek, Gibson, and Tucker found that TxDOT partnering was generally beneficial but that the process used in Texas missed the opportunity to be truly transformative by failing to require follow-on sessions. Other departments of transportation have encountered similar problems in implementing their partnering processes.

Caltrans (California Department of Transportation)

The 2007 Caltrans Construction Partnering Steering Committee (CCPSC), which included construction leaders from Caltrans and the construction industry, provided recommendations to improve the Caltrans Partnering Program. The committee started work in October 2006 and has met quarterly since then. Indicative of the detail to which CCPSC delved into the process, five subcommittees were created to work on improvement efforts in concentrated areas. In September 2008, CCPSC issued and approved the new Caltrans specification and *Field Guide to Partnering on Caltrans Construction Projects.*[5] At the heart of the new process are the following six key lessons, upon which their program is based:

1. Follow-up and Measurement
2. Training and Empowerment of Field Staff
3. Project Stakeholder Partnering
4. Strategic Level Partnering
5. Decision Making and Risk Management
6. Recognition and Awards

These key factors are implemented as follows:

1. To encourage the use of project partnering, a change to the partnering specification has been proposed. The new partnering specification provides that professionally facilitated project partnering is mandatory for all projects over $10 million and optional but encouraged on projects from $1 million to $10 million. In addition to requiring partnering, a separate and distinct session of project team training in partnering skills development is mandatory for all projects with a total bid of $25 million or greater and is encouraged on projects from $10 million to $25 million.

2. To encourage follow-through and dispute prevention, the project team will include a partnering maintenance and close-out plan in the partnering charter and be required to do monthly partnering evaluation surveys. The survey results will go to the project team, construction managers, and the partnering facilitator, providing feedback for course corrections as needed.

3. To encourage the use of project partnering in dispute resolution, the new specification allows up to a 20-day extension of the notice of potential claim (NOPC) timeline. The dispute resolution ladder (DRL) process looks to resolve disputes within six weeks prior to involvement of a dispute review board (DRB). The DRB, however, will remain in place, as it serves a valued purpose.

4. Caltrans uses partnering facilitators to encourage quality and consistency in Project Partnering statewide. A statewide team will assemble and review the information in an annual quality review to capture best practices and areas of needed improvement.

185

ODOT (Ohio Department of Transportation)

The Ohio Department of Transportation's 2001 strategic initiatives included the department's commitment to "embrace partnering with contractors to improve quality and to reduce disputes." In an as-yet-unpublished 2006 proposed redraft of its *Manual for Partnering on Construction Projects*,[6] ODOT recommended the minimum threshold for use of formal partnering be set at $5 million (and/or three funding sources for more than a one-year project duration), and suggested a broad spectrum of persons be invited from executives to managers to inspectors, estimators, foremen, and subcontractors (as appropriate).

There are common components of partnering workshops recommended in Ohio, including working from an agenda, keeping minutes of the meeting, developing partnership objectives (i.e., stakeholders' wants and needs), and defining an issue resolution process, as well as identifying obstacles and developing action plans. Ohio also recommends drawing up a "charter" with its mission statement and goals and advises that the team consider "[h]ow we work in terms of communication, sequencing, planning, coordinating, and general work flow."

Additional workshops are recommended "as necessary to facilitate the flow of the project . . . and ensure that the lines of communication are maintained and problems are addressed in a timely manner." On larger, multiyear, multiphase projects or projects with critical items of work or milestone dates, the *Manual* calls for a project milestone meeting, at which the following items would be considered:

- Partnering Project Rating Form evaluations
- A review of the partnering charter
- Items that could be improved
- Items that could be deleted
- Items that should be included
- Items that should be continued
- Things that did not go well
- Things that went very well
- Upcoming activities that could be challenging
- Roadblocks that are ongoing or anticipated
- Right of way or utility conflicts
- Public issues
- Finalization
- Performance of all parties

In survey responses to partnering sessions over the past 15 years, the authors have collected anecdotal responses concerning the effectiveness of partnering. In general,

participants were in favor of the philosophy but skeptical of the efficacy of the actual process. Their greatest skepticism concerned the ability of the participants to actually engage (e.g., ". . . success is directly dependent upon the integrity of the participants," "the parties lacked commitment," the "wrong people were involved"). Participants concluded that traditional partnering often fails due to the nature of the chosen process, not the underlying philosophy (e.g., "one-time opening session that is ineffectual," "failure to set up mechanisms for continuous issue review," and "failure to establish meaningful project teams at horizontal levels of competence").

Megaprojects Partnering

In megaprojects, this skepticism is further complicated by the clustering of projects and contractual relationships whose only real commonality is the owner. Megaprojects are often "partnered" only at the project level and not at the program level, resulting in a fragmentation of the effort to establish relationships that are focused on creating and nurturing an effective "whole project"—or even "whole program"—team throughout the megaproject.

The authors have seen megaprojects in which the discrete projects within the megaproject were treated as barely related planets in a common solar system whose only shared experience was the solar system owner at the center. Conversely, the authors have participated in two megaprojects whose leadership recognized the essential relatedness of all of the efforts and instituted a common, facilitated partnering program cutting across all contract lines and disparate sites (in one case, literally hundreds of miles apart).

The Fix for Megaprojects

Horizontality

We believe that one way to address each of the summarized reasons for failure in partnering is by establishing meaningful project teams across horizontal levels of competence. Traditional contractual relationships establish vertical silos of entities. The people on the project live and work in these vertical silos; their communication and responsibilities tend to be vertical—up and down each silo's chain of command, and then over and up/down to another organizational silo.

However, if a project is a network of complex commitments, those commitments need to be made by the people who actually carry out the work. Thus, executing the project requires effective horizontal relationships, i.e., people working at their levels of competence and authority with others of similar competence and authority. That means, for example, that field-level people (superintendents, inspectors, and field managers)

work together, forming a strong, cooperative bond. At the next level "up," it means that project managers, design managers, owner's representatives, and construction managers come together as a manager team. These teams work collaboratively, reporting to an executive team comprised of the top-level people from the owner, designer, contractor, major subcontractor, and construction manager organizations.

In this realigned mode of executive, manager, and field teams, the focus of each team is the project itself, not their intraorganizational or interpersonal relationships. Meeting commitments are based on shared experience and shared responsibility. Each of these teams focuses on its level of competence and authority. For example, executives do what executives do — they decide issues of overall cost, schedule, and contract. Project managers make decisions on project execution details, such as change orders or how the work is managed, and make recommendations to the executives on issues beyond their authority. In this scenario, those recommendations are *team* recommendations of all the players at a project management level. This provides the benefit of a well-thought-out collective decision to individual managers within their own organizational silos.

This reporting structure — both empowered and challenged by the executives — allows the manager team to pull together to meet the needs of the project. Knowing they must identify and resolve day-to-day issues, report regularly as a team to the executives, and generally behave responsibly and cooperatively, these managers use their shared experience to bond as a team. Field-level people typically live in this "get-it-done" real world, anyway. Thus, they operate well in such a horizontal atmosphere, with a corresponding alignment of managers and executives above them. This creates a more harmonious and efficient structure and positions the teams to handle disputes at the lowest level possible.

Simultaneity

In addition to forming horizontal teams at levels of competence, effective partnering also allows for impeccable coordination of efforts on the project. This frees project participants to think of the project as a group of simultaneous events that are not necessarily segmented or sequential. For example, although tunnel finishes naturally follow electrical system installation, impeccable coordination between trades may allow scheduling of simultaneous efforts in different areas of the project.

True collaboration (what the authors think of as "true partnering") has allowed managers to completely rethink how projects are sequenced. In a recent medical center project, for example, the planners were waiting for floor layouts to see what heavy equipment would be placed before they believed they could order steel for the building. But it turned out (after discussions with the steel subcontractor, the medical equipment subcontractor, and others in the *design* phase of the project) that a slightly larger steel order would hold heavy machinery wherever it was placed in the facility. The project was able

to place its steel order months in advance of the traditional time, resulting in huge savings in time and staging, and resulting in a budget that was more accurate earlier in the project. These savings more than offset the small additional cost of "extra" steel.

Partnering at the outset of the design phase of the job (even in a design-bid-build contract) can result in the development of efficiencies throughout the project. This allows several efforts to commence simultaneously, clipping large chunks of time out of the schedule. Continuous partnering, impeccable coordination, increased relatedness—all add to project efficiencies that reduce costs of construction and virtually eliminate claims at the end of the job.

Effective Partnering Can Make a Significant Contribution

Successful partnering acknowledges and manages the "political space" between and among the various individuals and horizontal teams within the megaproject. Regularly facilitated partnering sessions of the whole project team establish affinities, efficiencies, and relations between parts and pieces of the project that result in cost and time savings. For example, regular individual team meetings help the field-level delivery teams focus on the work 30 to 90 days out. Such meetings coordinate the efforts needed to accomplish the work and manage the commitments between the team and those commitments made by the team to other project teams. Beyond the daily and weekly check-in sessions, these partnering sessions also offer a regular forum for managers individually and collectively to monitor the effectiveness of the project's communication and decision-making systems (submittals, schedules, requests for information, and change orders). Trust is tracked on the project at each team level from month to month and recorded at these meetings. Teams can forecast risks, anticipate opportunities, and make action plans to minimize those risks and maximize the opportunities. By pulling these reports, assessments, and plans together in summary form every month, the manager team can then report their assessments and recommendations for further action in summary form, as a group, to the executive team.

Making Partnering "Scalable" to Megaprojects

As described above, fully effective partnering in a megaproject requires recognition of the essential relatedness of all of the individual projects or subprojects which make up the megaproject. A common, facilitated partnering *program,* cutting across all contract lines and disparate sites, is the key to maintaining the unity of interrelated efforts. The program must be seen as a whole and treated holistically.

Such "up-scaled" partnering creates "project first" horizontal teams at the field, manager, and executive levels. Each of these teams includes participants from the designer,

the contractor, trade partners, and suppliers, and these teams can be further broken down into responsible categories. Each horizontal team is then related across project lines into integrated mega-teams at their appropriate competence levels as well. The formation of these teams allows routine and meaningful communication and coordination among the various projects that form the program.

Because megaprojects may contain many different "projects," it is important that teams elevate their thinking from just "project first" (i.e., "What can I do to help my project?") to "program first" (i.e., "How does success on my particular aspect of the project affect success of the program?"). For instance, in a recent program to develop emergency stored water, several projects (dam raise, tunnel installation for transporting water between reservoirs, hydroelectric plant installation in large transport pipes) were covered in the program. The program can be thought of as a megaproject, and each of the component parts as a several-hundred-million-dollar project. Each of those projects had to be coordinated to make the overall program work; each participant on each project had to be cognizant of the effect of that project on the larger program and coordinate its work accordingly.

These "program" teams anticipate opportunities for improving program performance by looking at efficiencies across the program. They also resolve conflicts between various projects to enhance development of the program. This kind of collaborative partnering has also proven effective in dealing with large public agencies that need cooperation among departments, among project participants, and also across the entire capital improvement program.

Scaling the partnering effort to embrace the entire program and create what one program director called a "culture of facilitation"—in which the partnering facilitators mentor the program leaders in facilitating on-site team meetings at various levels—brings collaboration and teamwork into a megaproject, which is the real promise of partnering. In broadening the partnering scope across the entire program, there is a heightened, expanded role for the executive team. This larger role for selected company and agency executives offers a regular forum for high-level monitoring of the progress of the various projects. It allows for the monitoring of necessary interproject or all-program coordination. Further, it serves as a constant backstop for unresolved problems, unexpected negotiations, and those conflicts that ripen into disputes. It is the ultimate assurance that project activities are conducted as an efficient production organization, cutting across all company and project silos. The all-program executive team is empowered to make the decisions necessary to fulfill the program, and to review and, if appropriate, approve the recommendations of other all-project teams.

This structure also addresses the concern that construction partnering fails because it does not concentrate on the kinds of things partnering in the production business does, viz., on supply-side relationships that grow into long-term relationships. Often in megaprojects, teams are joint ventures of various organizations. The structuring of the

joint venture teams means that company silos must be broken down right away and that partnerships be made that may well have lasting effects on the relationships of the parties — even where the parties have been competitors in the past. Partnering those projects means that the parties have to address supply-side, ongoing shared relationships much as Toyota has addressed ongoing concerns with suppliers by partnering with those suppliers in developing leaner ways of supplying Toyota's needs.[7]

As new forms of agreement become more widely used, partnering and the ongoing collaboration it promises become even more important. In design-build contracts, for instance, the power of cooperation between the designer, the contractor, and the owner requires collaboration across company silos. Integrated project delivery on larger projects requires collaborative relationships in order to integrate the delivery of the project—the very essence of the promise of partnering is what allows such integration. The rapid development of single access points for design and building modeling (building information modeling or "BIM") for production and control of design sets implies a new level of collaboration on projects for the entire team. These developing project delivery systems demand impeccable coordination and defined relatedness and a project culture that breaks down the organizational silos and makes real collaboration possible. The true underpinnings of partnering, mindfully applied to these projects, will make these delivery systems viable, economically feasible, and culturally desirable.

Relevance of Older Contract Forms

Older contract forms often address partnering as a start-up effort with few or no expectations and deliverables. While this can be an adequate base on which to build a good foundation, partnering can use a contractual lynchpin to ensure its effectiveness. The basic framework should draw from the experiences of the California, Ohio, and Texas DOT programs and provide at least:

- A kick-off partnering session;
- Monthly or quarterly follow-up sessions (Caltrans recommends monthly evaluations);
- A close-out workshop; and
- A provision within the contract for facilitated dispute resolution processes that emphasize the importance of taking responsibility for the dispute and resolving it at the level closest to the work. This system is outside and in lieu of traditional claims procedures and should not merely include a rote dispute resolution step-ladder of options.

Most older forms of contracts, including public agency contracts, can be amended with a simple partnering section that incorporates the above language (in the last

bulleted paragraph). States that have allowed their contracting agencies to enter into design-build contracts already have the authority and often the mechanism in place to allow such amendments. Because transportation departments have been such advocates of partnering over the years, it is a good idea to check with the relevant state's department of transportation to see what agreements and specifications for partnering they may have adopted. These can be readily converted into a section on partnering.

The authors recommend that any partnering addenda to older contracts also modify the dispute resolution provisions of the contract to bring them into line with the idea of a facilitated, responsibility-based approach to problem-solving. Problem-solving is much more efficient, economic, and efficacious than dispute resolution and should be part of every partnering specification.

Reference Sources

Bayer, Richard S., and Fauchier, Dan. (2008) *Why Partnering Fails and How to Fix It,* privately published manuscript presented to Construction Management Association of America National Conference and Trade Show, San Francisco.

Bayer, Richard S., et al. (July 8–11, 2007). *Project Realignment—Partnering on Steroids,* 46th Annual Workshop on Transportation Law, Transportation Research Board, Washington D.C.

Bayer, Richard S., et al. (April 5–8, 2006). *Resolving Construction Disputes in the Change Order Spec,* paper presented at the 8th Annual ABA Section of National Dispute Resolution Spring Conference.

Construction Industry Institute. (1991). *In Search of Partnering Excellence*, Special Publication 17-1. Austin: University of Texas.

Cushman, Robert F., et al. (2001). *Proving and Pricing Construction Claims*, 3d edition, Section 9.03[C]. New York: Aspen & Business.

Thomas, George W., and Bayer, Richard S. (May 2005). "Cost Control in Dispute Resolution," Surety Claims Institute *Newsletter,* pp. 3–8.

Change Order and Claims Management for the Modern Megaproject

Changes during the construction process are inevitable. There is no such thing as a perfect design, and even if the design were perfect, owners often make significant changes during construction for a variety of reasons. Despite the occasional value engineering or other cost-saving change orders, changes typically result in a net increase to the cost of construction, and often increase the time required for performance as well. In the context of megaprojects, even a moderate rate of change orders, say 5 percent, on a $1 billion project can result in $50 million in additional costs. And because most

megaprojects are often financed, in whole or in part, with public money, transparency of the change order and claims settlement processes that increase the cost to the public is essential.

Unresolved change orders are fodder for construction claims and disputes that generally ripen (some would say "rot") over time. Resolving an aged claim after substantial completion becomes that much more difficult as institutional memories fade, staff is reassigned or relocated, and the incentive for partnering and good working relations has passed.

The sheer scale of megaprojects allows the potential for mega-problems, if appropriate care and attention are not properly directed to establishing a sophisticated and well-resourced change order process and to timely processing of the change order issues that are processed through the system. Also critical are the linkages of this change organization to the design clarification and construction administration elements of the project, including relationships to field change orders (FCO), construction change directives (CCD), architect's supplemental information (ASI), requests for information (RFI) or clarification (RFC), and other types of field communication and design clarification mechanisms used to support construction progress and identify possible change issues during construction.

A comprehensive and efficient change order system that captures all changes and claim information as early as practicable is imperative. Ideally, the change order system would be based on a comprehensive and "balanced" set of general conditions[8] and would be structured to require daily maintenance at the field level. This would afford the greatest potential for resolution at the lowest possible level, and, by definition, in the most efficient way with respect to time and money. The discipline reflected in the field management of potential change issues needs to be reflected and replicated in each successive level of the contract administration or construction management organization hierarchy to produce a smoothly operating system for issue identification, responsibility allocation, pricing and impact analysis, and commercial and legal closure.

Change Orders and Claims Management Overview

Change orders are executed to modify the contract documents for a variety of reasons, including but not limited to: owner directives related to function, performance, aesthetics or budget; design errors; design omissions; code compliance or building inspection issues; constructability issues; and alternative construction methods or materials. Regardless of the reason, all change order requests, documentation, and approvals should follow a consistent procedure that captures the merit determination process and the basis of cost and schedule impacts.

On a megaproject, the demands on the change order evaluation and claims administering staff are exponentially more complex when compared to simply a "large" con-

struction undertaking. The changes and claims staff must be qualified and capable of performing the following tasks on a routine basis: change estimating and credit evaluations; scheduling, which includes using critical path method (CPM) analysis, schedule development, status updates, and critical path review; damages quantification and evaluation; productivity and labor impact assessments; work disruption evaluations; and cost audits. Moreover, the team must be able to effectively prepare and present these evaluations to management in several project forums and before different audiences in order to facilitate and complete the often complex decision-making process established for administering a megaproject.

Construction Administration and Management Structure

Large construction management firms are aware of the importance of standardized procedures. Megaprojects, by definition, will tend to have project durations of five to ten years or more and large construction management organizations, which can, over time, be expected to have turnover of staff-level engineers whose duties include processing change orders. A construction manager (CM) organization is a virtual necessity for a megaproject.[9] Especially on a multiprime construction project, a common administrator must have the authority under a comprehensive set of commercial contract documents to fairly but aggressively administer the complex, competing, and highly coordinated design, construction, and support functions required of the typical megaproject.

A typical experienced CM organization will be comprised of at least a highly qualified resident engineering and inspection staff; a quality control and assurance team; project controls staff charged with closely monitoring manpower, budgets, and schedules; and a change order and claims staff responsible for administering contract changes and dispute resolution.[10] All of these departments are essential to a successful change order process, one that can promptly process routine change orders to a mutually acceptable conclusion and can reduce the scope of disputes over claims for extra monies or schedule time to only the most difficult and contentious matters. The latter issues, however, are also those matters that, rather than being allowed to fester, would be addressed early through the step-issue resolution models discussed elsewhere in this chapter. The primary objective of a professional contract management team comprised of change order specialists, claims analysts, and supporting schedule and estimating staff is to minimize unresolved issues that occur through the course of the project.

Development of Changes on the Megaproject

Many change orders arise from questions from the contractor regarding the intent or direction given in the design. These questions are often referred to as requests for

information (RFIs), requests for clarification (RFCs), change/clarification requests (CCRs), or requests for approval (RFAs), where the solution to the problem is submitted by the contractor to the owner for concurrence. For instance, the contractor may find that a particular detail is incomplete, ambiguous in context with other parts of the contract documents, or simply unbuildable as designed. A well-organized CM team will have standardized forms for the contractor's use to bring these issues immediately to management's attention. Typically, the contractor will submit the RFI to the resident engineer, who may answer the question directly or forward the question to the design team. Alternatively, the design management process has a mechanism for clarifying and further developing the design set out in the issued construction documents. If the design bulletin, architect's supplemental information, or response to the contractor's RFI acknowledges additional scope, the response should be accompanied by a request for proposal (RFP) to determine cost and schedule impacts, if any. For tracking purposes, the RFP should also include a proposed change order number.

Because of the sheer number of issues that can be expected on a megaproject — and for forensic purposes later in the job — it is recommended that the system track the change order development via a change order data log. A parallel log will often be established for contract "claims" that will be pursued (usually as disputed change requests) beyond the change order review, approval, or denial cycle and usually as an issue now subject to a structured general conditions provision enabling appeals on disputed matters. Once a potential change order (PCO) or change order request (COR) number is issued, that identifier can be entered into a log, listing the date of the RFP and associated RFIs/CCRs. As the proposed change develops further, the contractor's proposed price, the fair cost estimate price,[11] negotiated price, change order number, and date of execution can all be entered into the detailed issue-tracking log. Should the contract be the subject of a wrap-up claim or litigation, this data will assist the claims and legal professionals in understanding how the change order issue developed. As there is no guarantee that the change order administrator (or the scheduler or estimator) who prepared the change documentation will be available, sometimes years later, the change order log represents the best source of information and the "road map" to necessary records in the absence of institutional human knowledge.

Contractor's Submittal

The contractor's proposal should contain sufficient detail to determine material quantities, labor hours by trade and position, equipment required to perform the work, and a clear presentation of mark-ups on the contractor's own costs as well as subcontractors' costs.[12] When the resident engineer forwards the request for proposal to the contractor, a copy should also be forwarded to the CM's estimating staff requesting an independent

"fair cost estimate" or "independent assessment." If a schedule review is called for by the written protocol, the CM's schedule department will need to participate in the decision-making. Over the course of a megaproject, there could be thousands of requests for proposals and schedule impacts. The demand for independent fair cost and schedule assessments can overwhelm an underresourced technical staff of three or four estimators and schedulers, which in turn will slow down the entire change order process.

By way of example, on the $4 billion Boston Harbor Project (1989–2001), the CM organization at its peak consisted of more than 300 people, with as many as 8 full-time estimators. On the $15 billion Boston Central Artery/Tunnel Project (1990–2007), the changes and claims staff alone, including estimators, schedulers, and cost negotiators, reached approximately 110 full-time professionals and part-time technical and construction claims consultants.

It is a rare change order engineer, estimator, or scheduler, however, who is competent in all related change, estimating, and scheduling disciplines. As the project evolves, it may be necessary to adjust the staff to reflect the predominant type of work going on. For example, changes to the electrical and instrumentation systems can be expected to be one of the larger subjects of change orders during the later phases of the megaproject. To maintain the timely processing of estimates and change orders, the prudent CM's blend of professional staff will reflect the type of work being performed in the field. The key to maintaining a responsive team of issue resolution administrators is adequate initial organization staffing and budget, available contingency, and flexibility in supplementing the team as needs change and potentially problematic backlogs develop that can adversely affect job progress, contractor finances, and key participant attitudes about the project work.

Independent In-house Analysis

Obtaining an independent fair cost estimate (FCE) is essential to prepare the resident engineer or contract administrator for negotiations with the contractor on any but the most insignificant changes. Armed with the FCE, the resident engineer can quickly identify the differences between the contractor's proposal and the owner's cost assessment, and commence to negotiate. Additionally, the FCE will allow the resident engineer to identify any issues with the contractor's cost elements (as allowed by the contract), fee mark-ups, overhead, insurance, and bond.

Once the costs for a number of related proposed change orders have been successfully negotiated, a change order can be prepared incorporating several proposed change orders into a single contract amendment. The aggregation of smaller individual change orders into a larger, single change order (or contract amendment) will permit process efficiencies so that the usually complex and multitiered approval system will not get

bogged down having to address many small change orders. Public owners, however, may want to place limits on the value of individual change orders due to delegated spending approvals, signatory authority, or budget proscriptions and limitations. Change order files should be fully structured, complete, and clear in describing or depicting the basis for the change to the work, especially on megaprojects built with public funds. Cost overruns on large public projects make excellent fodder for either local newspapers or political platforms.[13] Transparency, the ability to document change order development, and routine exercise of the right to audit contractor and subcontractor books — including documenting the reason or need for the changes — not only are a necessity when building with public funds, but also represent good general construction administrative practice. Use of outside forensic claim auditors and consultants, where necessary (due to the size and complexity of a developing issue), can be a valuable strategy for supplementing the professional staff of the project management organization while providing an objective viewpoint of the merit and damages associated with a difficult issue. This tactic can help relieve change order administrators from bogging down on a potential large claim at the expense of processing newly developing and more routine job issues.

In summary, to be effective and to protect both the owner and the consulting parties administering the change and claims resolution processes, the change order control system must, at a minimum, provide for:

- An unambiguous set of technical guidelines spelling out what is compensable and what is not compensable; how schedule delays and request for time extensions will be measured; when forward lump-sum pricing, time and material, and other pricing mechanisms will be used; and what industry standards apply to pricing equipment use and for materials costs;

- Changes to be issued in writing, signed by the owner or an authorized representative of the owner, unless emergency action is necessary;

- Conformance to strict protocols for authorizing changes, so as to avoid waivers or constructive approvals by action of the design or construction management administrators;

- Contractor's contractual duty to proceed with the work in the face of a dispute or disagreement on any aspect of the alleged change;

- A defined process for timely administering of change issues, including merit determinations, fair cost estimates and schedule impact assessments, negotiations, and commercial closure; and

- Legally binding waivers of additional monies (or time extension) upon payment of agreed sums, including, as necessary, addressing cumulative impacts or the work disruption potential of the changes.

197

Allegations of Cumulative Impact Changes

The successful owner and construction manager are ever vigilant and constantly consider measures for claims avoidance. Careful attention to change order and contract language can help preclude certain "wrap-up" claims. The overwhelming demands of construction can sometimes consume the contractor's project manager, and there can be a tendency to assign a lower priority to the administrative tasks, including change orders. It is essential that both the contractor and construction manager have sufficient staff to remain current with the change order process.

To help stress the importance of timely change orders, the construction manager must enforce contractual time requirements for the submittal of information requests and change order proposals. The organizational structure should have requirements for weekly or biweekly change resolution meetings whose objective is to close out as many routine changes as possible for all cost and time extension impacts. Failure to keep pace with the issue identification, change order merit, cost and schedule impact assessment, and payment authorization dynamic will quickly devolve into issuance of unilateral change orders directed by contract, tracked by laborious time and material record-keeping (both by the owner/construction manager and the contractor) to be reconciled at some later time and place. On a megaproject in mid-construction, this collapse of the change order resolution system will signal the highest risk for receipt by the owner of a total cost or modified total cost wrap-up claim[14] at the job's end — or even earlier for a so-called "equitable adjustment" to the contract — and it often presages the eventual breakdown of the overall contractual dispute resolution process.

Even on the best managed megaprojects, it is not uncommon for owners to receive "wrap-up" claims or claims for equitable adjustment upon substantial completion of the multiyear construction project. Often these claims include issues that were previously denied as change orders or claims, delay costs, and/or lost productivity claims. Despite clear contract language barring the late submittal of such claims, these claims do arise and typically require some response on the merits — otherwise litigation may be the next step. Effective change order language and contract administration can help prevent or preclude these claims.

When the contractor claims an issue that has been the prior subject of a rejected change order proposal or claim, it should be a simple matter to locate the file on that proposal to review the original basis for denial. Often these claims are being responded to after the construction management staff has been relocated and the back-up documents are not in readily available files. A solid document control and log and filing system allows the late-arriving, and sometimes expensive, consultant to locate the file and related documents.

Most change orders contain language to the effect that the cost of the change order in-

cludes all direct and indirect costs. However, the long duration and complexity of mega-projects sometimes makes it difficult for contractors to capture all costs associated with a particular change order, especially where there is an overall high rate of smaller change orders. Despite the contract language releasing the owner from all direct and indirect costs, the federal government recently was found liable for cumulative impact costs.[15] Admittedly, this case is not representative of typical scope growth; here the government added a new floor to a building after nine months of construction, increasing the contract price by 34 percent. However, owners may want to consider including language that specifically mentions cumulative impact costs in the waiver provision. Among other strategies being explored is affirmatively including a nominal sum of money in a bilateral change order, identified as compensation for any unforeseen impacts due to the change.

Schedule Delay Issues

Construction delays can come from anywhere: lack of progress in the field, delays in procurement, delays in preparing/reviewing shop drawings, delays from additional scope correcting deficient or erroneous design details, and possibly delays in the processing of change orders (which is more likely to occur in the absence of strong partnering between the owner and contractor).

Well-written contract language will put the initial burden on the contractor to request a time extension or waive a time extension for that particular issue. An experienced project controls staff is essential in evaluating a contractor's request for time. It is not enough to look at the schedule's longest and most critical path; subcritical paths should also be examined to determine the presence of contractor-owned delays. The change order administrator should request an independent time extension analysis, similar to an FCE, for each substantive request for time. This analysis will determine whether the extension will impact a contract milestone and whether the delay is excusable. Then the analysis will identify the presence of any independent contractor-owned concurrent delay that would negate entitlement to supplemental delay costs. As with all claims documentation, this analysis should be properly filed in the record management system for future reference.

Importance of Binding Waivers for Settled Issues

Invariably, at the point when the change order and claims system fails to keep pace with the ongoing work changes on a megaproject, or when this development is combined with a set of costly change issues that are deemed the responsibility of the contractor, the fact that dozens or even hundreds of bilateral change orders have been mutually approved and settled by the parties will not guarantee they will not be resurrected

in the "wrap-up" claim. Aside from the numerous legal issues raised by arguments to "re-open" closed claims and changes, perhaps as part of a cumulative impact theory claim, the owner's best defense will be the quality of its settlement documentation. The waiver language should include time and delay costs whereby once the change order is executed, the contractor is contractually barred from raising the issue again.

There may be a catch, however. The contractor is often by general contract terms not supposed to proceed with the work until the change order is executed or affirmative authority is received from the appropriate level of the owner's management organization. If the change order is to be all-inclusive, then the magnitude of delay needs to be determined. Sometimes, usually with unforeseen conditions, the magnitude of the delay cannot be reasonably determined prior to the change order execution. In those instances, the issue may be addressed by multiple change orders, possibly including the initial change order based on recorded time and material costs with a "not-to-exceed" limit. Later, the balance of the costs and the substantiated time extension can be incorporated into a subsequent change order. Sometimes it is necessary to process change orders in multiple parts and defer the time portion of the change order. However, it should be considered an exception to the rule, as it inevitably leaves multiple issues open that are often difficult to reprioritize during a hectic construction schedule. Left unaddressed during the course of the project, these deferred change orders ultimately could end up in the cumulative impact or total cost claim filed at the end of a complex multiyear construction job.

Exculpatory Contract Language

"No damages for delay" clauses are common in public sector general conditions of construction contracts.[16] While there seems to be consensus that these clauses are enforceable, there are several well-settled exceptions that an experienced contractor may be able to use to circumvent the "no damages for delay" clause. Delay damages, delay costs, and supplemental costs all represent the contractor's cost of extending its site presence. When preparing the bid estimate, in addition to the contractor's direct costs of construction, the contractor needs to prepare a competitive price for its indirect administrative staff and associated equipment, office space, and utility needs. These costs are time based. The contractor's price depends upon how long certain staff are needed, how long the office space or trailers need to be rented, or how long insurance coverage is required.

Construction is one of the purest examples of the adage "Time is money." When the contractor is forced to extend its site presence, by definition it incurs additional time-based costs. When the delay is the result of the contractor's own performance, it would naturally follow that the contractor receives no relief in the form of additional supplemental costs. However, when the delay is the result of the act of the owner, and there

is no independent contractor-owned concurrent delay, it would seem to follow that the owner is responsible for paying the contractor's additional supplemental costs for extended site presence — that is, unless there is a provision limiting those additional costs or a "no damages for delay" clause. While the clause may offer some justification for the owner to execute a change order with a time extension to the contract schedule with no additional supplemental costs, the "no damages for delay" clause may be somewhat less effective when the contractor submits a claim for equitable adjustment after substantial completion and the contractor can show, for example, that hundreds of change orders were issued on the project, that the change orders were the cause of over a year of delay, and that the contractor incurred over $1 million in additional costs due to extended site presence.

Rather than rely on a "no damages for delay" clause, owners should consider contract language that clearly defines allowable supplemental costs in the instances of compensable time extensions. The typical megaproject contractor is going to be savvy enough to protect its interests, track all incurred costs, and have a decent chance of winning its claimed supplemental costs, even in the face of a limitation provision and "no damages for delay" clause. If so, it makes more sense to agree on a fair price on a discrete compensable time extension than to gamble and wait and then try to defend an aggressive, high-value claim comprised of a compilation of various actually incurred costs resulting from a contract's worth of delay issues that affected the contractor's performance of the work.

Strategies for Successful Megaproject Changes and Claims Management

Pre-bid Claims Avoidance Reviews

Whereas design development practices — including independent engineering peer reviews, independent design coordination technical reviews, and similar testing of the technical specifications and plans — are evaluated primarily for constructability and anticipated performance or function, the claims avoidance review should be performed by cost containment engineers and experienced claims professionals from an entirely different perspective.

The focus of these claims avoidance reviews is on the specification scope language and correlated drawing notes that may show discrepancies in responsibilities between different trades, raise ambiguous terms of performance quality or quantity, relate to unspecified quantities of material or equipment, or identify inconsistencies between plans and specification that will give rise to disputes. Claims avoidance evaluators also review and correlate the construction general conditions, supplemental, and special provisions of the contract with the specifications and plans to ensure the absence of discernible ambiguity in the final bid documents. Such reviews can be done late in the design development period and should be undertaken by a highly qualified construction claims consultant.

201

Escrowing Bid Documents

The use of escrowed bid documents for a competitively procured megaproject is the commercial equivalent to a prenuptial agreement. Though at first glance it may seem to be inconsistent with a partnering philosophy and to dim the passions of the awarded party going into a multibillion-dollar construction deal, it is intended to say, "Let's be open, honest and intelligent about the future possibility of complex claims," rather than "I simply don't trust you, Mr. Contractor." Escrow documents are prepared, packaged, and submitted to a neutral custodial party according to a detailed specification made part of the RFP process. Standard descriptions of the documents and necessary back-up detail are made available, along with qualifications of the trustee bank or document/records control firm. Protection for corporation trade secrets and confidentiality are also addressed.

The documents are accessible under specification terms that call for the existence of a dispute for which information in the bid documents could assist resolution. Both parties must generally agree to access the files, with or without the participation of a third party neutral. The objective is to verify contractor and major subcontractor bid assumptions on key issues, such as schedule progress, productivity, manpower, and other resource determinations. Where lump-sum items, such as gross excavation or dewatering quantities or tunnel water pumping capacity estimates, are involved, the escrow bid documents should specify the minimum level of detail required to understand the bidder's operating assumptions.[17]

Subsurface Conditions Allowances and Unit Price Items

To the extent consistent with the geotechnical baseline documents (addressing subsurface conditions to be expected for the project), line items in the bid should be considered wherever the expectation that certain conditions will occur is unpredictable and the bidders can reasonably estimate the cost given certain specified criteria. These line items can include allowances to cover removal of obstructions, unforeseen ground conditions, water control, etc., in lieu of multiple change orders based on possibly extensive differing site conditions investigations, preparation of cost, and impact submittals and negotiations.

Project-wide Hazardous Materials Remediation

Procurement of a dedicated contractor, qualified and hired by the megaproject owner, to address all contamination identification, testing, and remediation issues avoids the pitfalls of multiple prime contractors each addressing individual episodes of site contamination and remediation. Special care has to be taken to minimize impacts to the

ongoing construction in the event of an intervention by the owner's hazardous materials contractor, but generally speaking the owner or its construction manager are better suited to coordinate all work related to the incident and can better and more efficiently work to minimize disruption of the ongoing work, without the excessive risk of a third-party delay claim arising.

Third-party Impacts Task Force

Where the megaproject will affect nearby landowners, the general public, public services, or business areas, it may be prudent to commission a special review of the contract documents for possible impacts to abutters, adjacent businesses, and other third parties that could affect progress or costs of the work if not mitigated in advance. It is also prudent to enter into agreements with abutters (for example, major property owners) that can govern the relationship between the project and them. These agreements can deal with such issues as easements, traffic management, hours of operation, noise controls, and the like. These types of agreements can also provide protection against inverse condemnation claims.

Professional Liability Cost Allocation Process

Another strategy for avoiding post-project litigation—or at least for controlling the orderly resolution of alleged professional negligence issues in the megaproject context—is establishing a "Cost Recovery" or "Design and Construction Management Performance Review" program which, among other purposes, tracks the identification by administrators within the contract amendment organization of any possible errors and omissions that may result in change order requests or construction claims submitted by the contractors. A megaproject's overall management philosophy should recognize that professional services issues will arise with respect to substantive design, design schedule, construction management communications, on-the-job decision-making and field activities, and the administration of a sophisticated and multilayered project management bureaucracy. The primary purpose of a cost recovery or management review program is to avoid unnecessary dissension or finger-pointing during the project that could adversely affect the management team performance. A cost recovery program can accomplish these goals by providing all key parties to the program:

- Early notice of any performance issues to the party responsible, with an opportunity to place the issue's summary-level detail and a response from the identified responsible party in the record;
- Preservation of the record for review in scheduled periodic program meetings or

later in the project, as impacts of the alleged acts, errors, or omissions become apparent or are identified and recorded;

- Definition of a process for adjudicating the performance impact issues in an amicable and balanced process, emphasizing objective review and fair allocation of responsibility between the participants; and
- Opportunities for enabling constructive involvement of a professional liability issuer representative in the megaproject professional services performance review process.

To be effective as an early warning and issue preservation process, the program identifies contractor claims that may originate in part or in whole as a result of failure of any design, consultant, or construction management entity to completely meet its contractual obligations to the contractor, subcontractors, suppliers, or the project owner. Such claims may involve:

- Design defects, defective specifications, or errors or omissions on plans and drawings;
- Improper, delayed, or excessive inspection, review of materials, equipment, samples, or processing of submittals;
- Coordination issues;
- Misleading direction or misrepresentation reasonably relied upon by the aggrieved party;
- Abuse of authority or arbitrary and capricious decision-making ;
- Improper administration, direction, or supervision;
- Unreasonable rejection of value engineering cost proposals (VECPs), substitutions, or means and methods of construction; and
- Delay issues.

Reference Sources

Galloway, P. D. (June 5–6, 2006). "Cumulative Impact," *Current Trends in Construction Law, International Project Management and Dispute Resolution: The South Central American Project*, São Paulo, Brazil.

Howrey LLP. (August 21, 2006). "Recognizing and Managing Investment Risks on Global Megaprojects," *Construction Weblinks*. Retrieved July 17, 2009, from http://www.constructionweblinks.com/Resources/Industry_Reports_Newsletters/Aug_21_2006/reco.html.

Jervis, B, ed. (August 2005). *Construction Claims Monthly*, Volume 27, Number 8.

Levin, P. (1998). *Construction Contract Claims, Changes and Dispute Resolution*, 2d ed. Reston, VA: ASCE Press.

Long, R., and Carter, R. (2009). *Cumulative Impacts Claims*. Littleton, CO: Long International, Inc.

Massachusetts Accelerated Bridge Program Council. (December 15, 2008). *Project Controls Report*. Retrieved July 17, 2009, from http://www.eot.state.ma.us/acceleratedbridges/downloads/projectcontrols.pdf .

Massachusetts Turnpike Authority, Central Artery/Tunnel Project. (1996). *Construction Contract Administration Manual, 1996*.

Massachusetts Turnpike Authority, Central Artery/Tunnel Project. (1999). *PCA Cost Containment Lessons Learned, 1999 et seq.*

Ockman, S. (1986). "Measuring Success With Claims Management," in *Proceedings of the Project Management Institute*.

O'Leary, A. (July-August 2002). "Coping With Change Orders, Keeping Confusion Under Control and Limiting Disputes," *Design Cost Data*. Retrieved August 25, 2009, from http://www.dcd.com/oleary/oleary_ja_2002.html.

Prieto, R. (March 27, 2008). "Program Management Audit Checklist," Retrieved August 25, 2009. Available in document form from http://www.constructiontrends.com/categories/Project-Management/

Dispute Avoidance and Dispute Resolution

Dispute Avoidance

The Use of a Project Risk Profile

During the planning, permitting, and design phase, project management should perform a risk assessment of the most likely sources of disputes and claims. These can range from contractual allocation of risk issues, to project-specific engineering and construction challenges, to external regulatory or oversight risks. Based on this risk profile, project management should focus on ways to avoid and minimize the risks that may give rise to claims. For risks that cannot be avoided, project management should establish a dispute resolution process promptly to resolve issues as they arise during the course of the project.

"Appropriate" Risk Allocation

Risk allocation under the megaproject's contracts should follow the principle that risks should be assigned to the party or parties that can best avoid, manage, absorb, or transfer the risks. If there is thoughtful risk allocation, disputes and claims will be minimized; if there is risk allocation that does not meet this principle, there is a greater

likelihood that the party that cannot realistically shoulder the risk will try to shift that risk to some other party through a claim.

On megaprojects, risks will be enormous. These risks arise from the complexity of the relationships and the sheer size of the problem if something goes wrong, from catastrophic property or bodily injury losses, to economic losses from design problems, to schedule delays or unanticipated changes in the project due to such causes as differing site conditions. If careful consideration is not given to risk allocation, the likelihood is that there will be sizable claims on megaprojects.

Engineering/Constructability and Dispute Avoidance Reviews

Before contracts are put out for bid, they should be reviewed at two levels to avoid later problems that generate disputes and claims. The basic premise here is that if a problem is discovered before the project is in the execution phase, it is much easier and cheaper to fix than if it is discovered when the project is underway. First, there should be engineering/constructability reviews to pick up problems in specifications, plans, and drawings, and in more general subjects like cost estimates and projected schedules. Second, there should be dispute avoidance reviews focusing on the general conditions and the specifications to pick up errors, conflicts, and ambiguities. This review should also encompass cross-contract reviews to make sure, for example, that the owner-designer contract meshes with the owner-contractor contract.

On a megaproject, the complex interfaces among contracts, parties, and scopes of work are exponentially increased. Constructability and dispute avoidance reviews are even more critical, since the risk of errors is higher and the magnitude of the errors is larger. Often owners hesitate to spend the extra money on these types of reviews on the premise that it is "paying a checker to check the checkers." However, even the best quality control/quality assurance program can fail to pick up problems that a "fresh set of eyes" may find on an objective review of the contract documents. And a dollar spent to fix a problem before a job is bid is many factors less than fixing that same problem when a job is underway. Moreover, the higher the dollar cost of the "fix" to a problem discovered later, the greater likelihood that there will be a dispute or claim.

A constructability review should be done regardless of the type of project delivery method chosen. Under traditional design-bid-build projects, the constructability review is performed by the owner's designer before the project is put out to bid. The contractor typically then has the responsibility to prepare shop drawings, which is often where design coordination problems come to light—but by that time the costs to correct may be higher because the project is already underway. Some argue that design-build project delivery solves this problem because the designer and the builder are conjoined. This would theoretically eliminate design-construction coordination problems because the design can be developed

with the builder providing constructability input as the design is developed. It should be noted, however, that the designer may face some additional challenges in the design-build context, because often the design is being developed while the project may still be at an early stage with issues such as permitting. These later developments can materially affect the final design, notwithstanding efforts to avoid them through constructability reviews.

Partnering

As discussed in detail earlier in this chapter, project management must "set the scene," so to speak, by making it clear to project participants that whatever the contractual and risk allocation arrangements, the parties can avoid and resolve many disputes if they simply work in a collaborative manner. If project participants think first about resolving project technical problems together and then promptly thereafter sort out commercial issues while the parties are engaged collaboratively on "solving the problem," often it becomes a non-issue, or the negative effect is mitigated or compartmentalized so that any later formal claim is easier to resolve.

Dispute Resolution Process

Often one of the deliverables from a partnering program is an "issue resolution stepladder" that elevates disputes within organizations before the parties take an "official" position that may trigger a formal claim process. Thus, the issue resolution stepladder can function as a dispute resolution mechanism that precedes (and perhaps renders moot) the formal contract processes. This allows parties to elevate disputes quickly and informally within organizations before positions harden and while there is time to creatively resolve or mitigate the effects of the issue. What is important here is an informal agreement that issues that are not resolved within a set time period at the field level are elevated to the next management level, and if not resolved there, are elevated through successive management levels until either they are resolved or a decision is made that the issue must go through formal claim resolution processes. This may sound like another "parallel process" is being added to an already complex system, but in fact this type of dispute resolution process can be appended to regular project management meetings (with the only proviso that all appropriate management levels must be included and that any commercial agreement must be appropriately documented and approved through normal channels).

Relationships and Types of Parties

As part of project risk allocation, the contracts on the project will establish legal relationships among the project participants. However, some parties will have contractual

relationships with the owner, but they will not have contracts with other key project participants. For example, in a traditional design-bid-build megaproject, the owner will have one contract with the designer, another contract with the construction manager, and another with the general contractor. These same parties will have key non-contractual relationships with one another. The designer typically does not have a contractual relationship with the contractor, but the designer definitely has a relationship with the contractor through furnishing the design, reviewing and approving submittals, answering RFIs, and the like. Both contractual and non-contractual relationships are potential friction points for claims that need to be addressed by the dispute resolution process.

A related issue is the type of party and that party's relationship to the project. Direct project participants can be addressed through the project's contractual and management structure. But there are also indirect project participants, such as regulatory or permitting agencies, that affect the project but cannot be controlled in the same manner as direct project participants. These indirect project participants can generate friction points that should be addressed in any megaproject dispute resolution program. For example, agreements with permitting agencies could include a step resolution process for any permit violation issues before a stop work order is issued. Likewise, although persuasive power may need to be used, outside stakeholders may be persuaded to participate in project dispute resolution processes that involve their interests. For example, some projects enter into written agreements with key abutters that include mechanisms for identifying and elevating disputes for resolution between the project and the abutter before the abutter goes to a permitting agency and files a formal complaint for permit violations.

Step Elevation Processes—Both Internal and External to the Project

The use of "step elevation" of issues is fundamental to all megaprojects. Step elevation refers to the concept of requiring issues either to be resolved at the lowest project management level possible within a defined time frame or to be elevated to the next management level. This promotes "real time" resolution by requiring line management personnel to try to resolve issues or to explain to more senior managers why the issue has not been resolved and what impact that may have on project progress. When presented with an issue from lower levels, more senior managers can make a rational decision to leave the issue at the lower level, resolve it at their level, or send it up to a higher management level.

Step elevation should also be encouraged in relationships with external project participants, since these issues can have as much effect on project progress as internal project disputes. As noted, these are harder to dictate to external parties, but they still should be sought in agreements or procedures established with those parties (e.g., utility "force account" agreements).

Step elevation processes can be used both for issues (questions that may impede progress) and for disputes (matters on which the parties disagree). As to disputes, the step elevation process can effectively be used to resolve disputes before parties take formal positions that result in claims. The step elevation process can be based in the project contracts (which typically provide for early verbal notice, written notice, and a written response from the owner) or on the informal partnering issue stepladder model. Whichever path is used, the concept is the same—get issues and disputes resolved as quickly as possible at the lowest level of the organization, but have a fail-safe mechanism to move it up the management chain if it is not getting resolved in a timely manner.

Claim Resolution

Claim Risk Assessment

As part of the project risk assessment (discussed above as to dispute avoidance), a similar risk assessment should be performed to identify the most likely source and types of claims. Then, depending on the potential source and types of claims, the appropriate claim resolution tools should be put in place at the beginning of the project. The key issue is to ensure that "off the shelf" claim resolution processes are not being used; instead, the megaproject management team should carefully craft the claim resolution process and tools to be tailored to the specific risk profile of the project.

Based on the type of contractual arrangement and corresponding risk allocation, there may be potential claims at "friction points" of responsibility for schedule and costs. For example, the more there is a complete transfer of risk from the owner to the contractor, the more likely that this will be a friction point that will generate claims. Thus, this friction point should be a focus of any claim resolution process, with attention given to the type, size, number, and complexity of the claims that can be expected. However, on any megaproject the manager should expect, at a minimum, that the primary sources of claims will occur between the owner and the contractor, between the owner and the designer, and between the contractor and its subcontractors. In addition, depending on the type of project, the risk assessor may be able to predict the type of claims that may arise and the type of technical expertise that may be required (e.g., tunneling vs. structures).

Claim Resolution Tools

There are a few basic principles that should be applied to all claim resolution processes: First, claims should be resolved in "real time." Claims do not age well—they cause parties to focus on positions, not work progress; they sour relationships and build mistrust; the longer they linger, the more that memories fade, knowledgeable people leave,

documents are lost, and the reality of what actually happened becomes foggy. In addition, in "real time" claim resolution, the parties' incentives are aligned: everyone wants to complete the project per the contract at the lowest cost to all project participants. Those incentives can help motivate the parties to focus on solutions and provide more options for the parties to resolve the claims. For example, during the course of the project there may be more flexibility to "re-baseline" the project, which gives the owner the opportunity to close out past issues and get the contractor's resource-loaded commitment to a "to-go" schedule, while enabling the contractor to get a monetary settlement (and perhaps some time relief) to deal with cash flow issues and close out subcontractor claims. This type of creative solution would not be possible at the end of the project, when the delay has been incurred, the money spent, and the parties' positions staked out (sometimes for years).

There are many tools in the claim resolution tool box. The key is selecting the right ADR tool and effectively applying it to the type of project, the project risk profile, the project contractual relationships, and the project parties and participants (both direct and indirect). A combination of claim resolution tools can be used, and they can vary from one contractual (or noncontractual) relationship to another.

Dispute Review Boards

Dispute review boards (DRBs) consist of an outside panel of experts (usually three) who are appointed at the beginning of the project, who periodically visit and receive updates about the project, and who hear claims in an informal process that results in detailed, nonbinding recommendations. The advantage of DRBs is that they are comprised of impartial construction-industry–savvy experts who are familiar with the project, the parties, and the issues as they wend their way through the stepladder issue resolution and claim resolution processes. DRBs can also serve a dispute prevention function by asking the project participants hard questions about what they are doing to resolve pending disputes that might ripen into claims.[18]

On claims, DRBs hold informal fact-gathering hearings with the parties. The DRB then deliberates in private and issues detailed, nonbinding findings and recommendations that analyze the issues, the parties' positions, and the relative merits of the claim based on the contract and project circumstances, and then provides a recommended resolution that the parties can accept, reject, or use as the basis of further negotiations. DRBs will cost more due to the carrying costs of site visits and the like, but the timing of resolution is quick and the costs are minor compared to an arbitration or litigation process. DRBs have been used mostly on heavy civil projects where technical expertise in a particular type of construction is most valued, e.g., they were first used in the tunneling sector because of the view that tunneling experts could deal best with typical claims for differing site conditions.[19]

Standing Neutrals

Standing neutrals essentially act as "single person DRBs." Depending on the size of the project, they can either conduct periodic site visits as a regular DRB would, or they can be called in only when a dispute or claim arises for which the parties want input. Additionally, standing neutrals may be hired for their specific technical expertise to resolve technical issues that may arise based on the project's risk profile. For example, if the megaproject involved tunneling as the major risk factor, the standing neutral could be a tunneling expert. The advantage of this ADR technique is that it is less expensive, but the disadvantage is that the standing neutral may not have the same breadth of knowledge about the project and his or her expertise may not be tailored to the type of claim (e.g., technical vs. legal).

An example of a "standing neutral" is the dispute resolution advisor (DRA) used by Caltrans on some projects. The DRA is appointed at the beginning of the project and then is available if called upon by the parties to review an issue and provide recommendations for resolution.[20]

Jointly-Hired Experts

Sometimes parties will agree to jointly hire an expert to give them a recommendation on the resolution of a particular claim. For example, if there is disagreement on the status of the job schedule, an independent scheduling consultant may be hired to review both parties' positions and give an opinion on the job status. The advantage of this process (in addition to cost savings) is that it allows the parties to "partner" in having a project-hired (vs. party-advocate-hired) expert provide a neutral opinion.

Facilitators and Mediators

Facilitators and mediators are third-party neutrals often jointly hired (and paid for) by two or more project participants. Facilitators focus more on process issues, such as communication, collaborative problem solving, and claim process management. Mediators usually are jointly retained to assist the parties in resolving specific claims.

Facilitators can also be helpful in managing external project relationships, since they are seen as "nonthreatening" due to their neutrality and lack of a stake in the outcome of the process. For example, if an issue arises involving abutters, a facilitator can assist the parties in exploring acceptable solutions. Likewise, in permitting or enforcement issues, facilitators often can manage the discussion in a way that a direct project participant with a stake in the outcome cannot.

Mediators can also be used to manage claim processes, for example, to assist in a negotiated step process on large, complex claims. Likewise, mediators can be used to assist the parties to negotiate the merits of specific claims. They can be particularly

helpful in assisting the parties in "interest based" as opposed to "position based" negotiation because mediation processes are usually confidential and privileged in order to enable the parties to candidly assess the merits of their positions without fear of attribution in later legal processes if a negotiated resolution is not reached. Mediators are most effective when they are brought in at the beginning of a negotiation process where they can assist the parties on process issues as well as on the substantive merits of the claim.[21]

Arbitrators

Arbitration is well-established and widely used in the construction industry. Arbitration involves the engagement of one or more construction-knowledgeable arbitrators to hear and finally decide a claim. Arbitration usually involves a formal, lawyer-driven process, including document production, depositions, and a formal hearing. The arbitrator ultimately issues either a standard award (e.g., one party owes a sum certain to another party) or a reasoned award (explaining the reasoning and detailing the basis for the award). Except for limited circumstances, the arbitrator's award is not appealable and typically becomes the final outcome of the process.

Because the arbitration process in practice has become more complicated and expensive (often referred to as "litigation light"), many projects no longer favor its use, especially on large, complex claims. It is, however, available as a claim resolution tool and is mandated by some state statutes or standard contracting practices. Even if arbitration is the selected or required claim resolution technique, however, it can be fit into the claim resolution process as a "last resort" after other proven methods. And even in arbitration the parties can agree in their contracts to streamline the process to make it more expeditious and cost-effective.[22]

One Size Does Not Fit All

Dispute avoidance and claim resolution programs need to be tailored to fit the specific needs of the project. Often owners put in "boilerplate" claim resolution provisions without careful thought being given to what tools are available and which fit the actual risk profile of the project. Generally speaking, the larger and more complex the project, the more layers and options there may need to be on dispute avoidance and claim resolution tools. For example, there can be a multilayer approach that includes, first, a traditional notice of claim and negotiation process within a set time frame. Second, this can be supplemented by a partnering overlay that provides for senior management review before a formal position is taken by either party. Third, there can be a further process of mediation or a dispute review board where the parties get outside, objective advice but continue to control the outcome because they still must reach agreement for the pro-

cess to end. Fourth, there can be a binding process using third-party decision-makers, such as arbitrators or judges. In the experience of the authors, the use of a third-party decision-maker should be the last resort on any project because of the additional costs, diversion of resources, and loss of control of the outcome.

Implementation of a Dispute Avoidance and Claim Resolution Program

Dispute avoidance and claim resolution processes work only as well as the parties' commitment to and implementation of them. The best process on paper can work only if all levels of management adhere to their principles and processes. Moreover, the processes must be carefully incorporated into all of the project contracts and into the project management plan. The following are the areas that megaproject managers need to address in their project management plans in order to have a truly effective dispute avoidance and claim resolution program.

Resources and Training

The corollary to the parties' management commitment to the process is the need to provide the resources for and training of the personnel who must use the system. The authors' experience has shown us that staffing a dispute-resolution process with the right number and type of personnel is vital to the success of the program. The project team also should be trained on the processes and expectations of management in the implementation of those processes. Megaproject managers also should consider providing some sort of training to the contractor team so that owner expectations on processes, documentation, and expectations are clearly communicated to the most likely source for disputes and claims. Some owners may say, "Isn't this training the contractor to make claims?" The authors' response is that, first, contractors do have rights within the contract terms to make claims; second, that claims will be inevitable; and, third, that a properly and carefully presented claim is much easier to deal with and resolve if it meets the owner's needs and expectations to permit the owner to make a fairly considered, prompt, and merits-based determination.

There is no doubt that a comprehensive dispute avoidance and claim resolution program takes a heavy commitment of resources. However, resources invested in a robust, transparent, and merits-based process that resolves issues, disputes, and claims as they occur will assist project managers in ensuring that the project stays on track. Moreover, the investment in these resources is much less than the resources that would be needed for traditional adversary processes, which are more expensive (small armies of lawyers, consultants, and experts), take much longer, and are resolved in a win-lose outcome years after the fact.

Utilization and Monitoring

The dispute avoidance and claim resolution systems must constantly be monitored with "feedback loops" of whether the selected process is actually working. For example, senior management should receive periodic reports that track the progress of disputes and claims to verify that the program is functioning as planned. The key issue is to ensure that disputes and claims are prioritized (with issues that impact project progress being given top priority), they are moving up levels of management in accordance with the step resolution process (aging reports can be good a bellwether here), and the tools selected are in fact resolving issues.

Responsive Evolution

Based on the feedback loops, megaproject management must be willing to modify its program to fit evolving needs or to make adjustments if the processes originally selected are no longer working. For example, some claim resolution processes, such as DRBs, are very helpful for "one-off" claims that involve discrete issues. If, however, the owner is faced with a complex cumulative impact claim, a structured negotiation within an overarching mediation process may be more effective.[23] Thus, if certain dispute avoidance or claims resolution processes have been ineffective in resolving disputes or claims, project management must be prepared to explore other approaches and implement them with the concurrence of the contractor or other parties.

Reference Sources

Kelleher, T., Corgan, D., and Dorris, W. (2002). *Construction Disputes: Practice Guide With Forms,* 2 vols., 2d ed., New York: Aspen Publishers.

O'Leary, A., and Acret, J. (2002). *Construction Nightmares: Jobs From Hell and How to Avoid Them,* 2d ed., BNI Publications, Inc.

Loulakis, Michael C. (2005). *Design-Build Lessons Learned: Case Studies from 2004,* 10th ed. Vienna, VA: Wickwire Gavin, PC and A/E/C Training Technologies, LLC, pp. 41–43 and 223–238.

Sweet, Justin. (1997). *Sweet on Construction Law,* American Bar Association.

Notes

1.   The authors define a "dispute" as a difference of opinion on a project issue. A dispute becomes a "claim" when it is elevated to a demand for monetary or other relief under a contract. Most project specifications require the filing of a claim in order to trigger the process for resolution of the issue by whatever means are specified in the contract or, in some jurisdictions, by statute.

2. Cushman, R. (2001). *Proving & Pricing Construction Claims*, 3d ed., pp. 301–302. New York: Aspen Publishers, Inc.

3. Grajek, K. M., Gibson, Jr., G. E., and Tucker, R. L. (June 2000). "Project Performance in Texas Department of Transportation," *Journal of Infrastructure Systems*, 6:9, 73–79.

4. Construction Industry Institute. (1991). *In Search of Partnering Excellence,* Special Publication 17-1. Austin: University of Texas.

5. California Department of Transportation, Division of Construction. (September 2008), p. v.

6. See "Strategic Initiative Seven" in the Ohio Department of Transportation *Strategic Initiatives 2001*, p. 66.

7. See Liker, J. (2004). *The Toyota Way: 14 Management Principles from the World's Greatest Manufacturer.* New York: McGraw-Hill.

8. By "balanced," the authors mean using modern general conditions for construction that represent the industry's more progressive contract documents. These terms and conditions are even-handed in setting forth duties and responsibilities between the owner and contractor, they fairly allocate risk of loss, and they establish clear and consistent mechanisms for issue identification, change order administration, and management of claims and dispute resolution.

9. The authors recognize that several alternative procurement strategies may be applied to the contemporary construction megaproject, including design-bid-build, design-build, design-build-operate, build-own-operate-transfer, CM at-risk, and CM-advisor, as examples. The construction management tasks recommended for the megaprojects organization discussed herein apply to some degree in each model, but the authors' discussion is based on extensive experience in design-bid-build, CM at-risk, and CM-advisor type construction.

10. The CM organization will usually include other key departments such as safety, quality control, information systems technology, and document control. Megaprojects set in urban and other developed areas where impacts on third parties are anticipated may also have public relations, community outreach, and ombudsperson teams.

11. A "fair cost" or "independent" estimate is usually an estimate prepared by qualified in-house or consulting change order staff to validate and verify a contractor change order pricing. It is used to validate the contractor's proposed costs and as a negotiating template for the CM team.

12. One strategy that the authors recommend is to publish a simplified but highly detailed "how to" guidebook for contractors and subcontractors on contractual requirements for pricing and submitting change orders (and claims) for extra time and money. The booklet does not substitute for the general and special conditions, but focuses on practical submittal basics for issue merit determinations and quantum calculations otherwise buried in the formulas contained in hundreds of pages of general conditions.

13. See the Big Dig, Boston's Central Artery/Tunnel, where initial costs were estimated at less than $5 billion in the early 1990s and grew to nearly $15 billion over the course of 15 years of construction.

14. A Total Cost (or Total Delay) approach to proving a contractor's claim damages asserts that the total cost of performance minus all contract payments (or time extensions) received from the

owner equals the measure of damages caused by the impacts alleged to be the owner's fault. Courts are extremely critical of using this method and generally may allow its application only if five conditions are met: (1) actual damages are impractical to segregate or itemize; (2) contractor's estimated costs at bid time were reasonable; (3) contractor's actual performance costs were reasonable; (4) contractor was not responsible for the increase in contract costs; and (5) a reasonable cost accounting system has been used to track job costs. Modified Total Costs method of claim damages proof anticipates the challenges to the approach by starting with total cost and then deducting any cost overruns, underestimates, inefficiencies, and other self-inflicted damages from the total.

15. Madigan, T. (Summer 2008). "United States Court of Federal Claims Recognizes General Contractor's Claim for Cumulative Impact Despite Seemingly Broad Release Language in Contract Modifications," *Claims Resource*, San Francisco: URS Claims and Dispute Resolution Group, p. 3. Retrieved April 29, 2010, from http://www.pepperlaw.com/publications_update.aspx?ArticleKey=1287.

16. Depending on the jurisdiction, common exceptions to enforcement of no damages for delay include evidence of procurement fraud, intentional misrepresentation, and intentional or grossly negligent interference by owner.

17. Specifications writers should be careful when drawing up the qualifications for the bank or records management firm to specify adequate requirements for experience and long-standing presence in the commercial marketplace (and liability provisions if possible), since years later, on a project this author worked, a fiduciary firm "lost" the escrow bid file document boxes during office transitions and storage moves. Fortunately for the banking institution, a liquidated damages provision limited the custodian's liability to the contracting parties.

18. See Dettman, K. (2008). "The Role of Dispute Review Boards in Dispute Prevention," *DRBF Forum*.

19. The website of the Dispute Resolution Board Foundation provides a very good summary of DRB practice and procedure, including a *Dispute Review Board Manual*. See www.drb.org.

20. See Caltrans' standard specification 5-1.12.

21. See Dettman, K., and Harty, M. (July 2008). "Mediators as Settlement Process Chaperones: A New Approach to Resolving Complex, Multi-Party Disputes," *The ADR Quarterly*, Alternative Dispute Resolution Section of the State Bar of Michigan, .

22. See Dettman, K., and Miers, C. (2007) "The Use of 'Adjudication DRBs' Where Parties Are Subject to Adjudication or Arbitration Processes," *DRBF Forum*.

23. For example, on the CA/T Project, the original DRB process was replaced with a structured negotiation/mediation process to handle the "end of the contract" claims on several major construction packages. See Dettman and Harty, "Mediators as Settlement Process Chaperones," cited above in note 21.

CHAPTER 11

Insurance Issues

Robert Rogers, Lexington Insurance Company
Donna M. Hunt, Esq., Lexington Insurance Company
Sue E. Yoakum, Esq., Donovan Hatem LLP

Overview

Insurance coverage is an important early planning component for a successful megaproject. The intent of this chapter is to provide owners, design professionals, and contractors an overview and understanding of insurance needs, concerns, and options related to megaprojects. Insurance requirements for megaprojects are different from those for other projects because the recommended coverage limits are higher and many design professionals and contractors do not carry the insurance coverage limits that megaprojects require. In addition, risks in a megaproject are qualitatively and quantitatively different, often requiring specialized insurance coverage and risk management programs. In the early planning stages of the megaproject, owners, design professionals, and contractors need to consider insurance options and obtain an understanding of the implementation of such insurance options.

Insurance: A Review

There are different types of insurances available to design professionals and contractors that owners need to consider for megaprojects. In this chapter, "designer" will be used instead of "design professional," which includes architects, engineers, and other categories of design professionals. The typical types of insurance necessary for megaprojects include professional liability insurance, builder's risk insurance, environmental liability, commercial general liability, automobile insurance, and workers' compensation.

Professional Liability Coverage

For the designer's risk exposures, the focus is on the professional liability coverage commonly known as "errors and omissions" insurance. The trigger for payment under the designer's professional liability policy is negligence of the designer in the performance of professional services. To prove negligence, a claimant must establish four ele-

The Oresund Bridge, connecting Malmö, Sweden, and Copenhagen, Denmark, seen from Malmö. The combined rail and vehicular bridge consists of a central cable-stayed span between two viaducts and a tunnel (at extreme right), which completes the link to Copenhagen. The total length of the bridge is almost 8 kilometers and the tunnel is another 4 kilometers. Opened in 2000. Photo by Jonas Ericsson.

ments: (1) the designer had a *duty* to perform relevant professional services, (2) the designer *breached* that duty, (3) the designer's breach is the *cause* of the claimed damages, and (4) the claimant suffered those *damages*. All four elements of negligence must be proven for recovery under a designer's professional liability policy.

Professional liability policies generally define "professional services" as those services that the insured is legally qualified to perform for others in their capacity as an architect, engineer, land surveyor, landscape architect, construction manager, or as specifically included by endorsement to the policy.

Generally, professional services are those services for which special training, education, or licensing is required. In particular, professional services can include: design; preparation of reports and studies; observation of contractor's performance and resident engineering services; review and evaluation of contractor shop drawings and other submittals, change order proposals, value engineering proposals, etc.; recommendations regarding rejection of contractor work and/or acceptance of work; and forensic engineering/expert services.

"Claims Made" Policy

Professional liability policies are "claims made" policies, meaning the policy in effect when the claim is made against the designer is the policy that provides coverage. Because claims may be made against a designer years following a project's completion, insurance coverage should be maintained for several years after its completion. Designers must be certain to notify their insurance providers of all claims they are aware of during a policy period; otherwise the claim may be barred under a later policy.

Additional Insureds

Some professional service agreements include a requirement for the designer to include the megaproject owner or contractor as an "additional insured" on the designer's professional policy. However, this cannot be provided through the designer's professional policy. A designer cannot add owners or contractors as additional insureds on its professional policy because such policies are specific to licensed design professionals, which protect designers from claims to the extent caused by their negligent performance. Professional liability insurance is not an option or a benefit available to owners or contractors because the owners and contractors are not the licensed party nor are they providing professional services. Therefore, it is impossible for a megaproject owner or contractor to be named as an additional insured under a designer's professional policy. In addition, because most professional policies contain an "insured vs. insured" exclusion, a megaproject owner or contractor should *not* want to be named as additional insureds, because if they were, they would be unable to recover under the policy. The bottom line is a professional policy provides coverage for professional services and cannot be extended to cover others unless they are providing the same kind of professional services.

Some contractors carry professional liability insurance coverage for professional services (i.e., design services) that they may provide from time to time, especially if they work on design-build projects. A contractor's professional liability policy operates the same as a designer's professional liability policy. Therefore, whether the insured on the professional policy is a designer or a contractor, the discussion above pertaining to recovery and additional insureds is applicable.

An alternative available to owners or design-builders to being named as an additional insured on the designer's professional liability policy is an owner's and/or design-builder's indemnification endorsement added to certain project-specific professional liability policies. This type of endorsement allows an owner or design-builder to be specifically named as an "indemnified party." As an indemnified party, they can seek recovery from the insurance company providing this professional coverage for damages or judgments, including reasonable attorneys' fees and reasonable costs incurred by them from third-party claims asserted against an owner or design-builder to the extent caused by a breach of the designer's professional duties. This type of endorsement is the appropriate option for owners and design-builders, rather than an additional insured, because it allows owners and design-builders to recover damages they incur to the extent caused by the designer's breach of professional duties.

Builder's Risk Insurance, Commercial General Liability Insurance, and Other Insurance Coverage

Insurance coverage concerns for the contractors are different from those for the designers. These differences derive from the different risk exposures related to the different services provided by the contractors. Typically, contractors see claims being made against their builder's risk insurance, commercial general liability insurance, and automobile insurance, or workers' compensation insurance policies.

Builder's Risk Insurance

A builder's risk insurance policy provides coverage for direct physical damage to the project that may occur during construction. Builder's risk insurance is considered all risk coverage, and coverage is afforded unless excluded. Builder's risk insurance typically covers "hard costs" associated with the repair of the project and "soft costs" such as design fees, testing and inspection services, and legal expenses.

Builder's risk policies cover property and materials while the structure is under construction. More specifically, the policy covers materials at the job site prior to installation, materials in transit intended for the job, and the value of the property while under construction. Covered perils include: fire, lightning, hail, windstorm, theft, and vandalism. Most policies carry limited coverage for collapse. Standard exclusions in builder's risk policies include earthquake, employee theft, war, government action, mechanical breakdown, or intentional acts of the owner. In addition, because the intent of a builder's risk policy is to provide coverage for sudden or accidental events, damages resulting from faulty design, planning, workmanship, and materials are excluded.

Commercial General Liability Insurance

Commercial general liability insurance is the primary insurance for bodily injury and property damage. Again, both designers and contractors carry this coverage. Typically, contractors carry higher liability limits than the designers because the work of the contractor generally results in a greater risk of occurrence of bodily injury or property claims. Because the contractor is in control of, and responsible for, the site and workers' safety, the majority of claims against them relate to bodily injury and property damage that occur on the site during construction.

Automobile Coverage and Workers' Compensation

Automobile and workers' compensation coverage is necessary coverage and dictated by state law. With increased construction activity and large numbers of construction workers and vehicles on site during construction, one of the most important elements of this coverage is limits. Megaproject participants must recognize and accommodate for the reality that the coverage limits required by state law may not be adequate for a megaproject.

"Occurrence-Based" Coverage

Builder's risk, commercial general liability, automobile, and workers' compensation coverage operate on an "occurrence basis," meaning that coverage attaches at the time the damages or injury occurs, not at the time the claim is made.

Types of Insurance Coverage for Megaprojects

Two types of insurance coverage options will be outlined here: coverage under designers' and contractors' practice policies, which are typically maintained in the ordinary course of business by the designers and contractors, and project-specific insurance coverage. Currently, the most desired option for megaprojects is project-specific insurance coverage because of its ability to be dedicated and specially tailored to the specific project and policy holder.

Practice Policy

Risks on most projects are insured under liability coverage afforded by practice or corporate policies maintained by the designers and contractors in the ordinary course of business, whether the coverage is for professional liability, builder's risk, environmental liability, commercial general liability, automobile, or workers' compensation. There are many reasons why megaprojects necessitate insurance options beyond designers' or contractors' practice policies. Usually, practice polices carry inadequate insurance limits for megaprojects, are subject to eroding limits that are not dedicated to the megaproject, and must be renewed annually. Project-specific insurance can address all these insurance concerns.

Coverage Limits

Typically, designers do not carry the coverage limits recommended for, or come close to covering, the risks associated with a megaproject. Most designers do not have limits in the $10 million range or greater. In addition, if the prime designer does have coverage with limits of $10 million or above, then typically the design subconsultants and lower-tier design consultants will also be required to provide such limits regardless of the size or dollar value of their scope of work. However, very often, design subconsultants and lower-tier design consultants are smaller firms who do not typically work on large projects or megaprojects requiring such high limits. Of course, there are designers who have professional practice policies with limits higher than $10 million, but they are the exceptions. When dealing with megaprojects, most if not all of the designers working on the megaproject will be *underinsured*—a frightening realization for many megaproject owners.

Most providers of professional liability insurance do not have underwriting capacities of more than $5 million. There are some providers who do have capacity over $5 million, but they are in the minority. In addition, typically designers have policy limits of under $5 million and deductibles below $250,000. The average designer carries $2 million in professional liability coverage. These low coverage limits are unacceptable and unrealistic for megaprojects.

Eroding Limits

Another consideration for megaprojects related to the designer's professional insurance is that the practice policy covers risks on all projects on which the designer is currently providing, or previously provided, professional services. In any given year, the designer's policy may have claims already made against it, reducing the amount of policy coverage available for the megaproject.

This is called "eroding limits," and it is of particular concern because designers who are working on one megaproject are more than likely providing design services to other megaprojects, and the $10 million in professional coverage, which seemed like enough, is subject to erosion from claims on the other projects. The designer's $10 million in professional liability coverage can be quickly eroded by a megaproject.

In view of the foregoing, owners, designers, and contractors should not count on the designer's professional practice policy to have adequate coverage for megaproject risk exposures.

Annual Renewal

Designers annually renew their professional practice policies. Most insurance providers of professional policies will only write these polices for one year. Although it is common for the designer's agreement with the owner to require coverage for a number of years during and after construction, such coverage is dependent on future renewals. The professional liability market can be volatile. Over the life of a megaproject, terms and conditions may become more restrictive and high limits may become cost-prohibitive. There is the possibility designers will reduce coverage, cancel, or not be able to obtain professional coverage during future renewals.

The three factors discussed above—coverage limits, eroding limits, and annual renewal—apply to all practice policy coverage, from professional liability to builder's risk, environmental liability, commercial general liability, automobile coverage, and workers' compensation. These policies are placed with aggregate limits and are subject to eroding limits and annual renewals. Again, on most projects, the practice or corporate insurance coverage that designers and contractors carry is adequate, but this is not the case for megaprojects. A claim under a megaproject can quickly erode the average practice policy limits.

Project-specific insurance is an available option to secure adequate project coverage with acceptable limits dedicated to the significant risks associated with megaprojects. Project-specific insurance can be purchased with limits appropriate to megaprojects, are not subject to erosion by other projects, and do not require annual renewal.

Project-Specific Insurance Coverage

Many megaproject owners decide early in the insurance planning process that project-specific insurance coverage is their answer to the major insurance concerns discussed above and purchase project-specific insurance coverage for the megaproject for the designers and contractors working on the megaproject. Project-specific coverage is a recommended insurance solution for megaprojects because it is currently the only available way to provide coverage in the amount and nature that the megaproject requires.

If the owner chooses project-specific insurance for the megaproject, this choice must be communicated to the covered parties, usually the designers and contractors, early in the planning stage. Preferably, the decision to implement a project-specific policy is included in the request for proposals (RFP) process. This is important because it puts the covered parties on notice that there will be project-specific coverage and their practice policies will not be utilized to provide primary coverage for issues covered by the project-specific policy. When the selection of project-specific insurance occurs after the RFP or after the selection of the designers or contractors, there can be confusion. On occasion, a designer or contractor may desire to "opt out" of the project-specific coverage. This is not the way project-specific coverage is intended to work. All designers and contractors working on the megaproject are provided coverage under the project-specific policy and there can be no "opting out." Unless all covered parties fully participate in the project-specific policy, many of the policy's benefits will not be realized. Early planning and education to remind each party of the benefits of the project-specific policy is crucial.

This section will address the benefits and challenges for megaprojects of project-specific insurance policies. Project-specific policies are an investment to ensure success of the megaproject, and the owner should understand the mechanics of and be prepared to purchase these project policies early in the process so that the premium costs can be included in the pro formas as a cost of the megaproject. The premium for these project-specific policies is not insignificant and should be understood early so that the costs can be anticipated.

Advantages

Dedicated limits. For both the project-specific professional liability policy and the commercial general liability policy the advantage of the project-specific policy is similar. The greatest benefit is the availability of dedicated insurance limits appropriate for a megaproject. Because project-specific policies are dedicated to the megaproject, there are no claimants or owners from other projects making claims against these policies, and limits are dedicated and preserved for the megaproject for which they are purchased. These dedicated limits provide coverage for all participants working on a megaproject.

Coverage and triggers similar to practice policies. In general terms, project-specific policies include coverage and payment triggers for claims similar to those found in the designers' and contractors' practice policies. Almost all claims (subject to certain exclusions stated in the policy) that arise out of the negligent performance of professional services by the designer (or its employees) working on the megaproject are covered under the project-specific professional liability policy. Similar to a practice policy, a project-specific policy covers "professional services," defined as "architectural, engineering, surveying, cost estimating, and scheduling, if provided by a firm that is not also providing the construction services."

Risk management incorporated into the project-specific policy. Special attention should be paid to the selection of the insurance company providing the project-specific professional liability policy. Not all project-specific policies and offering insurance companies are the same. Be sure to review and understand the risk management services that may be included with the purchase of the project-specific policy. Good project-specific risk management programs from a professional insurance provider can be valuable during a megaproject in assisting with claims mitigation, management, and monitoring. Some project-specific liability providers offer risk management programs and others do not.

All insurance companies and attorneys who defend designers know that risks can be managed, if allowed, during the project. If an insurance company requests certain risk management procedures be implemented during the megaproject as a part of their project-specific coverage and placement, this request should be embraced by the owners, designers, and contractors. Risk management programs tailored to project-specific policies are designed to be minimally intrusive on project members, and the benefits can be huge. A common form of risk management is a formal process of project monitoring. Project monitoring requires megaproject participants to report periodically on project schedule, construction costs, financing, and changes in megaproject team members. These reporting requirements are useful in discussions during the project when costs, schedule, financing, and other changes occur on the project. There are certain project "markers" that, if followed and monitored, can give early warning of future problems and allow for real-time collaborative resolution between the owner, designers, and contractors. Real-time resolution is always less expensive and more efficient than later litigation.

Joint defense. A benefit of the project-specific policy is the requirement that the insured parties use a joint defense approach. Because all designers receive their professional liability coverage under the project-specific professional liability policy, this policy requires the designers to defend negligence-based claims in a joint defense approach. The joint defense requirement should not be perceived as a negative, but rather a positive, aspect of the project-specific policy.

A joint defense is designed to achieve the commitment and alignment of the parties in the defense of the claim. It is effective to have all designers aligned, rather than potentially working against each other, when answering and defending professional liability claims. Under a joint defense approach, the designers can be provided an efficient and effective defense of the negligence-based claims against them while at the same time effectively managing their legal expenses.

A joint defense addresses the following: exchange of information, identification and isolation of privileged communications, pooling of resources or sharing of legal costs, tolling of limitations/repose statutes, and dispute resolution among the joint defense parties. Some project-specific policies require that a joint defense approach be implemented in the defense and settlement of professional liability claims.

Litigation of claims in a megaproject can be extremely expensive, particularly because of the number of potential defendants. Megaproject owners benefit from the cost efficiency of the joint defense approach because dollars that could easily have been spent supporting multiple defense teams for the designers on the project are instead preserved to pay claims.

Waiver of subrogation. A subrogation action is a follow-on claim that an insurance company makes to recover money it paid out on a claim. A waiver of the subrogation clause is the relinquishing, by an insurer, of the right to collect money previously paid. Waiver of subrogation clauses are recommended for all megaproject agreements because the waiver effectively curtails ongoing litigation between insurance companies. Additionally, while initial claims on megaprojects take more time and more money to resolve than non-megaproject claims, the addition of a subrogation claim on a megaproject could take years, if not decades, to conclude.

Placement of project-specific policies for both designers and contractors allows the insurance companies who provide such coverage to require that waiver of subrogation clauses be inserted and coordinated in all megaproject agreements. An administrative benefit of project-specific coverage is that because there are fewer insurance companies involved in insuring the designers and contractors, it is much easier to coordinate and confirm that all insurance companies accept the waiver of subrogation approach.

What Must Be Done

Coordination. When project-specific coverage is selected, there are several issues that must be addressed for successful implementation of the policies. The first is the coordination and confirmation that the megaproject owner is paying the premium for all policies. Remember, because project-specific policies contain long policy terms and high limits, the premiums can be expensive.

SIR/deductibles. The second issue is to understand application of the self-insured retention (SIR) or deductible. When reviewing an SIR/deductible, the first issues to ad-

dress are the amount of the SIR/deductible and whether the SIR/deductible applies on a per-claim basis or in the aggregate. A per-claim SIR/deductible may result in a lower premium for the owner, but the designers/insureds under the policy assume more risk because of the potential application of multiple SIRs/deductibles. Project-specific policies that have an aggregate amount cap the SIRs/deductibles at a certain amount, and thus the designers/insureds can understand their maximum exposure.

A word of caution: Be certain that all parties know the amount of the SIR/deductible that will be applied per claim and/or in the aggregate for the project-specific policy being considered as early as possible so that the exposure relating to the SIR/deductible can be coordinated among the designers/insureds. The SIR/deductible for a project-specific professional policy is typically much higher than the SIR/deductible a designer would pay under its professional practice policy. Deductibles or SIRs for project-specific policies can range from $250,000 to $2 million per claim. Of course, the exact SIR/deductible amount depends on many factors, including coverage limits, the premium, and the risk of the designers/contractors insured under the policy. Megaprojects, with construction costs of at least $1 billion, could expect and anticipate SIRs/deductibles in the range of $2 million per claim.

Because there are multiple possibilities when it comes to allocating project-specific SIRs/deductibles, the time to define and describe the SIR/deductible allocation plan is at the beginning of the planning stage of the megaproject. All details relating to SIR/deductible allocation should be included in each designer's agreement. If for some reason the SIR/deductible for the project policy is not confirmed before the execution of the designer's agreement, the parties should come to a conceptual agreement of the SIR/deductible allocation, which will then be incorporated by amendment into the designer's agreement at a later date.

Prime designers listed as the "first named insured" on a project-specific professional liability policy should be aware of the additional responsibilities of the first named insured. The first named insured is responsible for the payment of the project-specific policy premium, the satisfaction of the per claim SIR/deductible, and the reporting of claims. Most often, it is stated in the agreement between the first named insured and the megaproject owner that the owner will directly pay the premium of the project-specific policy. This is very important, because otherwise, the first named insured will be responsible for the premium payment. With premiums for project-specific professional liability policies for megaprojects in the seven-figure range, there is motivation for the first named insured designers to reach agreement with the megaproject owners that the owners will make the premium payment.

Options for deductible allocation strategies include deductible sharing, where it is anticipated that each designer will pay a portion of the deductible based on a fault percentage allocation if its services were involved in the claim allegations. For larger deductibles (in the $1 million to $2 million range), a megaproject owner may allocate a maximum amount that each designer whose services are involved in the claim will pay, on a per-claim basis, and the owner pays the difference if there is a deductible amount that must be satisfied before payment under the project-specific policy occurs.

It is important to coordinate the deductible allocation for the lower-tier designers who often have practice policy deductibles of $50,000 or lower. This may seem like an awfully small deductible for a designer working on a megaproject, but remember that many megaprojects are publicly funded and often require participation by a mix of local and minority-owned businesses, whose scope of work, firm size, and receivables often support lower deductibles and limits. On average, lower-tier designers carry liability coverage in the range of $1 million, and occasionally up to $2 million. It is not unusual for a designer on a megaproject to be looking at a project-specific deductible that is larger than the fee they will receive, especially if they are a lower-tier or specialty designer.

Understanding the details relating to project-specific insurance policies that will be implemented for a megaproject is important for designers and contractors, so they and their insurance brokers can evaluate and understand how their practice policies work or do not work with the project-specific policies provided on the megaproject. For designers and contractors, the understanding and tracking of projects that have project-specific coverage is important so they do not include these projects under their practice policies.

Policies As "Claims Magnets"

Some owners, designers, and contractors are less than enthusiastic about project-specific professional policies because they are under the mistaken belief that such policies are "claims magnets." This is not necessarily the case with today's project-specific professional policies. The ability to bring a claim against the policy is dependent on meeting the terms of the project-specific policy. The frequency of claims activity on today's project-specific policies is curtailed by tighter policy terms and conditions and the inclusion of risk management programs.

Some claims activity can be attributed to the specific language in the project-specific policies. The first project-specific policies did not include an "insured vs. insured" exclusion. This resulted in the deteriorating of relationships among insureds and an increase in claims, especially on design-build projects where the design-builder was covered under the project-specific professional policy and allowed to sue its designers. Some design-builders viewed the policies as a vehicle to seek recovery for increased costs and treated the project-specific professional policies as "cost overrun insurance." The claims against the project-specific policies sought recovery not for negligent performance on the part of the designers, but for cost increases that probably should have been anticipated by the design-builder and therefore included as a contingency in the design-builder's budget.

The "good" project-specific policies placed today do not allow one insured to sue another insured. An "insured vs. insured" exclusion in the policy is an effective way to preserve the policy for the owner's assertion of negligence-based claims and also to preserve the relationships of the policy insureds.

Another concern that arises on projects, particularly on design-build projects, is how to determine which project party should be the first named insured on the project-specific professional policy. There is debate in the industry as to whether the design-builder or the prime designer on a design-build project should be the first named insured on the project-specific policy. Since the design-builder is contractually responsible for the design of the megaproject, it is reasonable for the design-builder to be the first named insured. From a megaproject owner's perspective, having the design-builder as the first named insured lends assurance that the design-builder's professional design services are insured. On occasion, a design-builder may request an indemnification endorsement allowing them to recover under the project-specific professional policy for a designer's negligent performance.

Conclusion

Project-specific professional policies are a recommended solution to megaproject owners for dedicated coverage for the professional negligence of designers and contractors. Megaprojects owners should investigate project-specific policies in the early planning stages of the megaproject in order to understand the premium costs, extent of coverage, deductibles, and placement of project-specific policies. The project-specific professional policy and build insurance coverages that start at the primary layer are the best option for good and dedicated coverage for the designers and contractors working on megaprojects.

Owners' Protective Professional Indemnity (OPPI)

Another option is available to owners seeking professional liability coverage for their megaprojects and not willing to purchase a project-specific policy that attaches at the "primary" coverage level. This option is an "owners' protective professional indemnity" (OPPI) insurance policy. An OPPI policy protects an owner in the case where a designer's practice policy is insufficient or exhausted by other claims. It is important to note that OPPI is for the owner's, not the designer's, benefit.

The placement of the OPPI can be less expensive for the megaproject owner because it provides less coverage. An OPPI functions somewhat as an excess policy and is the second policy to be accessed in the event of a professional liability claim. The megaproject owner, by contract, requires the designers to carry certain professional policy limits. These limits may be different for the prime designer than for the lower-tier designers.

One negative that designers and their professional liability insurers should be aware of is that occasionally the owner or the OPPI insurer may be in a position in a particular claim situation to exert downstream pressure on the designer and its professional liability insurer to pay more than fair value of a claim against a designer in order to trigger or access OPPI coverage for the project owner.

What Must Be Done

In some years a designer's professional practice policy will be depleted by claims activity, and in other years it will be preserved. Because of this unknown but constant exposure to the designer's professional practice policy, it is recommended for a designer's contract to provide a layer of coverage less than the total amount of their professional practice policies. In any given year, the full amount of coverage afforded under their professional practice policy may not be available. If the designer is contractually responsible to provide and maintain a specific amount of coverage, the designer may be required to pay the difference out of pocket. In other words, the dedicated limit for the primary layer provided by the designer's professional practice policy needs to be an amount the designer reasonably believes will be available in any given year. For example, if the designer carries $10 million in professional practice limits, it is not unreasonable that they allow $2.5 to $3 million to be exposed as a primary layer for the megaproject. However, in any given year the designer may or may not have this amount of available limits.

What to Avoid

In the past, designers were typically not informed when an OPPI policy was purchased by an owner, but this has changed. In recent years, the placement of OPPI policies has been communicated to the designers who are providing the primary layer of professional coverage. There is really no reason why a megaproject owner purchasing an OPPI would not communicate this information to the designers so that the designers can coordinate their professional practice coverage with the OPPI.

If a designer places too much of their practice policies at risk, then in a "heavy claims year," when the claim from the megaproject is made against the designer's professional practice policy, the designer may not have the coverage limits available that they contractually agreed to carry.

Furthermore, on future renewals of their professional practice policy, the designer will not be able to reduce limits, because of the contractual obligation to provide the

dedicated limits for the megaproject. This may not be of concern at this time for a designer involved in megaprojects, but the monitoring and tracking of this obligation is important and, if not properly managed, designers may find themselves underinsured, or worse, facing a contractual insurance obligation for which they are not properly insured.

OPPI policies do not work exactly like the designer's professional practice policy. The first named insured on an OPPI is the owner, not the designer. Therefore, the policy does not provide coverage for the designers, but rather seeks to reimburse the megaproject owner if a designer is negligent and the designer has exhausted a certain amount of its professional practice coverage.

In addition, the terms and conditions of an OPPI do not necessarily, and will less than likely, follow the terms and conditions of the designer's underlying professional practice policy. OPPIs do not lend themselves to a joint defense approach. Designers should also be aware that a megaproject owner may want to access the OPPI that they purchased, causing tremendous pressure from the owner to settle negligence-based claims at underlying limits. Of particular concern is the ability of the OPPI insurance provider to reserve its right to subrogation against the designer to collect the money the OPPI insurance provider paid. If the designer did not contract for a waiver of subrogation (which stops follow-on litigation) in its agreement with the owner, a subrogation action is very much a possibility, and the designer may pay again on a subrogation claim.

OCIP or CCIP

Another insurance option for owners, which will be only briefly mentioned here, is the purchase of OCIP or CCIP policies that include insurance coverage for builder's risk, environmental liability, commercial general liability, automobile insurance, and workers' compensation and typically do not provide professional liability coverage. As generally understood when discussing project-specific insurance, OCIP stands for "owner-controlled insurance program" and CCIP for "contractor-controlled insurance program." For clarity, "controlled" in the descriptions above means "procured" or "purchased by."

It is important to understand the specific coverage provided under an OCIP or CCIP. Typically, OCIPs and CCIPs do not include professional liability coverage. This is not to say they cannot include professional liability coverage, but it is important to emphasize the specific coverage provided for the megaproject under an OCIP or CCIP.

Megaproject Delivery Options and Impact on Insurance

Megaprojects lend themselves to the implementation of various forms of project delivery methods. When selecting insurance, it is crucial to have a thorough understanding of the project delivery methods, which include design-bid/negotiated bid-build, design-build, integrated project delivery (IPD), or public-private partnership (PPP). There are insurance decisions to make about each project delivery method. In addition, joint ventures, while not a project delivery method, are included in this discussion because they are commonly found on megaprojects and come with their own specific insurance concerns.

Does insurance work differently for different project delivery methods? First, project-specific insurance remains the recommended insurance for megaprojects, regardless of the project delivery method. IPD lends itself to needing project-specific insurances. IPD contemplates the owner, designers, and contractors all working together and legally liable to deliver the megaproject in accordance with a schedule and budget. With the unique risks and liabilities associated with IPD—which increase for megaprojects—IPD is a good candidate for project-specific coverage.

Design-bid/negotiated bid-build and design-build are also good candidates for project-specific coverage. As previously mentioned, there are some advantages of project-specific insurance that are particularly well-suited to design-build. A design-builder can purchase an indemnity endorsement allowing it to collect money for damages caused by the negligent performance of the designers. However, this does not mean the design-builder can use the professional project-specific policy as "cost overrun" insurance.

Joint ventures. Designers and contractors often form joint ventures in order to create a team with the experience, size, and strength needed for a megaproject. However, of concern for the firms forming a joint venture is what practice policy insurance limits will be required of each firm in the joint venture. Typically, megaprojects require joint and several liability from each of the joint venture firms. This is important because this requirement makes each firm individually responsible to the owner to deliver the megaproject, including providing the required insurance coverage.

The firms in a joint venture may have different coverage limits, different deductibles, and different insurance providers. The coordination of the different coverage limits, deductibles, and providers is important and must be addressed by each joint venture firm. The coordination effort includes determining the coverage limits for each firm in the joint venture, determining the deductible amounts for each firm, and identifying differing coverage requirements, if any. Coordination of insurance should *not* be undertaken when the first claim is made against the joint venture. This is too late and is ripe for unexpected surprises. Joint ventures lend themselves to project-specific coverage so that the coverage limits, deductibles, and insurance are the same for each firm and are coordinated among them.

Public-private partnerships (PPP). Public-private partnerships are typically utilized on projects where federal, state, and local governments are unable to meet the funding demands required to build large infrastructure projects. The public-private partnership approach allows private capital to be invested in project construction in return for future income after completion of the project, during the ownership and maintenance phase.

PPPs present substantial risk exposure and complex contractual relationships among the project stakeholders and require careful attention to risk management and insurance. Project-specific coverage is recommended to ensure adequate coverage for all parties working on a PPP megaproject. Insurance coverage is typically the responsibility of the private party to provide. Remember, even though a PPP is a partnership between a public and private entity, public sovereign immunity does not extend to the private entity.

Conclusion

Insurance for megaprojects is as important as the selection of the designers and contractors, and early adequate planning and strategies can reduce the risks of under-insured projects, enhance risk management processes on the project, and increase the likelihood of a successful megaproject.

CHAPTER 12

International Perspective

David Caiden, Arup
Peter Chamley, Arup

The authors of this chapter are civil engineers who have lived and worked on many continents and have had particular experience of civil engineering megaprojects. By counting "project countries," meaning countries where they have had some involvement on projects without being fully resident, it is fair to say that they have had some experience of the way things work in well over 30 different countries. The views and opinions expressed in this chapter are therefore those absorbed from personal familiarity based on a combined professional working experience of some 60 years. As such, they may be considered subjective, but nevertheless the writers feel that the sharing of these views can only be helpful to those considering embarking on a megaproject outside of the United States.

What Cannot Be Exported Overseas

The first thing to understand is that the experience from one location cannot necessarily be directly translated and used in a new location. There are many issues to consider that may or may not be unique to a particular country. The main issues can be categorized under the following headings:

- Political issues
- Cultural issues
- Labor custom and practice
- Finance processes
- Procurement processes
- Legal issues (which include custom and practice on styles of contract as well as what the authors call "enabling legislation")

Political Issues

Political issues cover the style and system of government at both national and lower levels and how these different levels interact and work in practice. Other chapters in this volume have explained that a full democracy may perhaps create the most difficult

Aerial view of the north entrance to the Gotthard Base Tunnel, a 35-mile rail tunnel through the Swiss Alps, part of the Swiss AlpTransit project to build faster north-south rail links across Switzerland. The Gotthard Base Tunnel will reduce the travel time between Zurich and Milan by almost half. Completion is now projected for 2018. Photo © 2009 by Klaus Foehl.

233

climate for getting things done. A good comparison here of the typical extremes might be the United States versus Singapore. In the United States we find there are not only state and federal governments to be dealt with but also city and county rules and regulations. The political path to project completion is a maze of obstacles from conception of the idea onward. Any single project may have politicians at up to six layers of elected bureaucracy to deal with and from differing political parties, each with his or her own interests. This is not a recipe for rapid and objective decision-making. Conversely in Singapore, working with a single level of government means that things can get done and get done quickly and there will not be layers of government with conflicting requirements. The contrast in time from inception to construction of large projects in, for example, New York and Singapore can be explained in very large measure by the differing political environments.

Above all, one of the political essentials with respect to accommodating megaprojects is the degree of transparency within the system. This means, *inter alia*, having rules for procurement by the governments and their bureaucracies that are clearly understandable and publicly available. Absence of transparent mechanisms can lead to corruption, which is discussed further in the closing section of this chapter. Environments that promote a protectionist policy by introducing hurdles to prevent non-local participation are clearly directly responsible for cost increases to projects. The intent of favoring local industry is undoubtedly well-intentioned in terms of providing wealth and jobs, but once schemes reach megaproject proportions all bets of this type are off. Megaprojects by their very nature — and remembering they are usually a "one-off" — cannot be entirely serviced by local firms and local skills, and thus importing expertise and technology is a prerequisite. Trying to restrict out-of-town, out-of-state, or out-of-country competitors only encourages a closing of ranks, which often results in cartels forming to carve up the work and a failure to adopt the most appropriate technology. The sad result is that the public pays too much for the end facility and that facility may not be as good as it could have been.

The same is true for specifications and supply rules that prevent foreign products from being incorporated. The "Buy America" legislation is an example of a political policy which can prevent the American public from enjoying the benefits of overseas development in certain technical areas of expertise, and it can also result in the public paying more than necessary for the end product.

Cultural Issues

Cultural issues comprise a very deep subject. They embrace the psyche of a nation or people, and in some societies there are different cultural groups with different feelings and aspirations that need to be accommodated in the planning of the project. One of

the most elemental issues is the extent to which a people or nation can accept the ben-efits of the many against the disbenefits of the few, which in turn impinges on issues such as individual rights and the importance they are given in the big picture. For exam-ple, in the United States the right to own property is a fundamental precept with links back to Colonial and Revolutionary days. This makes the implementation of the "emi-nent domain" principle far more difficult than in most other countries. Further, the his-tory of the abuse of eminent domain has made public opinion support the individual's rights even more strongly. The other extreme of this issue might be found in a country like Italy, which permits project-enabling legislation to allow the compulsory acquisi-tion of real estate to fit the project schedule — the difference in the Italian model being that if a property owner feels he has been unfairly compensated, his claim is dealt with *after* the acquisition. Some countries have reached compromise methods between these two extremes. For example, the Hong Kong Special Administrative Region has a history of the government or a quasi-government project promoter negotiating compensation payments with building owners, resulting in payments that many have considered to be above market rate. Thus, by making property owners more than happy, the projects proceeded on time or ahead of schedule and consequently were completed within the overall budget.

Other important elements are project statutory approval processes and the require-ments for consultation. The ability of the public to question and protest plans is long enshrined in many democracies, although the extent of this consultation and the speed of the process vary significantly. For example, the United Kingdom's Public Inquiry sys-tem for major projects is similar in many ways to a court procedure, with an Inspector (the "Judge") presiding over an inquiry closely resembling a court of law and with pro-ponents and opponents lined up on either side with their respective lawyers. The pro-cess can be extremely lengthy in hearing all the "evidence" for and against the proposed project before the Inspector reaches a decision. In fact, although this gives the public (and particularly opponents to the scheme) a fair opportunity to be heard, it is widely acknowledged that the process has become too lengthy, time consuming, and costly.

The public's attitude to development, change, environmental impact, and big busi-ness are all fundamental to how a project will be perceived. The acceptance of projects and the ability of the public to protest in an influential way can have a significant im-pact on the speed and success of any large project. A culture of protest, rather than simply accepting the imposition of change, can frequently influence the outcome. In many Western nations there has grown a strong environmental lobby that opposes megaprojects, which are seen as having negative environmental impacts or as pro-moting the interests of "Big Business." Making rational and objective decisions on the project benefits and the handling of environmental impacts can often become mired in irrational debate.

235

Labor Custom and Practice

Although labor custom and practice may be considered a subset of "cultural issues," it deserves a special heading because of its overwhelming importance. Megaprojects require mega-labor forces. This includes not only the various levels of construction workers, from unskilled labor to highly skilled craftsmen, but also the layers of professional staff necessary for design and implementation. For most territories the days of labor abuse, thank goodness, are long gone. It is important that the training and, if necessary, importation of labor and professional staff to be planned. Successful projects in the modern world rely on a well-trained and happy labor force. Putting arrangements in place that give this result requires an understanding of the local practice and customs as well as knowledge of available skills. This applies whether "union shops" are operated or not, though a history and a custom of a labor force capable and willing to multitask, rather than needing individual workers for individual tasks (demarcation), has a significant impact on the type and size of workforce required

Many arrangements for certain trades or skills have evolved over history. A good example of this evolution, because of the linear nature of tunneling, is that of tunnel miners. Tunnel miners need skills involving both brawn and brain. The key issue is that tunnel projects can proceed no faster than the face mining. This would seem to give the miners a position of complete power in terms of wage negotiations, and hence tunnel workers are indeed usually well paid. The traditional structure that has developed in almost all countries of the world (but notably not in all of the United States) is for miners to work on a target-bonus system. In such a system, it is imperative to set the progress targets fairly so that the base wage rate (paid when targets are not met) provides a sufficient living income and that bonuses (paid when daily or weekly targets are met or exceeded) provide extra money which the individuals perceive is well worthwhile for them to make. The gang has to work as a team to earn the bonuses, which means the "leading miner" has to control, supervise, and discipline his own gang to make sure everyone gets the bonus benefits; slackers will soon get dropped from his team. By setting targets and bonuses correctly, it is usually possible to optimize progress to match the capabilities of the available plant and equipment. Fixing a problem that is delaying production becomes everyone's problem. Contrast this to a fixed-wage agreement where there is no incentive for a miner to achieve a higher output level. In fact, the reverse is true: the longer the project lasts, the longer the miner will be employed at that same location. In this example, a fixed-wage agreement becomes a disincentive to progress.

It is important to understand the various trades, skills, and professions that will be required for a project, as well as their history and the local labor law context. To this must be added an understanding of the current market for those trades, skills, and professions and whatever mechanisms for training a new labor pool or importing the skills

that are available and could be made to work in the particular locality. When training is deemed necessary, the source of the new recruit trainees must also be identified. For example, there might be a local smelting plant scheduled to close or perhaps one closing in a nearby town. Maybe the local sea is "fished out" and fishermen are desperate to find alternative sources of income. In all cases, it is necessary to think about available accommodation where an influx of people is required. For remote locations, this may mean building a "construction town" that provides family facilities. The whole of this process takes detailed planning, and promoters usually understand well that resourcing the people for a project is basic. It is important for project promoters to get their governments to understand this also, and they usually do. For example, labor and immigration departments may need to have regulations changed by legislation to facilitate an influx of foreign workers.

Lastly, the understanding of labor custom and practice goes hand in hand with project estimating. International price benchmarking is frequently recommended for megaprojects. However, it is usually the case that the labor element within a project is large. If the manning levels used internationally do not translate to the specific country, then the benchmark estimates will need to be modified. For example, as a result of existing union agreements covering the eastern seaboard area of the United States, underground construction employs approximately four times the number of personnel as in similar jobs in Asia, Australia, or Europe. Obviously. therefore, an international benchmark price for a tunnel from those continents cannot be used as a comparison for underground work in New York. The authors are proponents (particularly in countries with a strong trades union establishment) of negotiating project wage agreements with unions and trade organizations. Setting in advance the wage level mechanisms and, if possible, such things as strike-prevention measures will give a far more reliable project cost estimate. If undertaken professionally by all those involved, a project wage agreement can eliminate practices that may have become outdated or inapplicable for a megaproject.

Finance Processes, Procurement Processes, and Legal issues

These three categories are dealt with at length in other chapters of this volume and so will not be discussed in detail here. The important issue in all cases is always to "think local" and not to try to impose a model used in another country when that model does not fit the local circumstances. Some countries have unique ways of doing things while others use approaches that are common, or at least similar, to a group of countries sharing a related culture. The history of "common country groups" often goes back to the days of a colonizing power and its legacy of legal, commercial, and linguistic frameworks. For example, French-speaking countries will often share ways that are based on Napoleonic

standards, and Spanish-speaking countries will likewise share their own commonalities, which well pre-date modern day Spain. Of course, the situation gets more complicated when a megaproject crosses country borders, which is often the case. This sometimes requires new sets of rules to be created specifically for the project, rules that need to be compatible or acceptable within the existing frameworks of the different countries. Labor and immigration law issues frequently require governments to pass new legislation. For everything mentioned in this chapter, local knowledge and understanding are essential, and this means having local people within the project implementation team in senior positions.

The ability to acquire the real estate and property necessary for a project to proceed is clearly of fundamental importance, and differing legal frameworks and property rights can make this a key project risk. As stated previously, in democracies that highly value the rights of the individual property holder over the needs of the wider community, simply obtaining the property necessary for the project can be become a long and involved process.

Obtaining statutory approvals and being able to remove any obstructions, such as utilities, is fundamental to maintaining the progress of any project; but for megaprojects, the risks can be enormous when parties with no intrinsic interest in the project are involved. In countries where utilities are state owned or heavily regulated, the facilitating work may be relatively straightforward. This is particularly the case where the government or the utility owner is the project sponsor. In countries where the utilities are owned by private companies, the ability to have these companies engage in the project may be severely limited. A particularly stubborn or slow-moving utility company can seriously delay a project or may even hold an owner to ransom.

What Must Be Exported Overseas

Conversely, there are some universal rules that not only cross boundaries but are required fundamentals in all locations. The two most important are:

- "Time is money."
- "Quality endures long after price is forgotten."

Time Is Money

This old adage would seem to be a statement of the ever-so-obvious. Yet on megaprojects the authors have found that time and again this simple rule gets overlooked in the fog of huge organizations and project teams. Earlier chapters make reference to the infamy of megaproject time and budget overruns. We believe that the budget overruns are almost always the outcome of the time overruns.

An issue that frequently gets lost in both the analysis and the outturn sums is that "the project" is not simply the construction phase or construction contracts. "The project" is something that starts with a dream, moves to an idea, and then usually progresses to a feasibility study. Even after that point, "the project" is still a very long way from the building stage. Options have to be priced, conceptual designs developed, detailed designs worked up, and contract documents drafted long before procurement processes can be started. This whole incubation stage costs money. The longer it takes, the more it costs. The longer it takes, the higher will be the bids when contracts eventually reach the street. This is the outcome of the way world economies work on a continuing inflationary basis. So all delays, even before any contracts are let, result in the owner (and that usually means, ultimately the public) paying more dollars. Every time a decision is delayed, at every stage and for whatever reason, the price goes up. Every time a previous decision is rescinded and changes are made, the price goes up. The key to delivering a megaproject within budget (and there actually are examples of this happening) can be summed up in one word: speed.

As the project moves through its various stages, the cost of every week of delay rises on an exponential curve. The delays late in construction, or worse, after construction (such as in the commissioning stage of a railway), are *hugely* expensive. Usually in the final reckoning, true cost increases are neither calculated nor revealed: the true cost increase, of course, would include the unavailability of the facility for public use, which means the additional costs incurred, for example, in people's travel times or for using alternative facilities.

The trick is to spend a good deal of money wisely in the early days. This should include things such as real estate acquisition and utility diversions. Putting off getting the land for work sites or buying the buildings that need clearing does not save money. In the final reckoning, delaying the acquisition costs more money than the real estate costs alone, because delayed acquisitions usually result in delay to the construction work itself, and the costs of construction delays are dear. This is difficult to explain to budget holders when there is no overall budgetary link, and this is also why a single organization should be made responsible for realizing the project. Unfortunately, because of the processes required for large infrastructure spending in the United States (budgets coming from different purses, an ROD, or record of decision, being needed before the real spending starts), the recommended seamless approach is not usually possible here. However, it has been achieved in other countries. As an illustration, it may be useful to compare two similar large projects with which the authors are familiar (see Table 1, next page).

The primary reason that the Hong Kong Island Line metro project was able to be built at this speed was that the entire planning cycle took cognizance of the "time is money" maxim by adopting the following principles:

Table 1. **A comparison of factors that affect subway construction in New York and Hong Kong.**

PROJECT 1—Second Avenue Subway, New York City, USA	PROJECT 2—Hong Kong Island Line, Hong Kong SAR
This subway (metro, or underground urban railway) project has been divided into phases to suit funding requirements. The whole project is over 8 miles (13 km) long and will have 16 stations and the publicized estimated cost was about $16 billion. The project has been split into four phases and the construction contract mentioned here is in the first phase. The first phase is therefore only about 2 miles (3.2 km) long with only 4 new stations and connection to an existing station. The authors have been working on this project for over six years and the first construction contract for Phase 1 (tunnel boring) was let in March 2007. At the time of writing (2009, that is, two years after contract award) tunneling has not yet started.	This similar metro project was also about 8 miles long having 12 stations. The design consultancy was let in December 1980 with design work starting in January 1981. The first trains were carrying passengers in May 1985, that is, less than four and a half years after the detailed design was awarded. The project was completed within the budget. Both projects are in complex and dense cities, but this project was far more technically challenging with more congested (narrower) streets and difficult granular soil below the water table. This required open-faced shields (pressure tunnel boring machines were still in their infancy) for compressed-air mining in up to 3.5 bars pressure. Extensive chemical ground treatment was also required.

1. The government had enacted enabling legislation (called "the Railways Ordinance") years in advance. This legislation empowered the Mass Transit Railway Corporation (MTRC) to acquire whatever land was necessary for the project and fairly compensate owners. In most cases owners were more than happy with the compensation received.
2. The government enacted compressed-air working legislation years in advance after it was established by consultants that compressed-air mining would be the principal method required for tunnel construction.
3. The areas required for the project (mostly for the off-line stations) were identified at the concept stage before detailed design was started. This allowed the acquisition process to be started early so that all properties were acquired before construction contracts were put out for bids.
4. Previous lines had been constructed using cut-and-cover station boxes in the

main roads. This had caused immense disruption, and the public had been out-raged by the inconvenience caused. The entire concept was changed for this new railway so as to minimize taking space in the streets and largely to do away with cut-and-cover construction in the road. This was achieved by siting stations "off-line" (that is, to one or other side of the running tunnels) in city blocks. The areas needed were created by demolishing acquired buildings. Deep basements were built on the demolished sites and these became the station concourses, linked to the platform tunnels by hand-mined passenger adits. Each concourse basement was topped by a thick, heavily reinforced transfer slab that was capable of sup-porting practically any design of high-rise building. The MTRC subsequently built tower blocks atop these slabs, and the revenue generated from this real estate fi-nanced the entire railway.

5. Obviously, some street shafts were required for launching the tunneling shields, and the locations for these, as well as the boundaries for each individual contract, were finalized at the concept stage. This allowed the street shafts to be designed in the first few months, and let and built as advanced contracts while the remain-der of the designs was being completed.

6. Utility diversions were also negotiated in advance and let and completed in those first few months.

7. The design consultants had extensive local experience and were able to specify in detail the method to be used for ground treatment areas. This had to be carried out from the surface to start and complete the compressed-air soft-ground tunnel drives, to protect fragile buildings, to construct sumps and cross-passages, and so on. Deviations from the specified approaches were not allowed.

8. Similarly, ground treatment to be carried out underground for junctioning compressed-air work was specified in detail (sodium silicate and bentonite-cement grouting combinations), and deviations from what was shown on the drawings were not permitted.

9. Trucking of spoils was allowed only at night so as not to interrupt the regular traf-fic on the already highly congested streets. This meant daytime stockpiling (tun-neling projects are nearly always worked on a continuous 24-hour basis for safety reasons). Where necessary, work sites were decked to make multilevel space avail-able in the restricted ground areas acquired.

10. The savvy contractors mitigated complaints and objections by liberal use of cash and by promptly fixing any damage caused to private property. For example, on one station where the top of a mountain had to be demolished with explosives, many building windows were broken as a result of the thousands of blast rounds fired. By replacing all damaged windows with superior quality double-glazed units on the same day that a breakage occurred, and even paying disgruntled residents

additional money "for their trouble" where it appeared appropriate, there were no work interruptions and no legal actions started.

No matter where a project is in the world, the enemy is always time. Lost time can hardly ever be recovered. When acceleration processes do recover some time, it always comes at a premium cost. The primary reasons that megaproject outturn costs become so high are that insufficient attention to detail is spent in the planning and concept stages and owners do not stick with the decisions made in those stages. For example, it is always too late to leave property acquisitions and utility diversions to the detailed design stage. Every "repackaging" iteration at the design stage (which is a frequent occurrence in large projects) causes delay and increases costs. Contract packaging and the contract boundaries need to be finalized at the concept stage and fully adhered to in the following stages. Packaging changes interfere with concept principles and cause a cascade of future problems.

Quality Endures Long After Price Is Forgotten

Most megaprojects are about constructing facilities for the public benefit that have to last a very long time. No one driving over a 200-year-old bridge that was originally designed for horse traffic will be dismayed to learn that the bridge's reconstruction to accommodate modern traffic went over budget. Yet this budgetary control is what we tend to concentrate our efforts on in modern times. Even more important to remember is the lifetime cost of maintaining the facility. Skimping on small elements to save capital budget can result in maintenance spending that swamps the savings. This old maxim remains valid today and has to be taken in conjunction with the "time is money" adage. This is particularly true for moving and wearing parts of machinery, for finishes in public areas, and for most electrical and mechanical elements, which usually have to endure for longer than the originally specified design life. On many big projects there will be research undertaken and committee meetings held to decide on something basic, such as what paint or finishes should be applied to walls in public areas, and the ranking often revolves around the capital cost. Imagine having a tooth filled at the dentist: the patient expects the filling to last a very long time and does not ask the dentist, "Do you have anything cheaper?" The situations are exactly comparable. Even when the rankings are done correctly and the lifetime maintenance is factored in, an absurd decision can still be made because the owner's representative only has direct control of the capital budget. The paradox is that the process of making these decisions consumes time — and remember that the time-and-money curve has an exponential form. So choosing plain steel washers over stainless steel, for example, may actually cost more (even if that decision time takes only one day) than selecting stainless at the

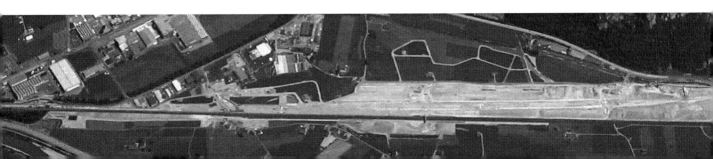

outset. In reality, decision times for components and products usually take a lot longer than a day. Thus, for expensive elements, such as escalators in a rail station, there is little point in wasting thousands of man-hours deciding what to specify. The product with the highest specification is probably the cheapest overall, and making that decision quickly can give the discount in time savings that actually pays for the superior product. Designers and project promoters have a duty to future generations and this duty should not be taken lightly.

Corruption

The closing section of this chapter briefly addresses a worldwide issue that is the cause of much wasted funding from governments, lending banks, and ultimately the general public. Corruption is something that consistently seems to creep into megaprojects and becomes one of the major reasons for budget explosions. Once corruption is allowed to occur it becomes insidious and begets corruption at further levels. Inevitably, if the corruption starts at the highest level, such as in countries where a ruler or minister or politician requests a "'facility fee" for awarding a contract, it cascades down to the lowest level and some form of bribery or kickback pervades all activities. There is no substitute for maintaining a high ethical standard, and excuses such as "That's the way business is done here" do not need to be tolerated. The authors' view is that it is better to walk away and let someone else play that game: there is sufficient work available in the world for those who wish to live with principles of decency and fairness.

There is a wealth of literature relating to corruption on public projects. One of the best summaries with respect to the high-level issue of the procurement process itself is the Norwegian report "Corruption in Public Procurement; Causes, Consequences and Cures," by Tina Søriede (Bergen, Nor.: Chr. Michelsen Institute, 2002). This report distinguishes between *political* or *high-level* corruption and *administrative* or *bureaucratic* corruption. It points out that in countries with a fully corrupt system the contract is awarded to the best briber, not the company best experienced or equipped to do the work. It further makes reference to the Organisation for Economic Co-operation and Development's year 2000 recommendations (*No Longer Business As Usual: Fighting Bribery and Corruption*, Paris: OECD, 2000). Here, OECD recommends what it calls a "white list" approach. Companies self-certifying that they comply with all antibribery laws can get their names put on an approval list. In the event that any audit or other inspection or investigation reveals their certifying statements are false, their contracts become automatically terminated and their names struck off the list. Søriede goes on to make certain recommendations for strategies to combat procurement corruption. Below in paraphrased (and sometimes amplified) form is a numbered list of what we view as the top ten recommendations from the OECD report.

1. An independent procurement unit with professional, knowledgeable, and adequately paid officials should be established.
2. Rotation of officials responsible for procurement should be considered.
3. Access to information is of primary importance in the bidding process.
4. Procurement rules must be clear and simple.
5. Performance or quality ratings must form a part of the assessment process.
6. Separating bid assessments into technical and financial evaluations using different panels of people is strongly recommended. Thus a "two-envelope" system is preferred.
7. A high number of bidders is no assurance of a competitive result and does not ensure a clean process, especially where local, state, or national market protection rules are applied. International bids need to be facilitated and encouraged for megaprojects. This may mean modifying a traditional procurement process so it becomes tailored to accommodate international bidders.
8. The period allowed to submit bids must be reasonable and adequate for bidders to undertake the work and should not be skewed by public holidays. Where multiple contracts are to be let, or coexistent projects have overlapping schedules, procurement agencies and/or their subgroups need to cooperate to ensure that bid intervals do not overlap.
9. There must be strict adherence to the time limits set for submittals and also for assessments, decisions, and awards.
10. Rules and routines for communication during the bidding process need to be set and enforced.

However, the direct form of corruption in procurement is not the only type of corruption that is seen on large projects. Some forms of corruption are more subtle and less easy to walk away from because they are culturally ingrained and need not directly involve the foreign backer, contractor, or individual worker. For example, there are many places where the "conflict of interest" principle does not seem to apply. In such locations one might find that the same academic is working as a consultant to a government, a contractor, and a designer on the same project. When working in these circumstances, it may not be necessary for the U.S. company or individuals to discard their own ethical standards. In such situations, having a required person on the payroll need not compromise making the right decisions. Nevertheless, this practice and the use of compulsory "agents" and middlemen needs to be handled very carefully to ensure it does not develop into something worse.

Other forms of corruption are even less obvious. For example, one country has a method of bidding contracts where the bidder has to put a discount percentage against a number of standard government unit price rates. In a tunnel job, the bid calculation

is based on the bid quantities, but it is recognized that quantities will change, especially for initial steel supports such as arch ribs and rockbolts. However, payment is made on an admeasurement basis. The highest discounter wins the contract but then has to design the initial support for which he has safety responsibility. Normally the contractor subrogates this responsibility to a design consultant. The design consultant gets paid as a percentage of construction payments. Thus, why should the designer produce an economic design? He is incentivized to overdesign, eliminate risk, and maximize fee. This might result in double the tonnage of steel being used. The contractor does not object, as he gets paid by the ton and so is able to increase his own profit. Thus the public gets duped out of millions of dollars.

Somewhat more malicious is the falsification of quality, testing procedures, or inspections and verifications. Stories abound of steel rebar being removed after inspection to be refixed in the next concrete pour. Another popular legend exists of a place where concrete test cubes could be bought at a market stall as substitutes for the real samples that go to the testing laboratory. In a similar vein is the diluting of concrete mixes or the falsification of batch labels on delivered materials. Unfortunately, the increasing trend of "self-certification" allows these practices to be perpetrated, and random sample quality checks can never substitute for full-time independent inspectors. In general terms, the less sophisticated the country, the more stringent the testing process needs to be, and the old style of contract, where the engineer from the design firm actually administers the construction contract with his own team of staff, still works best.

Closer to home, corruption takes many more twists. Vested interests, pork-barrel politics, and plain vanity from politicians who wish to add their name to a bridge or road before they die result in much wastage of public funds. Unfortunately the complexity of approvals and funding for public infrastructure makes the audit trail difficult to follow and makes controls hard to enforce. In such cases the benefit of the many gets brushed aside for the benefit of the few—the few being those who walk the corridors of power.

Conclusions

All countries have their own way of doing things and it is wrong to believe that outside experience may easily be adopted to "improve" the in-country methods. For this reason it is necessary to be very wary of "international benchmarking," especially when this is of a financial nature. While it may be true that lessons learned elsewhere *could* improve designs, procurements, and construction contracts, the existing cultural, political, and legislative frameworks may not allow necessary modifications to existing practices that would allow such changes. That is not to say that governments should not look to methods used elsewhere in order to consider making political and legislative changes where clearly these might lead to a better enabling structure for a megaproject.

Indeed, the authors encourage such an approach, but only those in positions of authority or power are able to make such changes — and even they will have some limitations.

On the other hand, there are some golden rules that apply everywhere when it comes to giving the public value for money. The most important of these is that "time is money." Any approaches that are able to shorten the whole life cycle of a project from feasibility to commissioning will result in lower cost. A "time is money" point of view needs to be instilled in both governments and owner agencies in order to benefit the public purse. Agency staff need to be trained to understand the cost of indecision and backtracking on previous decisions. There are examples in the world of big projects that do *not* exceed original budgets, and usually these exist where the culture of "sticking with the plan" is inherent within the owner or client organization.

CHAPTER 13

The Future of Megaprojects

Patricia B. Gary, Esq., Donovan Hatem LLP
Stephen D. Butler, Parsons Brinckerhoff

Introduction

If the future of megaprojects were predicted solely in terms of their past development and delivery process, it would be a bleak future indeed. The history of megaprojects reveals their poor economic track record. Megaprojects cost mega-dollars and often involve mega-disappointments. Megaproject scholar Bent Flyvbjerg notes that the Suez Canal exceeded cost estimates by 1,900 percent and the Channel Tunnel between Britain and France cost 80 percent more than originally estimated.[1] Boston's "Big Dig" Central Artery/Tunnel project replaced an elevated highway with 7.5 miles of underground expressway and a new bridge. An engineering marvel, the project faced enormous challenges from the start, as it was constructed underground in a congested urban area, among existing subway tunnels and utility pipelines, and inches away from historical buildings and skyscrapers in the heart of Boston's financial center. But its price tag also rivaled anything in the history of megaprojects and ultimately affected the public's perception. Regardless of the public's initial enthusiasm for these big projects, their record of actual or, in some cases perceived, cost overruns — 100 percent cost overruns are not unusual — threatens their future, as history leads many to question whether the magnitude of resources committed to these projects, when coupled with their environmental risks and impacts and disruption to the public, simply outweighs their benefits.

Despite their megacosts, however, the reality is that more and more of these large infrastructure projects are needed to meet our nation's growing transportation needs. Although some may label these new projects as grand ambitions gone astray, tragedies including the collapse of the I-35W Minneapolis bridge in 2007 illustrate the deteriorating condition of the public infrastructure in the United States. These tragedies serve as a wake-up call that our bridges and tunnels are aging and crumbling and that major improvements are needed. Upgrading, rehabilitating, and replacing our existing infrastructure is a priority, and new megaprojects designed to enhance or replace the existing infrastructure are necessary.

The bigger problem confronting the infrastructure development process in the Unit-

The Itaipú hydroelectric dam on the Paraná River between Brazil and Paraguay, seen from the Brazil side. It is the largest operational hydroelectric dam in generating capacity, second only to the Three Gorges Dam in total capacity. It is 7,700 meters in length and 196 meters in height. Photo ©2007 by Martin St.-Amant.

ed States is a lack of funding. As the demand for these projects increases, there is simply not enough transportation funding available to state agencies to finance them. And the history of megaprojects is a mixed legacy. The size and scope of the cost overruns and history of project delays has led the public to question whether cost and schedule estimates can be trusted. Critics suggest a need for more accountability in the project development and delivery process, including increased transparency, with a focus on the public's ability to scrutinize all of the information. As a result, the industry is reevaluating methods of project delivery and finding new technologies and financing tools to improve the cost-effectiveness of megaprojects.

President Obama's $787.2 billion economic stimulus package, entitled the American Recovery and Reinvestment Act of 2009 (ARRA), provides nearly $50 billion in federal funds for transportation and infrastructure projects. Of these funds, approximately $29 billion will be distributed by the Federal Highway Administration (FHWA) to states and local communities for highway and bridge projects. In keeping with the intent of Congress to provide capital funding to projects as quickly as possible to create jobs and stimulate both local and national economies, projects eligible for ARRA funds must be "ready to go." Much of the infrastructure stimulus money will be spent on smaller projects, such as the widening, repairing, and resurfacing of roads and highways, as well as for safety enhancements and bridge rehabilitation, rather than for new infrastructure megaprojects. States will have 120 days to obligate the first 50 percent of these funds and up to one year to allocate the balance. The ARRA stimulus funds could be transformational in the area of high-speed rail, as the initial $8 billion slated for high-speed rail projects and the $8.4 billion allocated to transit projects will provide a unique opportunity to jump-start high-speed rail and transit megaprojects that have been held back by the recession and federal rules requiring substantial levels of state matching funds. In the short term, the ARRA funds should provide a down payment to advance the engineering and design of high-speed rail projects but will not be enough to address future funding needs.

In the United States, large infrastructure projects have traditionally relied exclusively on public financing and have been paid for through federal and state funding. Although most public projects are still funded with public money, a lack of public-sector capital threatens the future of megaprojects. Federal, state, and local governments simply do not have enough funding available to undertake more new megaprojects with their associated mega-costs. In response to the very real concern that much-needed infrastructure projects will never get approved or built using traditional delivery and financing methods, the industry is searching for alternative delivery methods and sources of capital. "An emerging trend in the transportation community is to use private-sector dollars to partially or totally finance megaprojects," explains J. Richard Capka, Acting Federal Highway Administrator.[2] Historically, the FHWA financed highways through

the Federal-Aid Highway program, covering up to 80 percent of intrastate project costs and 90 percent of interstate project costs, but today's megaprojects cannot expect the same level of federal funding participation. "In many cases, smaller projects that have captured the interest of local or political stakeholders use up the available Federal funding in a given fiscal year," says Capka. An emerging trend is to leverage private sector capital to partially finance megaprojects. Public-private partnerships are a promising new development in the industry, which already seeks to utilize private-sector financial resources, as well as technical and management resources, to achieve more effective megaprojects. In the face of overwhelming statistical evidence that, historically, project sponsors have underestimated the cost of projects at the time of the decision to build, out of a concern that the project would not be approved if its true cost were known, public-private collaboration may provide a welcome solution. In effect, public-private partnerships transfer the cost of risk on a megaproject to private financiers instead of taxpayers. By putting private capital at risk, instead of relying on public sector funds, the risks shift to the entities best able to understand and protect against them. The belief is that greater private financial participation and risk assumption will lead to increased transparency and a renewed focus on accountability. By transferring the risk of cost overruns to private stakeholders and making private stakeholders bear the consequences of miscalculated cost estimates or forecasts, the theory is that there will be more accountable decision-making.

New Technologies Promise to Provide Solutions for Information Deficits

Issue

At the end of the first decade of the new millennium and the uncertainty of a global economic recession, there is a consensus in the architecture, engineering, and construction (AEC) industry that the future success of megaprojects will depend upon innovative approaches to project delivery. Building information modeling (BIM) has gained the attention of the industry, and the shift in technology is being heralded as a "BIM revolution." Based on parametric CAD technology, the BIM technological evolution in software and data systems utilized by the AEC industry is changing the way both vertical and horizontal projects are being designed, constructed, and delivered.

BIM modeling allows all participants to operate directly from a virtual model that is a central information resource, which increases efficiency by requiring fewer drawings and reduces the potential for errors or inconsistencies. The full potential of BIM is realized when all project participants collaborate in developing a central model. As public and private project owners and sponsors of megaprojects compete for increasingly

limited capital, BIM promises the ability to more efficiently control costs and schedules. If utilized effectively in the future, BIM has the power to reverse the negative image of megaprojects by enabling owners to accurately predict costs, quality, schedule, and sustainability. The criticism of megaprojects — that information about the costs of the projects is not always available — clashes with the "I" (information) in BIM. The BIM database provides the truth at any given time about the project and encourages information sharing and transparency.

Analysis and Discussion

Historically, design professionals relied upon a 2-D drafting design process and physical models.[3] Coordination of different systems was accomplished by overlaying physical drawings on light tables to see if key systems would fit together in the defined space. Drawings for each discipline were viewed on the light table and eventually merged into a composite drawing. On a megaproject, there could be tens of thousands of individual documents for each project, which together would comprise its design, but there would be no way to fully integrate the information in these systems. This process often resulted in design conflicts that would be brought to the designer's attention through a request for information (RFI) process. In the field, for example, the contractor may find that ductwork is hitting pipes or beams. As a design proceeds through development stages, changes made to individual sets of drawings must be reflected in other parties' updated drawings and documents, and errors can occur given the sheer volume of the data. Human interpretation is necessary to coordinate redesign between the various disciplines on a project and update the project drawings. This time-consuming process, where paper must pass through many sets of hands, is eliminated with BIM, since the key concept of BIM is that information is available in a database instead of drawings. With the advent of BIM, the inefficient paper-driven process of the past is becoming obsolete.

One of the advantages of BIM is that it allows the virtual model to automatically adjust to design changes by updating any section or process affected by a change. In "Building Information Modeling: A Framework for Collaboration," Howard W. Ashcraft explains that "because the BIM is a 'computable representation,' every manifestation of the BIM is automatically current. For example, section or elevations are just different manifestations of the BIM information. If you make a change in plan view (and, therefore, to the underlying BIM data), the elevation and sections views that are built from the same BIM data will automatically reflect the changes."[4] Since all other related data in the model automatically reflects the updated information, BIM can detect internal conflicts or "clashes" in the interfaces between building systems, which are commonly the source of contractor claims.[5] Using BIM as a clash-detection tool can provide enormous benefits to a project by reducing RFIs, which in turn reduces costs and delays.

BIM is an emerging innovative technology that can optimize efficiency and minimize waste in the design, building, and operation of a facility or infrastructure by promoting coordination between the different disciplines. BIM utilizes a virtual model and information databases as a central informational resource, allowing all stakeholders and participants in a project to utilize coordinated, reliable information about a project beginning at the design phase. The National Institute of Building Sciences describes BIM this way:

> A Building Information Model, or BIM, utilizes cutting edge digital technology to establish a computable representation of all the physical and functional characteristics of a facility and its related project/life-cycle information, and is intended to be a repository of information for the facility owner/operator to use and maintain throughout the life-cycle of a facility.[6]

Apart from 3-D visualization of a project, the model can leverage data for use in 4-D (scheduling) and 5-D (cost estimating). Three federal agencies — the General Services Administration, the U.S. Army Corps of Engineers, and the U.S. Coast Guard — have instituted an organizational transformation by requiring the use of BIM on all projects.[7] These federal agencies are tapping the potential of BIM to provide construction scheduling as part of a 4-D model, and cost data and estimating functions as part of a 5-D model.

Recommended Practices

BIM promises to transform the way the AEC industry does business. The aerospace, automotive, and shipbuilding industries have utilized virtual building technologies for decades to achieve a high level of quality and exact physical compliance with the model. While the full impact of BIM in the construction industry may not become apparent for another decade, the most immediate implication for megaprojects is that owners can expect much more clarity about cost and schedule in the earlier stages of design development. BIM speeds up the design and construction phases of a project by optimizing efficiency and minimizing waste. The benefits of the BIM model continue for the entire life cycle of the facility or transportation project because the model allows owners to access, extract, or update its information during all phases of the project's existence to make reliable decisions regarding operations and maintenance.

If construction is perceived as a team sport, one of BIM's key benefits is that it allows project participants to view the building model and make changes on the fly. As a result, construction schedules can be reduced significantly, and this speeds the project. Historically, many of the cost overruns on a project occur when information errors create change order requests during construction, resulting in both delays and waste — wasted time, wasted natural resources, wasted energy — which translates into environmental and economic consequences. A report issued by the U.S. National Institute of Standards

Exterior of the Beijing National Aquatics Centre (the "Water Cube"), designed by Arup, PTW Architects, China Construction Design Institute, and China State Construction Engineering Company for the 2008 Summer Olympics. Photo 2008 by Charlie Fong.

and Technology (NIST) in August 2004 quantified interoperability costs for the U.S. capital facilities supply chain in 2002 and estimated "the cost of inadequate interoperability in the U.S. capital facilities industry to be $15.8 billion per year."[8] Although there are costs associated with buying new software and training BIM users to become proficient, the payback in cost savings is large and immediate, as BIM reduces costly change orders by dramatically reducing RFIs and field coordination problems, thereby improving efficiency, productivity, and quality control. Ultimately, BIM will play a role in winning all kinds of projects, including megaprojects.

BIM has already changed the way engineering firms deliver stadium megaprojects. In 2005, engineering and design firm Arup won AIA's Technology in Architectural Practice (TAP) BIM award for its visually stunning and intellectually challenging design concept in the Water Cube project. The Beijing National Swimming Center, known colloquially as the "Water Cube," was the design selected in an international competition for an aquatics stadium to host the 2008 Summer Olympics. The creative force behind the Water Cube was a team comprised of Ove Arup Pty Ltd and PTW Architects, both of Sydney, Australia, and the China State Construction Engineering Corporation (CSCEC) from Beijing. The proposal for the winning entry included requirements for "extensive use of digital technology, energy-reduction, water savings, and use of new construction materials."[9] Dubbed a "masterpiece of structural engineering" and the "cool" building of the 2008 Summer Olympic games, the Water Cube is based on a formation of blue-tone translucent soap bubbles and a natural pattern of organic cells. The Water Cube was designed to be a greenhouse that captures heat energy in the form of solar radiation and optimizes energy use. Constructed of approximately 6,500 tons of steel and clad in a plastic material called ETFE (ethylene tetrafluoroethylene), the soap-bubble building envelope housed the pools for the Olympic swimming and diving competition and seating for 17,000 spectators.

Arup was able to demonstrate the design through the use of BIM and rapid prototyping, a technique drawn from the manufacturing industry.[10] By working with digital 3-D models that were "essentially 'printed out' on-demand in epoxy," the design team was able to present competition judges with a "kit of models." In honoring Arup for the in-

novative project, the AIA noted that "[t]he firm used off-the-shelf software augmented by some custom interfaces, as well as stereolithography, to produce a physical model. The project is a tour de force in the use of 21st century technology."[11]

In the United States, there are a growing number of new stadium and arena megaprojects that use BIM technology. The successful stadium megaprojects recently delivered with BIM include two new professional baseball stadiums: the Washington Nationals ballpark, which opened on March 30, 2008, and the $1.3 billion Yankee Stadium, which opened on April 3, 2009. Other stadium megaprojects being delivered with BIM are the $998 million Meadowlands Stadium in New Jersey, which is slated to open in time for the 2010 football season and will be home to the New York-based Jets and Giants professional football teams, and the new Brooklyn Nets Arena, the future home of the New Jersey Nets basketball team, scheduled to open in 2011.[12] In each of these megaprojects, the project teams utilized BIM for visualizing design and fabrication, detecting clashes, ordering steel, creating bills of materials, and expediting schedule. The project participants found that "sharing a building information model has been a 'win-win' for the whole project team."[13]

Apart from offering the benefits of automatic clash detection and precise quantity takeoffs, which results in better-coordinated construction documents, BIM also allows designers to analyze the environmental performance of a project in the early stages of a design.[14] For example, the building model can be linked to energy analysis tools to determine the building's energy usage.[15] By leveraging information in the model — such as site orientation, mechanical system performance, lighting density, heating and cooling load calculations, ventilation airflow, envelope insulation properties, and building-construction thermal properties — and then linking the building model to energy analysis tools, a consultant can analyze alternative green designs and technologies during the early design phases. The model facilitates the use of "what if" design options and simulations to predict how changes will effect energy usage, and it can help to guide a design to optimize energy performance. This type of energy evaluation is not possible using traditional 2-D tools without a great deal of human intervention and interpretation. Thus, compliance with performance-based criteria such as the U.S. Green Building Council's Leadership in Energy and Environmental Design (LEED) rating system can be difficult to assess at the beginning of a project using traditional methods.

The capability to link the building model to various types of analytical tools provides more insight into the project, encouraging collaboration among project participants for improved environmental performance.[16] The result is better outcomes that are more accurate, predictable, and sustainable based on factors such as water savings, energy efficiency, and materials selection. Sustainable design is no longer just an interesting concept — states and countries around the world are enacting sustainable-design legislation that requires compliances with performance-based criteria. California, Australia, and the

Artist's depiction of One World Trade Center, designed by Skidmore, Owings & Merrill, under construction and projected to be completed by 2013. Image courtesy of SOM.

European Union have already implemented building regulations that mandate sustainable design for new construction.

In July 2008, California became the first state in the nation to adopt a green building code. The California Green Building Standards Code, Title 24, Part 11, will be voluntary until 2010, when its provisions are expected to become mandatory.[17] The standards apply to all commercial and residential construction in the public and private sectors, including all schools, hospitals, and other public institutions. In New York City, Local Law 86, also known as the Green City Buildings Act, became effective on January 1, 2007, and requires new municipal buildings and renovations to existing municipal buildings in the five boroughs to meet LEED Silver certification standards.[18] In Washington, D.C., the Green Building Act of 2006 requires that all District public buildings meet the LEED certification standards.[19] As architects and engineers strive to provide more energy-efficient buildings and more accurate building performance analyses, BIM technology allows them to simulate, analyze, and document their designs more efficiently and can accelerate the process for LEED certification.

The $3 billion One World Trade Center in New York City, due to be completed in 2013, is an example of a megaproject that is using BIM to achieve LEED Gold certification. After the tragic events of September 11, 2001, rebuilding at the Ground Zero site of the World Trade Center Twin Towers became a matter of national pride. Reminiscent of historic New York skyscrapers, One World Trade Center will evoke the slender tapering form of the Empire State Building (designed in the Roaring Twenties and completed in the Great Depression year of 1931) but it will "speak about the future and hope as it rises into the sky in a faceted crystalline form filled with, and reflecting, light."[20] The mast at the top, which contains a television and communications antenna[21]—called the "Beacon of Freedom"—will emit light and rise to a final height of 1,776 feet, symbolic of the year of America's independence.

The architectural firm Skidmore, Owings & Merrill (SOM) used BIM technology to create a design with cutting-edge innovation in air quality, energy efficiency, daylighting, water conservation, materials conservation, and clean construction. One World Trade Center will achieve LEED Gold certification by:

- Collecting rainwater for cooling and irrigation
- Using recycled-content building materials
- Using wind turbines and solar panels to generate energy
- Enhancing the collection and use of daylight[22]
- Using one of the world's largest fuel cell installations, totaling 4.8 megawatts of clean, quiet, efficient, on-site energy capacity[23]

SOM is using BIM technology to coordinate systems from the basement of One World Trade Center to the top of the communications spire in order to minimize environmental impact and maximize operational efficiency. The building will also include state-of-the-art security and safety design. LEED Gold certification assures that when it is completed, One World Trade Center will stand as a national symbol of hope, commitment, and belief in a sustainable future.

Civil Engineers Can Implement BIM for Highway and Road Projects

Issue

BIM is still in its infancy, but forward-looking engineers already realize that it applies not just to buildings. Although the benefits of the BIM model and its new approaches to delivery were first applied in vertical construction, civil engineers are responding by incorporating BIM into horizontal construction projects. The idea that BIM's benefits extend to civil, environmental, and transportation engineering is sound thinking, because this segment of the industry can leverage the information model in the same way to optimize road and highway projects from the preliminary design through construction and into operations.

Analysis and Discussion

The domain of civil engineering has traditionally been on the outside of the building, and for this reason, civil engineers have not embraced BIM as quickly as architects. BIM evolved from the aerospace, automotive, and shipbuilding industries and has its conceptual roots in architecture in the AEC industry. But it is only a matter of time before the BIM concepts and model are adopted for everything that is megacostly to build. In this sense, the "B" in BIM should not be perceived as vertical building, but all kinds of building projects, including road, highway, underground transportation, and tunnel projects.

With more public owners challenging the delays and cost overruns that plague megaprojects, the AEC industry is searching for better methods of project delivery. In the road and highway design process, BIM allows coordination of reliable design information about the project, and enhances constructability, sustainability, road safety, and

environmental protection. The same principle of entering data-rich information and then linking it to a model to coordinate all of the elements of design and construction can be applied to road and highway design. In "What Does BIM Mean for Civil Engineers?" Adam Strafaci explains, "The most immediate benefits of BIM for road and highway design are better designs and increased efficiency and productivity. Because design and construction documentation are dynamically linked, the time needed to evaluate more alternatives, execute design changes, and produce construction documentation is reduced significantly. This is particularly important for transportation agencies because it can shorten the time to contract letting, resulting in projects being completed sooner and within more predictable timetables."[24]

For highway and road projects BIM allows data about site grades and slopes, vertical curves, geotechnical information, road geometry, parameters related to sight distances, traffic capacity, stormwater drainage, noise, and lighting to be integrated in a central database so that engineers can optimize their designs by evaluating more design alternatives. BIM allows an engineer to more effectively analyze sustainability at the design phase, with the aim of reducing the environmental impacts of construction projects. The U.S. Green Building Council's Leadership in Energy and Environmental Design for New Construction (LEED-NC) has developed rating systems that include credits for the "smart location" of projects in order to conserve natural resources and reduce environmental impacts. As LEED and green design become the standard, BIM will enhance the ability of engineers to leverage all of the information from the model to achieve the optimal design.

Finally, BIM has the potential to reduce RFIs on horizontal projects in the same way as vertical projects, by revealing discrepancies or clashes during the design phase, before errors are made after construction begins.

Recommended Practices

Innovative engineers are starting to apply BIM to highway, road, and underground transportation projects such as subways and tunnels, as well as to sanitary, sewer, and water distribution systems. Apart from its benefits in design, BIM enables the project team to better track the schedule. As owners demand more clarity about costs and schedule, BIM promises more predictability about budgets and cost estimates and will provide a competitive edge in the business of megaprojects.

Since BIM is a new, cutting-edge technology, there are relatively few megaproject case studies demonstrating how it can create value for stakeholders and transform the industry. Educators and academic institutions are just beginning to discuss ways to incorporate collaborative modeling into the undergraduate civil engineering curriculum. In "Work in Progress: How Building Informational Modeling May Unify IT in the Civil

Engineering Curriculum," Michael J. Casey of George Mason University points out the need to keep the undergraduate curriculum in line with the needs of the industry. He suggests "embedding BIM in the civil engineering curriculum with the goal of defining and promoting an extensible skill set that is reinforced through a comprehensive transportation design problem."[25] Casey comments that "If BIM emerges as the lingua franca for building design and construction, and evidence of that trend is increasing, then the need for civil engineers to participate in the interdisciplinary design process using the common BIM skill set will be important." The message from educators seems clear: the next generation of engineers will need to embrace both the concept and technology.

Liability Concerns Arising from Building Information Modeling and Industry Responses

Issue

BIM makes it possible for all of the information about the design, construction, and operations of a project to be exchanged from each project participant's own model and integrated into one unified data source, sometimes referred to as the "federated model" for the project.[26] The "M" in BIM refers to this federated model, which consists of linked but distinct component models that can all exchange information between their software platforms and the one federated model for the project. Despite the advantages of sharing information, the liability implications are numerous. Along with the rapidly evolving technology, concerns emerged that BIM might blur the boundaries between the project participants. With growing collaboration, industry leaders questioned whether regulatory controls, which protect the public through the requirement of "responsible control," would be sufficient to govern contributions to and use of the model.

The architect and engineer are the only registered professionals in the construction process, and the public relies on these registered professionals to safeguard the public's interest. The National Council of Architectural Registration Boards (NCARB) has promulgated a legal standard of responsible control for an architect of record who signs and seals documents.

Most states have adopted the "responsible control" standard as part of their professional licensing statutes. With the advent of BIM, an issue arose about the degree to which design professionals can rely upon model information provided by other project participants, or even changes made by the modeling software itself. Industry experts questioned how the architects' standard of care would evolve with BIM, when the project is not designed or delivered in the traditional way. Recognizing that new technologies such as BIM are changing the way projects are designed, constructed, and delivered, the NCARB established an Integrated Project Delivery (IPD) Task Force,

which held a hearing in October 2008 to address these issues and to determine whether changes were needed in the current Model Law in response to BIM and the IPD project delivery process.[27] The NCARB task force was charged with determining whether existing professional licensing statutes should be modified to reflect the realities of our new digital age.

In 2008, the NCARB standard provided that "[a]n architect may sign and seal technical submissions prepared by non-architects only if the technical submissions were prepared by persons under the architect's responsible control." The NCARB Rules of Conduct[28] defined "responsible control" to mean:

> That amount of control over and detailed professional knowledge of the content of technical submissions during their preparation as is ordinarily exercised by architects applying the required professional standard of care. Reviewing, or reviewing and correcting, technical submissions after they have been prepared by others does not constitute the exercise of responsible control because the reviewer has neither control over nor detailed knowledge of such submissions throughout their preparation.

The 2009 NCARB task force recommended modifications to the NCARB's Legislative Guidelines and Model Law to more explicitly address how BIM technology and IPD may affect responsible control by architects. At the NCARB's Annual Meeting and Conference in Chicago in June 2009, the Council's 54 member boards voted to pass Resolution 2009-01 and amend the definition of "responsible control," as follows:

> That amount of control over and detailed professional knowledge of the content of technical submissions during their preparation as is ordinarily exercised by a registered architect applying the required standard of care, *including but not limited to an architect's integration of information from manufacturers, suppliers, installers, the architect's consultants, owners, contractors or other sources the architect reasonably trusts that is incidental to and intended to be incorporated into the architect's technical submissions if the architect has coordinated and reviewed such information.* Other review, or review and correction, of technical submissions after they have been prepared by others does not constitute the exercise of responsible control because the reviewer has neither control over nor detailed professional knowledge of the content of such submissions throughout their preparation [emphasis added].[29]

The NCARB's new definition of responsible control recognizes that when there are more collaborators on a project, the concept of responsible control becomes critically important. Responsible control remains the mandatory duty of all licensed design professionals irrespective of whether they are sharing a federated model with contractors or other project participants through new tools such as BIM, or whether a new project delivery method is being utilized. Issuance of a building permit presumes that stamped

and sealed documents were prepared under the responsible control of a licensed design professional.

Analysis and Discussion

Industry groups representing both architects and contractors are responding to these concerns and have recently developed standard form contract documents that propose best practices for the use of BIM. The ConsensusDOCS group, which represents owners, contractors, subcontractors, and sureties, released the first standard contract document addressing the use of BIM. In September 2007, ConsensusDOCS, a coalition of 22 leading construction industry groups including the Associated General Contractors of America (AGC), jointly published the ConsensusDOCS family of standard construction documents. Subsequently, ConsensusDOCS began working on a BIM Addendum to provide contractual procedures for utilizing BIM on a project. On June 30, 2008, ConsensusDOCS released the BIM Addendum, the first standard form document to address BIM.[30] The BIM Addendum has been endorsed by 17 construction associations, including the AGC.

The creators of the BIM Addendum describe it as a fair document and not geared to any industry constituency. It establishes a detailed framework of contractual issues to be considered by the parties but also leaves many decisions regarding these issues up to the contracting parties. Article 3 (Information Management) requires the "Owner or its designated representative" to appoint one or more information managers for the project and provides three checkboxes to specify the entity selected, whether "architect/engineer," "contractor/construction manager," or "other." The information manager is a gatekeeper responsible for controlling access to the model, performing backup, maintaining model security, maintaining system logs, and providing authorized users with access instructions and system requirements. Liability concerns have been a disincentive to design professionals embracing BIM, but if they are not willing to do so in the future, the BIM Addendum contemplates that owners may seek BIM delivery methods that are contractor-driven.

Within 30 days after contract execution, the BIM Addendum requires all project participants to meet and use their best efforts to consider a checklist of 29 issues, procedures, and protocols for implementing BIM and then agree upon the terms of a BIM Execution Plan. The parties must establish a schedule for BIM development and coordination, including clash detection meetings among the project participants. Under the risk allocation principle set forth in Article 5 (Risk Allocation) of the BIM Addendum, each party is responsible for its own contributions to a model. Lastly, the BIM Addendum addresses intellectual property rights by clarifying that the BIM contributors retain a copyright to their own contributions, but grant to each other a limited nonexclusive

license to use each other's contributions for the sole purpose of work on the project, until final completion of the project.

Three months after the BIM Addendum was released, the design side of the industry released its own standard form of contract addressing the use of BIM. In October 2008, the American Institute of Architects (AIA) released AIA contract document E202-2008, a standard form Building Information Modeling Protocol Exhibit.[31] The AIA E202-2008 form focuses on the Levels of Development of a model. These levels of development, or LODs, describe the level of completeness to which a model is developed at each phase of the project and establish authorized uses of the information. The LODs are useful in establishing a line between the designer of record and the other project participants supplying information.

Article 3 of AIA E202-2008, for example, identifies the specific content requirements and authorized uses for each model element at five progressively detailed levels of completeness. In early levels of development, the model is in a conceptualization phase. Each progressive level builds on the previous level and includes all the characteristics of the previous level. At LOD 200, the criteria design phase, model elements are required to be "generalized" systems or assemblies with "approximate" quantities, size, shape, location, and orientation, and may be used for analysis, cost estimating, and scheduling based on this approximate and generalized data. At LOD 300, the detailed design phase, the model elements are required to be "specific assemblies accurate in terms of quantity, size, shape, location and orientation," and are then authorized for use in the generation of traditional construction documents and shop drawings. At LOD 400, the implementation documents phase, the model contains complete fabrication, assembly, and detailing information, and at LOD 500, at the conclusion of the construction phase, the model shows a virtual as-built likeness of "constructed assemblies actual and accurate." If implemented effectively, the LODs contemplated by AIA E202-2008 will provide snapshots of the model at different design phases that can be archived for record-keeping purposes and to demonstrate responsible control.

A Model Element Table in AIA E202-2008 (Article 4, § 4.3) identifies the LOD required for each model element at the end of each phase of the project. The Model Element Table also identifies the Model Element Author (MEA) for each element, who is the party responsible for developing the content of a specific model element to the LOD. The abbreviations "A-Architect," or "C-Contractor" are to be used to identify the MEA in the Model Element Table. The AIA form clarifies that the architect will be the model manager from the inception of the project, but this responsibility may be assigned to another party at another phase of the project. AIA E202-2008 assigns to the model manager the ongoing responsibilities to collect, log, and coordinate submission and exchange of models, validate that files are complete and usable, and maintain archives and backup. Similar to the BIM Addendum, AIA E202-2008 views the model manager as a

gatekeeper. But unlike the BIM Addendum, developed by the construction side of the industry, AIA E202-2008 contemplates that the architect will, at least initially, be the model manager and explicitly assigns to the model manager the responsibility to perform clash detection and issue periodic clash detection reports.

Recommended Practices

The construction and design sides of the industry have produced separate standard contract documents in response to the demands of these different industry segments for guidance in how to contractually address the legal uncertainties and risks associated with using BIM technology. Public and private owners are beginning to require the use of BIM on their projects, and these new standard documents can assist parties on all types of projects, including megaprojects, in developing their own contractual language. Each of these standard forms offers a useful checklist to consider in developing and defining the business relationship and clarifying the responsibilities of the parties. One consideration identified in the BIM Addendum, "the expected content of each Model and the required level of detail at various Project milestones," is more fully addressed by the AIA E202-2008 standard form, which outlines specific LOD content requirements and associated uses of model elements at five project phases. The LOD approach to BIM promotes the concept of responsible control because the architect or engineer may create an electronic record of how the project developed through different milestones to demonstrate that he or she exercised continuous and thorough involvement and maintained close coordination and control during a project.

On other issues, such as who will manage the model during the different phases of a project, the BIM Addendum provides choices, whereas AIA E202-2008 clarifies that the architect will manage the model from the inception of the project. Because roles and relationships can become blurred with the use of BIM, it is critical that agreements spell out the roles, duties, rights, and obligations of the parties using this new technology.

New Project Delivery Methods Encourage Collaboration, Team Building, and Open Information Sharing

Design-Bid-Build

Issue

In the United States, the design-bid-build (DBB) delivery model is currently the most widely used, particularly in state construction projects. State-legislated bidding processes typically require that open bidding be used in public construction projects because competitive bidding achieves the lowest possible price and fosters open market com-

petition, where there is less political pressure to select a given contractor.[32] The traditional DBB project delivery approach involves separate contracts between the owner and architect for design, and between the owner and the constructor for construction of the project. Each discipline operates independently of the other. The architect might hire specialists for the design of each building system by, for example, contracting with a consulting engineer for design of the mechanical system and with different engineers for design of the electrical systems and plumbing. These designs are provided in specification sections for the contractor and its subcontractors to construct and install, but the constructor is not involved until the design is complete. Each of these disciplines — designer, engineers, consultants, contractor, and subcontractors — is contractually walled off from the others.

Analysis and Discussion

In the vernacular of the AEC industry, traditional delivery and contracting approaches are characterized by "silos," which can be viewed as each project participant protecting its own financial interests, in part by maintaining its own information. Drawing bright lines between these silos has been a hallmark of construction law, where clear delineations of responsibility are used to control risks and determine both liability and insurability. Because of its structure, the DBB delivery model does not foster early involvement of the constructor in the design process. Constructability problems are often not discovered until the construction phase, when issues regarding design, coordination, unanticipated site conditions, new client requirements, or previously unknown errors need to be resolved through a request for information (RFI) process. This is a notoriously slow and time-consuming process. RFIs may begin to pile up, and the accompanying change order (CO) process, by which the RFI may be resolved, can take weeks or months and frequently leads to legal disputes, sometimes causing the project to reach a standstill.[33]

Traditional "silo-thinking" chills communication and information sharing, and the result is that projects often take too long and cost too much. Owners' demands for improved project performance have led industry participants to seek alternative project delivery methods to overcome the problems of cost overruns, waste, and inefficiency.

Integrated Project Delivery

Integrated project delivery (IPD) has emerged as a new method of organizing project teams guided by principles of trust, collaboration, information sharing, shared rewards and liabilities, and shared risk, with team success tied to project success. In June 2007, the American Institute of Architects California Council issued *Integrated Project Delivery:*

A Guide, a comprehensive study of IPD and the many variations of multiparty agreements. The *Guide* defines IPD as follows:

> Integrated Project Delivery (IPD) is a project delivery approach that integrates people, systems, business structures and practices into a process that collaboratively harnesses the talents and insights of all participants to optimize project results, increase value to the owner, reduce waste, and maximize efficiency through all phases of design, fabrication, and construction.

IPD principles can be applied to a variety of contractual arrangements and IPD teams can include members well beyond the basic triad of owner, architect, and contractor. In all cases, integrated projects are uniquely distinguished by highly effective collaboration among the owner, the prime designer, and the prime constructor, commencing at early design and continuing through to project handover.[34]

IPD has an advantage over previous team-oriented project delivery models, such as partnering, because it can leverage new technologies, such as BIM, which when utilized with a collaborative process, may forever change the way projects are designed and delivered.

Building a collaborative team of key project participants, including the three major stakeholder groups, i.e., owners, designers, and constructors, is the core principle of IPD. Collaboration is built on trust, with responsibilities defined in a "no-blame culture leading to identification and resolution of problems, not determination of liability."[35] The key participants may be contractually bound together by signing a multiparty agreement, such as the AIA C191-2009 Standard Form Multi-Party Integrated Project Delivery Agreement, or key participants may decide to form a single purpose entity (SPE), such as a limited liability company (LLC) established for the project. Both arrangements align individual success with project success, which is the heart and soul of IPD. Internal disputes are resolved by a dispute resolution committee, or the parties may utilize a "project neutral" to reach a consensus in the best interests of the project. Most IPD form agreements, including the AIA C191-2009, require the participants to agree to a "no suit" provision in their contract, in which they waive first-party claims among each other except for willful default. In all IPD contracts, a project contingency is utilized and must be of a sufficient amount in relationship to the estimated construction costs to fund the decisions of the dispute resolution committee. This contingency covers increases in construction costs that may arise from errors and omissions in the project documents, incorrect construction cost estimates, construction resequencing, and other events. The IPD approach allows the project parties to share risk and eliminates the traditional adversarial approach to liability that creates inefficiency and waste.[36]

IPD contracts are more complicated than traditional construction contracts and require project participants to "do the tough homework" on the project prior to entering

into an IPD arrangement. Many project-specific questions must be answered prior to the execution of an IPD contract, such as project contingencies, incentives, and goals. In October 2009, the AIA issued a new standard form agreement, the AIA C191-2009, for use on IPD projects. The AIA C191-2009 is a standard form multi-party agreement through which the owner, architect, contractor, and other key project participants execute a single agreement for the design and construction of a project. This newest IPD document differs from the AIA C195-2008, Standard Form Single Purpose Entity (SPE), which was released in May 2008, because the parties do not form an LLC under the new C191-2009 and instead continue to operate as separate entities. Under the new C191-2009, the parties continue to play their traditional roles but execute one coordinated and integrated agreement that clearly sets forth their roles and responsibilities in delivering the project consistent with the principles of IPD. The AIA's new Standard Form Multi-Party Agreement for IPD is premised on delivery of the project through shared effort, risk, and reward, and reflects the industry's shift away from working in silos. IPD contemplates collaboration among owners, architects, and contractors and allows project teams to harness the full capabilities of collaborative methods and tools such as BIM. Although the C 191-2009 form does not require use of a building information model, it envisions that the parties will employ BIM and IPD together. Section 1.14 provides:

> The Parties agree, where practicable, to employ collaborative technologies such as Building Information Modeling (BIM) and digital collaboration tools. The Project Management Team may choose to augment Models with additional materials including, but not limited to, physical models, renderings, sketches, drawings, reports, or specifications.

If the parties are using BIM, they may utilize Exhibit D, Target Criteria Amendment, or Exhibit FF, Digital Data Protocol. These exhibits allow the parties to identify how electronic data will be used and exchanged on the project and suggest that the parties attach a completed AIA E201-2007 Digital Data Protocol Exhibit or similar document to their agreement. Additionally, the parties may utilize Exhibit GG, Building Information Modeling Protocol, which allows the parties to identify and determine how they will utilize building information modeling on the project and suggests that the parties attach a completed AIA E202-2008 Building Information Modeling Protocol Exhibit or similar document to their agreement. The AIA's new IPD standard form documents will assist parties who are interested in negotiating and executing an IPD agreement.

As contractual frameworks are developed for IPD, it can be expected that integrated multiparty agreements will continue to vary in form and be customized to respond to the specific needs of a project and its participants.[37] Negotiating and drafting a multiparty agreement is a time-consuming and costly process, and it is typically used only on larger projects. The *Guide* points out three general forms of multiparty agreements that have already emerged: project alliances, single-purpose entities, and relational con-

tracts.[38] In each, the primary project participants execute a single contract, whereby they are bound together in a team environment to achieve team goals and some portion of compensation is tied to project success. Team process design is critical, with incentives, compensation, accountability, decision-making, and other factors determined on a project-by-project basis.[39] Project alliances were developed in the North Sea oil industry to support oil exploration, and have been used extensively in Australia.[40] In an integrated single purpose entity, the SPE bears unlimited responsibility for project outcomes, although key participants have an equity interest in the SPE and could lose their equity contributions if a major loss occurs.[41] Under relational contracts, the owner bears the risk that the project does not meet financial goals.[42] Each form of multiparty agreement calls for integrated processes that rely on a collaborative team approach to achieve a successful project.

Recommended Practices

IPD methodologies require a change in industry culture because they break down the traditional silos of responsibility. IPD projects embrace openness and transparency by blending the design and construction process, restructuring the form and relationship of the parties, and redefining the financial rewards and risks for all project participants. However, in many states, public entities cannot use the IPD format unless new legislation is enacted, due to state-regulated bidding requirements.[43] Parties wishing to use IPD will need to identify the business model that is best suited to their needs, and IPD may be accomplished by transitioning existing project delivery models to enhance the level of integration and collaboration on the project.

Design-Build

The design-build (DB) process is well suited to increasing collaboration between the design and construction teams because it already places responsibility for both design and construction activities in one contractual entity.[44] The DB model is becoming more popular in the United States, and the Design Build Institute of America (DBIA) estimates that in 2006, at least 40 percent of U.S. construction projects relied on a DB procurement approach.[45] Some governmental organizations, such as the Army, Navy, Air Force, and GSA, are reporting even higher rates (50–70 percent) of reliance on DB.[46] Under the DB model, the owner contracts directly with the design-build team to develop a project design. By combining design and construction in one entity, a higher level of coordination is achieved. The design-builder accepts the owner's design criteria, and after the owner's design modifications are implemented a final cost estimate for the project is established. The owner's role is then diminished, as the design-builder

becomes responsible for any further design changes. The design-builder accepts most of the risk, and the project can be completed faster because construction begins before the design is complete and construction drawings are finalized.

The federal government has used design-build extensively for over a decade, based on the authorization granted by the Federal Acquisition Streamlining Act of 1994 (FASA) and the National Defense Authorization Act of 1996.[47] In 1997, the Federal Acquisition Regulations were amended to incorporate design-build procedures.[48] A decade ago, DB procurement was still in conflict with most states' low-bid statutes for construction of public projects, as well as state professional licensing statutes, and there was little authority to use DB in the public sector.[49] That has now changed, and most state legislatures have passed laws that enable public agencies to use DB on public projects.

In delivery methods such as DB, where the constructor is brought into the project early, there are increased opportunities for implementing IPD methods and a new technology such as BIM to promote better outcomes for both public and private projects. Design-build agreements can be modified to reflect an integrated delivery approach by clarifying the roles of participants and their scope of services. The compensation model may be altered to create incentives for increased collaboration and the sharing of risk, and requirements may be added for design consultants to transfer BIM model data and incorporate information from related trade contractors and vendors.[50] In this sense, BIM would serve as a platform for collaboration and would work hand in hand with IPD methods to achieve the DB project goals.[51]

Transitioning to Public–Private Partnerships for Highway and Transit Infrastructure

Issue

Public-private partnerships (PPPs) are another new model of project delivery that emerged recently in response to owner and client demands. A public-private partnership is a contractual arrangement between public and private sectors to privately deliver a service or project that is traditionally provided by the public sector. The federal government has recognized that traditional approaches to funding and procuring highway and transit projects are failing and it is encouraging PPPs as an innovative approach that can reduce project costs, accelerate project delivery, and transfer project risks to the private sector.

The PPP model allows transportation agencies to tap private sources of capital that would otherwise be unavailable to improve the financial performance and schedule of highway and transit projects. PPPs are innovative contractual arrangements between public and private sector entities that leverage private-sector capital as well as techni-

cal and management resources. Unlike the traditional design-bid-build form of procurement, in which the public agency contracts with an engineering firm to perform design work and then separately contracts with a construction firm through a competitive low bid process, PPPs are based on a single private entity assuming the contractual risk and responsibility for performing all or many project functions.[52]

Analysis and Discussion

The private partner in a PPP is typically a consortium of private companies, or a private concessionaire. Prior to 2005, long-term concession-based PPPs were rarely considered or implemented in the United States, but subsequently they have become more prevalent.[53] In July 2008, the United States Department of Transportation (USDOT) issued the report, *Innovation Wave: An Update on the Burgeoning Private Sector Role in U.S. Highway and Transit Infrastructure*, a comprehensive examination of the unprecedented use of PPPs in the United States over the previous three years. The report attributes the growing number of PPPs in the U.S. to a government and industry response to failures of the traditional approaches to transportation funding and procurement. On a more positive note, however, USDOT advises that "a staggering amount of private capital has been raised over the last two years for investment in global infrastructure."[54] USDOT reports that there are currently more than 20 long-term concession-based PPP projects at various stages of procurement in the U.S. and that the value of each of these PPPs ranges from a few hundred million dollars to billions of dollars. By 2008, a total of 25 states had enacted legislation authorizing public authorities to enter into PPPs for highway or transit projects.

Public-private partnerships make sense on many levels, and in the immediate future we can anticipate there will be an increased utilization of long-term concession-based PPPs to finance megaprojects. Transportation resources are scarce and there is not enough public-sector capital to undertake the backlog of critical highway, bridge, and transit projects that are needed to enhance and rehabilitate the existing infrastructure. The unsustainability of the fuel tax has also been an important factor in the government's decision to consider alternative sources of revenue. Historically, revenue from the gas tax has been the principal source of funding for the Highway Trust Fund, but it can no longer keep pace with the need for refurbishing and improving transportation infrastructure. The government relies on fuel taxes to fund transportation projects, and the National Commission on Surface Transportation is urging Congress to raise federal gasoline and diesel taxes by 50 percent. This creates a conundrum because federal tax revenue does not increase unless gas consumption increases — which conflicts with national efforts to reduce emissions, promote alternative energies, and seek alternative fuel development. Additionally, rising fuel prices have already caused motorists to drive

less, resulting in less tax revenue to fund transportation improvements. PPPs help to align transportation policy with energy and environmental policies by substituting private capital for fuel-tax revenue.

The federal government is encouraging PPPs through a number of initiatives designed to increase the role of the private sector in highway and transit projects, and help state and local agencies to fund megaprojects. These initiatives include the Private Activity Bonds program, the Transportation Infrastructure Finance and Innovation Act (TIFIA) program, Interstate Tolling programs, the Special Experimental Project Number 15 (SEP-15) program, the Corridors of the Future Program, and FTA's PPP Pilot Program.[55] PPPs are emerging as a good fit to provide a solution to the failings of the traditional transportation funding system. A recent GAO report explains that "[p]rivate companies, driven by the need to make a return on investment, are incentivized to manage assets and provide services in efficient ways."[56] Consolidation of design, construction, and operation in one private entity can result in enormous cost savings efficiencies. Additionally, by raising private capital instead of public debt, PPPs can free up public funds for other purposes.

Recommended Practices

The United States Department of Transportation is encouraging use of the PPP model of delivery for highway and transportation megaprojects. The three most prominent PPPs in recent years to reach a commercial close are the landmark $3.8 billion Indiana Toll Road PPP, the $1.8 billion Chicago Skyway PPP, and the $1.8 billion Capital Beltway HOT Lanes PPP.[57] The momentum toward PPPs is increasing, and in 2008 there were more than 20 major highway and transit PPP projects at various stages of procurement.

The Chicago Skyway PPP was the first long-term concession of an existing toll road in the United States.[58] In January 2005, after a competitive bidding process, the city of Chicago closed a deal on a $1.8 billion concession to operate and maintain the Chicago Skyway, a 7.8-mile toll road, with a private consortium made up of Cintra Concesiones de Infraestructuras de Transporte S.A., a Spanish toll road developer, and Macquarie Infrastructure Group, an Australian toll road developer and operator. The concessionaire paid the city of Chicago the full $1.8 billion up front.[59] The concessionaire was granted the right to collect all toll revenue during a 99-year term in exchange for operating and maintaining the toll road for 99 years. Following this PPP transaction, the Indiana Finance Authority initiated a competitive bidding process for a concession to operate and maintain the Indiana Toll Road, and a private consortium of Cintra and Macquarie was also awarded this concession. These two landmark deals in 2005 drew attention to the amount of private capital that can be raised up front through PPPs.[60]

Texas is also at the forefront of the nation's current trend to use PPPs for new capital improvements to transportation infrastructure. In 2002, the Texas Department of Transportation (TxDOT) entered into a design-build agreement (PPP/concession agreement) with a consortium made up of Fluor Corporation, Balfour Beatty Construction, and T.J. Lambrecht for the $1.5 billion Central Texas Turnpike toll road project.[61] More recently, Texas committed to using concession-based PPPs for the design, construction, financing, operation, and maintenance of a new proposed network of superhighway corridors called the Trans-Texas Corridor (TTC) projects. In 2005, TxDOT signed an agreement with a private consortium made up of Cintra and Zachry Construction Corporation for the design, construction, and operation of the first Trans-Texas Corridor. The Cintra-led consortium submitted a proposal specifying that it would invest $6 billion to design, construct, and operate a portion of TTC-35 and would make a payment of $1.2 billion for the right to build and operate this segment of the road as a toll facility.

In addition to the TTC corridors, TxDOT is considering PPPs for several other projects that are at various stages of development — but one of these projects has already provided a significant "lesson learned" about the federal requirement to conduct a fair, open, and competitive PPP procurement process.[62] The PPP procurement for the SH-121 project, a 25.9-mile electronic toll road in Collin, Dallas, and Denton counties, was cancelled due to the actions of the Texas State Legislature in compromising the integrity of the public procurement process. In August 2006, the North Texas Tollway Authority (NTTA) signed an agreement that it would not bid on the project. Afterwards, TxDOT approved a private proposal worth over $5 billion submitted by a consortium made up of Cintra and JP Morgan Asset Management. However, notwithstanding TxDOT's initial selection of the private consortium, the Texas State Legislature was determined to have NTTA win the contract, and it enacted legislation directing TxDOT to waive the NTTA agreement and allow NTTA to submit a competing proposal for the SH-121 project. When NTTA subsequently offered a much higher concession fee, it was awarded the contract to build and operate the new tollway for 50 years. In June 2007, the Texas Transportation Commission approved the award of the SH-121 project to NTTA instead of the competitively selected consortium.[63]

The Federal Highway Administration advised TxDOT that the procurement process committed at least two violations of federal laws. First, allowing NTTA to submit a proposal after the selection process was completed violated the federal requirement under 23 U.S.C. § 112 to conduct a fair and open competitive process.[64] FHWA regulations set forth in 23 C.F.R. § 636.103 define "competitive acquisition" as an acquisition process which is designed to foster an impartial and comprehensive evaluation of offerors' proposals, and regulations 23 C.F.R. §§ 636.115 and 636.507 prohibit disclosure of information to one bidder that would create an unfair competitive advantage.[65] In a letter written by FHWA Administrator J. Richard Capka, the FHWA stated that TxDOT's

procurement process was an egregious violation of these provisions, because NTTA was given the unfair advantage of analyzing the Cintra-led consortium's publicly disclosed submission, including the final bid and many proprietary details, prior to submitting its own proposal. Second, a public entity such as NTTA is prohibited by FHWA regulations 23 C.F.R. § 635.112(e) from bidding against a private entity.

The FHWA threatened to impose serious sanctions, including: withdrawals of approvals for TIFIA federal loan and Private Activity Bonds support pursuant to the Safe, Accountable, Flexible, Efficient Transportation Equity Act: A Legacy for Users (SAFETEA-LU); withdrawal of the special exceptions program (SEP-15) waiver granted to expedite SH-121 and two other projects for accelerated environmental clearance; a request for reimbursement of all expenses incurred in considering the proposed TIFIA loan; and no future allocation of any federal-aid funds for projects associated with SH-121. To avoid these sanctions, TxDOT took actions to cancel the procurement for the SH-121 project. There are many lessons to be learned, but USDOT has stated the message simply: "[w]hen introducing private sector involvement in transportation projects through PPPs, state and local entities need to be vigilant to ensure that the procurement process is, and is perceived to be, fair and competitive."[66]

Not all states have enacted legislation enabling PPPs. In Massachusetts, for example, a Transportation Finance Commission has only recently issued a report recommending that the state consider PPPs as an alternative to traditional funding approaches.[67]

American Recovery and Reinvestment Act of 2009

Issue

During the presidential campaign, President Obama spoke about his vision for a future high-speed passenger rail network as part of his plan to "rebuild America." He spoke of relieving congestion, reducing greenhouse gases, and improving energy conservation by launching a new era of clean, safe, sustainable high-speed rail transportation. Although plans for high-speed rail have languished for years in America due to lack of funding,[68] high-speed rail service exists in France, Spain, Italy, China, Korea, and Japan, where trains now move at speeds of 200 miles per hour, compared with the average speed of 80 miles per hour for American trains.[69] These European and Asian countries have invested hundreds of billions of dollars to develop high-speed rail systems (Japan is already working on a new line to connect Tokyo and Osaka at 300 miles per hour). As noted by one commentator, "[h]igh-speed trains use one-third as much energy as comparable air travel and consume less than one-fifth as much energy as driving. This is a proven technology that America can adopt and protect its status as a mobility super power."[70]

Nevertheless, when the House Appropriations Committee was drafting its bill to re-

suscitate the economy in January 2009, funding for a high-speed rail was not included in the stimulus bill.[71] White House Chief of Staff Rahm Emanuel first asked House and Senate negotiators for $2 billion in funding just days before the Senate Appropriations Committee met, and then increased his request to $10 billion in the final closed-door bargaining.[72] When President Obama signed the $787.2 billion American Recovery and Reinvestment Act of 2009 (ARRA) on February 17, 2009, it dedicated $8 billion to high-speed rail. The surprise decision by the House-Senate conferees to quadruple funding for high-speed rail projects means many states will be in line to compete for this funding. The intent of this landmark investment in green infrastructure is to create jobs, reduce America's dependence on foreign oil, reverse global climate change, and build a green economy. It is a symbol of the Obama administration's new vision for America.

Analysis and Discussion

In total, the economic stimulus bill allocates nearly $50 billion in federal funds to transportation. The National Railroad Passenger Corporation (Amtrak), created by Congress in 1970, will receive $1.3 billion of the stimulus funds. The money dedicated to Amtrak is slated primarily for infrastructure repair and improvement. In addition to the $8 billion allocated for future high-speed rail corridors, approximately $29 billion will be used to make badly needed repairs to the aging and deteriorating bridges, highways, and roadways across the country, which have not been systematically upgraded in decades.[73] Another $8.4 billion is allocated for upgrades of subways, trams, and light-rail systems, and $2.1 billion is earmarked for airports.[74]

President Obama's economic stimulus package is already being compared to President Franklin D. Roosevelt's New Deal. During the Great Depression, the Public Works Administration of 1933 was a New Deal agency that funded more than 34,000 projects, resulting in numerous civil works masterpieces. Engineering marvels such as the Golden Gate Bridge in California, Camp David in Maryland, the Hoover Dam in Colorado, the Grand Coulee Dam in Washington State, and the Lincoln Tunnel, LaGuardia Airport, and the Triborough Bridge in New York City are a few examples of the public works projects that put people to work and brought economic relief.[75] Although similar public works monuments are not expected to arise out of Obama's economic stimulus plan, it is an opportunity to make high-speed rail a reality in America and at the same time create tens of thousands of jobs in the technology, engineering, and construction industries. Less glamorous than the New Deal megaprojects, the national network of high-speed passenger rail lines proposed by Obama will make travel "leaner and cleaner" and create an infrastructure that responds to today's economic, energy, and environmental challenges. Vice President Joe Biden explained the green goals of these high-speed rail megaprojects:

With [a] high-speed rail system, we're going to be able to pull people off the road, lowering our dependence on foreign oil, lowering the bill for our gas in our gas tanks. We're going to loosen the congestion that also has a great impact on productivity . . . the people sitting at stop lights right now in overcrowded streets and cities . . . [a]nd we're going to significantly lessen the damage to our planet. This is a giant environmental down payment.[76]

Historically, this is the most ambitious plan for public infrastructure since President Eisenhower's vision in the last century to build a national interstate highway system.[77] After 60 years, the United States' current air and land transportation system "consumes 70% of our oil demand—much of it from overseas sources—and contributes 28% of greenhouse gas emissions."[78] Obama's legislation recognizes that a new approach is needed. Apart from the $8 billion provided by the ARRA, the president proposed a high-speed rail grant program of $1 billion per year in his fiscal 2010 budget, for a total of $13 billion in funds allocated to the project over five years.

In April 2009, the U.S. Department of Transportation issued *Vision for High-Speed Rail in America*, which outlined a strategic plan for high-speed rail and identified 11 high-speed corridors as potential recipients of federal funding. Ten of them are the California, Pacific Northwest, Gulf Coast, Chicago Hub Network, South Central, Florida, Southeast, Keystone, Empire, and Northern New England corridors. The report also recognized opportunities for improvement to the Northeast Corridor from Washington to Boston—the nation's only existing high-speed rail service (because it operates above 90 mph). The strategic plan issued by USDOT contemplates that states will need to show leadership in requesting and preparing projects for funding, and in coordinating with Amtrak and other rail providers. The report further suggests that public-private partnerships will be needed: "With the prospect of significant public funding flowing through States to support capital investments—often in existing, privately owned rail lines—for expanded and improved passenger services, partnerships will be needed between States and the private railroads that own the infrastructure. Whether for comprehensive corridor improvement programs or discrete projects, State-railroad agreements will be needed to ensure that public investments will fulfill, and continue to be available for, their intended purpose."[79] Since many of the high-speed rail corridors cross state boundaries, the strategic plan also anticipates that the states involved will need to enter into multistate partnerships.

Recommended Practices

The Passenger Rail Investment and Improvement Act of 2008 (PRIIA) establishes three new competitive grant programs for funding high-speed and intercity rail capital improvements—Section 301 (IPR projects),[80] Section 302 (congestion projects),[81] and

Figure 1. **U.S. Intercity Passenger Rail Network**

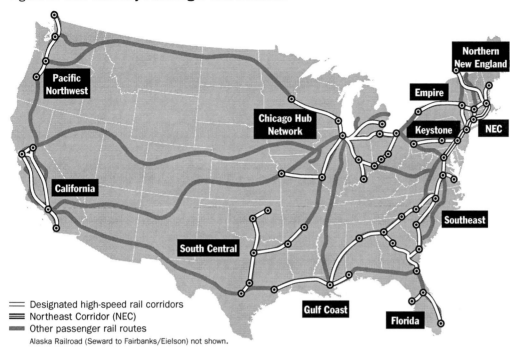

Designated high-speed rail corridors
Northeast Corridor (NEC)
Other passenger rail routes
Alaska Railroad (Seward to Fairbanks/Eielson) not shown.

From U.S. Department of Transportation, Federal Railroad Administration, *Vision for High-Speed Rail in America: High-Speed Rail Strategic Plan*, Washington, DC: Author, April 2009, p. 8.

Section 501 (HSR projects).[82] The ARRA's $8 billion HSR/IPR funding represents the first appropriations for Sections 301, 302, and 501 of PRIIA.[83] Under Sections 301 and 302, grant conditions include nonfederal matching funding requirements, but the ARRA waives the nonfederal matching requirements and directs the Secretary of Transportation to give priority to high-speed rail projects. However, not all states and cities are good candidates for grant money—only projects that have completed preliminary engineering and environmental work will be eligible for the first round of ARRA grants. To meet the ARRA's purpose of aiding near-term economic recovery, USDOT's strategic plan identifies three "tracks" for grants under the ARRA and annual appropriations that favor states and cities that have high-speed rail projects "shovel-ready." In order to qualify for grants under Section 301 (IPR projects) and Section 302 (congestion projects), eligible projects must be "ready to go"—meaning that environmental work required by the National Environmental Policy Act (NEPA) and preliminary engineering (PE) are complete—and they must also demonstrate "independent utility."[84] For projects that are not shovel-ready, funding will be available to stakeholders to conduct NEPA and PE work to make them ready to go and thus be eligible under a subsequent grant solicitation.

273

Projects that were well positioned to request a portion of the funding under the ARRA by the expected August 1, 2009, submittal deadline are:

- Chicago to St. Louis
- Chicago, Milwaukee, and Madison
- The "3-C Corridor" that would link Cincinnati, Cleveland, and Columbus, Ohio
- California
- Tucson to Phoenix
- Charlotte to Washington, D.C.[85]

Governor Arnold Schwarzenegger of California has declared that his state "will be in the front of the line in submitting its application" for federal funds.[86] California has a $30 billion plan to create a bullet train line to take passengers from Los Angeles to San Francisco in two hours, and to link all major cities in California. In November 2008, voters in California approved $10 billion in state funding toward development of a high-speed rail route. In January 2009, the state's High-Speed Rail Finance Committee approved the High Speed-Rail Authority's $29.1 million bond request, which will cover engineering design to be conducted in the current fiscal year.[87]

The stimulus monies alone will clearly not be sufficient to cover the cost of these high-speed rail megaprojects, but the federal funding will provide an opportunity to advance the development of particular projects. ARRA grants can support the critical design, engineering, and environmental work necessary to develop firm cost estimates and construction plans, so that a project can be ready to go in future rounds.

Sustainability and Green Design: The Future of Megaprojects

Issue

The term "sustainability" arrived on the world political stage in 1983, when the United Nations General Assembly established the World Commission on Environment and Development (WCED).[88] The WCED was commonly known as the "Brundtland Commission" because it was chaired by Gro Harlem Brundtland, Norway's former minister of the environment who later became prime minister. The commission was asked to examine the world's environmental problems and propose a global agenda addressing them. In 1987, after three years of public hearings on five continents, the Brundtland Commission published a report, *Our Common Future*, which coined the term "sustainable development." In a now-famous quote, the Brundtland report defined sustainable development and urged the world to take heed: "Sustainable development is that which meets the needs of the present without compromising the ability of future generations to meet their own needs."[89]

The report alerted the world to the global character of major environmental problems and the common interest of all countries to pursue policies aimed at environmentally sound development in order to reduce the effects of human activities on the environment for future generations. The report issued a call to action:

> Over the course of this century, the relationship between the human world and the planet that sustains it has undergone a profound change. When the century began, neither human numbers or technology had the power radically to alter planetary systems. As the century closes, not only do vastly increased human numbers and their activities have that power, but major, unintended changes are occurring in the atmosphere, in soils, in water, among plants and animals, and in the relationships among all of these. The rate of change is outstripping the ability of scientific disciplines and our current capabilities to assess and advise.[90]

Gro Harlem Brundtland's report opened up a broad international discussion of sustainability. Soon after publication of the Brundtland report, the term "sustainability" came into general use and helped to shape social consciousness in the United States.

The sustainability movement has had an enormous impact on the AEC industry in the United States. In 1993, amidst heightened anxiety about global warming and dwindling supplies of natural resources, David Gottfried founded the U.S. Green Building Council (USGBC), a Washington, D.C.–based nonprofit organization committed to sustainability through cost-efficient and energy-saving green building.[91] Buildings account for approximately 38 percent of greenhouse gas emissions, 39 percent of the total energy used, and 68 percent of electrical consumption in the United States. As a result, a major focus of green building is the reduction of energy use. The USGBC sought to forge strategic alliances with industry and government in the United States through educational workshops and conferences. The USGBC's green vision led to the development of the Leadership in Energy and Environmental Design (LEED) Green Building Rating System, which is used to measure and evaluate environmental performance of green buildings.

Analysis and Discussion

LEED development began in 1994, led by Robert K. Watson of the Natural Resources Defense Council (NRDC), the founding chairman of the LEED Steering Committee.[92] LEED is a voluntary, consensus-based system in which credits are earned for satisfying criteria that address specific environmental impacts inherent in the design, construction, and operation of buildings. The first LEED pilot program (LEED Version 1.0) was launched in 1998, and after modifications the LEED Green Building Rating System Version 2.0 was released in March 2000.[93] On April 27, 2009, the USGBC released LEED Version 3.0 (LEED 2009), an improved version of the green-building rating system, and

beginning in June 2009, all new LEED projects in the United States will be required to register for LEED 2009. More than a decade after LEED was born, the green building movement is no longer operating at a grassroots level. The government and its public agencies are now key drivers in the green building movement.

Certification under LEED provides a standardized method for measuring the "green-ness" of a project, and it is now a nationally accepted benchmark for sustainable design and construction. Projects earn points for each criterion that they fulfill, and projects that receive a higher level of points are awarded a higher level of certification. The rating system offers four certification levels for new construction: Certified, Silver, Gold, and Platinum. Each level corresponds to the number of credits accrued in six green design categories: Sustainable Sites (SS), Water Efficiency (EF), Energy and Atmosphere (EA), Materials and Resources (MR), Indoor Environmental Quality (IEQ), and Innovation in Design (ID). The LEED 2009 Green Building Rating System adds a seventh topic, Regional Priority (RP). A Platinum rating is the ultimate level attainable under LEED. Owners and institutions may choose a LEED goal at the beginning of a project, and then design and build with the intention of demonstrating that level of sustainability when construction is completed. Certification was initially administered by the USGBC, but in 2008 that responsibility was passed to USGBC's sister nonprofit corporation, the Green Building Certification Institute.[94]

LEED certification offers proof to clients, stakeholders, and the public at large that environmental goals have been met. As the green movement continues to gain momentum, government owners have begun to equate "green" design with "good" design. Policy-makers in government are now among the key drivers for sustainability and green building and they have begun to use sustainable design as a statement of their mission in publicly financed projects. State and local governments have adopted LEED incentive programs including tax credits, tax breaks, reduced fees, and priority or expedited permitting, and many state governments are mandating minimum LEED certifications for new state-funded construction. Government has the ability to raise the bar on sustainability to a higher level by implementing policy through laws and its own initiatives. The AEC industry can anticipate that in the near future, government funding of megaprojects will depend more often upon proof of sustainability.

Many federal agencies and departments have already adopted energy-reduction policies by mandating LEED certification and are committed to incorporating principles of sustainable design and energy efficiency in all of their building projects.[95] The nation's largest landlord, the General Services Administration, made the first official commitment to going green by adopting LEED with a stated goal of achieving Silver certification for all projects. The Department of the Navy and the Army Corps of Engineers also require LEED certification. The Department of Agriculture requires all new construction to achieve a minimum of LEED Silver, and the U.S. Forest Service requires LEED Silver

certification for construction of all facilities 2,500 square feet or larger. The Department of Energy mandates that construction projects exceeding $5 million in costs must be LEED Gold certified, and the Environmental Protection Agency requires all new construction in excess of 20,000 square feet to earn LEED Gold certification.[96]

Table 1. **Comparison of LEED point levels for new construction for versions 3.0 and 2.2**

	Points	
LEED Certification Level	**LEED 2009 for New Construction, Version 3.0**	**LEED 2005 for New Construction, Version 2.2**
Certified	40 — 49	26–32
Silver	50 — 59	33–38
Gold	60 — 79	39–51
Platinum	80 and above	52–69

Recommended Practices

Sustainability is one of the most important concerns at the beginning of the twenty-first century, and sustainable design is quickly becoming a requirement for institutional and government clients and owners. As government agencies begin to insist upon environmentally responsible public construction projects, it will become more and more important for professionals such as engineers, architects, and construction managers to be LEED-accredited and familiar with LEED requirements. The final LEED requirement—innovation and design process—awards one point for the use of a LEED-Accredited Professional (LEED AP).[97]

If a megaproject owner wants to effectively promote public trust and confidence throughout the life cycle of a project, issuing a vision statement that encompasses the organization's green goals and that describes the environmental sustainability the project seeks to accomplish can be a powerful public relations and marketing tool in winning public attention and support. Megaprojects sometimes take as long as 20 years to complete. Cost, quality, and schedule are important considerations throughout the life cycle of a project. But a long-term strategy for environmentally sound development that aspires to the highest possible standards of sustainability should be the paramount policy that guides the design and construction of all future megaprojects.

In January 2009, New York City became the first U.S. city to win the international Sustainable Transport Award, which was presented at the Transportation Research Board's annual conference held in Washington, D.C. The annual award "honors a city

that uses innovative transportation strategies to enhance the sustainability and livability of its communities, while also reducing greenhouse gas and air pollution emissions."[98] New York is taking a leadership role in promoting the sustainability of its transportation infrastructure and reducing its carbon footprint. New York City Transit, through its Department of Capital Program Management (CPM), is the first public agency in America to have an Environmental Management System (EMS) certified to ISO 14001 to "ensure our projects conform to international standards for environmental sustainability."[99] In 2007, New York's Metropolitan Transportation Authority (MTA) created a Commission on Sustainability and the MTA, with the goal of making the city's transit system "not only the largest public transit system in the U.S. — but the greenest."[100]

New York's Blue Ribbon Commission recently published a major report, *Greening Mass Transit & Metro Region: The Final Report of the Blue Ribbon Commission on Sustainability and the MTA*. The ambitious plan seeks to reduce oil dependency, limit the CO2 emissions that contribute to global warming, and carry the New York metropolitan area into the next half century.[101] Aimed at expanding the "greening power of transit" while at the same time reducing per-rider energy consumption and environmental footprint, four key areas of sustainability planning are covered by the report: Energy/Carbon, Facilities, Smart Growth/Transit-Oriented Development, and Materials Flow and Water Management. Nearly 100 recommendations and projects are identified in the report. The MTA's commitment to energy efficiency includes: deriving 7 percent of its energy needs from solar, wind, and other renewable sources by 2015; generating 80 percent of total electrical energy needs from clean, renewable energy by 2050; powering the Roosevelt Island Subway Station with renewable tidal energy generated in the East River; evaluating the feasibility of wind turbines as a power source; collecting ground and storm water for use in operations; utilizing green roofs; implementing weight-reduction and regenerative braking technologies; seeking LEED Silver certification for transit facilities where LEED standards apply; and for rail stations and power stations (where LEED standards do not substantially apply) developing green standards for transit facilities based on the LEED ratings. The MTA is drafting *The MTA Green Building Guidelines*, which will incorporate LEED criteria and serve as an industry model for green transit facilities. Once developed, it is anticipated that the guidelines will be submitted to the USGBC for "potential adoption as a *LEED for Transit* standard."[102]

New York transit is committing itself to these green goals in the belief that "green mass transit is the key to a green future."[103] The Commission believes that a $75 billion to $100 billion spending program will be required during 2010–2019, the time period covered by the report, and is seeking some of the ARRA stimulus money to push its green agenda forward. It views the current financial crisis as a "unique opportunity to frame stimulus actions in a way that will redirect public investment over the long term" to focus on three concerns: climate change, energy security, and infrastructure renewal

and expansion. If implemented, New York's lofty green goals will provide a promise of sustainable infrastructure for future generations. The New York model may serve as a blueprint for greening transit agencies and other metropolitan regions nationwide.

The future of megaprojects worldwide depends upon a vision that promotes the concept of sustainability, not just for a particular community but for the common good of the whole planet. Long before the Brundtland report, the Iroquois Nation articulated the concept of sustainability and for over 1,000 years lived by its creed: "In our every deliberation we must consider the impact of our decisions on the next seven generations." For the good of future generations, megaproject planners must aspire to the highest standards in which design goals are driven by concerns such as climate change, energy efficiency, and protection of natural resources.

Conclusion

Megaprojects attract a high level of public attention and political interest because of impacts on the community, environment, and both state and federal budgets. New technologies and project delivery models are changing the way megaprojects are delivered, and promise to improve their cost effectiveness and sustainability. Firms that are implementing new technologies such as BIM are finding it plays a role in winning projects. Projects are being delivered with new approaches that integrate people, systems, and business practices into a collaborative process that maximizes project results, increases value, and reduces waste. The future of megaprojects will be defined by these new pactices.

Notes

1. Flyvbjerg, B., Bruzelius, N., and Rothengatter, W. (2003). W. *Megaprojects and Risk: An Anatomy of Ambition*. New York: Cambridge University Press.

2. Capka, J. R. (January/February 2006). "Financing Megaprojects." *Public Roads*, 69:4, p. 2.

3. See generally *Building Information Modeling (BIM), Transforming Design and Construction to Achieve Greater Industry Productivity*. (2008). New York: McGraw Hill Construction SmartMarket Report.

4. Ashcraft, H. W. (Summer 2008). "Building Information Modeling: A Framework for Collaboration." *Construction Lawyer* 28: 6.

5. There is no single BIM software tool that performs every function. However, Autodesk Navisworks is an example of a 3-D visualization software program that permits model viewing.

6. Miller, R. "National BIM Standard Version 1, Part 1 — Out for Industry Review," *National Institute of Building Sciences*. Retrieved February 20, 2009, from http://www.nibs.org/nbims.html.

7. See Miles, M. K., III. (n.d.) *A Path Forward in BIM: A Road Map for Implementation to Support MILCON Transformation and Civil Works Projects Within the U.S. Army Corps of Engineers*. (PowerPoint presentation). Miles illustrates BIM examples including the Information Technology Laborato-

ry, Engineer Research and Development Center; Army Reserve Center, Louisville District; Iraq Prison, Gulf Region Division. Discussing BIM in civil works, he states that "BIM models can feed computer-aided facility management systems . . . [and] BIM can support asset management efforts." Miles sets forth the USACE challenge to the industry as follows: "We expect our design and construction contractors to develop BIM capabilities. We expect software vendors to use Industry Standards (e.g., NBIMS) and achieve interoperability. We expect BIM-based deliverables." See also Hammond, David M., *BIM: Agency-wide Actions, A Mission-centric Look at Portfolio and Asset Management*; U. S. General Services Administration, Public Buildings Service, Office of the Chief Architect, *Building Information Modeling: Agency-wide Actions*. All three were presented at a National Academy of Sciences Forum, *Engineering, Construction, and Facilities Asset Management: A Cultural Revolution*, October 31, 2006. The documents were retrieved March 9, 2010, from http://sites.nationalacademies.org/DEPS/FFC/DEPS_049447.

8. Gallaher, M. P., O'Connor, A. C., Dettbarn, J. L., Jr., and Golday, L. T. (2004). *Cost Analysis of Inadequate Interoperability in the U.S. Capital Facilities Industry*, Washington: National Institute of Standards and Technology, Advanced Technology Program, Information Technology and Electronics Office, p. iv. Retrieved July 6, 2009, from http://www.bfrl.nist.gov/oae/publications/gcrs/04867.pdf .

9. jonasrisen, "Kelvin's Conjecture: The Sustainability of Optimization and Integration," *Greenline*. Retrieved February 20, 2009 from http://greenlineblog.com/kelvins-conjecture-the-sustainability-of-optimization-and-integration/ .

10. Hill, D. (March 31, 2008). "The New Engineering: A Discussion With Arup's Tritram Carfrae," *City of Sound*. Retrieved February 20, 2009, from http://www.cityofsound.com/blog/2008/03/this-discussion.html.

11. American Institute of Architects. (June 2005). "Arup Honored for Innovative Swimming Center in Beijing," *Edges, Newsletter of the Technology in Practice Knowledge Community*. Retrieved February 20, 2009 from http://info.aia.org/nwsltr_tap.cfm?pagename=tap_nwsltr_20050630.

12. Squarzini, M., Tamaro, M., Kadakia, A., Hatfield, E., and Scarangello, T. (July 31, 2008). "Changing the Way We Deliver Stadiums: Successes with the Washington Nationals, Yankees and Meadowlands Projects," *GoStructural.com*. Retrieved July 6, 2009, from http://gostructural.com/article.asp?id=3049.

13. M. Squarzini et al., "Changing the Way We Deliver Stadiums."

14. Middlebrooks, R. E. (October 21, 2008). "Sustainable Design Through BIM and Analysis," *HPAC Engineering*. Retrieved July 6, 2009, from http://hpac.com/fastrack/Sustainable-Design-Through-BIM-and-Analysis.

15. "New Autodesk Tools Help Simplify Energy-Efficient Building Design and Renovation." Retrieved April 30, 2009, from http://www10.aeccafe.com/nbc/articles/view_article.php?articleid=687699.

16. Rundell, R. (April 10, 2007). "BIM and Analysis for Sustainable Design (1-2-3 Revit Tutorial)." *Cadaylst*. Retrieved July 6, 2009, from http://aec.cadalyst.com/aec/article/articleDetail.jsp?id=417408.

17. Guevarra, L. (July 17, 2008). "California Adopts Green Building Code for All New Construc-

tion," *GreenBiz.com*. Retrieved July 6, 2009, from http://www.greenbiz.com/news/2008/07/18/california-adopts-green-building-code-all-new-construction.

18. Howrey LLP. (January 15, 2007). "New York City Enacts Broad Green Building Law for Its Projects," *Construction WebLinks*. Retrieved July 6, 2009, from http://www.constructionweblinks.com/Resources/Industry_Reports__Newsletters/Jan_15_2007/newy.html.

19. Howrey LLP. (April 16, 2007). "Washington D.C. Enacts Green Building Requirements for Private Projects," *Construction WebLinks*. Retrieved July 6, 2009, from http://www.constructionweblinks.com/Resources/Industry_Reports__Newsletters/Apr_16_2007/wash.html.

20. Skidmore, Owings & Merrill. "World Trade Center Tower One Freedom Tower, Architectural Fact Sheet, June 2005." Retrieved July 6, 2009, from http://www.renewnyc.com/content/pdfs/freedom_tower_fact_sheet.pdf.

21. Day, M. "BIM and the Freedom Tower," *AEC Magazine*. Retrieved July 6, 2009, from http://aecmag.com/index.php?option=com_content&task=view&id=13&Itemid=35.

22. Beidler, A. (May 8, 2007). "New York's Freedom Tower: New World Trade Center Emphasizing Safety & Design," *Suite101.com*. Retrieved July 6, 2009, from http://modern-us-history.suite101.com/article.cfm/freedom_tower.

23. Murray, J. (June 12, 2008). "Freedom Tower to Tap Green Fuel Cell Power," *BusinessGreen.com*. Retrieved July 6, 2009, from http://www.businessgreen.com/business-green/news/2218895/freedom-tower-tap-green-fuel.

24. Strafaci, A. (October 2008). "What Does BIM Mean for Civil Engineers?" *CENews.com*. Retrieved February 20, 2009, from http://www.cenews.com/bimchannel/article.asp?id=3232.

25. Case, M. J. "Work In Progress: How Building Informational Modeling May Unify IT in the Civil Engineering Curriculum." Paper delivered at the 38th ASEE/IEEE Frontiers in Education Conference, October 22–25, 2008, Saratoga Springs, N.Y., p. S4J-5.

26. The ConsensusDOCS 301 *Building Information Modeling (BIM) Addendum* defines "federated model" as "a Model consisting of linked but distinct component Models, drawings derived from the Models, texts, and other data sources that do not lose their identity or integrity by being so linked, so that a change to one component Model in a Federated Model does not create a change in another component Model in that Federated Model." § 2.8.

27. "NCARB Holds Hearing on Integrated Project Delivery (IPD)," *NCARB News*, November 2008. Retrieved July 6, 2009, from http://www.ncarb.com/newsclips/nov08_1.html.

28. National Council on Architectural Registration Boards. (2008). *2008–2009 Rules of Conduct*. Washington: Author. Retrieved March 9, 2010, from http://www.ncarb.org/Getting-an-Initial-License/~/media/A836D00432E147CEA35199081D6F7A02.ashx.

29. National Council on Architectural Registration Boards. (2009). *2009–2010 Rules of Conduct*. Washington: Author. Retrieved March 12, 2010, from http://www.ncarb.org/~/media/Files/PDF/Special-Paper/rules_of_conduct10.pdf .

30. ConsensusDOCS, *ConsensusDOCS 301: BIM Addendum*, 2008. Available on-line at http://www.consensusdocs.org.

31. American Institute of Architects, *E202–2008 Building Modeling Protocol Exhibit*. Retrieved July 6, 2009, from http://www.aiacontractdocuments.org/e202_faq.cfm.

32. AIA National/AIA California Council. (2007). *Integrated Project Delivery: A Guide*. Washington, D.C.: American Institute of Architects; Eastman, C., Teicholz, P., Sacks, R., and Liston, K. (2008). *BIM Handbook, A Guide to Building Information Modeling*, Hoboken, N.J.: John Wiley & Sons, Inc. (hereinafter, *BIM Handbook*).

33. Fortner, B. (May 2008). "Special Report: Are You Ready for BIM?" *Civil Engineering, The Online Magazine of the American Society of Civil Engineers*, 78:5.

34. AIA, *Integrated Product Delivery: A Guide*, p. ii.

35. AIA, *Integrated Product Delivery: A Guide*, p. 6.

36. Lichtig, W. A. (Summer 2006). "The Integrated Agreement for Lean Project Delivery." *Construction Lawyer*, 3:26, p. 31.

37. AIA, *Integrated Project Delivery: A Guide*, p. 32.

38. AIA, *Integrated Project Delivery: A Guide*, p. 33.

39. AIA, *Integrated Project Delivery: A Guide*, p. 32.

40. AIA, *Integrated Project Delivery: A Guide*, p. 33.

41. AIA, *Integrated Project Delivery: A Guide*, p. 40.

42. AIA, *Integrated Project Delivery: A Guide*, p. 41.

43. "Integrated Project Delivery Improves Efficiency, Streamlines Construction." *Tradeline, Inc.*, July 16, 2008. Retrieved July 6, 2009, from http://www.tradelineinc.com/reports/0A03D1C0%2D2B 3B%2DB525%2D85702BCEDF900F61.

44. AIA, *Integrated Project Delivery: A Guide*, p. 47.

45. Eastman et al., *BIM Handbook*, pp. 6–7.

46. Eastman et al., *BIM Handbook*, pp. 6–7.

47. Quatman, G. W. (March 2, 2007). "Design-Build Legislation Sweeps the Nation," *AIA Industry News*.

48. FAR, 36.3. *See also* 10 U.S.C. 2305a and 41 U.S.C. 253m.

49. Parvin, C. (January 1997). "States Enact Design-Build Legislation," *Roads & Bridges*. Retrieved July 7, 2009, from http://www.roadsbridges.com:80/States-enact-design-build-legislation-article587.

50. AIA, *Integrated Project Delivery: A Guide*, p. 32.

51. AIA, *Integrated Project Delivery: A Guide*, p. 32.

52. United States Department of Transportation. (July 18, 2008). *Innovation Wave: An Update on the Burgeoning Private Sector Role in U.S. Highway and Transit Infrastructure*. Retrieved July 6, 2009, from http://www.fhwa.dot.gov/reports/pppwave/ppp_innovation_wave.pdf (hereinafter, *Innovation Wave*).

53. USDOT, *Innovation Wave*, p. 3.

54. USDOT, *Innovation Wave*, p. 5.

55. USDOT, *Innovation Wave*, pp. 3-4.

56. United States Government Accountability Office. (July 2007). "Surface Transportation: Strate-

gies Are Available for Making Existing Road Infrastructure Perform Better," GAO-07-920. Washington, D.C., pp. 33–34 (hereinafter "GAO Congestion Report").

57. USDOT, *Innovation Wave,* pp. 11–13.
58. "GAO Congestion Report," p. 11.
59. "GAO Congestion Report," p. 11.
60. "GAO Congestion Report," p. 11.
61. "GAO Congestion Report," p. 17.
62. "GAO Congestion Report," pp. 19–20.
63. "GAO Congestion Report," pp. 19–20.
64. Capka, J. R., Administrator, Federal Highway Administration, letter to Michael W. Behrens, P.E., Executive Director, Texas Department of Transportation, August 16, 2007.
65. Capka, letter to Michael W. Behrens.
66. Capka, letter to Michael W. Behrens.
67. Massachusetts Transportation Finance Commission. (September 17, 2007). *Transportation Finance in Massachusetts: Volume 2, Building a Sustainable Transportation Financing System, Recommendations of the Massachusetts Transportation Finance Commission* (hereinafter, "Massachusetts Report").
68. In October 2008, President George W. Bush signed The Clean Railroads Act of 2008 (PL 110-432), which authorized $1.5 billion for high-speed rail through 2013.
69. "A Vision for High Speed Rail," *The* [White House] *Blog,* April 16, 2009. Retrieved July 6, 2009, from http://www.whitehouse.gov/blog/09/04/16/A-Vision-for-High-Speed-Rail/.
70. Gertler, P. (April 27, 2009). "High Speed Rail Is a Game-changer." *ENR.com* [*Engineering News-Record*]. Retrieved July 6, 2009, from http://enr.construction.com/opinions/viewpoint/2009/0427-HighSpeedRail.asp.
71. Rogers, D. (February 17, 2009). "Major Rail Expansion on Track with Stimulus Plan." *USA Today.* Retrieved July 6, 2009, from http://www.usatoday.com/news/washington/2009-02-17-obama-railroads_N.htm.
72. Rogers, "Major Rail Expansion on Track with Stimulus Plan."
73. Armstrong, D. (February 19, 2009). "How the Stimulus Will Change Your Travel Plans," *Mainstreet.* Retrieved July 6, 2009, from http://www.mainstreet.com/article/lifestyle/travel/how-stimulus-will-change-your-travel-plans.
74. Armstrong, "How the Stimulus Will Change Your Travel Plans."
75. Schubert, P. (February 2, 2009). "A Stimulus for Good Design," *ENR.com* [*Engineering News-Record*], http://enr.construction.com/opinions/viewPoint/2009/0211-StimulusforGoodDesign.asp.
76. "A Vision for High Speed Rail," *The Blog,* April 16, 2009.
77. Gertler, "High Speed Rail Is a Game-changer."
78. U.S. Department of Transportation, Federal Railroad Administration. (April 2009). *Vision for High-Speed Rail in America: High-Speed Rail Strategic Plan.* Washington, D.C.: Author, p. 1.
79. USDOT, *Vision for High-Speed Rail in America,* p. 9.

80. Intercity Passenger Rail Service Corridor Capital Service (Section 301), 49 U.S.C. Chapter 244.

81. Congestion Grants (Section 302), 49 U.S.C. § 24105.

82. High Speed Rail (Section 502), 49 U.S.C. § 26101 *et seq.*

83. USDOT, *Vision for High-Speed Rail in America*, p. 11.

84. USDOT, *Vision for High-Speed Rail in America*, p. 12.

85. Craver, M. (March 20, 2009). "High-Speed Rail Projects Get Big Boost," *The Kiplinger Business Resource Center*. Retrieved on July 7, 2009, from http://www.kiplinger.com/businessresource/forecast/archive/High_Speed_Rail_Projects_Get_Big_Boost_090320.html.

86. Conkey, C., and Roth, A. (April 17, 2009). "U.S. Commits $13 Billion to Aid High-Speed Rail," *Wall Street Journal*. Retrieved July 7, 2009, from http://online.wsj.com/article/SB123989461947625407.html.

87. McKenna, C. (April 7, 2009). "California High Speed Rail Gets Funds to Continue Engineering Design," *Government Technology*. Retrieved July 7, 2009, from http://www.govtech.com/gt/636429.

88. Duncan, A. "This Norwegian's Past May Connect With Your Future," *Oregon State University Extension Service*. Retrieved July 7, 2009, from http://oregonfuture.oregonstate.edu/part1/pf1_03.html.

89. World Commission on Environment and Development, *Our Common Future*. New York: Oxford University Press, 1987.

90. *Our Common Future*, p. 22.

91. For more information about the U.S. Green Building Council, see "About USGBC" at their Website, http://www.usgbc.org/DisplayPage.aspx?CMSPageID=124.

92. "Leadership in Energy and Environmental Design," *Absolute Astronomy.com*. Retrieved July 7, 2009, from http://www.absoluteastronomy.com/topics/Leadership_in_Energy_and_Environmental_Design.

93. "History of LEED," *AccessPoint, Business Continuity & Recovery Services*. Retrieved July 7, 2009, from http://www.businessrecovery.ws/leed-certification/history-of-leed.

94. U.S. Green Building Council. (2009). *LEED 2009 for New Construction and Major Renovations*, Washington, D.C.: Author, p. xi.

95. U.S. General Services Administration. (April 8, 2009). "Sustainable Design Program." Retrieved July 7, 2009, from http://www.gsa.gov/sustainabledesign.

96. Mikalonis, S. "LEED as an Emerging National Symbol." *Greening of the Great Lakes*. Retrieved July 7, 2009, from http://www.greeningofthegreatlakes.com/public_policy/leed_emerging_standard.php.

97. U.S. Green Building Council. (April 8, 2004). "Guidance on Innovation & Design (ID) Credits." Retrieved July 7, 2009, from http://www.usgbc.org/Docs/LEEDdocs/IDcredit_guidance_final.pdf.

98. "New York City Wins Sustainable Transport Award," *Embarq*, January 27, 2009. Retrieved July 7, 2009, from http://www.embarq.org/en/news/09/01/27/new-york-city-wins-sustainable-transport-award.

99. "New York City Transit and the Environment," *New York City Transit*. Retrieved July 7, 2009, from http://www.mta.info/nyct/facts/ffenvironment.htm.

100. Metropolitan Transportation Authority. (April 14, 2008). "Governor Paterson and MTA Announce Sustainability Initiatives" (press release). Retrieved July 7, 2009, from http://www.mta.info/mta/news/releases/?agency=hq&en=080414-HQ9.

101. Blue Ribbon Commission on Sustainability and the MTA. (February, 2009). *Greening Mass Transit & Metro Regions: The Final Report of the Blue Ribbon Commission on Sustainability and the MTA,* New York: Author, p. 6.

102. *Greening Mass Transit & Metro Regions*, p. 35.

103. Jonathan F. P. Rose, Chairman of the MTA Sustainability Commission, April 14, 2008, quoted in "Governor Paterson and MTA Announce Sustainability Initiatives," cited above, n. 100.

PART II

Risk Management and Professional Liability Issues for Consulting Engineers Involved in Megaprojects

Preceding page:
Photograph from the
mid-1880s of the
construction of the
Forth Bridge. The
three main towers
are 330 feet tall,
and the roadway is
150 feet above the
water at high tide.
The bridge uses
58,000 tons of
steel.

CHAPTER 14

The Project Owner: Expectations and Relationship Issues

David J. Hatem, PC, Donovan Hatem LLP

Part II of this book addresses some of the more significant risk management and professional liability issues for consulting engineers involved in megaprojects.[1] While these issues are prominent and present in virtually all megaprojects, by no means is their occurrence or relevance restricted to megaprojects. These issues are important and relevant in the context of most projects — of many types, sizes, and degrees of complexity — and, hence, the discussion and recommendations set forth here have relevance and application in a context significantly broader than megaprojects.

However, what is characteristically different about megaprojects is that these risk management and professional liability issues are more certain to arise and their occurrences, if not prudently and timely anticipated and addressed, are more likely to lead to significant professional liability exposure for consulting engineers and, potentially, to project failure and severely disappointed expectations for all project participants. In addition, there are dimensions to the discussion of these issues that have specific application only in the megaproject context.

Part II will discuss these risk management and professional liability issues, with particular attention paid to the perspective of the consulting engineer involved in, or contemplating an involvement in, a megaproject. This discussion will be of benefit to the project owner and consulting engineer. The project owner will gain an enriched sensitivity to, and appreciation of, the risks and professional liability concerns and exposures facing the consulting engineer, while the consulting engineer will gain more guidance on how to improve its professional practices in meeting reasonable client expectations and in identifying, anticipating, and managing its professional liability risk exposure.

Part I contains analysis, discussion, and recommended practices regarding a variety of issues important to the successful planning, design, and construction of megaprojects. Implementing those practices should promote the realistic achievement of reasonable expectations of all project participants and thereby significantly reduce the potential of professional liability exposure for the consulting engineer. As such, the discussion in Part II should be read and understood in the broader context of the subject matter and recommendations set forth in Part I.

Panoramic view of the new Forth Road Bridge (left) and the 1890 Forth Rail Bridge (right), south and west of Edinburgh, Scotland. Designed by Sir John Fowler and Sir Benjamin Baker and built by Sir William Arrol & Co. between 1883 and 1890, the original dual carriageway rail bridge was built entirely of steel, the first major structure in Britain to use it. The bridge consists of two central spans of 1,710 feet each and two side spans and approaches. In 1964, a companion suspension bridge was built for road traffic. Its central span is 3,298 feet long, making it the fourth longest suspension bridge in the world when it was opened. Photo © 2006 by Greg Barbier.

Introduction

Mutual respect and trust and a recognition and appreciation of the respective interests and expectations of the client and the professional lie at the core of most profitable and positive client-professional relationships.[2] The achievement of these objectives depends upon a clear and realistic understanding of the risks, expectations, roles, and responsibilities of each party. For the consulting engineer,[3] the continuous process of managing the expectations of its client (typically the project owner, which is the term used in this book) and the ability to engage in candid discussions with the project owner about project risk issues are essential components of a healthy client-professional relationship. On megaprojects, there are substantial and unique challenges in the achievement of these objectives.

One of the most challenging aspects of managing client expectations on a megaproject arises from the dynamic, complex, and evolving character of the project participants' identities, roles, and responsibilities throughout the project's extended duration. These characteristics derive from the fact that megaprojects require flexibility in delivery approach in order to adapt to a wide range of factors and influences, including the variability of budgets and resource availability considerations, the political environment, evolving stakeholder interests, and changes within the project owner's organization. Typically, the extended duration of the megaproject (often a decade or longer) and the need to respond to "lessons learned" have an effect on these characteristics, which pose significant challenges for the consulting engineer in managing its own risk and the expectations of the project owner, the disappointment of which underlies most professional liability claims. The preceding points will be a common and dominant theme of discussion and demonstration throughout this chapter.

1.0   Project Owner Identity

Issue

On megaprojects, the consulting engineer's client (the project owner) may be one or more public entities, and the client's identity and its organizational and management structure may fundamentally evolve over the typically long duration of the project. Project stakeholders, such as grantors or funding sources, abutters, and project overseers — while not the client *per se* — often have significant interests in key elements of the planning, funding, program definition, design, and construction of the megaproject, and the respective interests of the project owner and other project stakeholders may conflict continually or at various intervals.

Analysis and Discussion

In most "non-mega" projects, the project owner is readily identified and remains essentially constant in organizational and management structure through planning, design, and construction execution. This general observation and expectation, however, is significantly less accurate and applicable to a megaproject. The reason is that the often very extended duration of a megaproject, changes in political administrations, political pressures and compromises having to do with the project, funding and interfaces/interferences with the public, the need to serve multiple core constituencies (e.g., state, local, and federal), budgetary constraints, the need for significant continuous and stable funding commitments during the project, and the number of stakeholders and project overseers having or claiming an interest in how the project is planned and delivered all typically combine to produce a higher probability and frequency of fundamental organizational and management evolution in the project owner. Moreover, the project owner who originally made the critical program and design decisions may not be the owner at the time of the project's turnover or completion, and these two different owners may have significantly divergent or conflicting expectations and interests (e.g., reduced design and construction costs on the front end in exchange for higher operations and maintenance costs on the back end may serve the original owner but not its successor).

In many instances, the interests of the project owner may conflict or otherwise be at variance with those of other project stakeholders. This situation may create ethical challenges and problems or, at a minimum, "discomfort" when the consulting engineer has professional relationships with both the megaproject owner and other stakeholders (on other projects) during the megaproject. To further complicate matters, over the duration of a megaproject the project owner's personnel will probably change, causing the consulting engineer to continuously reestablish bonds with, and manage expectations of, the new client representatives. By the same token, employees at all levels within the consulting engineer may also change, requiring the consulting engineer to take special steps to orient and reassign its personnel in such a way so as to maintain regularity in the service it provides to the project owner, consistent maintenance of the client relationship, and continuous management of expectations.

Recommended Practices

- Learn as much about the client as is practicable, including any future plans for project ownership or management transition. This should be a continuous learning process on megaprojects because the identity of the project owner may vary or change over the duration of the project.

291

- Stay informed about changes within the project owner's organization and be attentive to the continuous need for client expectation "maintenance" and relationship-building as personnel changes occur.

- Identify all of the important project stakeholders and overseers to ascertain their present and potential future interests and views regarding the multitude of planning and delivery issues for the megaproject. Determine whether the consulting engineer has any present or potential future conflict in representing the project owner in relation to the roles and interests of the various stakeholders and overseers. A conflict of interest, in a legal sense, is any actual or apparent divergence of interest between one client and some other client that impairs the consulting engineer's ability to serve either client in accordance with professional and ethical standards.[4] Short of the strict legal sense of "conflict," in a broader sense, a conflict of interest may be perceived to exist (as distinct from actually existing) in any situation in which a discomfort occurs because of a professional's simultaneous representation of two clients with actual or potentially divergent interests. In this situation, the "conflict" should be managed and resolved primarily through good practice judgment rather than by strict or rigid legal rules or constraints.

- The point to emphasize is that in a megaproject, the opportunities for real and apparent conflicts, whether strictly or broadly defined, are many, and they change and need to be constantly identified, monitored, evaluated, and reassessed as the project progresses, given the potential for change in project owners, the number of stakeholders and overseers, and the various existing or potentially divergent interests and views of all of them.

- Document all discussions and communications with the project owner about important project planning and design and construction expectations and implementation decisions. This is especially important, given the typically long duration of megaprojects and the relatively high potential for changes in project owner identity and personnel. The documentation should list the basis of the project owner's decisions, including the options presented by the consulting engineer and its comparative analysis thereof (including an analysis of the degrees of potential project risk associated therewith), the consulting engineer's recommendations and rationale, and the reasons why the project owner made its decisions. Documenting these facts is important regardless of whether the project owner ultimately decides to accept or reject the consulting engineer's recommendation, and this type of documentation should be shared with the project owner and become part of the project record.

- In this specific context, creating and maintaining such documentation is essential to achieving continuity and objectivity in the project record regarding critical project decisions, recommendations, communications, and discussions. This is espe-

cially important because changes in the project owner's organization or personnel are likely to occur over the project duration. Megaprojects provide ample opportunities during their long time span for second-guessing or "Monday-morning quarterbacking" by project overseers, investigators, those pursuing professional liability claims against consulting engineers, funding agencies, auditors, the public, the press, and politicians, to name but a few. Documentation will, at a minimum (and for better or worse), set the record straight as to what the project owner was told, the recommendations the consulting engineer made, the basis of these recommendations, what the project owner reasonably should have expected, and why the decisions of the project owner were made. In defending a subsequent professional liability claim against the consulting engineer, this documentation is extremely useful in showing that the project owner had an informed basis for making decisions on subjects at issue in the claim. Conversely, just as adequate documentation may be a shield in defending a professional liability claim, inadequate or non-existent documentation may be a sword that can be used against the consulting engineer. For example, professional liability exposure may exist if the documentation demonstrates that the consulting engineer did not adequately identify the available options or prudently assess their respective risks and benefits or did not exercise sound judgment in making a recommendation to the project owner. In the experience of this author in defending consulting engineers involved in megaprojects against professional liability claims, serious problems are created when no documentation exists because this allows others more "creative" opportunity and liberty to second-guess on the basis of no factual or documented record. In many such situations, so-called engineering "experts" are often eager to opine that, without considering the adequacy or appropriateness of the consulting engineer's judgments and recommendations themselves, the absence of such documentation *in itself* is evidence of substandard professional performance.

2.0 Consulting Engineer Scope of Services: Roles and Responsibilities

Issue

Commercial disputes and professional liability claims between the project owner and the consulting engineer often arise on megaprojects either because the services to be provided and the roles and responsibilities of the consulting engineer are not clearly or consistently defined or because the reality of actual service performance does not align with or conform to the contractually defined service scope, roles, and responsibilities.

In some instances, the latter situation results when there are delays between the project owner's request for a change in services or roles of the consulting engineer and the negotiation and execution of contractual amendments, or when no one has addressed the need for such amendments.

In yet other situations, the project owner may choose not to retain the consulting engineer to perform certain services or roles that the latter initially recommended. In addition, as the megaproject attains certain objectives or milestones, the scope of services previously required of the consulting engineer may diminish, with the project owner assuming responsibility for performing those services or hiring other consulting engineers to perform them.

Analysis and Discussion

In evaluating project-specific risk exposure for consulting engineers, especially on megaprojects, one should carefully examine the requested or contemplated scope of services and the expected roles and responsibilities of the consulting engineer. The scope of services of the consulting engineer should be clearly and consistently defined in the agreement with the project owner.

As with virtually all aspects of megaprojects, owners have and exercise many options in the retention and assignment of professional service scope to consulting engineers, and initial owner decisions in that regard are prone to change during the course of the project. These decisions and their evolving character pose the potential for professional liability exposure for the consulting engineer, as there is a correlation between service scope and professional liability exposure. In addition, the scope of services required of the consulting engineer will affect the application of the professional standard of care.

The resolution of most professional liability claims involves an understanding of the scope of services that the consulting engineer is contractually obligated to provide to the project owner.[5] Applying the professional standard of care typically and primarily depends upon such a contractual scope analysis. Hence, it is important that the contract accurately and contemporaneously reflects and demonstrates the scope of services required and expected of the consulting engineer. Changing schedules, variable funding pressures or constraints, desires to experiment, design innovation, or implementing new contract delivery or management approaches (e.g., fast-track) over the duration of a megaproject account for why engineering service scope and corresponding professional liability risk exposure may (after the execution of the owner-consultant agreement) increase significantly on a megaproject. In other circumstances, the project owner may contract for professional services among multiple consulting engineers to achieve a degree of independence or "checks and balances" in service delivery. In the alternative, the owner may choose to assume or perform portions of the scope previously contracted

to the consulting engineer in order to reduce outside consultant fees.[6] In other circumstances, scope addition may be requested by the project owner.

In many situations, "doing less" in service scope translates to more—rather than less—professional liability risk exposure. For example, geotechnical engineers have long recognized the importance of recommending that service scope include not only design but also engineering and observational services during construction. Commissioning a more encompassing service scope typically results in a significant risk reduction for both the geotechnical engineer and the project overall because the continuity of the engineer's involvement provides timely and meaningful opportunities to identify and mitigate design and construction risk exposures. Put another way, in many instances there is an inverse relationship between risk and professional service scope: the greater the service scope, the less the risk exposure. In addition, when the consulting engineer's scope is overly limited by the project owner, it may not be possible to develop appropriate, corresponding, effective, and legally enforceable contractual limitations on professional liability risk and exposure.

Following contract execution, the project owner may elect to delete services from the consulting engineer's scope, perform these services on its own, or independently contract with other consulting engineers to perform them. These service delivery variations may be problematic for a number of reasons, including the fact that the consulting engineer may have initially evaluated its risk and compensation, or accepted certain contractual risk allocation provisions, based upon the originally contracted service scope. Another problem may be the qualifications and experience of the project owner to perform the services in question. Also, when other consulting engineers are engaged by the project owner to perform these services, coordination difficulties, lack of continuity and consistency, and potential service scope gaps pose increased risk. The project owner's retention of another consulting engineer to perform the services may create additional risk for the new consulting engineer. The latter may lack familiarity with the design or other services performed by the initial consulting engineer, and when multiple engineers are performing overlapping services, there is coordination risk, potential conflicts in advice, and delayed, indecisive, and inconsistent directions or communications to others, such as the constructor. Also, in a megaproject where design and construction management consistency, coordination, and interface are critically important, such division and distribution of service responsibility between different consulting engineers may lead to fragmentation in professional accountability and responsibility, constructor claims, diminution in project quality, and compromise in the implementation of uniform design standards and other project policies.

In all instances, it is important that contractual amendments are executed in a timely manner and describe the services required of the consulting engineer accurately, due to the likely variability in service scope definition on megaprojects. For the reasons previ-

ously discussed, the need for contract modifications or amendments and identification and evaluation of the corresponding risk potential arising from changes to the service scope should be regularly undertaken by the consulting engineer.

Recommended Practices

- Clear, accurate, and consistent definitions of service scope and the roles and responsibilities of the consulting engineer are critically important steps in managing professional liability risk exposure. This process should commence with the consulting engineer's recommendation to the project owner regarding appropriate service scope and the roles and responsibilities for the specific megaproject engagement. The consulting engineer should recognize that, due to a variety of factors, its service scope, roles, and responsibilities may evolve during the extended course of the megaproject and, hence, it is important that such evolution be tracked and periodically evaluated from a risk exposure perspective and that scope changes be contractually and contemporaneously conformed through timely contract amendments.[7]

- There should be a correlation between contractually undertaken scope, roles and responsibilities, and risk and reward (compensation) for the consulting engineer.

- Contractual risk allocation and commercial terms should be negotiated in a manner that corresponds with the required service scope and roles and responsibilities of the consulting engineer. The contractual service scope should establish a primary baseline for (a) risk allocation between project owner and the consulting engineer and (b) the evaluation of whether (in any specific professional liability claim context) the consulting engineer complied with the professional standard of care.

- Changes in service scope — additions or deletions — need to be evaluated against this risk allocation baseline. Reductions in service scope do not necessarily translate into a reduction in professional liability risk exposure for the consulting engineer; in fact, the inverse is often the case.

- Any scope changes should be contemporaneously evidenced by contract amendment. In addition, the consulting engineer should obtain the legally required confirmation that funds have been appropriated and are available to subsidize payment for any scope addition. The amendments should address not only compensation and commercial arrangements related to scope change, but also any corresponding need to modify or develop special risk allocation provisions based on scope alteration. In this regard, it must be emphasized that the scope and fee may decrease but professional liability risk exposure may increase.

- Document recommendations to the project owner regarding changes to the ser-

vice scope and roles and responsibilities, as well as project owner requests for deletion or reduction in service scope. The recommendations and the reasons for them should be documented and communicated to the project owner. This can become awkward and sensitive in circumstances in which the project owner intends to reduce the consulting engineer's scope and perform the services itself, especially if the owner is not qualified, experienced, or otherwise capable of doing so. While the consulting engineer's recommendations against such a course may appear to be self-serving, the consultant should document and communicate its recommendations in that regard, lest the consultant be exposed to "scapegoat" liability exposure and damage to its reputation.[8]

- Services should be performed in a manner described in the contractually-defined scope. Performing services beyond that scope may create increased liability exposure, an imbalance in contractual risk allocation, and compensation inadequacies.

3.0 Project Owner Expectations: Reasonable Definition and Management

Issue

Project owners on megaprojects have grand designs and program "wish lists" that often do not align with budgetary, schedule, and other realistic program constraints or with the interests of other important project stakeholders. Programs need to be flexibly defined and periodically redefined in response to evolving planning, operational, and other needs (and wants); to budget and schedule pressures, external stakeholder input, interests, and required compromises; to funding limitations; to permit and regulatory limitations; and to other variables, constraints, and considerations. In addition, the intense competition for funding at federal, state, and local levels often leads megaproject owners to pragmatically and publicly define project profiles and funding strategies in an artificially minimalist manner designed to secure funding and "get the first shovel in the ground" rather than to reflect and comprehend the complete and realistic dimension, cost, or schedule of the project scope.[9] Moreover, as discussed previously, the potentially evolving nature of the identity, organization, management, and personnel of the project owner on a megaproject over its extended duration may create changing project owner expectations.

Analysis and Discussion

Much has been written in recent years about the apparent disconnect and lack of realism between the publicly defined programmatic expectations of the project owner

on megaprojects and the actual limitations and constraints on the ability of the project owner to achieve these expectations. This disconnect and lack of realism is driven, in significant part, by the way that megaprojects are funded and is exacerbated by the lack of transparency and accountability of the project owner in the execution of the mega-project. If project owners understate risks and costs or fail to disclose them, eventually, when the project reality is known or disclosed, stakeholders may form the perception that the project's "over budget" status is due to service deficiencies of the consulting engineer, and the owner may not have the interest or incentive to correct this perception. All too often, the consulting engineer is "caught-up" and blamed as complicit with the project owner's lack of transparency and accountability or is otherwise held responsible for the disconnect and lack of realism — a convenient "scapegoat." Many of the recommended steps discussed in the preceding chapters, if implemented, will go a long way in substantially reducing these problems on megaprojects. While admittedly the development and successful implementation of these recommended practices lies in significant part beyond the initiative and control of the consulting engineer — and primarily rests with the project owner, funding and oversight agencies, and, to a degree, politicians — there are important risk management measures that the consulting engineer may undertake to significantly reduce the risk of professional liability exposure directly resulting from these disconnects and lack of realism.

Recommended Practices

- Document the project owner's expectations as they are developed and defined, including the owner's decisions, and communicate to the project owner the anticipated cost and schedule implications of these decisions.
- Document advice to the project owner regarding the project's costs and schedule, risk exposure associated with various program options, and project owner decisions.
- Recommend the development and periodic monitoring and updating of a risk register to be used to make and validate realistic estimates of project cost and schedule.
- Recommend that the project owner carry adequate contingency for both known and unknown risk exposures.
- Recommend the advisability of conducting an independent review and validation of the project budget and schedule and key project management programs, initiatives, and systems. Document these recommendations.
- Encourage the project owner's transparency, accountability, and periodic updating and reporting to stakeholders and overseers on the cost and schedule estimates and the current status of the project.

- Learn about the project owner's funding strategies, sources of funds, and stability of funding considerations, all of which may impact the professional liability risk exposure of the consulting engineer if a project is suspended or curtailed for funding-related reasons.
- Educate the consulting engineer's staff about the need to constantly manage the project owner's expectations and document recommendations and advice given to the project owner. Emphasize the importance of this to the staff.
- Understand and be responsive to the owner's preferences (attitudes) toward risk assumption and tolerance and incorporate those views into the design and construction process and contractual risk allocation provisions.
- Recognize that the organization, management, or personnel composition of the project owner is likely to change over the extended duration of the megaproject and, accordingly, understand the importance of continuous management of client expectations and maintenance of documentation in order to preserve an objective project record.

4.0   Project Owner–Consulting Engineer Relationship Issues

Issue

Megaprojects constantly challenge the traditional definition and structure of the project owner–consulting engineer relationship. In the traditional owner-engineer relationship established on most conventional projects, the consulting engineer functions as an independent contractor of the project owner. In that arrangement, a significant degree of professional independence exists between the structure, organization, and functions of both parties. In addition, the consulting engineer is selected and retained by the project owner to perform certain services based on the former's expertise and experience. Thus, it is reasonable to identify, by the discrete and contractually defined function or organizational sources (i.e., between project owner and consulting engineer), who did what and, therefore, who is responsible and accountable for derelictions or deficiencies in the performance of respective roles, obligations, and scopes.

In a megaproject, there are often sound and compelling reasons to consider the potential integration or merger (homogenization), both structurally and functionally, of the project owner's and the consulting engineer's organizations. In some cases, the consulting engineer functions as an extension of the owner's organization. These homogenized units are often labeled "integrated project organizations" (IPOs). The project owner may implement an IPO for a number of reasons, including the goals of minimizing project cost by reducing the need for project owner redundancy or oversight (shad-

owing) of the consulting engineer; increasing and streamlining efficiency and resource utilization; future training of the project owner's internal staff; and, on the more subjective end, achieving complete unification and alignment of project interests of both the project owner and the consulting engineer.

Integrated project organizations often achieve the management goals of efficiency, cost effectiveness, collaboration, alliancing, and team building. However, particularly in the context of a megaproject involving the integration of a public sector project owner and a private sector consulting engineer, sufficient attention needs to be dedicated to developing appropriate standards for evaluating and determining professional accountability of the consulting engineer in connection with services performed on an integrated basis with the project owner. Unless that occurs, questions will be raised subsequently (and, potentially legitimately) about the ability of the project owner to monitor and manage the consulting engineer's performance and accountability.

Analysis and Discussion

On megaprojects, there are a variety of project owner–consulting engineer relationships, some of which are defined by contract and some of which functionally evolve in a more informal manner. In some instances, the contract defines one type of relationship and the actual or functional relationship deviates in material respects. This is yet another manifestation of the dynamics and flexibility inherent in a megaproject that develop from the changing roles and responsibilities of the participants over the duration of the project.

In view of the changing character of project owner–consulting engineer relationships on megaprojects, how does the consultant best manage risk and professional liability exposure and make sure that contracts, which, by definition, are more formal, static, and slower to evolve, adapt appropriately and promptly to any such changing relationships — i.e., to fairly and reasonably reflect the degrees of risk assumption resulting from varying and evolving project owner–consulting engineer relationships?

On most project engagements, the consulting engineer has a traditional "independent contractor" relationship in which roles and responsibilities are clearly defined by contract. The consulting engineer is expected to exercise independent professional judgment and make prudent recommendations, has the ability to control and supervise the quality of its service performance, is responsible for the supervision and quality control of its service performance (and that of its subconsultants), and is retained for its recognized and demonstrated qualifications, experience, and expertise in the relevant project context. In this traditional independent contractor relationship, the project owner generally is responsible for final decision-making and independent oversight and management of the consulting engineer and primarily (or exclusively) relies upon the consult-

ing engineer for independent service performance and judgment on matters within the consulting engineer's contractually defined scope, roles, and responsibilities.

This traditional independent contractor relationship has as its principal characteristics a clear delineation and assignment of the consulting engineer's service scope, roles, and responsibilities; independence in the performance of its services and ability to supervise and control the quality of that performance; definition of standards to evaluate its professional accountability; and the project owner's reliance upon the consulting engineer (and its subconsultants) for the exercise of sound professional judgment and adequate performance of the contractually-assigned service scope consistent with contractually-defined standards. In the independent contractor relationship, determining the consulting engineer's accountability — typically under the professional standard of care measurement — centers on evaluating the performance of the consulting engineer. In the event of a proven departure from the professional standard of care, the consulting engineer may be held accountable, in which case its professional liability insurer generally will indemnify the project owner for the resulting damage caused by the consulting engineer's deficient performance.

The contractually defined and assigned service scope, the independence of the consulting engineer and its ability to control and manage its own performance, and the degree of independent professional discretion and judgment of the consulting engineer are critically important factors in the evaluation of the consulting engineer's professional liability risk exposure and its professional accountability and responsibility. Simply put, the greater the degree of specificity and clarity in the definition of the consulting engineer's service scope obligations and its independent ability to control its service performance, the greater the degree of professional responsibility and accountability. At the same time, the greater the degree of control over the quality and other aspects of its service performance, the more manageable the consulting engineer's risk exposure.

In a megaproject, it is not uncommon for the project owner and consulting engineer to assume, contractually or otherwise, relationships that vary in significant ways from this traditional independent contractor model. Many of these variations involve some form, and differing degrees of, organizational and functional integration between the project owner and the consulting engineer.

The collaboration or integration between owner and consultant may be achieved in a more or less formal (contractual) manner through so-called IPOs or by a variety of "secondment" relationships. The IPO and secondment relationships may involve, more or less, the integration of owner and consultant roles in areas such as project planning, design, project management, and construction management. Although IPOs have been used in the purely private sector context, the use of these integrated roles and relationships in public sector design and construction raises special issues, as discussed below. In many of these instances, the IPO or secondment–consulting engineer relationship

301

commences in a more conventional independent contractor structure and subsequently—due to such factors as the stage of the project's design and construction or the project owner's desire to reduce costs (by reducing consultant fees) by a supposedly more efficient use of project personnel—transforms into an IPO or secondment relationship. When such evolution occurs, in-place (executed) contracts (in conventional independent contractor terms) may not, and often do not, reflect the reality of the actual and respective roles, responsibilities, or relationships of the project owner and consulting engineer.

At one end of the "integrated" spectrum is "secondment," which is defined as "the state of being released or transferred from a regularly assigned position for temporary duty with another organization." In a megaproject, secondment approaches include both the temporary assignment of consulting engineer personnel to the project owner and, in the reverse direction, the temporary assignment of project owner personnel to the consulting engineer. To a degree, both of these secondment approaches may (and often do) result in a diminished ability of the consulting engineer to direct, supervise, control, and manage the quality of its service performance. In addition, conflicting allegiances and loyalties among seconded personnel may arise, and the defense of professional liability claims against the consulting engineer may be complicated by such issues. In circumstances in which personnel of the consulting engineer are seconded to the project owner, contractual risk management responses for the consulting engineer may include releases, indemnification, and limitation of liability for claims and liabilities arising out the performance of services of the seconded personnel. In a related vein, if the consulting engineer is not able to effectively control the performance of project owner personnel seconded to the consulting engineer, similar contractual responses are appropriate.

At the other and more aggressive end of the "integrated" model spectrum is the IPO. To date, the most publicized example of using an IPO on a megaproject is the Central Artery/Tunnel (CA/T) Project in Boston, in which, commencing around 1997, the Massachusetts Turnpike Authority (MTA), the project owner at that time, and its private sector program management consultant functioned in an IPO relationship. This relationship had been preceded by a somewhat conventional independent contractor relationship and was followed by various secondment relationships.[10] In varying forms and structures, IPOs currently are being utilized on other megaprojects, such as the Panama Canal and the East Side Access Project in New York.

There are many reasons that account for project owners choosing to use the IPO approach on megaprojects. Some project owners perceive that combining their own internal personnel with the consulting engineer's staff will produce efficiencies with respect to resources, talent, and budget control (by reducing the consulting engineer's fees). In addition, combining or merging the owner's and consultant's personnel may result in more collaboration, a unification of project goals, directness in communication, and transparency in service performance. In theory, integration—in structure, attitude,

and physical co-location—will serve to build a team spirit and reduce adversarial interactions, tensions, and balkanization that sometimes develop in the more traditional independent contractor arrangement, especially on public sector projects.

IPO formation may be achieved contractually (de jure) or in organizational and functional practice (de facto). In some instances, the project owner–consulting engineer relationship may commence as independent contractor in character through some project milestone, such as completion of design development, and then evolve into an IPO. In any event, it is important that the consulting engineer make certain that the risk allocation provisions contained in its agreement reflect the reality of the present nature of its relationship with the project owner.

As previously discussed, the relationship between a project owner and a consulting engineer has traditionally been legally characterized as "independent contractor" in nature, given the professional expertise and degree of control in judgment expected to be exercised by the consulting engineer in providing its services and that "Professionals, such as Architects and Engineers, perform their design tasks as independent contractors due to the highly specialized skill and license requirements of their work."[11] The degree of professional and legal responsibility assumed by, or imposed by law upon, the consulting engineer as an independent contractor typically is contractually defined in provisions such as the following:

> The Engineer is an Independent Contractor, and nothing contained in the Contract Documents shall be construed as creating or constituting any relationship with the Owner other than that of an Independent Contractor. In no event shall the relationship between the Owner and the Engineer be construed as creating any relationship whatsoever between the Owner and the Engineer's employees. Neither the Engineer nor any of its employees is or shall be deemed to be an employee of the Owner. Except as otherwise specified in the Contract Documents, the Engineer has sole authority and responsibility to employ, discharge, direct, and otherwise control its employees and has complete and sole responsibility as a principal for its agents, for all Subconsultants, and for all other persons that the Engineer or any Subconsultant hires to perform or assist in performing the services. Any review, approval, or acceptance of the Engineer's services or work product by the Owner shall not relieve the Engineer of its responsibility and liability under this Agreement and/or the Contract Documents.

As a general matter, in the traditional independent contractor model the roles, responsibilities, and service scope of the consulting engineer, and its ability to manage and control the quality of its service performance, typically are aspects of the professional relationship and the consultant is obligated to indemnify the project owner for failure to satisfy the professional standard of care or for a breach of professional duty in the performance of contractually-assigned scope.

Figure 1. **Typical Responsibility-Control Relationships**

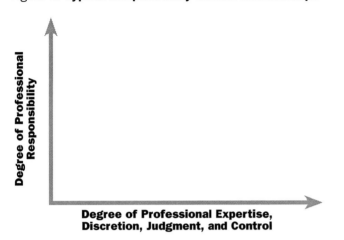

There is, and should be, a correlation between the consulting engineer's (a) ability to supervise and control its service performance and ability to exercise independent professional judgment and (b) degree of professional accountability. The greater these abilities, the higher the degree of accountability. The degree of professional accountability should correspond with the degree of professional service control (see Figure 1).

These aspects of the independent contractor relationship and the corresponding degrees of professional accountability and professional liability risk exposure of the consulting engineer are more or less significantly and fundamentally altered, undermined, and eroded in IPO and secondment relationships. In IPO relationships, the consulting engineer typically has less ability to direct, supervise, control, and manage its personnel and service performance and, as such, the legal result should be a diminished degree of professional accountability and liability responsibility or risk for the consulting engineer.

Moreover, in an IPO, roles, relationships, and service scope performance are shared between the project owner and the consulting engineer, often with no specific delineation between them. In some important respects, this collaboration represents the very essence of the integrated nature of the IPO. If these relationships are addressed contractually (as they should be), then the release, indemnification, and limitation of liability provisions (which protect or limit the professional liability exposure of the consulting engineer) are appropriate adjustments. For example, in addressing the secondment of the private sector management consultant personnel to the public sector authority on the CA/T Project, the relevant contractual allocation of liability provisions stated:

> Because the [seconded Management Consultant employees] will be under the Authority's exclusive supervision, direction and control in their performance of the Services, the Authority and the Department hereby agree to release [the Management Consultant] from any and all liability to the Authority and the Department, to the extent permitted by law, for any claims, liabilities, costs or expenses arising out of or relating to (i) any act or omission of the [seconded Management Consultant personnel] within the scope of their performance of the Services; (ii) the technical, economic and environmental feasibility, effectiveness, and consequences of any decision, procedure, method, or process implemented by the Authority, the Department or third-parties as a result of the activities of the [seconded Management Consultant personnel] within the scope of their performance of the

Services; and (iii) any personal injury or death, loss or damage to property, economic loss, indirect or consequential damages, such as loss of use, or incidental expenses of whatever nature, arising out of or in connection with the activities of the [seconded Management Consultant personnel] within the scope of their performance of the Services.

The IPO may be defined and structured in various ways, including a "salt and pepper" approach in which the respective project owner and consulting engineer personnel, depending upon their expertise, technical skill, or mere resource availability, combine (integrate) and may be supervised by, and report to, their non-employer. From a legal perspective, the IPO may well result in joint and shared control and responsibility in service performance between the project owner and the consulting engineer and, consequently, a blurring of otherwise clear and traditional roles and responsibilities that underlie the conventional independent contractor structure.

In the public sector megaproject context, the reduced accountability of the private sector consultant in an IPO has raised substantial legal and public policy concerns, both as a matter of perception and reality.[12] As the Report of the Massachusetts State Senate Committee on Post Audit and Oversight, "Road Blocks to Cost Recovery: Key Findings and Recommendations on the Big Dig Cost Recovery Process,"[13] December 2004, stated:

> Under the Integrated Project Organization, state employees were integrated with employees of [the management consultant] with the goal of creating a more seamless project management structure. It was to be a "dynamic, flexible and harmonious whole [to enable state employees and management consultant employees to work together cooperatively, without duplication of efforts] . . . designed to match staff members' technical skills to jobs without regard for the organization paying their salaries."
>
> At the time, benefits of an IPO had been realized primarily in the private sector and were largely untested in the public sector where different levels of review and safeguards are necessary and paramount to insure efficiencies and accountability in state government. In many cases, public projects face strict mandates under state law that is inapplicable and not analogous to the private companies. . . .
>
> The Committee, however, has substantially larger concerns with the IPO's effects on project management and its impact on the cost recovery process. . . . [T]here was a remarkable lack of discussion in any legal agreements made between [the management consultant] and the Commonwealth on the significant issues related to adopting an IPO on a public contract. Based on the Committee's investigation, it appears the following critical questions were never addressed:
>
> - What effects will this have on public accountability of the parties?
> - Will it affect the legal relationship between [the management consultant], the Massachusetts Turnpike Authority and the State?

- If so, how—who will assume professional and contractual accountability for the varying aspects of the project?
- How will the work programs (the contracts of the Big Dig) be impacted by the IPO?
- Will they have to be amended to mirror the realities of the new organizational structure?
- If not, is it not the case that [the management consultant's] contractual obligations are out of step with the professional liability standards of the organizational structure adopted?
- What does it mean when [the management consultant] is acting effectively as the State, and the State as [the management consultant] under the IPO?

It is the understanding of the Committee that these questions were never appropriately addressed prior to or subsequent to adopting the IPO. . . .

Therefore, it is the conclusion of the Committee that because these larger liability issues were apparently never addressed, adverse behavioral issues ensued. As a direct consequence, there was an absence of the "arms length" transactional relationship that typifies a project owner/consulting engineer relationship. This resulted in a project that lacked adequate public oversight, putting cost recovery on a back burner in favor of state and [Management Committee] employees "getting along to go along" under the IPO, and [the Management Consultant's] stunning lack of referral of itself to the cost recovery process. . . .

Many commentators on the CA/T Project have identified issues surrounding the relationship between the project owner and the private management consultant as some of the more important "lessons learned" from that project experience, including the need of the project owner "to keep a tighter check on the private firms it uses to manage such projects."[14] "All along, a problem for the Project [had] been a degree of closeness, where the people who were supposed to be doing the watching and blowing the whistle were holding hands with the people making those decisions at the project management level and at the [management consultant] level."[15] "As the Public Agency, you need to be a strong owner and understand that while you share certain goals and objectives with the project manager, it is not complete alignment. You need to balance the concept of teamwork with an appropriate professional relationship and distance. . . ."[16] "The first lesson of the Big Dig is that you need a balance between efficiency and oversight."[17] This same group of commentators noted that these "relationship" issues and the ensuing problems—in both reality and perception—are exacerbated when the project owner places too much emphasis on a "culture" of cost-control, efficiency, and lack of accountability and transparency. "With the Big Dig, because of state and federal pressures on costs, the other set of issues—disclosure and checks and balances and quality control—were subordinated over time. Increasing costs distorted the balance needed between trans-

parency and accountability and quality control on the one side, and the cost issue, which had too much focus. Efficiency won over oversight and that had a consequence, some of which we are seeing now."[18]

Fundamentally, these relationship issues and the associated problems (in perception or reality) are not at all solved by the retention and layering of private sector consultants on top of or beside each other. For example, the practice of retaining an agency construction manager independent of the design team—while facilitating checks and balances over other project participants (including the consulting engineer responsible for design)—does not substitute for the project owner itself adopting an appropriate distance and independence in the management of its relationship with the consulting engineer. Nor does it substitute for the need for the project owner to have its own internal qualifications, capability, and credibility to manage the project, including overseeing and evaluating the consulting engineer's performance and implementing robust programs for its own accountability and transparency. Moreover, if the scope of services and responsibilities of the agency construction manager relative to other project participants is not clearly defined and allocated, the project owner's ability to enforce accountability of its multiple private sector consulting engineers may be significantly compromised and undermined. Ambiguity, redundancy, and conflict in the definition of service scope and allocation of risk and responsibility among such consulting engineers also increase their professional liability exposure.

Implementing an IPO relationship poses substantial issues and challenges to many aspects of the project, including the distinction among roles and responsibilities, the differentiation between the public owner and consulting engineer, the ability of the consultant to control the adequacy of its service performance and exercise independent professional judgment, professional accountability (i.e., between the public owner and consulting engineer, who is responsible for what, and to whom, and on what basis such determinations are made), potentially conflicting allegiances and loyalties, and the ability of the public owner to credibly demonstrate (realistically and by perception) that it has adequate and independent qualifications to manage and oversee the consulting engineer who is part of the IPO. In addition, there are important practice and project-specific professional liability insurance implications posed by an IPO, more specifically: whether the consulting engineer is assuming non-traditional "professional services"; whether any claim or liability results from professional services performed by the consulting engineer as distinct from services performed by the project owner or its employees; whether the consulting engineer is able to defend a claim on the basis that its ability to exercise independent professional judgment was impaired or adversely influenced or impacted by virtue of the IPO structure; and whether the consulting engineer has potential conflicting loyalties between obligations owed to the IPO and those owed under the professional liability policy.[19]

There are a number of important implications of risk allocation, potential professional liability, and professional liability insurance for the consulting engineer functioning in the IPO approach. The most fundamental transformation from traditional independent contractor to IPO is that in the latter, the project owner and consulting engineer, by definition, function and interact in an integrated mode—internally and from the external perspective. This integration results in the fusion and collaboration in service performance between the project owner and consulting engineer. An IPO results in a significant de-emphasis in the need for identifying the entity performing the service. The IPO functions in a "salt and pepper" manner which, by design and intent, typically is structured and organized to minimize any emphasis on identification and segregation of the project owner and consulting engineer in the actual performance of service activities. Also, the IPO results in shared and collaborative responsibility for control, management, and decision-making that results from the "team" effort. In some circumstances, consulting engineers are empowered to make decisions (not simply render advice or recommendations) that typically are reserved for the project owner alone and, at times, in subject areas outside the scope of traditional engineering services as defined in most professional liability insurance policies.

For obvious reasons, this transformation in roles and responsibilities creates significant challenges to the process of determining the consulting engineer's professional accountability and responsibility. In a corollary respect, the application and availability of the consulting engineer's professional liability insurance is complicated because insurance presumes and depends upon the ability to identify and evaluate fault or breach of professional duty *of the consulting engineer* (as distinct from others, including the project owner).[20] In addition, the IPO structure may result in the consulting engineer's involvement in matters that go beyond the scope of traditional professional services (as defined in a professional liability insurance policy) and create *owner* risk and liability exposures for the consulting engineer that are not covered under professional liability insurance.

Project stakeholders and other third parties may not see any external differentiation and distinction between the project owner and consulting engineer in the IPO approach. This obliteration of independent identities may result in the consulting engineer becoming subject to third-party and public law liability exposures that typically would not exist in the traditional independent contractor relationship. For example, on some projects, the project owner and consulting engineer collectively and publicly are referred to as the "project."

In the public sector megaproject context, the integration of the project owner and consulting engineer in an IPO may create perceived conflicts of interest or related problems due to the "closeness" of the project owner–consulting engineer relationship in an IPO. Connected to this concern is the ability of the project owner to credibly demon-

strate that it has the incentive and adequate, qualified, and independent ability to manage and oversee the consulting engineer who is part of the IPO.

Deficiencies in project owner accountability often lead to unwarranted and unfair criticism of the consulting engineer:

> The reality of the Big Dig [CA/T Project] is that from the start, schedule compliance was favored over budget adherence. Management spent money to keep the project moving, knowing that failure to overcome obstacles in individual contracts would have a ripple effect throughout the project. In the megaproject environment, the whole is split into many smaller parts that must fit together in both space and time. If one contractor's schedule slipped, several other contractors could claim a delay. Public sector and political accountability also would have gone a long way to address the continuing issue of cost escalation. The decision to blame the management consultant for underestimating true project costs during the project planning may have provided a convenient scapegoat to deflect political accountability. However, it also had the long-term detrimental effect of exposing the management consultant to media pressure in which it could not respond and eroding the public confidence in the privatized program management of the Big Dig. When a technical problem occurs that rightly requires the management consultant's action, even their best efforts are met with skepticism. The lesson learned is that you can't have it both ways. If you use your program manager as a scapegoat in the media, you can't expect the public to accept your total reliance on him when problems arise.[21]

As previously noted, in an IPO the consulting engineer, by virtue of the integrated nature of the relationship, may be exposed to risk and liability that are traditionally borne by the project owner alone.[22] This will result not only in increased exposure in non-traditional areas, but also in circumstances in which the consulting engineer is exposed to liability while the project owner may be entitled to sovereign or governmental immunity.[23]

IPO Implementation: Some Risk Management and Professional Liability Implications

Recognizing that many project owners involved in megaprojects are inclined to implement — or at minimum, explore the implementation of — the IPO approach, what are some proactive risk management steps that the consulting engineer may pursue in the IPO relationship?

The foregoing discussion amply demonstrates that a consulting engineer functioning in the context of an IPO faces professional liability exposure beyond the realm of that traditionally assumed in the more conventional independent contractor relationship. As

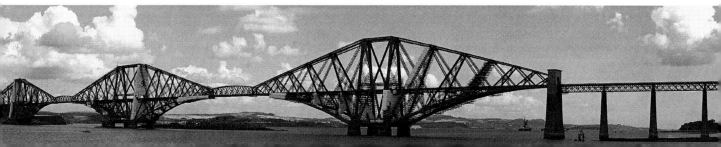

such, it is important that the consulting engineer in an IPO relationship be aware of the potential for liability exposure posed by the "integrated" nature of the organization. At some point, for different purposes, the public, project stakeholders, or others may seek to hold the consulting engineer accountable for services it performed as part of an integrated organization. As such, while it is less important operationally during the functioning of the IPO that differentiation and attribution of service performance occur, ultimately, in any subsequent investigation to determine liability and accountability, it is important that the consulting engineer be in a position to distinguish, define, and demark its role and responsibilities and to document the bounds of its actual service performance. Demarcation and documentation are critically important both to evaluating the adequacy of professional service performance and to the defense and adjudication of claims involving professional accountability.

In the IPO context, there are contractual and risk management responses that may be effective in reducing the professional liability exposure of the consulting engineer. For example, consider the following contract provisions:

- *Threshold Exemption*

  Project Owner recognizes and expects that certain claims, liabilities, and costs (direct, indirect, special, incidental, and consequential) may result from the Project Owner's decision to implement, primarily for its benefit, an Integrated Project Organization ("IPO") relationship with Engineer and that, given the nature of that relationship, it may be difficult, if not impossible, to specifically identify and allocate risk or responsibility for such claims, liabilities, and costs. Accordingly, the Project Owner agrees not to sue and otherwise will make no claim directly or indirectly against the Engineer on the basis of professional negligence, breach of contract, breach of fiduciary duty, indemnification, or otherwise, to the extent that any such claim allegedly or actually arises out of or relates to the services provided by the Engineer as part of the IPO unless such claims exceed $_____ in the aggregate as determined at substantial completion of the Project.

- *Indemnification*

  The Project Owner agrees to defend, indemnify, and hold harmless the Engineer for all claims, liabilities, settlements, judgments, costs, penalties, and attorney's fees, to the extent caused or alleged to be caused by acts or omissions of the Engineer while functioning as part of an Integrated Project Organization with the Project Owner.[24]

- *Limitation of Remedy*

  The Consulting Engineer should consider the inclusion of a limitation of remedy provision in its agreement with the Project Owner, pursuant to which the

latter agrees that any recovery by the Project Owner (or anyone claiming by or through the Project Owner) shall be limited to a specified dollar amount if based on claims arising out of services performed by the Consulting Engineer as part of the IPO.

- *Covenant Regarding Constructor Releases and Same Protection as Project Owner*

  The Project Owner will use reasonable efforts to afford the Consulting Engineer the same protections as the Project Owner receives in releases, remedies, and indemnities in contracts, modifications, and/or settlement agreements with Constructors entered into by the Project Owner during the term of this Agreement.

- *Constructor Release and Covenant Not to Sue*

  The Constructor, or any subcontractor, successor, assign, subrogee, or surety of the Constructor, agrees to release and not to bring any civil suit, action, or other proceeding in law, equity, or arbitration against the Engineer, or the officers, employees, agents, or consultants of the Engineer, for the enforcement of any action which the Constructor may have arising out of, or in any matter connected with, the Work. The Constructor shall assure that this release and covenant not to sue is contained in all agreements with subcontractors and sub-subcontractors of every tier, and shall assure its enforcement. The Consulting Engineer, its officers, employees, agents, and consultants are intended third-party beneficiaries of this release and covenant not to sue and are entitled to enforce this release and covenant in law or equity.

In addition to contractual responses, there are a variety of risk management admonitions that can and should be implemented on any project utilizing the IPO approach. For example, the consulting engineer should maintain documentation of the basis of project decision-making and train its personnel on special precautions to take in an IPO, including ethical issues and the balancing of tensions between the management objectives of, and allegiances to, the IPO on one hand and the consulting engineer's obligations under public laws (including registration laws), its own corporate policies, and obligations to its professional liability insurer on the other.

Even when not involved in a strictly formal integrated relationship with the project owner, the consulting engineer is often legally or contractually characterized as possessing a "special relationship" of trust, confidence, and loyalty with the owner. These characterizations may lead to the legal conclusion that a fiduciary relationship exists between the project owner and the consulting engineer, thereby giving rise to claims of breach of fiduciary duty by the former against the latter.[25] The intimacy and prolonged nature of the project owner–consulting engineer relationship on megaprojects may be more likely to give rise to fiduciary duty claims, especially in circumstances in which the

owner and consulting engineer function in an IPO; the project owner becomes wholly or predominantly reliant or dependent upon the consulting engineer; or the project owner has inadequate resources, qualifications, or experience to efficiently and independently monitor, manage, or supervise the performance of the consulting engineer.

In other circumstances, the consulting engineer may be viewed as an agent of the project owner or otherwise so clearly aligned as to be legally considered "one" with the project owner. This "agency" relationship may subject the consulting engineer to liability that derives from wrongdoing predominantly or exclusively on the part of the project owner. In yet other circumstances, this agency relationship may confer upon the consulting engineer certain defenses — such as derivative sovereign immunity — that typically and traditionally have been available only to the public project owner.[26]

A fair question is whether in an IPO — in which schedule or cost predominate — there is a greater risk that quality, and perhaps even safety, may be compromised. Will a consulting engineer's professional obligations to the public become subordinated to more project-specific and programmatic objectives of the IPO? The transformation of allegiances can be ever so gradual and subtle in an IPO, and checks and balances between the project owner and consulting engineer may be relaxed or become significantly less of a priority. The consulting engineer's allegiance to its public and professional responsibility may also be overridden or compromised by a sense of loyalty and commitment to the "integrated project organization." While achieving efficiency and cost effectiveness, does the IPO ultimately undermine public confidence in the engineering profession by subordinating public interest and promoting a predominant sense of loyalty to the "project" and the "IPO"? In the final analysis, do the public interest and integrity of the engineering profession suffer? Is the consulting engineer's accountability undermined or compromised or, in some instances, completely eroded in either perception or reality, or both?

Are consulting engineers to be blamed for all of these potentially adverse consequences of an IPO? Certainly not. In the first instance, the consulting engineer rarely initiates or proposes the IPO approach. But in the final analysis, consulting engineers are (for the most part) registered professionals who owe obligations to the public, and, in some applications, the IPO approach may present evident and heightened risks in terms of the consulting engineer's ability to fulfill those public obligations.[27] In no circumstances, however, should the consulting engineer subordinate its professional and public (registration) law obligations to the sense of allegiance owed to the IPO.

Increasingly, project owners are motivated to experiment with, or implement various forms of, IPOs with their consulting engineers. The project owner's decision to proceed in that organizational direction typically is driven by the desire to reduce costs (i.e., private consulting engineer fees) and promote the more efficient utilization of owner and engineering resources. Also underlying such project owner decisions is the objective to develop a "team" approach to project delivery.

These objectives underlie most project owner decisions to utilize the IPO approach. They certainly have positive components and offer significant opportunities for improved and more efficient project delivery. However, the IPO approach also has certain inherent risks, especially for the consulting engineer. The consulting engineer may be required to perform services or engage in activities that go beyond the traditional practice of engineering. In addition, the public, the constructors, and others may perceive the project owner and consulting engineer as "one" and view each as completely responsible for the acts of the other. The project owner may be protected from liability claims by virtue of sovereign immunity in circumstances in which the consulting engineer does not have the benefit of that defense. The consulting engineer may also be subjected to pressure—however subtle in nature—to subordinate sound engineering judgment and recommendations for the "good of the IPO." In the event of a claim against the consulting engineer arising out the performance of services in an IPO, it may not be possible or feasible to differentiate services performed or supervised by the project owner from those performed or supervised by the consulting engineer. Moreover, the public and other project stakeholders may lose confidence in the ability of the project owner to effectively manage the consulting engineer because of the "intimacy" of the IPO relationship, which can lead to an increased focus on professional liability claims against the consulting engineer.[28]

These and related risks for the consulting engineer in an IPO need to be identified and evaluated on a project-specific basis and the consulting engineer should develop a risk management plan to address them, commencing with the drafting and negotiation of appropriate contractual risk allocation provisions. These provisions should reflect the basic position that the consulting engineer's liability exposure in an IPO should be limited because the consultant takes on significant degrees of risk for the project owner's benefit. Put another way, in an IPO, the consulting engineer may end up with a reduced fee and may also lose a significant degree of its traditional ability to control and supervise the quality of its service performance, exercise independent judgment, and otherwise manage its risk exposure. Thus, at a minimum, this diminished supervision and reduced degree of control should result in a *higher* threshold of liability for the consulting engineer and limitations on remedies and recovery from the consultant.

Recommended Practices

- Obtain legal review of structural/functional and contractual aspects of any IPO and make certain that risk allocation provisions of the consulting engineer's contract reflect the reality of the relationship and appropriately balance risk and reward.
- Obtain contractual indemnification, limitation of remedy, release, and covenant

not to sue protections for professional liability exposure resulting from services performed by the consulting engineer on an integrated basis, especially in circumstances in which those services are directed, controlled, or managed by the project owner.

- The consulting engineer should not assume liability of the project owner's employees or representatives, even those performing services directly or under the supervision of the consulting engineer.

- Limit liability to third parties (such as constructors) arising from consulting engineer services performed as agent for the project owner.

- Notwithstanding the collaborative nature of service performance in an IPO, at some point efforts may be made by the project owner or others to independently hold the consulting engineer accountable for the adequacy of services performed as part of the IPO.

- Performance of services in an IPO will not excuse or relieve the consulting engineer of its professional responsibility to perform its services in accordance with requirements of registration and other public laws. Public health, safety, and welfare should never be subordinated or compromised, especially in an IPO.

5.0   Balancing Risk and Reward

Issue

Megaprojects pose substantial professional liability risk exposure for consulting engineers. Chapter 4 focused on the subject of specific contract issues for the consulting engineer in the megaproject context. This section addresses the need for balancing risk assumption with reward in a more general sense.

Analysis and Discussion

There is, and should be, a balance and correlation between, on one side, the consulting engineer's contractual service scope, defined roles, responsibilities, and risk and, on the other, its compensation (reward). For example, performance of a study or preparation of conceptual or preliminary design (which generally involves fairly limited service scopes) should represent limited risk and liability exposure and, therefore, liability should be contractually limited to a specified dollar amount and any consequential damage exposure should be either eliminated or limited. Contracts should be negotiated and agreed in a manner that is cognizant of the basic principles that:

- The more limited the consulting engineer's scope, the greater the need for liability limitation.
- The lesser the ability of the consulting engineer to control its service performance and exercise discretion and independent professional judgment in the execution thereof, the greater the need for liability limitation.
- The more that factors and variables outside the consulting engineer's control may influence or impact professional liability exposure, the greater the need for liability limitation.
- The greater the degree of distribution and dispersal of professional scope and responsibility among multiple professionals by the project owner without overall "prime" responsibility in one of them, the greater the need for liability limitation.

Megaprojects present many and varied opportunities for all of the foregoing heightened risk exposure scenarios for the consulting engineer due to their many stages (studies, preliminary design, final design, construction), complexity, number of project participants, use of innovative design and alternative project delivery approaches (such as fast-track), number of design and construction contract interfaces and interdependencies, and quest for independence in the design and construction management functions.[29]

Recommended Practices

- Negotiate contract terms that reflect an appropriate balancing of professional liability risk exposure with contractually defined scope, roles, responsibilities, and agreed compensation.
- Manage risk through contract language, such as clearly defined scope, indemnification limited to professional negligence of the consulting engineer, limitations on liability, and consequential damage disclaimers. Similarly, and especially in subsurface megaprojects, manage risks through an adequate and timely commissioning of the consulting engineer's involvement during the construction phase.

Notes

1. There are various definitions of what constitutes a "megaproject." In terms of whether a project is considered "megaproject" in nature and subject to special oversight processes and mechanisms, the Federal Highway Administration (FHWA) has suggested that the following be considered: whether the project has an estimated cost of at least $1 billion; whether it involves a high level of interest on the part of the public, the Congress, or the Administration; or, in the case

of a Federal-Aid Highway and Mass Transit project, whether it may have a significant effect on the recipient's financially constrained overall transportation program of projects. FHWA, "Major Project Program Cost Estimating Guidance," January 2007. Elsewhere, it has been stated: "There is currently no standard definition of what constitutes a 'major' project. The definition has been applied to projects ranging from those with a total cost of as little as $10 million to those estimated to cost $1 billion or more." Government Accountability Office (GAO), "Cost and Oversight of Major Highway and Bridge Projects—Issues and Options," GAO-03-764T, p. 1, n. 1. (5-8-3). The Federal Highway Administration defines a megaproject as a major infrastructure project that costs more than $1 billion or a project of a significant cost that attracts a high level of public attention or political interest because of its substantial direct and indirect impact on the community, environment, and state budgets. "Mega" also connotes the skill level and attention required to manage the project successfully. J. Capka, "Megaprojects—They Are a Different Breed," *Public Roads* 68(1) (July/Aug. 2004) : 3. In "Report of the OIG DOT Task Force on Oversight of Large Transportation Infrastructure Projects" (July 11, 2005), the Office of Inspector General (OIG), DOT, defined megaprojects as "transit, highway and aviation infrastructure projects that (1) will cost at least $1 billion, or (2) are financed with at least $250 million of federal funding, including direct loans and loan guaranties, or (3) have significant congressional or departmental interest." *See also* "OIG Methodology for Reviewing Transportation Megaprojects," p. 3 (Nov. 28, 2005); *see*, K. Frick, "The Cost of the Technological Sublime: Daring Ingenuity and the New San Francisco–Oakland Bay Bridge," Chapter 12 in H. Priemus, B. Flyvbjerg, and B. Van Wee, eds., *Decision-Making on Mega-Projects: Cost Benefit Analysis, Planning and Innovation*, Cheltenham, UK: Edward Elgar Publishing Ltd., 2008, §12.2, 240–41 (hereinafter *Decision-Making*).

2. *See* J. Dunnicliff and H. Parker, "The Care and Feeding of Individual Consultants and Their Clients," *Geotechnical News* 20 (Dec. 2002): 26–30; J. Dunnicliff and H. Parker, "Discussions of 'The Care and Feeding of Individual Consultants and Their Clients,'" *Geotechnical News* 21 (June 2003): 28–36; J. Atkins and G. Simpson, Chapter 2, "Clients," in *Managing Project Risk: Best Practices for Architects and Related Professionals*, Hoboken, NJ: Wiley, 2008.

3. For the most part, the term "consulting engineer," as employed in this chapter, refers to a private sector engineering (or other design, program, or construction management professional) firm engaged by the project owner to provide specified engineering services connected with the planning, design, management, and construction of a megaproject.

4. *See* "ASCE Code of Ethics, Professional and Ethical Conduct Guidelines," *Engineering Inc.* 14 (Sep./Oct. 2003); M. Iqbal, "Ethics and Rules of Conduct Governing Design Professionals" ("§IV. ASCE Code of Ethics and Rules of Professional Conduct"), in S. Hess et al., eds., *Design Professional and Construction Manager Law,* Chicago: American Bar Association, 2007, 32.

5. The terms of the consulting engineer's contractual obligations—particularly with respect to service scope, roles, and responsibilities—are critically important and often dispositive in determining professional liability exposure of the consulting engineer both to clients and third-parties. *See* D. Hatem, "Design Professional Legal Responsibility-Construction and Completion

Phases," in S. Hess et al., eds., *Design Professional and Construction Manager Law*, 93–122; Parent v. Stone & Webster Eng'g Corp., 408 Mass. 108, 556 N.E. 2d 1009 (1990); Note, "Architectural Malpractice: A Contract-Based Approach," *Harv. L. Rev.* 92 (1979): 1075; P. Jackson, "The Role of Contract in Architectural and Engineering Malpractice," *Ins. Counsel J.* 51 (1984): 517.

6.   This type of distribution of professional services itself poses a risk potential due to dispersion and ambiguity of roles and responsibilities.

7.   There is an increasing recognition on megaprojects of the need for project management plans that contain, among other things, a clear and consistent definition of roles and responsibilities of all major project participants, including the consulting engineer. Among other things, the inclusion of such definitions in project management plans promotes accountability and facilitates the evaluation of standard of care compliance and legal responsibility. *See The Alaskan Way Viaduct and SR 520 Bridge Projects: Expert Panel Review, Revision 1*, Spokane: Washington State Department of Transportation, 2006, pp. 1-2, 1-3, 3-4. The latter report admonishes that the project management plan must "clarify roles and responsibilities with respect to decision-making and any subsequent liability" (p. viii). J. Capka, in "A Well-Conceived Plan Will Pull It All Together," *Public Roads* 68 (July/Aug. 2004): 7, stated:

> The project management plan should provide a clear description of the project management team's composition and organization and how it will conduct business. Roles and responsibilities need to be easily understood. Large projects, more often than not, will reduce the skills and talents of the private sector to augment those in the public sector's management organization. The plan should describe how those skills will be integrated to provide management with efficient decision-making while insuring that public oversight is — and is perceived to be — appropriate and effective.

8.   *See* below, note 28.

9.   *See* discussion of external risk factors in § 3.4, below.

10.   Prior to the implementation of the IPO on the CA/T Project, a relationship between the project owner and its private sector management consultant was intended to be somewhat of an "agency" in character, in the sense that the management consultant was retained to augment the project owner staff required to manage the design and construction of a project of such complexity and size. As has been stated,

> At the inception of the project, the Massachusetts Highway Department needed additional engineering and construction management help for the duration of the proposed CA/T project. This help could be obtained by hiring additional staff at MassHighway or by retaining assistance from consulting firms in the private sector. The decision taken by then–Secretary of Transportation Fred Salvucci and Governor Michael Dukakis was to conduct a procurement for a design and construction management firm (or firms) who would temporarily, during the term of the CA/T project, serve as an extension of MassHighway staff, under its direction and control. . . .

The December 9, 1987, Agreement between MassHighway and the [Management Consultant] (Work Program 4) explicitly confirmed these arrangements. Section IV of the Agreement incorporates a Scope of Work that was attached to the Agreement as Exhibit A. In the Definition of Services, the term "management" was defined to mean all services described in the scope of work, subject to the Department's (MassHighway's) "direction and approval." Throughout the Agreement various provisions confirmed that the Management Consultant was to act as an agent of the Department, an extension of its employees, without actual or apparent authority to bind the Department.

Section III of the Agreement, at Section E, at Subsection 3, includes a release by the Department of the Management Consultant (and a Covenant Not to Sue by the Department in favor of the Management Consultant) for any liability in excess of available insurance proceeds plus 200% of the Management Consultant's portion of the Net Fee under the Agreement, except to the extent that any claim is attributable to the willful misconduct, gross negligence, . . . fraud, or active concealment of the Management Consultant.

Subsection 6 confirms that the Management Consultant "shall be deemed to be acting as the Department's agent in its dealing with third parties . . . , provided however, that the Management Consultant shall have no real or implied authority to bind the Department in contract or by declaration of admission." J. Miller, "Lessons Learned: An Assessment of Select Public-Private Partnerships in Massachusetts," *Pioneer Institute White Paper* No. 45, Dec. 2008, p. 20 (hereinafter Miller, "Lessons Learned").

Notwithstanding the "agency" character of the relationship between the project owner and the management consultant, the various agreements between them made clear that the management consultant would be held accountable for its failure to satisfy contractual and professional standards of performance. In that important respect, the management consultant accountability conformed with accountability standards in a conventional independent contractor relationship. In addition, in 1994, the CA/T Project implemented a cost recovery program which detailed a process for the evaluation of the adequacy of the professional performance of the management consultant (as well as other consulting engineers) and provided a vehicle for the assertion and resolution of professional liability claims in the event that performance failed to meet required standards and resulted in economic damage to the project owner.

11. Chapter 17, "Design Professionals: Roles and Responsibilities," in *Bruner & O'Connor on Construction Law*, § 17.4, Eagan, MN: West Group, 2002 (hereinafter, *Bruner & O'Connor*).
12. *See* Committee for Review of the Project Management Practices Employed on the Boston Central Artery/Tunnel ("Big Dig") Project et al., *Completing the "Big Dig": Managing the Final Stages of Boston's Central Artery/Tunnel Project*, Washington, DC: National Academies Press, 2003.
13. Available on-line at http://www.mass.gov/legis/senate/bigdig.htm.
14. P. Primack, "Learning from the Big Dig: How to Manage Megaprojects and How Not To," *Com-

monWealth 11 (Fall 2006): 58 (hereinafter, *CommonWealth*). In commenting on the IPO implementation on the CA/T Project, one commentator has stated:

> In retrospect, the Integrated Project Organization is now perceived to have created more problems than solutions with respect to the completion of the Project, and it certainly seems to have affected the results of settlement discussions among the parties, the Attorney General of the Commonwealth and the U.S. Attorney. There is little doubt that the IPO increased costs and time for project completion because it blurred responsibility and accountability between the public and private sectors. (Miller, "Lessons Learned," 21.)

See, H. de Bruijn and M. Leijten, "Management Characteristics of Mega-Projects," chapter 2 in Priemus et al., eds., *Decision-Making*, p. 37 (commenting that on the CA/T Project, the intimate nature of the IPO relationship between the public owner and private sector management consultant jeopardized the former's ability to control and manage the latter and resulted in "a situation where nobody could offer any counterweight to the [management consultant] on the basis of (technical) expertise").

In an April 13, 2009, *Engineering News Record* article entitled "Special Inspector General Recommended for Stimulus," William Angelo commented on the need for accountability in government spending on public projects funded by federal economic stimulus legislation and emphasized the need to learn from lessons on other projects, such as the Central Artery/Tunnel Project, stating:

> Stimulus-delivery officials can learn from [the CA/T Project]. . . . As part of [a settlement agreement the project management consultant] agreed to file separately to the Federal Highway Administration "lessons-learned" reports about operational problems delivering the project.
>
> Faced with removing a 50-year old viaduct running through the heart of the city without disrupting traffic, the joint venture oversaw the design and construction of a $15-billion, 7.5-mile bridge/tunnel complex linking two Interstate highways and Logan International Airport. At the same time, [the management consultant] had to deal with evolving owners— from the Massachusetts Dept. of Public Works to the state highway department to the state Turnpike Authority and finally an Integrated Project Organization (IPO). Political deadlines, differing subsurface conditions, scope growth and interest payments, among other factors, all contributed to cost growth. "At the time that the project owner decided to implement the IPO on the CA/T project, there was no significant precedent in the application of the IPO approach to public sector construction or with respect to the potential impact that the IPO approach may have on issues of performance standards, the evaluation and determination of professional accountability of the private sector consulting engineer or overall project objectives such as quality control," notes [the management consultant] in its report.
>
> What [the management consultant] learned was that accountability, particularly in cost recovery, suffered in that the IPO blurred the independent roles of the consultant and

merged them with the owner. Integrating roles and responsibilities exposed both the consultant and owner to risks typically assigned to the other, such as design defects and project financing. "Clear roles and responsibilities definition are important not only in terms of accountability, but quality control and safety as well," says [the management consultant] in its report. Issues of allocating risk, determining professional-liability accountability and conflicts of interest also must be addressed, it says.

The IPO also strained independent professional judgment, in that shared responsibilities "diminished and compromised" the ability of the consultant to control its performance. One overriding concern was the need to structure the IPO to respect the professional obligations of the consultant in matters of public health, safety and welfare. Finally, shared decision-making causes problems because the consultant is not entitled to sovereign immunity and thus could face potential civil liability issues.

In its lessons-learned report, [the management consultant] says an IPO should have clearly defined responsibilities with sufficient authority and control, uniform work processes and procedures, and external oversight. Key decisions include "establishing a clear scope of work and responsibility for each party and ensuring that responsibilities, authority and accountability are well thought through and specifically defined in any contractual agreements," it notes."

See D. J. Hatem, "Megaproject Issues and Challenges: Some Informal Remarks," *Design and Construction Management Professional Reporter*, Donovan Hatem LLP (Boston, Nov. 2009).

15. *CommonWealth*, K. Mead, p. 59.

16. *CommonWealth*, J. Rooney, p. 61.

17. *CommonWealth*, A. Natsios, p. 62.

18. *CommonWealth*, A. Natsios, p. 63.

19. *See* D. Hatem, "Developing Risk Indicators for Evaluating Professional Liability Exposure on Major Public Projects: A Broader Dimensional Approach," *Design and Construction Management Professional Reporter* (Feb. 2004), 1–13, 21–22.

20. The project owner typically is not an insured under the consulting engineer's professional liability insurance coverage. *See, e.g.*, D. Hatem, "The Owner As 'Additional Insured' Under the Design Professional's Professional Liability Policy: Can It Be Done and, if So, How?" *The CA/T Professional Liability Reporter* (Sep. 1996).

21. D. Baxter, "Big Believer," *Roads & Bridges* 45 (June 2007): 00–00.

22. The case of *In re* Massachusetts Turnpike Authority and James J. Kerasiotes, U.S. Sec. & Exch. Comm., Administrative Proceeding File No. 3-11198, Cease and Desist Order, Release No. A260/7-31-3 demonstrates this point. In that case, the project owner was held accountable for a Securities and Exchange Act violation in connection with the publication of a prospectus regarding funding for the Central Artery/Tunnel Project. Although the private sector management consultant was not found to be in violation of Securities Rules and Regulations, given the inte-

grated nature of the relationship between the public owner and the management consultant, the latter was exposed to an investigation and potential liability.

23. The issue as to whether, in such circumstances, a consulting engineer is, by extension, entitled to derivative immunity when it performs services or functions that traditionally have been reserved to or performed by the public owner is predominantly dependent upon the vagaries of state law and is without much legal precedent in most states. *See, e.g.,* GLF Construction Corp. v. LAN/STV, 414 F. 3d 553 (5th Cir. 2005) (holding that under Texas statute an engineer, as an independent contractor of public transportation authority, is liable only to the extent that the authority would be liable if it were performing the same service function; therefore, the engineer was entitled to derivative sovereign immunity in defense of construction contractor negligence and negligent misrepresentation claims against the engineer; noting that the Authority would have a remedy against the engineer for deficiencies in the latter's performance); Estate of Theresa E. Lyons & William Lyons v. Strand Assoc., Inc. et al., 207 Wis. 2d 446 (Wis. App. 1996) (holding that the design engineer who was directed by DOT to implement alleged faulty aspects of bridge design was entitled to sovereign immunity; design decision at issue was made and directed by a DOT designer in order to reduce overall project cost; in extending immunity the court found, on the record, that it was satisfied that the engineer demonstrated that it had informed the government about hidden or potential flaws associated with the DOT design directive and that the DOT had all of the information necessary to support a proper discretionary design choice; in legal effect, an independent professional contractor, such as an engineer, who follows the official directives of a public owner is an "agent" and therefore entitled to sovereign immunity and (i) the governmental authority approved and issued reasonably precise specifications and directives, (ii) the engineer conformed to those specifications and directives, and (iii) the engineer warned the supervising governmental authority about the possible dangers/risks associated with those specifications and directives that were known to the engineer but not necessarily to the governmental authority); KiSKA Constr. Corp. USA v. Washington Metro. Area Transit Auth., 321 F. 3d 1151 (March 11, 2003) (holding that WMATA's discretionary decision to exclude certain subsurface reports and design documents from tunnel project's bid package was susceptible to policy judgment and discretionary and, therefore, outside sovereign immunity waiver for tort committed in proprietary function and, thus, construction contractor negligent misrepresentation claim against WMATA was barred; United States *ex rel.* Ali v. Daniel, Mann, Johnson & Mendenhall, 355 F. 3d 1140 (9th Cir. 2004) (ruling that district court erred in granting summary judgment dismissing False Claims Act allegations against consulting engineer for public owner; the alleged false statements were provided by the consulting engineer to FEMA in support of funding request, by the engineer on behalf of the public owner, and were based solely upon information furnished by the public owner; determining that even though public owner was not a "person" subject to liability under the FCA statute, the private consulting engineer was neither statutorily exempt from potential FCA liability nor entitled to a sovereign immunity defense); United States v. Sequel Contractors, Inc., 402 F. Supp. 2d 1142

(C.D. Cal. 2005) (ruling that project management firm hired by public owner to manage airport construction projects and review construction contractor pay applications may be liable under the California False Claims Act for overpayments made to construction contractor based upon overstatements made in contractor payment application; declining to dismiss project management firm's counterclaim against public owner for negligence on the theory that, assuming the validity of the False Claims Act allegations, the owner was negligent in supervising employees that the project management firm provided to the owner and that these employees were "special employees" of the owner because they were directly controlled and supervised by the owner). Note Eby Construction Co. v. LAN/STV, 205 S.W. 3d 16 (Tex. App. 2006) (declining to apply the defense of derivative sovereign immunity to the private sector engineering firm with respect to a constructor's claim against the latter in circumstances in which the engineering firm failed to provide adequate proof that the public transit authority would have been similarly immune from the constructor's claims).

24. The enforceability of such an indemnification provision will be subject to any applicable state law.

25. *See* discussion below in §5 of chapter 16.

26. *See* note 22, above.

27. *See* S. Allen and S. Murphy, "Cheaper, Faster Path Led to Failure, Ceiling Design Was Weakened," *Boston Globe*, Dec. 24, 2006, A1.

28. *See* discussion, § 3.4 below.

29. For an excellent discussion of the need to balance risk and reward, *see* Dunnicliff & Parker, "The Care and Feeding of Individual Consultants and Their Clients," cited in full at n. 2, above; D. Thompson, "Client-Consultant Selection," in D. Hatem, ed., *Subsurface Conditions: Risk Management for Design and Construction Management Professionals*, Hoboken, NJ: Wiley, 1998 (hereinafter *Subsurface Conditions*). J. Monsees and T. Smirnoff have stated:

> Consideration of risk is necessary, essential and proper when determining fee and profit. Innovative and/or state of the art designs require a higher level of effort and risk for the design professional and, therefore, a higher fee for the services rendered. . . .
>
> Many times, the issues of risk and liability are determined by the level of insurance required by the owner or agency contracting for the service. The larger the project, the larger the errors and omissions (E and O) and liability insurance requirement. While such insurance is a necessity, it must be recalled that it does not cover the engineering for all occurrences and project liability exposures. . . . Many larger projects may include an owner-directed insurance program or wrap-up policy that covers all the firms involved in the project; designers, construction managers, contractors, and subcontractors. Many contracts require indemnification of the owner/client by the engineering/geotechnical engineer. This indemnity is the shifting of liability risk from one party to another, usually from the client to the engineer. For a price, insurance shifts this risk from one party to another—e.g., from the engineer to an insurance company.

The current trend in litigation is to go for the deep pockets, generally the largest firms and those with the most money. A small firm may not present a large enough target for a law suit, but this is not a shield to hide behind. Depending upon the firm structure (be it a sole proprietorship, partnership, or corporation), the level of joint and several responsibilities may vary considerably. J. Monsees and T. Smirnoff, "The Professional Services Agreement," in Hatem, *Subsurface Conditions*.

In a lecture titled "Consultants or Scapegoats," delivered on October 23, 1957 (reprinted in 1958 in the *J. of Boston Soc'y of Civ. Engineers*), Professor Karl Terzaghi addressed a number of important aspects of the relationship between consulting engineers — especially "earthwork," now geotechnical engineering, consultants — and their clients on subsurface projects. Terzaghi stated:

The assignments referred to under the preceding headings have one essential feature in common. In each case an engineering organization was in serious trouble and therefore, willing to accept the consultant's recommendations. If the consultant is invited to cooperate on a project before unanticipated difficulties have been encountered, conditions may be radically different. This is due to the fact that some engineering organizations are subdivided into three independent compartments — the survey, design, and construction departments — or else they assign the supervision of construction to inspectors who have neither the duty, nor the qualifications to judge whether or not the design assumptions are compatible with the field conditions. . . .

In connection with structural engineering, this administrative set-up is perfectly satisfactory, provided the engineers in charge of design are reasonably familiar with the methods of construction. On the other hand, in the realm of earthwork and foundation engineering, the absence of continuous and well organized contacts between the design department and the men in charge of the supervision of the construction operations is always objectionable and can even be disastrous. This is due to the fact that boring records always leave a wide margin for interpretation. If the site for a proposed structure is located on a deposit with an erratic pattern of stratification, such as a marginal glacial deposit, the boring records may not disclose a single one of the vital subsoil characteristics, and the real subsoil conditions may be radically different from what the designer believed them to be. Therefore, the design assumptions may be utterly at variance with reality.

The consequences of these conditions depend on the qualifications of the personnel engaged in the supervision of the construction operations. If the supervision is in the hands of a construction department, it also depends to a large extent on whether or not design and construction departments are on friendly terms with each other. More often than not the two departments despise each other sincerely, because their members have different backgrounds and different mentalities. The construction men blame the design personnel for paying no attention to the construction angle of their projects, but they are blissfully unaware of their own shortcomings. The design engineers claim that the construction men

have no conception of the reasoning behind their design, but they forget that the same end in design can be achieved by various means, some of which can be easily realized in the field, whereas others may be almost impractical. If none of the men in charge of design has previously been engaged in construction, the design may be unnecessarily awkward from a construction point of view. In any event, the construction men have no incentive to find out whether or not the design assumptions are in accordance with what they experience in the field during construction, and various discrepancies may pass unnoticed. If conditions are encountered which require local modifications of the original design, the construction engineer may make these changes in accordance with its own judgment, which he believes is sound, although it may be very poor. Important changes of this kind have even been made on the job without indicating the change on the field set of construction drawings.

In another passage, Terzaghi stated:

[I]t is evident that the success of large-scale earthwork operations depends on many factors other than the adequacy of the original design. This fact introduces serious complications into the relationship between the client and a consultant who was retained in an advisory capacity in the design stage of the project.

The incentive for retaining a consultant commonly grows out of the fact that the functions of most engineering organizations cover a very broad field, including earthwork, structural, hydraulic, mechanical and electrical engineering. Few, if any of the members of such an organization have the time and the opportunity to specialize. Hence, if a new project assigned to such an organization involves design problems of an unusual character, a consultant is retained who is expected to cooperate in the solution of the problems.

In engineering organizations with a watertight partition between designers and the personnel engaged in construction, the consultant is quite obviously placed at the disposal of the design department. After the design is completed his service period on the project, like that of the design department, is considered terminated. He has no control over what the inspectors and the contractor chose to make out of the drawings and specifications, and he cannot even know whether or not the men on the job are competent enough to notice significant differences between design assumptions and field conditions. If the engineering firm does not maintain a construction department, or if the owner reserves a right to supervise construction, conditions may be even worse. The consequences depend on the type of service the consultant was asked to render, as shown by the following examples:

(a) The client requests the consultant to participate in the design of a structure and in the drafting of the specifications. He has the sincere intention of acting in accordance with the consultant's recommendations, but the service period of the consultant ends as soon as construction starts. The consultant's advice cannot be sounder than his knowledge of the subsoil conditions at the time when the advice was rendered. If these conditions are radically different from what the boring records indicated—which is by no

means uncommon — the structure may fail in spite of conscientious adherence to the consultant's advice.

(b) The client invites the consultant to make proposals concerning design and construction, but he reserves — or assumes — the right to deviate from the recommendations as he deems fit, without informing the consultant about the final decision concerning the design. If this decision is the result of misjudgment or ignorance, the consultant is unable to prevent its consequences.

(c) The consultant gets the assignment of participating in the design of a small portion of a large unit, e.g., the design of the core of an earth dam which has been designed by others. If the structure fails on account of conditions which have no bearing on the performance of the portion investigated by the consultant, this portion goes with it, and after failure, it may be impracticable to find out which part failed first.

(d) The consultant is asked to express an opinion concerning the design of a structure without being given an opportunity to make a thorough investigation of all those conditions which determine the performance and safety of the structure. The consultant's opinion may be sound or unwarranted, depending on circumstances unknown to all the parties involved.

(e) An engineering firm requests a consultant to participate in the preliminary stage of a large project merely for the purpose of using his name as window dressing. If and when the firm gets the job, the consultant is shelved and remains in his state of retirement until something goes wrong. After the shortcomings of the design have become noticeable, it may be too late to correct the mistakes.

In each of these five cases, the name of consultant remains permanently associated with the project. Proceeding from case (a) to case (e) the hazards to the good reputation of the consultant increase. In any event, if the project ends in disaster, the consultant will find himself in the front row of scapegoats, because he was introduced to the owner as the foremost authority among the persons who participated in the design.

Terzaghi, "Consultants, Clients, and Contractors," 45.

CHAPTER 15
Risk Allocation

David J. Hatem, PC, Donovan Hatem LLP

1.0 Basic Risk Allocation Principles

The process and decisions on how risk is allocated—contractually and in actuality—are important determinants of success on all construction projects, especially megaprojects. "Success" in this context occurs when the contractual and functional relationships among project participants enables them to meet their respective expectations and achieve their common goals in a manner appropriately sensitive to their individual interests and risks, and that minimizes the potential for protracted and adversarial disputes among them. In these respects, "success" depends upon effective risk allocation.

In order to allocate risk effectively, it is necessary to implement processes for identifying and registering specific risks that can be anticipated on the megaproject. There are several excellent resources available on these subjects, which are addressed in preceding chapters. Risk identification and risk registers are essential to effective, fair, and "successful" risk allocation decisions.[1]

The process of identifying and registering risk is an important part of developing a realistic budget and schedule for a megaproject. The occurrence (likelihood and frequency) of risk and the resultant impact (severity) in most instances will have a significant potential for affecting project cost and schedule and, depending upon the reliable predictability and degree of that impact, there will be a substantial probability that the expectations of project owners and other project stakeholders involved in megaprojects will not be met.

The technical processes for identifying and registering risk have significantly improved over the last decade. However, the more important development in recent years has been the near-universal recognition in megaprojects of the need for project owner realism, accountability, and transparency in the development and execution of these processes. Unless the processes of risk identification and registering are comprehensive and objective in the assessment and evaluation of risk exposures, any megaproject budget or schedule based upon them will start on a suspect and vulnerable foundation. Risk identification, assessment, and budget/schedule preparation should be validated

The Hangzhou Bay Bridge, completed in 2007 but not opened until 2008, is a 22-mile, 6-lane road bridge across Hangzhou Bay at the mouth of the Yangtze River, greatly shortening the travel distance between Ningbo and Shanghai. It is the longest transoceanic bridge in the world, second only to the Lake Pontchartrain Causeway as the world's longest bridge. Photo © 2007 by Jürgen Zeller.

by qualified "third parties" independent of the project owner and the consulting engineer. In the opinion of this author, all of these improvements are positive and should be implemented by the megaproject owner. Moreover, these developments should serve to reduce the professional liability risk exposure of the consulting engineer for the reasons more particularly addressed in chapter 16.

The next important set of issues relates to how project-specific identified risk should be allocated among project participants. The project owner's risk allocation decisions will probably be influenced by the choice of delivery method for the megaproject. Certainly, the owner's decisions regarding allocation of risk between it and the consulting engineer will influence the latter's professional's liability exposure. In addition, the project owner's decisions regarding allocation of risk between the constructor in design-bid-build and the design-builder in design-build will influence the professional liability of the consulting engineer.[2]

Risk allocation directly relates to professional liability exposure of the consulting engineer. When risk is unfairly or ineffectively allocated, the result is disputes and claims among project participants. Moreover, the failure to effectively allocate risk between the project owner and the constructor significantly increases the potential of the consulting engineer's professional liability exposure to *both* the project owner and the constructor.

Issue

Once project-specific megaproject risks have been identified and registered, how should the cost and time impacts of risk materialization be allocated among project participants?

Analysis and Discussion

There are numerous excellent publications that address the important subject of risk allocation methodology. Four basic principles predominate in these publications:

- *Control:* Risk should be allocated to the project participant in the optimum position to control and manage the variables relevant to that identified risk. Allocating risk to a project participant who is not in a position to technically, legally, or otherwise control and manage the occurrence or impact of that risk will lead to significant frustrations, conflicts, and disputes derived from a fundamental sense of unfairness.

- *Clarity:* The project owner's risk allocation decisions should be clearly articulated and defined in relevant project contracts and contract documents. Ambiguity as to

how risk is allocated will lead to otherwise avoidable conflicts and disputes among project participants.

- *Consistency:* Risk allocation decisions need to be expressed in all relevant contract documents in a consistent manner. Conflicting or contradictory expressions will result in disputes and complicate and protract their resolution.

- *Fairness:* Achieving the preceding three fundamental principles will go a long way in achieving the fourth, fairness in risk allocation, inasmuch as achieving and expressing the risk allocation decisions in a balanced, clear, and consistent manner promotes fairness.[3]

Recommended Practices

- Precedent to any risk allocation decisions, the project owner should conduct or commission a comprehensive process of risk identification and registration.

- Consider retaining a qualified professional, independent of the project owner and consulting engineer, to validate the identification and registering process and the assessment of project-specific risk.

- Allocate risk to the project participant in the optimum position to control risk variables.

- Clearly and consistently define and articulate risk allocation decisions in contract documents and implement those decisions in a manner consistent with contractual articulations.

- Be fair and balanced in risk allocation decision-making and implementation.

- Develop contingency plans to address and mitigate the materialization of identified risks.

- Consider procuring project-specific professional liability insurance to cover risk that may impact professional liability exposure of the consulting engineer.[4]

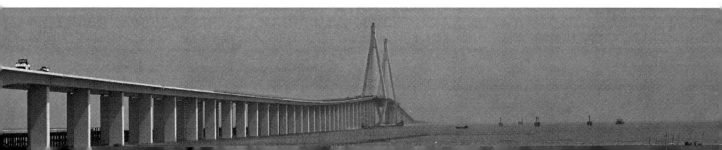

2.0   Project Owner as Risk Allocation Decision-Maker

Issue

Who is responsible for risk allocation decisions?

Analysis and Discussion

The project owner is responsible for making the critical decisions regarding allocation of risk between it and other project participants. While, in some instances, risk allocation decisions may be informed by or predicated upon technical, consulting, or legal advice and recommendations or be the product of some degree of negotiation among affected project participants, the general proposition holds that the ultimate decisions regarding how risk is allocated fall within the initiative, province, and responsibility of the project owner in the public megaproject context.

Risk allocation decisions may be directly or indirectly expressed in various procurement solicitations, contract documents (such as legal terms and conditions), technical provisions of the contract documents, and geotechnical baseline or other reports. As noted previously, these decisions should be preceded by an adequate risk identification, assessment, and registration process and guided by the basic principles discussed in the preceding section.

The consulting engineer serves an important advisory and consulting role to the project owner in the latter's risk allocation decision-making. Legal advice to the project owner about the extent to which legal rules or contracts may limit or otherwise govern risk allocation decisions provides further important guidance in informing the project owner's risk allocation decision-making. However, the consulting engineer's advice based on a technical understanding of the risk variables and factors, the respective project participants' ability to control project-specific challenges and issues, risk allocation coordination and alignment issues, and experience, provide equal, if not more valuable, guidance to the project owner. What the law (i.e., legal advice) permits and what amounts to good and prudent management regarding risk allocation (i.e., consulting engineer advice) may be two fundamentally different things. The law typically may allow for several risk allocation options, but few of these may be advisable as a matter of prudent and realistic project management. For example, an option that allocates risk aggressively to the constructor may be legally enforceable but may also serve to reduce the field of bidders or, even if accepted, may be prone to disputes and claims. The essence of the consulting engineer's contribution and value in this advisory role is its ability to temper and interject into the project owner's risk allocation decisions appropriate and adequate consideration of technical, sensible, pragmatic, and realistic factors that should inform and influence the project owner's decision regarding risk allocation.

Megaprojects provide numerous opportunities for considering innovative and non-traditional design and construction approaches. For example, megaprojects may consider relatively innovative design (e.g., NATM tunneling, soil mix) or design and construction approaches (e.g., fast-track). While such approaches, in appropriate circumstances, may represent significant potential advantages in terms of cost reduction and schedule compression for the project owner, there are important risk factors and potential impacts that must be technically understood and translated by the consulting engineer into informed risk allocation advice and recommendations to the project owner and eventually communicated in contract document requirements. The consulting engineer serves an important role in identifying and evaluating the potential feasibility of such approaches and in advising and implementing the project owner's risk allocation decisions.

Such decisions must be documented and communicated clearly and consistently to all affected project participants. In many instances, the consulting engineer will be requested to prepare portions of the contract (general conditions or technical terms) or reports (e.g., geotechnical baseline reports) that document and communicate these project owner risk allocation decisions. In doing so, it is important that principles of clarity and consistency be maintained. For example, risk allocation provisions of technical sections should be coordinated and reconciled with the general conditions of the contract documents. Consideration should also be given to prioritization or order of precedence provisions in the event of potential conflicts and inconsistencies. In most instances, it is advisable to obtain independent legal review by respective and independent counsel for the consulting engineer and project owner. Unfortunately, professional liability claims have been made against consulting engineers based upon allegations that claims and disputes needlessly arose between the project owner and the constructor due to conflicts, ambiguities, and inconsistencies in risk allocation provisions prepared by the consulting engineer.

Recommended Practices

- The project owner's risk allocation decisions should be clearly and consistently articulated and documented.

- The consulting engineer should provide technical and consulting advice to the project owner regarding risk allocation issues in order to inform the project owner's decisions.

- The consulting engineer's advice and recommendations should be based upon an identification and assessment of underlying risk factors, the ability of project participants to control and manage specific risk, the potential impact of risk occurrence, and mitigation or contingency plans.

- The consulting engineer's advice and recommendations should be clearly and

consistently communicated in understandable terms to the project owner and documented.

- Consideration should be given to obtaining independent legal review of risk allocation provisions by respective and independent counsel for the project owner and consulting engineer.

3.0 Risk Allocation and Professional Standard of Care for Consulting Engineers

Issue

How does the subject of risk allocation between the project owner, consulting engineer, and other project participants relate to the professional standard of care for the consulting engineer?

Analysis and Discussion

The professional standard of care is a form of allocating risk between project owner and consulting engineer for certain potential deficiencies in service performance of the consulting engineer. Typically, under the professional standard of care, only the risk of deficient professional service performance that falls below the professional standard of care (or negligence) is allocated to the consulting engineer. More specifically, under that risk allocation standard, perfection in the performance of the consulting engineer's services is neither expected nor required and the project owner retains the risk of deficient engineer performance that does not amount to professional negligence (i.e., breach of the professional standard of care). The broad scope of services typically required of the consulting engineer on megaprojects, the number and complexity of design and construction interfaces, and the challenge to consider and implement innovative and non-traditional design and construction approaches (as well as other factors discussed in chapter 16)—all serve to render risk assessment and allocation for professional services on megaprojects (i.e., professional standard of care application) more challenging, variable, less predictable, and, hence, more risk-prone. In some instances, the variables affecting risk for deficient service performance may be identified, defined, and specifically allocated and documented when the project owner–consulting engineer agreement is executed. In other situations, the risk variables may arise due to changes, events, or needs for flexibility in the design and construction approach that subsequently occur. The latter situation is more common in the dynamic context of megaprojects than on more conventional projects. Open-mindedness, experimentation, design innovation,

and flexibility are necessary attitudes of the consulting engineer involved in a mega-project. In some instances, consulting engineers are requested to become involved in non-traditional risk (e.g., designing construction means and methods) or innovative design approaches. In other instances, schedule or program scope changes or other factors may result in modifications to originally-contemplated delivery methods. The latter includes implementation of fast-track or other non-traditional contracting or project delivery approaches that may directly or indirectly increase the risk of professional liability exposure beyond that reasonably contemplated at the point of contract formation.

In the megaproject context, the project owner may request (or require) that the consulting engineer agree to indemnify third parties, such as project stakeholders or abutters, for certain risks and exposures sometimes having nothing directly to do with the service scope, roles, or responsibilities of the consulting engineer and to a degree of risk and damage exposure (direct or consequential) far beyond that required of the consulting engineer under its agreement with the project owner. Alternatively, the consulting engineer may be requested or required by the project owner to issue certifications (or "collateral warranties") to such third parties. The principal concern in this context arises when the indemnification obligations or certifications involve areas beyond the range of the consulting engineer's scope, roles and responsibilities, or its ability to control risk, and the indemnification obligations represent an assumption of legal responsibility or risk exposure beyond that reasonably contemplated under the consulting engineer's agreement with the project owner. Suffice it to say, such requests or requirements should be carefully evaluated by the consulting engineer and reviewed with its legal counsel.

The key to successful client service and prudent risk management for the consulting engineer is to recognize the potential — if not probability — that, after contract award/execution, the consulting engineer will find itself in the position of assuming greater risk than contractually contemplated due to the dynamics and evolutionary characteristics of megaprojects and the variations in the design and construction approaches that may be required on the megaprojects. Simply saying "no" to the project owner may be the simple and most risk-averse answer in such circumstances; however, that simple answer may be neither prudent from a professional "business" relationship standpoint nor necessarily required as a matter of appropriate risk management.

As discussed in chapter 16, the professional standard of care is intended to be flexible and adaptive in its definition and application (reasonable care under the circumstances). As post-contract-execution variations in design and construction approach are presented, the normal and residual operation of the professional standard of care should adjust to take into account any heightened professional liability risk exposures. Notwithstanding, it is advisable that contract modifications be negotiated and executed to address specific risk allocation adjustments that are required due to such altered or heightened risk exposures.

333

Recommended Practices

- Be attentive to the need for contractual risk allocation adjustments due to evolving variations in planned design and construction approaches.

- Modify contractual risk allocation and professional standard of care provisions to specifically account for altered professional liability risk exposure due to innovations and variations in planned design and construction or project delivery approaches.

- Be flexible and adaptive in serving the project owner's evolving needs and requirements, while being equally attentive to consequential changes in potential professional liability risk exposure and the need for adequate contractual and risk management practice responses.

- Consider the advisability of project-specific professional liability insurance for risk exposures of the consulting engineer involved in a megaproject.

4.0 Project Owner–Constructor Risk Allocation and Consulting Engineer Professional Liability

Issue

To what extent do the project owner's decisions regarding allocation of risk with the constructor affect the professional liability exposure of the consulting engineer?

Analysis and Discussion

Clearly risk allocation—professional standard of care/indemnification—provisions in the project owner–consulting engineer agreement directly affect professional liability exposure of the consulting engineer. Less apparent and more subtle and indirect—but very real—is the extent to which risk allocation between the project owner and constructor may affect the professional liability exposure of the consulting engineer. On most megaprojects, the process of risk allocation is dynamic and complex; evaluating one's risk exposure discreetly, statically, rigidly, and in isolation from the risk exposure of other project participants can lead to a serious underestimation of realistic risk exposure.

The question remains, however, as to how risk allocation between the project owner and constructor may affect the professional liability risk exposure of the consulting engineer.[5] There are a number of ways in which this may occur. As a general proposition, the answer largely derives from the risk allocation principles discussed above in § 1.0.

If risk is not clearly, consistently, or fairly allocated between the project owner and constructor, or if it is allocated in a manner inconsistent with the risk assumer's ability to control and manage risk, there is a relatively high probability that expectations among those parties will be significantly disappointed and that disputes and claims will arise between them.

There are several examples that demonstrate this proposition. When economic damage risk for schedule delay is allocated between project owner and constructor such that the constructor bears the entirety of that risk, there is a significant potential for serious and substantial disputes and claims between the project owner and the constructor. Similarly, when the time/cost risk of unforeseen subsurface conditions is allocated by the project owner entirely to the constructor, the potential for disputes and claims substantially increases.[6]

In these two examples—no damage for delay and no differing site condition remedy—the law recognizes exceptional circumstances in which, despite these onerous risk allocation decisions, a constructor may be entitled to equitable (or extra-contractual) relief. In general, some of these exceptions are based on proof of some deficiency in the services or work product of the consulting engineer. Put another way, onerous project owner–constructor risk allocation provisions often instigate direct (project owner) or indirect (constructor) claims against the consulting engineer.

In many jurisdictions, the so-called economic loss doctrine precludes third-party (e.g., constructor) claims against the consulting engineer. In general, the economic loss doctrine is premised on the notion that rights and remedies among project participants should be allocated, contractually defined, and exercised only directly against those parties based upon their direct (privity) contractual terms and relationships.[7] While this is a sensible rule that comports with economic and contractual expectations, the consulting engineer should be aware that it does not always apply. In fact, allowing third-party claims—in circumvention of the economic loss doctrine—is more the rule than the exception.

In addition, onerous risk allocation between project owner and constructor will increase the likelihood of project owner indemnification, professional negligence, or other claims against the consulting engineer, given the constructor's need to resort to legal theories that focus upon alleged deficiencies in the consulting engineer's performance. Thus, the consulting engineer should advise the project owner to adopt fair and reasonable risk allocation contractual terms and agreements between the latter and the constructor.

Project owner–constructor agreements contain numerous provisions that allocate project risk between the owner and constructor. Some of these provisions may directly affect the constructor's ability to recover time or cost due to delay, defective design, or differing site or concealed conditions, among other risks. Moreover, contracting practices surrounding the procurement of the construction contract (e.g., low bid competi-

tive and fixed price) may also directly affect risk allocation between the project owner and the constructor. These risk allocation provisions and associated contracting practices indirectly impact and increase the professional liability exposure of the consulting engineer beyond that typically contemplated under the consulting engineer's agreement with the project owner.

There are some fundamental risk allocation principles that apply, including the guiding principles that risk should be allocated to parties in the optimum position to control and manage risk (the "control principle") and that risk should be fairly allocated (the "fairness principle").[8] As a general observation, the more these fundamental principles are ignored or violated in the allocation of risk between the project owner and constructor, the greater the likelihood that the consulting engineer will become embroiled in claims and disputes that otherwise should rest exclusively (or, at a minimum, predominantly) with the project owner and constructor.[9] Claims and disputes in the construction process should be directed toward, and resolved between, contracting parties or those in "privity," viz., the project owner and constructor. However, when risk has been unfairly or otherwise inappropriately allocated between them, the likelihood is that the constructor will seek remedies or recourse against a non-contracting party, notably the consulting engineer.

For this basic reason, the consulting engineer should have more than a casual interest in how risk is allocated between the project owner and the constructor. Indeed, the consulting engineer has a very direct interest in this issue, given the heightened risk of professional liability exposure that can result if project owner–constructor risk is inappropriately addressed between the project owner and constructor. To the maximum achievable extent, the consulting engineer should endeavor to influence the project owner to adhere to sound risk allocation principles and appropriate contracting practices in connection with the procurement and negotiation of project owner–constructor agreements.

Project owner–constructor agreements contain numerous provisions that serve to allocate various types of risk between them. For example, the agreement may include the following types of risk allocation provisions, the effect of which is to disclaim project owner responsibility for certain types of risk ("risk disclaimer provisions"):

1. *Delay Damage Risk Disclaimer:* This provision typically provides that in the event that the constructor is delayed due to causes outside its control, the constructor's exclusive remedy against the owner will be an extension of time and the constructor shall not be entitled to any damages or other economic adjustments due to the delay. Subject to limited exceptions, this type of provision is legally enforceable in most jurisdictions. A related provision is a consequential damage waiver, under which the constructor agrees to waive the right to recover consequential damages, including delay damages against the owner. As in the case of a no-damages-for-

delay provision, the consequential damage waiver provision is enforceable in most jurisdictions.

2. *Design Inadequacy Risk Disclaimer:* Under this type of provision, a constructor is required to relinquish, release, and waive any right that it would otherwise have to recover against the project owner under the so-called *Spearin* implied warranty doctrine[10] for defects or other inadequacies in the constructability of project owner–furnished design and contract documents. As a general principle, this type of provision will be enforceable if it clearly and specifically articulates its intent and effect.[11]

3. *Subsurface and Concealed Conditions Risk Disclaimer:* There are several provisions in the project owner–constructor agreement that may impact allocation of risk for subsurface and/or concealed conditions. As a general rule, absent a differing site conditions provision, the constructor accepts and undertakes the risk of additional cost and time due to differing site conditions.[12] Based upon a number of sound economic and contracting policy reasons, many project owners typically include differing site condition clauses to more equitably allocate the risk of differing site and concealed conditions. In addition, under state and federal law, and/or as a requirement of grants or other public funding, many project owners are required to include differing site condition clauses in the project owner–constructor agreement. However, many private and public owners have the choice or option whether to include a differing site condition clause and those owners exercise a number of options in that regard.[13]

One such option is not to include a differing site condition clause. Other options are to include a differing site condition clause but to disclaim the accuracy of site information; not to include certain site data or related geotechnical reports within the definition of contract documents; and to classify certain site data as information that the constructor is not entitled to rely upon in bidding and performing the work. Yet another option, while considered more risky for the project owner, is to withhold such data or reports from the constructor.[14] The point to emphasize in this context is that the project owner has options regarding risk allocation for differing and concealed conditions risk and, if properly and legally implemented, the options will (and should) be respected and enforced by courts and other dispute resolution mechanisms.[15]

In addition to the utilization of risk disclaimer provisions in the project owner–constructor agreement, the project owner makes a number of decisions about contracting practices that may impact risk allocation between the project owner and constructor and may also serve to heighten the professional liability exposure of the consulting engineer to both the project owner and the constructor or other third-parties.

A recent case—*KiSKA Construction Corp. U.S.A., and Kajima Engineering and Construction, Inc., a partner in KiSKA-Kajima, a Joint Venture v. Washington Metropolitan Area Transit Authority*, 321 F. 3d. 1151 (D.C. Cir. 2003)—demonstrates this point. *KiSKA* involved claims by a tunneling joint venture constructor (KiSKA-Kajima, the "constructor") against the Washington Metropolitan Area Transit Authority ("WMATA") arising out of excessive dewatering required in connection with the construction of two subway tunnels—the Green Line Extension—in Washington, D.C. (the "project"). Prior to bid, WMATA engaged a geotechnical engineering firm (the "geotechnical engineer") to investigate and evaluate subsurface conditions at the project site and to evaluate the feasibility of various tunneling methods, tunneling equipment, and dewatering systems. In November 1992, the geotechnical engineer submitted its first Tunnel Alternative Report ("TAR"), in which it reported that "[g]roundwater for most of the [tunnel] alignment is anticipated to be above the crown [i.e., the top of the tunnel]," and that, in light of this soil condition, "even . . . fairly extensive dewatering" was not likely to be entirely "[e]ffective." Accordingly, the geotechnical engineer recommended not only that "some type of closed face tunnel boring machine" be used for the project, but also that "[o]pen face tunneling be strictly prohibited on this [c]ontract." In January 1993, the geotechnical engineer submitted a revised TAR. The second TAR reaffirmed the conclusions of the first, noting that "dewatering considerations dictate closed face mining methods" and "[o]pen faced tunneling in conjunction with dewatering is not judged a viable construction technique on this [c]ontract." After reviewing the second TAR, WMATA's board of engineers met with the geotechnical engineer and, shortly thereafter, the geotechnical engineer issued a third and final TAR, which authorized the use of an open face machine but cautioned that "[e]xtensive dewatering will be an essential element of the open faced shield option." Noting that, "effective dewatering of the alignment is at best going to be difficult," the third TAR recommended that "an extensive pre-support grouting/ ground improvement program . . . be required for most of the alignment."

Following issuance of the third TAR, the geotechnical engineer advised WMATA that even extensive pre-support grouting would not permit open-faced tunneling "if ground-water is not depressed [through dewatering] the recommended two feet below tunnel invert [i.e., the bottom of the tunnel]." WMATA then directed the geotechnical engineer to design an appropriate dewatering system for the project. The geotechnical engineer produced a dewatering design that included over 300 dewatering wells.

Following the completion of that design, WMATA issued an invitation for bids, which set forth the detailed design specifications and required bidders to submit lump-sum bids for executing the work based upon those specifications. WMATA did not include the geotechnical engineer's TARs in the bid package, however, nor did WMATA conform the design specifications to the geotechnical engineer's recommended dewatering system. Based upon the specifications provided by WMATA, KiSKA-Kajima submitted

a lump-sum bid of approximately $43 million, which WMATA accepted. In early 1994, WMATA and KiSKA-Kajima entered into a construction contract.

During construction, the constructor experienced a number of difficulties with both the dewatering system and the excavation methods required by the contract. Two complications proved particularly troublesome: (1) the dewatering system specified by WMATA failed to lower the groundwater table two feet below the tunnel invert and (2) the great majority of surface grout holes could not be drilled vertically at their specified locations without damaging underground utility lines. The constructor claimed that, in order to overcome these difficulties, the cost would almost double its $43 million lump-sum bid. Eventually, the constructor filed suit against WMATA in federal court alleging fraudulent misrepresentation, negligent misrepresentation, and unilateral mistake, among other claims. Prior to trial, the federal district court issued several pre-trial rulings. The district court dismissed the constructor's tort claims on sovereign immunity grounds on the basis that certain owner decisions are "susceptible to policy judgment, and, therefore, immune from judicial review because they involve planning and design rather than implementation or operation." In other rulings, the district court rejected the constructor's claim that WMATA breached implied warranties with respect to the design of the dewatering system contained in the contract documents.

The issue in the district court's first ruling was WMATA's decision not to include the various TARs in the bid or contract documents or otherwise to make the same reports available to the bidders. The constructor claimed that the failure to disclose or make available the TARs constituted both fraudulent and negligent misrepresentation on the part of WMATA. The constructor contended that WMATA fraudulently and negligently misrepresented that WMATA would implement an effective dewatering system and that the tunneling methods prescribed by the contract were feasible, while concealing the geotechnical engineer's TARs and recommendations that closed-face minings should be used, dewatering would be costly and ineffective, and pre-grouting would be ineffective if the dewatering was not effective. The constructor contended that as a result of WMATA's misrepresentations and failures to disclose, it labored under a unilateral mistake as to the cost, duration, and feasibility of the project and that WMATA materially breached the contract, including various express and implied warranties.

WMATA defended itself on the basis that its decision was immune from liability. The district court concluded that WMATA had "broad discretion in defining the contours of the invitation for bids" and, therefore, dismissed the constructor's claims against WMATA. On appeal, the constructor contended that WMATA lacked the "discretion" to conceal and/or misrepresent material information from constructors and that such conduct does not involve the exercise of a policy judgment. The constructor contended that the district court erred in ruling that sovereign immunity shields WMATA from the constructor's tort claims. On appeal, the United States Court of Appeals for the District of

Columbia affirmed the district court's dismissal of the constructor's tort claims on the basis of sovereign immunity. In doing so, the appellate court stated:

> This case poses the following question: does WMATA's discretion to select a particular project design encompass the discretion to determine the content of that project's bid package? On appeal, KiSKA answers this question in the negative, arguing that (1) WMATA lacks the discretion to "conceal and/or misrepresent material information" from contractors and (2) "such tortious conduct does not involve the exercise of a "policy judgment". . . . [W]e conclude that WMATA had broad discretion to determine the contents of the tunnel project's bid package.
>
> While KiSKA's claim presents a closer question than those decided in cases past, we believe that the district court correctly held that WMATA's discretionary decision to exclude certain design documents from the tunnel project's bid package is "susceptible to policy judgment.". . . Specifically, WMATA's decision required consideration of budgetary constraints and economic expediency. While at first glance WMATA's fiscal considerations may appear to pale in comparison to those implicated in hiring decisions . . . those considerations involve more than simply packaging, duplication and distribution costs. If WMATA were to release unreliable or mistaken reports indicating an inflated need for the dewatering wells, for example, the reports could cause contractors to similarly inflate their bids. Of course, WMATA may not withhold all unfavorable information from Constructors; if it did, WMATA might soon find few firms willing to submit bids on its projects. WMATA must therefore exercise its policy judgment to balance the goal of fair disclosure against the sensible withholding of unreliable information.[16]
>
> Although KiSKA argues that WMATA's position "assumes the *merits* of the issue, i.e., that the information concealed from bidders was not 'material,'" . . . KiSKA's position, in contrast — given that the merits of a claim will rarely be known before a court establishes its jurisdiction over that claim — would permit endless contractor challenges to WMATA's final specifications. While KiSKA may disagree with WMATA's decisions regarding the materiality of a given set of documents, such judgments are, in our view, WMATA's to make. We therefore conclude that the content of the tunnel project's bid package is a discretionary decision susceptible to policy judgment and, accordingly, affirm the district court's dismissal of KiSKA's tort claims on sovereign immunity grounds.

The appellate court also affirmed the district court's dismissal of the constructor's breach of warranty claims regarding the design of the dewatering system and surface free-grout holes, ruling that the contract documents did not create any warranty that the specified dewatering system would maintain the groundwater level two feet below tunnel invert or require the constructor to drill surface grout holes vertically.

The application of the sovereign immunity defense to preclude constructor tort claims against a project owner — such as occurred in the *KiSKA* case — does not arise often.[17]

However, the sovereign immunity defense is available to immunize the public project owner's liability resulting from decisions based on its exercise of policy judgment and discretion.[18] In *KiSKA*, the court determined that WMATA's judgment and discretion as to the contents of the bid package—i.e., specifically the decision not to include the TARs—represented an exercise of policy judgment and discretion and, therefore, the constructor's claims predicated upon a challenge to that judgment and discretion were barred by the doctrine of sovereign immunity.

A more common aspect of the *KiSKA* case is the constructor's combination of a claim based upon differing site conditions (i.e., excessive dewatering due to site conditions) with a claim for defective design and/or breach of the *Spearin* implied warranty obligation (discussed in more detail in Chapter 17).[19] More specifically, in circumstances in which a constructor's ability to recover against the project owner for differing site conditions is precluded or otherwise severely restricted under the project owner–constructor agreement, it is likely that the constructor will concurrently and/or alternatively seek recovery under a theory of defective design and, in many such cases, directly sue the consulting engineer. In addition, in such circumstances the constructor's assertion of defective design claims may well result in the project owner's assertion of a professional negligence or indemnification claim(s) against the consulting engineer.[20]

The foregoing examples of risk disclaimer provisions that may be contained in project owner–constructor agreements are by no means exhaustive and are offered for the purpose of demonstrating two points:

1. Project owners and, to a lesser degree, constructors have options with respect to the allocation of risks in a number of significant areas of potential exposure.

2. As a general proposition, the contractual decision to accept the various options will, in most cases, be legally enforced.[21]

These fundamental points, however, raise some broader questions:

1. Is the project owner's utilization of such risk disclaimer provisions—which have the legal and practical effect of allocating to the constructor all, or the majority of, the risk and consequent financial exposure—consistent with the fairness and control principles of sound risk allocation decision-making?

2. To what degree will the project owner's utilization of such risk disclaimer provisions and related contracting practices potentially impact professional liability exposure of the consulting engineer?

The first question is addressed in section 4 of this chapter.[22] However, there are certain points to emphasize in this regard:

1. The *project owner* is the principal risk allocation decision-maker.
2. Although, as a *legal* matter, the constructor must voluntarily agree to the risk

allocation provisions (as well as all other terms) of the project owner–constructor agreement, in a variety of public and private procurement contexts the *reality* is that the opportunity for negotiation is limited or non-existent and the constructor must accept those provisions as tendered by the project owner or not bid on the project.

3. Although the project owner is the principal risk allocation decision-maker, others may have a role in advising the project owner, including its legal counsel and the consulting engineer. Legal counsel typically may be asked to address the legality and/or enforceability of risk allocation provisions and related contracting practices while the consulting engineer typically may be requested to provide advice of a broader nature, such as whether such provisions and practices are customarily utilized by other owners in similar circumstances, whether they are likely to prevent or lead to post-award claims and disputes, and whether the consulting engineer has had any experience dealing with claims or disputes on other projects in which such provisions and practices have been utilized.

There appears to be no published empirical data conclusively establishing that utilization of these types of risk disclaimer provisions and related contracting practices in project owner–constructor agreements increases the risk of professional liability exposure for the consulting engineer. However, logic (and the experience of the author) definitely supports the conclusion that a constructor will pursue a professional liability claim against the consulting engineer — or perhaps more precisely, transform what would have been a contractual claim against the project owner into such a third-party professional liability claim — to recover costs incurred by the constructor but not recoverable against the project owner due to risk disclaimer provisions.[23] Put another way, the constructor will pursue such claims against the consulting engineer because it "has no other place to go," given the contractual preclusion on recovery interposed by the risk disclaimer provisions.

Certainly, in some jurisdictions, some of these third-party professional liability claims pursued by a constructor against a consulting engineer (with whom the constructor has no contractual privity or direct relationship) are barred by the so-called economic loss doctrine. In substance, the economic loss doctrine is based on the principle that one who claims pure economic loss (i.e., loss other than personal injury or property damage), such as additional construction costs, disruption, delay, or other consequential damages, may not legally recover on the theory of negligence against a party with whom it has no contract. The basic rationale is that the third party's remedy (if any) in such a situation should be defined by, and confined to, whatever rights and remedies it has under its agreement with its contracting party (e.g., the project owner–constructor agreement) and that to allow the third party to pursue recovery against the consulting

engineer (with whom the constructor has no contract) under the theory of negligence in such circumstances would circumvent the contractual exchange of economic benefits and burdens embodied in the agreement between the constructor and the project owner. It would also subject the consulting engineer to imposition of an unfair risk of liability to persons with whom the professional has no contractual relationship.[24] However, the economic loss doctrine has not been accepted by appellate courts in many jurisdictions and, even in those jurisdictions in which the defense has been adopted, there are exceptions that are well-known and available to the constructor in pursuit of professional liability claims against the consulting engineer. The bottom line is that the consulting engineer, in most jurisdictions, should not comfortably rely upon the economic loss defense to preclude constructor claims incited by using risk disclaimer provisions in the project owner–constructor agreement.

Third-Party Negligence Claims Against Consulting Engineers for Economic Loss

Whether third parties who have no privity or contractual relationship with a consulting engineer may assert, and recover on, negligence claims for economic loss (not bodily injury or property damage) against the consulting engineer has been a controversial issue over the last 50 years for the courts to address and resolve. Underlying this issue are a number of competing policies and considerations regarding the legal duties owed by consulting engineers and the parties to whom those duties are owed. The ability of a claimant to assert a viable negligence claim depends upon, and presumes, the existence and breach of a legal duty of care owed by the consulting engineer to the claimant. Unquestionably, consulting engineers owe to their client (typically the project owner) a duty to act with reasonable care and diligence in the performance of those services for which the client has engaged the consulting engineer, subject to the terms of that engagement. The scope of services and other relevant terms and standards of performance are defined in the contract between the project owner and the consulting engineer.[25] The project owner–consulting engineer contract typically includes provisions that the consulting engineer perform its services as a representative of and for the benefit of its client and negates the implication of any duty or third-party beneficiary obligations owed to third parties.

It is generally recognized that the consulting engineer performs its services in the context of a network of interrelated contractual and transactional relationships between the project owner and others, such as the constructor, construction manager at risk, or their subcontractors (collectively the "constructor"), in which rights, duties, obligations, risks, and remedies are respectively defined between the project owner and those other parties. These contractual terms are (or are presumed to be) the product of negotiation between the project owner and the constructor and are intended to evidence their

various agreements, including limitations on risks, rights, and remedies. Moreover, contracts between the project owner and those other parties explicitly allocate risks and responsibilities, sometimes on an exclusive basis (e.g., construction means and methods and safety) and sometimes on a shared basis (e.g., differing or concealed site conditions).[26]

Given the foregoing background and the centrality of contracts in defining risk, rights, obligations, and remedies among the various project participants in the design and construction process, courts have struggled with whether or not the law should impose a duty upon the consulting engineer to act with due and reasonable care for the benefit of third parties, notably constructors.[27] In this area, courts grapple with a number of challenging conceptual and policy issues:

- While a consulting engineer may owe a primary duty to its client (with whom it has a contractual relationship), a breach of that duty may cause economic damage to a foreseeable class of third parties. Should these third parties be able to pursue a negligence claim against the consulting engineer for this economic damage?

- How should that foreseeable class of third parties be limited to avoid exposing the consulting engineer to the risk of indeterminate liability exposure?

- Should third parties be allowed to pursue negligence claims against the consulting engineer without regard to limitations of liability or other risk allocation provisions negotiated and contained in the project owner–consulting engineer contract? Would recognizing such a duty owed to, and right of action by, third parties impose upon the consulting engineer obligations that exceed and potentially conflict with the roles, responsibilities, and primary duties and allegiances owed by the consulting engineer to its client?

- In determining whether any such duties and claim rights should be established in favor of third parties, should the respective provisions contained in (i) the consulting engineer's agreement with its client and (ii) the third party's contract with any other party be determinative, consultative, or otherwise relevant?

All of these issues are critically important in the context of third-party negligence claims against consulting engineers seeking recovery for economic damage.

The Economic Loss Doctrine

As a general matter, the economic loss doctrine precludes recovery by a third party based on the negligence of a professional in the performance or discharge of duties owed by the latter to its client. In various forms, and to varying degrees and extents, the economic loss doctrine has been adopted in many jurisdictions in the United States.

As has been noted by an authority in this area, "Courts divide on the application of the [economic loss doctrine], but it has been applied in several jurisdictions to limit actions by participants in the construction process against architects and engineers, typically, for negligent design or supervision."[28]

Especially in the design and construction context, the rationale for the economic loss doctrine is predicated upon the sound proposition that rights, responsibilities, obligations, risks, and remedies by and between project participants primarily and predominantly should be defined and enforced according to the terms and limitations set forth in their respective contracts, and those terms and limitations should not be circumvented or subverted by the judicial application of the general law of negligence in the third-party liability context.[29] As Jay Feinman stated:

> The construction process presents one of the most complex settings in which third-party professional liability cases arise. . . .
>
> Every construction project in which a claim against a third party may arise is characterized by an extensive set of intertwined relationships. These relationships originate in the parties' contracts; the owner contracts with the design professional and the general contractor, the general contractor engages subcontractors, and the subcontractors contract with suppliers, for example. Each contract is likely to contain complex terms about performance obligations that contemplate the performance of other participants in the project. The owner's agreement with the architect, for example, may specify the extent of the architect's duty to coordinate or supervise the work of contractors and subcontractors, and the agreements of the contractors and subcontractors in turn may specify the duty to cooperate and to submit to the architect's control. These contracts may also contain risk allocation terms, defining the scope of liability to contracting parties and other participants, either in detail or by a general provision or limitation. . . .
>
> The law's role in this process is to support the parties' private ordering by using contract law to interpret and enforce their contracts. In defining obligations and allocating risks and benefits, the parties create expectations. The function of the law is to fulfill those expectations by enforcing the contracts as the parties have made them. It is inappropriate for the courts to impose liability outside the contracts, as through tort [i.e., negligence] law. Tort law is better suited to the redress of accidental physical harm than to the regulation of the kind of consensual economic relationships present in the construction process. If the courts were to impose liability, you would upset the parties' own allocation of rights and duties, diminish their ability to regulate their own affairs, and introduce inefficiencies into the process. A particular concern is the threat of indeterminate liability; when the parties cannot accurately predict to whom and for what they will be liable, it is impossible for them to plan appropriately for performance and risk in the course of construction. . . .

345

Among all the areas of professional liability, the contractual approach to third-party liability is particularly well suited to construction industry cases. Participants in the construction process typically use extensive contracts to form their relationships. Both at the level of the trade groups which promulgate form contracts and the individual transaction for which the parties negotiate a unique contract, serious allocation of the costs and benefits of the construction process, including the costs and benefits of contracting with respect to risk, characterize the contracting process.[30]

Negligent Misrepresentation Exception to Economic Loss Doctrine

In some claims, the constructor alleges that it was economically damaged as a result of its reasonable reliance upon information negligently prepared or furnished by the consulting engineer pursuant to a contract between the latter and the project owner. In the design and construction context, for example, a constructor may allege that it sustained economic damage due to its reasonable reliance upon subsurface data negligently investigated, prepared, or described by a geotechnical engineer pursuant to the latter's agreement with its client (typically the project owner or another prime design professional).[31] In these claims, the constructor typically alleges that it is entitled to recovery against the consulting engineer based on the legal theory of negligent misrepresentation. In many states, the courts recognize an exception to the economic loss doctrine to allow constructor negligent misrepresentation claims.

The *M. Miller Co. v. Central Contra Costa Sanitary District*[32] and *Texas Tunneling Company v. City of Chattanooga*[33] cases were two of the earliest cases charting the course for the so-called negligent misrepresentation exception to the economic loss doctrine, under which constructor claims predicated upon allegations that a design professional negligently prepared or furnished information (subsurface data, site conditions, survey results) could provide the foundation for an actionable negligence claim for economic damage against the design professional.

In *Miller*, the court allowed an action by a constructor on a sewer project against the engineer who conducted the soil tests and provided a report on which the constructor relied in bidding on the project. During construction it was determined that the material underlying the construction site was unstable in a manner not indicated in or anticipated by the subsurface report, resulting in the constructor's performance costs being greater than it had projected at the time of bid. The court held that the constructor stated a viable negligence claim against the soil engineer because it determined that the engineer had knowledge that its report would be relied upon by prospective bidders.

In *Texas Tunneling*, a subcontractor was allowed to assert a claim against an engineer on a sewer project based on allegations that the bid documents failed to include certain information about test bore drillings and that the subcontractor therefore underesti-

mated its performance costs. The court held that an action for negligent misrepresentation was available to the subcontractor.

In applying this negligent misrepresentation exception to the economic loss doctrine, most courts utilize the formulation set forth in the *Restatement (Second) of Torts*, Section 552, which states:

> § 552. Information Negligently Supplied for the Guidance of Others
>
> (1) One who, in the course of his business, profession or employment or in any other transaction in which he has a pecuniary interest, supplies false information for the guidance of others in their business transactions, is subject to liability for pecuniary loss caused to them by their justifiable reliance upon the information, if he fails to exercise reasonable care or competence in obtaining or communicating the information.

Constructors and other third parties (not in privity with the consulting engineer) have sought to expand the negligent misrepresentation exception on the theory that not only negligently-furnished *information*, but also negligently-furnished *designs, reports,* or other *communications* expressing or evidencing an exercise of professional interpretation, application, judgment, or opinion should form the basis of actionable negligent misrepresentation claims for economic damage by a constructor against the design professional. Notably, under such an expanded theory of liability, a constructor may seek to recover economic damages against a design professional on the basis that the latter's negligently-prepared design contained errors or other deficiencies that delayed or increased the constructor's cost of performance.

Certain recent court decisions show a more specific focus and analysis regarding the scope and application of the negligent misrepresentation exception to the economic loss doctrine, resulting in more constraint in recognizing third-party claims against design professionals. Specifically, these decisions concentrate on the underlying basis of the alleged negligent misrepresentation in the context of the § 552 *Restatement* formulation. Is the alleged misrepresentation one of *information* (as literally and explicitly required by § 552 of the *Restatement*) or of some other *communication* or *work product* attributable to the professional's performance, including the exercise or expression of professional interpretation, judgment, opinion, or design?

Two recent (non-appellate) court decisions are instructive in this regard — *Delaware Art Museum v. [Architectural Firm]*, U.S. District Court for the District of Delaware, Civil Action No. 06-481 GMS (D. Del. 2007) ("Delaware Art"), and *KDK Enterprises, Inc. v. [Architectural Firm], Commonwealth of Massachusetts*, Middlesex Superior Court, Civil Action No. 04-1305, Memorandum of Decision and Order, June 1, 2006 (KDK).

In the *Delaware Art* case, the museum asserted a negligent misrepresentation claim against a consulting engineer (the "consulting engineer") with whom it had no contract

(the consulting engineer had contracted with the project architect who, in turn, had contracted with the museum). The consulting engineer filed a motion to dismiss on the basis that the economic loss doctrine barred the museum's claims against it. In opposing that motion, the museum relied upon the negligent misrepresentation exception to the economic loss doctrine. According to the museum's allegations, the consulting engineer "produc(ed) drawings that resulted in incorrect clearance heights for ceilings, structural steel with insufficient support, mechanical rooms that are inaccessible to maintenance personnel, and other material flaws and inefficiencies." The museum contended that these deficiencies were the result of the consulting engineer's negligence and resulted in additional project costs to the museum.

The federal district court dismissed the museum's claims, stating:

> [The museum] does not dispute that only economic damages are claimed. Accordingly, in order to survive a motion to dismiss, [the consulting engineer] would have to fall within the exception to the Economic Loss Doctrine [under Section 552 of the *Restatement*].
>
> For a . . . defendant to be considered in the business of supplying information [under Section 552 of the *Restatement*], a "case-specific inquiry" must be made, "looking to the nature of the information and its relationship to the kind of business conducted.". . . When information is the "end and aim" product of a defendant's work, Delaware Courts have found the potential for liability. . . .
>
> A designer's end product is considered to be the tangible end of their design . . . thus, "the provision of plans and design drawings used to construct the project do not constitute the business of supplying information.". . .
>
> As a class of defendants, engineers fall on both sides of the § 552 exception, as their "business has dual purposes, one of which may shield them from liability, the other of which may expose them to liability.". . . The mere provision of calculations, specifications or reports for a project will result in an engineer being considered a pure information provider. . . . When an engineer's responsibility involves more, such as designing components of a project, however, his role will not fall within the exception to the economic loss doctrine. . . .
>
> In the present case, it is clear from the pleadings that [the consulting engineer] was responsible for designing particular components of the renovation and expansion of the museum, and as such, did not act as a pure information provider. [The museum's] complaint states that [the consulting engineer] "produc[ed] drawings that resulted in incorrect clearance heights for ceilings, structural steel with insufficient support, mechanical rooms that are inaccessible to maintenance personnel and other material flaws and inefficiencies.". . . As a party responsible for the design of certain components of the renovation and expansion of the Delaware Art Museum, [the consulting engineer's] "end and aim" was to provide [the museum] with certain completed systems that they designed, and any information provided was ancillary to the same.

KDK involved a negligence claim for economic damage by a subcontractor against an architect who was under contract with the project owner. The subcontractor claimed that, while the project specifications prepared by the architect called for a "Level 4" drywall vertical surface, during the punch list process the architect required that the subcontractor achieve a Level 5 drywall surface. Thus, according to the subcontractor, the architect's specification calling for a Level 4 drywall vertical surface constituted a negligent misrepresentation. In rejecting and dismissing the subcontractor's claim against the architect, the Massachusetts Superior Court stated:

> KDK is seeking recovery from [the Architect] for pure economic loss. However, KDK and [the Architect] are not in contractual privity. Therefore, the Economic Loss Doctrine is applicable to the claims. The Economic Loss Doctrine, which is recognized in Massachusetts, prohibits recovery on negligence claims for purely economic loss where there is an absence of contractual privity. . . . However, a narrow exception to the Economic Loss Doctrine has been carved out for claims of negligent misrepresentation. . . . In other words, a complainant may recover his economic losses from one who has made a negligent misrepresentation to him, even in the absence of contractual privity. . . . Thus, the critical question before the Court is whether KDK has a reasonable expectation of proving the essential elements of a negligent misrepresentation, in view of the undisputed facts set forth in the summary judgment record. . . .
>
> To recover for negligent misrepresentation, a plaintiff must prove that the defendant (1) in the course of his business, (2) supplied false information for the guidance of others, (3) in their business transactions, (4) causing and resulting in pecuniary loss to those others, (5) by their justifiable reliance upon the information, and (6) with failure to exercise reasonable care or competence in obtaining or communicating the information. . . .
>
> The Court is mindful of the notion that an Architect may not escape liability for a negligent misrepresentation merely because he is not in the business of supplying specific information for the guidance of others. . . . However, false information in an Architect's plans and specifications is only actionable as a misrepresentation if the information concerns a matter that is "susceptible of actual knowledge." . . . In other words, information provided by an Architect in plans and specifications that concerns a matter of judgment is not actionable as a misrepresentation. . . .
>
> KDK's claim of negligent misrepresentation is premised on the specification calling for a Level 4 drywall surface in view of the other specifications set forth in the Contract Documents. In essence, KDK argues that had [the Architect] exercised due care, [the Architect] would have realized that a Level 4 drywall surface would not achieve a satisfactory surface finish in combination with the required painting and lighting specifications. The determination as to what combination of drywall surface would produce an acceptable surface finish in view of the painting specifications and critical lighting

requirements is, in the view of the Court, a matter of judgment. It is a specification upon which the Architect is asked to render his professional opinion, given his education, training, and experience. It is not akin to a statement concerning the location and quality of subsurface ledge, or the description of an area of land for construction of a road. Having premised its negligent misrepresentation claim on specifications concerning a matter of judgment, rather than on specifications that are susceptible to actual knowledge, KDK's claim fails as a matter of law. . . .

KDK's reliance on *Alpert v. Commonwealth*, 357 Mass. 306 (1970) is unavailing. In *Alpert*, the Court noted "where one party furnishes plans and specifications for a contractor to follow in a construction job, and the contractor in good faith relies thereon, the party furnishing such plans impliedly warrants their sufficiency for the purpose intended." . . . However, the specification at issue in *Alpert* also concerned a matter susceptible of actual knowledge. It involved a positive representation as to the amount of unsuitable material that [the excavator] could expect to encounter. . . . The Department of Public Works set forth a figure in bidding specifications that was based on allegedly deficient boring tests that the Department had completed. Unlike the specifications here, which concern a matter of judgment, the specifications in *Alpert* were susceptible of actual knowledge. . . .

Moreover, according to the Court in *Klein v. Catalano*, 386 Mass. 701, 719 (1982), an Architect does not generally warrant that his work is fit for its intended purpose. Rather, an Architect impliedly promises to exercise a standard of reasonable care that is required of members of his profession. . . . The *Klein* Court concluded that the plaintiff's claim against an Architect for breach of an implied warranty was tantamount to a claim for professional negligence. . . .

Therefore, to the extent that KDK's claim concerns the failure of [the Architect] to exercise reasonable care in determining what level of drywall surface would produce an acceptable surface finish, in view of the painting and critical lining specifications, the claim actually amounts to one of negligence and, as previously discussed, it is barred by the Economic Loss Doctrine.

The *Delaware Art* and *KDK* decisions provide support for the position that the negligent misrepresentation exception to the economic loss doctrine does not apply in circumstances in which the alleged misrepresentation relates to communications and representations of non-factual and non-informational subject matter but, rather, involve representations that reflect or express (a) a professional opinion or judgment, such as design (rather than pure objective fact or information), or (b) a representation relating to a design process (construction documents that reflect or express the exercise of professional acumen, judgment, skill, or opinion) intended to achieve an end result (a completed construction project). On the other hand, the exception would apply in cir-

cumstances in which the representation is based on statements of fact or other matters susceptible of actual knowledge, as distinct from professional opinion or judgment. These are important and positive distinctions and limitations on the negligent misrepresentation exception.[34]

Of course, one approach to mitigate this potential professional liability exposure would be for the risk disclaimer provisions to be written so as to extend to the consulting engineer the same protection afforded to the project owner—i.e., in the event of the risk occurrence, the constructor would be precluded from recovering against *both* the project owner and its consulting engineer. While some project owners adopt this approach, others are reluctant to do so, apparently because of concerns that it will result in some loss or diminution of accountability for the consulting engineer. In any event, from the constructor's perspective, this approach is hardly a desirable solution in that it exacerbates the perceived unfairness resulting from the use of such risk disclaimer provisions in the first place by precluding *any* remedy against *any* project participant.

Under another mitigation approach, the consulting engineer would advise the project owner against using such risk disclaimer provisions and related contracting practices. This advice typically is predicated upon the following points:

1. While such risk disclaimer provisions may be legally enforceable, the practical experience and reality is that if risk is disproportionately or unfairly allocated to the constructor, there is a substantial probability that claims and disputes will result because the degree of risk and cost impacts allocated to the constructor will be too onerous, perhaps even placing in jeopardy the project owner's ultimate goals of completion on schedule and within budget in the event of constructor default.

2. When constructors are not able to recover against a project owner due to contractual barriers, they will often assert so-called "extra contractual" claims against the project owner (as well as negligence and/or negligent misrepresentation claims against the consulting engineer) based upon the legal theories of fraud, fraudulent inducement or misrepresentation, deceit, mutual or unilateral mistake, and/or superior knowledge. While proof of such extra-contractual claims is stringent and recovery difficult for the constructor, these claims are often prompted by risk disclaimer provisions and related contracting practices and, despite the legal burdens and challenges, constructors out of desperation often pursue such claims in litigation during the progress of the work (the timing of the claim assertion often corresponds with the occurrence of the relevant risk), thereby jeopardizing the project's completion on schedule and within budget.

The project owner's decision to adopt such risk disclaimer provisions should be based on considerations that are significantly broader and more pragmatically based than a pure legal analysis as to the enforceability of such provisions. While the legal enforce-

ability advice is important, the consulting engineer's advice adds an equally important and valuable dimension to the risk allocation decision-making process.

A fair question is whether the consulting engineer's advice, solicited or unsolicited, is self-serving in this context. Admittedly, there is a self-serving element to such advice — i.e., to the extent that project owners decide not to utilize such risk disclaimer provisions and related contracting practices, the consulting engineer will want to significantly reduce its heightened risk of professional liability exposure from constructor claims, if not to eliminate it entirely. However, for other reasons that are definitely in the project owner's best interest, it is important that the project owner appreciate the pragmatic factors surrounding the use of such risk disclaimer provisions and practices and the potential for claims, disputes, project disruption, and schedule and budget jeopardy that they pose. Simply put, the project owner's risk allocation decision should be informed and predicated upon sound and established risk allocation principles, including the control and fairness principles. In the final analysis, *all* project participants benefit from such seasoned, enlightened, and universal advice.

Often toward the conclusion of the project, a constructor may assert significant claims against the project owner and/or the consulting engineer, alleging that the constructor incurred unanticipated economic damage due to excessive changes and cumulative schedule impacts (acceleration or delay). In some instances, these claims may be asserted solely against the project owner based upon the project owner's alleged breach of its *Spearin* implied warranty obligation to furnish contract documents that may be used to construct the project within the required cost or time requirements. In other situations, the constructor may assert such claims against both the project owner and the consulting engineer, with the claims against the latter being typically predicated upon professional negligence. Depending upon the law of the particular state, professional negligence claims by the constructor may be barred by the economic loss doctrine.[35]

These claims often seek recovery in substantial amounts, with the result that many project owners become unwilling to proceed to trial or other modes of formal dispute resolution and often are quite anxious to settle. In such circumstances, the consulting engineer may be pressured into contributing towards a settlement. The project owner may be unwilling to accept the legal reality that the consulting engineer's risk exposure derives from its compliance with the professional standard of care and, in most instances — especially in those jurisdictions adopting the economic loss doctrine — the constructor's ability to recover against the consulting engineer (i.e., a non-contracting party whose performance is judged by the professional standard of care) is more legally burdensome than its ability to recover under its contract with the project owner. Notwithstanding these important legal distinctions, the consulting engineer may be subjected to significant pressure from the project owner — for "client relationship" or "share the pain" reasons — to contribute to a settlement of such constructor claims.

In this type of situation, the consulting engineer's response should be based upon an evaluation of the risk allocation (standard of care and indemnification) provisions of its agreement with the project owner in relation to its actual performance, measured by its standard of care compliance. Certainly "client relations" considerations are a pragmatic factor that should be taken into account in this evaluation process, but they should not be the predominant or controlling factor (absent very compelling circumstances that justify that "client relations" factors override). This is because a consulting engineer needs to evaluate such risks and professional liability exposure in a balanced and somewhat uniform manner across the firm's "book of business," measuring both specific clients and projects. Exempting any specific client or project from such a balanced and uniform process may create a firm "precedent" and, with it, expectations for other clients that they will be similarly and "specially" treated.

At an even more fundamental risk-reward evaluative level, these types of claims of cumulative economic loss and impact are to be expected from many constructors involved in megaprojects. Thus, the risk and cost of resolving such claims is inherent in the megaproject and is one that the project owner should accept and address either by resolution or defense. Of course, to the extent that the consulting engineer's deficient performance has contributed to the cost of resolving the constructor's claim, the consulting engineer should be held accountable to the project owner under the risk allocation terms of the agreement between them and under the residual professional standard of care principles. In most situations—even those involving demonstrable and plausible proof of the consulting engineer's deficient performance—the project owner and consulting engineer are better served by a joint defense of the constructor's claims.

Professor Sweet has made a rather compelling case as to why consulting engineers should be interested in the subject of constructor claims for unanticipated economic loss, which he labels as "post completion" claims:

> To the contractor, [post completion] claims [are] needed to make the owner pay for planning and executing the project so badly that the Constructor spent money it should not have had to spend. To the Owner, these claims [look] like a desperate attempt by the Constructor to bail itself out of a losing contract caused by its poor bidding or inefficient performance. . . . Why should the Engineer concern himself with these post completion claims? Often, the bases for such claims are poor planning and administration by the Engineer. Commonly, these claims are made against the Owner; the assertion is that the Owner is responsible for the Engineer it engaged, and some claims target the Engineer directly. More commonly, even if the claim is made against the Owner, the Owner may assert an indemnification claim against this Engineer if the Engineer's conduct is the principal basis for the claim. Even if the Engineer or other design professional is not a party to the litigation, he is sure to be called as a witness by one or more parties. If

he is, he will have to search his records, produce them to any party that requests them, and search his recollection of events that may have occurred many years in the past. He is likely to be called to testify at lengthy discovery procedures and be a witness at an arbitration or litigation. Whether as a party or as a witness, litigation will cost the engineer time and money. Also, his involvement may create a psychological nightmare. His conduct is under review and usually challenged. This can affect his professional reputation and undermine his confidence. Finally, the engineer will face the uncomfortable and dispiriting background of conflict in the inhospitable atmosphere of the lawsuit. We are all aware of the law's influence on professional practice. It goes with the territory. The engineer must be aware of the legal backdrop against which he performs his work. These post completion claims are increasingly part of that backdrop.[36]

Several factors on public projects that indicate that such constructor economic loss claims may be asserted include the

- Quality and completeness of the design;
- Competence of project management by both the consulting engineer and the project owner (or independent construction manager);
- Sophistication and experience of the project owner;[37]
- Size and complexity of the project, including the use of innovative design and construction approaches;
- Site conditions, especially the extent of subsurface investigation, the contractual approach to risk allocation, and disclosure of subsurface investigation results to bidders;
- Type of contracting approach (single versus multiple prime, number and complexity of contract interfaces, fast-track); and
- Fairness and clarity in contractual risk allocation between project owner and constructor.

Unquestionably, all of these factors are present in most megaprojects, thereby posing a significant risk that the constructor's cumulative impact claims against the owner, which directly or indirectly involve the consulting engineer, will, as Sweet characterizes it, become "part of the construction landscape."[38]

At the root of the economic loss doctrine is the recognition that allocation of risk between contracting parties — e.g., the project owner and the constructor — should not be circumvented or subverted by the allowance of recovery by the constructor against the consulting engineer. Anthony Meagher and Michael O'Day note that allowing a constructor's claim of economic loss — non-contractual claims against consulting engineers — "not only affects constructors and design professionals, it also directly affects the bargain of the project owner, which might be implicated in such a claim, or any litigation that may ensue by virtue of increased project costs."[39] They continue:

> [C]ourts often have failed to lead parties to the "terms of their own agreements" and have not shared the [United States] Supreme Court's reluctance to "intrude into the parties' allocation of risk."[40]

Notwithstanding, many courts have allowed constructors to assert non-contractual economic loss claims against consulting engineers. So why should the project owner be interested or concerned about the consulting engineer's exposure to constructor non-contractual economic loss claims?

> A project owner retains more than a passing interest in the debate over whether its contractors and their subcontractors should be permitted to sue the design professional(s) who designed the project and administered the construction contract. Such claims raise at least three concerns for owners. First, allowing such actions can draw the owner into litigation. Although the owner's interests generally align with the design professional's, the latter may point to the owner as an independent cause of the contractor's damages. Second, permitting such claims likely increases the owner's design costs because of the increased insurance expenses to the design professional. Third, and perhaps most importantly, allowing such claims may do violence to the owner's contractual bargain by permitting the contractor to circumvent the construction contract, such as limitations on the recovery of damages, waiver of jury trial, dispute resolution provisions, and jurisdiction and venue clauses.[41]

In addition, the allowance of such claims may impair the consulting engineer's ability to protect and represent the interests of the project owner due to concerns about potential liability exposure to the constructor:

> An Architect has a duty to administer construction as set forth in its agreement with the Owner. Permitting a Contractor's direct claims in tort against the architect muddies the water. Now the architect owes contractually defined obligations to the owner and an additional duty of care, enforceable in tort, to the contractor. Those requirements may conflict during the project, forcing the architect to choose one liability over another. For example, an architect that requires too much performance of a contractor may be liable in tort for the excess, while an architect that requires too little may be in breach of the contractual duties owed to the owner.[42]

Recommended Practices

- Project owners should strive to allocate risk with constructors in a manner that is clear, consistent, and fair.

- Consulting engineers should recognize the potential for heightened professional liability risk exposure in circumstances in which the project owner and constructor unfairly allocate risk between themselves.

- Consulting engineers should encourage the project owner to include provisions to minimize the risk of third-party claims in its agreement with the constructor.[43]

5.0 Project Delivery Methods and Contracting Approaches: Professional Liability Implications

Issue

How does the project owner's choice of a project delivery method and contracting approach impact consulting engineer risk and professional liability exposure?

Analysis and Discussion

The project owner's choices and decisions regarding selection of a project delivery method and contracting approach have a definite impact upon the professional liability exposure for the consulting engineer. The ultimate determination of professional liability depends, as discussed in Part 3 of this chapter, upon the application of the professional standard of care and consideration of the consulting engineer's contractual service scope and other obligations, all of which must be evaluated in the context of these project owner decisions.

On megaprojects, the project owner's initial decisions regarding delivery method and contracting approach represent a critical step in the project planning process.[44] However, it is generally more the exception than the rule that these initial decisions will hold constant throughout project execution. Megaprojects require flexibility in project execution so as to be able to adapt and adjust to, for example, new or innovative design approaches, constructor-proposed (value engineering) design changes, implementation of fast-track due to schedule recovery pressures, and construction means and methods design requirements due to critical third-party or abutter concerns or issues. Thus, the project owner's initial decisions regarding project delivery method and contracting approaches, and the corresponding impact upon the consulting engineer's professional liability exposure for defective design, are not static. On megaprojects, these decisions

are influenced by a number of dynamic and variable factors and by considerations that may result in changes in those methods or approaches, which will consequently affect the consulting engineer's professional liability risk exposure.

The prospect and occurrence of this type of change—inherent in megaproject planning and execution—are not necessarily problematic for the consulting engineer so long as the consultant anticipates and is aware of the change event in a timely manner, has the ability to evaluate its risk exposure that may result therefrom, and has an opportunity to negotiate any appropriate contractual or other risk allocation adjustments or modifications that may be needed as a result of these changes, and implements appropriate risk management practices.

To say it another way, the choice of a project delivery method on a megaproject does not necessarily ultimately resolve risk allocation for defective design of permanent project work or construction means and methods. Given the dynamic and flexible needs of megaprojects, changes are likely to occur that will influence such risk allocation. While there is nothing inherently problematic about this type of change, the consulting engineer should be attentive to it and the implications which result regarding professional liability risk exposure.[45]

5.1   Design-Bid-Build

In the design-bid-build delivery method, generally the engineer of record (EOR) is responsible for the design of permanent project work and the constructor (by and through its design professional subconsultant) is responsible for the design of construction means and methods. The project owner impliedly warrants to the constructor that the design it furnishes to the latter is constructible and that, if the constructor executes the work in accordance with that design, the completed work will achieve its intended function or purpose.[46]

These generalizations apply on most design-bid-build projects, including many megaprojects utilizing the design-bid-build delivery method. However, on megaprojects, there is an increased likelihood that various aspects of design responsibility may be fragmented and/or assigned, delegated, or distributed to multiple project participants and accomplished in such a manner that ambiguity exists as to risk allocation and responsibility for defects in the final design, as well as for construction means and methods design. This type of ambiguity may arise due to the involvement of multiple parties in the design process: (a) preliminary design: the progression of design development (say, to the 15 percent to 20 percent level) by the in-house engineer or independently-retained engineer prior to, and as a basis for, the selection of a final designer, who will be responsible for the final design (consistent with the preliminary design concept);

(b) project-wide standard details or requirements: limitations on the final designer's discretion and flexibility by owner-imposed project-wide standard design requirements; (c) design management and design development reviews and approvals: the process by which design development submissions are reviewed and approved and the entire design development process is managed by the project owner; (d) design delegation: the delegation of the design of certain aspects of permanent project work to the constructor (to be accomplished by and through a specialty designer); (e) use of detailed design or prescriptive criteria for construction means and methods: the project owner, often influenced or required by third-party or abutter agreements, may restrict the constructor (who otherwise has generally broad discretion in selecting and designing the construction means and methods) through the use of contract requirements or limitations on design choices and approaches or, in some instances, by the owner's potential removal of the constructor's responsibility for designing specific means and methods and the assignment of those responsibilities to the engineer of record; (f) constructor-proposed value-engineering or other changes to permanent project work; and (g) project owner purchase of equipment to be used in the construction process: the project owner may decide to purchase certain equipment, such as a tunnel boring machine, to be used in the construction process and furnish that equipment to the constructor.

Thus, even in design-bid-build, the most conventional and traditional project delivery method, there are numerous circumstances on megaprojects in which issues of design responsibility are complicated by the number of participants involved in the design development and approval process –involving both permanent project work and construction means and methods—and the respective roles and responsibilities of each of those participants. In some important respects, megaprojects require that participants assume non-traditional roles and responsibilities due to special project requirements. Moreover, the roles and responsibilities assigned and established at the project's inception are likely to evolve during its execution. There is nothing inherently surprising in all of this; the key for the consulting engineer is to identify in a timely manner the professional liability risk exposures associated with assigned roles and responsibilities (both initially and as they evolved) and to develop contractual and other risk management practices to control that risk exposure.

5.1.1   Conceptual Design; Uniform Design Criteria, Standards, Details, or Requirements

On megaprojects, the project owner may seek to establish project-wide uniformity in final design approach or requirements to the maximum extent permissible. This objective may be accomplished through issuance of preliminary design, standard design

details, performance requirements, or design criteria, compliance with which is mandatory by the final designer (or the constructor's designer) unless specific components of the final design require modifications or adjustments. Ultimately, of course, the final designer is responsible for preparing a design that satisfies the professional standard of care and other legal requirements (code and regulatory), including the exercise of prudent judgment in evaluating the appropriateness of standard or other project-wide prescribed design standards or criteria in any specific design application. Accordingly, while the project owner (or its consulting engineer) may seek to mandate or otherwise maximize the use of such project-wide design standards, details, or criteria, the consulting engineer who prepares and stamps the final design will always have professional responsibility for that design and the obligation to exercise sound professional judgment in the application of those standard details or criteria.[47]

If the project owner has retained a consulting engineer to prepare the preliminary design or project-wide standard design or criteria, the consultant may (depending upon contractual terms of engagement) have some degree of professional liability exposure to the project owner for the adequacy or appropriateness of that preliminary design or the project-wide design standards or criteria. The application of the professional standard of care in such circumstances is generally more forgiving than the application of the standard of care to the adequacy of final design. Notwithstanding the more forgiving application of the professional standard of care to the adequacy of preliminary design, professional liability may still attach to a consulting engineer who prepares or furnishes preliminary design or project-wide standard design or criteria.

5.1.2 Design Management and Design Development Reviews and Approvals

On megaprojects, the design development submissions prepared by the consulting engineer responsible for final design typically undergo review and approval by the project owner or another engineering firm engaged by the project owner to represent its interests. Review and approval by the project owner or its independent engineer do not relieve the engineer of record (EOR) of responsibility for the final design. In this process, it is important that the EOR exercise independent professional judgment and not succumb to any undue influence in the review and approval process that could compromise its judgment.

Conversely, over-intrusiveness and dominance by the project owner or its independent consulting engineer in the design development and finalization process may result in shared responsibility of the former for defective final design risk, especially risk resulting in property damage or economic loss.

5.1.3 **Design Delegation**

Design of components of the megaproject is often specialized, complex, and innovative in nature. In addition, megaprojects require keen attention to both constructability and cost efficiency of design. These characteristics often result in design responsibility being allocated and delegated among several parties for specific components of permanent project work (as distinct from construction means and methods). These parties may include constructors or, more precisely, design professionals engaged by such constructors.

Specifically, the contract documents may delegate to the constructor responsibility (through a qualified and registered design professional) for the design of a specific permanent work component. Alternatively, a constructor may propose, as part of a substitution process, value engineering, constructability review, or otherwise alternative designs of permanent project work. In either of these scenarios, however, the constructor (or its designer) becomes responsible for the design of specific components of permanent project work. In these circumstances, the constructor typically must adhere to certain prescribed preliminary design performance criteria or standards in the design of the permanent project work.

In relation to design delegation, there are principal areas of concern that must be adequately addressed to achieve the objectives of a clear and pragmatic definition of design responsibility consistent with public law requirements and fair risk allocation.

Public Law Considerations

In the more general context of this discussion, "public law" refers both to laws enacted by the various state legislatures and regulations promulgated by agencies or registration boards of these states. In contrast, contract or private law deals with the ability of parties to define and provide a mechanism for regulating their relationships, affairs, risk assumptions, commercial expectations, and legal obligations through a "private" ordering and arrangement (e.g., contracts). As a general rule, in the United States' legal system, parties have significant autonomy to define and structure the terms of their contracts, subject to compliance with any applicable (usually relatively minimal) public law requirements, such as professional registration laws and regulations.[48]

In the specific context of design delegation, the principal registration/licensure issues relate to (1) the qualifications of the person performing the design and (2) the person who, in the context of distributed and delegated design, is in charge of that design and the coordination and integration of the design with other components of the project. Does the distribution and delegation of design responsibility result in adequate protection of public health, safety, or welfare? In the context of collaborative design, can or

should more than one person or entity be responsible for the entirety of the project design? Could design responsibility be compartmentalized in some manner such that multiple parties share design responsibility or several different parties have responsibility for respective portions of the permanent project design? These are all important design delegation issues.[49]

Public law — especially professional registration laws and regulations — is governed by the sovereign jurisdiction of each of the 50 states,[50] and various states regulate design delegation in significantly divergent ways, with most not having specifically addressed the practice.[51] As such, predictability in the determination of acceptable delegation practices is generally uncertain and the development of standard contract provisions that comply with applicable public laws is a significant challenge. Moreover, resolving the design delegation issues mentioned above in a uniform (or "national") manner from the public law perspective is an additional challenge.[52]

Questions have been raised about the legality of design delegation under certain laws and regulations. These questions and their answers depend largely upon the laws and related regulations of the 50 states. Due to the variations and peculiarities in those laws and regulations among the various states, no attempt will be made here to survey or discuss them comprehensively. In general, however, there are two broad classifications of law and regulations that typically present issues for the application of design delegation: registration laws and public competitive bidding laws.

The central issue raised by design delegation under many state laws regulating the registration (or licensing) of design professionals is whether design services may be delegated to a non-professional (i.e., a constructor). Another issue is what types of design services must be performed by a registered professional. It is important to address these and related issues in design delegation because the consequences of failing to do so could lead to the voiding of contract obligations (i.e., a contract may be declared legally unenforceable), payment problems for the constructor (especially if payment for an "illegal" service is implicated), and the imposition of civil and criminal fines and penalties resulting from violation of state registration laws.[53]

Most states have enacted competitive bidding laws that are applicable (subject to certain limitations) to the procurement of constructors on publicly-awarded or publicly-funded projects. An underlying assumption of these laws is that multiple constructors will bid on a project based upon a set of contract documents that represent a "complete" design for all components of the permanent work. Thus, the scope of the work to be bid and constructed (at least in theory) will be clearly and comprehensively defined so that the bidder's price is the controlling factor in a low-bid competitive award (which, many times, is the only real consideration in the absence of conscientious attention to pre-qualification and prior performance experience factors, if appropriate under state law).

Under the design delegation approach, the design of one or more components of the

permanent work may not be complete at the time of bid and award and, under such circumstances, will be left or delegated to be performed by the successful bidder. Thus, in a public competitive bid process on a project using the design delegation approach, different constructors may formulate their bids with different expectations and judgments about how to fulfill the delegated design obligations. In this respect, the bid comparison will not be "apples to apples" in character (since not only price, but also work scope related to the delegated design, may vary among bidders) and, therefore, this result could undercut the policies and objectives that underlie the public competitive bid laws of many states. In fact, it is for this same reason that the design-build delivery method poses a problem under some state competitive bidding laws. As has been stated:

> Another argument raised against design delegation is that it undermines competitive bidding laws for public construction projects. The goal for such laws is to facilitate public construction of maximum quality products at the lowest possible cost. For that to happen, it is argued, all bidders must bid on the same work, that is, the same plans and specifications. But that cannot happen, it is argued, if the design is not complete because the principal design professional is going to delegate the responsibility and cost for portions of the design through a Constructor or SubConstructor. While scrupulous Constructors will retain quality design professionals to perform delegated design, less scrupulous Constructors motivated by economic incentive will retain design professionals who under-design the work or simply "sell their stamp," thereby impacting public safety and confidence in construction. Further, any expected cost savings are lost if the cost of design is delegated along with the responsibility for such to Constructors and SubConstructors who will reasonably mark-up for overhead and profit.[54]

Clearly, for these reasons, a project owner and/or its consulting engineer contemplating the design delegation approach on a public project should consult with knowledgeable counsel regarding the legality of that approach under public bidding laws in the state in which the project is to be located.

The relatively undeveloped state of public law requirements pertaining to design delegation practice provides courts, in third-party personal injury and wrongful death tort cases, with a fair degree of discretion to adjudicate design responsibility issues. In the absence of clearly-defined public law requirements, and without constraint by contractual provisions relating to design delegation (as the third party, by definition, is not a party to such contracts),[55] especially in the context of often highly-sympathetic facts and circumstances (including serious personal injury and death), this judicial (and jury) discretion can be quite significant, relatively unbounded, and legally or pragmatically immune from appellate review.

Private Law—Contractual Risk Allocation

In the absence of public law limitations or regulatory constraints, parties have significant autonomy to allocate risk associated with design delegation. To be effective as reliable predictors of risk allocation consequences, contracts must be developed, negotiated, and finalized with due regard for the regulations of public law. Moreover, contracts must enable the parties to perform within the design and construction process.

Do contractual risk allocation approaches adequately, responsibly, and realistically address the practice of design delegation? Conventional wisdom says no, that matters of contractual risk allocation have not been adequately addressed, particularly when evaluated for proper regard for policies or requirements that underlie relevant public law. In Carl Circo's article (note 51, above) on design delegation contracting approaches in the years following the Hyatt Regency catastrophe, the author stated:

> Unfortunately, the primary legacy of the 1981 Kansas City Hyatt Regency Hotel catastrophe is not more aggressive legal controls over specialty design practices; it is, instead, contracting practices that more aggressively insulate project design professionals from specialty design errors. There is growing evidence that specialty design practices since 1981 portend increasingly troublesome questions of contractual responsibility and legal liability.[56]

Many contractual approaches to risk allocation in design delegation operate under the assumption that applicable state public law allows design responsibility for distinct portions of permanent project work to be assigned, distributed, delegated, or shared among multiple project participants, provided that those participants are qualified and licensed to provide such a contribution to their respective portion of the permanent project design work. This assumption may not be consistent with the public law requirements of applicable state law. For example, in some states, design responsibility may not be distributed or delegated, notwithstanding the parties' desire to divide and allocate design responsibility among qualified professionals for portions of the permanent project work. The permissibility of allocating and distributing design responsibility typically must be determined by reference to applicable state public law. However, given the limited number of states that have chosen to directly address the practice of design delegation, parties are often left without an adequate public law framework within which to navigate, negotiate, and establish contractual risk allocation terms that would predictably, reliably, and realistically define their rights and obligations.

To contractually address design responsibility in the design distribution or delegation context, the American Institute of Architects (AIA) has explicitly approved the practice of design delegation since the introduction of related provisions in the 1997 edition of the AIA standard documents. Paragraph 3.12.10 of the 2007 edition of the *General*

Conditions of the Contract for Construction (AIA Document A201-2007) essentially tracks the language of the cognate paragraph in the 1997 predecessor document:

> § 3.12.10 The Contractor shall not be required to provide professional services that constitute the practice of architecture or engineering unless such services are specifically required by the Contract Documents for a portion of the Work or unless the Contractor needs to provide such services in order to carry out the Contractor's responsibilities for construction means, methods, techniques, sequences and procedures. The Contractor shall not be required to provide professional services in violation of applicable law. If professional design services or certifications by a design professional related to systems, materials or equipment are specifically required of the Contractor by the Contract Documents, the Owner and the Architect will specify all performance and design criteria that such services must satisfy. The Contractor shall cause such services or certifications to be provided by a properly licensed design professional, whose signature and seal shall appear on all drawings, calculations, specifications, certifications, Shop Drawings and other submittals prepared by such professional. Shop Drawings and other submittals related to the Work designed or certified by such professional, if prepared by others, shall bear such professional's written approval when submitted to the Architect. The Owner and the Architect shall be entitled to rely upon the adequacy, accuracy and completeness of the services, certifications and approvals performed or provided by such design professionals, provided the Owner and Architect have specified to the Contractor all performance and design criteria that such services must satisfy. Pursuant to this Section 3.12.10, the Architect will review, approve or take other appropriate action on submittals only for the limited purpose of checking for conformance with information given and the design concept expressed in the Contract Documents. The Contractor shall not be responsible for the adequacy of the performance and design criteria specified in the Contract Documents.[57]

Paragraph 3.12.10 assumes that, so long as its requirements are met, design responsibility for portions of permanent project work may be distributed or delegated among qualified project participants and that the design responsibility may be allocated to each such participant for its respective portion(s) of the distributed or delegated design and/or specific and defined contributions to the design development process. Under paragraph 3.12.10 — and in similar contractual approaches — the project owner's design professional (i.e., the consulting engineer) is required, or likely, to provide some or all of the following services in the design delegation context:

- Developing and specifying the conceptual basis of the delegated design (e.g., design criteria or performance standards);
- Defining the qualifications of the constructor's design professional;

- Reviewing (and, in some instances, approving) the design development submissions of the constructor's design professional;
- Coordinating the delegated design with the overall project design;
- Reviewing shop drawings or other constructor submittals regarding the delegated design; and

Observing construction, reviewing and certifying payment applications, and making recommendations regarding acceptance of completed construction work relating to the delegated design.

In the context of the AIA contractual approach to design delegation, questions about design delegation practices have arisen among project participants in disputes and claims. Consider the following representative issues:

- Does the consulting engineer remain responsible for the permanent design delegated if that design falls within the scope of the EOR's original design responsibilities?

- Is the consulting engineer required to furnish design criteria or performance standards for the development of the delegated design, and to what degree and under what professional standard of care is the consulting engineer responsible for the adequacy of those criteria and standards?

- Who is responsible for specifying and verifying the qualifications and experience of the constructor's design professional?

- What is, or should be, the scope of the consulting engineer's review of the constructor's design professional's design submittals? Should it be limited to conformance with specified or furnished design criteria or performance standards or be a more expansive review? In paragraph 3.12.10 of the AIA Document A201-2007, what does "for the limited purpose of checking for conformance with the information given and the design concept expressed in the Contract Documents" mean, and how effective is this provision in limiting the consulting engineer's review scope and responsibility?

- Who is responsible for the coordination and compatibility of the consulting engineer's design of the non-delegated portion of the project permanent work with the delegated design portion?

- Who should review the constructor's shop drawings related to the delegated design? The consulting engineer, constructor's design professional, or both? And, for what purpose(s)?

- How does the *Spearin* implied warranty doctrine apply in the context of delegated design responsibilities?

- How does design delegation reconcile (or not) with professional registration and licensure laws for design professionals?
- Do the constructor, its trade subcontractor, and/or the constructor's design professional have adequate professional liability insurance to cover risk associated with defects or negligence in the delegated design?
- Does the blending of design functions representative of collaborative and shared design processes blur lines of legal responsibility and increase the risk of compromise in public safety, health, or welfare?
- How does one reconcile contractual allocation of design adequacy risk and responsibility among those participants functioning in a collaborative and shared design mode with countervailing public law requirements such as registration or licensure laws and OSHA? Can these conceptually distinct spheres of legal responsibility really be compartmentalized, or does one impact or override the imposition or assignment of legal responsibility in the other?[58]
- These issues typically are resolved under applicable public law requirements, contractual risk allocation, and other relevant provisions, as well as prevailing professional and industry practices. As a general observation, predictability of results in the resolution of such disputes — particularly in litigation and arbitration and by juries in sympathetic personal injury and death tort cases — is a highly uncertain proposition for all project participants, especially the consulting engineer, thus posing significant risk for all participants.[59]

The goal of any contract is to structure commercial and legal (risk) matters in a way that promotes certainty, predictability, and realism in the enforcement of rights and obligations among the contracting parties, but the contractual risk allocation approach in design delegation practice has not been adequate to the task. In part, this results from unclear public laws in many states, as well as from unclear contract provisions that raise more issues, disputes, and conflicts than they solve.

In July 2000, the British Health and Safety Executive (HSE) issued *The Collapse of NATM at Heathrow Airport,* its report on the investigation into the October 1994 collapse of tunnels being built at Heathrow Airport (the HSE Report). The failure of project participants to clearly identify and effectively allocate and manage risk were predominant factors cited by the HSE Report as contributing to the collapse.

The HSE Report provided a tremendous service to those involved in the design and construction of subsurface projects, especially for those owners (and consulting engineers who advise them) contemplating the use of the design-build approach in its entirety or the delegation by the constructor of the design of a portion of the permanent project work on a design-bid-build project. Although cast in the specific context

of a NATM tunnel collapse, the lessons learned as described in the HSE Report have far broader application to all megaprojects. However, as noted in the forward to the HSE Report, despite the complexity of the events, circumstances, and contractual roles and relationships involved in the Heathrow tunnel collapse, "the lessons are relatively straightforward." Some of the principal lessons for owners and consulting engineers (working for constructors) may be summarized as follows:

For the Project Owner

1. Carefully consider the implications of delegating design responsibility to the constructor, especially in circumstances in which the integration of the constructor's design into the overall project design is essential.

2. Retain geotechnical consultants with a scope of services adequate to undertake a reasonable level of subsurface investigation that can support contemplated design and construction approaches and methodologies.

3. Retain qualified consulting engineers with substantial experience in subsurface projects to advise and assist the project through the design development and finalization, which should include an appropriate level of review of the design submissions by the constructor's engineer.

4. Obtain independent, adequate (in terms of defined scope and compensation), and qualified professional and technical advice (including geotechnical services, testing, construction, and quality control monitoring) during construction.

5. Avoid the risk of conflicting roles and responsibilities for project participants, which leads to confusion and ambiguities, and of fragmentation and diffusion of roles and responsibilities by clearly defining roles and allocating risk and responsibilities in agreements and contract documents.

For the Consulting Engineer to the Constructor

1. Do not accept an inadequate contractual scope (or compensation) for design or construction administration phase services.

2. Hold paramount the need to exercise independent professional judgment in the discharge of contractual and other duties and obligations (especially to the public in the area of safety).

3. Proceed with design only upon being satisfied that an adequate level of subsurface investigation has been undertaken to support the contemplated design and/or anticipated construction approach or methodology.

4. Endeavor to be directly involved in all important meetings and communications that relate to the development and execution of project design.

5. Do not proceed with construction until the design has reached an appropriate degree of development; do not use the "observational approach" during construction (which is important) as a substitute for incomplete or inadequate pre-construction design.[60]

There are several risk management/allocation considerations pertaining to design delegation that should be conscientiously evaluated by the consulting engineer in connection with effective structuring and the implementation of design delegation. These considerations will be addressed from the perspective of the consulting engineer engaged by the project owner, as well as from the perspective of the consulting engineer engaged by the constructor to design a portion of the permanent work.

Design Delegation in Context

In the design-bid-build delivery method, the consulting engineer (i.e., the engineer of record) typically and traditionally is engaged by the project owner to design most, if not all, components of the permanent work. [61] The constructor is obligated to build in accordance with the EOR's design; the constructor does not have responsibility for the design, nor is it required to take the initiative in identifying any perceived deficiencies in the design or in proposing improvements or other changes to the design prepared by the EOR.

Especially during the last two decades, the design delegation approach has evolved to the point where in many design-bid-build projects, the constructor is delegated or, as a result of some other means, actually undertakes (typically by retaining a registered and qualified design professional as a subconsultant) the design of a portion of the permanent work, collectively and broadly referred to as "design delegation." In some instances, design delegation is done expressly; in other instances, by implication or subtly through, for example, the issuance of design criteria or performance standards in the contract documents that, while not explicitly imposing a design obligation on the constructor, in practical effect require the constructor to design a component of the permanent work.[62] As has been observed, "[w]hether Constructors like it or not, whether it is valid in all jurisdictions or not, design delegation is an increasing reality in today's construction industry."[63]

Reasons for Design Delegation

A number of reasons have been identified for the increasing use of the design delegation approach, including:

1. The design complexity of certain components of the permanent work and the special expertise required for that design, which is considered by some in the industry

to be beyond the acumen and skill of many consulting engineers (i.e., many consulting engineers are perceived not to be qualified to provide the complete design required in complex projects, and therefore the owner looks to others to provide the professional and practical design expertise that complicated construction projects, or systems within those projects, require).

2. Pressures to reduce the cost of the design and construction of the permanent work.

3. The increasing emphasis on the constructability of the design of permanent work (a factor often not sufficiently considered by design professionals).[64]

Design Delegation Applications

In general terms, design delegation may be initiated by either the project owner (directly or through its consulting engineer) or the constructor. In either event, the delegation may occur explicitly or implicitly. Regardless of how it is initiated, one of the constant objectives in the process should be clarity and specificity in the delegation, not to mention fair and balanced allocation of risk and responsibility for the delegated design.[65]

A project owner may explicitly delegate design (typically through its EOR) when it includes a provision in the contract documents obligating the constructor (typically by a qualified and registered professional) to furnish the design of some component of the permanent work or when it invites a constructor to submit value-engineering proposals for the modification of the design of permanent work contained in the bid and/or contract documents. In both of these examples, the project owner explicitly initiates the design delegation process. A constructor may explicitly invite (and undertake) design delegation responsibility when it initiates or proposes (in response to a project owner solicitation or otherwise) modifications or substitutions to the design of a component of the permanent work. In other circumstances, the delegation may be implicit (or certainly less clear and explicit), as when a project owner includes in the contract documents performance standards or design criteria regarding a component of the permanent work and obligates the constructor to provide submittals and/or perform the work consistent with those standards or criteria.

There are several examples of the types of permanent work components (as distinct from construction means and methods) that can be considered appropriate candidates for design delegation. One example of design delegation in civil or horizontal construction projects is the design of tunnel lining systems, and there are several examples from the building or vertical construction process. The AIA New York State Task Force on Delegation of Design developed a list of "ancillary components"[66] — defined

as "components which are subordinate, supplementary or accessory to the main project components and which are provided by another [registered professional] licensee with special expertise" — and gave the following examples:

- Curtain walls
- Precast concrete panels (e.g., walls, floors)
- Proprietary exterior walls, windows, and floor systems
- Handrail, guardrail systems
- Steel attachments
- Pre-engineered systems, including elevators, escalators, lifts, conveying equipment
- Gorilla glass
- Sprinkler systems
- Fire suppression/smoke systems
- Exhaust systems
- Fire proofing materials and assemblies (ul assemblies)
- Electrical systems, lighting fixtures
- HVAC systems
- Ceiling support systems
- Components to meet performance criteria stated by a manufacturer or a testing laboratory
- Steel connections consistent with a fabricator's shop practice
- Conformance to industry standards
- Prefabricated, pre-engineered components
- Lead/asbestos/pollution control delegation and hazardous abatement
- Handicapped/accessible components
- Special, high tech components: computerized systems that run conveyor systems (airports), computerized control systems for security, and emergency power systems (proprietary items)
- Stair systems.[67]

Issues Raised by Design Delegation

There are numerous issues raised by design delegation: as an initial matter, determining whether design delegation is appropriate on the project; the role (if any) of the project owner in that decision; the technical and contractual implementation of such a decision; whether to include design criteria and/or performance standards that set forth the parameters of the delegated design; how risk and responsibility are defined and allocated for the delegated design; and the project implementation through activities such as design and submittal review and performing administrative and observational roles by the consulting engineer related to the construction of the delegated design. Most, if not

all, of these issues may have professional liability implications for consulting engineers engaged by either the project owner or the constructor.

Unclear design delegation leads to unfair risk allocation and unknowing assumption of responsibility by the constructor. Lack of clarity, specificity, and explicitness in the delegation of design can result in confusion and ambiguity about who is responsible for the adequacy and/or performance of the delegated design and the likelihood that "something will fall between the cracks" in the allocation of that responsibility. It can also lead to a constructed design that may not be as safe because more than one entity is responsible for the design. The project owner may not be aware that its consulting engineer is delegating to the constructor responsibility for some component of the permanent work (leading some owners to question whether design delegation results in their paying twice for the design of the delegated component). Those who identify these and related issues typically rely upon the *Hyatt Regency* case as a tragic demonstration of the worst fear of what could happen when design responsibility is not clearly delegated and allocated among project participants.[68]

Design Criteria and Performance Standards

In most situations in which design delegation is effectuated (either by contract document requirement or invitation, i.e., solicitation of a value-engineering proposal), the contract documents typically contain certain design criteria and/or performance standards (collectively "criteria or standards") that define the basic elements that must be incorporated into the design and/or the performance, objectives, or other standards that the completed design must achieve. The purpose of these standards is to communicate minimum characteristics of the delegated design, to limit the discretion and judgment of the constructor's design professional in certain defined respects in developing the delegated design, and, finally, to provide the requirements against which the consulting engineer will review the design or other related submittals of the constructor (or its designer) concerning the delegated design. In circumstances in which the design is delegated without such criteria or standards, there is a significantly increased potential for disputes and conflicts between (a) the project owner and/or the consulting engineer and (b) either of them and the constructor, or its design professional, about the quality, characteristics, or other important features of the design that reasonably should be sufficient or adequate to satisfy the design delegation obligation.

When the criteria or standards are defined in the contract documents, an issue may arise as to whether the project owner (and/or the consulting engineer) or the constructor (and/or its design professional) is responsible for the adequacy and/or appropriateness of those criteria or standards. This is important and should be addressed in the contract documents so as to avoid (or, realistically, minimize the risk of) ambiguity, confusion, and associated disputes about allocation of risk and responsibility for deficiencies in the

specified criteria or standards. One approach is to require that the preparer/issuer of the performance criteria or standards (typically the project owner and/or its consulting engineer) be responsible for the adequacy and appropriateness of the specified criteria/standards. Yet, it is difficult to understand or accept from a professional registration or liability perspective how the constructor's design professional — who will stamp the design — can entirely disclaim responsibility or be relieved of liability for its design submitted for a project-specific application while knowing of its inadequacy or having reservations (where one reasonably should have them) about the adequacy or appropriateness of the criteria or standards which form the basis of that design. Contract provisions appearing to provide that protection may be ineffective and, hence, afford illusory protection.

Registration, Qualifications, and Experience of the Constructor's Design Professional

Consider a design delegation process that includes contractual requirements about the professional registration status, qualifications, and experience of the design professional who will be proposed by the constructor to perform the delegated design. The failure to address these factors on the front end, in the contract documents and through early submittal requirements, could lead to disputes with the constructor regarding those issues at a later, untimely point in the construction process — i.e., after designs have been completed and submitted and the clock is ticking on the response period. It can also lead to claims by the project owner against its consulting engineer that the constructor's design professional was not qualified to undertake the design and, thus, the design professional should be responsible for failing to specify those qualifications or for negligence in approving the qualifications of the constructor's design professional. The point to emphasize here is that the time to address the qualifications of the constructor's design professional is in the beginning, when the contract documents and qualification requirements and submittals are set out, and not for the first time upon review of the constructor's completed design submission.

Project Owner's Consulting Engineer's Review of Delegated Design

Assuming that the project owner's consulting engineer has clearly communicated and defined the criteria or standards governing the delegated design, the consultant should reasonably be expected to review the designs submitted by the constructor's design professional for conformance with those criteria or standards. As noted above, in those circumstances in which such criteria or standards are not clearly or effectively communicated and defined (or not communicated or defined at all), there is a substantial probability that conflict and dispute will arise concerning the consulting engineer's appropriate scope of review of the delegated design submission and of other issues related to the adequacy of the delegated design. The consulting engineer should develop a stamp and related transmittal review language clearly stating the limited purpose of its review of the delegated design submittal.

Disputes and claims arise in situations in which the consulting engineer (or one of its consultants) engages in a review beyond contractual limits and attempts to intrude into the discretion or professional judgment of the constructor's design professional. In doing so, it is probable that the consulting engineer will assume some degree (if not all) of the responsibility for the adequacy of the delegated design (i.e., responsibility not only for the concept but also for the development of design details), which may result in claims from the constructor for additional time and/or cost due to "intrusion" or "unwarranted interference" by the consulting engineer in its ability to reasonably fulfill its design delegation obligation.

In addition to authorizing the consulting engineer to review the constructor's design for compliance with the defined criteria and standards, the contract also typically extends the review to determining whether that design "conforms to information provided in the contract documents and the overall project design" or contains words to that effect. The latter language could be construed to impose upon the consulting engineer responsibility for assuring that the delegated design properly integrates and coordinates with the overall project design. Therefore, the consulting engineer should make a conscientious effort to integrate and coordinate the delegated design with the overall project design and to clearly and fairly allocate responsibilities to the appropriate project participants according to the guiding principle that risk be allocated to the party in the best position to control the variables that may affect or impact that risk potential. Specifically in this case, the constructor should not be allocated the responsibility for design integration and coordination if it (or its designer) is not in a position to control or influence design decisions that are necessary to fulfill its responsibility for integrating and coordinating the design.[69]

Constructor's Responsibility for Delegated Design

When the design has been delegated along with the criteria or standards to the constructor, the constructor has the obligation to develop and furnish a design that meets those criteria and standards, which is then typically stamped and sealed (depending upon state law requirements) by a registered design professional. In addition, the constructor's design professional may be required to furnish a certification that, to the best of its knowledge, information, and belief, the design conforms to governing codes applicable at the time of submission and has been prepared in accordance with appropriate and reasonable standards of professional practice, with a view toward the safeguarding of life, health, property, and public welfare, and that the certifying professional is professionally responsible for the design. In delegating the design, the consulting engineer should require that the design submission be stamped and sealed and that a certifica-

tion substantially similar to that outlined in the preceding sentence be submitted by a qualified and registered design professional engaged by the constructor. It is also recommended that the contract documents include prequalification and early submittal requirements regarding the qualifications of the constructor's proposed design professional consistent with the certifications discussed in the preceding sentences.

In addition, the contract documents should clearly state that the project owner and the consulting engineer (and its consultants) are entitled to rely upon the adequacy, accuracy, and completeness of the services, design, calculations, other work product, reviews, certifications, or other approvals performed or provided by the constructor's design professional.

In implementing design delegation, it is important that the contract documents (and the consulting engineer's agreement with the project owner) clearly define the respective roles of the consulting engineer and the constructor's design professional with respect to the performance of administrative services relating to construction of the delegated design. More specifically, once the delegated design has been submitted and approved, who has responsibility—i.e., the owner's consulting engineer and/or the constructor's design professional—for the following administrative services in connection with the construction of the delegated design: review of shop drawings and related submittals; observation of construction work; review and approval of constructor or subconstructor payment requisitions; evaluations and recommendations regarding claims in dispute relating to construction; preparation and execution of opinions, certifications, affidavits, or other statements to construction lenders or funding authorities and building code or other regulatory authorities concerning the status, quality, or contact compliance of the construction work. If a system of primary and secondary review is contemplated or expected among those design professionals, their respective roles, responsibilities, and any applicable limitations should be clearly defined and communicated to all project participants so as to minimize the risk of any ambiguity or confusion.

Risk Allocation, Professional Liability, and Design Delegation

Project Owner's Consulting Engineer

Typically, the consulting engineer who implements the design delegation (on behalf of the project owner) through the preparation and issuance of criteria and standards and other services in connection with the review and construction of the delegated design will be required to perform those services in accordance with the professional standard of care. Specifically, and in the absence of contractual provisions imposing a higher obligation, design professionals are obligated to perform their services, including preparation and development of design and construction administration services, in accordance with the standard of care required of another professional possessing similar skills, qualifications, and experience and performing its services at the same time and under similar circumstances, including scope and other related contractual limitations (the "professional standard of care"). If claims are made against the consulting engineer by the project owner or others alleging deficiencies in the performance of any such services (e.g., in the preparation of inadequate or inappropriate criteria or standards), the validity of any such claims generally will be determined in accordance with the professional standard of care. Compliance with that standard does not require perfection or "error free" services; rather, the standard tolerates a level of imperfection.[70]

Although the professional standard of care for the consulting engineer remains unaltered in the context of design delegation, application of that standard may be complicated under the following circumstances: when responsibility for the delegated design has not been clearly allocated; when problems result from alleged or actual combined or contributory deficiencies in the underlying criteria or standards (developed by the consulting engineer) and in the details of the final design (as developed by the constructor's design professional); and when there is an overlapping or unclear assignment of roles and responsibilities or "ambiguous" conduct by the consulting engineer (or conduct that exceeds contractually-specified limitations) in the performance of its responsibilities to review and approve the delegated design and in conducting administrative services regarding the construction of the delegated design.

Project Owner and Constructor

In general, a project owner who furnishes to a constructor a complete and detailed design impliedly warrants the accuracy, suitability, completeness, and constructability of that design. This well-established risk allocation principle for design adequacy was first recognized by the United States Supreme Court in *United States v. Spearin*, 258 U.S. 132 (1918),[71] and typically is referred to as the *Spearin* or implied warranty obligation.

The rationale for allocating the risk of defective design to the project owner under the *Spearin* or implied warranty obligation is based on the principle that since the project owner (typically, through its consulting engineer) is in control of the design process and undertakes to prepare and furnish the "entire and complete" design to the constructor, the project owner should be responsible for the accuracy, suitability, completeness, and constructability of that design. Simply put, responsibility for risk should follow actual control of, or ability to control, that risk. As Sweet has stated:

> As a basic principle, responsibility for a defect rests on the party to the construction contract who essentially controls and represents that it possesses skill in that phase in the overall Construction Process that substantially caused the defect. Usually defects caused by design are the responsibility of the owner in a traditional construction project and the Constructor who both designs and builds. Control does not mean the *power* to

make design choices. Usually every owner has the power to determine design choices. For example, an owner may require a particular tile to be used, a power within its contract rights. But the control needed to invoke the basic principle means a skilled choice, either one made by an owner who has professional skill in tile selection or an advisor such as an architect with those skills. This principle recognizes that the owner who supplies the design is responsible for design that does not accomplish the owner's objective and may not have a claim against the design professional. Usually the standard to which the design professional is held is whether she would have performed as another design professional similarly situated would have.

Under this principle, the owner, through faultless, bears the cost of correcting defects. The owner has the principal economic stake in the project and will benefit from a successful project. There is no reason why it cannot be responsible for project failures even though it is blameless and cannot transfer the loss. . . .

Risk allocation is based on the probable intention of the parties, the greatest skill possessed or supplied by the owner, the Constructor's lack of discretion and the owner's being in the best position to avoid the harm, as well as the owner's ability to spread, absorb, or shift the risk to the design professional. . . .[72]

In the context of design delegation, this basic principle, however, may be displaced or, put another way, the risk of defective design may be reallocated to the constructor. Sweet suggests that this displacement should occur when the party who would normally have the risk (i.e., the project owner in the context of furnishing a completed design) "clearly communicate[s] to the [Constructor] that the latter must and does assume responsibility for defects that the basic principle would [otherwise] place on the [owner]. Attempts to displace the basic principle must meet the standards of good faith and fair dealing and not be unconscionable."[73]

The traditional rule that the project owner bears the risk of "defective" design is predicated on the rationale that the project owner (typically by and through its consulting engineer) prepares and furnishes the design and contract documents and that the project owner is in control of the design process. Generally speaking, (a) the more extensive and substantial the involvement of the constructor in the development and finalization of the design and related documents, (b) the greater the degree of discretion given to the constructor in the development and finalization of the design, and (c) the greater the expertise of the constructor as a reason for delegating a design role to the constructor, then the greater the probability that the risk for "defective" design will be allocated to the constructor or, alternatively, will be shared in some fashion as between the owner and constructor. However, for any such "displacement" or "reallocation" of the design adequacy risk to occur, the constructor must have *significant* involvement in the development and finalization of the design.[74]

For example, in *Johns-Manville Corp. v. United States*,[75] the Claims Court stated:

> [For the warranty to apply, it must be determined] that the design specifications [were] devised and drafted by the Government. Because of the often extensive interplay between Constructors and the Government during the development, modification, and purchase of products, it must be determined whether design specifications are truly the Government's own, or whether the Constructor has assisted in their drafting and provided such expertise as to negate the Government's implied warranty, because the Government specifications, in effect, endorse the Constructor's product or input.

In *Austin Co. v. United States*, 161 Ct. Cl. 76, 314 F. 2d 518, *cert. denied*, 375 U.S. 830 (1963), the constructor's implied warranty claim failed because its proposed technical modifications were incorporated into the government's specifications. The constructor's voluntary preparation of the specifications for what was essentially a new product indicated to the court that the constructor had assumed the risk of impossibility of performance, and the Court found no implied warranty by the government. In *Bethlehem Corp. v. United States*, 199 Ct. Cl. 247, 462 F. 2d 1400 (1972) (per curiam), the Court also denied a warranty of specifications claim. Although the government had drafted the specifications for an environmental test chamber, it did so in reliance on extensive information provided by the constructor and with the constructor's full knowledge that the government was relying on its expertise. The Court held that the constructor had assumed the risk of non-performance.[76]

In general, the allocation of risk to the project owner for "defective" design exists primarily in those circumstances in which the project owner furnishes to the constructor a detailed, fully developed, and completed design. In this specific context, allocation of risk principles often turn on the distinction between "design" and "performance" specifications, the former typically resulting in allocating the defective design risk to the owner and the latter typically in allocating the risk to the constructor.[77]

In some instances, courts undertake a detailed and complex analysis to determine whether the specification is design or performance in nature and, therefore, whether responsibility and risk for design inadequacy should be allocated to the project owner or the constructor. For example, in *Fruin-Colnon Corp. v. Niagara Frontier Transportation Authority*, 585 N.Y.S. 2d 248 (App. Div. 1992), the constructor entered into a contract with the Niagara Frontier Transportation Authority to excavate and construct twin subway tunnels, each approximately two miles long, as part of the Buffalo Light Rail Rapid Transit System. During the course of performance, several disputes arose between the constructor and the Authority. In particular, the constructor alleged that it encountered a differing site condition during excavation, entitling it to recover $3,255,150 in excess of the contract price of $38,948,800. The second dispute concerned whether the constructor or the Authority bore responsibility for addressing the infiltration of water

into the tunnels — the so-called watertightness dispute, for which the constructor was claiming $568,297.80 as reimbursement for remedial grouting.

When the Authority appealed the trial court award in favor of the constructor on the watertightness claim, the appellate court affirmed the decision. In its appeal, the Authority contended that the trial court erred in awarding judgment in favor of the constructor on the watertightness claim since the contract contained a performance specification that imposed the responsibility for achieving watertightness on the constructor and, consequently, the constructor was not entitled to extra payment for grouting. The constructor contended that the trial court erred in concluding that no differing site condition existed. In affirming the judgment in favor of the constructor on the watertightness claim, the appellate court engaged in an extensive analysis of the Authority's contention that the contract documents constituted a "performance" specification, as distinct from a "design" specification. In addressing this distinction in the specific context of the watertightness claim, the appellate court stated:

> A performance specification requires a Constructor to produce a specific result without specifying the particular method or means of achieving that result. . . . Under a performance specification, only an objective or standard of performance is set forth, and the Constructor is free to choose the materials, methods and design necessary to meet the objective or standard of performance. . . . Concomitant with control over the choice of design, materials and methods is the corresponding responsibility to ensure that the end product performs as desired. . . . In other words, the contractual risk of non-performance is upon the Constructor. . . . That is in contrast to a design specification, where the owner specifies the design, materials and methods and impliedly warrants their feasibility and sufficiency. . . . A Constructor must follow a design specification without deviation and bears no responsibility if the design proves inadequate to achieve the intended result. . . . Whether a provision is a performance specification or a design specification depends upon the language of the contract as a whole. . . . Other factors to consider include the nature and degree of the Constructor's involvement in the specification process, and the degree to which Constructor is allowed to exercise discretion in carrying out its performance under the contract. . . .
>
> In arguing that the watertightness requirement was a performance specification that [the Constructor] assumed the responsibility of meeting, [the Authority] relies primarily on the language of [the watertightness clause]. Read in isolation, [the watertightness clause] appears to be a performance specification; it specifies the end objective (watertightness) and the standards for measuring that objective, but does not specify the methods of achieving watertightness. Nevertheless, the language and structure of the contract as a whole, as well as the parties' usage and course of performance under the contract, support the conclusion that a design specification was created.

Although the watertightness clause itself does not set forth a particular method for achieving watertightness, the contract as a whole establishes complex and exacting standards for design and construction of the tunnel. [The Constructor] was to construct an unreinforced, cast-in-place concrete liner of precise dimension. The type and mix of the concrete was precisely specified, as were detailed requirements for placing, curing, protecting, and furnishing the concrete. [The Constructor] was given no discretion to deviate from those specifications, whether for the purpose of water proofing or otherwise. For example, [the Constructor] had no discretion to install an impermeable outer liner to resist the hydrostatic pressure that both parties knew would exist following completion of construction. Other provisions of the contract contemplated that waterproofing would be accomplished by means of fissure grouting, which also was to be carried out pursuant to detailed specifications. Additionally, the payment and warranty provisions of the contract support the conclusion that, as a whole, it created a design specification. The contract explicitly provides that "all measures necessary for achieving the degree of watertightness specified in [the watertightness provision] including remedial treatments to stem leaks," would be paid for at the contract unit prices. It is unlikely that [the Authority] would have agreed to pay [the Constructor] on a per unit basis if, as [the Authority] contends, [the Constructor] had assumed the responsibility of achieving watertightness. Further, unlike the general warranty set forth in the contract, the extended watertightness warranty did not provide that [the Constructor] would remedy water leaks at its own expense, as it would have if [the Constructor] had assumed the responsibility of achieving watertightness.

In addition to its examination of the contract documents as a whole in determining whether the specification was "design" or "performance" in nature, the appellate court also considered significant the course of dealing, communications, and conduct of the Authority and the constructor prior to, during, and following construction. Specifically, the appellate court stated:

The parties' course of dealing prior to construction also supports the inference that a performance specification was not intended. Bidders had no input into the design of the tunnel, nor did [the Constructor] exercise any independent design judgment after it was awarded the contract. [The Authority] relies heavily on [the Constructor's] March 5, 1980 letter submitted in support of its Value Engineering Change Proposal (VECP), a type of bilateral change order. In that letter, [the Constructor] asserted, as a reason why it should be permitted to change the design of the tunnel liners to a "full circle pour," that [the Constructor] bore the risk of meeting the watertightness requirement. In relying on the language of that letter, [the Authority] overlooks the context in which it was sent. If the contract had created a performance specification with respect to watertightness, it would have been unnecessary for [the Constructor] to obtain [the Authority's]

approval for a design change, and it would have been impermissible for [the Authority] to withhold such approval. Similarly, the parties' course of dealing during and following construction illustrates that the contract did not establish a performance specification. As evidence that [the Constructor] undertook the responsibility of waterproofing, [the Authority] cites that [the Constructor], on its own initiative, developed and carried out a course of chemical grouting, a method not mentioned in the contract and for which [the Constructor] did not bill [the Authority]. It is far more significant, however, that [the Authority] routinely denied [the Constructor's] numerous requests to implement various other waterproofing methods. Even before the concrete liners were put in place, and while the water diversion system was operating, [the Constructor] repeatedly requested permission to grout the numerous water-bearing fissures that were present in the exposed rock. Those requests consistently were denied based on [the Authority's] erroneous view that fissure grouting was not intended to achieve watertightness. After the tunnel was constructed and the water diversion system turned off, [the Constructor] unsuccessfully requested permission to fissure grout, plug the deep wells with piezometer testing holes and construct a permanent dewatering system. Those requests were denied by [the Authority] which maintained an uncooperative and obstructive attitude. [The Constructor] nonetheless proceeded to fissure grout under protest, based on its proper interpretation of the contract. It would have been unnecessary for [the Constructor] to seek [the Authority's] consent for such measures, and contractually impermissible for [the Authority] to withhold such approval, if [the Constructor] were in fact responsible for achieving watertightness and had discretion to chose the means to achieve that objective.[78]

The degree of involvement of the project owner or its consulting engineer in the review and evaluation of the constructor's delegated design and/or in the performance of administrative services regarding the construction of that delegated design may complicate the process of determining risk allocation and legal responsibility for deficiencies in that design. Despite a general transference of design adequacy risk from the project owner to constructor through the design delegation approach, there may be circumstances in which the project owner retains that risk or the risk is reallocated to the project owner. These circumstances can arise when a project owner furnishes specifications or criteria (whether prescriptive or performance) and/or the conceptual design to the constructor as part of a design delegation process. The *more detailed* the specifications and design criteria furnished by the project owner, and the *less discretion* given to the constructor to deviate from those specifications or criteria, the more likely that the project owner will retain some level of risk and responsibility for the adequacy of that design.[79] Similarly, the more involved the project owner becomes in reviewing, commenting on, or directing changes to the design developed by the constructor, the greater the likelihood that the

project owner will assume some degree of risk for design adequacy. The degree of the owner's involvement during construction in the submittal review and/or proposed substitution review/approval process may also affect the design risk exposure of the project owner. Simply put, the greater the degree of involvement of the project owner in the design development process or in the review, evaluation, and direction of the design of the constructor (or that of its design professional), the greater the risk of project owner responsibility for design adequacy in the design delegation context.[80]

Thus, it may generally be stated that the risk of design adequacy transfers to the constructor when the latter has the responsibility as well as a reasonable degree of discretion (in developing the design under the design delegation principle) for preparing and furnishing a complete design. Although the project owner or its consulting engineer may be responsible for the adequacy of any contractually-specified criteria or standards, the constructor will have a significantly more difficult burden in proving claims based upon defects in those criteria and standards than it would in proving defects or breaches of implied warranties with respect to a completed design prepared by (or by the consulting engineer on behalf of) the project owner and furnished by same to the constructor.[81]

The case of *Guy F. Atkinson Construction Co.*, ENG BCA 6145, 98-1 BCA §29582 ("Atkinson"), decided on December 29, 1997, demonstrates that a constructor who provides the design of a portion of the permanent work will be responsible for the adequacy of that design, as well as any constructability problems associated with its implementation. The project at issue in *Atkinson* involved the construction of 5,620 linear feet of twin subway tunnels under a fixed-price contract between the Washington Metropolitan Area Transit Authority ("WMATA") and Atkinson. Bidders were given two options as to the method of constructing the tunnels: one option called for a single-pass method using conventional shield mining with a 4-foot pre-cast, segmented, unreinforced concrete liner 10 inches thick and sealed and gasketed into place; the second option employed the New Austrian Tunneling Method, consisting of mining with initial support provided by a lining of concrete reinforced by metal followed by installation of a non-reinforced, cast-in-place final liner not less than 12 inches in thickness. Atkinson's successful bid was based on the conventional single-pass earth tunneling method utilizing a 10-inch bolted and gasketed pre-cast concrete tunnel liner.

The contract documents included a "Value Engineering Incentive" clause that allowed the constructor to pursue changes to the contract document design through value engineering change proposals (VECPs), with the understanding that, should the so-called VECPs be accepted by WMATA, the constructor would assume the risk that the VECPs would be successful and produce a result at least equivalent to the design included in the bid and contract documents.

Approximately one month after the contract award, Atkinson submitted a VECP that included extensive changes in the tunnel design specified in the contract documents.

Atkinson's VECP called for the installation of a 7-inch-thick pre-cast, reinforced concrete initial liner that would be unbolted but expandable against the walls of the newly mined tunnel. Following the placement of a waterproof membrane, a cast-in-place concrete lining of 12-inch thickness would be installed inside the pre-cast support. Ultimately, WMATA and Atkinson entered into an agreement (after extensive revisions to the original VECP), subject to several technical requirements, including that the final tunnel liner must be designed with a factor of safety not less than 2.5. In addition, in a Memorandum of Agreement concerning approval of the VECP, WMATA and Atkinson agreed to several conditions, including the following:

1. Atkinson shall submit a final design which is to be reviewed and approved as design documents by WMATA if such documents comply with WMATA standards and criteria (subject to certain minor exceptions); and Atkinson's design documents shall be prepared and stamped by a registered professional engineer for the State of Maryland for that purpose and shall be responsive to the detailed comments of WMATA and its consultants.

2. Any delays in obtaining WMATA approval of the design submission shall not be cause for any adjustment in price or time under the contract.

3. Notwithstanding any review, approval, acceptance, or payment by WMATA, Atkinson:

   3.1 Shall be responsible for the professional and technical accuracy of all designs, drawings, specifications, and other work or materials furnished under the VECP and shall, without additional cost or fee, revise any errors or deficiencies in its performance.

   3.2 Shall be liable to WMATA for all costs to it of any kind caused by or resulting from Atkinson's negligent performance and preparation of the revised design, or performance of the work.

   3.3 Shall be liable for all integration of the revised design with all other aspects of the original design.

   3.4 Shall save, hold harmless and indemnify WMATA against liability claims and the cost of bodily injury and property damage occurring in connection with or in any way incident to or arising out of the occupancy, use, service, operations, or performance of work under the VECP modification resulting in whole or in part from acts, errors, or omissions of Atkinson, or any representative of Atkinson for a maximum of $3 million dollars, which indemnification shall remain operative for a period of three years following acceptance of the work under the contract.

During construction, Atkinson's failure to excavate the tunnels to specified line and grade rendered it impossible to maintain the final liner thickness at 12 inches, resulting in the need for Atkinson either to reinforce the final liner up to its design strength with a safety factor of 2.5 or to reline the misaligned segments. In this context, WMATA reminded Atkinson that its acceptance of the VECP with an unreinforced, cast-in-place final tunnel liner was conditioned upon a design that could provide for a final liner with a minimum thickness of 12 inches, thus insuring a safety factor of 2.5. In response, Atkinson submitted a "factor of safety claim," seeking to recover the cost it incurred in constructing the final subway tunnel liners to a safety factor of 2.5. The practical effect of the 2.5 safety factor was that the liners of the subway tunnels had to be constructed with a much greater length of steel reinforcement and, consequently, at greater cost than would have been the case had a lower safety factor been utilized. Affirming the rejection of this claim, the Board of Contract Appeals stated:

> The contract provisions applicable to VECPs place the risk that the proposal will be successful and will yield a result at least equivalent to what was required by the original contract specifications squarely on the proposing Constructor. . . .
>
> Substantive evidence in this appeal is conclusive that the terms VECP agreed to by the parties required that the thickness of the final tunnel liner was not to be less than 12 inches and that any parts of the tunnel liner where the thickness was less than 12 inches would have to be reinforced with steel to a safety factor of 2.5, which would then be equivalent to the strength of the unreinforced tunnel liner with a thickness of 12 inches. When [Atkinson] was unable to install a substantial part of the final tunnel liner to a thickness of 12 inches because of misalignment of the tunnels during construction, [Atkinson] became responsible for the cost of reinforcing the undersize tunnel liner to the specified 2.5 Factor of Safety.[82]

Finally, warranties or certifications that may be required of the constructor and/or its design professional may impose upon it/them liability standards for the adequacy of the delegated design that exceed the negligence-based professional standard of care.[83] On the other hand, provisions in the contract documents, such as a waiver of consequential damages, may serve to limit the potential liability of the constructor for certain types of economic or consequential damages due to deficiencies in the delegated design.

Constructor's Design Professional

As a general rule, the adequacy of the constructor's design will be governed by the professional standard of care unless that constructor (or its design professional) agrees to a higher or other standard. Although the contract documents may state that the constructor is not responsible for the adequacy of criteria or standards relevant to the delegated design furnished in the contract documents, the constructor's design professional

who stamps, seals, or provides certifications regarding the delegated design may become implicitly responsible for the adequacy of those underlying criteria or standards, especially in those circumstances in which that design professional, at the time of undertaking that design, is (or reasonably should have been) aware of and/or has reservations concerning the adequacy of those criteria or standards.

Similarly, as noted above, the constructor's design professional may assume liability or responsibility for the integration and coordination of the delegated design with the overall project design, unless the latter responsibility is specifically addressed and allocated in the contract documents. Finally, while the constructor may be entitled to the benefit of certain "contractual" defenses based upon provisions in the contract documents, such as a waiver of consequential damages, these provisions may not extend these contractual protections to the constructor's design professional.[84]

Design Delegation: Some Risk Management/Allocation and Professional Practice Observations

Risk Management/Allocation

The preceding discussion hopefully has demonstrated the need for conscientious attention to the risk management and allocation considerations and associated professional liability implications of design delegation. There are several points that should be emphasized:

- Design delegation should be utilized only in those situations in which a good reason exists to do so, such as the need or advisability of obtaining the constructor's design expertise (or special access to same). In those limited situations, the design delegation should be accomplished in such a manner as to provide the constructor and/or its design professional with reasonable discretion to develop the delegated design, and use of unduly restrictive and detailed criteria or standards generally should be avoided. Ideally, design delegation should not be employed in situations involving complex and intricate relationships and dependencies between the delegated design and the overall project design.

- The project owner should be informed of the intention to delegate design of a component of the permanent work to the constructor and, ideally, be given a timely, meaningful, and informed opportunity to participate in approving the use of design delegation.

- In the contract documents, design delegation should be clearly, fairly, and explicitly expressed, the area of design delegated to the constructor should be specifically defined, and risk for the adequacy of the delegated design should be clearly allocated. These are very important concerns because design delegation inherently

poses a substantial potential for fragmentation and diffusion of design responsibility among several project participants, the effect of which could negatively impact not only the quality of the completed project, but also public safety.

- In addition to clearly and fairly delegating and allocating responsibility for design of a specific component of the permanent work, the contract documents should also similarly define and allocate responsibility for (a) the adequacy of any contractually-specified criteria or standards applicable to the delegated design and (b) the integration and coordination of the delegated design with the overall project design. The "fragmentation and diffusion" concern (discussed in the preceding paragraph and elsewhere in this section) is exacerbated when responsibility for criteria and standards and for design integration and coordination are not clearly defined and allocated in the contract documents. In many situations, design professionals — even in the absence of the design delegation approach — are more than sufficiently challenged to coordinate the design produced by *their own subconsultants,* over whom they possess contractual and other lines of authority, influence (e.g., payment), and direct communication and control. Satisfactorily assigning responsibility for the adequacy of the criteria and standards and for design integration and coordination in the context of design delegation is even more challenging due to the sometimes dysfunctional, diffused, and non-privity relationship between those who will be actually undertaking design.

- Even in circumstances in which the contract documents clearly, fairly, and explicitly allocate risk for the delegated design, for the adequacy of criteria or standards and for design integration and coordination, the extent to which these risk allocations will be recognized and respected depends, in substantial part, on the context in which claims or disputes arise that involve or implicate these risk allocations. For example, it should reasonably be expected that risk allocations will most likely be recognized and dispositive if the claims are between the owner and constructor and involve equitable adjustments (time and/or cost) or other commercial or contractual disputes between them. At the other end of the spectrum, risk allocations are less likely to control in a dispositive manner in the context of bodily injury or other third-party claims against the project owner, the constructor, and/or their respective design professionals, or in public enforcement or regulatory proceedings against those parties, such as an OSHA proceeding. In addition, even with clear risk allocation to the project owner (and/or its consulting engineer) for the adequacy of contractually-specified criteria or standards, it is not likely that the constructor's design professional will be able to entirely avoid liability or responsibility for deficiencies in those criteria and standards that are incorporated into the delegated design stamped by the constructor's design professional, especially

in situations in which the design professional has (or knows about or reasonably should know about) reservations concerning the adequacy of the criteria or standards and/or in which the design deficiencies are raised in the context of bodily injury or other third-party claims, or in an OSHA or board of registration proceeding against the design professional.

- Assuming that clarity and specificity in the risk allocation of the design delegation has been achieved in the "front-end," confusion and ambiguity may be interjected in the contract documents and the lines of responsibility blurred through the conduct of the project participants in implementing the design delegation approach. This may occur, for example, when the owner's consulting engineer assumes an "aggressive," overly ambitious, or "extra-contractual" review role over the delegated design submitted by the constructor (through its design professional).

- The contract documents should contain appropriate and fair indemnification or other risk allocation provisions that are consistent with the manner in which risk has been defined and allocated in the contract documents relating to the delegated design.

- Attention should be given to the need for adequate professional liability insurance for the professional liability risk associated with design delegation. On larger projects — particularly those involving $50 million dollars or more in construction value — serious consideration should be given to the purchase of project-specific professional liability insurance.

Professional Practice

In some respects, many of the risk management/allocation issues pertaining to design delegation may be *reasonably* — but not perfectly or entirely — addressed through both appropriate provisions in the contract documents and adequate project-specific professional liability insurance coverage. However, in addition to risk management/allocation issues, the design delegation approach also raises a number of important questions about the professional practice of design professionals, their present and future role in the design and construction process, and their present and future relationships with project owners.

In the past several years, we have heard certain "complaints" fairly consistently from many project owners about their design professionals. A number of these complaints appear to be the driving force underlying the tremendous surge of project owner interest in the design-build delivery method. It may be productive to review some of these complaints in the context of design delegation:

- Some project owners complain that *their own design professionals* do not pay sufficient attention to the cost and constructability implications of their design and that many constructors (and their design professionals) have demonstrated a better comprehension, aptitude, ability, and willingness to be attentive and sensitive to those considerations.

- Some project owners complain that *their design professionals* should be providing a broader range of design and professional services — e.g., that the prime design professional should retain more disciplines than traditionally has occurred, including geotechnical engineers, cost estimators, and specialty designers.

- Some project owners complain that *their design professionals* shift too much design responsibility away from them to others who are not as qualified to undertake that design or shift risk in a manner that fragments, diffuses, dislocates, and unfairly allocates responsibility for design of the permanent work. In turn, this leads to contentious and adversarial relationships between project participants, as well as to disputes, arbitration, litigation, etc. — all of which these owners find distasteful. When this occurs, project owners get frustrated, and sometimes angry, especially when the fragmentation and diffusion of design responsibility was initiated by *their design professionals* and impaired the quality of the completed project. These complaints are shared by many more project owners than had been believed and, in significant part, are a driving force underlying popular support for "single-point responsibility," which is a distinguishing hallmark of the design-build delivery method.

Another matter to consider about project owner complaints is the emerging interest in constructor-led design-build (under which the constructor retains and controls the design professional and design process and has a direct relationship with the project owner) and the corresponding and contrasting temerity and reluctance (primarily due to liability and related concerns) of design professionals to assume the prime position in the design-build delivery method. Also, some representatives of constructors have expressed a substantial interest and enthusiasm in design delegation and sense an enormous business opportunity for the construction industry associated with design delegation.

For example, one such commentator, speaking on behalf of constructors, stated:

- Throughout the constructor community, we hear nothing but criticism about architects and their work. Many say bad documents are the root cause of all our problems. Design delegation will provide constructors with a role in improving these bad documents and perhaps even place constructors in a leadership position with owners.

- Constructors must realize they may now be obligated to provide design.

387

- The A/Es [architects/engineers] are clearly trying to establish their ability to delegate portions of design now. They are absolutely correct when they say they are not now providing comprehensive design and should not be viewed as the A/E of record for the complete design. Design has been diffused for years, and it's better to clarify who is providing it rather than to fool ourselves.

- The architects are abdicating their historical role in the construction industry by taking this stand. We told them this would happen way back in 1966 when they changed from "supervise" and "inspect," to "observe" and "endeavor to guard." Constructors are tired of warning them; they feel it's now time to take matters into their own hands. If the architect wants to pass off their duties to constructors more and more, so be it.

- Constructors have always shown great ingenuity. This is a great opportunity to alter the course of the construction industry for the betterment of our clients and their projects.

- Insurance is available, although it may be expensive and available on only a limited basis. Many constructors are taking on design liability as a business risk whether they know it or not.

- The whole thing is really a macro issue. If the architects are unable or unwilling to step up to the plate, we owe it to the industry to take charge. Design will be done by architects and engineers, but under the auspices and direction of a constructor.[85]

Similarly, it has been stated:

> Some view the trend toward greater design delegation as a long-term market advantage for Constructors, arguing that over time Owners will realize it is the Constructor who brings real value to the project. With this recognition, the Constructor's role in the construction project will expand so much so that the Constructor will be responsible for selecting the designer, and even for selecting the project delivery system to be used.[86]

So what does all of this mean for consulting engineers? Specifically, does design delegation address or fuel project owner complaints about their consulting engineers? Is design delegation yet another method by which project owners are becoming further detached from their consulting engineers as the single-source and prime provider of professional services on a construction project? These questions are hard, penetrating, and perhaps even disconcerting, but are worth pondering. However, for risk management/allocation reasons alone (discussed above), this author would recommend that the design delegation approach, if selected, be "used sparingly and with caution."

5.1.4 Use of Detailed Design or Prescriptive Criteria for Construction Means and Methods

Generally, the constructor (through a qualified or registered design professional) is responsible for the design and implementation of construction means and methods.[87] However, on megaprojects there may be a number of reasons why the project owner may elect to exercise greater control over the constructor's selection, design, and implementation of construction means and methods. The owner may exercise this control affirmatively (by prescribing specific means and methods) or negatively (by limiting or precluding certain constructor discretion or options regarding means and methods). These reasons include potential damage to adjacent structures and physical or environmental constraints or limitations imposed by permits or other project approvals.

In such circumstances, the project owner may include in the contract documents detailed, mandatory, or prescriptive elements of the constructor's design of construction means or methods or, alternatively, in implementing these approaches the owner may request that the consulting engineer develop criteria or standards for, or design, specific construction means and methods.[88]

This raises several issues about potential professional liability exposure, starting with whether the consulting engineer is qualified and sufficiently experienced to undertake the design of construction means and methods. By designing the construction means and methods, does the consulting engineer become responsible for the specification and/or implementation of safety precautions or programs associated with that design? What if the construction means and methods design suggested by the consulting engineer and adopted and implemented by the constructor is not constructible or fails to achieve its intended performance result? Who is responsible — project owner, consulting engineer, or constructor? Does the project owner impliedly warrant the adequacy and constructability of suggested construction means and methods contained in the contract documents?

The point to emphasize is that, in a megaproject, the general rule that the constructor is responsible for the design of the construction means and methods does not universally apply and, in fact, there is a significantly greater than normal possibility that the project owner, through its consulting engineer, will assume responsibility for influencing the design of the construction means and methods and, in some instances, for prescribing the actual details of the construction means and methods. The extent of the project owner's and consulting engineer's involvement in the construction means and methods will vary according to a range of options, including:

- Specifying suggested design or performance criteria.
- Mandating and prescribing design or performance criteria.

389

- Including a suggested and fully detailed design in the contract documents.
- Specifying and mandating adherence to a fully-detailed design included in the contract documents.
- Performing construction-phase services — e.g., submittal review and field observation — relating to construction means and methods.

These options carry varying degrees of professional liability risk exposure for the consulting engineer. Because generalizations in this context are not especially meaningful, an appropriate risk assessment should be undertaken for each project-specific situation. However, one should not necessarily assume that the greater the degree of the consulting engineer's involvement in construction means and methods design the greater the degree of its professional liability exposure. In fact, the inverse may be a more accurate risk assessment: the greater the degree of its control over the design development process and its ability to mandate compliance with the design, the greater the ability of the consulting engineer to control and manage risk variables, and thus the lesser the degree of its liability exposure.

In addition to professional liability risk exposure associated with influencing or prescribing/mandating the design of construction means and methods, the consulting engineer should be attentive to risks associated with the review of constructor submittals of construction means and methods design. In general, the admonitions discussed above regarding the consulting engineer's review of the constructor's design submissions in a delegated design (*see* § 5.1.3 above) are applicable in circumstances in which design criteria or performance standards are provided (as distinct from a fully detailed design) for construction means and methods design.

5.1.5 Project Owner Purchase of Construction Equipment to Be Used in the Construction Process

Typically, the contract documents contain performance requirements for certain equipment to be used in the construction process (as distinct from equipment to be part of the permanent and completed project). The constructor has some degree of discretion in the initial selection (subject to submittal review/approval) of the equipment manufacturer, and the latter assumes responsibility for and warrants that the design and manufacture of the equipment will meet the performance or other requirements specified in the contract documents. If the equipment fails to meet these requirements, the constructor assumes the risk and economic consequences and may have a remedy against the manufacturer from whom it purchased the equipment in warranty.

On megaprojects, project owners sometimes chose to pre-purchase construction

equipment and, upon award of the construction contract, assign the equipment to the constructor. Under these circumstances, who is responsible if the equipment fails to achieve the specified or required performance objectives?[89]

The analysis required to answer this question can be quite complex. The functioning and productivity of the equipment may be dramatically influenced by the constructor's means and methods of construction, maintenance of the equipment, the experience of the equipment operators, and the skill and quality of the constructor's labor force. In addition, differing site conditions — the risk of which should otherwise be allocated under the contract documents — also may impact the functioning and productivity of the equipment. Thus, the mere fact that the owner-furnished equipment is not functioning as expected does not necessarily mean that the project owner is responsible for the cost or time implications.

5.1.6 **Fast-Track**

On megaprojects, there is immense pressure to maintain the schedule, especially in the progress of work in a manner that will meet contract package interfaces and interdependencies. In some instances, these objectives are accomplished by allowing the constructor to proceed procuring materials and commencing construction even though design is not actually finalized and coordinated in all respects. In general, this approach is termed "fast-track." If the fast-track approach is successfully implemented, there could be significant schedule benefits, including not only schedule maintenance, but also compression and acceleration. Also, using the fast-track approach may assist project owners in accelerating funding decisions or in strategies to overcome potential abutter or stakeholder opposition. However, even in these scenarios, the benefits may result in growth in both design fees and construction costs that manifest themselves during the construction process. Depending upon the degree of design finalization, coordination, or modification that occurs during the construction process, this cost growth can be substantial and represent a significant percentage of the total cost when measured in relation to the initial construction contract award amount.

In a fast-track project, there is a significant potential — especially with the degree of oversight on megaprojects — for questions to be raised, such as: Did the public know in an informed and realistic way about the risk of substantial increase in cost due to using the fast-track approach?[90] Was the documentation that the consulting engineer gave appropriate and balanced advice to the project owner regarding the benefits and risks associated with fast-track?

Of course, if the expected benefits of the fast-track approach are never realized, or if the detriments outweigh any of the realized benefits, then it is probable that a host of even more penetrating questions will be raised and that the owner may pursue a professional liability claim against the consulting engineer.

Even within the traditional design-bid-build delivery method there is more than ample opportunity on megaprojects for variations in project design approach to result in different and/or increased professional liability exposure for the consulting engineer.

5.2   Design-Build

In the last decade, project owners have exhibited a significant degree of interest in the design-build approach to the delivery of all or portions of megaprojects. Schedule compression and greater opportunities for cost containment and significant risk transfer are among the reasons prompting project owner interest in the design-build delivery method. Moreover, many public-private partnership arrangements utilize the design-build delivery method and, given the increasing governmental authorization and interest in the public-private partnership approach, it is expected that design-build will receive even more attention in the years to come.[91]

Project owner decision-making in the selection of any project delivery method or approach — in design-bid-build (see preceding discussion) or in design-build — should be well-informed and based upon considerations that include the need to fairly and realistically balance risk allocation of all project participants. The consulting engineer often is in the position to provide valuable advice to the project owner in that decision-making process. Assuming that the project owner decides to utilize the design-build method, there are several options specific to the implementation approach that must be considered and chosen.

However, as a general matter, in the context of design-build projects, risk should be fairly allocated as between the project owner and design-builder. Subsurface information disclosure by the project owner, use of differing site conditions and other risk-sharing contract provisions, and utilization of the geotechnical baseline report are all recommended.[92]

Design-build, from a professional liability perspective, represents exposure and risk for the consulting engineer, depending upon contractual risk allocated among project participants and the respective roles and responsibilities of the consulting engineer and other project participants.

In the design-build delivery method, the project owner typically furnishes to the design-builder preliminary design criteria and standards, including performance specifications ("preliminary design"), which the design-builder is required to utilize in developing and finalizing the project design.[93] The design-builder is responsible for the adequacy and performance of the completed project design and construction. What are

the responsibilities and professional liability exposure of the consulting engineer who will prepare the preliminary design? And what are the responsibilities and professional liability exposures of the consulting engineer who will be retained as a subconsultant by the design-builder to prepare and stamp the final design? To a degree, the answers to these questions are guided by the same general principles discussed in § 5.1.3. However, the contractual terms will also need to be considered in responding to these questions.

An important and unfortunately increasing area of exposure for the design-builder's consulting engineer is the design-builder's claims for cost growth due to the consulting engineer's errors in estimating and/or interpreting and developing the owner's preliminary design requirements. A first line of defense against such claims involves examining the consulting engineer's scope of services: to what degree was design to be developed prior to the design-build award? Based on what information and studies? With what opportunity to verify or validate project owner-furnished data or information, including preliminary design? What was the consulting engineer's responsibility (if any) for cost estimating? The answers to these questions will help determine whether or not the consulting engineer met the professional standard of care. In many instances, these types of claims are based on the consulting engineer's allegedly deficient pre-award services derived from the design-builder's failure to carry adequate design development contingency in its contract price with the project owner.

To assist in the management of this professional liability risk exposure, the consulting engineer should consider including the following provisions in both pre-award teaming and other agreements, as well as in the post-award agreement between the design-builder and the consulting engineer:

- *Responsibility for Cost Estimating/Quantity Surveys*

  The Engineer shall provide the following specific services solely for the use and benefit of the Design-Builder in connection with preparation of the response to the RFP: [here define services]. The Design-Builder shall be solely responsible for all cost estimating, quantity surveys, or other predictions of expected project cost. While the engineer may provide estimates regarding quantities or units of scope components, the Design-Builder acknowledges that such estimates are (a) based upon only limited and conceptual design development derived from the contents and requirements of the RFP and (b) likely to significantly increase based upon the post-award design development and finalization process.

  The Design-Builder shall verify quantities or other information furnished by the Engineer, shall use its knowledge and experience as a construction professional in developing its bid and pricing for the work, and shall include in such bid an appropriate degree of contingency for additional cost resulting from the post-award design development and finalization process. The Engineer shall not be responsible for project costs, direct, indirect, or consequential, that result from the design development and finalization process.

- *Liability Threshold*

  Agreement Not to Claim for Certain Costs. Design-Builder recognizes and expects that it may incur or expend direct or indirect costs in excess of the fixed contract amount specified in its Agreement with the Owner due to a number of reasons, including (i) the design development process; (ii) Owner review of design development submissions; (iii) quantity or cost estimating issues or variations; (iv) inaccurate or otherwise unattainable concepts, assumptions, details, or other information underlying or embodied in deliverables, including schematic design, prepared by Engineer during the Proposal Phase; or (v) for other reasons, and for which the Design-Builder may be unable to obtain any cost or time adjustment or relief from the Owner (the "Additional Costs"). Design-Builder agrees not to assert any claim against the Engineer unless and until such Additional Costs exceed _____; and, in such event, the Design-Builder's entitlement to any recovery shall be based on a breach of the professional standard of care.

The difference in roles and responsibilities for project owners, consulting engineers who prepare preliminary designs, constructors who lead the design-build team, and consulting engineers engaged by those constructors result in different risks and liability exposures. In addition to the legal dimensions of this discussion, the behavioral dimensions of these differences must also be assessed.[94]

The "behavioral" dimensions of this discussion are critically important. Simply because the design-build delivery method has been selected does not necessarily mean that project participants will be in a position to adjust to their seemingly new roles and responsibilities. More specifically, in design-bid-build:

- Project owners typically control the process of permanent project work design: they select the design professional and review and approve design development submissions and any substitutions to the approved design.

- Design professionals are responsible for the preparation and finalization of the detailed design of permanent project work and for exercising professional judgment in that process.

- The constructor is responsible for constructing in accordance with the contract document design and is not responsible for defects or inadequacies in the design of permanent project work.

Design-build represents a fundamental change in these more traditional roles and responsibilities. Effecting these changes through contract terms is relatively simple; alter-

ing the behavior of project participants to conform to these relatively new changes in their roles and responsibilities has proven to be more challenging.

For example, in a design-build project, the project owner may seek to control the design development and finalization process by issuing mandatory and detailed prescriptive designs as part of the RFP process, and may seek to assert plenary authority in the review and approval of the design-builder's design development submissions. In substance, such an approach would contradict one of the primary reasons for selecting the design-build delivery method, namely, to assign and confer substantial discretion and professional judgment to the design-builder in order to develop a design consistent with limited design and performance criteria specified and mandated by the project owner, in exchange for the design-builder's assuming responsibility for the adequacy and quality of that final design.[95] This is an example of the control principle regarding risk allocation: in exchange for the design-builder's assuming greater control over the design development process, it also assumes the risk of the adequacy and quality of final design. When project owners impermissibly intrude into the design development process in design-build, or attempt to override the exercise of professional judgment and discretion of the design-builder's designer, while at the same time insisting that the design-builder and its designer assume responsibility for the adequacy and quality of final design, the control principle in risk allocation is subverted.

In addition, in design-build the consulting engineer, who serves as the project owner's preliminary design consultant and representative, may intrude itself into the design development and review/approval process by imposing its professional judgment over that of the design-builder's design professional. Also, some constructors leading the design-build team may not fully appreciate their integrated responsibility for both design and construction of permanent project work.

Efforts need to be initiated to make certain that project participants understand their differing roles and responsibilities in design-build and "behave" in conformance with them. The more that project participants, by actual conduct, deviate from contractually-defined roles, the more likely that ultimate issues of risk and liability will not be determined in accordance with contract terms. In addition, the more that the owner (and its design professional) prescribes and limits design discretion and judgment of the design-builder (and its design professional), the more likely that the design-build objective of transferring single point responsibility to the design-builder for both design and construction of the project will be frustrated.

What are some of the professional liability risks and exposures for consulting engineers functioning in the design-build delivery method?[96] There are a number of contractual terms in the design professional's agreement with the design-builder that may influence professional liability risk exposure. In addition, how risk is allocated between the project owner and design-builder (constructor-led) may also impact professional

liability exposure. Here are some of the more important contract provisions relevant to this discussion:

- Standard of care
- Warranty obligations
- Performance guarantees — extent and qualifications
- Scope of services
- Responsibility for coordination of multiple design disciplines
- Time for service performance/liquidated damages
- Extent of cost guaranty
- Risk allocation provisions
    - Differing site conditions
    - Site information responsibility
    - Design responsibility — preliminary and final
- Redesign obligation within basic service obligation
- Responsibility for consequential damages
- Design to cost obligation — fixed limit
- Effect of flow-down provisions of prime design-build agreement
- Responsibility for permit, regulatory, and code issues — obtaining/compliance, changes in laws and regulations
- Degree of project owner involvement in review/approval of design-builder's design development submissions.

In addition to contractual terms, there are other factors that may influence professional liability risk exposure on design-build projects:

- Degree of project owner's (or project owner's consulting engineer's) *actual* involvement in the development and approval of the final design
- State of "completion" of the design and construction documents
- Design and construction concurrency (a/k/a "fast-track")
- Constructor influence in design — its impact on quality
- Unfair/unbalanced risk between the design-builder and project owner (for example, differing site conditions and site information disclosure)
- Scope and timely involvement of the constructor's design professional during construction
- Timely involvement of the constructor's design professional in communications relating to design (especially those involving the project owner's consulting engineer)
- Identifying, accepting (in practice, not simply contractually), and becoming comfortable with new design and construction risk
- Clearly defining and managing the project owner's expectations about reasonable limits of risk transfer and project objectives

- Prior experience of the design-build team in working together on design-build projects (or otherwise)
- Project type (e.g., complex, unique, demanding schedule, stringent performance requirements) may suggest higher risk in use of the design-build approach
- Reasonableness of the project owner's expectations regarding the schedule and the degree of involvement of the project owner and its consulting engineer in the design development, review, and approval process
- Reasonableness of the project owner's expectations about the role of the professional design member of the design-build team
- Timeliness of the project owner's decision-making
- Inadequate qualifications, experience, or financial capability of the design-builder (especially a problem in design-build joint ventures)
- Adequacy of insurance and surety protection
- Dispute resolution mechanisms with the project owner and among the design-build team

Examples of claims by design-builders against its design professional include:

- Deficient or inadequately developed design in accordance with project owner–furnished preliminary design or performance specifications
- Errors, omissions, or other inadequacies or deficiencies in the development and finalization of the design
- Failure to coordinate the performance of its multiple prime design professional consultants
- Failure to perform on time
- Error/omissions in preliminary design evaluations, estimating, and recommendations upon which design-builder relied in negotiating prime agreement
- Error/omissions in understanding/interpreting project owner–furnished preliminary design, performance specs, or information (such as site information) furnished by the project owner
- Construction means and methods design
- Geotechnical and environmental exposure
- Cost estimating during design development
- Indemnity and warranty claims
- Field advice/decision-making
- Failure to cooperate or efficiently manage the design professional subconsultant(s)

Examples of project owner claims against its consulting engineer include:

- Defects in the preparation of geotechnical and other reports and the preliminary design/performance specifications

- Defective review/approval of the design-build design submissions
- Negligent recommendations in the project owner's selection of the design-build team
- Impossible/impracticable performance specification
- Inadequacies or inaccuracies in the site/environmental information
- Failure to diligently/adequately represent the project owner's interest during construction regarding the payment process, quality of work, and/or work conformance with contract document requirements
- Intrusion/interference into the design-builder's design development process

Examples of claims involving deficiencies in preliminary design/performance specifications include:

- Errors or omissions
- Inappropriateness of preliminary design criteria for project-specific application or compliance with codes, standards, or other governing requirements
- Conflicts and inconsistencies between the preliminary design, the performance specifications, and some other mandatory criteria or standards furnished and required by the owner
- Impossibility or impracticability of achieving required performance standards or requirements
- Conflicts or inconsistencies between the preliminary design and standards required by applicable code, governmental, or regulatory authority
- Incompatibility of the preliminary design with the project geography or site-specific constraints

The professional standard of care is flexible in application to the preliminary design. The fact that the preliminary design, by definition, is incomplete and based upon limited information and developmental effort is a significant consideration in defining the latitude for the acceptable standard of care governing it and in evaluating responsibility for the adequacy of that design. In addition, the preliminary design is prepared in the expectation that the design will be further questioned, validated, developed, and finalized by a qualified design professional who, ultimately, will stamp the final design and that, during this design development process, the design will undergo constructability and related reviews by the design-builder who will be responsible for the design and construction of the project.

Examples of preliminary design/performance specification deficiency issues:[97]

- Was the deficiency due to some inadequacy in the development or definition of the preliminary design and/or performance specification?

- Did the project owner inappropriately intrude upon the design-builder's design development and finalization process or discretion or change the design criteria or performance standards required of the design-builder during that process?
- Did the project owner assume responsibility for defective design due to the scope and nature of its role in the review and approval of the design-builder's design development submissions?
- Did the design-builder fail to develop the design in accordance with the preliminary design?
- Is the deficiency due to the design-builder's failure to detect errors or omissions or the lack of coordination or other problems during procurement or the design development process?
- Did the design-builder perform adequate constructability reviews during design development?
- Did the design-builder's failure to construct in accordance with the approved final design cause or contribute to the deficiency?

Recommended Practices

- The project owner's choice of a delivery method will impact the definition of roles and responsibilities of the respective project participants, including the consulting engineer, and will therefore affect professional liability risk and exposure.

- Understand how delivery method selection relates to professional liability risk and exposure.

- Amend contractual and risk allocation terms of your agreement to reflect any changes in roles or responsibilities that may occur subsequent to the owner's selection of the project delivery method.

- Be flexible in agreeing to modify roles and responsibilities to accommodate evolving project delivery approaches but understand, assess, and contractually account for professional liability risks and exposure that results from any such modifications.

- If you are preparing and expected to stamp the final design based upon preliminary design criteria or project-wide standards furnished to you, satisfy yourself as to the adequacy and appropriateness of the criteria and standards to the specific application of your design.

- Do not be bullied into accepting revisions to your design development submissions by the project owner or its representative.

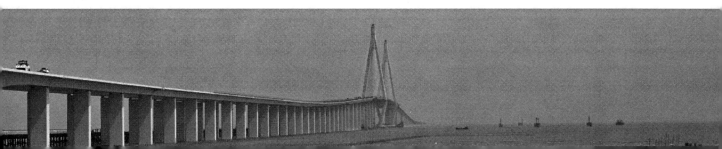

- If you are implementing design delegation, it should be accomplished in a manner that clearly and consistently defines and allocates design responsibility among the involved project participants and addresses responsibility for integration of delegated design with other aspects of permanent project work design.

- If you are prescribing detailed requirements of, or limitations to, the constructor's means and methods, understand that you are likely assuming some degree of responsibility for the adequacy and constructability of the construction means and methods; this also applies if you exercise dominant control and direction in the review of the constructor's proposed means and methods of construction.

- Make certain that you adequately explain and document risks associated with the use of the fast-track approach. The project owner needs to understand that both design fees and construction costs will likely increase during the construction phase due to untimely completion, modification, and coordination of design, resulting in change orders and potential demolition and reconstruction of work in place.

- Understand the difference in roles and responsibilities of project participants associated with the design-build delivery method and "behave" in accordance with contractually-defined roles and responsibilities.

- Provide the design-builder with sufficient discretion and judgment to develop and finalize the project design, consistent with preliminary design criteria or standards furnished by the owner.

- Include in the agreement between the design-builder and its consulting engineer substantial provisions that acknowledge that the latter's assumption of the design (as contemplated at the time of the design-builder's response to the RFP) will evolve during post-award design development and that this process of design evolution may well impact cost and schedule, and therefore the design-builder should carry adequate design development contingency to account for this.

Notes

1. *See* J. Reilly, "Probable Cost Estimating and Risk Management," *North American Tunneling 2008 Proceedings*, p. 576.
2. *See* discussion below, § 4.
3. *See* P. Mead, "Current Trends in Risk Allocation in Construction Projects and Their Implications for Project Participants," *Construction L. J.* 1 (2007): 23.
4. For a more detailed discussion of this point, *see* § 1 of chapter 18.
5. The term "decisions" may not be precisely accurate in connection with the public procurement

process in which the constructor often does not have the ability to participate—i.e., negotiate—in the risk allocation decision-making process.

6.   For more detailed discussion, *see* § 2 of chapter 17.

7.   W. R. Allensworth, R. Altman, A. Overcash, C. Patterson (eds.), *Construction Law*, chapter 23, Chicago: American Bar Association Publishing, 2009 (hereinafter *Construction Law*).

8.   *See* §1, above. For a more detailed discussion of these control and fairness principles, *see* D. Hatem, "Risk Allocation and Dispute Resolution on Construction Projects: Roles and Challenges for Legal Counsel," *The CA/T Professional Liability Reporter* (June 1997), and sources referenced therein (hereinafter "Risk Allocation and Dispute Resolution").

9.   Hatem, *Subsurface Conditions*, § 10.1.2.1, 269–72.

10. Under the *Spearin* implied warranty doctrine, the party which furnishes detailed, prescriptive, and final design (typically the project owner) to another (typically the constructor) for use in construction implicitly warrants that the design is complete, accurate, adequate, and suitable for construction of the project and that if followed and found to be deficient in any of those respects, the recipient of that design will not be held responsible for the consequences thereof and may be entitled to a remedy for damages incurred as a result. Significantly, the *Spearin* implied warranty obligation for defective design is broader than design liability predicated upon the negligence-based professional standard of care (*see* § 2 of chapter 16). Under the latter standard, a design professional is expected to exercise reasonable care, skill, and diligence in the preparation of design documents and neither impliedly warrants, nor is obligated to produce, an error-free or perfect design (unless it has contractually agreed to do so). The *Spearin* implied warranty obligation is substantially more expansive, requiring, in effect, that the design be defect-free and stating that liability attaches regardless of whether the design was prepared in accordance with the professional standard of care.

The origin of the implied warranty of design adequacy is the landmark United States Supreme Court case United States v. Spearin, 248 U.S. 132 (1918). In that case, the government's detailed plans and specifications required Spearin, a constructor, to excavate the site and to relocate and reconstruct a six-foot brick sewer line that intersected the site. After the sewer was relocated and reconstructed, heavy rains caused it to back up which, in turn, created water pressures which broke the line in several places and flooded the dry dock excavation. The government insisted that Spearin clean up the site and reconstruct the damaged line at its expense. The Supreme Court ruled that the government was liable for breach of its "implied warranty" of the adequacy of the final design depicted and described in the plans and specifications and that Spearin was not obligated to perform or pay for the corrective work. *Spearin* has been adopted by the vast majority of courts in the United States. *See* J. Sweet & M. Schneier, eds., *Legal Aspects of Architecture, Engineering and the Construction Process*, 8th ed., § 23.05(E), Florence, KY: Cengage, 2009, pp. 515–21 (hereinafter *Legal Aspects of Architecture*); for a summary of recent case law addressing the *Spearin* doctrine, *see* T. Marcey, "Does The *Spearin* Doctrine Live On," *Construction Briefings*, No. 2009-12 (Thomas Reuters Dec. 2009).

Although *Spearin* was initially used in the defensive context by a constructor (i.e., to avoid performing or paying for corrective work), that original application was later expanded to utilize *Spearin* as the basis for offensive or affirmative claims by constructors against project owners for additional costs for direct or indirect impacts incurred by the constructor based on defects in project owner–furnished detailed design. *See, e.g.,* Big Chief Drilling Co. v. United States, 26 Cl. Ct. 1276, 1304 (1992) (stating that if defective design specifications issued by the project owner prevent or delay completion of the contract, the constructor is entitled to recover damages for the project owner's breach of the *Spearin* implied warranty obligation). The court in *Big Chief* stated that it is well-established that the project owner warrants the adequacy of design to the extent that compliance with the design will result in "satisfactory performance." In circumstances in which a constructor is delayed or incurs additional costs due to design deficiencies, the constructor is allowed to recover additional costs resulting from delays due to such design deficiencies.

The *Spearin* doctrine has been extensively discussed and clarified over the years, often with the words "design" and "performance specifications" used to differentiate between the circumstances in which the design warranty does and does not apply. *See* Stuyvesant Dredging Co. v. United States, 834 F. 2d 1576, 1582 (Fed. Cir. 1987); J. D. Hedin Constr. Co. v. United States, 171 Ct. Cl. 70, 76–77, 347 F. 2d 235, 241 (1965); Utility Contractors, Inc. v. United States, 8 Ct. Cl. 42, 50–51 (1985), *aff'd.*, 790 F. 2d 90 (Fed. Cir.), *cert. denied,* 479 U.S. 827, 93 L. Ed. 2d 53, 107 S. Ct. 104 (1986). The warranty applies only to "design specifications" because only by utilizing specifications in that category does the government deny the constructor's discretion and require that work be done in a certain way. Fruin-Colon v. Niagara Frontiere Trans. Auth., 585 N.Y.S. 2d 248 (App. Div. 1992). When the government imposes such a requirement and the constructor complies, the government is bound to accept what its requirements produce. "Design specifications explicitly state how the contract is to be performed and permit no deviations. Performance specifications, on the other hand, specify the results to be obtained, and leave it to the constructor to determine how to achieve those results." *Stuyvesant Dredging,* 834 F. 2d at 1582. Thus, whether the specifications are design or performance specifications is critically important for an understanding of the existence of any "warranty" claims and the parties' respective rights and obligations. The United States Court of Appeals for the Federal Circuit spoke to this issue, as follows:

> Performance specifications "set forth an objective or standard to be achieved, and the successful bidder is expected to exercise his ingenuity in achieving that objective or standard of performance, selecting the means and assuming a corresponding responsibility for that selection." . . . Design specifications, on the other hand, describe in precise detail the materials to be employed and the manner in which the work is to be performed. The Constructor has no discretion to deviate from the specifications, but is "required to follow them as one would a road map." Blake Constr. Co. v. United States, 987 F.2d 743 (Fed. Cir. 1992).

11. Disclaimers of design adequacy will be upheld if specific and clear. *See* Mass. Bay Trans. Auth. v. United States, 129 F. 3d. 1226 (Fed. Cir. 1997) (construing specific design warranty disclaim-

er to exclude owner liability for negligence); J. F. White Contracting Co. v. Mass. Bay Trans. Auth., 40 Mass. App. Ct. 937 (1996) (owner's implied warranty obligation effectively disclaimed by clear and specific language); Wunderlich v. California, 65 Cal. 2d 777, 785 (1967). *See generally*, E. Diepenbrock, C. McCandless, & J. Dorso, "Restrictions on Risk Allocation for Unexpected Conditions," *Passing the Buck: Legal Limitations on Transferring Construction Risk*, American Bar Association, New York, Jan. 24, 2002. Some states prohibit such disclaimers by statute. For example, California Public Contract Code #1104 provides that:

> No local public entity, charter city, or charter county shall require a bidder to assume responsibility for the completeness and accuracy of architectural or engineering plans and specifications on public works projects, except on clearly designated design build projects. Nothing in this section shall be construed to prohibit a local public entity, charter city, or charter county from requiring a bidder to review architectural or engineering plans and specifications prior to submission of a bid, and report any errors and omissions noted by the constructor to the architect or owner. The review by the constructor shall be confined to the constructor's capacity as a constructor, not as a licensed design professional.

Short of a provision that explicitly and entirely negates the project owner's otherwise applicable *Spearin* implied warranty obligation, there are other provisions in a project owner–constructor agreement that accomplish, more or less, the same objective. *See* A. Tramountanas, "Affirmative Defenses to the *Spearin* Doctrine: Government Attempts to avoid the Implied Warranty of Specifications," *Construction Briefings* (May 2003). Provisions such as those dealing with design omissions and misdescriptions, patent and obvious defects, the verifications clause, and the duty to coordinate clause illustrate this point. *See* M. Lineberry, "Restrictions on Risk Allocation for Design Inadequacies and Changes in the Law," *Passing the Buck: Legal Limitations on Transferring Construction Risk*, American Bar Association, New York, January 24, 2002. *See generally Bruner & O'Connor*, § 9:80; *Construction Law*, chapter 3, § 3.04; chapter 22, § 22.04 (ABA Forum on the Construction Industry Jan. 2009).

12. *See* Diepenbrock, McCandless, & Dorso, "Restrictions on Risk Allocation for Unexpected Conditions," cited in full in n. 11, above. In addition to establishing the project owner's implied warranty obligation (*see* above, note 10), *Spearin* reaffirmed a basic "common law" contract law principle: where a party agrees to do, for a fixed sum, an act possible to be performed, it will not be excused from performance or be entitled to additional compensation merely because unforeseen difficulties are encountered. In the context of subsurface conditions and/or concealed conditions, this principle means that, absent a contractual differing site/concealed conditions clause granting equitable relief, constructors generally do not have recourse for increased costs due to differing site or concealed conditions encountered in the performance of their work. *See* Hatem, *Subsurface Conditions*, § 10.2.1.1. However, in addition to this established common law principle, it is equally established that unless prohibited by sovereign immunity doctrine, a public owner may be held liable, to the same extent as a private owner, for the concealment or withholding

of material facts known by it but not disclosed to the constructor directly and resulting in additional construction costs or performance problems. However, as in *KiSKA*, discussed in the text below, where the challenged owner actions underlying the constructor's claim involved design, planning, and discretionary decisions, the sovereign immunity doctrine may bar the claim. KiSKA Constr. Corp. USA v. Wash. Metro Area Transit Auth., 321 F.3d 1151 (D.C. Cir. 2003). All of these issues are discussed in more detail in Part 4 of this chapter.

13. *See generally*, Sweet & Schneier, *Legal Aspects of Architecture*, Chapter 25; H. G. Beh, "Allocating the Risk of the Unforeseen Subsurface and Latent in Construction Contracts: Is There Room for the Common Law?" *U. Kan. L. Rev.* 46 (1997): 115–54. *See also* Diepenbrock, McCandless, & Dorso, "Restrictions on Risk Allocation for Unexpected Conditions"; G. Brierley & J. Smith, "Contracting Practices for Underground Projects," in N. Sweeney, ed., 2002 *Construction Law Update*, New York: Aspen, 2002; J. Grove, *Consultant's Report on Review of General Conditions of Contract for Construction Works*, The Government of the Hong Kong SAR, 1998, 15–17. Risk allocation for differing site conditions on design-build projects is explored in more detail in G. Brierley & D. Hatem, eds., *Design-Build Subsurface Projects*, Scottsdale, AZ: Zeni House, 2002, and in D. Corkum & D. Hatem, "A Contracting Strategy for Managing Risk on Subsurface Projects Delivered Using Design-Build," 2003 *RETC Proceedings*. In the latter article, the authors state:

> Engineers working as part of the Design-Build Team need to exercise particular caution . . . where an Owner has attempted to shed all risk of DSCs [differing site conditions]. The Engineer's concern is simply that with the Design-Build Constructor precluded from seeking recovery from the Owner for a damaging DSC, the next most likely target will probably be the Engineer that performed the investigation and provided the interpretations. This shifting of targets for cost recovery is readily apparent in the recent trend of instances of defective design claims that are no longer viable against the Owner, but may be enforceable against the Design-Builder's Engineer. Moreover, the Engineer, because its contractual relationship is directly with the Design-Builder, will find itself without the benefit of some of the usually available defenses, such as the doctrine of betterments. Because of this tension, the Engineer may be less likely to suggest innovative and efficient techniques that are at the very core of the rationalization to proceed using Design-Build. "A Contracting Strategy," p. 814.

14. *See* D. Federico Co. v. New Bedford Redev. Auth., 723 F. 2d. 122, 125 (1st Cir. 1983); Diepenbrock, McCandless, & Dorso, "Restrictions on Risk Allocation for Unexpected Conditions"; G. Sarno, Annotation, "Public Contracts: Duty of Public Authority to Disclose to Constructor Information, Allegedly in Its Possession, Affecting Cost or Feasibility of Project," *A.L R.* 3d 86 (1978): 182. On this subject, one commentator has stated:

> Whilst the principle that the risk should be allocated to the party best able to manage the risk is well understood, in practice, many client organizations seek to pass on most risks to the Constructor. It is understandable that any principal would wish to have a clear un-

derstanding and quantification of the cost of a project before a commitment is made to commence the work. Increasing public scrutiny requires public clients, in particular, to be openly accountable for the consequences of cost overruns and this places considerable pressure on those responsible for the management of the project to "offload" the project risks. Consequently, invitations to tender often indicate that the Constructor is to ensure that the contract price should include all manner of risks. These include the "classic" issues such as unforeseen ground conditions, unknown utilities, inclement weather, etc.

The Constructor can only price these risks if he is given access to the relevant information that will allow him to assess their potential impact. Such is the "paranoia" that surrounds this issue that some principals who hold information such as geotechnical reports, services/utilities details, etc., will even deny the Constructor access to this information on the basis that the Constructor may later take action against the principal due to the information being misleading or inaccurate.

Whilst such an argument may have some legal justification, we need to ask ourselves — where are we going here? Have we become so insecure that we will knowingly withhold information which we know will be of real value and assistance to a tenderer on the basis that they may use it against us later?

The author suggests that such behavior is in direct conflict with the fundamental risk sharing principle. If the principal wishes to retain the knowledge of ground conditions, he should retain ownership of the risk and provide for an appropriate contingency in the stated cost of the project. If the Constructor is required to assume the risk, all information must be made available "warts and all" to ensure that the Constructor is given every opportunity to assess the risk.

There is an onus on all parties to genuinely shoulder appropriate responsibilities for risk. Clearly, this is a "two-way street" and principals will only be comfortable in assuming responsibility for risk if Constructors take real responsibility for the issues which they can assess and price. However, it is vitally important that principals do not adopt what the author terms the "Pontius Pilate" approach to risk allocation, which seems to be the preferred approach of many latter-day principals in relation to major infrastructure projects.

C. MacDonald, "Allocation of Risk in Major Infrastructure Projects—Why Do We Get It So Wrong?" *Int'l Construction L. R.* 1 (2001): 345.

15. *See* Sweet & Schneier, *Legal Aspects of Architecture*, p. 562.
16. WMATA had argued on appeal that it had the right to exercise judgment when it decided that the bid package would not benefit from the inclusion of superseded and discarded design concepts.
17. In many instances, however, sovereign immunity is not available to a public owner as a defense to a constructor claim based upon the owner's failure to disclose subsurface information. For example, in D. Federico Co. v. New Bedford Redevelopment Authority, 723 F. 2d 122 (1st Cir. 1983), a public entity failed to disclose an engineering report that would have put the construc-

tor on notice as to the nature of unusual subsurface material. During the project, the constructor was required to perform extensive extra work as a result of the inadequate description of the material to be excavated and was required to remove approximately 20 times more material than originally anticipated. Had the constructor been aware of the withheld information, it would have at least been on notice of the unusual conditions. The court granted an equitable adjustment to the constructor, thereby imposing on the public owner an affirmative duty to disclose relevant subsurface information. However, despite such a failure to disclose relevant subsurface information, in order for the constructor to recover, its claims for damages must directly result from the failure to disclose. In Fondedile, S. A. v. C. E. Maguire, 610 A. 2d 87, 96 (R.I. 1992), the Supreme Court of Rhode Island distinguished *Federico* on precisely the latter basis. In *Fondedile*, the owner had knowledge concerning subsurface conditions of a seawall (the repair of which was the subject of the project) but did not disclose those conditions to the constructor. After construction commenced, the constructor received a surveyor report showing movement of the seawall. As a result, the constructor requested permission to change certain grouting procedures but did not request additional payment for those changes, nor did the constructor cite movement of the wall as the cause for the grouting changes. Based on this evidence, the court found that the knowledge of subsurface conditions withheld by the owner was not the cause of the additional costs claimed by the constructor and, accordingly, the *Federico* holding did not apply.

Constructors have been allowed recovery due to the project owner's failure to disclose information when the contract documents do not fully and accurately define the work to be performed; the constructor had no reason to know the work omitted would, in fact, be necessary and the project owner did have such knowledge; the project owner had reason to know of the constructor's ignorance; and the project owner's failure to disclose directly caused the constructor's claimed damage. Although in many of these cases recovery has been allowed under the theory of misrepresentation or superior knowledge, usually the constructor also claims that the project owner breached its *Spearin* implied warranty obligation by furnishing a defective design that failed to inform the constructor of the work requirements. *See generally* P. Latham, "Kaplan Constructors Inc., and the Superior Knowledge Doctrine, What Must the Government Disclose and Why?" 4 ABA, *Pub. Cont. L. J.* 191 (1971).

18. *See* R. Cushman & G. Hedemann, *Architects and Engineers Liability: Claims Against Design Professionals*, 2d ed., § 18.2, New York: Aspen, 2005. In some instances, the sovereign immunity doctrine may also protect the project owner's independent consulting engineer from civil liability. *See* Texas Transportation Code § 452.052, which provides:

    If an independent Constructor of the authority or entity is performing a function of the authority or entity, the Constructor is liable for damages only to the extent that the authority or entity would be liable if the authority or entity itself were performing the function.

19. For further discussion of this subject, *see* § 4.6.2 of this chapter and D. Hatem, *Subsurface Conditions*, pp. 313–40. A recent case demonstrating this combined approach is PCL Construction Ser-

vices, Inc. v. United States, 47 Fed. Cl. 745 (Ct. Cl. 2000), which is discussed in Brierley & Hatem, *Design-Build Subsurface Projects* § 3.2.4.1 and n. 58, pp. 63–65, and in *Bruner & O'Connor* § 14.28.

20. D. Hatem, "Errors/Omissions Cost Recovery Claims Against Design and Construction Management Professionals," *The CA/T Professional Liability Reporter* (June 1996); *Bruner & O'Connor on Construction Law*, §14:22; S. Stein & C. Popovsky, "Design Professional Liability for Differing Site Conditions and the Risk-Sharing Philosophy," *Construction Lawyer* 20 (Apr. 2000): 13; D. Hatem, *Subsurface Conditions,* §10.2.4.

21. Some may appropriately comment that these types of risk allocation options and decisions, even though embodied in contracts executed by the constructor, are, in reality, not a matter of "free choice" for the constructor in the public procurement and contracting context. More specifically, the constructor, in that context, typically has no or limited opportunity to negotiate contract risk allocation provisions and its only real option is whether or not to pursue or enter into the contract. There is much legitimacy to this comment. As far as the impact of onerous or unfair risk allocation provisions on the bidding environment, *see* discussion in § 2 of chapter 17.

22. *See* § 2 of chapter 17. *See also* D. Hatem, "Risk Allocation and Dispute Resolution."

23. *See* D. Hatem, *Subsurface Conditions*, § 10.2.4.

24. *See* D. Hatem, *Subsurface Conditions*, § 10.1.2.1.

25. If the project owner–consulting engineer contract does not explicitly define the applicable standard of performance, the law implies that the engineer will be obligated to perform its services in accordance with the professional standard of care. Klein v. Catalano, 386 Mass. 701, 718–19 (1982). The common law functions, in the absence of a more specific contractual performance standard, as a "default" standard that may be stated as follows:

> As a general rule, "[a]n architect's efficiency in preparing plans and specifications is tested by the rule of ordinary and reasonable skill usually exercised by one of that profession. . . . [I]n the absence of a special agreement he does not imply or guaranty a perfect plan or satisfactory result . . ." Architects, doctors, engineers, attorneys and others deal in somewhat inexact sciences and are continually called upon to exercise their skilled judgment in order to anticipate and provide for random factors which are incapable of precise measurement. The indeterminable nature of these factors makes it impossible for professional service people to gauge them with complete accuracy in every instance. . . . Because of the inescapable possibility of error which inheres in these services, the law has traditionally required, not perfect results, but rather the exercise of that skill and judgment which can be reasonably expected from similarly situated professionals. *Klein*, 386 Mass. at 718. For further discussion, *see* § 2 of chapter 16.

26. For a discussion as to how these risk allocation provisions may impact professional liability exposure of design professionals, *see* D. Hatem, "The Relevance and Potential Impact of Risk Allocation Provisions in Owner-Contractor Agreements on Professional Liability Experience of Design Professionals," *Design & Construction Mgmt Prof. Rep.* 1 (Oct. 2003): 1; D. J. Hatem,

27. The difficulty that the courts have in addressing and resolving this issue generically extends to third-party claims against other professionals, such as accountants and lawyers. While many of the underlying legal concepts and policies are similar in dealing with the issue of third-party negligence claims against all such professionals, what is characteristically different about the design and construction process context is the predominance and centrality of a network of contractual relationships that typically and explicitly define and allocate (and/or negate or limit) risks, rights, obligations, and remedies among the various parties (including the consulting engineer and these third parties, respectively) involved in the design and construction process.

28. J. Feinman, *Professional Liability to Third Parties*, 2d ed., Chicago: American Bar Ass'n, 2007), 26 (hereinafter, "Feinman").

29. *See, e.g.*, Blake Constr. Co. v. Alley, 353 S.E.2d 724, 727 (Va. 1987); Berschauer/Phillips Constr. Co. v. Seattle Sch. Dist. No. 1, 124 Wash. 2d 816, 881 P.2d 986 (1994).

30. Feinman, pp. 276, 278.

31. *See, e.g.*, M. Miller Co. v. Cent. Contra Costa Sanitary Dist., 18 Cal. Rptr. 13 (Cal. Ct. App. 1962); Texas Tunneling Co. v. City of Chattanooga, 204 F. Supp. 821 (E.D. Tenn. 1962), rev'd in part, 329 F.2d 402 (6th Cir. 1964); Nota Constr. Corp. v. Keyes Assocs., 694 N.E.2d 401 (Mass. App. Ct. 1998).

32. *See* above, note 31.

33. *See* above, note 31.

34. S. Stein, *Construction Law*, Albany, NY: Matthew Bender & Co., 2006, § 5A.06[4], 5A-83.

35. As a general rule, in asserting such claims against the consulting engineer, the constructor must establish that the consulting engineer departed from the professional standard of care. Evidence of an economic loss or damage — even one caused by the consulting engineer — is insufficient as a matter of law to establish professional liability of the consulting engineer unless the constructor demonstrates that the consulting engineer failed to comply with the professional standard of care required under these circumstances. Typically, such a demonstration requires that the constructor retain an expert who is qualified to provide such an opinion. In this regard, the constructor's legal burden of proof in establishing professional negligence on the part of the consulting engineer is significantly more onerous than the constructor's burden in proving a breach of implied warranty (*Spearin*) claim (*see* note 11, above) or differing site condition claim (*see* § 6.2 of chapter 17) against the project owner.

36. J. Sweet, "Contractor Postcompletion Claims: Advice to Engineers," *J. of Prof. Issues in Engineering Edu. & Prac.* 130 (Oct. 2004): 298.

37. On this factor, Professor Sweet has commented:

> . . . [T]here is a downside in dealing with some professional owners, mainly on the public side. They may lack wisdom and good sense. They may lack the discretion to bend the rules. Even if

they have flexibility, they may be so glued to their rules that they cannot recognize concepts of fundamental fairness and the need for the public entity to have a good reputation.

While following clear rules generally leads to a well-run project, there are times when rules must be bent or even ignored. Rules are designed for ordinary events. When something quite out of the ordinary occurs rigid adherence to rules can produce an unfair outcome. Failure to administer rules wisely can create an adversarial mood. This can cause unneeded conflict, generate disputes, and produce claims, yet the key factor is consistency. Blowing hot and cold creates disaster and post completion claims. Here reputations are crucial. . . .

Public projects carry other risks that most private projects escape. Public projects are in the public spot light. Awards can and often are challenged or become hot public issues. This can create delays. Anything that has a strong possibility of causing delay is surely a negative factor and the precursor of a post completion claim. Public projects are more likely to generate post completion claims than private projects. This is the reason for greater use of 'no damage' or 'no pay for delay clauses' in public contracts. . . .

Sweet, "Contractor Postcompletion Claims," 298.

38. Sweet, "Contractor Postcompletion Claims," 303.

39. A. Meagher & M. O'Day, "Who is Going to Pay My Impact? A Contractor's Ability to Sue Third-Parties for Purely Economic Loss," *The Construction Lawyer* 25 (Fall 2005): 27.

40. Meagher & O'Day, "Who Is Going to Pay My Impact?"

41. Meagher & O'Day, "Who Is Going to Pay My Impact?" pp. 27, 31.

42. Meagher & O'Day, "Who Is Going to Pay My Impact?" pp. 31–32.

43. Meagher & O'Day, "Who Is Going to Pay My Impact?"

44. *See* F. Oksuz, R. Goodfellow, & C. Meueller, "The Owner's Manual on Contracting Strategies for Large Projects," 616–623; W. Edgerton & G. Davidson, "Getting the Right Contract Package," 624–30; J. Reilly, "Alternative Contracting Practices — An Update," 631–69, all in M. Roach et al., eds., *North America Tunneling 2008 Proceedings*. Project owners have many delivery method choices, traditional and non-traditional in nature. *See* R. Altman, "Project Delivery Systems," Chapter 4 in W. R. Allensworth, R. Altman, A. Overcash, C. Patterson, eds., *Construction Law*, Chicago: American Bar Ass'n Publishing, 2009, chapter 4; Sweet & Schneier, *Legal Aspects of Architecture*, chapter 17.

45. In addition to the project delivery approaches discussed in this chapter, there are various innovative forms of project delivery that focus on collaboration and sharing of risk among primary project participants and which establish direct and non-traditional contractual (privity) relationships among those participants. With respect to design, the hallmark characteristics of these innovative approaches involve collaborative and simultaneous involvement of the prime project participants (i.e., project owner, design professional and constructor) in the design development process and in the sharing — as distinct from allocation according to the principles discussed in § 1 of this chapter — of risk among those participants. These approaches typically may be classified as integrated project delivery or various forms of "alliancing."

Detailed discussion of these innovative approaches is beyond the scope of this chapter. However, it should be noted that the collaborative and risk sharing characteristics of these innovative approaches do pose substantial and non-traditional professional liability risk exposures for design professionals and professional liability insurability concerns. *See* H. Ashcraft, "Building Information Modeling: A Framework for Collaboration," *The Construction Lawyer* 28 (Summer 2008): 5, 11; D. Hatem, "Design Responsibility in Integrated Project Delivery: Looking Back and Moving Forward," (Donovan Hatem, LLP, Jan. 2008); W. J. Bender, "Defining and Allocating 'Design Responsibility' in Complex Projects," Skellenger Bender, P.S. 2007; D. Larson & K. Golden, "Entering the Brave New World: An Introduction to Contracting for BIM," Jan. 2008, retrieved April 19, 2010, from http://www.mortenson.com/Resources/Images/6102.pdf; D. Hatem, "Roles and Responsibilities, Risk Allocation and Professional Liability Exposure in Collaborative World of Building Information Modeling and Integrated Project Delivery: Business as Usual or Fundamental Change?" (Donovan Hatem, LLP, Nov. 2008). In addition, green and sustainable design involves many of the same professional liability risks associated with integrated project delivery. *See* D. Hatem, "Green and Sustainable Design: Part I: Professional Liability Risk and Insurability Issues for Design Professionals," *Design and Construction Management Professional Reporter,* Donovan Hatem LLP (June 2010).

Public-private partnerships, in the specific context of subsurface megaprojects, are discussed in § 7 of chapter 17.

46. *See* discussion of *Spearin* doctrine, note 10, above.

47. Brierly & Hatem, *Design-Build Subsurface Projects* § 3.2.4.2.2, pp. 76–82; C. Hammond, "Dealing with Defects: Defective Owner-Provided Preliminary Design in Design-Build Contracting, Pt. 2," *International Construction Law Review* 15 (1998): 193.

48. Sweet & Schneier, *Legal Aspects of Architecture,* § 5.02, p. 32.

49. Certainly, no legitimate question may be raised about the importance of these issues in light of the severe consequences that may result when insufficient attention is directed to them. The 1981 collapse of the Hyatt Regency Hotel walkways in Kansas City, resulting in the death of 114 people, amply and adequately demonstrates this point. For a discussion of the Hyatt Regency matter, *see* M. Iqbal, "Ethics and Rules of Conduct Governing Design Professionals," in S. Hess et al., eds., *Design Professional and Construction Manager Law,* Chicago: American Bar Ass'n, 2007; Duncan v. Missouri Bd for Architects, Prof'l Eng'rs & Land Surveyors, 744 S.W. 2d. 524 (Mo. Ct. App. 1988); J. Gillum, "The Engineer of Record and Design Responsibility," *Journal of Performance of Constructed Facilities* 14 (May 2000): 67–70 (stating that: "While the Engineer of Record may share some of his or her responsibility in accord with the standard of practice in his/her area of the Country, overall responsibility should not be delegated! In other words, *the buck stops with the Engineer of Record*").

50. *See generally* Sweet & Schneier, *Legal Aspects of Architecture,* Chapter 10. While registration laws and regulations are "public" laws in the sense of being enacted or promulgated by the various state legislatures, there can be legal relationships between the determination of public law viola-

tions and professional liability based on "private law," or contractual or common law principles. *See* D. Hatem, "Administrative, Regulatory and Registration Proceedings Involving Design Professionals," *Wiley Construction Law Update*, Hoboken, NJ: Wiley, 1991. Also, when state legislatures or licensing boards do not act or act timely enough to address a professional matter otherwise subject to regulation, courts in the professional liability (notably, tort) context often "can supplement or even replace the regulatory licensing process. . . ." Sweet & Schneier, *Legal Aspects of Architecture,* chapter 10, p. 129.

51. For an excellent summary and discussion of relevant state law pertaining to design delegation practice, *see* C. Circo, "When Specialty Designs Cause Building Disasters: Responsibility for Shared Architectural and Engineering Services," *Neb. L. Rev.* 84 (2005): 162–246.

52. Only a few states have directly addressed the practice of design delegation in state registration laws and regulations, with Florida and New York having well-developed regulatory schemes.

53. E. Kelley, *Division of Design Responsibility: A Specialty Constructor's View*, Chicago: American Bar Ass'n, Oct./Nov. 1997); W. Bender, "Defining and Allocating 'Design Responsibility' in Complex Projects," Skellenger Bender, 2007.

54. Ernstrom & Dreste, LLP, "The General Conditions of the Contract for Construction A201 — It Isn't What It Used to Be," p. 5, ABA/AIA Oct./Nov. 1997, A201 Program.

55. Although contracts and contract documents among project participants are relevant in the context of determining civil liability of those participants to third parties (*see* D. Hatem, "Design Professional Legal Responsibilities — Construction and Completion Phases," chapter 4 in S. Hess et al., eds., *Design Professional and Construction Manager Law*, Chicago: American Bar Ass'n, 2007), they are not always determinative in that context, particularly when public law requirements are not clearly defined or, worse yet, are not defined at all. Moreover, while it is "well accepted that a design professional sealing and signing the design does not hold a monopoly on all design knowledge necessary to complete a successful, modern construction project, and it is often prudent for him or her to rely upon the expertise of experienced contractors or suppliers to design certain components of the required work. . . , design delegation does not imply design abdication. The licensure statutes permitting design delegation regulate the process by which a licensee may delegate design tasks." M. Iqbal, "Ethics and Rules of Conduct Governing Design Professionals," p. 50.

56. Circo, "When Specialty Designs Cause Building Disasters," 164.

57. For a good discussion of contract provisions in the context of design delegation, *see* chapter 29, "Design Delegation," in D. Brenan et al., eds., *The Construction Contracts Book*, 2d ed., Chicago: American Bar Ass'n, 2008.

58. Circo has summarized some of the scenarios involving claims against the EOR in the design delegation context:

> . . . [I]n some cases the owner may have a claim against the project architect or the architect's consulting engineer for specialty design defects. The owner may establish a profes-

sional negligence claim against the project architect by proving the project architect's professional negligence in performing services under the architect's contract that relate to the specialty work. Several factual possibilities might emerge.

The owner might be able to show that the project architect or the architect's consulting engineer negligently approved the specialty engineer or negligently failed to review or question the qualifications of the specialty engineer. The contract for the project architect's services is likely to leave considerable doubt about the role of the architect and its consultants in selecting or approving design professionals retained by a design-build subcontractor. In an appropriate circumstance, however, the owner might successfully argue that either the contract language or the surrounding circumstances imply a role. For example, if the plans provided by the owner's architect and its consulting engineers provide that a subcontractor must furnish critical structural design details, a court might conclude that the project architect's professional responsibility includes, by necessary implication, at least the obligation to confirm that the subcontractor retains a qualified structural engineer.

The project architect and its consulting engineer might also incur liability if they failed to convey adequately to the design-build subcontractor the design concept, or inadequately established the design criteria for the subcontractor to meet. It is difficult to assess in the abstract how to address claims of this nature because it is not clear how a court should interpret a contractual requirement that the project architect must provide the design concept and the design criteria. Presumably, even though the project architect's design services agreement completely excludes the specialty design, the project architect and its consulting engineer still may need to specify certain critical details. For example, if the specialty work involves structural components, the owner's design team may be responsible to provide such critical design details as the load-bearing requirements of connections or the materials to be used. In some cases, the design professionals on the owner's design team might be subject to liability for failing to specify that the specialty engineering submittals must meet certain industry standards or must include certain supporting documentation or calculations.

The process involved in approving or otherwise permitting the specialty design to become final may provide the most fertile ground for a claim against either the project architect or its consulting engineer. No matter how the contract documents describe the actions of the owner's design team in relation to the specialty work, one or more members of the team will probably have some responsibility with respect to a significant number of submittals that require action on behalf of the owner. Each of those responsibilities must be performed in conformity with the professional standard of care. For example, the architect might incur liability based on a limited obligation to review the construction drawings for conformance with the requirements or information the architect furnished or based on an obligation to coordinate the specialty design documentation with the other design documents for the project. A claim of that nature might succeed, for example, if the architect's plans show inadequate details to guide a manufacturer in the manufacturing process or if the architect accepts drawings submitted by the subcontractor that bear no professional seal, or if a process or documents essential to proper coordination are missing or inadequate.

The owner might even be able to develop evidence that the project architect breached the professional standard of care by leaving responsibility for this specialty design to a design-build subcontractor in the first instance. This would probably require expert testimony that under the circumstances it was not professionally prudent to divide design responsibility in the manner contemplated by the project architect's plans. There must be circumstances in which a project architect should not allow division of design responsibility or should do so only with the added protection of a comprehensive review on the owner's behalf by an independent engineer who is part of the owner's design team. At a minimum, the project architect should be responsible in most cases to establish a process that assures that appropriately licensed professionals provide or approve all critical design services and that coordinates all design services for the project.

In some situations, a court might identify a non-delegable duty of the project architect or one of the architect's consulting engineers. Even if a court would recognize a non-delegable duty of a member of the owner's design team for certain aspects of the project, one might question whether that duty should extend to a specialty design that is expressly excluded from the contract between the owner and the project architect. In an appropriate case, a court might explicitly or implicitly impose a non-delegable duty on the project architect or the architect's consulting engineer as the design professional of record for the project or on the basis of ordinances governing approval of design plans under the applicable building code."

Circo, "When Specialty Designs Cause Building Disasters," 239–41.

59. Again, Circo, "When Specialty Designs Cause Building Disasters," 211–12, states:

Although specialty design-build practices have yet to produce many reported decisions, these cases show that any shared design process may blur conventional liability boundaries. Even in the relatively rare instance in which the circumstances or the contracts clearly delineate the distinct responsibilities relating to the specialty work, it may be difficult to characterize each step in the process as exclusively within one scope or the other. Often, the project A/E, the prime contractor, and the specialty designer (and, perhaps, others) will have overlapping responsibility for interdependent aspects of the process by which the specialty design is developed, approved, coordinated, and integrated into the project. All of these factors will tend to distribute to several participants some risk of liability associated with specialty design.

60. For a more detailed discussion of the HSE Report, *see* A. Muir, "Coda: The Heathrow Tunnel Collapse," *Tunneling: Management by Design*, London: E+FN Spon, 2000, 271–288; D. Hatem, "Oct. 1994 Collapse of NATM Tunnels at Heathrow Airport: July 2000 Report on the Investigation by the Health and Safety Executive," *The CA/T Professional Liability Reporter*, No. 2 (Boston: 2000).

In contrast to the project owner's general obligation to furnish design for permanent work,

typically, the constructor is responsible for the design of the temporary or incidental means and methods of construction ("construction means and methods") and discharges that obligation by retaining qualified design professionals to undertake that design. D. Hatem "Risk Allocation for Design Adequacy and Construction Means/Methods," *The CA/T Professional Liability Reporter*, Vol. 1, No. 2 (Boston: Jan. 1996), pp. 10–11. "Design Delegation," as discussed herein, does not refer to the design of such construction means and methods but, rather, is confined to the design of work that will become incorporated as part of the permanent and completed project — i.e., permanent work.

61. The topic of design delegation is addressed here in the context of the traditional design-bid-build delivery method in which the project owner independently contracts with (a) a consulting engineer for the design of the permanent work and (b) a constructor to build the project in accordance with that design. In the alternative delivery method of design-build, the project owner typically contracts with a single entity that is contractually responsible for both the design and construction of the project. In large part due to the fusion of the design and construction functions and obligations in a single entity, many of the risk management and allocation considerations presented by design delegation in the design-bid-build delivery method are not presented in Design-Build, or are not as critical in relation to the latter delivery method. More specifically, those considerations are most likely to be important when the design and construction contractual responsibilities are independent and distinct and where the constructor undertakes responsibility for the design of permanent work and engages a design professional different from the EOR to prepare that design. In design-build, since the design and construction activities are integrated and since virtually all of the design of the permanent work will be done by a design professional in contractual privity with the constructor (whether part of the design-build prime entity or a subconsultant to the constructor as prime), these considerations have less criticality and relevance.

62. D. Hatem, "Changing Roles of Design Professionals and Constructors: Risk Allocation, Management and Insurance Challenges," *The CA/T Professional Liability Reporter* (Boston: May 1998).

63. Ernstrom & Dreste, LLP, "The General Conditions of the Contract for Construction A201 — It Isn't What It Used to Be," p. 5.

64. One commentator has stated that the purpose of design delegation is "to achieve safe, efficient and cost-effective design solutions to construction problems." N. Potter, "Design Delegation Provisions of AIA Document A201, 1997 Edition," *Construction Lawyer* 18 (July 1998): 27.

The cost pressures in the construction process certainly and most obviously emanate from the project owner due to funding or other budgetary constraints and limitations. In addition to the project owner, however, constructors and design professionals are also influenced by cost pressures to utilize the design delegation approach. Specifically, one form of design delegation occurs when a constructor proposes "value engineering" or substitutions to the contract document design, specified materials, systems, or other components of permanent work, sometimes on the basis of anticipated cost savings. Design professionals, increasingly under contractual obligation to design within a fixed limit of construction costs, may seek to "fulfill" that obligation by delegating design to the constructor, producing a bid within that limit but eventually resulting in a design (prepared by the constructor or a professional on its behalf) that is not consistent with the project owner's quality standards or other requirements and potentially resulting in costs beyond the project owner's budget.

65. Due to a lack of clarity and specificity, implicit design delegation — whether initiated by the project owner (through its EOR) or the constructor — certainly and substantially increases the risk of disappointed expectations of and/or unknowing assumptions by the owner, consulting engineer, and the constructor arising out of ambiguity, confusion, or uncertainty in undertaking responsibility for the adequacy of the delegated design. D. Cohen, "Minimizing Conflicts Between Design Professionals and Constructors," *Construction Briefings*, 2d Series, No. 95-11 (Washington, DC: Federal Publications, Inc., 1995); J. Sweet, *Sweet on Construction Law*, Chicago: American Bar Ass'n, 1997, § 7.8, 244.

66. Commenting on this list, one author, writing on behalf of the General Building Constructors of New York State, Inc., stated "We call it the 'A to Z' list. Almost every major and some minor components of a building are listed. Every project is different, and it would be unfair to suggest that all these items would be delegated on a single project. However, for us, this is an incredible list. What's left for the architect to do — draw the artistic rendering and pick the color schemes?" J. Zogg, "A201 Division of Design Responsibility — Are the Owner and Public Well Served by Delegation of Design?" ABA/AIA Oct./Nov. 1997, A201 Program.

67. Letter dated August 12, 1996, from Barbara J. Rodrigues, Executive Vice President, AIA New York State, NYS Education Department.

68. The *Hyatt Regency* case is discussed in D. Hatem, "Administrative, Regulatory and Registration Proceedings Involving Design Professionals," *Wiley Construction Law Update*, Hoboken, NJ: Wiley, 1991. In addition, lack of clarity in design delegation responsibility which results in an actual or heightened risk of impairment to public safety, especially in circumstances in which the design professional authors or issues the contract documents that create the ambiguity or confusion, also results in increased exposure under OSHA. D. Hatem, *OSHA Liability for Design and Construction Management Professionals Involved in the Design and Construction Process* (Boston: June 1997). Commenting on the 1997 AIA document revisions dealing with design delegation, one noted commentator, Milton Lunch, stated:

> These conditions for design delegation leave unanswered a host of questions that ultimately will be resolved by court decisions. For example, how broad may the delegation be in defining what functions can be delegated? How are "design criteria" to be determined? What guidelines will be used to determine whether the submitted design conforms to the "design concept" — a term that is not defined? Finally, how will potential liability be allocated among the prime professional, the Constructor-delegator, and the licensed professional-delegatee?

M. Lunch, "Revised A201 Leaves Many Design Delegation Issues Unclear: General Conditions of the Contract for Construction," *Building Design & Construction* (Dec. 1997).

69. For a discussion of principles applicable to risk allocation in the construction process, *see* D. Hatem, "Risk Allocation and Dispute Resolution on Construction Projects: Roles and Challenges for Legal Counsel," *The CA/T Professional Liability Reporter*, Vol. 2, No. 4 (June 1997): 1–15.

70. *See* § 2 of chapter 16. Of course, the consulting engineer can agree to (or warrant) performance in accordance with a standard of care higher than the professional standard of care. For example, the client may request that the design professional perform its services "in accordance with the highest standards," without or free of any deficiency, and/or "to the complete satisfaction of the client." Alternatively, the client may request that the consulting engineer be "fully and legally responsible in all respects for the technical accuracy and completeness of all design" and/or "be legally responsible for all acts, errors or omissions." These requirements would, if accepted by the consulting engineer be tantamount to imposition of an obligation to perform in a perfect manner and to be legally responsible for any imperfection whatsoever in the performance of services, regardless of whether the professional standard of care (or negligence) had been or could be demonstrated or proven (by expert opinion or otherwise) to be satisfied. In addition, the assumption of such a heightened standard of care by contract will pose substantial insurability concerns under most professional liability insurance policies.

71. *See* note 39, above. For a discussion of the implied warranty principle in the context of subsurface projects, *see* D. Hatem, *Subsurface Conditions*, 313–40.

72. Sweet & Schneier, *Legal Aspects of Architecture*, Chapter 24, § 24.02, p. 528.

73. J. Sweet, *Construction Law*, p. 236 (American Bar Ass'n 1997).

74. For example, it has been held that a constructor's participation in "panel discussions" during the design development process was insufficient to shift the risk of defective design to the constructor. Haehn Mgmt. Co. v. United States, 15 Ct. Cl. 50, 56 (1988), *aff'd* 878 F. 2d 1445 (Fed. Cir. 1989). Moreover, a constructor was determined not to have assumed the risk of defective design when the government amended a specification using a constructor's suggestion that had been submitted in a value engineering proposal but withdrawn by the constructor before the government acted upon it. Tranco Industries, Inc., ASBCA No. 22379, 78-2 B.C.A. (CCH) P13, 307, *reconsideration denied*. 78-2B.C.A. (CCH) P13, 552.

75. Ct. 13 Cl. 72 (1987), *vacated for lack of jurisdiction*, 855 F.2d 1571 (Fed. Cir. 1988).

76. *Johns-Manville*, 13 Ct. Cl. at 119–20. In circumstances in which a constructor develops its own design (especially where the constructor is given the option to do so by virtue of its expertise, qualification, and/or specialized experience), the constructor alone should be responsible for that design. Austin Co. v. United States, 161 Ct. Cl. 76, 314 F.2d 518, *cert. denied*, 375 U.S. 830 (1963); Hawaiian Bitumuls & Paving v. United States, 26 Ct. Cl. 1234, 1240 (1992) (". . . when [the owner] has provided design specifications and drawings, and [the Constructor] persuades [the owner] to change them in favor of [the Constructor's] preferred specification, [the Constructor] assumes the risk that performance under its proposed specifications may be impossible. In general, the party originating the design specifications is responsible for losses suffered by the other parties due to defects in the specifications").

77. *See* Universal Contracting & Brick Pointing Co., Inc. v. United States, 19 Ct. Cl. 785, 793–95 (1990); Aleutian Constructors v. United States, 24 Ct. Cl. 372, 379–80 (1991) (when the contract documents delegate design responsibility to the constructor and obligate the constructor to use its expertise and ingenuity to fulfill that obligation, the owner does not have a *Spearin*-type implied warranty obligation; in such circumstances, the constructor is required to select a roofing manufacturer who will exercise skill and judgment in designing and providing instruction for attaching a rubber membrane to a hangar roof in a way that would achieve the wind uplift tolerance criteria specified in the contract documents); M. A. Mortenson Co., ASBCA No. 3944190-2 BCA (CCH) § 22,831, 1990 WL 101357 (1990) (constructor not entitled to equitable adjustment for a constructive change, as contract contained merely performance specifications); Stuyvesant Dredging Co. v. United States, 11 Cl. Ct. 853 (1987), *aff'd,* 834 F.2d 1576, 34 Cont. Cas. Fed. (CCH) § 75,414 (Fed. Cir. 1987) (constructor not entitled to additional compensation for excessive dredging material as contract contained performance specifications and allowed the constructor to choose the means to achieve the result intended); C. Foster et al., *Construction and Design Law*, Chapter 20, § 20.2d.1 (Lexis Law Publishing, 1998). However, if the constructor is confused or misled by unclear or incomplete design criteria, it may be able to successfully establish that the owner breached an implied warranty, thereby transferring the risk of design inadequacy to the owner. Haehan Mgmt. Co. v. United States, 15 Ct. Cl. 50 (1988), *aff'd,* 878 F.2d 1445 (Fed. Cir. 1989). In a related vein, a constructor may claim that the performance criteria or standards specified in the contract documents are defective because it would be futile, impossible, or commercially impracticable to develop a design that would be capable of meeting those criteria or standards. The constructor making such assertions bears a heavy burden of proof. *See, e.g.,* Concrete Placing Co., Inc. v. United States, 25 Ct. Cl. 369, 374 (1992) ("only in the relatively rare case where the specifications call for a performance which is impossible to achieve can a Constructor obtain an equitable adjustment for defective performance specifications").

78. For a detailed discussion of the design versus performance specification distinction and the consequences thereof in the context of subsurface construction, *see* D. Hatem, *Subsurface Conditions,* 313–40.

79. For example, in Appeal of M. A. Mortenson Co., 93-3 B.C.A. (CCH) § 26, 189 (June 30, 1993), the board found the government liable for estimated quantities of material indicated in conceptual design drawings, even though the contract awarded was a design-build contract under which the constructor had responsibility for completing the design and preparing the construction drawings. The board reasoned that the constructor had no choice but to rely on conceptual drawings in preparing a firm price for the work.

80. *See* M. Loulakis & O. Shean, "Risk Transference in Design-Build Contracting," *Construction Briefings,* 2d Series, Washington, DC: Federal Publications, Inc., 1996.

81. In addition, since the constructor furnishes the completed design and may control or have the ability to control the design development process when design responsibility is delegated, the constructor, not the owner, assumes the legal obligation of the implied warranty for that design.

417

Mobile House Envtl. v. Barton & Barton, 432 F. Supp. 1343 (D. Col. 1977). Typically, the constructor will be able to "pass along" its implied warranty liability to its design professional only if it can establish that the latter violated the professional standard of care.

> The implied warranty risk is not necessarily or always the equivalent of the design professional's risk associated with a departure from the professional standard of care. Unlike the design professional's more limited negligence-based professional standard of care obligation, the implied warranty risk implies a warranty that the design is virtually perfect and adequate in all material respects. Specifically, a party — e.g., owner or Constructor — which has an implied warranty obligation will be liable for virtually all design defects, but may be unable to obtain indemnification, cost recovery, or other recourse against the design professional who prepared that design absent satisfactory proof (typically required in the form of expert testimony) that the design professional failed to adhere to the professional standard of care.

See D. Hatem, "Risk Allocation for Design Adequacy and Construction Means/Methods," *The CA/T Professional Liability Reporter*, Vol. 1, No. 2 (Boston: Jan. 1996).

82. In Sehulster Tunnels/pre-Con v. Traylor Bros., Inc/Obayashi Corp., 111 Cal. App. 4th 1328 (2003), the constructor requested design changes to the tunnel ring segments as shown on the contract documents. The constructor had difficulty and ran into cost overruns with respect to the design substitutions it had proposed and which were accepted by the project owner. In denying the constructor's claim, the court stated:

> The parties agree that under the Prime Contract, City had design responsibility for the tunnel ring segments. TBO acknowledges that it was responsible for providing a tunnel-boring machine compatible with the original tunnel ring segment design that met all of the performance requirements of the specifications it had at the time of bidding. TBO was responsible for designing and manufacturing the tunnel-boring machine. In July 1995, after learning it was the low bidder, TBO discovered the potential conflict between its design for the tunnel-boring machine and the City's design for the tunnel ring segments. TBO discovered that to install the ring segments as designed would require the boring machine to be lengthened, increasing the "skin friction" between it and the tunnel with a resulting risk that the boring machine could become permanently lodged in the tunnel, jeopardizing the entire project. However, TBO advised City of its discovery in late September before City had issued the notice to proceed but after TBO had prematurely ordered the tunnel-boring machine. TBO recommended using an alternative tunnel ring segment design that would avoid lengthening the boring machine. City's engineers did not concur with TBO's assessment, but did agree that the longer shield on the boring machine would increase skin friction and *might* increase the difficulties in advancing the shield. . . . In early October 1995, TBO advised City that if City did not agree with its suggestion of pursuing an alternative tunnel ring segment design, it would immediately start work on an extended length version of the tunnel-boring machine to be compatible with the original ring segment design.

TBO's construction manager acknowledged at trial that a tunnel-boring machine could have been designed to be compatible with the original tunnel ring segment design and stringent performance requirements, but he believed that such a machine would increase the risk of failure. For whatever reason — whether it was amiable partnering among contractual parties at the onset of a lengthy contractual relationship or simply risk avoidance — City decided to redesign the tunnel ring segments so they could be installed with the shorter tunnel boring machine ordered by TBO. Parsons developed the new design in November 1995 and the following month City instructed TBO to proceed with the construction of the redesigned tunnel ring segments. . . .

Although the City was solely responsible for the tunnel ring segment redesign, TBO requested the redesign, was significantly involved with its preparation, and was primarily responsible for its implementation. Further, because of TBO's oversight at the bidding stage and premature ordering of the tunnel-boring machine, it sought to persuade City to change its tunnel ring segment design before manufacturing commenced so it could avoid up to $1 million in modification costs to lengthen the tunnel-boring machine. In this context, it can be reasonably inferred that TBO expressed concern for the potential risk of the tunnel-boring machine becoming lodged in the tunnel was exaggerated, especially considering its expressed willingness to proceed with the boring machine modification and the original ring segment design if City did not agree. Absent *definitive* evidence, the original design for the configuration of the tunnel ring segments was unworkable and incorrect, City may have ordered the design change as a 'good partner,' not anticipating that the redesign would increase the cost of manufacturing the tunnel ring segments.

111 Cal. App. 4th at 1346-1348

A constructor's proposal of an alternative design in lieu of the design prescribed and detailed in the owner-furnished contract documents, if accepted by the owner, should serve to negate any implied warranty obligation of the owner associated with the original contract document design. This conclusion derives from the fact that the basis of the implied warranty obligation is both negated and overcome by the constructor's voluntary decision not to rely upon the owner-furnished design and, instead, to use its own design to construct. However, it should be noted that there could be a number of contractual and other circumstances that potentially may alter that result. For example, if contract documents do not clearly evidence the intention that the constructor will be responsible for its alternative design, do not require that the alternative design be prepared and stamped by a registered professional, suggest that the alternative design is merely a product or material substitution (i.e., not a design change), or create ambiguity in the submittal process as to the constructor's design responsibility due to the nature and extent of the owner's (or its consulting engineer's) review of the proposed design or the stamp or other terms evidencing acceptance or approval of the constructor's alternative design. *See* Kiewit-Atkinson-Kenny v. Mass. Water Resources Auth., Massachusetts Superior Court No. 011920-BLS, Memorandum and Orders on Various Motions for Partial Summary Judgment, Sep. 3, 2003, pp. 8–9, 15–16.

83. D. Thomson & M. Vorbrich, "A Guide to the 1997 AIA Document A201," *Construction Briefings*, 2d Series, Washington, DC: Federal Publications Inc., 1997.

84. In addition, the design professional retained by the constructor may be required to indemnify the latter for claims and damages due to any deficiencies in the delegated design and/or the failure of that design to meet requirements, express or implied warranties, or other obligations imposed upon the constructor by law or under the contract documents. As in the case of any design professional's indemnification obligation, the design professional retained by the constructor should limit its indemnity obligation to only those situations caused by or resulting from its negligence and/or failure to meet the professional standard of care.

85. J. Zogg, "A201 Division of Design Responsibility—Are the Owner and Public Well Served by Delegation of Design?" p. 5.

86. Ernstrom & Dreste, "The General Conditions of the Contract for Construction A201—It Isn't What It Used to Be," 5–6.

87. D. Hatem, *Subsurface Conditions*, § 10.2.2.1(B).

88. D. Hatem, *Subsurface Conditions*, § 10.2.2.2, pp. 296-312; T. Tirolo & G. Almerarls, "Suggested and Prescriptive Means and Methods—Are They Really in the Owner's Interest? A Contractor's Perspective," *2005 RETC Proceedings*; D. Hatem, "Design Professionals and Construction, Means, Methods, Techniques, Sequences, and Procedures: Are the Lines of Responsibility Really That Absolute and Clear?" *33rd Annual Meeting of Invited Attorneys*, (Victor O. Schinnerer & Co., Inc., 1989).

89. *See* A. Biggart, G. Krainer, & A. Walters, "Owner Procured Tunnel Boring Machines—A Discussion," *2005 RETC Proceedings*.

90. G. Simpson & J. Atkins, "Managing Risk in Fast-Track Projects," in J. Demkin, ed., *AIA Handbook of Professional Practice, Update 2006*, Hoboken, NJ: Wiley, 2006, 91–102. Simpson and Atkins extol the importance of explaining challenges and risks of fast-track to the project owner:

> It is essential for architects to inform their clients of the challenges and risks of fast-track delivery. Some clients, however, will not be willing to accept that a higher incidence of design and construction changes is normal and should be anticipated, even when the architect has fully explained the potential downside of fast-track. These clients often believe that architects are using fast-track as a lame excuse to justify poor quality design services. Architects must carefully consider the risks involved in working with clients who cannot or will not accept the realities of the fast-track environment.
>
> When architects choose to engage in fast-track project delivery, they should take steps to manage client expectations of the architect's performance. To begin with, the design professional can advise owners of the following differences between fast-track delivery and traditional project delivery methods:
> - Some construction will be based on incomplete designs and documents.
> - Uncertainty about construction costs will be greater and last longer.
> - Design assumptions and decisions will need to be revisited more often.

- There will be a greater number of requests for information and change orders.
- The incidence of changes, and the consequent perception of errors and omissions, is likely to be greater.
- Overall construction cost will probably be higher.
- There is a potential for a longer construction period.
- The owner must be willing to tolerate risk and be continually involved in the design and construction process.
- Use of complex architectural design "features" and unique materials may be limited due to the overlapping sequencing of work activities.

A good way to communicate these and other aspects of the fast-track approach is in a letter. . . . For projects where use of the fast-track method is a certainty or an absolute requirement, the letter can be modified to review the inherent risks in the approach, especially in cases where the client has no prior experience with this form of project delivery.

Owners who have been informed of the realities of fast-track delivery and the stamina required to work in this environment will find it more difficult to justify that they did not know what they were getting into.

91. For more detailed discussion of public-private partnerships in the specific context of subsurface megaprojects, *see* § 7 of chapter 17.

92. D. Hatem, *Design-Build Subsurface Projects*, chapter 2.

93. *See* L. Hauser & W. Tinsley, "Eyes Wide Open: Contractors Must Learn to Identify and React to Design Risks Assumed Under Performance Specifications," *The Construction Lawyer* 27 (Summer 2007): 32, 35–37; H. Hamersmith & E. Lozowicki, "Can the *Spearin* Doctrine Survive in a Design-Build World: Who Bears Responsibility for Hybrid Specifications?" *J. of Am. C. of Construction Lawyers* 2 (Winter 2008): 123.

94. These issues are extensively discussed in D. Hatem, *Design-Build Subsurface Projects*, chapter 3 (G. Brierley & D. Hatem, eds., Zeni House: 2002). Design-build certainly is not a panacea for resolving all disappointed expectation and professional liability concerns in the megaproject context. *See* "The Big Dig Disaster: Was Design Build the Answer?" *Suffolk U. L. Rev.* 40 (2007): 909–30.

95. *See* P. Cullinan, "Design Liability," *Tunnels & Tunneling International* 27 (June 2005): 45–47; *see* British Tunneling Society, "Tunneling Contracts Are Best Implemented Based on a Detailed Design procured by the client before tendering the construction contract," *Tunnels & Tunneling International* (Mar. 2009), pp. 27–29.

96. These issues are extensively discussed in D. Hatem, *Design-Build Subsurface Projects*, chapter 3.

97. D. Hatem, *Design-Build Subsurface Projects*, §§ 3.2.4.2.1, 3.2.4.2.2; L. Hauser & W. Tinsley, "Eyes Wide Open: Contractors Must Learn to Identify and React to Design Risks Assumed Under Performance Specifications," 232; H. Hamersmith & E. Lozowicki, "Can the *Spearin* Doctrine Survive in a Design-Build World: Who Bears Responsibility for Hybrid Specifications?", 123.

CHAPTER 16

Professional Accountability

David J. Hatem, PC, Donovan Hatem LLP

1.0   Introduction

There are a variety of ways in which the adequacy of a consulting engineer's performance may be evaluated on a megaproject and in which deficient performance may be addressed. Contracts typically define specific deliverables and services to be performed, prescribe schedules or deliverable submission due dates, billing, payment, and audit requirements, and standards according to which the consulting engineer is obligated to perform and that will be used to evaluate the adequacy of the consulting engineer's professional service performance. This section will focus on the latter subject, i.e., the standards used to evaluate the adequacy of consulting engineer professional service performance on megaprojects.

As discussed below in § 2, while the appropriate standard for consulting engineer performance on megaprojects is the negligence-based professional standard of care generally applicable on all projects, megaprojects certainly involve a specialized application of that standard, given their size, complexity, special "one of a kind" or unique nature, duration, organizational and functional relationships, evolving roles and responsibilities of project participants, the complexity and number of design and construction interfaces, increased use of innovative design approaches and non-traditional project delivery approaches, and other heightened risk variables. Moreover, given the dollars involved and the project's visibility, there is a significant potential, if not probability, that on megaprojects the project owner or other stakeholders will initiate efforts to hold the consulting engineer professionally accountable for cost overruns, schedule delays, and other major events of disappointed expectation in circumstances in which the consulting engineer was not able to control the factors or variables that caused such events.

Megaprojects — for obvious and understandable reasons — attract significant public attention. Project cost and schedule — especially given the size, cost and duration of the megaproject — are constant subjects of public interest. When the megaproject exceeds the published budget or schedule, the public rightfully asks about the reasons and seeks to hold any potentially responsible party accountable. The public waits (and typically is

The Interstate Highway system in the United States is a 47,000-mile system of limited-access, high-speed highways, the longest such system in the world. Authorized by the Federal-Aid Highway Act of 1956 and championed by President Eisenhower, the Interstate system was initially projected to cost $25 billion over 12 years but wound up costing $114 billion over 35 years. This photo shows a portion of I-84 near Mitchell Point, and the Columbia River in Oregon. Photograph from the Library of Congress, Historic American Engineering Record.

423

inconvenienced) for a long time for the completed project, and when it is finished but does not meet their expectations of quality or functionality (on top of substantially exceeding cost or schedule), the public will demand answers and accountability. Moreover, many mistakes made on the megaproject will tend to be highly visible. For these and other reasons, there is an increased focus on the accountability of the consulting engineer on a megaproject. The public funding agencies and other stakeholders need to have confidence in the process by which the project owner (or its designees) oversees, investigates, and evaluates the consulting engineer's performance.

This section will address the subject of the professional accountability of the consulting engineer on a megaproject. As we shall see, while the same basic principles of a professional standard of care apply in the evaluation of the consulting engineer's performance, megaprojects pose some very special challenges in applying that standard, given the high potential for disappointed project expectations of the project owner and other stakeholders and the high degree of public and political attention to the megaproject, including the process utilized to evaluate professional accountability, especially when cost overruns occur.

2.0   Professional Standard of Care

Issue

The consulting engineer's professional services on a megaproject impact the most important expectations of the project owner — cost, schedule, and quality. Some project owners perceive that the practice of engineering is pure science and expect virtual perfection in service performance. However, neither that perception nor the resulting expectation comport with the reality of engineering or reasonable standards upon which to evaluate the adequacy of the consulting engineer's judgment or performance. What is the standard that should be applied?

Analysis and Discussion

The professional standard of care for consulting engineers has generally been defined as follows:

> As a general rule, "[a]n architect's efficiency in preparing plans and specifications is tested by the rule of ordinary and reasonable skill usually exercised by one of that profession. . . . [I]n the absence of a special agreement he does not imply or guarantee a perfect plan or satisfactory result. . . ." Architects, doctors, engineers, attorneys and others deal in somewhat inexact sciences and are continually called upon to exercise their skilled judgment in order to anticipate and provide for random factors which are incapable of

precise measurement. The indeterminable nature of these factors makes it impossible for professional service people to gauge them with complete accuracy in every instance. . . . Because of inescapable possibility of error which inheres in these services, the law has traditionally required, not perfect results, but rather the exercise of that skill and judgment which can be reasonably expected from similarly situated professionals.[1]

The application of the professional standard of care is highly dependent on fact and circumstance. In applying the standard to a specific professional liability claim, one should consider, among other factors and circumstances, the following:

- The experience and qualifications of the consulting engineer
- The consulting engineer's scope of services and other terms of engagement
- Roles and responsibilities of other project participants
- Innovative versus traditional design
- Fast-track approach[2]
- Judgmental nature of service activity
- Complexity of project
- Time/schedule constraints
- Influence of risks or variables beyond control of the consulting engineer
- The number and complexity of design and construction interfaces

Professional Standard of Care

Regardless of how risk is allocated to the consulting engineer, there is a fairly universal principle of contractual and professional practice that the occurrence of risk or consequent adverse impact (e.g., cost and/or schedule), standing alone, does not amount to a legal liability of the professional; rather, the legal liability of the professional depends upon adequate proof that the professional failed to meet contractually defined and professionally required objective standards of performance (the "professional standard of care").[3] This standard does not require perfection in the performance of professional services. Rather, the test is whether the consulting engineer's performance met the standard reasonably and objectively expected of another similarly qualified and experienced professional functioning under the same or similar constraints and contractual obligations (e.g., service scope, schedule, risk allocation contractual terms), considering the totality of other relevant factors and circumstances.[4]

In order to demonstrate that the consulting engineer did not meet the professional standard of care, the claimant—typically the project owner, but sometimes a third party or other project participant—must prove the following:

1. The professional standard of care required under the specific circumstances involved, including the scope and limitations of the professional's contractual obligations;

2. That under the totality of circumstances, the professional failed to meet that standard;

3. That the failure of the professional to meet that standard caused damage to the claimant; and,

4. The amount of such damage.

These are *conjunctive* requirements, in the sense that proof of *all* is necessary to recovery and the failure to prove *any* such requirement is fatal to recovery.

In general, it is fair to say that the proof required to establish the legal liability of the consulting engineer derives from a "bottom-up" process — i.e., a process in which specific claimed deficiencies in the professional's performance are identified, measured against the objective professional standard of care, and then evaluated to determine whether any such deficiencies that failed to meet the standard actually caused damage and, if so, to what degree or extent.

While it is important to evaluate professional liability risk exposure in the manner described above, with the focus primarily centered upon the contractual risk assumption and actual performance of the professional,[5] it is equally important to recognize that whether risk is appropriately and timely identified and appropriately allocated among other project participants may impact the professional liability risk and exposure of the consulting engineer.[6] The point to emphasize, however, is that risk and professional liability exposure for the consulting engineer may be affected by factors and variables beyond the control or influence of the professional. Specifically, the extent to which risk has been appropriately allocated between the project owner and the constructor may impact the risk of professional liability exposure. For example, when project owners include "no damage for delay" provisions in the construction contract or do not include differing site condition clauses, the risk of claims and disputes arising that implicate "third-party" targets, such as the consulting engineer, is substantially increased, leaving the constructor with "no other place to go."[7]

Similarly, when things "go wrong" on a megaproject, such as major cost overruns or schedule delays, the unfortunate reaction of many project owners is to look for "culpable" parties without using a defined and fair process, based on objective performance standards, for establishing their legal liability. In such circumstances, it is appropriate for the project owner to question and evaluate the performance of all project participants to determine whether, under contractual or other applicable standards (such as the professional standard of care), the participants have performed in a substandard manner that caused some or all of the cost overrun or schedule delay. However, that inquiry should be undertaken in a fair and published process, in which specific allegations of deficient service performance are evaluated in accordance with contractual or other objectively defined and applicable standards.[8]

Take as an example a situation in which a major public infrastructure project is substantially "over budget" and is believed to be experiencing a significant "cost overrun." Assume further that the project is extremely visible and subject to criticism in the public and political arenas, as are most megaprojects. In such a situation, it would be entirely appropriate for the project owner to identify and evaluate the causes of the "cost overrun" to determine any responsibility of the various project participants, including the consulting engineer, as well as the project owner itself.

Why the project owner? The answer starts with the fact that the entire inquiry in this hypothetical, but very real, scenario on a megaproject is triggered by the significant difference between the project "budget" and the actual project cost that resulted in the "cost overrun." Was the project owner's "budget" accurate and realistic? Do the actual costs genuinely reflect a "cost overrun," or do they simply reflect the realistic project cost? Does the "cost overrun" result from initial cost underestimation? Is it cost underestimation that then leads to the perception that one or more project participants are responsible for the "cost overrun"? These are often complex, challenging, and sensitive questions that typically do not lead to simple analysis or answers. In this circumstance, there is a significant potential for the consulting engineer to become a convenient scapegoat. In addition, these questions typically are raised in a highly-charged (sometimes hysterical) political atmosphere in which the opportunity for rational analysis and dialogue may not be present. What is the key, however, is that the project owner is a central subject and main figure in the analysis and answers.

Why are these inquiries relevant to the consulting engineer? Many project owners — prompted, instigated, or challenged by politicians, the media, project stakeholders, and external project overseers — are seeking to hold consulting engineers responsible for "cost overruns." "Cost overrun" is a pejorative term. You might hear some of these project owners (or their surrogates) saying: "Just look at the numbers — they speak for themselves. How can we be so far over budget and someone not be responsible? Cost overruns like this should not be normal or expected — no one can deny that! So who is to blame and how much of the 'cost overrun' can be recovered (cost recovery), and from whom? It would defy logic to think that 'cost overruns' like this just happen, that no one is responsible, and that a substantial portion of the 'cost overrun' may not be reimbursed through cost recovery from the responsible project participants."[9]

The following passage from Sweet demonstrates some of these points:

> An Ohio public entity made a proposal requiring design professionals to pay the cost of construction change orders caused by the design professional. The professional societies and professional liability insurers objected, saying that the policy erroneously assumed that change orders are necessarily caused by negligence of the design professional and that the professional liability insurance policies would not cover such a form of strict

liability. After these objections were made, the Ohio agency withdrew the proposal. However, this is probably not the last such attempt to charge cost overruns to the design professional.

Attempts have been made — mainly by clients but also by design professionals — to recognize the likelihood of cost overruns due to design and to deal with them in various ways in the contract. One public contract in Virginia specified that the design professional would be responsible for cost overruns related to design if the overruns exceeded 3 percent of the contract price, without any need to show that the design professional had not performed in accordance with the professional standard. Even more, as noted in the preceding paragraph, some clients insist that all overruns due to design be the responsibility of the design professional whether or not the designer has failed to perform in accordance with the professional standard. This form of strict liability would almost certainly not be insurable under normal professional liability policies.

It would be unfair to the contractor if the contractor submitted its bid without knowing that the architect was strictly responsible for all design overruns. If the contractor knew of such strict liability, it could infer that all questions of interpretation that arise during performance would be resolved against the contractor. This would affect its bid.

Looking at this problem from the standpoint of a design professional, people interested in limiting design professional liability have suggested including provisions stating that the design will inevitably contain errors, omissions, conflicts, and ambiguity, all of which will require clarification and correction during construction. They suggest the client be advised that producing perfect documents is impossible and that some design decisions are more efficiently deferred for the benefit of the client until construction is underway and actual field conditions exist. . . .[10]

In effect, such an approach to professional liability claims is "top-down" in nature, in the sense that the claimant starts with the total amount of the "cost overrun" and then assumes that the "cost overrun" must necessarily be due to the deficient performance of the consulting engineer. This top-down approach fundamentally disregards and contradicts the application of the professional standard of care and all traditional principles associated with the determination of professional liability.

Things are far more complicated than suggested by a top-down approach, and all professionals should be grateful for that complexity! Let us start the process of rational analysis.

Megaprojects are different in so many significant ways from traditional projects. Accordingly, it is fair to ask whether the professional standard of care should correspondingly be different as applied in the context of megaprojects. The answer is "no" because the application of the professional standard of care is always adaptable to project-specific factors and circumstances, including those involved in megaprojects. Put another way, the same type of bottom-up evaluation of professional standard of care compliance that is utilized in a traditional project should apply to a megaproject, albeit in a different fact and circumstance context.

Many project owners and federal and state grantors and regulators of megaprojects implement, or mandate the implementation of, a "cost recovery" program to periodically evaluate the adequacy of consulting engineer performance. These cost recovery procedures should be developed in a manner consistent with contractual terms pertaining to risk allocation and performance standards and should take into account the range of appropriate and relevant facts and circumstances discussed above. In addition, any such cost recovery program should be implemented through a fair and balanced process. More specifically, while the project owner should control the process and be responsible for its prudent and diligent implementation,[11] the consulting engineer should be informed of the "ground rules" governing the process and be afforded a reasonable, timely, and meaningful opportunity to respond to allegations of deficient performance. In ideal circumstances, the consulting engineer should be afforded an opportunity to provide input regarding the proposed cost recovery process.[12]

Recommended Practices

- All parties should negotiate appropriate standard of care and indemnification contract provisions that are negligence-based.

- Project owners should develop fair cost recovery procedures that utilize the professional standard of care as an evaluative base.

3.0 Professional Standard of Care Application in the Megaproject Context

Issue

On a megaproject, there are many project risk parameters (some constant, others evolving), including project owner identities, expectations, and personnel changes; design innovation; design, code, or other standards that may change over the duration of the project and design details and production expectations that may evolve, based on "lessons learned" on the project or otherwise; discontinuity in the consulting engineer's involvement during design and construction; risk associated with project suspension or disruption; the number of critical project design and construction interfaces and interdependencies; fast-track approach to design and construction; bifurcating design and construction professionals' roles and responsibilities through the hiring of an indepen-

429

dent construction manager; and non-traditional relationships between project owner and consulting engineer, such as integrated project organization. How does one fairly apply the professional standard of care, given all of these (and other) risk factors and variables and the dynamic interaction, complexity, and design and construction interface challenges?

Analysis and Discussion

The foregoing factors and variables are but a few of the many that influence the application of the professional standard of care on a megaproject. Due to the sheer complexity of a megaproject, there is a substantial and heightened risk that professional liability claims may be asserted by the project owner and a variety of third parties against the consulting engineer. A number of the more risk-prone services of the consulting engineer are judgmental in nature and therefore not susceptible of "precise" evaluation in terms of clear or scientific principles of what absolutely is "right" or "wrong." Moreover, under the professional standard of care, some degree of imperfection should reasonably be expected and tolerated in the consulting engineer's performance of these services.

The key is to develop a contractual and attitudinal approach, reflected in a fair, published, and objectively-based review process that adequately balances these factors in evaluating the consulting engineer's performance on the megaproject. An integral part of such an approach is acknowledging that there are very significant risks, outside and beyond the control of the consulting engineer, that may materially impact the owner's expectations of project cost, schedule, or quality. Because of the pervasive role of the consulting engineer, there is a near-automatic reaction by some project owners (and project stakeholders, members of the public, and others) to want to hold the consulting engineer accountable for virtually everything that goes wrong, especially events that fail to fulfill the owner's quality, cost, or schedule expectations. However, such an overreaching and overly-simplistic reaction is fundamentally unfair to the consulting engineer and ignores the proper application of the professional standard of care, i.e., to objectively evaluate the relevant consulting engineer's performance measured against the performance reasonably expected under the same or similar (i.e., megaproject) circumstances.

In many instances, project risks on megaprojects are greater for reasons that are intended to advance or benefit the project owner's internal needs or programs, constraints, or public or political objectives. Examples include:

- Consideration and use of innovative design approaches that have limited proven application on similar projects in an effort to reduce cost or schedule.[13]
- Consideration and approval of innovative value engineering proposals in order to encourage the constructor's ingenuity and to reduce project cost or compress

schedule in circumstances in which the contract document design embodies a more conservative and traditional (time-tested and proven) design approach. [14]

- Receptivity to experiment with new products or design approaches even though the project has experienced satisfaction with existing products or approaches.
- Encouraging and implementing partnering and more flexible attitudinal approaches to relationships and roles among project participants, in circumstances in which the project owner otherwise would be entitled to strictly enforce contractual obligations.
- Use of innovative and non-traditional contracting practices
  - Fast-track approach
  - Design-build
  - Value engineering
- Need for independent design and management reviews (which typically lead to constructive criticisms but can be taken out of context in a retroactive cost recovery process).
- Availability and stability (continuity) of public funding
- Contractual risk allocation between project owner and constructor, and project owner and third parties.

There are a number of factors beyond the direct ability of the consulting engineer to control.[15] These include:

- Increase or changes in project scope/program
- Timing of increase or change in scope/program
- Deficient scope of subsurface investigation program
- Inadequate or faulty risk assessment
- Differing site conditions
- Acceleration to meet project milestones or political needs
- Fast-track to maintain, recover, or accelerate schedule
- Law or regulatory change or interpretation
- Labor availability
- Cost escalation
- Delay in owner decision-making and in addressing issues and problems
- Third-party impacts
- Funding issues and suspension
- Loss of public support or confidence in project management/leadership
- Inadequate project owner accountability, transparency, and reporting to project stakeholders

In addition, change of personnel within the owner's organization can create a high

431

Cascade Locks 15
Troutdale 43
Portland 58

potential for inconsistent and changing expectations, culture and philosophy, and subjectively different understanding of what project success means when evaluating consulting engineer performance.[16]

These and related factors need to be taken into account when applying the professional standard of care in a megaproject.

Recommended Practices

- Document recommendations and communications by the consulting engineer to the project owner, especially disclosures of risk and benefits associated with innovative design or construction approaches.

- Conduct an assessment of the risk implications of the various project-specific factors and variables that may affect the application of the professional standard of care and professional liability exposure.

- Develop contract terms and a risk management plan that address risk implications of factors and variables identified in such an assessment.

- Consider the availability of project-specific professional liability insurance to transfer some of the identified professional liability risk exposures.

4.0 External Risk Factors on Megaprojects and the Professional Standard of Care

Issue

What factors on megaprojects are outside the ability of the consulting engineer to control or manage — i.e., "external risk factors" — but may lead to professional liability claims asserted against the consulting engineer, and how do these external risk factors affect the application of the professional standard of care?

Analysis and Discussion

A number of characteristics inherent in megaprojects result in risk factors that may form the bases of professional liability claims against a consulting engineer. These risk factors have significantly less to do with the adequacy of the consulting engineer's performance (i.e., internal risk factors), but rather derive from, or are significantly influenced by, the character of a megaproject, that is, from risk factors *external* to the consulting engineer's performance. The issues, analysis, and recommended practices associated with many of these "external risk factors" are addressed in Part I of this book. This section will address how these external risk factors, if not adequately addressed and managed, can lead to increased professional liability exposure for the consulting engineer.

Major public projects typically pose significant and complex technical and management challenges for design and construction management professionals, requiring substantial skill and experience in order to successfully achieve the project's objectives and programs. Public projects also pose relatively high degrees of professional liability risk exposure, thus requiring appropriate contractual risk allocation provisions and effective risk management practices to anticipate and limit such exposure.

The conventional approach to risk identification for professional liability exposure for design and construction management professionals has focused primarily, and in some instances exclusively, on factors *internal* and *technical* in nature. *Internal* and *technical* factors include the qualifications and experience *of the professional team*, its ability to meet the anticipated project-specific program, and design and construction challenges and requirements. This conventional approach, which centers on the *internal* and the *technical*, does not adequately focus on the extent to which factors *external* to the design and construction management professional ("external risk factors") may impact the risk of potential for professional liability exposure. The most important of these external risk factors involve matters primarily within the control and influence of the project owner.

The Design and Construction Process: Risky and Dispute-Prone

Unquestionably, the design and construction process poses substantial risk for all project participants. Much has been written about the need to identify risk on a project-specific basis and to allocate risk in accordance with sound principles, such as the control and fairness principles.[17] In general, these principles counsel that risk should be allocated to the project participant in the best position to control and manage the risk and that risk should be clearly and fairly allocated in a manner that results in risk sharing rather than total and absolute risk transfer. Similarly, if risk is not appropriately allocated in accordance with such principles, there is a greater probability that significant disputes will arise among project participants, the resolution of which is less predictable, more contentious, more protracted and, hence, more costly.[18]

For the consulting engineer, risk factors include the contractual service scope, performance standards, and indemnification obligations; the adequacy, accuracy, and constructability of the project design; the ability to administer or manage (depending upon contractual scope) the construction of the project in the manner consistent with the project owner's expectations, as defined in the contract documents; and the ability to effectively communicate with the project owner in a timely manner and to manage the

owner's expectations (especially about cost, schedule, and quality) of both the professional's performance and the completed project. Depending upon contractual engagement terms, most of these risks are to a greater or lesser degree within the control of the consulting engineer.

External Risk Factors

What are these external risk factors? What types of problems may result from such external risk factors? How do these external risk problems affect the application of the professional standard of care and the professional liability exposure for the design and construction management professional?

External risk factors are those risk factors that are *external to* the qualifications, capabilities, and experience of the professional and/or the *internal* and/or *technical* ability of the professional to control or manage in accordance with required standards and the reasonable expectations of the owner. These external risk factors typically include the project budget and schedule; the project contingency; funding availability and stability; the project owner's management structure, governance, and decision-making; experience and qualifications of the project owner; the project owner's realism and transparency in the management of the project; the project owner's contracting and planning decisions and policies (risk allocation, delivery method, integrated project organization, and dispute resolution); the extent of the project owner's involvement in the design and construction process; and the structure and implementation of the project owner's cost recovery program for evaluating adequacy of professional service performance.

It Starts and Ends with the Project Owner

All of these external risk factors fall primarily, if not exclusively, within the control and responsibility of the project owner. The manner in which the project owner addresses and makes decisions about external risk factors may result in serious disappointment of its own, and stakeholders', expectations and, therefore, may also have a significant secondary impact on the professional liability exposure of the consulting engineer.

Project owners define and decide most of the basic parameters of the entire project: the program, scope, aesthetics, functionality, budget and schedule, strategies for obtaining and sustaining funding, risk allocation approaches, policies for project transparency (e.g., cost and schedule reporting/disclosure) and accountability, management structure, contractual roles and relationships, and delivery method. These decisions are within the control of the project owner and constitute risk factors *external* to the design and construction management professional. Certainly consulting engineers serve an important consulting role in advising and making recommendations to the project owner about these subjects; however, the project owner is the ultimate decision-maker. Yet, project owners do not make these decisions in a vacuum; for example, the availability and stability of project funding or required project completion dates will constrain project owner options regarding these various subjects and, therefore, limit, if not in some cases dictate, decision-making. In almost all situations, however, the project owner does have options and the ability to choose and decide among those options. The manner in which decisions regarding external risk factors are made, and the validity and prudence of these decisions, has the potential for dramatically impacting the professional liability risk exposure of the consulting engineer.

Strategic and deliberate underestimation of costs by the public owner of a megaproject—motivated by funding or by political or related objectives—can result in public policy demands for the accountability and transparency of the public owner regarding the preparation, periodic updating, and reporting of cost estimates. However, typically what proximately follows the owner's underestimation of cost is the demand for accountability of private sector consulting engineers involved in the megaproject, especially in circumstances in which the public owner has failed to accurately report project cost estimates in a timely manner. While it is certainly fair and appropriate that the consulting engineer be held accountable for its failure to adhere to the professional standard of care in cost estimating (or in the performance of its other services), it is not appropriate to hold the consulting engineer responsible for the political and economic consequences of the project owner's conscious and strategic decisions governing the cost estimating methodology, reporting, updating, and disclosure. However, in the politically-charged environment of megaprojects, these distinctions often are blurred or cynically merged into each other. In other words, the public owner's inappropriate handling of cost estimation and reporting inevitably leads to professional liability claims against the consulting engineer.

As has been stated:

> Enron and its successor scandals have shown that one should be skeptical of professionals and officials who promise to regulate themselves. This skepticism must now be applied to those involved in promoting and building large public works projects. In addition to the war on corporate deception, we need a war on deception in government, and with the same objective: to curb multimillion-dollar financial waste. Government ethics stand as much in need of betterment as corporate ethics.
>
> Key weapons in the war on deception will be accountability and critical questioning. The professional expertise of engineers, economists, planners and administrators is certainly indispensable to building the infrastructures that makes society work. Our studies show, however, that their claims about costs and benefits mostly cannot be trusted and should be carefully examined by independent specialists and organizations and should

435

be open to public scrutiny. The same holds for claims made by politicians and officials. Institutional checks and balances — including financial, professional, or even criminal penalties for consistent and unjustifiable biases in claims and estimates of costs and benefits — should be developed and employed in the campaign against deception.

Many of the experiments with new governance currently emerging in large construction projects and in other parts of government contain more and better financial checks and balances than previous institution set-ups. This is a step in the right direction, but should be no cause for repose. The lying game has long historical roots and is deeply ingrained in professional and institutional practices. It would be naive to think it is easily toppled. Given the stakes involved — including billions of dollars worth of misinvestments in underperforming projects — this shouldn't deter us from trying.[19]

Project Cost

As a starting point in the discussion of project cost as an external risk factor — especially as it relates to potential professional liability risk and exposure — it is helpful to focus on this simple formula which provides the impetus for much of the cost recovery efforts against consulting engineers on megaprojects in circumstances in which actual project cost significantly exceeds the budget:

$$\text{Actual project cost} - \text{Project budget} = \text{"Cost overrun"}$$

In this simple formula, "cost overrun" has an inciteful connotation. More specifically, "cost overrun" (especially a significant one) suggests that something negative and abnormal has occurred, given the substantial disparity between the project's budget (expected or planned) and actual cost. This negative and pejorative connotation fuels the search for the "wrongdoers" who caused the "cost overrun" to occur and who are responsible for paying damages.[20]

Again, things are not so simple and one needs to engage in a process of logical analysis to examine the components of the formula because they provide the foundation (and are key to the dismantling) of the perception that a "cost overrun" has actually occurred and warrants cost recovery because of the supposed failure of the consulting engineer.

Actual and budgeted project costs, and the differential expectations that flow therefrom, may be defined follows:

> Actual costs are defined as real, accounted construction costs determined at the time of project completion. Estimated costs are defined as budgeted, or forecasted, construction costs at the time of decision to build.
>
> . . . Various cost estimates are made at different stages of the process: project planning, decision to build, tendering, contracting, and later renegotiations. Cost estimates

at each successive stage typically progress toward a smaller number of options, greater detail of designs, greater accuracy of quantities, and better information about unit prices. Thus, cost estimates become more accurate over time, and the cost estimate at the time of making the decision to build is far from final. It is only to be expected, therefore, that such an early estimate would be highly inaccurate.[21]

Some preliminary points and definitions are in order. John Reilly has correctly overviewed the following considerations regarding major project cost estimating:

- The final cost of a project is subject to variables, assumptions, and conditions.
- These influence significantly the range of "probable projected cost."
- A single cost number represents only one possible result and is dependent upon the variables.
- The variables are not all directly controllable or absolutely quantifiable.
- Better cost estimating must include potential risks and opportunities.[22]

The budget and most of the underlying assumptions and parameters are established by the project owner. In many important respects, the budget defines the cost expectations of the project owner as well as other important project stakeholders, such as funding sources, taxpayers, legislators, the media, and the public at large.

The goal of the consulting engineer is to fulfill the defined and reasonable expectations of its clients in matters within its scope and responsibility. Disappointed expectations typically lead to conflict and disputes — the pathological side of project relationships.

Project owners also strive to fulfill expectations. Delivering a project on time, on budget, and consistent with contract requirements and operational and user needs are the most important of such expectations. Unmet expectations can be devastating and, in some cases, fatal for the project, especially in terms of public, political, stakeholder, and funding support.

The seeds for disappointed expectations about the project's cost are planted when the budget is unrealistic from the start. An unrealistic budget is one based upon a faulty or incomplete set of parameters or underlying assumptions, which, in some cases, may result from estimating or technical deficiencies and errors. In many cases — perhaps significantly more than we would like to think — budgets are unrealistic for other, deliberate, strategic reasons.

Recently, a number of studies and published articles have focused on the reality that budget costs of major public infrastructure projects — of all types, both domestic and international — are systematically and significantly underestimated. These studies and analyses, however, did not focus on the "collateral" or "downstream" effects of such underestimation on professional liability risk and exposure.

As noted above, the basic, overly simplistic — and hence deceptive — formula that leads to the "cost overrun" conclusion relies on a comparison (subtraction) of actual project costs and budgeted or estimated costs. This comparison, without elaboration or explanation, consists of merely subtracting one number from the other, with the difference representing nothing more than the net actual costs and budgeted project costs.

The sustainability of this formulaic approach to determining whether the consulting engineer is responsible for any portion of the "cost overrun" depends upon a detailed analysis of the extent to which (a) the budget reflects the complete and realistic assumptions, scope, and anticipated costs of the project, based upon an adequate risk assessment, and (b) the actual costs are due to the failure of the project participant to meet required performance standards.

Actual Project Costs

Actual project costs are often compared with the project's budget for the purpose of determining that the difference represents a "cost overrun." From that determination, the next step, fueled by the inciteful label of "cost overrun," is to conclude that the "cost overrun" must be something abnormal, unexpected, or the responsibility of some culpable project participant. Often, the consulting engineer is the prime target among potentially responsible parties who are blamed for causing the "cost overrun."

To what extent, if any, was the actual project cost caused by or due to the consulting engineer's departure from the professional standard of care or due to some other cause or explanation? There are many reasons why the actual cost may exceed the project budget (even assuming that the budget is reasonable, accurate, complete, and otherwise realistic). These reasons include increases in the project scope, differing site conditions, cost of accelerating work, the project's delivery method (e.g., fast-track approach), omissions from the original project scope, deficiencies in the project design that may not necessarily constitute a departure from the professional standard of care, changes in laws and regulations, availability of skilled labor, market cost escalation in labor and materials, delays in the owner's decision-making and in addressing issues and problems, and third-party impacts, considerations, and/or challenges to project implementation. Most of these reasons have nothing whatsoever to do with the performance of the consulting engineer, yet some may potentially give rise to professional liability, assuming adequate proof of a departure from the professional standard of care. The point to emphasize here is that in order to hold the consulting engineer legally responsible, the reasons for actual cost impacts must be analyzed in detail and the professional's performance measured or evaluated in relation to the professional standard of care.

A More Detailed Analysis of the Project Cost External Risk Factor

Research amply supports the conclusion that "cost underestimation" is not the result of technical or estimating errors or miscalculation. Cost underestimation represents a major problem that heightens professional liability exposure. Some of the more important aspects of this problem may be summarized as follows:

Lack of Realism in Initial Cost Estimates

Researchers have concluded that:

> Cost overruns on major transport infrastructure projects are widespread. The difference between actual and estimated investment cost is often 50–100 percent, and for many projects cost overruns end up threatening project viability. . . .
>
> A main cause of overruns is a lack of realism in initial cost estimates. The length and cost of delays are underestimated, contingencies are set too low, changes in project specifications and designs are not sufficiently taken into account, changes in exchange rates between currencies are underestimated or ignored, so is geological risk, and quantity and price. Changes are undervalued as are expropriation costs and safety and environmental demands. Many major projects also contain a large element of technological innovation with high risk. Such risk tends to translate into cost increases, which often are not adequately accounted for in initial cost estimates.[23]

The problem of unrealistically low initial cost estimates inevitably and necessarily leads to the perception of a "cost overrun," and the collateral effects of heightening professional liability exposure are put in play. The correlation of lack of realism in initial cost estimates and the "cost overrun" perception is logical and established. As one noted commentator has stated:

> [I]t is inevitable if the real scope (including the effects of risk events) is greater than that envisioned by the estimator, then no manager, however excellent, can manage to an impossibly low estimate.[24]

Cost Underestimation and "Cost "Overruns"—Influence of Owner Strategic Considerations

Noted commentators have concluded that "[c]ost underestimation and overrun have not decreased over the past seventy years. . . . Cost underestimation and overrun cannot be explained by error and seem to be best explained by strategic misrepresentation, namely lying, with a view toward getting projects started."[25] The same commentators have elaborated on this conclusion:

> We . . . conclude that cost overrun has not decreased over time. Cost overrun today is in the same order of magnitude as it was ten, thirty or seventy years ago. If techniques

and skills for estimating costs in avoiding cost overrun in transport infrastructure projects have improved over time, this does not show in the data. No learning seems to take place in this important and highly costly sector of public and private decision making. This seems strange and invites speculation that the persistent existence over time and space and project type of significant and widespread cost overrun is a sign that an equilibrium has been reached: strong incentives and weak disincentives for cost underestimation and thus for cost overrun may have taught project promoters what there is to learn, namely that cost underestimation and overrun pay off. If this is the case, cost overrun must be explained and it must be expected to be intentional.[26]

Elsewhere the same commentators, after reviewing the pattern of "cost overruns" on certain major projects, have similarly observed:

> Cost overruns of 50 to 100 percent in fixed prices are common for major infrastructure projects, and overruns above 100 percent are not uncommon. . . . Our assessment was that the difference between forecast and actual costs revenues and viability could not be explained primarily by the innate difficulty of predicting the future. The differences are too consistent and too one-sided for this to be the case. Instead, our conclusion was that the differences must be explained by project proponents succeeding in biasing forecasts in ways that make decisions to go ahead with projects more likely than decisions to stop them. The key problem is a lack of accountability.[27]

Commenting on the pervasiveness and commonness of the strategic cost underestimation approach, one researcher has noted that this is a "pattern . . . well established for decades, [which] has been subject to surprisingly little scrutiny by political scientists or scholars of public administration. Forecasts are presented to the public as instruments for deciding whether or not a project is to be undertaken; but they are actually instruments for getting public funds committed to a favored project. Once the decision to build the project is made, the realization that the initial cost estimates were too low, or that the patronage estimates were too high, will rarely stop the project. Somehow, more money will always be found to complete a project which is already underway."[28]

Costs Are "Highly, Systematically and Significantly Deceptive"

Flyvbjerg et al. have concluded that:

> On the basis of the evidence . . . , we conclude that cost estimates used in public debates, media coverage and decision making for transport infrastructure development are highly, systematically and significantly deceptive. So are the cost-benefit analyses into which cost estimates are routinely fed to calculate the viability and ranking of projects. The misrepresentation of cost is likely to lead to the misallocation of scarce resources which,

in turn, will produce losers among those financing and using infrastructure, be they taxpayers or private investigators.

An important policy implication for this highly expensive and highly consequential field of public policy is for the public, politicians, administrators, bankers and media not to trust the cost estimates presented by infrastructure promoters and forecasters. Another important implication is that institutional checks and balances—including financial, professional or even criminal penalties for consistent or foreseeable estimating errors—should be developed to insure the production of less deceptive cost estimates. . . .[29]

The same authors summarized that "[c]osts are underestimated in about 9 out of 10 projects" and that "[u]nderestimation of costs at the time of decision to build is the rule rather than the exception for transportation infrastructure projects. Frequent and substantial cost escalation is the result."[30]

"Salami Tactics"

The selective and strategic inclusion/exclusion and sequencing in the disclosure of the project's scope during the budget process is another major problem in the project cost external risk factor.

[E]xisting research indicates that project promoters routinely ignore, hide or otherwise leave out important project costs and risks in order to make total costs appear low. . . . [Ignoring] or underplaying geological risks may be helpful in getting projects approved, and no other risk is more likely to boomerang back and haunt projects during construction. "Salami tactics" is the popular name used to describe the practice of introducing project components and risks one slice at a time in order to make costs appear low as long as possible. If such tactics are indeed a main mechanism in cost underestimation, as existing research indicates, then, clearly, comparing actual project costs with estimated costs at the time of decision to build does not entail the error of comparing apples and oranges, but is simply a way of tracking how what was said to be a small, inexpensive apple turned out to actually be a big, expensive one.[31]

Project Owner Lack Of Accountability and Transparency in Developing and Reporting Realistic Project Budget and Actual Project Costs

The lack of accountability of the project owner both facilitates and is a central reason for the underestimation of the initial budget cost. This lack of accountability is aggravated by the (intentional and strategic) failure of project owners to report to project stakeholders and the public in a transparent, timely, and credible manner developments that can, did, or will impact the ultimate and actual cost of the project.[32]

Consulting engineers involved in all projects or client engagements are ethically obligated to maintain loyalty to and the confidences of their clients. In fact, it is fairly

441

common for agreements between consulting engineers and clients to recognize such obligations and, more specifically, to prohibit the consulting engineer from disclosing confidential information regarding the project to anyone other than the client (except as compelled or required by law or with the client's consent).

On megaprojects, there are a myriad of non-clients who may have a legitimate interest in being informed, on a reasonably current basis, about the status of major project parameters such as cost and schedule (i.e., not health, safety, or public welfare). The project owner–client, however, for equally legitimate reasons, may wish to limit, constrain, or prohibit the consulting engineer's ability to communicate with third parties regarding such issues. If the inquiring party is a political branch of government or governmental agency, the consulting engineer often will find itself in an untenable position and under fire — between the proverbial "rock and a hard place." Whatever the traditional ethical standards or constraints may stipulate or require, the pressure upon the consulting engineer to disclose details of project cost and schedule in such circumstances to the political branch or governmental agency is real and possibly significant. The tension created by this pressure should be addressed through enactment of laws and promulgation of regulations that mandate certain disclosures to the public and thereby override contractual or otherwise applicable ethical restraints upon the consulting engineer.

Virtually all of the researchers and commentators who have analyzed the correlation between initial budget cost underestimation and "cost overruns" have understood and focused on the associated problem of lack of project owner accountability and transparency in developing and reporting project costs. Bruzelius et al. stated:

> The test of publicity is the main means of enforcing accountability in the public sector. The role of government is, in principle, to represent and protect the public interest and it must, therefore, at all times be possible for the public to verify whether this is indeed the case. The transparency requirement means, inter alia, that all documents and other information prepared or commissioned by the government and its agency should be made available to the public.
>
> In addition, public hearings and other means of communicating with a wider public should be considered and used from an early stage and independent groups of experts should be used to carry out peer reviews of the important aspects of the project. . . .[33]

Flyvbjerg et al. have similarly commented:

> Whatever the reasons are for cost increases after decision makers give the go-ahead to build a project, or however large such increases are, legislators and citizens — or private investors in the case of privately funded projects — are entitled to know the uncertainty of budgets. Otherwise, transparency and accountability suffer.[34]

The same authors elsewhere have noted:

[P]roject promoters often avoid and violate established practices of good governance, transparency and participation in public and administrative decision making, either out of ignorance or because they see such practices as counterproductive to getting projects started. . . .[35]

The Failure to Adequately Identify and Evaluate Project Risk and the Impact of That Failure on Cost

In order to arrive at a fair and realistic estimated or initial budget cost, it is important to develop a comprehensive and conscientious plan for the identification and management of project-specific risk.[36] In addition, it is equally important that risk be allocated to project participants in a clear and fair manner. The project owner is the central decision-maker in the risk allocation process. The owner plays the major role in defining the scope of the investigation of issues or conditions that may impact project risk assessment and in being open to an independent review of the project's risk assessments, project budget, and schedule projections. The failure to identify and manage project risk and to allocate risk appropriately among project participants will impact ultimate and actual project cost.[37]

Flyvbjerg et al. concluded that:

> The megaprojects paradox consists in the irony that more and more megaprojects are built despite the poor performance record of many projects. . . . [W]e link the idea of megaprojects with the idea of risk and we identify the main causes of the megaprojects paradox to be inadequate deliberation about risk and lack of accountability in the project decision making process. . . . [I]n terms of risk, most appraisals of megaprojects assume, or pretend to assume, that infrastructure policies and projects exist in a Newtonian world of cause and effect where things go according to plan. In reality, the world of megaproject preparation and implementation is a highly risky one where things happen only with a certain probability and rarely turn out as originally intended. . . . [I]t is untenable to continue to act as if risk does not exist or to underestimate risk in a field as costly and consequential as megaproject development. . . . We do not believe risk can be eliminated from society. We believe, however, that risk may be acknowledged much more explicitly and managed a great deal better, with more accountability, than is typically the case today.[38]

The same authors have correctly observed that the "first step in reducing cost overrun is to acknowledge that a substantial risk of overrun exists and cannot be completely eliminated; but it can be moderated. A next step is to allocate the risk of overruns to those best able to manage it."[39] Reasonably comprehensive and accurate risk identification and analysis should provide the foundation for a sound, realistic, and achievable

project risk management plan that includes "the identification of strategies to reduce risks, including how to allocate them to the parties involved and which risks to transfer to professional liability risk management institutions, namely insurance companies."[40] Risk identification and management should address not only the technical risk, but also macro and longer-term non-technical risk factors such as project governance and management, availability and stability of project funding, and general political considerations that may influence project planning and decision-making.[41]

Other External Risk Factors

In addition to the project cost external risk factor and its associated problems, there are other external risk factors that may impact professional liability exposure for the consulting engineer.

Inadequacies in the Experience, Qualifications, and Policies of the Project Owner

John Reilly has noted that two factors which "most commonly influence the success or failure of a project are (1) the expertise and policies of the project owner and (2) the management structures of the project owner and stakeholder management of the project."[42] Reilly concludes that on major public infrastructure projects, cost overruns and related "problems may lie primarily with the ability of the Owner to lead and/or manage the complex implementation process."[43]

Fred Salvucci, who oversaw the promotion of the Boston Central Artery/Tunnel Project as former Secretary of Transportation for the Commonwealth of Massachusetts, recently made a number of important observations on this subject in an article entitled "Big Dig, Boston — Lessons Learned," published in *T&T North America* (May 2003). Salvucci concluded that the state's reduced public management capacity undermined its ability to manage final design decisions and "to make informed judgments on 'value engineering' opportunities proposed by third-parties." Reflecting on the cost growth of the Central Artery/Tunnel Project, Salvucci observed:

> As the costs mounted, the Weld administration hid the increases by shifting anticipated toll revenue from operation and maintenance to servicing debt and by shifting costs to the future through the issue of bonds and revenue anticipation notes. These "creative financing" policies left the project with no operation and maintenance plan and were adopted without honest disclosure of problems that would have been required by the then since abolished FHWA biennial. With no honest disclosure to stimulate timely search for solutions, problems were hidden for as long as possible and to the point where no options were available. . . . At the same time, while the policy management of the Big Dig suffered under the extreme privatization theories of the Weld administra-

tion, the sheer dedication, creativity and skill of the public and private sector engineers and construction managers, who have been building the Big Dig since I left, are a credit to the profession. It is easy to take pot shots at Big Dig cost increases, but maintaining an extremely high safety standard and solving hundreds of near-impossible challenges while conducting the equivalent of open-heart surgery on the City's center should be respected and celebrated.

Finally, Salvucci noted that "[u]nforeseen conditions and circumstances, changes in government administration — often accompanied by major shifts in political philosophy, as well as changes in the economic context will always occur during implementation of such large projects."

The Essentially Public and Political Nature of the Megaproject

Megaprojects are conceived, developed, and delivered in public in a big and notorious way and in a relatively constant state of political controversy. Competition for funding of a megaproject typically is both intrastate and interstate; funding for the megaproject may preclude other project options in a state, and states themselves compete for federal funding.

The scope and program of megaprojects are often the subject of as much "political" negotiation and compromise as they are the subject of technical judgments and decisions. The political nature of megaprojects is continuous in nature; it hardly ends with funding and the conceptual phase.

Due to their political and highly public nature, megaprojects require a substantial degree of transparency to engender, maintain, and restore public trust and confidence. On most "ordinary" construction projects, project owners and consulting engineers are accustomed to operating under a fair degree of independence, intensity, "need to know" and controlled communications, and confidentiality. Megaprojects do not follow this operating assumption. Key issues for project owners and consulting engineers involved in megaprojects over the last five years demonstrate that, to be successful in terms of maintaining and restoring public support, trust, and confidence, megaprojects must function within a virtual "fish bowl." The public, including all project stakeholders, have a "right to know" about the planning, design, and execution of the megaproject, as well as a right to have input in all of those issues. Megaprojects produce a significant impact (e.g., inconvenience, economic disruption, environmental and safety issues) upon the public. The public has a strong and legitimate interest in knowing all important aspects of the megaproject in a timely manner, as well as having input in the decision-making. Moreover, megaprojects involve and depend upon "mega" dollars. The public has a right to know how those dollars are being spent — i.e., the public needs to know that the megaproject is being competently and prudently planned, overseen, designed, managed, and execut-

445

ed by qualified professionals and in the best interest of the public trust. Given the substantial public funds involved in megaprojects, there is a significant potential for waste, abuse, and fraud—all of which serve to heighten such needs. The public expects and is entitled to candid and timely information and communications about the megaproject, which serves to enhance the integrity and credibility of the project owner.

The U.S. Department of Transportation Task Force on Oversight of Large Transportation Infrastructure Projects has stated:

> Given the complexity of megaprojects, DOT recipients frequently hire professional contractors and consultants to provided needed services on these megaprojects. In many cases, in the course of their work, these outside experts acquire intimate knowledge of potentially serious difficulties, including cost overruns and scheduling difficulties. However, this critical information may go unreported to DOT. Specific requirements should be set forth in the written agreement with the recipient to make clear that outside professional experts providing services under a DOT-assisted megaproject have an independent duty to report circumstances that could have a material effect on the scope, cost or schedule of the megaproject.[44]

Politicians need to secure public support for the megaproject—elections may be won or lost and political careers jettisoned or terminated based upon a politician's position regarding a megaproject. Megaprojects pervade both the state and federal political spectrums, and they often attract national attention. In this predominantly politically-charged environment, it does not take much for the project owner's discontent to get transformed into allegations about the adequacy of the consulting engineer's performance and to become greatly publicized, exaggerated, and politicized, and for the consulting engineer to become the convenient scapegoat and "victim" of the crushing forces of divergent political interests and agendas.

Management of Public Expectations

At the outset of the megaproject, expectations (of cost, schedule, and quality) need to be realistic, clearly defined, and communicated, and they need to be continuously adjusted, managed, and monitored throughout project execution. Change will happen. Surprises and disappointments, especially major ones involving time or money, need to be anticipated, avoided, and properly managed. The public needs to understand the risks and variables associated with the complexity of megaprojects. Estimates are just that—predictions. Contingency should be planned for, realistic, periodically updated, and explained to the public based upon informed and independently-validated risk assessments.[45]

Nature of relationship between project owner and consulting engineer

Megaprojects require and depend upon a close working and professional relationship between the project owner and consulting engineer — significantly more so than on most conventional projects. Further, on many megaprojects the owner implements, in varying degrees, forms of integrated relationships with the consulting engineer.[46] However, in order to maintain public trust and confidence, megaprojects also require and depend upon an appropriate degree of independence between the project owner and the consulting engineer and upon qualified oversight and management by the former over the latter. As R. Capka has stated:

> The project management plan should provide a clear description of the project management team's composition and organization, and how it will conduct business. Roles and responsibilities need to be easily understood. Large projects, more often than not, will require the skills and talents of the private sector to augment those in the public sector's management organization. The plan should describe how those skills will be integrated to provide management with efficient decision-making while insuring that public oversight is — and is perceived to be — appropriate and effective.[47]

External Risk Factors and Professional Liability Exposure

So what does all of this discussion about external risk factors mean in terms of the professional liability exposure of the consulting engineer? Given that most, if not all, of the identified problems resulting from these external risk factors are largely, if not exclusively, within the control of the project owner, is there anything — short of declining to participate in a project — that such a professional may do to limit or contain any professional liability exposure resulting from such external risk factor problems?

What is the evidence of any correlation between the external risk factor problems and professional liability exposure? In response, it is difficult to establish a direct causal link between them. By way of contrast, in a situation in which a specific error or omission in the performance of professional services occurs ("conventional errors/omissions claim"), it is generally quite feasible to evaluate that claim in relation to scope and performance of services and the professional standard of care to determine whether any departure from that standard caused damage or additional project cost and, if so, the amount of any such damage or additional cost. Professional liability claims arising out of external risk factors are more complicated, more subjective, less specific, involve substantial alleged damages, and, hence, are more difficult to resolve according to the traditional analysis utilized in a conventional errors/omissions claim context. This is so for several reasons:

- Typically, external risk factor problems—such as those that result in the perception of a "cost overrun"—result in the assertion of professional liability claims that otherwise would not have been asserted against a consulting engineer. Often, in circumstances in which a significant "cost overrun" occurs, a project owner will assert a generalized claim against the consulting engineer, alleging that the latter must be responsible in some general or unspecified manner for the "cost overrun," given its magnitude and unexpected nature. This claim assertion approach may be characterized as "top-down" in the sense that the project owner starts with the top or "cost overrun" number. Typically, the claim is asserted without much foundation, discrimination, or specifics in terms of professional responsibility and then, over a contentious and protracted process, the number is significantly negotiated *down* to a number that derives from the more traditional, or "bottom-up," analysis based on identifying and evaluating specific errors/omissions issues to determine the nature and extent of responsibility, if any. The "top-down" approach is akin to a constructor's total cost claim approach and, as in the case of a total cost claim, "top-down" claims typically are based on faulty and unsubstantiated assumptions as to responsibility, causal effect, and amount of damage or cost, and, accordingly, professional liability claims based on the "top-down" approach are (like constructor total cost claims) appropriately regarded as more suspect and difficult to resolve.

- Most of the external risk problems result from the project owner's direct decision-making role and involvement in various activities, such as developing and approving the project budget; defining the project program; defining the scope and sequencing of project scope and the cost estimating process; defining and implementing cost reporting procedures, transparency, and accountability to project stakeholders; decision-making regarding risk allocation, dispute resolution, delivery method, and project management structure; and amount of cost contingency. In circumstances in which these problems lead to professional liability claims, resolution of such claims becomes more difficult and challenging due to the project owner's direct and primary involvement and decision-making role, the subjective factors that must be evaluated regarding that role, and the project owner's exercise of judgment in the problem areas. As one might expect, the evaluation of these types of factors and considerations is more complex and sensitive than the evaluation of the purely technical issues that typically underlie the conventional errors/omissions professional liability claim. Moreover, when these types of claims are asserted during the progress of the megaproject, the consulting engineer's assertion of defenses that point to the project owner's own involvement and responsibility will inevitably create tension and conflict in the existing client-professional relationship. In the context of an *integrated* relationship with the project owner (see § 4 of chapter 1), these tensions and conflicts are exacerbated and the ability to segregate project owner actions and responsibilities from those of the consulting engineer will be more challenging. Also, for the consulting engineer, what is at stake is more than money; depending upon the rationality of the process and/or the result, the reputation and the ability of the professional to do further projects with the project owner may be impaired in this type of claim scenario in which the project owner's actions and judgments are "front and center."

• Particularly on public projects, especially those subject to external oversight (governmental, political, media, or public in nature), problems with external risk factors may impel a project owner to assert professional liability claims as a "cover," leaving the consulting engineer in somewhat of a "scapegoat" position. Specifically, left to itself, the project owner may genuinely understand the reasons for the "cost overrun" and recognize that the professional is not totally or even primarily responsible, but may feel — or perceive the need to assert — a professional liability claim due to project oversight, public, or political pressures. This may explain why many project owners pursue professional liability claims predicated on external risk factor problems, knowing that the claims will "boomerang" back at them.

5.0 Heightened and Non-Traditional Professional Liability and Other Risk Exposure of Consulting Engineers on Megaprojects

Issue

Beyond the traditional professional liability risk exposure based upon legal theories of professional negligence and breach of contract, megaprojects expose the consulting engineer to non-traditional professional liability and other risk exposures. The amount of public money, the number of project overseers, external risk factors, the sheer importance of the ultimate stakes, and the opportunity to use and publicize events on megaprojects to demonstrate a point or establish a "precedent" or "example" — all account for the heightened and non-traditional professional liability and reputational risk to consulting engineers involved in megaprojects.

Analysis and Discussion

There are a variety of legal claims and governmental investigations that may involve the consulting engineer on a megaproject and expose the latter to professional liability claims beyond those typically asserted in the conventional project context, as well as to significant damage to their reputation.

Breach of Fiduciary Duty

In general, a breach of fiduciary duty claim is predicated upon the basis that the consulting engineer, by virtue of its specialized knowledge, expertise, and skill, owes a fiduciary duty to the claimant. On a megaproject, a fiduciary or confidential relationship may derive from the degree of trust and confidence between the project owner and the consulting engineer, especially in circumstances in which the consulting engineer possesses superior knowledge, skill, or expertise.[48] More specifically, in a breach of fiduciary claim, the project owner typically alleges that this special duty is breached when the consulting engineer fails to apply this knowledge, expertise, and skill in a manner consistent with the owner's best interest.

The relatively substantial degree of interaction and integration between project owners and consulting engineers on megaprojects, the significant degree of specialized knowledge and experience of consulting engineers typically involved in megaprojects, and the significant extent to which confidential information is shared between them combine to create a higher expectation that the relationship between them be founded and maintained on trust and confidence—the predicates of a fiduciary duty claim. This expectation is further heightened in circumstances in which the project owner predominantly or entirely depends upon the expertise and judgment of the consulting engineer or in which the consulting engineer functions as an agent or extension of, or is integrated with, the project owner.

Breach of fiduciary duty claims typically do not require proof of a departure from the professional standard of care or expert opinion in order for the claimant to recover. In addition, the allegations made in such a claim generally are designed to question the integrity, ethics, or professionalism of the consulting engineer and, as such, the mere assertion of such allegations has the potential for attracting significant negative attention and publicity for the consulting engineer and for impairing the prospect of future project opportunities.

Is the relationship between a consulting engineer and its client "fiduciary" in nature, such that the engineer owes a *fiduciary* duty to its client? As a general matter, a relationship is "fiduciary" when one party has superior knowledge and authority and that person is in a position of trust and confidence over the subordinate party. Not all client-professional relationships are fiduciary in character. In the pure design professional — client service context, courts have been reluctant to automatically find that the design professional owes a fiduciary duty to the project owner. However, in the project manager or management consultant context, in which the consulting engineer contractually assumes a position of trust and confidence, some courts have been more receptive to finding such a duty. Moreover, in the integrated project organization context, given the closeness of the relationship, courts have been even more receptive to finding that such a fiduciary duty exists.[49]

Thus, while in most conventional project contexts a fiduciary duty relationship generally does not exist, in the megaproject context courts may be more receptive to finding that such a duty is owed by the consulting engineer to the project owner based on the factors and considerations discussed in this section. The legal answer to whether such exposure may exist depends upon the applicable state law and the specific facts and circumstances at issue, including the contractual terms governing the relationship between the project owner and the consulting engineer. In the event that a court determines that such a fiduciary duty existed and had been violated by the consulting engineer, proof of that violation generally does not depend upon a breach of the professional standard of care (see § 2 below) and the consequences of such a determination — i.e., that the consulting engineer breached the trust and confidence it owed to its client — may have a serious and adverse impact on further project opportunity procurements.

False Claims Statutes

The federal government and an increasing number of states have enacted false claims statutes, which, in general, are intended to impose civil liability upon a party who makes false statements in order to secure payment from public funds or who causes such payments to be made by false statements. Notable examples of the latter are situations in which a consulting engineer provides a statement or certification (a) in support of a project owner's request for federal or state funding or (b) in connection with the review, evaluation, or recommended disposition regarding a constructor's requisition or application for payment. Assuming that a violation of a false claims statute is determined to exist, the consulting engineer may be found liable for actual and punitive damages and, under some state statutes, consequential damages as well. The fact that the consulting engineer did not economically benefit from the payment is immaterial.

The significant potential for waste, fraud, and abuse on megaprojects, as well as the amount of public funding, expenditures, and oversight, substantially increases the risk of false claims act exposure for the consulting engineer. In general, the purpose of the false claims legislation is protection of the public from false or fraudulent claims by those involved in publicly-funded projects or contracts. The federal False Claims Act (FCA, Section 3729 of Title 1 of the U.S. Code) has been in existence since 1863. Approximately 15 states have enacted their own form of FCA legislation. While the FCA has been in force for almost 150 years, only recently have design professionals been the focus of FCA investigations and claims, and that focus has been particularly acute — for the foregoing reasons — on megaprojects.

The False Claims Act imposes liability for knowingly (a) presenting, or causing to be

presented, false claims (§ 3729 (a)(1)); and (b) using false records or statements to get false claims paid (§ 3729 (a)(2)).

Precisely what "false" or "fraudulent" means in the context of an FCA statute depends upon the particular statutory language. In general, "false" or "fraudulent" implies that the claim as submitted does not comply with contractual, regulatory, or statutory requirements. Misrepresenting the percent complete of service performance, misrepresenting compliance with contractual or other required standards, and submitting overcharges are typical examples and prime candidates for FCA exposure. In general, for conduct to be "knowing" within the meaning of an FCA statute, the respondent must act either with actual knowledge of falsity, in deliberate ignorance, or in reckless disregard (often described as "gross negligence plus") of the truth or falsity of the statement. In general, innocent mistakes or mere negligence in furnishing the information or providing the claim statement is not sufficient to establish liability. However, no specific intent to defraud is required for FCA liability to result.

Typically, FCA claims may be asserted by the government (federal or state, depending upon statutory scheme), as well as *qui tam* claimants (i.e., private party whistle-blowers).

What are the scenarios that may lead to FCA liability for consulting engineers involved in megaprojects?

Direct claim submissions of consulting engineers

Progress and final payment requests

- Misrepresenting percentage of services complete
- Overbilling
- Misrepresenting facts or matters susceptible of objective validation or verification

Certifications or statements accompanying consulting engineer payment requests

- In general, certifications or statements about matters that are objectively ascertainable or quantifiable, if falsely stated, are more prone to potential FCA liability. In contrast, certifications or statements that services were performed in accordance with the professional standard of care, the making of which requires some degree of subjective evaluation and judgment, are less prone to provide a sustainable basis of FCA liability.

Certifications or statements regarding constructor performance or compliance with contractual obligations[50]

Certifications or statements of the consulting engineer regarding:

- Constructor progress or final payment requests
- Quality, quantity, or progress relative to constructor performance

- Constructor requests for equitable adjustments or claims

Certification or statement content

- The content of the certification or statement signed by the consulting engineer with respect to constructor performance or entitlement to payment is extremely important in determining the potential for FCA liability. The more the statement is qualified and judgmental in nature, the less likely that the statement will provide the basis of FCA liability. The more the statement addresses objective or quantifiable terms or representations, the more likely the statement may provide an actionable basis for FCA liability.[51]

- Certifications or statements made to support or assist the project owner in obtaining funding or grant authorization, or in the disbursement, or eligibility determination for disbursement, of public funds.

In a recent case,[52] a state university engaged an agency construction manager (CM) to provide professional consulting services in connection with reconstruction of buildings damaged by an earthquake. The university sought and obtained Federal Emergency Management Agency (FEMA) funding. The CM submitted a memorandum and letter to FEMA stating that one of the buildings, although unoccupied at the time of the earthquake, had been closed because of modifications to bring the building into compliance with current code requirements and that an architectural report commissioned by the university "clearly indicates the university's intention to re-occupy the facility to its intended use. It was, at the time of the earthquake, conducting due diligence studies to bring the facilities back into operation." These statements were material and critical to FEMA funding because "applicable FEMA regulations provided that buildings not in use at the time of the earthquake were ineligible for funding unless, before the disaster, the owner had an intent to re-occupy them within a reasonable time." The building at issue had been closed in 1991, in part because of declining enrollment, and it was left unoccupied for more than two years before the earthquake. The CM did not mention in its statements submitted to FEMA that the feasibility study reports were rejected by the university in December 1993. Instead, the CM stated that the university did not appropriate funds for the restoration of the facility based on the outcome of the study because of the earthquake in January 1994. The CM predominantly relied upon information provided by the university in making all of these statements. A FEMA representative testified that had he been aware of all the facts (i.e., that the university had rejected the study and had no intention prior to the earthquake of re-occupying the building), he would not have approved the funding request and that he would have found the building ineligible for FEMA funding. The federal dis-

trict court concluded that this evidence could allow a factfinder to conclude that the CM made misrepresentations to FEMA in violation of the California FCA. The court addressed whether there was evidence that the CM presented a false claim knowingly. Under the FCA, a defendant must be shown to have known that the claim was false, acted in deliberate ignorance of the truth or falsity of the claim, or acted in reckless disregard of the falsity of the claim. Negligence and innocent mistake are insufficient to meet the intent requirement under the FCA. Neither of the CM employees responsible for preparing the materials inquired about the university's intentions regarding the feasibility study. The CM drafter of the letter never discussed the study with anyone other than his superior. The superior acknowledged he had never read the feasibility study and said that although he was aware the feasibility study had been discussed at the meeting (where it was rejected), he made no effort to find out what had happened at that meeting. The court found that this evidence was sufficient to raise an issue of material fact as to whether the CM acted knowingly or with reckless disregard for or deliberate ignorance of the truth or falsity of the representations in the letter.

Consulting engineer certifications or statements regarding constructor requests for equitable adjustments or claims

Typically, a consulting engineer is contractually required or requested by the project owner to evaluate a constructor's payment request or claim for equitable adjustment. The consulting engineer's agreement or the contract documents should define the role of the consulting engineer in such an evaluative process. Typically, but depending upon specific contract terms, the consulting engineer provides a technical evaluation of the payment request or claim and a recommendation to the project owner with respect to disposition thereof.

Statements, certifications, and recommendations made by the consulting engineer with respect to constructor payment requests and equitable adjustment claims may provide the basis for FCA claims against the consulting engineer if they contain false information or are made in reckless disregard of the truth or falsity of the assertions made therein. FCA liability for the consulting engineer may result even though the consulting engineer does not economically benefit from the false statement, certification, or recommendation.

While the following cases involve FCA liability of constructors, note the implications for potential FCA liability for consulting engineers who issue certifications or statements in reliance upon representations made by the constructor in connection with such claims and who evaluate and make recommendations to the owner concerning such claims.

Daewoo Engineering & Construction v. United States, **73 Fed. Cl. 547 (2006)**

- In *Daewoo*, a constructor was found liable under the federal FCA for conduct including false representations about the quality of work it had performed, making misrepresentations about site conditions encountered, and submitting an inflated request for equitable adjustment.

- Daewoo claimed an entitlement to equitable adjustment due to problems in compacting the soils according to specification requirements.

- The court found that these statements were false and imposed FCA liability.

Commercial Contractors, Inc. v. United States, **154 F. 3d 1357, 1366 (Fed. Cir. 1998)**

- In *Commercial Contractors*, the Army Corps of Engineers had contracted with Commercial Contractors, Inc. (CCI) to build parts of a flood contract channel. CCI was to excavate, set up forms and pour concrete, test the concrete, and backfill the excavated areas. After completing performance, CCI submitted a certified claim seeking additional payment, and after the claim's denial, it filed suit in the Court of Federal Claims.

- The government asserted several counterclaims alleging FCA liability, and the trial court agreed that CCI violated the FCA.

- On appeal, the Federal Circuit first affirmed that CCI violated the FCA by submitting claims when it knowingly had failed to excavate in accordance with contract requirements and had knowingly backfilled the channel using construction debris, which was contractually prohibited because of concerns about adequate support for the channel. Second, the Federal Circuit upheld the trial court's finding that CCI had built one end of the channel shorter than specified in the contract to avoid construction difficulties and had knowingly submitted claims for this noncompliant work, thereby violating the FCA. Third, the contract requirements prohibited CCI from removing the forms used for pouring until the concrete had hardened 80 percent of the required strength, which was determined by simultaneously pouring test cylinders. The Federal Circuit determined that CCI improperly heated the test cylinders to accelerate the hardening and that CCI therefore had violated the FCA by knowingly submitting claims for work performed in violation of quality control standards.

United States v. North American Construction Corp., **173 F. Supp. 2d 601 (S.D. Tex. 2001)**

- In *North American*, a drilling company bid on a second-tier subcontract to drill wells on an Air Force base. The driller was provided a bidding package by the first-tier subcontractor that included certain inaccurate well-boring logs but did

not include government-generated logs that more accurately reflected subsurface conditions. After securing the subcontract, the driller encountered different drilling conditions than it expected, which caused substantial delays and cost overruns. After performing unsuccessfully, the driller drafted a request for equitable adjustment (REA) that blamed the first-tier subcontractor for failing to provide the government's accurate drilling logs as part of the bid package.

- The prime contractor allegedly realized that the REA would be denied unless it blamed the government for the delays and cost overruns, so it told the subcontractor to redraft the REA to cast blame on the government. The subcontractor complied with this request and redrafted the REA to allege that the government had withheld superior knowledge of subsurface soil conditions. The contractors then certified the accuracy of the REA, and it was submitted to the contracting officer. Soon afterwards, an employee of one of the contractors filed a *qui tam* lawsuit alleging the REA was knowingly false, and the government joined the lawsuit, alleging that the defendants omitted relevant factual information from the REA and made several affirmative false statements in the REA.

- The district court denied the defendants' motion to dismiss, ruling that the allegations in the complaint stated a claim for relief.

Defenses to FCA False Certification and Statement Claims Against Consulting Engineers

Courts are disinclined to find FCA liability where relative truth or falsity of the claim involves a matter open to opinion, judgment, or interpretation.

- In *Tyger Construction Co. v. United States*, 28 Fed. Cl. 35, 45 (Cl. Ct. 1993), FCA liability was denied based on a certification that construction had achieved substantial completion, because certification of substantial completion constitutes an opinion and is subject to the exercise of professional judgment.

Good faith disagreements over contract interpretation are not actionable under the FCA.

- In *Commercial Contractors, Inc. v. United States*, 154 F. 3d 1357, 1366 (Fed. Cir. 1998), contractual claims based on "a plausible but erroneous contract interpretation" are not actionable under the FCA.

Engineering judgment is not actionable under the FCA.

- Courts have consistently declined to find that "exercise of scientific or professional judgments as to an applicable standard of care falls within the scope of the FCA." *Luckey v. Baxter Healthcare Corp.*, 2 F. Supp. 2d 1034, 1047 (N.D. Ill. 1998); P. Comodeca & K. Carter, "The Defense of False Claims Act Suits by Federal Subcontractors," *Construction Lawyer*, 29, 33 (Spring 2009).

- Proof of one's mistakes or inabilities is not evidence that one is a cheat. "Without more, the common failings of engineers . . . are not culpable under the [FCA]. The phrase 'known to be false' does not mean 'scientifically untrue'; it means 'a lie.' The [FCA] is concerned with ferreting out wrongdoing, not scientific errors. What is false as a matter of science is not, by that very fact, wrong as a matter of morals." *Wang v. FMC Corp.*, 975 F.2d 1412, 1421 (9th Cir. 1992).

Failure to meet the professional standard of care does not constitute an FCA violation.

- In *United States ex rel. Mikes v. Straus*, 84 F. Supp. 2d 427, 432–33 (S.D.N.Y. 1999) (footnote omitted), the district court explained that the failure to perform to a professional standard of care, without more, is not a violation of the FCA:

  > The parties do not appear to dispute that Defendants made "claims" within the meaning of the FCA when they submitted claims for Medicare reimbursements for the spirometry tests that they performed on patients at PCCA. Rather, Defendants challenge Mikes's contention that the Medicare claims made by Defendants were false or fraudulent. Defendants correctly point out that Mikes is unable to point to a single identifiably false claim made during her employment at PCCA. Instead, she cites a number of documentary sources describing the standard of care for the administration of spirometry tests, most prominently, the guidelines promulgated by the American Thoracic Society (ATS), which recommend daily calibration of spirometers using a three-liter syringe. Mikes claims that Defendant's failure to follow the ATS recommendation amounts to a breach of the applicable standard of care, so that Defendants' Medicare submissions were based on negligently performed spirometry tests. For this reason, she argues, Defendants' Medicare claims were fraudulent within the meaning of the FCA. I note first that Mikes has failed to demonstrate that the ATS guidelines in fact constitute the standard of care for operation of spirometers, let alone that Medicare claims for spirometry not performed in compliance with those guidelines may be deemed fraudulent under the FCA. But even had she made this showing, her proposition that Defendants' alleged professional negligence is actionable under the Act is incorrect. Submitting a claim to the Government for a service that was not provided in accordance with the relevant standard of care, however, without more, does not render that claim false or fraudulent for FCA purposes.

457

See *Hagood v. Sonoma County Water Agency*, 81 F. 3d 1465, 1478 (9th Cir. 1996); *United States ex rel. Milam v. Regents of the Univ. of Cal.*, 912 F. supp. 868, 886 (E. Md. 1995) ("Disagreements over scientific methodology do not give rise to False Claims Act liability"); *Boisjoly v. Morton Thiokol*, 706 F. Supp. 795, 810 (D. Utah 1988) (Engineering judgment "is clearly not a statement of fact that can be said to be either true or false, and thus cannot form the basis of a FCA claim"); *Reynolds v. Science Applications International Corp.*, United States District Court, Southern District of New York, Memorandum Decision and Order, 07 CV 4612 (June 26, 2008) (". . . purported errors based on flawed reasoning, mathematic calculations, or scientific judgments are not false for purposes of the FCA").[53]

Lack of Materiality

- *"Lack of materiality* means whether an alleged falsity is capable of influencing the government's decision to pay." J. Boese, *Civil False Claims and Qui Tam Actions*, § 2.03A (2003). Remedial provisions, retainage and warranty, indemnification, and risk allocation provisions may evidence the government's intent to pay even if defective work is encompassed in-progress or final payment requests certified or approved by the consulting engineer. *See Allison Engine Co. v. United States* ex rel. *Sanders*, 553 U.S. 662, 128 S. Ct. 2123 (2008) (in which the Supreme Court held that the federal FCA requires proof that "the defendant intended that the false record or statement be material to the government's decision to pay or approve the false claim." Under this standard, liability is precluded where "the direct link between the false statement and the government's decision to pay or approve a false claim is too attenuated to establish liability").

Government knowledge of defective or incomplete construction work or other contractual non-compliance.

Government direction to constructor to perform work at variance with contractual requirements.

- In *United States* ex rel. *Durcholz v. FKW, Inc.*, 997 F. Supp. 1159, 1162–64 (S.D. Ind. 1998), the plaintiff alleged that the defendant constructor had violated the FCA by submitting invoices that falsely stated excavation work had been performed when, in fact, dredging work had been performed. The district court granted summary judgment to the contractor. It found that government officials had wanted dredging performed from the outset of the contract and had directed the contractor to dredge but to submit invoices stating excavation work had been performed to streamline the contracting process. The court noted, "[The Contractor's] actions were authorized by the Navy, known and approved of by the responsible govern-

ment officials, and carried out without knowingly misleading the government"
(997 F. Supp. at 1171). The Seventh Circuit (189 F.3d 542, 545 (7th Cir. 1999)) affirmed, stating that government knowledge can constitute a defense to liability by
negating the elements of falsity or knowledge.

Government knowledge that the constructor's claim was suspect.[54]

At present, there is limited legal precedent with respect to consulting engineer liability under the FCA. However, it is anticipated that, especially on megaprojects, there will
be a growing trend toward increasing assertion of claims by state and federal authorities
against consulting engineers under state and federal FCA legislation:

> Design professionals such as architects and engineers also can face FCA liability either
> in their capacity as consultants to owners or by virtue of their direct relationship with
> the federal government. In such cases, the types of activities that would impose liability
> on a contractor, such as overbilling, would result in liability on the part of the design
> professional. It is unlikely, however, that one could assert a false claim against a de-
> sign professional based on claims for payment based on what turn out to be defective
> designs. "Submitting a claim to the Government for service that was not provided in
> accordance with the relevant standard of care, however, without more, does not render
> that claim false or fraudulent for FCA purposes. This is because "[c]ourts have consis-
> tently declined to find that a contractor's exercise of scientific or professional judgment
> as to an applicable standard of care falls within the scope of the FCA. In one case, how-
> ever, an architect allegedly violated the FCA by certifying specifications as being appro-
> priate for the work when it supposedly knew they were defective. While the court dis-
> missed the suit on disclosure grounds, and did not reach the issue of the viability of the
> underlying claim, the case, nonetheless, shows that a designer can face an allegation of
> FCA liability for such false certifications. . . .
>
> . . . The FCA's reach is not confined to traditional targets such as construction and
> defense contractors. Almost any time federal funds are involved, there is the possibil-
> ity of running afoul of the FCA. Although many cases against owners eventually are
> dismissed, the ability of realtors to survive the initial pleading stage exposes owners at
> least to the costs of defending against the actions. Likewise, design professionals and
> construction managers must be cognizant of the very real threat of finding themselves
> involved in an FCA case based on their work on federally funded projects.[55]

The potential for FCA liability for consulting engineers has several important impacts
beyond increased risk and liability exposure. Typically, the mere pendency of an FCA
allegation or claim must be disclosed when the consulting engineer is seeking new project opportunities. In addition, the pendency of an FCA claim or allegation could have
adverse public relations/external affairs implications. In a number of situations, a public

project owner may be immune from liability under the FCA, but the consulting engineer is fully exposed to that liability. The latter situation is particularly problematic for the consulting engineer in circumstances in which the project owner was the principal actor with respect to the alleged FCA violation.[56]

As a general proposition, the consulting engineer should develop internal compliance programs to sensitize employees to the importance of potential FCA liability exposure. In addition, the content and subject of all certifications and statements executed by the consulting engineer should be carefully evaluated and qualified and limited so as to reduce the risk of exposure to FCA liability.

Securities Laws and Regulations

Funding for megaprojects is sometimes secured from bonds or other instruments which require public offerings or a prospectus in compliance with federal and state securities laws and regulations. The offering or prospectus typically will contain information and projections about the project that are material to the subscription effort — e.g., cost estimates, schedule, project management, project status, etc. In some situations, the consulting engineer may assist the project owner in the preparation or compilation of such information or projections. If it is claimed and determined that such information or projections were false or misleading, those who were involved in the process may be subject to liability to bondholders and others under federal and state securities laws.

On the Central Artery/Tunnel Project, the SEC issued a cease-and-desist order stating:

> This matter involves misrepresentations resulting from the delay in disclosing cost increases at the Massachusetts Central Artery/Ted Williams Tunnel Project (the "Project"), popularly known as the "Big Dig," by the Turnpike Authority and Kerasiotes in connection with three municipal bond offerings during 1999. The offerings were by the Turnpike Authority in March 1999, the Commonwealth of Massachusetts ("Commonwealth") in September 1999, and the Massachusetts Bay Transportation Authority ("MBTA") in December 1999. At the time of each of these offerings, the Project staff had projected cost increases exceeding $1 billion, which should have been disclosed to the public, including potential bondholders, underwriters, and credit rating agencies in connection with the bond offerings. However, because the cost increases had not been fully quantified or confirmed, the Respondents deemed them to be speculative and did not disclose them. Instead, beginning in the spring of 1999, the Project staff embarked upon an effort to quantify and confirm the specific amount of any cost increases, including a "bottom-up" review of every Project contract. As a result, the offering materials accompanying each of the bond offerings indicated that the Project was on budget and that it would cost only $5.5 billion to complete. The cost increases were ultimately disclosed to the

public in February 2000. Although Respondents' approach to dealing with projected cost increases was part of an effort to control project costs, their failure to disclose such cost increases did not take into account their obligations under the Federal Securities Laws. By their negligent conduct, the Turnpike Authority committed and Kerasiotes committed and caused violations of Sections 17(a) (2) and (3) of the Securities Act.

Governmental Investigations

The degree of external oversight of megaprojects fosters and generates a number of state and federal investigations relating to the funding, budget, cost, schedule, planning, design and construction, and quality of completed work, to name just a few areas. In some instances, the consulting engineer may be the target or focus of the investigations; in other situations, the consulting engineer may simply be requested to provide information; and in yet other situations, the consulting engineer may be requested by the project owner to assist it in responding to or defending against allegations made in such investigations. These investigations may be the prelude to cost recovery or other professional liability claims against the consulting engineer. While the consulting engineer certainly should endeavor to work cooperatively with the project owner in connection with such investigations, it should not lose sight of the fact that it needs to protect its own interest in connection with such investigations and that those investigations may ultimately lead to independent civil claims against it.[57]

Debarment/Disqualification

Virtually all states have procedures to debar or disqualify a consulting engineer from contracting with the public agency if the consulting engineer is found to have engaged in certain proscribed conduct that typically goes beyond simple professional negligence or breach of contract. Given the political and controversial nature of megaprojects, the "arsenal of weapons" that the project owner (or other project stakeholders) may chose to employ against the consulting engineer when "things go wrong" may include the initiation of debarment or disqualification proceedings. The mere pendency of such proceedings — almost independent of the end result — can do severe reputational and business (economic) damage to the consulting engineer.

Reputational Risks and Exposures

All of the foregoing types of claims, investigations, and other professional liability risk exposures — especially when coupled with the more traditional professional liability risks based on professional negligence — may result in severe reputational damage to

the consulting engineer. These risks are significant in view of the high public visibility of megaprojects. The ability to compete successfully for new project engagements may be negatively impacted, and otherwise positive relationships with existing clients may be damaged.

Recommended Practices

- Document advice and recommendations given to the project owner and the latter's decisions and basis thereof.

- Decline to provide statements or certifications for which the consulting engineer does not have adequate facts or ability or opportunity to ascertain and evaluate the accuracy and completeness thereof.

- Limit or qualify any statements or certifications, as appropriate.

- Conduct adequate due diligence prior to making certifications or statements.

- Decline to provide statements or certifications on subjects or matters beyond the consulting engineer's knowledge, service scope, qualifications, or experience.

- Understand the purpose for which the consulting engineer is preparing or compiling information and, as appropriate, limit, qualify, or disclaim the accuracy or completeness of that information.

- Understand that governmental investigations may target — presently or eventually — the consulting engineer and that the consulting engineer needs independent legal advice and representation in connection therewith. Reliance upon the project owner's legal counsel is imprudent, as the interests of the project owner and the consulting engineer are likely to diverge at some point. Moreover, governmental investigations may lead to subsequent civil proceedings against the consulting engineer.

- Maintain the appearance and reality of genuine independence from the project owner during any governmental investigations.

- Take seriously any intimation of potential debarment/disqualification proceedings and promptly retain legal counsel for advice and assistance therewith.

- Retain (or better yet, have your legal counsel retain) qualified external affairs or public relations consultants with experience, strategic advice capabilities, and "on the ground" knowledge of the relevant political and governmental environment.

6.0 Duties and Obligations of Consulting Engineers to Third Parties

Issues

There are a host of parties beyond the project owner who have a stake or interest, directly or indirectly, in the delivery or oversight of the megaproject. Does the consulting engineer owe any duties or obligations to such third parties? If so, how are such duties or obligations reconciled with the primary duty or obligations of the consulting engineer to the project owner?

Analysis and Discussion

Given the number of stakeholders, overseers, and participants involved in megaprojects, there is a significant potential, if not probability, for the consulting engineer to find itself "smack in the middle" of conflicting interests and agendas. In the general context of professional liability, the notion (and derivative legal defenses) that the consulting engineer owes duties and obligations to only those in privity or direct contractual relationship with the engineer has long since eroded. While a number of states limit the ability of non-clients to sue engineers based on the so-called economic loss doctrine, the courts have recognized fairly broad exceptions to that doctrine, particularly in circumstances in which the engineer has reported inaccurate or incomplete information about the project to third parties.[58]

In the design-bid-build delivery method, in which the project owner furnishes to the constructor detailed design documents which the constructor is obligated to follow in the construction of the project, the project owner legally (and impliedly) warrants to the constructor that the design is adequate and, if adhered to by the constructor, will result in an end result consistent with the objectives and requirements of the contract documents. This implied warranty of design adequacy obligation is often confused with the consulting engineer's obligation to design in accordance with the professional standard of care. The former obligation is a far more exacting standard and more encompassing obligation; the latter obligation is more forgiving and allows for some degree of imperfection measured against an objective professional standard of care obligation (see § 2 above). However, the confusion of these two obligations (the project owner's design adequacy implied warranty and the consulting engineer's professional standard of care) often results in constructor claims against the consulting engineer along with project owner claims for indemnification against the consulting engineer in circumstances in which the constructor alleges an underlying claim that the project owner breached its implied warranty obligation by furnishing defective design.

The implied warranty doctrine typically and primarily has been utilized in the context of competing claims between project owners and constructors. However, to the extent that a constructor's implied warranty claim against the project owner is based upon an alleged deficient design or other deficient work product or services of the consulting engineer, it is likely that the project owner may assert negligence or indemnification claims against the consulting engineer arising out of the constructor's underlying implied warranty claim against the project owner.[59] Thus, even though consulting engineers typically are not directly a party in constructor implied warranty claims, there is a distinct likelihood that such claims involving the consulting engineer's services may give rise to negligence or indemnity claims by the project owner against the consulting engineer. As such, the scope and contours of the implied warranty doctrine impact the potential professional liability risk exposures of the consulting engineer.

The origin of the implied warranty doctrine is the landmark United States Supreme Court case of *United States v. Spearin*, 248 U.S. 132 (1918).[60] In that case, detailed plans and specifications issued by the government required the contractor, Spearin, to excavate the site and to relocate and reconstruct a 6-foot brick sewer line that intersected the site. The contract documents did not disclose the existence of a dam on the site. Spearin had no knowledge of the dam and performed its work in accordance with the requirements of the plans and specifications. After construction of the new sewer, the dam (which was located in a connecting sewer) caused the new sewer to burst. The Supreme Court held that the government impliedly warranted the accuracy of plans and specifications that it issued to the contractor and, given the inaccuracy contained therein regarding the existence of the dam, the government could not hold the contractor responsible for the cost of repairing the damage.

As the case law has evolved since the *Spearin* decision, courts have recognized that the *Spearin* implied warranty doctrine encompasses two distinct implied warranties: (1) a warranty that site conditions exist as represented or indicated by the project owner in the contract documents (the "warranty of accuracy") and (2) a warranty that if a contractor follows detailed plans and specifications furnished by the project owner, the result will be a completed project suitable to the use as it was intended (the "warranty of suitability").[61]

A point of controversy and uncertainty in the *Spearin* implied warranty doctrine concerns its applicability in a claim in which the focus is not an inaccurate representation of existing site conditions or deficiencies in the suitability of the completed project (the end result) but a contractor's claim that it incurred delays or additional performance costs due to defects in owner-furnished detailed design and construction documents. In other words, does the *Spearin* implied warranty doctrine apply to a constructor implied warranty claim? Can *Spearin* be used in a claim seeking recovery of delay damages or additional *performance* costs rather than recovery (or avoidance of responsibility) for unanticipated (inaccurately represented) site conditions or costs of correction for some defect (or other unsuitability) in the attainability of the final and completed project work?

Although *Spearin* was initially used as a defense by a constructor (to avoid performing or paying for corrective work), that original application was later expanded to use *Spearin* as the basis for offensive claims by a constructor against the project owner based on defects in owner-furnished detail design that resulted in a failure of the completed project to achieve the intent or objective of the owner-furnished project design. For example, in *Big Chief Drilling Co. v. United States* 26 Ct. Cl. 1276, 1304 (1992), the court stated that if defective design specifications issued by the project owner prevent or delay completion of the contract, the constructor is entitled to recover damages for the owner's breach of the *Spearin* implied warranty obligation. In that case, the court stated that it is well established that the project owner warrants the adequacy of design to the extent that compliance with that design will result in "satisfactory performance." In circumstances in which a constructor is delayed or incurs additional costs due to design deficiencies, the constructor is allowed to recover additional costs resulting from delay due to such design deficiencies.

In the case of *PCL Construction Services, Inc. v. United States*, 47 Fed. Cl 745, 794–800 (2000), the United States Court of Federal Claims rejected a constructor's claims of breach of implied warranty with respect to government-furnished specifications. In that case, the court stated:

> The warranty of government specifications, also sometimes referred to as the "*Spearin* doctrine," provides that if the Government furnishes specifications for the production or construction *of an end product* and proper application of those specifications does not result in a *satisfactory end product*, the contractor will be compensated for its efforts to produce *the end product*, notwithstanding the *unsatisfactory results*. . . . PCL's focus on the performance of the contractor appears to try to expand the *Spearin* doctrine, which focused on the *final product* of the contract, *rather that on the contractor's performance*. It is established in government contract law that the government warrants the performability of the design specifications. . . .
>
> It is also well-established that a contractor cannot prevail by showing that the specifications were less complete than it would have preferred. The courts and boards of contract appeals have repeatedly rejected the notion that the government is liable for difficulties encountered by a contractor because performance specifications supplied by the government were insufficiently detailed to enable the contractor to perform the contract in an efficient or profitable manner. . . .
>
> Contrary to PCL's assertions that [the Government's] fixed price contract carried with it assurances regarding the "standards of care" used to design the project and the degree of certainty which was implied by the term "estimated" in the drawings, there can be no

doubt that PCL assumed substantial risk pursuant to the contract, especially because the contract was largely a performance specification and it was indicated regarding the design provided that supplementation was required. Although this contract, along with any contract that contains a changes and differing site conditions clause, whether fixed-price or not, guaranteed PCL that it would be compensated for costs incurred as a result of Government-directed contract changes and, for example, for material differences between the subsurface conditions depicted in the contract and encountered in the field, it is well-established that "absent unusual circumstances, a fixed-price contractor . . . shoulders the responsibility for unexpected losses, as well as for his failure to appreciate the problems of the undertaking. . . ."

This contract required the successful awardee to construct a complex set of structures in a logistically difficult site in a relatively short period of time. PCL knew this, or should have known this, when it submitted its proposal, and recognized that this project was going to be challenging. It, therefore, should have been evident to PCL that its proposal preparation demanded an especially careful evaluation of the solicitation. . . .

Thus, with regard to whether USBR's [U.S. Department of Interior, Bureau of Reclamation's] design was defective, and not as detailed and complete as PCL would have preferred, the level of detail and completeness was readily ascertainable by a bidder performing a detailed bid estimate, as PCL did. Therefore, PCL "took a calculated risk, the unfortunate consequence of which it must now bear alone. . . ."

Here, PCL's contractual responsibilities included coordinating and implementing a large array of tasks related to the construction of the project, the preparation of a large number of contract submissions and schedules, documentation of construction activities, oversight and inspection, and quality control to insure that its work was contractually compliant. PCL was obligated to perform these activities at a complex and difficult site within a specified time frame. Moreover, PCL was explicitly informed that its obligations would be governed by a contract package containing estimated information, that the contract package was imperfect, and that the contract package would be supplemented and refined as necessary during construction. All of these facts were fully disclosed to PCL during the bid preparation period in USBR's specifications and drawings that were part of the solicitation, and these facts were reiterated for all bidders at USBR's pre-bid conference. After reviewing the extensive evidence presented at trial through the witnesses and the voluminous exhibits, the court finds that the plaintiff's claim for breach of warranty is unsupported.

More recently, the Supreme Court of Ohio also grappled with the boundaries of the *Spearin* implied warranty doctrine. In *Dugan & Meyers Construction Co., Inc. v. Ohio Department of Administrative Services*, 113 Ohio St. 3d 226 (2007), a constructor asserted a claim against a project owner for additional performance costs and delays due to inaccurate, defective, and incomplete plans issued by the project owner. During the progression of the legal dispute, a court-appointed referee, relying upon the *Spearin* implied warranty doctrine, recommended that the constructor be awarded damages for the "cumulative impact" of the excessive number of design changes required during construction. The referee ruled that under the *Spearin* implied warranty doctrine, a constructor has a contractual right to expect complete, accurate, and buildable plans and may recover its damages resulting from the project owner's failure to meet the contractual obligation.

The Supreme Court of Ohio rejected the referee's decision, ruling:

> *Dugan & Meyers* raises as its primary issue the question whether a construction-law doctrine known as the *Spearin* Doctrine is recognized in Ohio and, if so, the parameters of the doctrine. *Dugan & Meyers* suggests that an Owner of a competitively bid construction project impliedly warrants that the plans issued are buildable, accurate, and complete and that a contractor may recover damages if the owner breaches that implied warranty, resulting in delay or increased cost to complete the contract. . . .
>
> *Spearin* involved the existence of a site condition that precluded completion of the construction project. Ohio courts have recognized that the "*Spearin* Doctrine holds that, in cases involving government contracts, the government impliedly warrants the accuracy of its *affirmative indications regarding job site conditions.*" . . . In contrast, the case before us concerns the allocation of damages flowing from *delay* in completion of a construction project due to plan changes. Despite the interest in the *Spearin* Doctrine and the arguments of counsel from the various amici, we decline the opportunity to extend the *Spearin* Doctrine from job-site conditions cases to cases involving delay due to plan changes. . . . This Court has long recognized that "where a contract is plain and unambiguous, it does not become ambiguous by reason of the fact that in its operation it will work a hardship upon one of the parties thereto and a corresponding advantage to the other [and] that it is not the province of courts to relieve parties of improvident contracts.". . .
>
> The Contract in the case at bar contained several relevant provisions, which were valid under Ohio law when the contract was signed. . . . The Contract also contained a no-damages-for-delay clause, which provided that "extension of time granted . . . shall be the sole remedy which may be provided by the Department.". . .
>
> In the case at bar, even if the plans required more changes than originally contemplated, the Contractor established a detailed procedure to be followed for all changes. In order to hold in favor of Dugan & Meyers, we would need, first, to find that the state had implicitly warranted that its plans were buildable, accurate, and complete, and, second, to hold that the implied warranty prevailed over expressed contractual provisions. To do so, would contravene established precedent, which we will not do.
>
> Our decision is in accord with numerous decisions throughout the country. . . .

113 Ohio St. 32 at 230–238

A justice of the Ohio Supreme Court issued a dissenting opinion, stating:

> I dissent. This case calls for an application, not an extension, of [*Spearin*]. As in all *Spearin* Doctrine cases, the fault in this case lies with the owner's plans. It requires no leap to find that the state implicitly warranted that its plans were buildable and that that warranty prevailed over general contract provisions. An owner's plans and specifications must be reliable for the contractual process to work. The majority seems to suggest that an owner need not be concerned with preparing accurate plans, since any deficiencies must be corrected by the contractor. As it turns out, the state could have saved a lot of money on blueprints and just submitted some sketches on the backs of a few cocktail napkins.
>
> In *Spearin*, the contract at issue required the contractor relocate a section of sewer piping as part of the construction of a dry dock. . . . Neither the Government, nor Spearin was aware that the design of the existing sewer system caused a large amount of water to be diverted into the pipe that was to be replaced during periods of heavy water flow. . . . Spearin complied with the contract requirements for the relocation of the sewer pipe, including the location, dimensions, and materials required by the government.
>
> The relocated sewer line proved inadequate and burst in several places after a heavy rainfall, flooding the excavation for the dry dock. . . . Spearin refused to continue working on the project until the government rectified the sewer-line situation. . . . The government argued that the responsibility of remedying existing conditions rested with the contractor. . . . Because Spearin refused to restore the sewer and continue work, the government annulled the contract. . . .
>
> *Spearin* sets forth the general rule of law that the contractor usually assumes the risk of work-site conditions. . . .
>
> But when the Contractor's difficulties are a result of faulty specifications by the Government, the burden changes. . . .
>
> Under *Spearin*, construction changes caused by unexpected site conditions remain the responsibility of the contractor. But when the government's plans themselves are the cause of turmoil, things change: Justice Brandeis recognized [in *Spearin*] that a contractor might well agree to assume risks relevant to design. By stating in his opinion that one who undertakes to erect a structure upon a particular site "assumes ordinarily the risk of subsidence of the soil,". . . Justice Brandeis recorded the obvious assumption that the contractor's responsibility for contract completion begins where the owner's detailed design ends. In essence, the Court recognized that the contractor's right to recovery for the owner's breach of its implied warranty of the adequacy of design was conditioned upon the contractor's reasonable reliance upon the owner's defective design in preparing its bid and in doing the work. 3 *Bruner & O'Connor on Construction Law* (2002), Section 9:78. . . .

Here, the principal cause of the delay, as determined by the finder of fact, was "an excessive number of errors, omissions and conflicts in the design documents furnished to bidders by the State and incorporated into [Dugan & Meyer's] Contracts." There were no shifting sands, no acts of God, no surprising aquifers. As in *Spearin*, the designs themselves were the root of the problem. Here, the contract contained procedures for dealing with design problems, but like the overburdened sewer pipe in *Spearin*, the procedure buckled under the torrent of required design changes.[62]

Id. at 234–238

In effect, these decisions, taken together, appear to be indicating a view that, outside the specific context of indicated or represented (and non-disclaimed) site conditions, the constructor should be responsible for the cost of performing its work and achieving the end result, with entitlement (if any) to additional time or compensation governed by the terms of the contract between the constructor and the project owner. Similarly, a constructor's entitlement to cost or time impact associated with differing or concealed site conditions should be governed by the risk allocation (differing terms, including any concealed conditions provisions) and other disclaimers contained in the contract between the project owner and the constructor.[63] These are fundamentally sound principles that recognize the centrality of contracts in defining and allocating duties, performance obligations, cost, time, site condition, and other risks between them. Third parties should not be allowed to circumvent and subvert their contractually-accepted risk by the assertion of negligent claims for economic damage against consulting engineers, and courts should not countenance such tactics.

7.0 Role of Consulting Engineer in Assisting Project Owner in Defending Third-Party Claims and Investigations

Issue

During the course of a megaproject, there are likely to be a number of events in which a variety of third-parties — e.g., abutters, environmentalists, constructors, public investigatory agencies or bodies — raise issues, commence investigations, or assert claims directly against the project owner that, to a greater or lesser degree, may involve the services or performance of the consulting engineer. To what degree can or should the project owner and consulting engineer work jointly in the defense or otherwise in responding to such third-party issues or claims?[64]

Analysis and Discussion

This is a complex topic, the resolution of which is dependent upon the specific issues, claims, facts, and circumstances presented. Often the resolution of these issues is enhanced by consulting with legal counsel. Consulting engineers have valuable information and perspectives about, as well as candid assessments of and general experience in, third-party situations which, when shared with the project owner or the owner's legal counsel or other independent advisors, provide extremely valuable strategic input that aid in the evaluation and resolution of third-party issues and claims. On the other hand, the issues or claims raised by such third parties may involve, to a greater or lesser degree, matters having to do with the performance of the consulting engineer. Thus, the ultimate interests of the project owner and the consulting engineer may actually or potentially diverge with respect to third-party issues or claims.

Thus, it is always appropriate for the project owner and the consulting engineer to be independently represented by separate legal counsel in connection with such third-party issues or claims. Specifically, it is not appropriate for the project owner to insist that the consulting engineer not involve its own independent counsel or to suggest that the consulting engineer's interests (present or future) may be adequately and jointly represented by the owner's legal counsel. Having said that, and recognizing the actual or potential divergent and conflicting interests of the parties, the consulting engineer's legal counsel should understand that their representation should be undertaken in a collaborative mode with the owner's legal counsel and that the traditional legal model of "zealous advocacy" of one's client must be moderated and tempered to fit the circumstances, given the ongoing and more pervasive professional relationship between the project owner and consulting engineer.[65] To conduct legal affairs otherwise would subvert and turn on its head the macro considerations involved in such a relationship in deference to the discrete and lesser-important third-party issue or claim.

Recommended Practices

- Develop a relationship with the project owner in which the owner recognizes and acknowledges the value that a consulting engineer typically contributes to the response to and defense of third-party issues and claims, and the need for the consulting engineer to have independent legal representation in such situations.
- While it is appropriate in certain situations for the consulting engineer to be reimbursed for its legal fees in such matters, the payment of such reimbursement does not establish an attorney-client relationship between the project owner and the consulting engineer's legal counsel, and the latter at all times represents only the consulting engineer.

- The fact that the project owner and the consulting engineer may align in the defense and response to third-party issues or claims should not impair the independent professional judgment or opinion of the consulting engineer.

- Early in the megaproject, establish a relationship with legal counsel who is experienced in the legal and related issues of megaprojects and who understands the importance of "working together" in alignment with the owner and its legal counsel generally, and especially on such third-party issues and claims. Often this is best provided by a combination of legal counsel with significant megaproject experience and qualifications and legal counsel with more local or political experience or contacts.

- Notwithstanding the potential that a third-party issue or claim involving the consulting engineer's performance may lead to an eventual professional liability claim by the project owner (or others) against it, the consulting engineer should always be candid in providing information and advice to the project owner concerning the subject at issue. However, in such situations, there must always be a tension and balancing between the obligation of the consulting engineer to professionally serve the project owner and the need to protect its own interest. In some circumstances, the actual or potential tension may warrant the advisability of the consulting engineer recommending that the project owner retain an independent professional consultant to provide specific assistance relative to the third-party issue or claim, especially if the consulting engineer's performance may impair the credibility or value of the consulting engineer in providing assistance to the project owner.

- Notwithstanding the importance of a strong and positive relationship between the owner and consulting engineer in a specific megaproject context, the consulting engineer should not lose sight of the importance of protecting its own interest with respect to third-party claims and investigations. While it may presently appear that the interests of the owner and consulting engineer are united, those interests may (and are likely to subsequently) diverge.

Notes

1. Klein v. Catalano, 386 Mass. 701, 718, 437 N.E.2d 514, (1982); Allensworth et al., *Construction Law*, chapter 6, § 6.04.
2. Under the fast-track approach, construction may start before the entire project design is completed. In substance, this results in the potential for both the design and construction phases to overlap. The expectation is that the collapsing of these two phases will shorten the overall project schedule. Notwithstanding schedule compression and other advantages to the project owner,

there are disadvantages to using the fast-track approach, particularly with respect to potential professional liability of the consulting engineer:

> The principal disadvantage of fast-tracking is the incomplete design. The contractor will be asked to give some price — usually after design has reached a certain stage of completion. Very likely the contract price will be cost plus overhead and profit, with the owner usually obtaining a guaranteed maximum price (GMP). However, the evolution of the design through a fast-tracking system is likely to generate claims. Completing the design and redesigning can generate a claim that the contract has become one simply for cost, overhead, and profit and that any GMP has been eliminated. The owner may be constrained in making design changes by the possibility that the contractor will assert that the completed drawings must be consistent with the incomplete drawings.
>
> Two other potential disadvantages need to be mentioned here. First, there is greater likelihood that there will be design omissions — items "falling between the cracks." Needed work is not incorporated in the design given to any of the specialty trade contractors or subcontractors. Although such omissions can occur in any design, they are more likely to occur when the design is being created piecemeal rather than prepared in its entirety for submission to a prime contractor.
>
> Second, in fast-tracking there is a greater likelihood that one participant may not do what it has promised, and thus adversely affect the work of many other participants. . . .

Sweet & Schneier, *Legal Aspects of Architecture*, § 27.04.B, 353; *see also* P. Halls, B. Nodzon, & N. Brennaman, "Design Professionals and the Design-Build Project," chapter 5 in Stephen Hess et al., eds., *Design Professional and Construction Manager Law*, Chicago: American Bar Ass'n, 2007, 126–27.

In an article by Tom Sorel, "The Life Cycle Continuum," *Public Roads* 68 (July/August 2004), Sorel, commenting on fast-track, stated that in the course of assessing a megaproject and its phases, a management decision may be presented as to whether to employ fast-tracking, which is usually defined as "compressing a project's schedule by overlapping activities that would normally be done in sequence. Early completion of a project can provide numerous cost and other benefits, but fast-tracking itself can have costs, such as those resulting from change orders associated with completing design after construction contracts have been awarded. The key is careful analysis, as well as managing the expectations of the public and other stakeholders."

In *Broken Buildings, Busted Budgets* (University of Chicago Press, 2007, pp. 171–72), B. LePatner made the following observations about fast-track:

> . . . Time is money and other arguments for commencing construction as quickly as possible are well known, but beware that the Owner's risk rises rapidly using fast-track. Under fast-track, no construction manager can or will provide realistic assurances that the initial proposed project budget or preliminary GMP will be finalized into a final GMP of the same amount, let alone that the final construction cost will be less than the GMP. Construction

Managers explain that they have no control over the material market place or over the cost of labor. Moreover, since fast-track construction commences before the project design is finalized, the Owner effectively loses the opportunity to re-bid the project if the final GMP prepared by the Construction Manager far exceeds the Owner's budget. Reducing scope at that point will have an enormous ripple effect that likely impacts the schedule, negating any advantage the fast-track process might have yielded.

By agreeing to a fast-track process, the Owner gives up control over the pricing and schedule to the Construction Manager who bears little risk if the budget is exceeded or the project encounters serious delays. By avoiding the fast-track and committing the Architect extra time to complete the critical construction documents, the Owner has the opportunity to secure a fixed price for the work shown on the drawings. If there are errors or omissions detected, the Construction Manager or Contractor will be given the time to assist in identifying them *before* they impact the schedule and lead to large claims.

3. D. Hatem, "Errors/Omissions Cost Recovery Claims Against Design and Construction Management Professionals," *The CA/T Professional Liability Reporter* (Boston: June 1996). Of course, it is possible, although not advisable, that the professional contractually agree to perform in accordance with a standard (such as a warranty of perfection) that exceeds the professional standard of care. Hatem, *Subsurface Conditions*, § 10.1.1.1, pp. 261–67.

4. D. Hatem, *Subsurface Conditions*, § 10.1.1.2, at 267–69.

5. Actual conduct of the professional in the performance of professional services may vary from the contractually required scope, obligations, and/or professional standard of care and, as such, actual conduct is a relevant factor to consider in determining legal liability of the professional. As a general matter, consulting engineers should perform services or otherwise conduct themselves in a manner consistent with their contractually-defined roles, responsibilities, and service scope.

6. *See* discussion in § 4 of chapter 15.

7. *See* discussion in § 4 of chapter 15.

8. For a discussion of project owner cost recovery, *see Highway Contract Claims Avoiding/Handling*, Vol. 1, Federal Highway Administration, Course No. 13437, Mar. 1991, pp. 47–48, and Appendix F, 48 CFR 52.236-23, "Responsibility of the Architect-Engineer Contractor"; M. Markow, "Best Practices in the Management of Design Errors and Omissions," NCHRP Project 20-07, Task 225, National Cooperative Highway Research Program, Transportation Research Board, Mar. 2009; F. E. William East, Construction Engineering Research Laboratory, *Opportunities for Design Quality Improvement Through Architects/Engineers (A/E) Liability Management* No. P-88/13t, Champaign, IL: CERL (NTIS Accession No. ADA199967), 1988; D. J. Hatem, "Errors/Omissions Cost Recovery Claims Against Design and Construction Management Professionals," *The CA/T Professional Liability Reporter*, Vol. 1, No.4 (Boston: June 1996).

9. *See, e.g.,* "Analysis of Bechtel/Parsons Brinckerhoff's Reply to *The Boston Globe's* Investigative

News Series Concerning the Big Dig," Office of the Inspector General, Commonwealth of Massachusetts, Feb. 2003, pub. no. 18327-50-02/03-IGO.

10. Sweet & Schneier, *Legal Aspects of Architecture*, § 14.04 F, p. 246.

11. Generally, a consulting engineer should not participate in a cost recovery matter regarding the performance or judgment of another consultant when the consulting engineer's performance itself (or the performance of others for whom it may be responsible) is or reasonably could be at issue. Given concerns about the perception of conflict, consulting engineers in this position should err on the side of non-involvement.

12. *See* D. Hatem, "Public Owner Programs for Design Professional Accountability and Project-Specific Professional Liability Insurance: Functional Alignment," *Transportation Research Board Presentation*, Jan. 2008; R. Fogle, "Managing Client Expectations," *Proceedings of the 46th Annual Meeting of Invited Attorneys*, May 18, 2007; ACEC National Risk Management Committee, "The Cost of Perfection in Public Works Projects and Cost Recovery Policy Issues for Department of Transportation," 2006; D. Hatem "Errors/Omissions Cost Recovery Claims Against Design and Construction Management Professionals," *The CA/T Professional Liability Reporter* (Boston: June 1996).

13. It has been observed that generally the more conservative, traditional and "robust" the design, the more manageable and predictable the risk exposures on a megaproject; conversely, the more innovative and unproven the design approach, the less manageable and predictable the risk exposures. H. Bruijn & M. Leijten, "Management Characteristics of Mega-Projects," chapter 2 in Priemus et al., *Decision-Making*, pp. 25–27.

14. For a discussion, the professional liability risk associated with innovative design approaches, products, processes and technologies, *see* D. Hatem, "Green and Sustainable Design: Part I: Professional Liability Risk and Insurability Issues for Design Professionals," *Design and Construction Management Professional Reporter* (June 2010).

15. In a series of articles, Bent Flyvbjerg has identified several factors and characteristics that account for risk and cost overruns on megaprojects; specifically: "[l]ong planning horizons and complex interfaces between the project and its context, and between different parts of the project"; "[d]ecision making, policy and planning are often multi-actor processes with conflicting interests"; "[o]ften the project scope or ambition level change significantly over time"; and "[u]nplanned events are often unaccounted for, leaving budget and other contingencies sorely inadequate." B. Flyvbjerg, "Truth and Lies About Megaprojects," inaugural speech to the Faculty of Technology, Policy, and Management, Delft University of Technology, Sep. 26, 2007. In other articles, Flyvbjerg added to these factors and characteristics that "[t]echnology is often not standard." B. Flyvbjerg, "Policy and Planning for Large Infrastructure Projects: Problems, Causes, Cures," World Bank Policy Research Working Paper 3781, Dec. 2005; B. Flyvbjerg, "How Optimism Bias and Strategic Misrepresentation in Early Project Development Undermine Implementation," *Concept Program*, No. 17, Chapter 3, The Norwegian University of Science and Technology, 2007, 41–55; B. Flyvbjerg, "Policy and Planning for Large-Infrastructure Projects: Problems, Causes, Cures," *World Bank Policy Research Working Paper* no. WPS 3781, Washington, DC, 2005.

16. According to R. Capka, megaprojects are different from the ordinary project in several important respects: size, complexity, complex procurement contracting, controversy, time, scope creep, urban setting, human and environmental impacts, risk and uncertainty. R. Capka, "Megaprojects — They Are a Differing Breed," *Public Roads,* July/Aug. 2004. In the same article, Capka states that megaprojects need to garner and maintain public support, emphasizing the requirement for project proponents managing the project in a "fish bowl," and "managing public expectations, being attentive to the potential for waste, fraud and abuse."

17. *See, e.g.,* D. Hatem, "Risk Allocation and Dispute Resolution on Construction Projects: Roles and Challenges for Legal Counsel," *The CA/T Professional Liability Reporter* (Boston: June 1997), and sources referenced therein.

18. R. Smith, "Allocation of Risk — The Case for Manageability," *Int'l Construction L. Rev.,* (1996): 549.

19. B. Flyvbjerg, "Machiavellian Megaprojects," *Antipode* 37 (Jan. 2005): 18–22. In another article, B. Flvvbjerg, has stated that "Professional and occasionally even criminal penalties should be enforced for planners and forecasters who consistently and foreseeably produce deceptive forecasts. An example of a professional penalty would be the exclusion from one's professional organization if one violates its code of ethics. An example of a criminal penalty would be punishment as a result of prosecution before a court for similar legal set-up, for instance where deceptive forecasts have led to substantial mismanagement of public funds. . . . Malpractice in planning should be taken as seriously as it is in other professions. Failing to do this amounts to not taking the profession of planning seriously." B. Flyvbjerg, "Policy and Planning for Large Infrastructure Projects: Problems, Causes, Cures," *World Bank Policy Research Working Paper* no. WPS 3781, 24-25. *See also* B. Flyvbjerg, "Public Planning of Megaprojects: Overestimation of Demand and Underestimation of Costs," in H. Priemus et al., *Decision-Making.*

20. On the CA/T Project, the project owner's cost recovery "team" referred to the recovery of such damages as "reparations."

21. B. Flyvbjerg, M. S. Holm, & S. Buhl, "Underestimating Costs in Public Works Projects Error or Lie?" *APA Journal,* 68 (Summer 2002): 279, 281. *See also* B. Flyvbjerg, M. Garbulo, D. Lavallo, "Delusion and Deception in Large Infrastructure Projects: Two Models for Explaining and Preventing Executive Disaster," 51 *Cal. Mgmt. Rev.* 170 (2009); B. Flyvbjerg, "Optimism and Misrepresentation in Early Project Development," in T. Williams, K. Samset, K. Sunnevag, eds., *Making Essential Choices with Scant Information; Front-End Decision Making in Major Projects,* New York: Palgrave MacMillan, 2009.

22. J. Reilly, "Towards Reliable Cost Estimates," *T&T North America,* Sept. 2003.

23. B. Flyvbjerg, N. Bruzelius, & W. Rothengatter, *Megaprojects and Risk: An Anatomy of Ambition,* Cambridge: Cambridge University Press, 2003, 11–12.

24. J. Reilly, "Towards Reliable Cost Estimates"; J. Reilly, "Probable Cost Estimating and Risk Management," *North American Tunneling 2008 Proceedings,* p. 576. Issues associated with lack of realism in cost estimating, lack of accountability and transparency, and conflicting interests of various project stakeholders have been cited as reasons why the World Trade Center rebuild project

in New York reportedly is several billion dollars over budget and will be delayed several years. *See* "World Trade Center Assessment Report, June 30, 2008," prepared by the Executive Director of the Port Authority of New York & New Jersey.

25. B. Flyvbjerg, N. Bruzelius, W. Rothengatter, *Megaprojects and Risk*; United States General Accounting Office, "Federal-Aid Highways: Cost and Oversight of Major Highway and Bridge Projects—Issues and Options," GAO-03-764T, Washington, DC, May 2003; Editorial, "Megaprojects Cause Megaheadaches When Focus In Lost," *Engineering News Record*, October 25, 2004, p. 82 (11).

26. Flyvbjerg, Bruzelius, & Rothengatter, *Megaprojects and Risk,* p. 16.

27. N. Bruzelius, B. Flyvberg, & W. Rothengatter, "Big Decisions, Big Risks: Improving Accountability in Megaprojects," *Int'l Rev. of Admin. Scis.* 64 (Sept. 1998): 424–25.

28. M. Wachs, "Ethics and Advocacy in Forecasting for Public Policy," *Bus. & Prof'l Ethics J.* 9 (1 & 2) (1991): 141, 145. Robert Caro, the biographer for Robert Moses, master planner for many of New York City's major bridges, tunnels, and highways, wrote:

> "Once you sink that first stake," he [Moses] would often say, "they'll never make you pull it up." . . . [I]f ends justified means, and if the important thing in building a project was to get it started, then any means that got it started were justified. Furnishing misleading information about it was justified; so was underestimating its costs.
>
> Misleading and underestimating, in fact, might be the only way to get a project started. Since his projects were unprecedentedly vast, one of the biggest difficulties in getting them started was the fear of public officials . . . that the state couldn't afford the projects, [which] beneficial though they may be, would drain off a share of the state's wealth incommensurate with their benefits.
>
> But what if you didn't tell the officials how much the projects would cost? What if you let the legislators know about only a fraction of what you knew would be the project's ultimate expense?
>
> Once they had authorized that small initial expenditure and you had spent it, they would not be able to avoid giving you the rest when you asked for it. How could they? If they refuse to give you the rest of the money, what they had given you would be wasted, and that would make them look bad in the eyes of the public. And if they said you had mislead them, well, they were not supposed to be mislead. If they had been mislead, that would mean they hadn't investigated the projects thoroughly, and had therefore been derelict in their own duty. The possibilities for a polite, but effective form of political blackmail were endless.

R. Caro, *The Power Broker: Robert Moses and the Fall of New York*, New York: Vintage Books, 1975, 218–19.

29. Flyvbjerg et al., *Megaprojects and Risk*.

30. Flyvbjerg et al., *Megaprojects and Risk*, 282.

31. Flyvbjerg et al., *Megaprojects and Risk*, 28.

32. This and related project owner practices may lead to public law liability exposures. *See In the*

Matter of the Massachusetts Turnpike Authority and James J. Kerasiotes, United States Securities and Exchange Commission, Order Instituting Cease-and-Desist Proceedings, Making Findings, and Imposing Cease-and-Desist Order Pursuant to Section 8A of the Securities Act of 1933, Administrative Proceeding File No.: 3-11198, Release No. 8260, July 31, 2003.

33. Bruzelius et al., *Big Decisions, Big Risks*, p. 423.

34. Flyvbjerg et al., *Megaprojects and Risk*, p. 281.

35. Flyvbjerg et al., *Megaprojects and Risk*, p. 5. *See generally* R. Shorland, "The Importance of Transparency and Communication in the Creation of Infrastructure Projects," *Int'l Construction L. Rev.*, 18 (2001): 386. In an article entitled "Towards Reliable Cost Estimates" (*Tunnels & Tunneling North America*, Sep. 2003, p. 4), John Reilly succinctly reinforced these points in stating that "more open transparency and accountability by public officials is needed to restore full credibility."

36. R. Smith, "Allocation of Risk — The Case for Manageability," *Int'l Construction L. Rev.*, (1996): 549.

37. In addition, the failure to timely, accurately, clearly, and fairly identify and allocate risk will lead to the higher probability of disappointed expectations of project participants and related disputes among them, resulting in negative consequences to both project cost and schedule. R. Smith, "Allocation of Risk — The Case for Manageability"; J. Diekmann & M. Girard, "Are Contract Disputes Predictable?" *J. of Construction Engineering & Mgmt* 121 (Dec. 1995): 355.

38. Flyvbjerg et al., *Megaprojects and Risk*, p. 6.

39. Flyvbjerg et al., *Megaprojects and Risk*, pp. 11–12.

40. Flyvbjerg et al., *Megaprojects and Risk*, p. 73. In the area of professional liability risk exposure, however, insurance should be considered a "default" mechanism, with the primary and most effective risk allocation and management issues being addressed through contractual provisions, risk management plans, and sound quality control and related professional practices. *See generally* Construction Industry Institute, *Allocation of Insurance-Related Risks and Costs on Construction Projects*, Pub. 19-1, Austin, TX: Construction Industry Institute, 1993, 102. For an excellent discussion of the importance of risk management practices in mitigating exposures due to external risk factors, *see* D. Lane, "Risk Management — A Practical View," *Tunnels & Tunneling Int'l* (Dec. 2003).

41. Reilly, "Towards Reliable Cost Estimates"; J. Reilly, M. McBride, D. Sangrey, D. MacDonald, & J. Brown, "The Development of a New Cost-Risk Estimating Process for Transportation Infrastructure Projects," *Civ. Engineering Prac.* (Spring/Summer 2004): 53–75.

42. J. Reilly, "Managing Costs of Complex, Underground and Infrastructure Projects," American Underground Construction Association Regional Conference, Seattle, Mar. 19, 2001.

43. Reilly, "Managing Costs of Complex, Underground and Infrastructure Projects."

44. *Report of the ONE DOT Task Force on Oversight of Large Transportation Infrastructure Projects* (July 11, 2005), p. 15.

45. Consulting engineers have limited ability to estimate project cost with precise accuracy that reflects market and other economic factors, even though "overbudget" projects often lead to professional liability claims against them. L. Melton & B. Autry, "Beyond His Power to Build It: Who Is to Blame for the Overbudget Project?" *The Construction Lawyer* 25 (Winter 2005): 20.

477

46. *See* discussion in § 4 of chapter 14.

47. R. Capka, in "A Well-Conceived Plan Will Pull It All Together," *Public Roads* 68 (July/Aug. 2004): 7

48. *See generally* T. Scanlan & L. Malone, "The Design Professional and Tort Liability," in Stephen Hess et al., eds., *Design Professional and Construction Manager Law*, 145, 151–52, Chicago: American Bar Association, 2007; Sweet & Schneier, *Legal Aspects of Architecture*, § 11.04B, pp. 160–63.

49. *See*, "Architects and Clients Do Not Per Se Have a Fiduciary Relationship," *Construction Litigation Reporter*, Sep. 2007, p. 356.

50. *See*, J. Atkins and G. Simpson, *Managing Project Risk: Best Practices for Architects and Related Professionals*, Ch. 5, pp. 174–76, Hoboken, NJ: Wiley, 2008; Sweet & Schneier, *Legal Aspects of Architecture*, § 22.07, p. 495.

51. In general, certification forms promulgated by the AIA, AIA Document B103–2007, should minimize the risk of potential FCA liability. *See also* AIA Document G702–1992.

52. United States *ex rel.* Ali v. [CM Professional Firm], 355 F.3d 1140 (9th Cir. 2004).

53. In other legal contexts — such as the ability of a constructor to assert negligent misrepresentation claims against a design professional (not in privity with the constructor) — recent court decisions have reached determinations that such claims lack merit as a matter of law based on reasoning similar to that expressed in these FCA cases. *See* D. Hatem, "The Pendulum Begins to Swing Back: Recent Judicial Limitations on the Negligent Misrepresentation Exception to the Economic Loss and to the *Spearin* Implied Warranty Doctrines," *Design and Construction Management Professional Reporter* (Jan. 2008), pp. 9–19 (hereinafter, "The Pendulum Begins to Swing Back").

54. Note the implications of a government knowledge defense for consulting engineer professional liability if the constructor alleges that the direction to deviate from contractual requirements came from the consulting engineer or that the latter was aware of the deviation and explicitly or implicitly waived the contract requirement.

55. C. Spink and K. Pages, eds., *False Claims in Construction Contracts*, Chicago: American Bar Ass'n, 2007, p. 67. In addition to traditional professional liability claims, the management consultant and various constructors involved in the Central Artery/Tunnel Project were subjected to FCA claims.

56. This was the situation in United States *ex rel.* Ali v. [CM Professional Firm], 355 F.3d 1140 (9th Cir. 2004).

57. *See* discussion in § 7 below.

58. *See* D. Hatem, "The Pendulum Begins to Swing Back," pp. 9–19.

59. See D. Hatem, ed., *Subsurface Condition*, §§ 10.2.4, 10.2.5.

60. Sweet & Schneier, *Legal Aspects of Architecture*, § 23.05E, pp. 515–21; W. Allensworth et al., *Construction Law*, §§ 3.04, 22.04.

61. S. Stein in *Construction Law*, § 18.02.

62. *See* M. Schneier, "No-Damages-For-Delay Clause Precludes a Contractor's Recovery of Delay Damages Under the Implied Warranty of Design," No. 6 *Construction Litig. Re.* 5 (2007): 28 (stating that *Dugan & Meyers* made clear that, under the *Spearin* implied warranty doctrine, the gov-

ernment [only] impliedly warrants the accuracy of its affirmative indications regarding *job site conditions*; the doctrine does *not* apply to a claim of delay damages caused by defective design where the design itself was buildable).

63. *See, e.g., S&M Constructors, Inc. v. City of Columbus*, 70 Ohio St. 2d 69 (1982) (holding that specific contractual disclaimers for accuracy of site conditions preclude recovery under more general *Spearin* implied warranty doctrine).

64. See R. Crist, R. Preston, and M. Eyth, "Joint Defense Agreements Between Owners and Design Professionals," *The Construction Lawyer* (American Bar Ass'n Spring 2009), p. 35. In a related context, there are many benefits to joint defense agreements among multiple design professionals. D. Hatem, *Joint Defense Agreements in Construction Disputes Involving Design Professionals: An Approach to Effective Dispute Management* (Victor O. Schinnerer, 2002).

65. *See*, D. Hatem, "Risk Allocation and Dispute Resolution on Construction Projects: Roles and Challenges of Legal Counsel," *The Central Artery/Tunnel Professional Liability Reporter*, Boston: June 1997; D. Hatem, "Megaproject Issues and Challenges: Some Informal Remarks," *Design and Construction Management Professional Reporter*. Boston: Oct. 2009.

CHAPTER 17

Subsurface Megaprojects

David J. Hatem, PC, Donovan Hatem LLP

Introduction

Subsurface megaprojects involve major subsurface or underground components. Why a special focus in this chapter on subsurface megaprojects?

All subsurface projects pose a substantial potential of encountering conditions different from those anticipated (so-called differing site conditions) that can (and often do) significantly increase the expected cost and/or time for the completion of the project and, hence, seriously disappoint programmatic, planning, schedule, cost, contractual risk, and commercial expectations of major project participants. Often, these differing site conditions are encountered early in the project schedule and result in substantial reduction or exhaustion of the planned or available contingency funds. On subsurface megaprojects — by virtue of their typically linear, sequential, and interdependent construction approach and components — these differing site conditions can have consequential impacts that manifest themselves early in the project work and have a significant negative impact on critical path, leading stakeholders to believe that they were seduced into supporting or funding a project that was destined — only shortly after the "first shovel is in the ground" — to be significantly over budget, behind schedule, and prone to disputes and claims among project participants because of seriously disappointed expectations.[1] Project owners and their consulting engineers, in these circumstances, soon become the target of allegations of poor project planning and design judgments.

The cost "added" to address and compensate for these differing site conditions — while necessary to implement and progress the project — is rarely viewed by the public, other stakeholders, and sometimes even the project owner as adding any value or benefit to the completed project. In addition, the construction process in subsurface megaprojects is often disruptive to the public; in such circumstances, continued public and stakeholder funding and support is difficult to sustain over the long haul, especially when the project is over budget and behind schedule.

Simply put, in general, subsurface projects pose the risk of serious disappointment in cost and schedule expectations and, on megaprojects, that risk (like virtually all fac-

High-speed Shinkansen ("new trunk line," also known as "bullet") trains at a facility in Hakata on the island of Kyushu. At the far left is a Series N700 engine. Next to it is a Series 500 train. The third train is a Series 700 engine (there are three others in the photograph). The fourth and seventh from the left are Series 300 trains. The trains' operating speeds vary from 270 to 300 km/hr. Photo © 2008 by Rsa.

ets of megaprojects) is significantly magnified. As will be discussed in this chapter, the probability of disappointed expectations that are inherent in subsurface megaprojects significantly increases the prospect of professional liability claims against the consulting engineer.

The key to the management of risk and realization of project participant expectations on subsurface megaprojects lies in the development of appropriate measures for the planning, design, construction, and risk allocation. The prudent and successful implementation of these measures can significantly reduce the potential professional liability risk exposure for the consulting engineer.

1.0   Risk Identification: Adequacy of Subsurface Investigation

Issue

How does a project owner's pre-construction subsurface investigation program relate to professional liability exposure of the consulting engineer?

Analysis and Discussion

The most prominent risk on subsurface projects is that the actual subsurface conditions encountered will materially differ from those anticipated in the design, cost estimating, planning, scheduling, selection of construction means and methods, and procurement of equipment. The materialization of this risk dramatically impacts—often negatively—the expectations of all major project participants. This risk can never be entirely eliminated; rather, the focus in project planning realistically should be directed to minimizing both the occurrence of the risk and its impact.

The planning, definition, and implementation of an adequate pre-construction subsurface investigation program is essential to minimizing and mitigating the occurrence and impact of encountering unanticipated subsurface conditions during the construction process.[2] Typically, on design-bid-build projects, the project owner has responsibility for planning, definition, and implementation of such a program.

The design and implementation of both permanent project work and construction means and methods depends upon reasonably accurate and reliable information about subsurface conditions expected to be encountered during construction. Encountering subsurface conditions materially different from those anticipated during the design phase may require redesign or, at a minimum, re-evaluation of initial design or planning and work method assumptions at an untimely point during the construction process.

In addition, the encountering of such conditions during construction often results in

equitable adjustment claims by the constructor for additional time and/or cost. While the extent to which such claims are made, and the degree of uncertainty and contentiousness associated with them, largely depends upon the contractual risk allocation and dispute resolution provisions, the adequacy of the pre-construction subsurface investigation will strongly influence the frequency, magnitude, and potential for the containment of such claims and disputes.

Undoubtedly, the extent of subsurface investigation will impact front-end project costs. However, the cost and schedule impact of addressing untimely design changes during construction, the revision of anticipated construction means and methods, and the resolution of constructor claims and disputes — due to differing site conditions encountered during construction — must be balanced in considering whether to expend those front-end costs. In virtually all cases, the expenditure of such front-end costs is well advised.

Once the subsurface investigation program is completed, the project owner needs to make important decisions about what to do with the products of that investigation. In general terms, those products fall into two classifications regarding anticipated subsurface conditions: (1) data and (2) interpretations (or opinions). Important issues for project owner decision at this point include:

- What subsurface condition data or interpretations should be provided to bidders?
- Should both data and interpretations be provided to bidders?
- Should any subsurface condition information be accompanied by disclaimers negating the bidder's right to rely upon the accuracy or completeness of the information?
- Should geotechnical baseline reports be prepared and provided to bidders?

These and related issues will be addressed in § 5. The point to emphasize here, however, is that the availability of options regarding decisions about these issues and the quality of any subsurface condition data and interpretations will be influenced by the adequacy and quality of the subsurface investigation.

In yet another important respect, the extent and nature of the subsurface investigation program will have an important, albeit indirect, impact on potential professional liability risk exposure of the consulting engineer.[3] As a general matter, the more information about subsurface conditions available, the more reliable the design assumptions and the more likely development of a design responsive to subsurface conditions. The less subsurface condition information available, the higher degree of uncertainty about the ultimate applicability of design assumptions or the ability to execute the design without significant revision caused by encountering unanticipated subsurface conditions encountered during construction. Moreover, the amount and quality of information about subsurface conditions available prior to the start of construction should better inform and guide the constructor's opportunity to reliably plan (and design) con-

struction means and methods and make prudent decisions regarding selection of construction equipment options.

The comprehensiveness and quality of the subsurface condition investigation can have an impact on the ability of the consulting engineer to perform its services and on the constructor to plan and perform its work. Although inadequate subsurface investigation may not necessarily be the responsibility of the consulting engineer, if inadequate information results in a need for design revision during construction or for material changes in the constructor's contemplated means, methods, or selected equipment, this often leads to claims against or involving the consulting engineer. These claims typically assert inadequate subsurface investigation, negligent interpretation or description of anticipated conditions in reports or in the contract documents, unconstructability, or design deficiencies.

Observations and Recommended Practices

- Project owners should request advice from their consulting engineers about the planning, definition, and scope of a subsurface investigation program. The cost of such a program typically is relatively small compared to the resultant costs that are likely to be incurred during construction and thereafter in the claims process due to inadequate subsurface investigation and the cost of addressing design revision during construction and differing site condition claims.

- No subsurface investigation program should be expected to be perfect or entirely complete in predicting anticipated subsurface conditions; however, the less subsurface investigation that is conducted, the greater the likelihood of disappointed expectations.

- On subsurface megaprojects, there is a significant potential for disappointed contractual and commercial expectations of both the project owner and constructor caused by differing site conditions resulting from inadequate subsurface investigation—a matter largely within the control and responsibility of the project owner's decision-making.

- Consulting engineers should make and document informed recommendations to project owners regarding the scope of subsurface investigation reasonably required to support the successful planning, reliable cost and schedule estimates, and the design and construction of the project.

- An adequate subsurface investigation program will maximize the opportunity for options requiring subsurface condition report preparation and information dissemination.

- Project owners should disclose to bidders all available subsurface condition data.

2.0   Risk Allocation for Subsurface Conditions

Issue

How should subsurface condition risk be allocated between project owner and constructor? To what extent do decisions regarding project owner–constructor subsurface condition risk allocation affect professional liability exposure of the consulting engineer?

Analysis and Discussion

Section 1 of chapter 15 addressed basic principles of control, clarity, consistency, and fairness that should govern project owner risk allocation decision-making. These principles apply with equal — if not paramount — relevance and significance specifically to risk allocation decision-making for subsurface conditions.[4] The manner in which these risk allocation decisions are made will influence the frequency and magnitude of project owner–constructor claims and disputes regarding differing site conditions, the impact of such differing conditions on the overall project cost and schedule, and the professional liability exposure of the consulting engineer.[5]

The adequacy of the subsurface investigation program is essential to effective risk allocation for subsurface conditions. More specifically, the degree to which informed decisions may be made about risk allocation for subsurface conditions by both the project owner and constructor depends upon the reliability, accuracy, and comprehensiveness of information derived from the subsurface investigation program.

Project owners have options in deciding how to allocate performance, cost, and time impacts associated with the encountering of differing site conditions.[6] On public projects, those options may be limited by state or federal laws that mandate the use of differing site condition clauses under which the project owner and constructor are entitled to claim equitable adjustments in cost or time due to the encountering of site conditions that are materially different from those indicated in the contract documents. However, in the absence of legal requirements mandating the inclusion of such differing site condition clauses, project owners have a range of available options with respect to subsurface condition risk allocation.[7]

These options include, from one end of the spectrum, the allocation by the owner of all subsurface condition risk to the constructor, to, on the other end, the contractual sharing of the risk with the constructor. Even when a differing site condition clause is utilized, there are several mechanisms available for its implementation. For example, a differing site condition clause may be used in conjunction with a baseline report, which sets forth an objective definition of subsurface condition "indications" contained in the contract documents. The contract documents may state or define whether the constructor may rely only upon data or interpretations as well; the use of disclaimers about the

accuracy or completeness of subsurface information or the ability of the constructor to rely upon that information; the method by which equitable adjustments will be determined (i.e., unit price); the extent to which consequential or impact costs may be recoverable; and the method by which differing site condition claims will be resolved. All of these contractual mechanisms (and the project owner's selection and decisions regarding the same) will have a significant effect on risk allocation for differing site conditions — even in situations in which a differing site condition clause or other form of subsurface condition risk sharing provision is included in the contract documents.

On a subsurface megaproject, decisions regarding risk allocation and the contractual mechanisms to implement them are among the most important decisions in the planning of the project. While these undoubtedly are the project owner's decisions, the consulting engineer in many instances has the ability and opportunity to advise and inform the owner in a valuable and meaningful way in the making of these decisions. From a purely legal perspective, the option of allocating all subsurface condition risk to the constructor (assuming it is legally permissible) may seem attractive to the project owner. Superficially, this "all risk to the constructor" approach is intended to insulate the project owner from all costs or time impacts attributable to differing site conditions.[8] However, this option *appears* to be a lot better than it may ultimately prove to be in reality for the project owner. Specifically, there are several potential adverse consequences associated with the "all risk to the constructor" approach:

1. Responsible constructors cognizant of the risk associated with this approach may well decline to submit bids.

2. Other constructors who elect to bid may attempt to hedge against the risk by including some undisclosed contingency to attempt to guess and thereby "address" the materialization of the risk.

3. There is a substantial risk that adversarial relations and ensuing disputes will arise if risk is disproportionately and unfairly allocated to the constructor.

4. While the constructor's contractual remedies may be negated or extremely limited under the "all risk" approach, constructors may resort to other "extra-contractual" remedies predicated upon legal theories of misrepresentation, fraud, superior knowledge, or breach of implied warranties.[9]

5. In the event that the burden of the "all risk" approach becomes too onerous in the performance and on the financial resources of the constructor, there is a significant potential that the constructor will default or otherwise become unable to complete its contract obligations, resulting in a late or over-budget completion of the project (particularly, if subsurface work is a major component of the project scope or performance).

These are but some of the potential adverse consequences associated with using the "all risk" approach. In many respects, the perceived risk-shifting benefit of the "all risk to the constructor" approach is more illusory than real in terms of the risk-insulating protection it affords to the project owner.

At the end of the day, project participants have a reasonable right to expect that their contractual risk allocation decisions will be respected by courts, arbitrators, dispute review boards, or others requested and empowered to resolve their differing site condition claims and disputes.[10] However, that expectation is not always realized. Dispute resolvers should not second-guess the wisdom or judgment underlying contractual risk allocation decisions of project participants, but that is more likely to occur when those dispute resolvers sense that risk has been disproportionately or unfairly allocated.

For this basic reason (which is more extensively discussed in § 5, below), the consulting engineer should take more than a casual interest in how risk is allocated between the project owner and the constructor. Indeed, the consulting engineer does have a very direct interest in that issue, given the heightened risk of professional liability exposure that may result if project owner–constructor risk is inappropriately addressed between the latter parties.[11] To the maximum achievable extent, the consulting engineer should endeavor to influence the project owner to adhere to sound risk allocation principles and appropriate contracting practices in connection with the procurement and negotiation of project owner–constructor agreements.

Recommended Practices

- Project owners should authorize an adequate subsurface investigation program to provide the foundation for informed subsurface condition risk allocation decision making and project planning.[12]

- Project owners should make subsurface condition risk allocation decisions in accordance with the recognized principles of control, clarity, consistency, and fairness.

- Risk allocation decisions should be expressed and implemented in a clear and consistent manner in the contract documents.

- Fairness in subsurface condition risk allocation will increase competition among responsible constructors who are considering bidding on the megaproject and will reduce the risk of constructors carrying undisclosed (and potentially, unrealized) contingency to anticipate increased cost due to differing site conditions.

- Fairness in risk allocation decision making will reduce the likelihood of contentious claims and disputes, increase the likelihood that dispute resolvers will adhere to those risk allocation decisions, increase the likelihood that the constructor will

achieve contractual performance, and maximize the likelihood that the project will be completed on schedule and within expected costs.

- Fairness in risk allocation between project owner and constructor should serve to reduce the professional liability risk exposure of the consulting engineer.[13]

3.0 Impact of Subsurface Problems on Megaproject Cost and Schedule

Issue

To what degree do subsurface problems, including differing site conditions and related constructor performance/productivity issues, impact cost and schedule on a megaproject?

Analysis and Discussion

Almost by definition, on a subsurface megaproject, subsurface problems, including differing site conditions, can and often do have a major impact on cost and schedule. As previously noted, the risk of unanticipated or adverse subsurface conditions on major subsurface projects typically manifest early in the construction process, thereby having the significant potential for negatively impacting (and potentially exhausting) project cost contingency and schedule critical path.

Clearly, the more reliable information available during design and disclosed during bid and construction planning (i.e., prior to the start of construction), the less likely that commercial and contractual risk expectations of all project participants will be disappointed to any significant degree. Moreover, the more that the anticipated differing site conditions are conscientiously and contemporaneously evaluated and considered, and design and construction contingency mechanisms are provided to address such conditions, the less severe and disruptive any impacts that result therefrom during the construction process.

The minimization of significant cost, performance, or schedule impacts of differing site conditions depends upon adequate planning. This planning process should start with the commissioning of an adequate subsurface investigation program and extend into the contractual expression of fair and balanced subsurface condition risk allocation and the development of design and construction contingency plans to address the occurrence of such conditions.

Recommended Practices

- Project owners should commission and undertake an adequate subsurface investigation program.

- Project owners should fairly allocate subsurface condition risk and implement risk allocation decisions consistently and in a manner designed to achieve the expeditious resolution of differing site condition claims and disputes.

- Expect the unexpected: plan for the contingency of differing site conditions.

- Investigate and try to resolve differing site condition claims in a timely manner consistent with contract document provisions.

- Consulting engineers should provide recommendations to project owners regarding risk allocation options and document those recommendations.

- Consider the use of unit price provisions to define and contain economic impacts—direct and indirect (consequential) of differing site conditions.

4.0   Consulting Engineer Involvement During Construction Phase of Subsurface Projects

Issue

Why and to what extent should consulting engineers be engaged by the project owner to provide observational and related services during construction on a subsurface megaproject?

Analysis and Discussion

Subsurface conditions influence in a dynamic and interactive way a number of factors in the design and construction process, such as assumptions regarding the design of permanent project work; design and implementation of construction means and methods; and equipment specification, selection, and use. Initial design and construction planning decisions are predicated upon data available from pre-construction subsurface investigation. Subsurface conditions encountered during construction that materially differ from pre-construction data may require that design and construction planning decisions be changed. Put another way, the successful design of a subsurface project will continue after the design is complete and construction commences, and the realistic expectation should be that design assumptions and components and the construction

means and methods for accomplishing the work may evolve and adapt due to subsurface conditions encountered during construction.[14] This expectation demonstrates the advisability of retaining the consulting engineer to provide a range of construction phase services, including observing the work and the subsurface conditions encountered. In addition, differing site condition claims should be promptly noticed and investigated, evaluated and resolved. In the latter regard, the consulting engineer engaged to provide such investigative and evaluative services during construction will be available to represent and protect the project owner's interest in the process of giving timely and knowledgeable assistance in evaluating and resolving differing site condition claims.

Recommended Practices

- Retain the consulting engineer to provide observational and related services during construction.

- Utilize and commission the consulting engineer to promptly investigate and evaluate differing site condition notices.

5.0   Contracting Practices

Issue

What contracting practices and provisions should be considered for inclusion in project owner–constructor agreements on subsurface projects?

Analysis and Discussion

The preceding discussion should demonstrate the importance of clear and fair risk allocation for subsurface conditions and contractual provisions for achieving the timely and effective resolution of differing site condition claims.

Since the early 1970s, the American Underground Association (AUA) has published a series of recommended and "improved" practices for contracting on subsurface projects.[15] Some of the principal components of these improved contracting practices include the following:[16]

Subsurface Information Disclosure

Typically, the project owner authorizes, subsidizes, and commissions the undertaking of the subsurface investigation program. The importance of an adequately defined and ex-

ecuted subsurface investigation program is discussed above in § 1. Assuming that such a program has been accomplished, the question becomes what to do with the products (generally classified above as "data" or "interpretation or opinions") of that investigation—more specifically, whether and to what extent those products should be disclosed to construction bidders. To a significant degree, this decision needs to be made consistently with the project owner's decision regarding risk allocation for subsurface conditions.[17]

Many project owners approach this subject out of concern that disclosure of subsurface information may carry with it liabilities or warranties to the constructor and, therefore, they seek either to withhold such information or to disclose it but disclaim its accuracy, reliability, or completeness.

As a general matter, it is recommended that all available and reasonably reliable subsurface information be disclosed and made available to bidders. To the extent that reservations exist as to the reliability of the information, the disclosure should be accompanied by appropriate qualifications or limitations or, alternatively, may be addressed through conferral of lesser priority status or non-contract document classifications, such as "reference" documents.

The practice of non-disclosure of known and available information is risky for the project owner (and the consulting engineer) and prone to subsequent claims against the project owner (and the consulting engineer) based upon fraud, misrepresentation, breach of implied warranty, or failure to disclose knowledge in the superior position of the project owner (i.e., superior knowledge). These types of allegations typically make dispute resolution exponentially more challenging and problematic, particularly when asserted against public sector project owners.

Disclaimers

In some instances, project owners may decide to disclose subsurface condition information but disclaim the accuracy, completeness, or reliability of the information. Project owners may elect to utilize such disclaimers for a variety of reasons, including:

- Due to genuine concern about the accuracy or reliability of the subsurface condition information.

- In order to limit liability exposure for constructor claims based on allegations that owner-furnished subsurface condition information was inaccurate or misleading.

- To limit risk-sharing exposure under a differing site condition clause by negating the constructor's reasonable right to rely upon project owner–furnished subsurface condition information.

The extent to which disclaimers are legally effective depends upon applicable laws governing project disputes; however, as a general matter, many states uphold the legal

enforceability of specific disclaimers.[18] In circumstances in which giving legal effect to a disclaimer subverts or renders illusory the risk-sharing intent of a differing site condition provision, courts may decide not to enforce the disclaimer. However, in at least one decision a federal district court enforced a specific disclaimer in a manner that negated a constructor's entitlement to an equitable adjustment under a differing site condition clause.[19]

As noted previously, risk should be allocated consistently in the contract documents. Using disclaimers of subsurface condition information should be carefully evaluated relative to their consistency with other subsurface condition risk allocation provisions.

In addition to disclaimers, statements of limitation or qualifications may be utilized in conjunction with disclosure of subsurface condition information.[20] The language of these qualifications and limitations should be specific and based upon some legitimate need to restrict reliance upon disclosed information.

Differing Site Condition Clauses

As previously discussed, differing site condition clauses are a contractual mechanism available for the allocation of subsurface condition risk between project owner and constructor. In the absence of a differing site condition provision, typically the constructor, under the so-called "common law" rule, bears all risk associated with subsurface conditions.[21]

A differing site condition clause represents a contractual risk-sharing mechanism that must be understood in the legal context or framework of the common law rule. More specifically, absent a differing site condition clause, the constructor assumes all subsurface condition risk under the common law rule. The differing site condition provision effects a qualified modification to the common law rule in the sense of providing a constructor with an opportunity for an equitable adjustment due to the encountering of differing site conditions in those circumstances in which the physical conditions encountered at the site differ substantially or materially from those "indicated in the contract documents" and the constructor has otherwise complied with notice and other procedural requirements of the differing site condition clause. Not all differing site conditions entitle a constructor to an equitable adjustment. In addition, to be entitled to an equitable adjustment (of cost or time), the constructor must demonstrate that the difference between anticipated conditions (i.e., indicated in the contract documents) and those actually encountered is material and that a causal connection exists between the claimed cost/time impact (forming the basis of the equitable adjustment request) and the substantial or materially differing site condition claimed. On public projects, courts are reluctant to find or infer a waiver of the conditions and requirements of the differing site condition provision.

Baseline Approach

The "baseline approach" is a method — often expressed in a "baseline report" — of objectively defining, describing, and/or quantifying physical conditions reasonably expected to be encountered during the performance of construction work.[22] The definition and/or quantification derives from the available subsurface data. The goal of the baseline approach is to provide an objective basis for the contractual expectation as to physical conditions "indicated in the contract documents" for purposes of subsurface condition risk allocation and differing site condition clause interpretation and application.

Subsurface megaprojects generally justify the cost of preparing a baseline report. However, it is neither realistic nor practicable to expect that all anticipated physical conditions may be the subject of "baseline" definition or quantification.

The baseline approach may be demonstrated by the following example. Assume that the subsurface investigation reveals the existence of boulders of a certain size in a specific portion of a planned tunnel alignment. A prudent constructor interpreting the data would form the reasonable expectation that a certain quantity of boulders possessing certain physical characteristics are likely to be encountered and that the cost and time of excavating and disposing of those boulders should be included in the contract bid price. In addition, the constructor will develop its means and methods, equipment choices, and other planning decisions based on that reasonable expectation. In effect, the constructor develops a *subjective* impression or expectation as to the type and amount of boulders expected to be encountered based upon "indications in the contract documents."

If the baseline approach were utilized in this example, the baseline report would contain a specific description of the physical characteristics of the boulders and a quantification of the number of those boulders expected to be encountered. In this respect, the baseline defines an *objective* expectation about the type and quantity of boulders "indicated in the contract documents" for the purpose of defining contractual expectations and the threshold (or baseline) for determining whether the conditions actually encountered are substantially or materially at variance with the "indications in the contract documents."

This distinction between a constructor's *subjective* expectation and the baseline *objective* statement (description and quantification of physical site conditions) is critically important. A substantial number of differing site condition claims, and the resolution thereof, depends upon whether the constructor's *subjective* expectation of anticipated site conditions was reasonable and grounded in the indications (explicit or implicit) contained in the contract documents. In most situations, there can be — and are — differing judgments about what is reasonable under the particular circumstances. By adopting an *objective* approach to site condition description and quantification, the baseline approach should serve to (a) reduce differing contractual expectations about the antici-

pated physical site conditions to be encountered and (b) streamline the evaluation and resolution of differing site condition claims.

In this context, the baseline may be established and defined in various ways, often reflecting the project owner's degree of cost and time risk tolerance or aversion. For example, suppose the data produced by the subsurface investigation program reasonably could support a predicted range of 100 to 200 boulders. Who should determine where in the range to define and quantify the baseline expectation statement about the boulders? As with most risk allocation issues, decisions of this sort should be made by the project owner after consulting with the consulting engineer. The lower the end of the baseline range, the lower the bid and the more likely the possibility of differing site condition claims; the higher the end of the baseline range, the higher the bid and the less likely such claims. Where to establish the range may be influenced by availability or stability (continuity) of project funding; generally, the more that funding availability is determined and committed prior to the start of construction, the more conservative (higher range) the baseline. The consulting engineer should document options and recommendations presented to the project owner regarding baseline definition and the potential cost or time implications of those recommendations.

Can using the baseline approach result in professional liability claims against the consulting engineer? While the baseline approach is relatively new, the answer is "yes."[23] First and foremost, the consulting engineer should make clear and certain that all project participants understand the purpose and objective of the baseline approach. Second, the project owner's decisions regarding the baseline approach, including the selection of a baseline range, should be well-informed based upon the consulting engineer's technical advice and recommendations and should be documented.

6.0   Professional Liability Issues for Consulting Engineers on Subsurface Megaprojects

Introduction

Many consulting engineers regard subsurface condition problems as resulting from many causes—construction performance or productivity issues, geologic conditions, project owner risk allocation decisions, contracting terms or practices, or other actions, events, or decisions—all of which are directly related to events or the decisions or conduct of others or otherwise beyond the control of the consulting engineer and, therefore (logically), viewed as having no impact or consequence on their professional liability exposure. Unfortunately, on subsurface megaprojects, as well as other subsurface projects, the experience has amply proven otherwise.[24]

Subsurface megaprojects hold out the potential of significant project owner–constructor contractual risk and disappointed commercial and other important expectations (e.g., project schedule, funding availability).[25] The central role served by most consulting engineers in subsurface investigation (planning, recommendations, report preparation), design, construction engineering, and observational services necessarily places the consulting engineer and its performance at the heart of most disputes and claims resulting from such underlying disappointed expectations.

Encountering unexpected obstacles often occurs early in the progression of project work, threatening to exhaust all project owner contingency, schedule float, and other planning expectations and contingencies. For the constructor, such early disappointments may likewise significantly erode construction contingency, anticipated profit, and schedule float.

In an ideal world, well drafted contract risk allocation provisions that appropriately anticipate subsurface conditions at variance with reasonable contractual expectations (and corresponding project planning and commercial expectations) should be the sole and definitive source for resolving claims of differing site conditions. Put another way, disappointed expectations, however severe, should be addressed and conclusively resolved in accordance with contractual risk allocation terms between parties in contractual privity (i.e., the project owner and constructor). Those with experience on subsurface projects know that things are not so simple, no matter how clear the contract terms — and especially if the contract terms are not clear. The higher (more severe) the level of disappointment, the greater the likelihood that it will lead to claims and disputes between the project owner and constructor.

When that occurs, given the central role of the consulting engineer in subsurface condition investigation — and, in many instances, in project design and construction phase services, including the investigation and evaluation of differing site condition claims — it is not by any means uncommon for the consulting engineer to be embroiled in such claims and disputes.

The resolution of these claims against consulting engineers often requires the retention of experts to evaluate the consultant's relevant performance in terms of professional standard of care,[26] especially in a project with subsurface conditions in which the consulting engineer's judgments play such a significant role. These judgments –when called into question in a claim — must be evaluated according to the professional standard of care. In this realm, there are rarely any absolute or definitive answers, no clear "right" or "wrong." As a practical matter, these observations mean that the ability to predict the outcome of such claims is less clear and certain than in other professional liability contexts and the cost of defense typically is greater. Put another way, this scenario for a professional liability claim can potentially pose significant, uncertain, and unpredictable risk exposure.

As if all of the above factors were not enough, when the project owner's disappointed expectation is significant—in the sense of imperiling major project goals (budget and schedule) and objectives—there will be substantial pressure on the consulting engineer (especially one who has a more long-term relationship with the project owner) to settle the owner's claim against the consultant. The consulting engineer's professional liability risk exposure in major subsurface projects is substantial, complex, and less predictable in terms of outcome. Moreover, in claims against the consulting engineer that derive from underlying subsurface condition claims of the constructor against the project owner, the consulting engineer's relationship with a project owner may be threatened by the owner's diminishing confidence in the consultant.

Consulting engineers involved in subsurface projects face substantial potential professional liability exposure to both their client and third parties directly or indirectly involved in those projects with whom the consultant has no contractual relationship (e.g., constructors, specialty trade constructors, adjacent property owners, members of the public). This potential professional liability exposure may arise out of acts or omissions of the consulting engineer in connection with a broad range of services: recommendations regarding site selection; adequacy of pre-construction site investigation; preparation of data, reports, opinions, and/or studies regarding actual or anticipated subsurface conditions; preparation of concept or other studies relating to preliminary design criteria or concepts; failure to adequately assess or communicate to the client relative degrees of costs, impacts, or risk associated with alternative design or optional construction approaches; problems or disappointments associated with innovative design or construction approaches (e.g., soil mix, ground freezing); preparation of design and contract documents and/or "reference" documents to be utilized in connection with bidding or construction of the subsurface projects; the administration and/or management of construction of subsurface projects, including the review and evaluation of constructor submittals, proposed value engineering or other constructor-proposed substitutions, proposed construction means and methods, and payment requisitions; the observation of construction work for conformance with the contract documents; and the investigation, review and evaluation of constructor differing site condition claims.

As one commentator has noted:

> [T]here is a clear negative aspect [to changed conditions claims] that puts the geotechnical engineer of a project at risk for failing to meet the standard of care in their site characterization. With a modest amount of imagination, an attorney can convert what is truly a [differing site conditions] claim into a suit against the project owner and design professionals. The owner's geotechnical engineers should recognize that it is greatly in their own interest to produce a pre-bid investigation that will avoid a claim. If a claim eventuates, then the engineer should strive to resolve that claim equitably and prompt-

ly and not encourage it to escalate to the next level. Note that Federal backers will often contribute to settlement of a [differing site conditions] claim, but they certainly will not choose to share the cost if the finding is of negligence and defective design.[27]

In the context of subsurface projects, claims are frequently asserted by project owners, as well as constructors (and their specialty trades) and other third parties, against consulting engineers arising out of the encountering of actual or alleged differing site conditions. As one commentator has observed:

> Other parties may be liable as well. The Architect or Engineer who prepared the plans and specifications is often named as a defendant in differing site condition cases. Because there is usually no contract between the contractor and the architect, the contractor's action is typically based upon negligence or some other tort, and cases are split regarding the liability of the architect in these circumstances. If the Owner is held liable to the Contractor as a result of an unforeseen differing site condition, the Owner may seek indemnity from the Architect, who prepared the plans and specifications or who communicated incorrect data to the Contractor. The ultimate liability for damages resulting from an unforeseen site condition may also rest upon consultants hired by the Owner, Architect or Contractor, who should have discovered the conditions at the site, but did not. These parties may be soil consultants, testing agencies or geotechnical engineers. Depending upon the jurisdiction, they may be held directly liable to parties with whom they have no privity of contract. In other jurisdictions, the parties may be subject to indemnity claims brought by those parties found liable to the Owner or Contractor.[28]

There are a number of appellate court decisions involving claims against consulting engineers based on differing site conditions. In general terms, such claims have been asserted against design professionals by project owners and third parties based on the following allegations: failure to undertake an adequate pre-construction investigation/survey of existing site conditions;[29] failure to accurately and/or completely describe existing site conditions in bid and contract documents;[30] failure to disclose information concerning existing site conditions that was generally (or otherwise) not available to bidders or not available within the time frame permitted for preparation of the bid;[31] negligence in the drafting of bid or contract documents with respect to the circumstances under which a constructor would be entitled to time or economic relief due to encountering differing site conditions;[32] failure to prepare accurate quantity or other estimates;[33] and failure to properly and/or timely address and resolve differing site conditions claims in accordance with the engineer's obligations under the contract documents or in accordance with the professional standard of care.[34]

Consulting engineers may also be exposed to professional liability claims that arise from purely administrative services performed during the construction phase.[35] Under

most standard general conditions of construction contracts, the consulting engineer has the obligation to fairly, promptly, and impartially administer the construction contract.[36] This obligation includes the interpretation of contract documents and resolution of disputes regarding differing site conditions claims between the project owner and constructor.[37] In the performance of this role, the consulting engineer must act fairly, impartially, and without unreasonable delay in addressing and resolving claims involving differing site conditions.[38]

There are a number of subsurface conditions issues and problems that may result in professional liability exposure for the consulting engineer, including:

- The failure to adequately investigate subsurface conditions at the site.
- The failure to adequately disclose or otherwise make available subsurface condition information.
- The failure to fairly allocate subsurface condition risk as between the project owner and constructor.
- The failure to timely anticipate and address differing site condition issues that arise during construction.
- The failure to timely modify or revise design assumptions based upon encountered site conditions.
- The failure of geotechnical reports to accurately or clearly address their subject matter.
- The inclusion of "overly optimistic" predictions of subsurface conditions in geotechnical reports.
- The failure to coordinate and prioritize (i.e., place in order of precedence) contract document and other information (or reference materials) available to the constructor.
- The failure to adequately and realistically assess project costs and schedule and potential risk factors associated therewith due to insufficient or inaccurate subsurface conditions data.
- "Suggesting" construction means and methods that are not feasible for site-specific application.
- The failure to timely resolve differing site condition claims and disputes.[39]

Some of these issues do not directly involve the performance of the consulting engineer but, rather, result from project owner planning, risk allocation, or contracting decisions or the latter's project management and dispute resolution decisions and practices. Some, of course, directly relate to the adequacy of the consulting engineer's performance. In many circumstances, however, decisions about whether to pursue a professional liability claim against a consulting engineer are not made on the basis of an analysis of whether the consultant caused or contributed to the subsurface condition

problem or its consequence but, rather, are motivated by the substantial degree of the project owner's and/or constructor's disappointed expectations. These types of claims against the consulting engineer are also motivated by the dominance and pervasiveness of the consultant's service involvement in most of the subject areas that underlie the disputes between the project owner and constructor over differing site conditions.

In this regard, it should be noted that, while recovery (assuming entitlement) under a differing site condition provision does not require proof of fault or other culpability on the part of the project owner or anyone else (including the consulting engineer), it is not unusual — especially in a highly contentious differing site condition claim — for allegations of fault and improper conduct and motivations to be asserted by the constructor against the project owner and its consulting engineer. To some degree, these types of allegations are incited, for example, by the project owner's and/or consulting engineer's non-entitlement position, which attributes the constructor's difficulties not to a genuine and material differing site condition but, rather, to other factors: the constructor's own inadequate, unreasonable, or unrealistic pre-bid expectation or understanding or inspection of site conditions, poor planning, and management of the work; inadequate contingency; improper selection, design, or implementation of construction means and methods; or the failure of the constructor to maintain and properly operate its equipment. These positions — while certainly appropriate responses to many differing site condition claims — all point to the conduct or responsibility of the constructor as the cause (in whole or in part) of its claimed differing site condition problem. As such, even though the differing site condition process is intended to operate in a no-fault way — at least in terms of the constructor's ability to prove entitlement — the constructor's rebuttal to such responses may be to "shoot back" allegations of improper decisions, conduct, or motivation of the project owner, or deficiencies in design or other service activities, or improper conduct in relation to the consulting engineer's performance.

In some situations, the constructor, in addition to asserting a differing site condition claim against the project owner and/or consulting engineer, may assert additional claims (derived from such fault-based allegations) seeking recovery for the differing site condition on theories of fraud, misrepresentation, breach of implied warranty, and defective design. Unlike the differing site condition claim, these other claims *do* require proof of fault or legal liability of the project owner, and depending upon the particular claim (e.g., breach of implied warranty, inaccurate description of interpretation of site data, or defective design), they may also call into question the adequacy of the consulting engineer's performance.

When constructors respond in this manner — especially when the response finds fault with the consulting engineer's performance — some project owners are inclined (some sooner, others later) to assert professional liability claims against their consulting engineer for indemnification, professional negligence, or other legal theories of re-

covery. Moreover, in such circumstances, constructors may assert direct claims against the consulting engineer based on theories of negligence (depending upon jurisdiction and availability of an economic loss defense), negligent misrepresentation, and other acts.[40]

A simplistic assessment of the professional liability exposure environment for the consulting engineer arising out of subsurface condition issues and problems may sound something like, "How can we be at fault? We didn't put the stuff in the ground." Or, "At the end of the day, if the constructor can prove entitlement for a differing site condition, then the project owner should pay because it would be work that, by definition, was not included in the original bid assumption." Or, "This claim against us is nothing more than the predictable and natural consequence of imprudent project owner decisions regarding the extent of pre-construction subsurface investigation, withholding, and non-disclosure of available subsurface information or unfair risk allocation."

To a significant degree, this assessment may in most cases be fair and accurate, but it should not detract from the reality that the consulting engineer will need to defend professional liability claims. In some circumstances, the effective defense to those claims may result in the consultant "pointing the finger" against its own client, the project owner, to which the owner may reply in like measure. In such scenarios, the constructor becomes the primary beneficiary.[41]

The bottom line is that project owners and constructors should not be allowed to avoid or circumvent their risk allocation decisions as described in their contractual provisions by asserting improper claims against the consulting engineer for risk or damage intended to be encompassed within those provisions. As Sweet has stated:

> [T]here has been the tendency to expose the design professional . . . to claims by other participants, particularly contractors. . . .
>
> For example, some courts allow a contractor to maintain a tort action against a geotechnical engineer for misrepresentation. The context was a transaction in which the construction contract clearly placed the entire risk of unforeseen subsurface conditions on the contractor. Allowing the tort action induces the geotechnical engineer to request indemnity from the client, to increase her contract price to take this risk into account, or to price her work to encompass performance designed to ensure that her representations are accurate even if "excessive" caution would not be justified. Either way, the system of allocating risks is frustrated, with the client paying twice for the same risk. . . .[42]

6.1   **Constrained Consulting Engineer Scope**

Issue

How does a consulting engineer's service scope affect its professional liability risk exposure and what can be done to manage that risk?

Analysis and Discussion

More so than in any other type of project, successful subsurface projects require significant and timely interaction between the design and construction processes throughout the entire project execution. Typically in the traditional design-bid-build delivery method — especially one that utilizes a sequential and non-collaborative design-then-construction approach with low bid competition in a public procurement — the ability to achieve constructability input during the design phase is precluded by public law requirements.[43] The development and decision-making of the final project design is likely to be influenced by constructability considerations, including the anticipated and available options for the constructor's construction means and methods and equipment selection.[44] Similarly, ground conditions actually encountered during construction and the behavior of those conditions due to interactions with the constructor's selected means and methods may impact the final project design or require its revision. In order for the consulting engineer to effectively anticipate and address these types of "interaction" issues, it is advisable that the consulting engineer have continuous involvement in the project throughout construction.

This type of continuous involvement allows the consulting engineer to anticipate and address design and other issues relating to subsurface conditions encountered during construction in a timely fashion. This involvement will also allow the consultant to represent and assist the project owner in a meaningful and effective way in addressing and resolving differing site condition claims.

As has been stated:

> Design is becoming increasingly fragmented, as specialist consultants and contractors are used, and as new forms of construction management are introduced. Design is a continuous process, requiring regular review to ensure that the client's needs are being met. It is important that arrangements are made to ensure that information on ground conditions is communicated to all of those involved in the project. Reassessment of the design should be carried out throughout construction and, where necessary, the operation and decommissioning phases of a project. Good communication between client, designers and Constructors, and a team approach to risk management are essential. . . . There is no longer, however, a clear and unambiguous relationship between [the roles

of owner, project manager, designer and Constructor] and the work carried out by each organization involved in construction. For example, a civil engineering contractor undertaking a DBFO (design-build-finance-operate) contract might reasonably consider himself to be the client for the work. He would typically undertake at least part of the design, and have other elements of design completed by design consultants, and by specialist subcontractors or subconsultants. Many clients employ a project manager to ensure that key systems are put in place, and larger clients may employ design specialists who, at least in the early stages of design development, will carry out particular elements of the preliminary design.[45]

Recommended Practices

- The project owner should retain the consulting engineer to provide services continuously from planning and design through the completion of construction. This continuity of involvement is especially important and advisable on subsurface projects.

- The lack of continuous involvement of the consulting engineer during construction increases the risk for the consulting engineer that subsurface condition issues and problems — especially, those that involve the need to revise the project design — will result in professional liability claims and that the consulting engineer will not be in a position to anticipate and thereby expeditiously address and mitigate such issues and problems.

6.2 Combined Differing Site Condition and Defective Design (Implied Warranty) Claims

Issue

Should a constructor be allowed to pursue recovery against the project owner based simultaneously upon combined theories of differing site condition and defective design claims, and what is the effect of the assertion of such combined claims on the professional liability exposure of the consulting engineer?

Analysis and Discussion

On most megaprojects, the contract documents include a differing site condition clause entitling the constructor (and the project owner) to an equitable adjustment for cost and time impacts sustained as a consequence of encountering physical site condi-

tions substantially or materially at variance from those conditions indicated in the contract documents. The differing site condition clause permits recovery in the absence of fault; all that generally is required to establish entitlement is a demonstration of a substantial or material difference in encountered physical site conditions from those indicated in the contract documents and that the difference caused the constructor to incur the claimed additional time or cost in the performance of its work.

Despite the fact that the constructor need not prove fault or some other violation of a legal obligation by the project owner, in some instances a constructor will combine or simultaneously assert both a differing site condition claim and a defective design claim against the project owner arising out of alleged unanticipated site conditions. Typically, in such circumstances, the defective design claim is based on breach of implied warranty and derives from some alleged defect in the project design, alleged inaccurate geotechnical data, contract document, or geotechnical report representation, or indication that pertains to the site condition at issue. The defective design and inaccurate data or report claim components most commonly involve services performed by the consulting engineer and allege some deficiency in the latter's performance of those services.

In the specific context of subsurface projects, constructors frequently assert claims for differing site conditions that are based primarily or alternatively on allegations of defective design ("combined" differing site conditions and defective design claims).[46] In other words, constructors claim that they are entitled to economic or time adjustments based on site conditions, asserting (simultaneously or alternatively) that: (1) the conditions actually encountered materially differed from those reasonably anticipated based on indications in the contract documents and/or (2) incomplete or inaccurate information, data, or interpretations regarding site conditions or defective design, relating to subsurface conditions or work, resulted in the claimed additional cost or time. Given the combination of such differing site condition claims with specific allegations of "defective" design or deficiencies in other professional services of the consulting engineer, it is not uncommon in these circumstances for claims to be asserted by either or both the project owner or constructor against the consulting engineer.[47]

There are several reported cases that involve combined differing site condition and defective design claims.[48] The results in those cases are somewhat mixed. In some of the cases, courts have ruled that the defective design claim is not actionable because the contract documents provide a specific remedy in the differing site condition clause and, therefore, resort to an independent and alternative defective design or breach of implied warranty claim as a predicate for recovery is unnecessary and unwarranted or otherwise intended to circumvent the contractually prescribed or limited remedy provided under the differing site condition clause. In other cases, the courts have allowed simultaneous pursuit of claims under differing site condition clauses and defective design or implied warranty theories.

In some situations, a constructor initially may assert a combined differing site condition and defective design claim against the project owner and at the conclusion (through adjudication or settlement) of that claim assert a claim against the consulting engineer based, for example, on legal theories of professional negligence and negligent misrepresentation. These sequential and strategic litigation tactics are viewed with disfavor by courts.

This scenario is exemplified in the context of claims sequentially asserted by Martin K. Eby Construction Co., Inc., a constructor, in connection with a bridge construction project for the Jacksonville Transportation Authority (JTA), and then subsequently asserted by Eby against JTA's consulting engineer, Jacobs Civil, Inc.. In its claims against JTA, Eby contended that it encountered a differing site condition consisting of soft soils that would require it to construct certain temporary access structures different from the manner it had anticipated in formulating its bid, resulting in over $10 million in additional costs. In addition, Eby contended that JTA breached its implied warranty of design adequacy by furnishing a design for certain dirt haul roads that could not be constructed as shown in the contract documents; specifically, Eby claimed the design drawings, in failing to depict or indicate necessary soil reinforcement or modification, led it to believe that it could construct the roads without the need for any soil reinforcement or modification. The differing site condition and defective design claim arose out of the same alleged differing soil conditions. The court rejected Eby's claims on the bases that (a) the soil boring information indicated in the contract documents and the contractually-required site inspection revealed wet and marshy soil conditions consistent with those encountered by Eby and, therefore, no differing site condition claim entitlement was established, and (b) Eby failed to establish any breach of implied warranty as to design adequacy because it did not prove that it relied upon the contract document design in formulating its bid and, in any event, Eby's bid assumptions were unreasonable given soil information and other indications contained in the contract documents.[49]

One month after entry of the final judgment dismissing Eby's combined differing site condition and defective design claims against JTA, Eby commenced a new action against Jacobs, JTA's consulting engineer. In that action, Eby asserted claims against Jacobs based on legal theories of negligence and negligent misrepresentation, which claims were principally derived from the same underlying claims that Eby had unsuccessfully asserted against JTA in the prior litigation between the latter parties. The court dismissed Eby's claims against Jacobs on the basis that since Jacobs and JTA were in contractual privity with each other (and shared a commonality of interest relative to Eby's respective claims), a judgment in the prior action in favor of JTA inured to the defensive benefit of Jacobs, and Eby could not relitigate (in the second action against Jacobs) its previously and unsuccessfully asserted claims against JTA "by re-casting and relabeling its claims and rotating defendants."[50]

What are the professional liability implications for the consulting engineer of combined differing site condition and defective design/implied warranty claims by the constructor against the project owner? In some situations in which a constructor asserts a differing site condition claim against the project owner, liability (albeit on a non-fault basis) of the project owner is based on the contract documents, i.e., entitlement under the differing site condition clause. As a general proposition, liability exposure of the consulting engineer *should* be relatively minimal, assuming that the consulting engineer's site investigation was adequately defined and properly executed and the results accurately, clearly, and consistently reported or portrayed to others. If the project owner expends additional cost or time in reimbursing the constructor pursuant to the differing site condition claim, those impacts generally are, and should be, regarded as inherent in the project owner's risk contingency exposure. Viewed from a somewhat different perspective, the conditions encountered are inherent in, incident to, and a part of the cost of constructing the project. In those respects, the liability exposure of the consulting engineer for impacts due to the differing site condition should be on the relatively low end of the scale, assuming that the consultant's performance met the professional standard of care. Most project owners accept this principle and do not pursue professional liability claims against the consulting engineer in such circumstances.

However, when a constructor combines a differing site condition claim with a defective design/implied warranty claim, the latter claim may independently and especially attract the attention of the project owner and could lead to the assertion of a professional liability (direct negligence or indemnification) claim against the consulting engineer. This occurs typically because the defective design/breach of implied warranty claim derives, to a greater or lesser degree, from services performed by the consulting engineer and typically calls into question the adequacy of that performance. However, there is a significant difference between the standard of proof and liability required to establish (1) a claim against a project owner for breach of implied warranty as to design and (2) a professional negligence claim against a consulting engineer. The former is a lesser standard of proof; the latter typically requires demonstration by expert opinion that the consulting engineer's services departed from the professional standard of care.

In general, a project owner who furnishes the design to the constructor impliedly warrants the accuracy, completeness, and constructability of that design. This now-established risk allocation principle for "defective" design — i.e., the implied warranty obligation — imposes on the project owner an implied warranty or promise that the design is free of material defects and is constructable.[51]

Notwithstanding that legal distinction, the constructor's assertion of a defective design (implied warranty) claim against the project owner may increase the risk of a professional liability claim by the project owner against the consulting engineer and, in

some cases, lead to a constructor's assertion of claims against the consulting engineer for negligence, negligent misrepresentation, and/or indemnification.

In most instances, the project owner and consulting engineer should (and do) work cooperatively in the investigation, evaluation, and, if necessary, defense of a constructor's differing site condition claims.[52] The consulting engineer often contributes valuable technical assistance and the ability to develop and define the constructor's reasonable bid expectation, based upon indications in the contract documents and how those expectations compare to the actual conditions encountered.

Unfortunately, in circumstances in which a defective design/implied warranty claim has been asserted by the constructor against the project owner, and the project owner is thereby instigated or otherwise reactively prompted to assert a professional liability claim against the consulting engineer, the ability of the project owner and consulting engineer to effectively collaborate in the defense of the constructor's differing site condition claim is often significantly undermined and compromised. Project owners should consider avoiding the assertion of such professional liability claims until plausible evidence exists to support the consulting engineer's departure from the professional standard of care or, at a minimum, defer the assertion of such claims pending resolution of the constructor's differing site condition claim.

Recommended Practices

- Constructor claims of defective design/breach of implied warranty that arise out of, or are combined with, differing site condition claims should be prudently and timely evaluated by the project owner prior to the owner's assertion of any professional liability claim against the consulting engineer. There are significant advantages to the project owner and consulting engineer working collaboratively in the investigation, evaluation, and defense of differing site condition claims that may be compromised or entirely eroded if the project owner and consulting engineer assume adversarial positions due to the project owner's premature or ill-considered reactive decision to assert a professional liability claim against the consulting engineer.

6.3   Special Project Owner Defenses to Subsurface Condition Claims

Issue

Are there legal defenses available to the project owner for differing site condition claims that generally are not available to the consulting engineer?

Analysis and Discussion

In many situations, a project owner's legal liability exposure for a constructor's differing site condition claim is contained or defined by the specific remedies prescribed in the contract documents and potentially further restricted or precluded by disclaimers or other provisions in the contract document. The consulting engineer may or may not be able to avail itself of such contractual defenses since it is not a direct party to the project owner–constructor agreement. In some circumstances, however, the project owner's contract defenses may explicitly extend to the consulting engineer (as a contract beneficiary) or do so by implication or specific reference to the consulting engineer as the project owner's agent.

Beyond the contract documents, a project owner may have available certain other legal defenses to differing site condition claims, such as the sovereign immunity doctrine. Under that doctrine, a project owner may be entitled to immunity from civil liability in circumstances in which the project owner is considered to be functioning in a discretionary, or policy-making, role or capacity. The *KiSKA-Kajima* case discussed in chapter 15 demonstrates the application of the sovereign immunity defense for a project owner in the context of a constructor's differing site condition claim.

Decisions such as *KiSKA-Kajima* raise certain important questions relative to the consulting engineer's professional liability exposure:

- To what extent may the sovereign immunity defense extend to protect the consulting engineer (so-called derivative sovereign immunity)?

- If not applicable, to what extent does the availability of the sovereign immunity defense for the project owner increase the professional liability exposure of the consulting engineer?

The analysis of the first question is dependent upon the application of state law.[53]

Assuming that the sovereign immunity defense is not derivatively available to the consulting engineer, there certainly does exist the possibility of increased professional liability exposure of the consulting engineer to the constructor. The analysis in this respect is quite similar to the analysis that underlies the observation of increased professional liability exposure of the consulting engineer when risk is unfairly allocated between the project owner and constructor.[54] The basic issue is that if a constructor is

precluded recovery for a differing site condition–based claim against the project owner, the risk of the consulting engineer's professional liability exposure to the constructor is significantly increased because that is the only avenue of recovery for the constructor. This explanation for the increased professional liability exposure of the consulting engineer is just that, i.e., an explanation, and by no means is that explanation offered as a rationale, justification, or defense of the practice of constructors asserting such claims.

6.4   Baseline Approach: Professional Liability Implications

Issue

What are the potential professional liability risk implications for consulting engineers in connection with use of the baseline approach.[55]

Analysis and Discussion

There are many salutary objectives to be achieved for both project owners and constructors associated with the use of the baseline approach, among which are facilitating the clearer contractual definition and fairer allocation of risk for subsurface conditions and the corresponding minimization of conflict, disputes, and claims arising out of differing site conditions claims.[56] For these and other good reasons, it is anticipated that many enlightened and sophisticated megaproject owners will encourage and promote the baseline approach and will want their consulting engineers to similarly embrace and implement the baseline approach. Consulting engineers involved in the preparation of baseline reports, however, need to be attentive to potential professional liability risks associated with the use of the baseline approach.

Certainly, serving the perceived best interest and desires of clients is the primary goal of most successful professionals; however, this goal must always be counter-balanced against the need for prudent and diligent attention to legitimate professional liability implications associated with the fulfillment of that goal. The baseline approach is no exception in this regard.

Given the relative novelty of the baseline approach, it is not possible at this time to predict precisely the professional liability implications for consulting engineers who elect to use that approach. However, reasonably accurate predictions may be made based upon professional liability experiences in related contexts.[57] This discussion will explore some of the professional liability implications associated with the baseline approach. The purpose is *not* to discourage the use of the baseline approach; rather, it is to increase awareness of the consulting engineer as to the potential risk management and profes-

sional liability risk implications associated with its use and to recommend risk management and contractual practices designed to manage that risk.

The Geotechnical Baseline Approach

Generally speaking, the baseline approach is utilized on subsurface projects "to set clear realistic baselines for conditions anticipated to be encountered during subsurface construction, and thereby provides all bidders with a single contractual interpretation that can be relied upon in preparing their bids."[58] Similarly, it has been stated that "[t]he basic purpose of . . . baselines is to define concisely the geotechnical 'indications of the contract' for administration of the DSC clause. These baselines establish a contractual basis for the allocation of geotechnical risk; they are not necessarily intended to define the 'single correct' interpretation of geotechnical conditions."[59] In substance, the purpose of the baseline approach is to assist in the allocation of risk for site conditions by facilitating the definition — qualitatively and/or quantitatively — of those site conditions which should be anticipated and included within the contractual obligations and contract price of the constructor.

The baseline approach primarily is intended to assist the project owner and constructor in more clearly defining and allocating risk for differing site conditions at the point of contract formation, thereby reducing the likelihood of misunderstandings, disappointed expectations, disputes, and claims (and associated project delays and disruptions) during the construction process. Assuming that the baseline has been clearly, concisely, and consistently expressed in the contract documents in descriptive terms that can be objectively evaluated and measured in the field during construction, the baseline approach can serve as a useful tool in several ways: in defining and allocating the risk to be included as part of the initial contractual undertaking and within the contract price; in administering the differing site condition clause; and in facilitating the resolution of differing site condition claims.

Generally speaking, most differing site condition clauses allow for an equitable adjustment for so-called "Type 1" conditions in circumstances in which the actual physical conditions encountered at the site during construction substantially or materially differ from the physical conditions indicated in the contract documents (i.e., "contract indications"). Contract indications may be either express or implied. Express indications typically are explicit statements or representations in the contract documents about anticipated physical conditions, such as ground water levels and soil and rock classifications. Implicit indications regarding physical conditions are derived through a process of (reasonable) logical deduction and inference from all of the information in the contract documents regarding those conditions.[60]

In many respects, the *baseline* may be considered as a consolidated or shorthand (al-

though generally not the exclusive) reference for the contract indications relevant to the physical conditions that are the subject of the baseline description. As such, the baseline approach is intended to aid in risk allocation and in the administration of differing site condition clauses by substituting a more certain and objective baseline description for the relevant contract indications (which typically are subject to subjective and variable, but reasonable, interpretations).

Educating the Project Owner: Understanding and Managing the Project Owner's Risk Preferences, Attitudes, and Expectations

Use of the baseline approach requires a certain degree of client education on the part of the consulting engineer. To successfully undertake this educational role, it is important for the professional itself to understand that approach, including its purpose and limitations, and to accurately and effectively communicate that understanding to the project owner.[61] The project owner's misunderstanding or unrealistic expectations about use of the baseline approach, as in other incidents of the professional-client relationship, substantially increases the risk of professional liability.

Professionals who are knowledgeable and experienced in the use of the baseline approach have observed:

> Owners/Clients must be educated regarding ownership and the assignment of risks for the project, the cost and likelihood of certain conditions being encountered, and the proper contingent planning for these events as regards schedule and cost. These events (risks) mean potential cost to the job, which may or may not occur, but must be understood as inherent in any underground project. . . .
>
> In accepting the principle of a GDSR [Geotechnical Design Summary Report], the owner must understand that it describes a contractual set of "baseline conditions" to be assumed during the bid and subsequent construction. That does not mean and should not be taken as a guarantee that "no risk exists." It is the designer's obligation to educate his owner client, and the owner's obligation in turn to recognize that encountering site conditions outside those delineated in the baseline GDSR are risks that the Owner must assume if they can be shown, in accordance with the contract documents, to have a negative impact on the construction. The designer must also understand his owner's tolerance for change orders, as compared to lower overall cost. An owner adamant against change orders may willingly prefer a more "conservative" set of baseline conditions even if it means a higher overall bid price and higher cost.[62]

The project owner should be directly involved in communications and discussions regarding the establishment of baselines and be advised of the consequences and implications on risk allocation, cost, and claims potential with respect to how the baselines are established.[63] The consulting engineer should document the project owner's

involvement and decision-making regarding the establishment of baselines. In addition, the consulting engineer must exercise due care in translating the project owner's risk preferences (i.e., degrees of risk tolerance/adversity for site conditions) into the definition of baselines.

Most standard differing site conditions clauses are capable of allowing for an equitable adjustment (assuming the requirements of the clause are met) to the constructor (for extra time or compensation) or to the project owner (schedule savings or credits). Despite this mutual capability in the potential for equitable adjustment — extra or credit — historically, project owners have rarely pursued "credit" differing site condition claims against constructors.

The baseline approach may, however, potentially influence some project owners to pursue such credit differing site condition claim opportunities due to the following factors:

1. Project owners who have been educated in the baseline approach and who have participated in establishing the baseline will have a greater focus on, awareness of, and sensitivity to the distinction (and associated economic consequences) between the anticipated conditions (as defined by the baseline) and the conditions actually encountered; and,

2. Some project owners traditionally have been disinclined to pursue credit differing site condition claims against constructors because: it is difficult to identify and prove what constitutes more favorable conditions; it is difficult (if not impossible) to reliably and expeditiously determine the reasonable bid and contractual expectations of the contractor with respect to the subject conditions; and utilizing baseline reports substantially alleviates, if not eliminates, these difficulties by introducing an objectively-defined and (ideally) clear definition of the baseline conditions upon which contractual obligations are undertaken, thereby facilitating pursuit of credit differing site condition claims.

In the event that a project owner utilizing the baseline approach seeks to pursue (or wishes to reserve the opportunity to pursue) credit differing site condition claims, it is important that this intention be ascertained by the consulting engineer well in advance of the start of construction. Additionally, the project owner should retain the consulting engineer to provide an adequate scope of services during construction so as to be in a position to identify "more favorable than baseline" conditions and to protect the project owner's right to pursue credit claims consistent with the requirements of the differing site condition clause in the contract documents. Just as failure to provide timely notice may be an effective defense to a constructor's differing site condition claims, a project owner's (or its representative's) failure to timely notify the contractor of a credit differing site condition claim may similarly be fatal to the pursuit of that claim. In such

situations, the consulting engineer must exercise due diligence and care in representing the project owner's interest, since failure to do so could lead to professional negligence or cost recovery claims by the project owner against the consulting engineer based upon deprivation of credit differing site condition claim opportunities.[64]

Relationship Between Scope of Engineering Services and Quality of Baseline Definition

In the related contexts of contracting for (a) performance of subsurface investigations, (b) preparation of geotechnical data and interpretive reports, and (c) the performance of services required to represent the interests of the project owner during construction, the consulting engineer devotes a substantial amount of time and effort impressing upon (educating) their client that their ability to adequately perform those services on behalf of it (the client) directly corresponds to the adequacy of the scope of services authorized and commissioned by the project owner. The same admonition is true in the context of preparing geotechnical baselines.

The quality of the baseline — defined as its reliability, definitiveness, and relative accuracy — in most instances will be significantly impacted and influenced by the nature and extent of the subsurface investigation and the quality and quantity of reliable data generated and made available as a result of that investigation. "The amount of geotechnical data that is available and usable for the interpretation and prediction of ground conditions and behavior for tunneling depends less on the expertise of the geotechnical engineer than on the budget and schedule allocated by the owner for site investigation."[65] The consulting engineer should advise the project owner regarding the correlation and interrelationship between the authorized scope of geotechnical subsurface investigation services and the quality of the baseline definition.

Establishing the Baseline: Distinction Between Geotechnical Data and the Baseline Approach

The project owner should understand that the same geotechnical data (typically developed as a result of subsurface and related investigation) could result in baselines being established and/or expressed in significantly different ways. The project owner serves an important and significant role in influencing how the baseline will be established. This observation largely derives from the distinction between a geotechnical baseline and the geotechnical data from which that baseline is derived. This distinction definitely leads to the possibility that the same geotechnical data regarding the same subsurface conditions could result in the establishment of materially different baselines for those same conditions.

The baseline is intended to state a contractual assumption about the anticipated site conditions for the purposes of defining contractual risk allocation and expectations and

administering the differing site condition clause. Contractual *assumptions* are to be distinguished from factual representations. As has been stated:

> The baseline is a representation of what is *assumed* will be encountered for the purpose of defining "the indications of the capital contract." Thus, the provision of a baseline in the Contract is not a warranty that the baseline conditions will, in fact, be encountered. It is therefore not appropriate for the Owner or Contractor to conclude that baseline statements are warranties. However, baseline statements in a Contract can be considered a contractual commitment by the Owner that those baseline conditions will be applied in the administration of the DSC clause. This understanding should be addressed in the Contract Documents.[66]

The baseline is not necessarily intended to reflect, represent, describe, or portray *actual* and *factual* geotechnical conditions and need not "rigorously" be grounded in geotechnical reality or precisely derived from or supported by data or other information available about physical site conditions. In fact, and to the contrary, it is quite conceivable that the same objective data (i.e., geotechnical reality) may result in materially different baselines, depending upon the project owner's subjective degree or level of risk tolerance/adversity with respect to site conditions.

Simply put, based upon the same geotechnical data, project owners may choose to define baselines in substantially different ways depending upon either their tolerance for risk (based upon attitudes, funding constraints, or other considerations) or other factors influencing their willingness or ability to retain risk for differing site conditions.[67]

From the standpoint of the consulting engineer, it is important both to understand and to adequately translate into the baseline formulation the project owner's attitude or philosophy toward risk tolerance/adversity.[68] In addition, to the extent that the baseline, as established, does not (by intention) reflect the available geotechnical data, it is important that the constructor understand the distinction (between geotechnical data and the baseline) since the baseline description may be important to the constructor in the planning of the work, including the design and implementation of construction means and methods required for the work. In other words, the constructor may draw implications or inferences from the established baseline with respect to the planning of the work and, if the geotechnical data does not precisely correlate with or support the baseline, this could lead to claims from the constructor based upon misrepresentation if the constructor reasonably understood the baseline to reflect geotechnical data. In addition, constructor misunderstanding as to the purpose or foundation of the baseline representations could lead to professional liability claims by the project owner or constructor against the consulting engineer.

There are several potential concerns with the lack of correlation or congruence between the baseline and geotechnical data, many of which may increase the risk of

professional liability for geotechnical and design engineers and construction management professionals.

As stated above, the baseline is intended to function as a substitute for the contract indications relevant to the physical conditions described in the baseline. As an indication — in fact an explicit statement — the baseline (absent any qualification or other disclaimer) constitutes a representation of physical conditions to be encountered in the performance of the work. If the baseline representation, however, is not correlated with or precisely supported by geotechnical data, a constructor that encountered conditions at variance with the baseline may claim that:

1. The project owner and/or the consulting engineer concealed relevant information about actual physical site conditions underlying the baseline definition. The legal articulation of this type of claim is based upon "superior knowledge" and typically is characterized as misrepresentation or fraud. The risk of this type of claim is heightened when the data report is not made a part of the contract documents, disclaimed, or not made available (for reference or otherwise) to the constructor.

2. The project owner and/or consulting engineer misrepresented (through the baseline articulation) the actual physical conditions that would probably and reasonably be encountered by defining the baseline in a manner inconsistent with the geotechnical data available at the time the baseline was established.

3. Although the constructor sustained no time or cost impact specifically related to the conditions described in the baseline, the constructor may claim that it sustained additional time or cost impact in performing other portions of the work due to implications that it derived from the baseline description upon which it based the planning (construction means/methods, sequences or procedures) of its work. In this type of claim, a constructor will contend that it inferred, derived, or based its selection, design, and/or implementation of construction means, methods, procedures, sequences, or equipment upon the baseline definition.

Although there appear to be no known reported legal appellate cases to date regarding the baseline approach, ample precedent exists in the related context of quantity estimates developed by a consulting engineer and furnished by the project owner to bidders.[69] This legal precedent involves issues pertaining to both liability of project owners to constructors, as well as potential liability of consulting engineers to constructors. Some of the lessons learned from that precedent are certainly potentially applicable to the baseline approach.

In many instances, the consulting engineer develops quantity estimates for items or components of work to be performed. The project owner, in turn, includes these estimates in the bid and contract documents. In some instances, the project owner requests

that the constructor bid the estimated quantities of work on a unit price basis. If there are significant overruns or underruns in the estimated quantities, the constructor may assert claims for adjustments in the unit price and/or otherwise seek to renegotiate the contract price based upon the theory of "cardinal change."[70] In this type of situation, the constructor typically alleges that the project owner made misrepresentations regarding the actual quantities, miscalculated the basis of the estimates, and/or concealed information which, if disclosed to the constructor, would have clearly demonstrated that the estimates were inaccurate. In some situations, constructors will assert negligence and/or negligent misrepresentation claims against the consulting engineer which developed the quantity estimates.

The result in many of these claims depends upon whether the accuracy of the estimates is limited or disclaimed and/or whether the constructor was admonished in the bid and contract documents that the estimates were solely *approximations* rather than *absolute representations of fact* as to the physical conditions which would be encountered in the performance of the work.

Although not addressing the precise subject matter of baselines, the case law regarding constructor claims against project owners and consulting engineers based upon inaccurate or misleading quantity estimates illustrates certain legal principles that will have equal applicability to constructor claims involving "inaccurate" or "misleading" baselines. For example, consider the following:

1. Constructor claims seeking adjustments in unit prices based upon inaccurate quantity estimates are more likely to succeed in circumstances in which the estimates are "grossly," "drastically," or "substantially" inaccurate, as represented to the bidders and the constructor.

2. Constructor claims seeking adjustments in unit prices due to inaccurate quantity estimates are more likely to succeed in circumstances in which the owner concealed (consciously or not) or otherwise failed to disclose data or other relevant information upon which the estimates were predicated.

3. Even in those circumstances in which the variation between estimated and actual quantities is not significant or substantial in nature, a constructor may be entitled to an equitable adjustment in the stipulated unit prices (which were based upon estimated quantities) when the variation in quantities necessitated a material change in the contractor's reasonably anticipated construction means, methods, techniques, procedures, or sequences, including equipment required for the performance of the work.

4. The use of appropriate disclaimers, limitations, and qualifications regarding the accuracy of estimates may be effective in defeating constructor claims against the

project owner and/or consulting engineer based upon inaccuracies in the estimates (except, possibly, in circumstances in which the project owner concealed or failed to disclose material information, including data or other information, upon which the estimate was predicated).

What can we learn from these principles regarding the use of the baseline approach, especially in circumstances in which the project owner or consulting engineer knew or reasonably should have known that the baseline as defined in the bid and contract documents did not reflect physical conditions (rigorously, strictly, or) objectively indicated by the available data but, rather, was the product of a "subjective" evaluation significantly influenced by the project owner's risk tolerance/adversity attitude (rather than a strict or rigorous foundation in the available geotechnical data)?

In circumstances in which the consulting engineer knows or reasonably should know that the baseline definition (for example, quantity of significant obstructions of a defined character or size or removable by specific construction means, methods or equipment) is not entirely congruent or strictly supported by objective data but, rather, is based more on the project owner's subjective risk tolerance/adversity attitude, it is recommended that the bid and contract documents contain a provision such as the following:

> The GBR [geotechnical baseline report] includes baseline statements with respect to certain subsurface and site conditions that may be encountered during the performance of the work. These baselines were developed based upon consideration of geotechnical information and data gathered through soil borings, predictions, and evaluations concerning anticipated means/methods that may likely be utilized by the constructor and the judgmental interpretation of that information, data, and other relevant factors. The objective of establishing these baselines is to provide an objectively-defined contractual basis for the allocation of risk for site conditions and to facilitate in the resolution of claims for differing site conditions.
>
> A description of the various subsurface and site conditions in the GBR, while based on substantial geotechnical investigations and analysis included in the data reports, should not be understood or interpreted as guaranteeing or warranting that those conditions actually will be encountered during the construction process. No amount of investigation and analysis can precisely predict the characteristics, quality, or quantity of anticipated subsurface and site conditions and/or the behavior of such conditions during construction operations, the latter of which varies greatly and may be significantly dependent upon and influenced by the specific construction means/methods, including equipment, actually selected and utilized by the constructor.
>
> The baseline is not intended to represent, describe, or constitute any warranty or indication, whether expressed or implied, of the actual conditions that will be encoun-

tered in the performance of the work, nor may the contractor rely exclusively upon the baseline as the sole input for the planning or performance of any aspects of its work, including without limitation the selection and/or design of the means, methods, equipment, techniques, sequences, and procedures of construction to be employed by the contractor and safety precautions and programs incident thereto.

This type of provision should serve to clearly communicate to the constructor (and bidders) that the baseline is purely a *contractual* baseline and does not necessarily reflect the available geotechnical data regarding the baseline conditions. In addition to providing the foundation for negating claims based upon inaccuracies — gross, substantial, significant, or otherwise — in the baseline, this type of contract language should serve to defeat or undermine constructor claims based upon additional cost due to changes in anticipated construction means, methods, techniques, procedures, sequences, or equipment (due to variations between the "baseline" and actual conditions) by negating any implication or warranty that the baseline conditions would actually be encountered, thereby undercutting any contention that the constructor reasonably relied upon the baseline to represent the actual conditions to be encountered.

Some have suggested that when the baseline approach is utilized, it is neither necessary nor advisable to include data reports or other information that may form the basis of the baseline within the definition of the contract documents.[71] Although, by establishing a clear and objective (baseline) definition of physical conditions, one of the primary purposes of the baseline approach is to minimize the possibility (or opportunity) of reaching different (albeit competing and reasonable) interpretations from indications of anticipated physical conditions, the concealing or failing to disclose relevant and material data (or other information upon which the baseline was established) may foster and facilitate a constructor's claim, predicated upon the theory of "superior knowledge," of "inaccurate" or "misleading" baselines, especially when the baseline does not reflect the available geotechnical data.

In addition, the baselines may not address all relevant physical site conditions and, therefore, the geotechnical data and related reports may separately have significance in the evaluation and/or resolution of differing site condition claims related to conditions *not addressed* in baselines. Serious and careful consideration should be given to these issues before making a decision either to exclude data and related reports from the definition of "contract documents" or not to disclose that information to the constructor.

Implementing the Geotechnical Baseline Approach

A preliminary but important question in implementing the baseline concept is "Who prepares the baseline?" The obvious candidates (assuming multiple professional firms are involved in the design and construction process) are the geotechnical engineer, the

prime design professional (if different from the geotechnical engineer), and the construction management professional (if different from either the geotechnical engineer or prime design professional). Although the baseline is to some extent predicated upon geotechnical data developed by the geotechnical engineer as a result of subsurface investigations, it is not necessarily the case in all instances that the geotechnical engineer will actually prepare the baseline. The baseline preparer will consult with other members of the design team, especially the geotechnical engineer, and will need to get, at minimum, the geotechnical engineer's review of the definition and expression of the baseline for (a) consistency with the geotechnical data or other geotechnical reports or information to be provided or otherwise made available to the contractor[72] and (b) conformance with the project owner's risk tolerance/adversity attitude or philosophy.

In addition to coordination issues among the various design and construction management professionals in preparing and reviewing the baseline, it is important that adequate consideration be given to the status of the geotechnical baseline report (GBR), specifically, will it be a contract document? If so, will other geotechnical reports, such as the geotechnical data report (GDR) or geotechnical interpretive report (GIR), be provided or otherwise made available to the constructor and, if so, will they be regarded as contract documents or reference documents or given some other designated status? If the GBR, GDR and GIR are all to be designated contract documents, will any order of precedence be established among them?[73] What if the baseline does not address all anticipated subsurface conditions? Will geotechnical data or other reports be made available and/or included as part of the contract documents so as to establish for purposes of the differing site condition (DSC) clause what is to be indicated in the contract documents regarding non-baseline subsurface conditions?

All of these questions are important not only for the purpose of establishing clarity in the definition and expression of the baseline, but also to minimize the risk of professional liability. Generally speaking, when risk is ambiguously or unfairly allocated for site conditions between the project owner and constructor, there is a significant increase in the risk of professional liability for the design and consulting engineer.[74]

In this regard, it is important to bear in mind that the primary audience (there may be secondary audiences, such as dispute review boards, courts, or other dispute resolvers) to whom the baseline is directed is the constructor, who must use the baseline in bidding, pricing, and planning the work. As such, the baseline should be written (expressed) not only clearly, but also in a manner that the constructor will understand from a cost and constructability standpoint. To accomplish that, it may be advisable to have someone with construction experience review the baseline prior to publication. In addition, legal review of the baseline, as well as other geotechnical reports, may be advisable. As one commentator has noted:

One often overlooked opportunity for reducing potential misunderstandings over the contractual status and meaning of geotechnical reports is to include an experienced construction attorney in the review effort. Owners regularly establish and deploy well compensated teams of highly qualified, experienced engineers on design review panels and consulting engineer boards. Such rigorous technical reviews by experienced individuals identify and prevent potential problems. However, it seems that it is anathema for them to consider the contractual component. Though no rational owner or design engineer would undertake a tunnel project without a geotechnical report and evaluation, many owners and engineers think nothing of adapting, without consultation with experienced counsel, and without regard to project risk, contract provisions which unfairly allocate risk and subjugate the carefully coordinated language of standard form contracts. (As the saying goes, there are more engineers practicing law than vice versa.) Apparently, only a few owners are enlightened enough to realize that properly selected and managed, lawyers can be constructive members of a team and provide added value and a real benefit during the planning, contract document preparation, and execution phases of a project. Indeed, one former major public owner from the Pacific Northwest consistently urges owners to "partner" *with* their lawyers.

This need not be a costly proposition, and will certainly be cost effective. A modest amount of lawyer involvement in offering suggestions for drafting a more usable and less ambiguous GBR [geotechnical baseline report], for example, will cost substantially less than the legal involvement that might be required for the formal negotiation for a major dispute. It is true that there is an obvious objection to lawyer involvement because so often the response from an unenlightened lawyer (one who does not understand risk allocation in construction) is "no you can't do that." The acceptable response of course is "I'll work with you to find a way that this *can* be done." Thus, owners should retain counsel with that attitude.[75]

Finally, it is important that the consulting engineer involved in the administration of the construction contract, especially in the review and evaluation of differing site condition claims, understand the purpose of the baseline approach and how the baseline relates to the statutory or contractual differing site condition provisions that are included in the contract documents. Specifically, will *any* variation in actual conditions encountered from the baseline expression of those conditions qualify as a differing site condition, or must the variation be *material* in nature? Specifically, most differing site condition clauses, whether statutorily mandated or otherwise, limit recovery to only those conditions that are *materially* different from those indicated in the contract documents. Although some of these issues may be addressed in the field during construction, it is highly preferable that they be anticipated and clearly addressed in the contract docu-

ments. In this regard, it is recommended that the baseline be reviewed by the project owner's legal counsel for conformity with statutory or contractual differing site condition provisions included in the contract documents. For the consulting engineer's own reasons, it should request that its own legal counsel review the baseline articulation for professional liability implications.

The Baseline Approach and Construction Means and Methods

Careful consideration should be given by the consulting engineer to professional liability implications and risk associated with using the baseline approach to address construction means and methods, equipment, and related constructor performance matters.

Although the baseline approach is relatively new, it is generally acknowledged that the use of baselines should be restricted to the definition (qualitative or quantitative) of *physical site conditions* anticipated to be encountered, as distinct from the definition and/or prescription of either (a) the construction means and methods to be utilized by the constructor or (b) the performance expectations, requirements, standards, or other related matters that may directly or indirectly implicate the constructor's construction means and methods, equipment, or safety precautions and programs. For example, it has been observed that:

> In general, a baseline report that predicts performance is asking for trouble, as this is only partly determined by geologic conditions, and is also partly determined by the contractor's means and methods, which the engineer can not predict. Items such as TBM production rate, utilization, penetration rate or cutter wear; overbreak; or a precise description of what will be encountered at a specific location or a level of detail beyond what is needed should not be given. There may be exceptions to this, but the owner needs to understand the risks involved in the detailed monitoring required to verify means and methods.[76]

While the establishment of a baseline may be predicated upon assumptions about the construction means and methods to be selected by the constructor,[77] or may be established in a manner intended to influence the constructor's selection of construction means and methods,[78] it is generally recommended by those with substantial experience in subsurface projects that the baseline not address construction means and methods, constructor equipment, or related constructor performance considerations.[79]

Despite the general admonition that baselines should relate solely to the definition of physical site conditions as distinct from constructor performance expectations, requirements, or standards, there will inevitably be circumstances in which project owners request (or, as a matter of professional judgment, engineers conclude) that base-

lines be developed for certain constructor performance expectations, requirements, or standards. Should the consulting engineer decide to utilize the baseline approach for such a purpose, the issue will become whether that can be accomplished in a manner that limits (in the sense of defining, restricting, qualifying, and managing) the project owner's and consulting engineer's risk exposure for construction means and methods and safety-related issues.

The case of *CH2M Hill, Inc. v. Herman* (the "*CH2M Hill* case"),[80] while not explicitly involving baselines, may be used to demonstrate some of the relevant points in this regard.

CH2M Hill Central, Inc. (CH2M Hill), a consulting engineering firm, entered into an agreement with the Milwaukee Metropolitan Sewerage District (the District) to provide services for the Water Pollution Abatement Project (the project). The project consisted of numerous tunnels, shafts, sewers, and other systems to collect and convey both storm drainage and sewerage to two wastewater treatment plants. At issue was a portion of the project known as the "cross-town collector" (CT), one of several 10-foot diameter sewers, which included construction of the CT-7 Tunnel. The Secretary of Labor issued citations following a methane gas explosion in the CT-7 Tunnel in which three employees of the general contractor died. CH2M Hill was cited for violations of construction standards based on allegations that the electrical equipment and circuits in the CT-7 Tunnel were not approved for hazardous locations, that employees were not trained in the explosive and toxic gas hazards associated with tunnel construction, and that the ventilation in the tunnel was not adequate. The OSHA Review Commission affirmed the issuance of those citations against CH2M Hill; however, on appeal, the United States Court of Appeals for the Seventh Circuit vacated the citations.

Much of the record in the *CH2M Hill* case centered upon CH2M Hill's role in connection with a modification to the construction contract relating to a differing site condition (DSC) involving methane gas. It may be helpful to focus more precisely upon the circumstances giving rise to that modification and CH2M Hill's role in relation to the modification, and then to revisit (with the benefit of hindsight) how the engineer's risk of OSHA exposure and potentially other forms of professional liability risk may have been mitigated and managed in such circumstances (recognizing, of course, that hindsight is "great").

The Methane Gas Differing Site Condition

CT-8 Tunnel

The project involved the construction of several tunnels in the Menomonee Valley, including the CT-7 Tunnel, which was directly involved in the *CH2M Hill* case and the so-called CT-8 Tunnel, the construction of which had commenced prior to the award of the CT-7 Tunnel Contract. During pre-construction activities in April 1987 in the Menomonee Valley, Jay Dee, the general contractor for the CT-8 Tunnel, encountered methane in a bore hole while drilling pre-construction surface test borings. Subsequently, in December 1987, during tunneling, Jay Dee shut down a TBM due to perceived explosive levels of methane. Jay Dee submitted notice of a differing site condition claim based upon the encounter of methane in the CT-8 Tunnel. In that differing site condition claim, Jay Dee sought an equitable adjustment for the cost of additional safety and other incidental construction means and methods, measures which it claimed it had not anticipated in its bid (based upon information in the contract documents) and considered necessary due to the discovery of the methane gas differing site condition. At or about the same time, Jay Dee hired Testing Service Corporation to investigate the methane gas condition.

The task order pertaining to the services on the CT-8 Tunnel between the District and CH2M Hill obligated CH2M Hill to investigate, evaluate, and make a recommendation to the District regarding any contractor claims, including differing site condition claims. In the process of evaluating Jay Dee's methane gas differing site condition claim, CH2M Hill retained Engineering-Science, Inc. to investigate the occurrence of methane along the alignment of the CT-8 Tunnel and also retained another independent consultant to advise on appropriate measures that could be taken to address that condition along the CT-8 Tunnel alignment.

The final report of Testing Service Corporation — Jay Dee's consultant — concluded that methane was present in the soil along the alignment of the CT-8 Tunnel, that there was a possibility that ignitable concentrations could exist for a few seconds, and that those conditions could lead to a serious methane incident. Engineering-Science's final report similarly concluded that the presence of methane in the soil along the CT-8 Tunnel alignment was possible, although its amount and location were unknown, and that there was a risk of ignitable concentrations.

Based upon these reports, CH2M Hill recommended to the District that Jay Dee's methane gas differing site condition claim be granted. The District agreed with that recommendation and, in accordance with its responsibilities under the task order, CH2M Hill prepared for the District's approval a modification to the CT-8 Tunnel construction contract, which the District approved and executed in March 1988.

CT-7 Tunnel

By the time the methane gas differing site condition had been identified and acknowledged on the CT-8 Tunnel, the District had awarded to S.A. Healy Co. the construction contract for the CT-7 Tunnel.

Based upon the investigation conducted in connection with the methane gas differing site condition claim on the CT-8 Tunnel, the District and CH2M Hill anticipated that a similar methane gas condition likely would or reasonably could be encountered at locations along the alignment of the CT-7 Tunnel. Investigations and resultant reports regarding the discovery of methane in the CT-8 Tunnel were considered relevant to the CT-7 Tunnel project because the "potential for encountering methane" was not perceived as materially different for the two tunnels, because both were soft ground tunnel construction work sites, the sites of both tunnels shared the same geologic setting, and both tunnels were located in the Menomonee Valley where organic soils are found and are "known to produce gas."[81] However, as in the case of the CT-8 Tunnel, the precise amounts and/or locations of such anticipated conditions could not be predicted or ascertained with any reasonable certainty.

Clearly, at this point the project owner had information about anticipated site conditions — specifically, the possible presence of methane gas in the CT-7 Tunnel — which (a) was either not available, indicated, or previously investigated to the extent now known prior to the award of the CT-7 Tunnel contract and (b) was not disclosed to the CT-7 Tunnel contractor at the time of bid. Since the CT-7 Tunnel contract had already been awarded at this time, the occurrence of methane gas in the CT-7 Tunnel would need to be addressed during the construction phase through the differing site condition provision. Also, since the project owner had acknowledged that the CT-8 Tunnel contractor was entitled to a differing site condition due to the presence of methane gas, it was probable that the same result would occur were a similar differing site condition claim made by the CT-7 Tunnel contractor.

Given these circumstances, what options were available to the District with respect to the possible methane gas condition in the CT-7 Tunnel?

1. Non-Disclosure Approach

In these circumstances, in which the project owner is aware (based upon the prior experience in the CT-8 Tunnel) of the possibility of methane gas in the CT-7 Tunnel, the owner faces the risk of claims from the CT-7 contractor based upon the theories of "superior knowledge," "fraud," "concealment," "misrepresentation," or "cardinal change" should the owner fail to disclose the potential methane gas condition to that contractor. For those reasons alone, non-disclosure of the methane gas condition is not an advisable option.

2. Disclosure and Deferral Approach

The project owner may choose to disclose the potential methane gas condition to the CT-7 Tunnel contractor and advise the contractor that in the event that methane gas were encountered along the alignment of the CT-7 Tunnel, the contractor should pursue the remedy provided under the differing site conditions clause in the contract documents. However, the contractor may be admonished to plan for the contingency that methane gas would be encountered so that the progress of the work would not be disrupted nor shut-downs occur should the methane gas condition be encountered. Presumably, this planning effort would include the identification and furnishing by the contractor (*after* bidding and award of the construction contract) of any appropriate temporary tunnel ventilation, equipment modifications, or other incidental means and methods to address the contingent risk of encountering methane gas. Any definitive resolution of a time or cost equitable adjustment due to any such methane gas differing site condition would be deferred.

In substance and effect, this option would defer addressing the methane gas condition until such a condition was actually encountered in the CT-7 Tunnel. The problems with this approach are several: the available information, including the prior actual experience of the same owner on the CT-8 Tunnel, indicates that methane gas is, at the very least, likely to be encountered in the CT-7 Tunnel given the location of that tunnel in the Menomonee Valley, and thus, deferral may result in avoiding the condition until some inopportune time during construction or tunneling operations; addressing the methane gas condition through the differing site condition claims process during the construction or tunneling operations may lead to conflict and associated delay and disruption and other (negative) consequential project impact that could have been avoided through an

effort to address the condition initiated prior to the start of those operations; encountering the methane gas condition during construction or tunneling operations may lead to the need to suspend or shut down the work or otherwise result in a negative impact on job progress or schedule; and simply informing the contractor to "plan for" potential methane gas conditions in an unspecified quantity somewhere along the CT-7 Tunnel alignment would not be especially meaningful to the contractor and could lead to the extremes of either wholly inadequate or substantially excessive planning by the contractor—the former of which would pose a substantial risk of negatively impacting job progress or schedule, while the latter would lead to potentially inflated contractor claims.

3. Baseline Approach

Acknowledging the likelihood that a methane gas condition may be encountered in various locations and concentrations along the CT-7 Tunnel alignment, the owner may opt to anticipate and address that condition through the issuance of a contract modification (given that the construction contract had already been awarded), which would acknowledge the existence of a methane gas differing site condition and establish a basis of compensation (i.e., equitable adjustment under the differing site condition clause) for equipment, temporary ventilation, and other incidental means and methods costs which the contractor should plan (expect) to incur in the expectation (contractual assumption) that methane gas will be encountered.

This baseline approach has the advantage of reckoning (prior to the commencement of tunneling operations) with the probable reality of a methane gas differing site condition in the CT-7 Tunnel and establishing some defined basis for compensation (equitable adjustment) for the contractor's costs in planning for and dealing with that condition. The primary potential concern with this approach may be the "dislocation" of previously established contractual risk allocation provisions, which assign exclusive responsibility for construction means and methods and safety precautions to the contractor. However, this concern may be mitigated through certain limiting language in the modification developed to effectuate the baseline approach.

What should be the project owner's objectives in these circumstances?

There are several objectives which should be considered by the project owner in these circumstances:

- Avoidance of constructor claims based upon theories of superior knowledge, fraud, concealment, misrepresentation, or cardinal change, given the

owner's awareness of the methane gas condition previously encountered on the CT-8 Tunnel located in the same valley as the CT-7 Tunnel.

- Avoidance of disputes, conflicts, claims, and associated delay, disruption, and other negative consequential impact on job progress or otherwise, if it becomes necessary to address methane gas differing site condition claims during the construction or tunneling operations.

- Avoidance of job shut down or suspension as a result of failing to adequately plan for the occurrence of methane gas during construction or tunneling operations.

- To develop a "baseline" approach to acknowledge, define, and establish a basis for compensation, in advance of commencement of construction or tunneling operations, due to a methane gas differing site condition, and thereby avoid and mitigate all of the above concerns.

- To accomplish and implement contractually the "baseline" approach without "dislocating" or disrupting previously established contractual risk allocation provisions, particularly those assigning to the constructor exclusive responsibility for construction means and methods and safety precautions and programs.

How Did the Project Owner in the CH2M Hill Case Choose to Address the Possibility of a Methane Gas Differing Site Condition in the CT-7 Tunnel?

The District sought to avoid differing site condition claims based upon the discovery of methane gas in the CT-7 Tunnel, as well as similar methane gas differing site condition claims expected from other Menomonee Valley tunnel contractors. Toward that end, the District requested that CH2M Hill evaluate the technical and financial issues associated with the preparation of a modification for the CT-7 Tunnel contract that would anticipate and resolve (at least to a degree) certain issues relating to expected methane gas differing site condition claims during construction. The objective of this process was to develop a contract modification that would specify *minimum* contractor performance requirements or standards for ventilation and other incidental means and methods to address the methane gas condition and to establish the basis for compensation thereof. While the word "baseline" was not used to describe this process, in substantive effect the owner was utilizing a baseline approach in proceeding in this manner.[82]

In January 1988 and during the next month, CH2M Hill held meetings with the CT-7 Tunnel contractor to discuss constructability issues related to the anticipated discovery of methane gas in that tunnel. In addition, at this time, CH2M Hill consulted the manufacturer of the LOVAT Tunnel Boring Machines, tunneling experts (including those from the United States Bureau of Mines), and also reviewed applicable OSHA and related state safety regulations. Based upon these consultations and investigations, and in accordance with its obligations under the task order applicable to the CT-7 Tunnel Project, CH2M Hill prepared a draft contract modification. The modification was entitled "Specification Modifications Pertaining to Methane Gas . . . Modifications to Specifications Section 01016 'Safety Requirements and Protection of Property.'" The modification specified the following performance requirements and stated that the contractor would be compensated for the cost of the additional equipment necessary to comply with those requirements, which included:

- An air supply of 200 cubic feet per minute per person.
- A linear velocity of 60 feet per minute (twice that required by the old tunneling standard).
- Ventilation to be adjusted to eliminate pockets of stagnant air.
- Continuous methane monitor to be at the muck discharge point on the TBM.
- The continuous monitor to sound an alarm at 10 percent of LEL [lower explosive limit] (not required by the old tunneling standard).
- The TBM to automatically shut down if methane levels reached 20 percent of LEL (the old tunneling standard required shut-down at 30 percent of LEL).
- The tunnel to be evacuated if methane levels reached 20 percent of LEL (the old tunneling standard required evacuation at 30 percent of LEL).
- Non-employee activated equipment (i.e., other than welders, lasers, pumps, etc.) to be approved for Division 2 from the face to the end of the trailing gear.

All of the expert witnesses in the OSHA proceedings testified that the above-stated combination of performance requirements set forth in the modification reflected sound engineering judgment.

On April 5, 1988, the District approved and issued the modification for the CT-7 Tunnel Contract.

Before the Review Commission, CH2M Hill emphasized that the record contained no evidence that:

- Healy believed that the contract modification or clarification prevented or relieved Healy from complying with OSHA requirements.

- The District or CH2M Hill in any way restricted or challenged Healy's ability or authority to install or use safety equipment required by OSHA standards, either directly or indirectly.

- Healy was in any manner restricted by the modification from installing additional safety equipment in the tunnel.

- The District or CH2M Hill purported to relieve Healy of any duty to comply with OSHA requirements.

- The contract modification stated or purported to state anything other than Healy's contractual obligations to the District.

- Healy could not have spent its own funds, or could not have requested additional funds from the District, to cover the cost of additional equipment and measures if it believed that OSHA standards required them.

In commenting upon CH2M Hill's role in connection with the modification process, the Secretary of Labor argued before the Review Commission that:

> Hill's leading role in the development and implementation . . . of the contract modification showed its in-depth role in safety at the site. . . . That modification addressed numerous safety issues regarding methane gas in the tunnel. . . . Moreover, the record shows that when methane threatened the project, Hill didn't just passively watch the schedule, it directed the construction management response to the hazard. It did not simply advise the owner or the contractor, it dictated the specific solutions to the methane problem by means of a contract modification that it wrote and which both the contractor and the MMSD referred to. Unlike a consultant, Hill did not simply provide data and assistance to Healy in determining what kind of equipment to use in the tunnel; rather, it supervised the research, analyzed the data, identified the required equipment, and then required Healy to enter into a contract modification. . . . In view of Hill's supervision of the project in the aggregate and its dominating role in determining the means of abating the specific methane hazard, Hill was clearly supervising the work in CT-7, and was therefore performing construction work under Part 1926.

The Review Commission substantially adopted the Secretary's arguments, in holding:

> In order to answer that question [relating to the relationship between contractual limitations on CH2M Hill's responsibility for safety and construction means and methods and other contractual provisions that granted certain administrative authority to CH2M Hill], we will review in some detail the circumstances of the Differing Site Condition ("DSC") contract modification. Broadly stated, from CH2M's perspective, the function of the modification was solely to determine whether or not Healy would be reimbursed for actions related to the potential methane gas hazard at CT-7. In the Secretary's view, the contract modification was not only about money, but necessarily implicated safety. We agree with the Secretary.
>
> Acting under the differing site condition and contract modification mechanisms, CH2M Hill implemented a contract specification directed specifically toward, and with the intent of eliminating, a substantial safety hazard at the site, the occurrence of methane gas. CH2M initiated a safety meeting with Healy and gave explicit safety instruction to the trade contractors, who in turn understood that CH2M was providing guidance and direction. CH2M's manager of the geotechnical office . . . initially formulated the contract modification, and it was communicated . . . through the resident engineer as a mandatory requirement. . . . In fact, the [District] and its approving official . . . relied on CH2M's expertise to determine what contractual provisions or specifications were necessary to meet the changed conditions encountered during the course of the work.

Accordingly, the Review Commission held that CH2M Hill was subject to Part 1926 of the OSHA Regulations and affirmed the issuance of the citations against CH2M Hill. In summarizing its conclusion, the Review Commission stated:

> The contracts here contain express language providing that the trade contractor, not CH2M, would have sole responsibility for safety precautions and programs. On the other hand, CH2M's many affirmative responsibilities and its authority clearly implicated safety, as did the exercises of its authority. In finding the construction standards applicable, we do not do so based on a presumption that a broad scope of duties necessarily implies responsibility for safety as well. Rather, we reach our conclusion based on an extensive record which illuminates specifically how safety concerns and safety issues were resolved in actual prac-

tice on the work site in question. As we have stated, in terms of its de facto actions, CH2M effectively was the nerve center through which means were developed and implemented for allowing the work to be conducted in light of a major safety hazard for a tunneling operation, the presence of methane gas. In terms of its contractual authority, CH2M was required to review and approve necessary actions, including Healy's safety program.

However, in a well-reasoned dissenting opinion, one Commissioner appropriately commented that:

> Having discounted the significance of the contractual provisions themselves, I now turn to the question of whether, through the Differing Site Condition (DSC) process and the issuance of a contract modification, CH2M in fact exercised control over Healy and other trade contractors with regard to matters of safety. There can be no dispute that safety issues were a necessary component of the contract modification, since the differing condition that created the need for the modification in the first place was primarily a safety hazard. However, all sizable construction projects require change orders at some point in time, and the implementation of this change order was nothing more than an exercise of CH2M's authority to draft contract language as agent for the MMSD. Viewed from the perspective of the DSC Process, and the primary objective of financial remuneration that it serves, there is little difference, if any, between the drafting of a contract specification to address a known condition at the site and the subsequent drafting of the same contract language to deal with the same condition as it becomes known. The majority does not contend, nor does our case law support the proposition, that drafting of contract language in itself constitutes the performance of construction work. In any event, the majority fails to specify any criteria by which we can identify those change orders that are so linked to safety as to bring the draftsman under the construction standards.[83]

In its brief filed with the Review Commission, CH2M Hill raised substantial issues about Healy's non-compliance with the requirements of the contract modification, such as Healy's reconfiguration of its ventilation system so as to permit methane gas to be recirculated in pockets rather than exhausted out of the tunnel; the TBM operator's alteration of the TBM in a manner that violated the contract modifications; and the fact that Healy did not comply with the evacuation plan, all of which directly related to the circumstances leading to the fatalities that occurred as a result of the methane gas explosion.

The Seventh Circuit vacated the citations issued against CH2M Hill, stating:

> In this case, no significant evidence in the record supports the factual findings of the Commission that CH2M Hill exercised substantial supervision or control. . . . The Secretary asserts CH2M Hill did engage in such activities based upon its responsibilities regarding the issuance of the contract modification with regard to discovery of methane gas in tunnel CT-8. Although the Secretary acknowledges that MMSD retained authority to determine the methods of construction and that MMSD asked CH2M Hill to investigate the problem, she argues that the Commission was substantially justified in *assuming* that the DSC procedures for contract modifications were the mechanism adopted by the parties to address safety concerns and that CH2M Hill must have exercised substantial control over the contractors in its fulfillment of duties related to the DSC procedure. She rests the remainder of her argument on the contention that the record supports the fact that the parties "perceived" CH2M Hill as the organization exercising authority over safety procedures, as evidenced by Healy's deferral to the firm with regard to its safety procedures in relation to the contract modifications for methane gas. This perception, according to the Secretary, stems from CH2M Hill's "hands-on" supervision of critical safety hazards (evidenced by CH2M Hill employees entering the tunnels), its authority to issue contract modifications (evidenced by its drafting responsibilities in the DSC procedures) and the fact that Healy looked to CH2M Hill for an explanation of the contract modification language (evidenced by the communication between the two explaining the contract modification regarding methane). From these conclusions, the Secretary argues that it is reasonable to assume that CH2M Hill could have required Healy to comply with the contract modifications, even though that did not in fact happen in this case.
>
> The problem with the Secretary's argument is that it only presents half of the picture of what was really happening with regard to the contract modifications. First, it is difficult to see how the contract language in Task Order 189 in which the MMSD contract with CH2M Hill to "[n]egotiate proposed contract modifications with the Contractor's representatives and make specific recommendations [and u]pon authorization by the DISTRICT, prepare and submit the contract modifications to the DISTRICT for submittal to the agencies for approval," contractually gives CH2M Hill direct authority over safety procedures in the tunnels. While some contract modifications may deal with issues that raise questions of safety, such as the one at issue in this case, contract modifica-

tion could occur for more mundane reasons as well, such as inclement weather or supply problems. In addition, any modification dealing with safety had to be approved by MMSD. CH2M Hill could not act on its own. A plain reading of this language does not support the Secretary's claims or the Commission's conclusions that CH2M Hill assumed ultimate responsibility for safety precautions in direct opposition to other language in its contracts with MMSD expressly disclaiming such responsibility.

The Secretary's contention that CH2M Hill's exercised de facto authority over safety in the tunnels also falls short of the mark. The Secretary seems to refuse to acknowledge that while CH2M Hill drafted the contract modification language and served as the contact person for Healy, the firm reported to and had to obtain the approval of MMSD before any modifications were incorporated into the existing contract. The Secretary makes much of the fact that Tom Lutzenberger, MMSD's director of construction, testified that he did not believe he had the knowledge base upon which to make recommendations regarding safety precautions and that although he was informed of CH2M Hill's meetings with Healy, he did not attend them. While it may be true that Lutzenberger did not exercise the control envisioned by the Task Order or that he simply did not have the qualifications to make such decisions, we will not predicate liability on CH2M Hill, who fulfilled its contract duties, because MMSD did not hire qualified individuals to oversee the process for which it had contractually retained responsibility.

In addition, the fact that Healy turned to CH2M Hill for advice does not indicate that CH2M Hill was acting as the de facto director of safety. Before it issued the clarification, CH2M Hill had to check with MMSD. From the record it is clear that CH2M Hill functioned as an intermediary between Healy and MMSD. MMSD directed the modifications; it ordered CH2M Hill to conduct an inquiry, reviewed CH2M Hill's suggestions and granted the final approval to the draft language, as well as the clarification of it requested by Healy. With this fuller picture, it would be disingenuous to say that the record supports the Commission or the Secretary's conclusion that CH2M Hill played a "central role" as the "nerve center" for developing and implementing safety practices for tunnel CT-7. . . .

CH2M Hill, while it exercised some authority, had only limited authority that was always subject to final approval by MMSD. While CH2M Hill drafted the DSC changes, MMSD (whether it exercised its responsibility attentively or not) had to approve any changes made. CH2M Hill was required to consult with

MMSD before such decisions were final. Unlike the employers found to come within the domain of the regulations, CH2M Hill lacked the necessary authority or supervisory responsibilities. CH2M Hill did not function as a coordinator of the safety program; the contract specifically removed this responsibility from CH2M Hill. Nor did it make representations that it would ensure the safety regulations were met. The firm through its drafting of contract modifications did not function in a manner that was "inextricably intertwined" with the actual construction. It could not instruct Healy how to perform the construction work, nor halt the work if the required regulatory safety measures were not met. In fact, it its explanation to Healy, it told the company to seek the advice of the manufacturer of the equipment for compliance. It did not accept that role itself. Thus, based on the Commission's own line of cases, CH2M Hill should not be subject to the construction standards for its work on the Program (*CH2M Hill*, 192 F. 3d at 721–724).

For the reasons previously discussed, the baseline approach was, in the opinion of this author, the appropriate response in the circumstances presented in the *CH2M Hill* case to address the anticipated methane gas condition in the CT-7 Tunnel. Since the construction contract had already been awarded to Healy, it was necessary to implement this baseline approach through a contract modification.

Reflecting on the contract modification process actually utilized, are there any risk management recommendations that may have mitigated, or improved the management of, the potential of OSHA and related professional liability exposure for the consulting engineer (understanding, of course, that "hindsight is great") in implementing the baseline approach in these circumstances?

At this point, it may be appropriate to revisit some of the objectives of a project owner opting to utilize the baseline approach in the circumstances presented by the methane gas condition in the Menomonee Valley. In substance, the project owner would be seeking a mechanism to anticipate and mitigate (or avoid) any negative impacts on project cost or schedule which could result if the methane gas condition were encountered along the CT-7 Tunnel alignment by establishing a baseline that would define *minimum* ventilation and associated performance requirements (i.e., incidental means and methods measures) that the contractor would be required to implement and for which the contractor would be entitled to an equitable adjustment (i.e., compensation). By addressing the potential methane gas differing site condition through a proactive base-

line approach, the project owner would also hope to reduce the risk of disruptive and costly differing site condition claims during the construction or tunneling operations and/or a work suspension or job shut down if such conditions were encountered without adequate contractual mechanisms requiring the constructor to anticipate and plan for (by furnishing incidental means and methods) those conditions. In addition, it would be important that the baseline approach be contractually implemented in a manner which did not "dislocate" or imbalance other contractual provisions allocating to the constructor exclusive control and responsibility for construction means and methods and safety precautions or programs.

What are the relevant risk management/professional liability considerations from the standpoint of a consulting engineer providing "traditional" engineering services on behalf of the project owner in these circumstances? Clearly, the project owner typically would need the services of the consulting engineer to advise and assist in the development and implementation (through document provisions) of the baseline approach and would request (if not require) that the consulting engineer provide the necessary services in those respects. Rejecting the project owner's request for such services may not be a viable or realistic option from a "client relations" or "business" perspective.

However, to a significant degree, providing the requested services may (a) constitute (or be deemed to constitute) an involvement of the consulting engineer in construction means and methods and safety precautions and programs; (b) require the consulting engineer to perform services or become involved in areas beyond those specifically required in its agreement with the project owner; (c) result in a "dislocation" or imbalancing of the constructor's otherwise exclusive responsibility for construction means and methods and safety-related issues due to the consulting engineer's involvement in the latter areas;[84] and (d) expose the consulting engineer to the risk of civil liability and/or OSHA exposure.[85]

Given the owner's objectives for using the baseline approach and the consulting engineer's risk and liability concerns, how can the baseline approach be developed and implemented in these circumstances in a manner that may reasonably accomplish the project owner's objectives, provide reasonable risk management controls for the consulting engineer's professional liability concerns, and potentially mitigate the consulting engineer's risk of OSHA exposure?

Documentation Between Project Owner and Consulting Engineer

The project owner's request to the consulting engineer for specific involvement in the development and implementation of the baseline approach should be documented, especially if compliance with this request is not within the scope of the basic services required of the consulting engineer. While such a request may have financial implications in terms of the consulting engineer's entitlement to additional compensation, there are other equally, if not more, important ramifications of a risk management/professional liability nature presented by such a request. Specifically, as noted above, such a request may result in (or may later be alleged to have resulted in) the consulting engineer's involvement in construction means and methods and/or safety issues, thereby subjecting the consultant to increased risk of both civil liability and OSHA exposure. The limited nature of the consultant's involvement should be documented so as to establish and memorialize the defined scope and extent of that involvement. In addition, the *purpose* of that involvement should be confirmed in writing. In relation to using the baseline approach in the differing site condition context, the specific purpose would be to advise and assist the project owner in developing, defining, and contractually implementing a basis for acknowledging a differing site condition and establishing the basis for compensating the constructor for certain *minimum*, or *baseline,* performance standards required to address that condition. In other words, the purpose is directed to the definition and implementation of a contractual baseline due to a differing site condition and the establishment of a basis for equitable adjustment under the contract due to that condition—not to safety-related issues *per se*.

This documentation between the project owner and consulting engineer may be effectuated by an amendment to the agreement between them or, at a minimum, through correspondence between them. The documentation should clearly state that the consulting engineer's specific, defined, and limited involvement in this particular issue does not create or imply any broader obligations of the consultant with respect to any other construction means and methods and/or safety-related matters; nor does the consulting engineer's involvement in the particular construction means and methods issue negate, diminish, or otherwise affect or alter the contractor's otherwise exclusive and complete responsibility under the contract documents for construction means and methods and safety-related issues.

Contract Document Provisions Relating to Baseline

Statement of Purpose of the Contract Document Baseline Provisions: The pertinent baseline provisions of the contract documents should contain an explicit statement as to the purpose of those provisions, i.e., to acknowledge the differing site condition and to define certain *minimum* or *baseline* performance standards that the contractor is required to implement for the purpose of addressing that condition and establishing the basis of an equitable adjustment. It may also be helpful to state that no differing site condition claim predicated upon the condition described in the baseline will be granted unless the contractor has fully complied with and implemented the minimum contractor performance requirements or standards set forth in the contract documents.

It may be preferable that the relevant contract document provisions (a) have a title or description that reflects the pertinent site conditions, rather than one that reflects safety-related requirements, and (b) be stand-alone in nature, i.e., not characterized as a revision to safety or related specifications or similar portions of the contract documents.

Text of Contract Document Baseline Provision: The text of the baseline provision should make clear that *minimum* or *baseline* performance requirements or standards are stated in order to establish a clearly defined basis for an equitable adjustment or compensation for certain (i.e., not the universe of) measures or standards required to be undertaken by the constructor. In this regard, (a) the more detailed or prescriptive the description of the minimum requirements or standards, the greater the risk that the consulting engineer may later be determined to have assumed responsibility for the adequacy (in a total or aggregate sense) of the measures required to address the differing site condition, and (b) the less discretion given to the contractor to develop supplemental and/or other necessary measures, the greater the risk of professional liability and potential OSHA exposure for the consulting engineer. As such, some may consider it preferable to express those *minimum* requirements or standards in a "performance" manner (leaving the development of complete details to the contractor's discretion within broad guidelines), even though that approach may result in a less precisely defined baseline for compensation purposes.

Contract Document Provisions Maintaining and Reinforcing Contractual Risk Allocation for Construction Means and Methods and Safety Precautions and Programs

The contract document provisions pertaining to the baseline should clearly state and emphasize that the constructor performance requirements and standards set forth therein to address the site condition that is the subject of the baseline are *minimum* (or baseline) in nature and that the constructor and/or its subcontractors remain solely and completely responsible for the design and implementation of all appropriate construction means and methods and safety precautions and programs, including without limitation compliance with all applicable federal, state and local, and industry rules and regulations regarding the safe conduct of the work and protection of persons and property. In this regard, it may be useful to explicitly reference, and thereby reinforce, the pertinent provisions in the contract document that allocate those responsibilities to the constructor and its subcontractors.

In addition, the contract document baseline provisions should also state that neither the project owner's issuance of the baseline nor any of the actions, performance of services, and/or recommendations of the consulting engineer in the development, negotiation, and/or preparation of the terms of the baseline shall relieve the constructor of its exclusive contractual responsibility regarding construction means and methods and safety precautions and programs.

The baseline approach is a relatively new, innovative, and somewhat controversial contracting practice. In many respects, the baseline approach, if prudently implemented, does represent a potentially and significantly positive and constructive opportunity to minimize conflict, disputes, and claims involving differing site conditions. However, the professional liability risk associated with the use of the baseline approach must be anticipated and recognized. As in the case of most risk, this professional liability risk can be effectively managed and contained.

Recommended Practices

- The consulting engineer should document recommendations made to the project owner, especially those relating to the scope of subsurface investigation and the establishment of the baseline, as well as all important decisions relating to those recommendations and the project owner's decisions regarding project subsurface work.

- In circumstances involving underlying constructor claims against the project owner, the consulting engineer and project owner should endeavor to work together in the joint evaluation, defense, and resolution of those claims.

7.0 Public-Private Partnerships: Opportunities and Risks for Consulting Engineers Involved in Subsurface Projects

Increasingly, public-private partnerships (PPPs) — a delivery approach under which a public owner engages a private sector entity to develop, fund, design, construct, operate, and maintain a public use project — are being explored and selected by public owners as mechanisms for realizing public projects for which public capabilities and resources are not available to support the funding, project management, operational, maintenance, and other traditional roles of the public owner. Tunnels for sewerage outfall and for transportation, as well as for other projects having significant subsurface work, are candidates for the PPP approach. Interest in, and utilization of, the PPP approach is expected to continue and increase, especially as public funding availability and public owner appetite for design and construction risk continue to decline.[86] Given the substantial project owner risk, funding contingency exposure, and management skill and experience involved in subsurface projects, it should not be surprising that the PPP approach will be attractive to public owners contemplating those projects. The future will present both significant opportunities and potential risks for consulting engineers who are interested in (and capable of) participating in PPPs.

7.1 Public-Private Partnerships: Definition, Contracts, and Relationships

Increasingly, projects are being developed, financed, designed, constructed, operated, and maintained under PPP agreements between the public and private sectors.[87] To date, approximately 25 states have legislation authorizing, in various forms, PPPs for

the delivery of public projects. PPPs started in the United States in the mid-1990s and, generally speaking, are still in their infancy. As of this date, not many have progressed through construction. Candidates for the PPP approach include an array of infrastructure projects ranging from toll roads, water and sewerage treatment plants, sewerage outfall tunnels, roadway and other transportation tunnels, power stations, hospitals, schools, and prisons. This section will focus on the use of the PPP approach on projects involving significant subsurface work.

Under the PPP approach, one or more private sector entities—the concessionaire—is responsible for the financing, design, construction, operation, and maintenance of the project. The principal objectives and drivers for these PPPs are the desire of the public (governmental) owner to deliver projects without recourse to public funding, to significantly reduce its risk exposure, and to improve the quality and efficiency in delivery of those projects and the ongoing operational service to the public.[88]

The concessionaire typically is a special purpose entity which has no assets other than the capital investments from shareholders and loan proceeds from a construction lender (the "lender") and the expectation of revenue from project post-completion operations (e.g., tolls from public roads or tunnels). As such and as a general matter, the concessionaire is a "special purpose vehicle," which is incorporated and funded solely for the purpose of holding the rights to develop, design, construct, operate, and maintain the project.

As a general matter of contractual structure, a PPP may involve:

- **A concession agreement** between the public owner and concessionaire, with the concessionaire (usually a special purpose entity formed solely for the project-specific purpose by the sponsors and having no substantial staff or physical assets) undertaking responsibility for the financing, design, construction, operation, and maintenance of the project.
- **A design-build subcontract** between the concessionaire and a design-builder (typically, constructor-led), pursuant to which the latter is responsible for the design and construction of the project.
- **One or more subconsultant agreements** between the design-builder and engineer subconsultants (the "engineer"), the latter of whom are obligated to design and provide other professional services relative to the project.
- **One or more trade subcontracts** between the design-builder and various trade subcontractors, which will be required to furnish labor or materials required to construct all or a portion of the project.
- **An operations and maintenance subcontract** between the design-builder and another entity, which will be responsible for post-construction operations and maintenance of the project.

Figure 1. **Typical Contractual Relationships in PPP Structure**

Public Owner

Shareholders ———— Concessionaire ———— Lender

Design-Builder   Operations and   Lender's
                     Maintenance Firm   Engineer

Engineer(s)   Trade
                     Contractor(s)

- **A lending agreement** between the concessionaire and a bank or other lending institution (the "lender") for the financing of the design and construction of the project.
- **A shareholder agreement** (often in the form of subordinated debt investment) between the concessionaire and various shareholders who will invest capital and hold equity positions in the PPP. The shareholders have an expectation to share in the operating revenue of the project once construction is completed; in some instances, the shareholders may also share in project risk and loss. As a general matter, the ratio of shareholder investment to project financing is relatively small.
- **A lender's engineer agreement** between the lender and a consulting engineer, pursuant to which the latter typically may be engaged on behalf of the lender to provide a variety of services, including due diligence, design review, evaluations of project technical feasibility, economic predictions, and evaluations of project design development and status of construction work.

7.2   Public-Private Partnerships: Risk Allocation Objectives

The first step in an effective risk management program for subsurface projects involves the planning and execution of an adequate subsurface investigation.[89] Subsurface projects inherently involve significant risk potential, given the inability to predict with precision ground conditions and the practical, economic, and technical limitations on

the ability to obtain complete or accurate information about those conditions or their anticipated behavior during construction operations. Uncertainty and relative unpredictability of subsurface conditions pose significant risk potential for all project participants, but especially the project owner and the constructor.

Assuming that a reasonably defined and adequate subsurface investigation has been planned and implemented, the next important step in an effective risk management program for subsurface projects involves the allocation of risk among project participants.[90]

As in any subsurface project, fair and equitable risk allocation among the major project participants in the PPP approach is critically important.[91] This has certainly proven to be the case in the context of the traditional design-bid-build delivery approach and in the context of design-build.[92]

Much has been written about the advisability of clear and fair allocation for subsurface condition risk in more traditional delivery method contexts. Project experience and the attendant "lessons learned" amply demonstrate that unclear and unfair allocation for subsurface condition risk has a number of potentially (if not probable) negative consequences, including reducing the number of willing and qualified constructors interested in pursuing such a project; the use of undisclosed contingency as a mechanism to "manage," or more accurately hedge, the heightened risk assumption; the probability of more conflict, adversity, and disputes among project participants; a significant increase in the inability of the constructor to meet performance requirements and expectations due to the disproportionate burden imposed by such risk assumption; and an increase in the risk of professional liability claims by the project owner and/or constructor against the consulting engineer, derivative of the increased conflict and dispute potential between the former.[93]

PPPs will prove to be no exception in terms of the need for clear and fair risk allocation for subsurface conditions among the major project participants. Simply put, the "lessons learned," namely, the advisability and prudence of clear and fair risk allocation for subsurface conditions, will prove to have equal applicability in a PPP subsurface project.

Design-Build Risk Allocation on Subsurface Projects

Most PPP projects are delivered using, in essence, the design-build approach under which a single entity—the design-builder (typically, constructor-led)—is solely responsible for both design and construction of the project (the "single-point principle").[94] As such, revisiting some of the basic risk allocation issues and recommendations applicable to design-build subsurface projects is appropriate at this point.

Some project owners, utilizing the design-build approach, expect that the single-point principle transfers to the design-builder (and its engineer and trade subcontrac-

tors) responsibility for all risk associated with subsurface conditions encountered at the site, which is an expectation that derives from the increased role of the design-builder in conducting subsurface investigations and in the design of the project. This approach could lead to significant—potentially boundless—risk assumption by the design-builder, given the design-builder's typical role in conducting or validating (and assuming responsibility for) subsurface investigation and in developing and finalizing the project design. This approach, however, is both misguided and unrealistic. While a design-builder may—depending upon contractual terms—have the obligation to conduct or validate the subsurface investigation and, hence, a greater responsibility for subsurface condition risk than may otherwise be applicable in the design-bid-build context (under which the project owner typically is responsible for the performance of subsurface investigation and the furnishing and reporting of relevant data), there should always be boundaries to and limitations on the design-builder's responsibility for cost and schedule impacts from differing subsurface conditions.[95] Put another way, while the design-builder's degree of risk assumption for subsurface conditions may be greater in the design-build context, there should be limits to that degree that are clearly communicated and understood, reasonably established, and contractually defined.

Similarly, the design-builder's risk for problems or defects associated with the constructability, achievability, and quality of the final design is greater than in the design-bid-build delivery method because the design-builder has responsibility for the development and finalization of that design. However, the design-builder's responsibility for the final design may not be absolute or unqualified in circumstances in which either (a) project owner–furnished and mandatory design criteria are overly-prescriptive or detailed or (b) the design-builder's judgment and discretion to develop the final design is limited or controlled by the project owner through the design development review and approval process or through some other mechanism.

As such, more enlightened project owners using the design-build approach recognize the advisability of fairness and balance in the risk allocation process, notwithstanding the increased role of the design-builder in subsurface investigation and in the development and finalization of project design.

PPPs and Risk Allocation on Subsurface Projects

Given that most PPP projects are delivered using the design-build approach, are there any reasons why different risk allocation objectives or principles should apply in the PPP context? In general, the answer should be "no."[96] However, there are several reasons that may account for why efforts are made in the PPP approach to transfer to the design-build team greater risk for subsurface conditions and defective design than may typically be assumed even in the more pure design-build context.[97]

As is typically the case in risk allocation, the direction starts (and in the public sector, for all practical purposes, ends) with the public owner's interests and objectives.[98] Risk allocation in PPPs is no exception. The public owner's risk allocation objectives in most PPPs may be summarized as follows:

1. The entire risk of delivering the project on time and within the fixed price should be transferred to the concessionaire by the fixed price/time terms of the concession agreement.

2. All substantial project risks, including subsurface and defective designs — once identified or assumed by the concessionaire — should be transferred or managed by a combination of either (a) insurance, (b) contractual risk assumption not transferable to insurance, and/or (c) assets of the concessionaire.

Of course, the character and extent of identified risk will be project-specific in nature and, therefore, generalizations are not especially meaningful in this context. However, as a general matter, the concessionaire may manage risk by (a) retaining and managing it; (b) transferring the risk, through indemnity or otherwise, to another project participant (such as the design-builder and/or engineer); or, if available, (c) transferring the risk to insurance.[99] The lender generally will require that the concessionaire transfer as much risk as possible "downstream" to the design-builder, engineer, and trade contractors and similarly will require that as much risk as practicable be transferred to available and adequate insurance coverages, including project-specific insurance. However, insurance is not available for a significant portion of the risk associated with subsurface conditions.

How are these objectives typically addressed in the various networks of PPP contracts?

Concession Agreement

In the PPP approach, the public owner relinquishes significant control over major aspects of the design and construction of the project; the transfer of that degree of control results in a commensurate degree of significant risk assumption by the concessionaire in the concession agreement.

In the negotiation of the lending agreement between the concessionaire and the lender, the concessionaire typically is required to demonstrate (credibly) to the lender that risk assumed by the concessionaire in the concession agreement will to the maximum extent either be transferred to insurance (often required to be project-specific in nature) and/or allocated downstream to other project participants, such as the design-builder (and its engineer). The inability to achieve this objective of maximizing risk transfer from the concessionaire may be a "deal-breaker" in obtaining a financing commitment

and, at minimum, the extent to which that objective is achieved will affect the cost of financing (and, hence, the competitiveness of the concessionaire's proposal to the public owner).

Even though neither the design-builder nor the engineer are direct parties to the concession agreement, the latter agreement will provide the risk allocation framework or context under which design and construction risk will be allocated to, and contractually assumed by, all downstream (lower-tier) design and construction firm project participants.

As has been stated:

> The Design-Builder in a Public-Private Partnership is expected to take all the risk associated with the design and construction of the project that the Concessionaire agrees to in the Concession Agreement. The Concessionaire is driven to shed all risk given that it is a special purpose entity created for this project and that the lenders will demand that such entity retain no significant risk. The result is that the Design-Builder will enter into a back-to-back design-build agreement and that the Concessionaire does not have the same motivation to achieve equitable risk allocation.
>
> If the Design-Builder understands that it will essentially assume all risks in the Concession Agreement associated with the design and construction of the project and the Concessionaire is not incentivized to aggressively negotiate equitable risk allocation, the Design-Builder will assume a prominent position at the negotiating table with the public sector owner. The Design-Builder will aggressively pursue contract comments and modifications and will attend all negotiations with the owner and assert its position. The astute Design-Builder will quickly identify the key risk allocation issues with the Concessionaire in the form of a term sheet so that the Concessionaire and the lenders understand the Design-Builder's risk position at an early point in time.[100]

As such, it is important that the constructor and its engineer carefully review the relevant provisions of the concession agreement that involve design and construction risk assumption and, if at all possible, be involved in the negotiation of that agreement. These provisions may address such subjects as risk and responsibility for accuracy and adequacy of subsurface investigation and data; the role and extent of the public owner in the review and/or approval of design development submissions of the design-builder; the standard of care or warranty applicable to the final design furnished by the design-builder and/or its engineer; and the indemnification obligations of the design-builder and/or its engineer. As to the latter, typically, the concession agreement will contain provisions obligating the concessionaire and other project participants (including the constructor and engineer) to indemnify the public owner and others for various risks, and legal liabilities, including breach of contract, breach of warranty, and negligence. These indemnity obligations generally are flowed-down by the concessionaire to the de-

sign-builder, engineer, and trade contractors, along with requirements that the latter parties also indemnify the concessionaire, the lender, and potentially other parties (e.g., shareholders) who are external to the PPP. Some of these indemnity provisions, as well as other provisions included in the concession agreement, may transfer risk not insurable under traditional design and construction insurance coverages.

The opportunities for additional compensation or time extension entitlements under the concession agreement generally are limited. In addition, if the public owner is obligated to grant such equitable adjustments to the concessionaire, typically those adjustments may take the form of extending the concession term or increasing the tolls or charges that the concessionaire may derive as revenue upon completion of the construction process. Thus, the compensation may actually flow to the concessionaire (and, therefore, downstream) significantly later than when it incurs the additional cost and time impact during the construction process. This potential "hiatus," coupled with the limited opportunities for entitlement to cost/time adjustments, could impose substantial economic drain on the finances of the concessionaire. On top of that, the hiatus could increase tension in the concessionnaire's internal operations and in project relationships among the concessionnaire, the design-builder, the engineer, and trade contractor participants during the design and construction process, increasing the risk of disappointed commercial expectations and claims, only some of which may be covered by available insurance coverages.[101] As has been noted, "There is a potential mismatch between what the concession company is likely to get from the governmental entity under the concession agreement, what it is able to procure from the project financiers and its liability to the construction contractors and operators under the various project agreements. The concession company should always attempt to ensure that there is no 'gap' between what it receives and what it pays out."[102]

Under the concession agreement, the concessionaire is obligated to produce a project designed and constructed in accordance with the quality, ultimate use, and performance standards specified in the concession agreement. That obligation not only exists upon completion of the project, but extends into the concession period, which typically could be as long as 25 to 35 years. Thus, the concessionaire has a "long tail" exposure for design and construction deficiencies that extends coterminous with the concession period which, in many cases, may be substantially longer than the applicable statute of repose/limitations, as well as the coverage duration of any procured project-specific insurance coverages.

Many concession agreements contain a mechanism under which the public owner and concessionaire appoint independent technical advisors to monitor the design and construction of the project and to make final and binding decisions as to whether the design deliverables and/or construction work meet the various requirements of the concession agreement. The design builder, engineer, and trade contractors may be required,

by virtue of flow-down provisions, to adhere to those decisions and accept them as final and binding.

From the perspective of the engineer, particular attention should be focused on provisions such as flow-down, indemnification, standard of care, warranty/guaranty, design development discretion/responsibility and scope of permissible design review by others, and the role of the engineer in providing services during construction, as well as the role of the engineer in cost estimating during the bid and pre-award phase. [103]

As a general proposition (and certainly in Australia), the underlying governmental rationale for public-private partnerships is that they must offer "value for money" (the "value criterion"). The value criterion typically is at the center of the factors considered by public owners in evaluating whether a project proposed for a public-private partnership is appropriate for delivery under that approach. Generally, the extent or degree of the public owner participant's ability to transfer or relieve the public of substantial development, funding, design, and construction risk associated with a proposed project is a very important factor in this evaluation: the greater the extent or degree of risk transfer, the more the "value criterion" is perceived to be satisfied. As has been stated, "a large component of the evaluation of the value for money concept is based on risk transfer to the private sector." [104]

In Australia, where — at least as of this date — the vast majority of PPP projects have occurred, private sector participants interested in PPPs maintain that risks should not be transferred to them until a rigorous risk identification program has been completed, and in no event should risks be transferred to them when they are not able to control and manage them, and that when such inappropriate risk transfer occurs, the result is higher risk premiums for that contingent exposure or, more drastically, the failure of the project or its private sectors participants (i.e., bankruptcy or other forms of financial insolvency). Lender requests have a major influence on risk allocation decisions in PPPs; the lenders must be comfortable (preferably, even more than comfortable) with the degree of risk to which their funds are exposed.

Of course, each project is different and the identification and evaluation of risk must be undertaken and understood in the specific project context. Generalizations are not meaningful in this context. As to risks associated with the design and construction process in PPPs, it has generally been stated:

> One of the key government objectives in PPP deals is to take advantage of the concession company's ability to bring design innovations and construction expertise to the delivery of the projects. In all PPP deals, the concession company will be required to assume the risk for the design, construction and commissioning of the infrastructure facilities. The concession company is also obliged to provide a fitness for purpose warranty to the government entity for the performance of the infrastructure facility during the

operational phase. The government frequently seeks an "output"-based fit-for-purpose warranty, which is linked to the government's service needs from time to time during the operational phase.[105]

The concessionaire generally is expected to assume significant risk, or the entire risk, of government approvals, *force majeure*, and subsurface, site and environmental conditions, unless the concessionaire can demonstrate that the degree of risk assumption would represent a significant risk premium cost (or project cost to the public entity) for those contingent risk exposures, to be paid by the public entity regardless of risk occurrence. As has been demonstrated in other non-public-private partnership contexts, the degree of risk assumption of constructors and/or design builders for differing site condition exposures indirectly impacts (and increases) the degree of professional liability exposure for design professionals on those projects.[106] In addition, driven by lender requirements, PPP projects typically contain relatively substantial liquidated damages for delayed completion.

In addition to the risk of exposure due to delayed project completion, the design-builder and its engineer also have substantial consequential damage exposure *following* completion of the project:

> [U]nder the PPP structure, the Concessionaire is reimbursed the project costs including financing in one of two ways in which repayment occurs over the life of the concession: (1) tolling revenues generated by the project or (2) a guaranteed revenue stream which is also frequently called shadow tolling. Repayment is typically tied to availability and condition of the infrastructure asset. If payments are reduced because of a defect in the asset, the Concessionaire will expect the Design-Builder to bear the risk of that lost revenue. As a result, in the financed PPP market the Design-Builder will assume an affirmative post-completion obligation for lost revenue (i.e., consequential damages) of the Concessionaire.[107]

Design-Build Agreement

Based upon the preceding discussion, the terms of the agreement between the concessionaire and the design-builder need to be evaluated according to the same standards utilized in reviewing a design-build prime agreement outside of the PPP context.[108] In addition, the substantial risks assumed by the concessionaire under the concession agreement and the concessionaire's (and its lender's) pressure to aggressively flow-down risk to the design-builder (and further down to sub-tiers of the engineer and trade contractors) emphasize the need for careful review of the prime design-build agreement in the PPP context.

The design-builder agreement should include a differing site conditions clause under

which risk is shared and allocated between the concessionaire and the design-builder. Use of geotechnical baseline reports are effective mechanisms to facilitate the definition of such risk allocation.[109]

Design-Builder–Engineer Subconsultant Agreement

Similarly, the design-builder–engineer subconsultant agreement should be reviewed using the same standards applicable in a pure (non-PPP) design-build project context,[110] with specific attention to scope of design development discretion and owner's approval standards, standard of care, warranty, performance (output) flow-down, insurance, and indemnity provisions. In addition, the agreement should be reviewed to determine the role, if any, of the engineer in cost estimating and in assisting the design-builder in agreeing to time and cost commitments in the prime agreement with the concessionaire. [111]

Lender's Engineer Agreement

This agreement should clearly define the scope of the lender's engineer's services and include other provisions that (a) define the role, duty, and scope of the engineer in review of design submissions and in the evaluation of construction work; (b) limit liability of the lender's engineer and waive responsibility for consequential damages; (c) limit the lender's engineer's duty to the lender; and (d) limit dissemination of and the right to rely upon the lender's engineer's reports and other deliverables.

The role and potential risk exposure of the lender's engineer is somewhat similar to that of an owner's engineer in the design-build context.[112] In general terms, the potential professional liability risk exposure could be substantial and significantly disproportionate when compared to the relatively limited role and compensation of the lender's engineer. This liability risk exposure exists with respect not only to claims by the lender, but also to third parties who receive and rely upon reports or other work product of the lender's engineer.[113]

The following case is instructive in terms of the potential professional liability exposure of a lender's engineer. In *Aliberti, LaRochelle & Hodson Engineering Corp., Inc. v. Federal Deposit Insurance Corp. (FDIC)*, 844 F. Supp. 832 (D. Me. 1994), the federal district court ruled that an engineer and a construction manager were liable to a bank (and, hence, the FDIC, which had succeeded to the bank's interest in the project) that loaned and advanced monies to a developer based on representations made by the engineer and the construction manager. In the *Aliberti* case, the developer retained an engineer and a construction manager, under separate agreements, to provide various professional services in connection with the developer's proposed construction of a condominium/

motel. The developer contacted a bank to obtain financing in connection with the project. In order to reduce project time and costs, the developer proposed to the bank that the project be designed and constructed in phases under the so-called fast-track method, in which it would not be necessary to have a complete set of detailed drawings prior to construction start. In addition, the developer reasoned that construction in phases would facilitate the ability to obtain financing within the lending limits of the bank.

In making its decision to commit financing for the project, the bank hired its own construction consultant, who had experience in the design and construction of similar projects, to verify financial and technical construction information provided to the bank by the developer and/or by the engineer and the construction manager. After some preliminary due diligence investigation, the bank issued a commitment letter to the developer that contained certain conditions. A budget prepared by the developer was appended to the commitment letter. After reviewing the budget, the engineer and construction manager notified the developer that the budget contained insufficient amounts for certain hard-cost line items and that there were scope of work items not included in the budget. In substance, the developer told the engineer and construction manager "that this was just an interim budget and not to worry about the missing budget items." At a subsequent meeting, the engineer and construction manager again expressed their concerns to the developer concerning the inadequacy and incompleteness of the budget and, again, were told "not to worry." Neither the engineer nor construction manager ever directly expressed their concerns about the budget to the bank. At a meeting with the bank, both the engineer and the construction manager were told that if, during construction, the project costs changed from the budget, then any such change in cost should be noted on the requisition form prior to submission to the bank and its construction consultant for review.

The loan closed and construction of the first phase of the project commenced. After the first month of construction, the bank's construction consultant became concerned that the project "was in trouble, but requisitions continued to display the [budget] number which was attested to by representatives of the engineer and construction manager." Shortly thereafter, it became apparent that the actual project cost would be nearly double the amount in the budget, and work on the project was suspended. The bank later purchased the project on a foreclosure bid.

After a trial, the district court found that the engineer and construction manager were liable to the FDIC (as successor to the bank's interest) based on four separate grounds: (1) inaccurate and false statements that the project could be completed for the amount stated in the budget; (2) failure to disclose knowledge of the missing line items contained in the budget; (3) failure to disclose the inadequacy of certain amounts for line items included in the budget; and (4) false statements of the total project cost on the requisition submitted to the bank. In making this determination, the district court

549

relied on several factors, including: (1) the fact that the developer's respective contracts with the engineer and construction manager obligated the latter firms to provide cost estimating services and to evaluate and update construction budget and anticipated costs; (2) the engineer and construction manager knew that the budget was inadequate and incomplete but failed to so advise the bank, despite their knowledge that the bank was relying on the information contained in the budget; (3) when the engineer and construction manager signed and submitted requisitions to the bank, they knew that the stated project cost was inadequate and substantially less than the amount needed to complete the first phase; (4) the bank justifiably relied on the representations made by the engineer and construction manager, which led the bank to wrongfully lend money and disburse loan proceeds to the developer; and (5) uncontradicted expert testimony established that the engineer and construction manager, as construction professionals, had responsibilities "to correct any misinformation, to disclose the absence of any familiarity with information, and to inform the Bank, if necessary, that estimating services which a bank would reasonably expect had not been undertaken," "that it is incumbent on the design professional to speak out," and "that construction professionals have an absolute obligation to clarify their involvement or lack of involvement in the project." After considering all this evidence, the district court ruled that the engineer and construction manager owed a legal duty to the bank to be honest and candid in communications with the bank despite the absence of a contractual relationship.

The preceding discussion should amply demonstrate that the process of risk identification and allocation for consulting engineers and constructors in PPP subsurface projects is complex and necessitates both a comprehensive and detailed project-specific risk assessment and evaluation, plus a review of a number of contracts beyond simply the design-build agreement and the subconsultant agreement between the design-builder and the engineer. In fact, there are many contractual documents that need to be reviewed at various iterative stages as the PPP project moves from the planning and procurement stages into realization. All of these documents and, in particular, the risk allocation objectives of the public owner and the concessionaire, can and will influence the pressures upon, and nature and degree of risk assumption by, the design-builder and its engineer.

In this regard, it has been recognized that the complexity in the various levels of contract negotiations and relationships among PPP participants results "in a proliferation of documents between all of the parties which can include lender direct agreements and interface agreements. The typical documentation of a PPP transaction is at a minimum triple that of more conventionally delivered projects. Risk issues for a design-builder can arise in any of those documents to which the design-builder is a party."[114] All of these legal documents—in and for whatever stage—most be carefully reviewed and understood from the legal and risk perspectives; no two PPP deals are exactly alike.

Consulting engineers involved in subsurface projects should expect to see a steadily increasing number of project opportunities that use the PPP approach. PPP project experience — especially from a risk-assessment perspective — has yet to develop to a point at which meaningful observations (much less lessons learned) can be stated. However, notwithstanding that limited experience, there is no good or logical reason to conclude that the salutary principles of fairness, clarity, and realism in subsurface risk allocation should not apply in the PPP context. PPPs pose substantial opportunities for the consulting engineer, as well as the opportunity to realize and achieve projects for the benefit of the public that otherwise would not be achievable with presently available public funding. These opportunities, however, must be understood, balanced, and fairly undertaken with an appreciation of the potentially significant risk which may be transferred to the consulting engineer. The analysis and informed discussion of this subject are in the early stages. We need to anticipate, capture, and communicate the experience, understand the relevant risk factors for consulting engineers involved in PPP subsurface projects, and develop guiding principles and standards to shape risk allocation in this relatively new frontier. In the final analysis, consulting engineers will benefit from this proactive approach.

Notes

1. *See* G. Anderson and C. Davis, "Winning the Risk Game," *World Tunneling*, June 2008, Issue 9, 34–36.

2. *See* W. Edgerton, ed., *Recommended Contract Practices for Underground Construction*, chapter 4, Littleton, OH: Society for Mining, Metallurgy, and Exploration, Inc., 2008; D. Hatem, "Professional Liability Risk and Project-Specific Professional Liability Insurance," *Chartis Tunneling Projects Seminar*, Donovan Hatem LLP, Boston/New York, Nov. 2009.

   Chapter 4 of this book addresses in detail the components of a subsurface investigation program. This chapter focuses on that subject as it relates to the professional liability exposure of the consulting engineer.

3. D. Hatem, ed., *Subsurface Conditions*, § 10.3.3, pp. 363–64.

4. *See* Hatem, *Subsurface Conditions*, § 10.2.1.1, 281–84; Brierley and Hatem, eds., *Design-Build Subsurface Projects*, §§ 3.1.1, 3.1.2, pp. 24–35, Scottsdale, AZ: Zeni House, 2002; Smith, Currie & Hancock's, *Common Sense Construction Law*, 4th ed., T. Kelleher, Jr., and G. Walters, eds., Hoboken, NJ: John Wiley & Sons, Inc., 2009, pp. 249–75.

5. The potential of constructor claims against the consulting engineer due to ineffective project owner–constructor risk allocation is discussed in chapter 15, above.

6. *See* Chapter 5, "Differing Site Conditions," in D. Brennan et al., eds., *The Construction Contracts Book*, 2nd ed., Chicago: American Bar Asso'n, 2008; J. Dorter, "Representations, Risk and Site Conditions," *Building & Construction L.*, 20 (2004): 7; J. Bailey, "What Lies Beneath," *Int'l Construction L. Rev.*, 24 (2007): 394; M. Branca, A. Silberman, & J. Vento, *Federal Government Construction Contracts*, 2d ed. (2010 American Bar Association), Chapter 9, pp. 247-272.

7. Sweet and Schneier, *Legal Aspects of Architecture*, chapter 25; Brierly and Hatem, eds., *Design-Build Subsurface Projects*, § 3.1.2.
8. Allensworth et al., *Construction Law*, §17.02A.
9. Allensworth et al., *Construction Law*, §17.02B.
10. Sweet and Schneier, *Legal Aspects of Architecture, Engineering and the Construction Process*, § 25.07, p. 562.
11. This topic is discussed in more detail in § 6.0, below.
12. *See* A. Wood, *Tunnelling: Management by Design*, London: Routledge, 2000; S. Eskesen, P. Tengborg, J. Kampmann, and T. Veicherts, "Guidelines for Tunneling Risk Management: International Tunneling Association, Working Group No. 2," *Tunnelling and Underground Space Technology* 19 (May 2004): 217–37; G. Arrigoni, "Contract and Construction Aspects," in V. Guglielmetti, P. Grasso, A. Mahtab, and S. Xu, eds., *Mechanized Tunneling in Urban Areas*, London: Taylor & Francis Group, 2007.
13. For more detailed discussion, see chapter 15.
14. The rationale for supporting the advisability of the design engineer's continuity of involvement during subsurface construction has been stated as follows:

> The design of a tunnel project, with its dependence on the ground conditions, is necessarily a prediction. Monitoring and observation of the ground and groundwater conditions and the performance of both the permanent and temporary works during the actual execution is essential, with feedback provided to the design team to confirm performance, optimize future designs, or to adjust the current design, if necessary, to reflect changed site conditions. This reinforces the ongoing role of the engineer during the construction phase, particularly in changeable ground conditions. This ongoing design role and the need for monitoring are also emphasized by the ITIG Code of Practice. In the UK there is tendency for division to be introduced between design and construction support, partly due to the length of time that major projects develop over, and partly due to various procurement rules. As discussed above, this division can be to the detriment of project success and needs to be dealt with in the project procurement strategy.

A. Alder and M. King, "The Delivery of Underground Construction Projects in the UK: A Review of Good Practice," 2009 *Rapid Excavation and Tunneling Conference Proceedings*, Society for Mining, Metallurgy, & Exploration, Inc., pp. 861, 869–70.

15. *See* "Introduction," in W. Edgerton, ed., *Recommended Contract Practices for Underground Construction*, Littleton, CO: Society for Mining, Metallurgy, and Exploration, 2008; *see* J. McKelvey, R. Goodfellow, & C. Hirner, "This Is Where the Money Is! The Impact of Contract Front End Documents on Tunneling Projects," in *North American Tunneling 2008 Proceedings*, 570–74; S. Lesser and D. Wallach, "The Twelve Deadly Sins: An Owner's Guide to Avoiding Liability for Implied Obligations During the Construction of a Project," *The Construction Lawyer* 28 (Winter 2008): 15.

16. For a detailed discussion of these improved contracting practices, *see* Brierly and Hatem, *Design-Build Subsurface Projects,* § 3.1.2.

17. See discussion in § 2.0, above.

18. *See, e.g.,* D. Hatem, *Subsurface Conditions,* 282–83 and n. 40, 382–88; Rapid Demolition Co., Inc. v. New York, 864 N.Y.S.2d 503 (App. Div. 2008).

19. Millgard Corp. v. McKee/Mays, 49 F. 3d 1070 (5th Cir. 1995). In contrast, *see* URS Group, Inc. v. Tetra Tech, Inc., 181 P.3d 380 (Colo. Ct. App. 2008) (expressing reluctance to frustrate purpose of differing site condition clause by disclaimers contained in contractual site investigation provision). As a general matter, disclaimers used in conjunction with differing site condition clauses typically are looked upon with disfavor by courts:

    > The obvious purpose of [disclaimer] provisions is to relieve the owner of liability for subsurface conditions. So, while the differing site condition clause places the risk of subsurface conditions squarely on the owner, disclaimer clauses . . . would shift that risk back to the contractor.
    >
    > There is an inherent conflict between the differing site conditions clause and disclaimers which instruct bidders that they will not be entitled to additional compensation if the subsurface conditions are different from what is indicated in the contract. In fact, it would appear that the public policy underlying the differing site conditions clause . . . would be defeated by such disclaimers. Public policy aside, many public entities continue to try to use various, and often creatively-worded, disclaimers in an attempt to defeat or limit the differing site conditions clause.
    >
    > As a result, many courts have had to resolve the conflict that is created when a contract includes a differing site conditions clause and one or more disclaimers that week to shift the risk of unexpected subsurface conditions back to the contractor. Most courts at the federal and state levels have held that such disclaimers cannot be used to defeat the differing site conditions clause. . . . M. Long and C. Rogers, "Unexpected Subsurface Conditions and the Differing Site Conditions Clause," § 2.7, p. 55, *Construction Law Update 2007,* New York: Aspen, 2007.

    See also Sweet and Schneier, *Legal Aspects of Architecture,* § 25.05, pp. 553–54. In Condon-Johnson & Associates, Inc. v. Sacramento Municipal Utility District, 149 Cal. App. 4th 1384 (2007), the contract included a statutorily-mandated differing site condition clause but also general disclaimers regarding the need for the constructor to conduct a site investigation and a disclaimer of subsurface condition information. The court ruled that general disclaimers would not override statutorily-mandated risk allocation provisions embodied in the differing site condition clause. E. Caplicki, "General Disclaimer Does Not Defeat Differing Site Conditions Claim," *J. of Prof. Issues in Engineering Edu. & Prac.,* 134 (October 2008): 368–70.

    In Justin Bryan; J&L Construction v. City of Cotter, 2009 WL 3337558 (Ark. Oct. 1, 2009), a constructor sued a consulting engineer for professional negligence in the pre-construction inves-

tigation of subsurface conditions allegedly encountered during construction. Although the special conditions of the contract documents stated that the constructor may not rely upon or make any claim against the consulting engineer with respect to "the completeness of soils reports," the court determined that the constructor's negligence claims against the consulting engineer should not be dismissed prior to trial because the meaning of "completeness" is not "plain or evident."

Also, in MasTec North America, Inc. v. El Paso Field Services, L.P, 2009 WL 2231802 (Tex. App. July 23, 2009), the court declined to dismiss a constructor's claim against an owner under a theory of breach of contract for defective specifications, notwithstanding lump-sum and pre-bid investigation provisions in the contract, where the owner was in a superior position to know whether its specifications were adequate for the intended scope of work and the contract evidenced that the owner made positive assurances concerning the reliability of those specifications. A dissenting opinion strongly disagreed with the majority's decision on the basis that the constructor voluntarily and contractually assumed the risk for which it was seeking recovery against the project owner.

20. The Engineers Joint Contracts Documents Committee (EJCDC), in its "Standard General Conditions of the Construction Contract," C-700, divides coverage into subsurface (§ 4.03) and underground facilities physical conditions (§ 4.04). Paragraph 4.02(A) provides that information is provided in the supplementary conditions; however, under § 4.02(B), the constructor may rely on the "general accuracy of the 'technical' data" even though that data does not constitute contract documents. However, § 4.02(B)(1) provides that the constructor cannot rely on the completeness of the information for purposes of execution or safety, nor, under § 4.0.2(B)(2), may the constructor rely on "other data, interpretations, opinions and information." Finally, § 4.02(B)(3) of the EJCDC documents precludes a constructor's claim against the project owner or consulting engineer with respect to the constructor's interpretation or conclusions drawn from the technical data.

21. *See generally*, J. Chu, "Different Site Conditions: Whose Risk Are They?" *The Construction Law.*, 20 (April 2000): 5; G. Brierley and J. Smith, "Contracting Practices for Underground Projects," *Construction Law Update 2002*, Hoboken, NJ: Wiley, 2002; Hatem, *Subsurface Conditions*, §§ 3.1.4, 3.1.4.1, 3.1.4.2, pp. 39–55; Brierley and Hatem, *Design-Build Subsurface Projects*, § 3.1.2.

22. R. Essex, *Geotechnical Baseline Reports for Construction: Suggested Guidelines*, § 1.3, p. 6, Reston, VA: ASCE, 2007; D. Hatem "Geotechnical Baselines and Geotechnical Reality: One and the Same, Similar or Not Even Close—Professional Liability Implications," *The CA/T Professional Liability Reporter* (Dec. 1996).

23. *See* discussion in § 6.4 of this chapter.

24. *See* D. Hatem, *Subsurface Conditions*, §§ 10.2.4, 10.2.5; D. Hatem, "Differing Site Conditions: Liability Precautions for Design Professionals," *Def. Couns. J.*, 61: 4 (Oct. 1994).

25. For a discussion of specific professional liability risk exposures for consulting engineers involved in various roles on design-build projects, *see* Brierly and Hatem, *Design-Build Subsurface Projects*, § 3.2.5.5, pp. 88–91.

26. *See* discussion in § 2.0 of chapter 16, above.

27. J. Gould, "Geotechnology in Dispute Resolution," *J. of Geotechnical Engineering* 121 (July 1995): 523–24. Another commentator has accurately noted:

> Although many claims paid by the owner in settlement or after adjudication give the appearance that the owner bears the risk of unknown subsurface conditions, the burden is distributed amongst all construction participants in many situations. Even though the owner may settle a subsurface claim, the contractor is likely to not receive full compensation in settlement for all of the increased costs of the changed subsurface conditions. Adjudication by the court process or by arbitration may award less than the full increased costs. . . . Even though it would appear that subsurface claims are reimbursable by the owner to the contractor, the true result is generally a sharing of the unexpected subsurface conditions. G. Jones, "The U.S. Perspective on Procedures for Subsurface Ground Conditions Claims," *Int'l Construction L. Rev.*, 155, 171 (1990).

> *See also* J. Dorter, "Representations, Risk and Site Conditions," *Building & Construction L.* 20 (2004): 7, 15.

28. C. Foster et al., eds. *Construction and Design Law*, VA: The Michie Company, 1989.

29. *See, e.g.*, Davidson & Jones, Inc. v. County of New Hanover, 255 S.E.2d 580 (N.C. Ct. App. 1979) (architect held liable to contractor in negligence for failing to make reasonable and proper examinations and inspections of soil conditions of the project site and of the foundations of adjoining structures), *cert. denied*, 259 S.E.2d 911 (N.C. 1979); Zontelli & Sons, Inc. v. City of Nashwauk, 373 N.W.2d 744 (Minn. 1985) (holding engineer is obligated to indemnify city for contract claims due to engineer's negligence in failing to conduct a proper investigation that resulted in drastic underestimates in the quantity of concrete and unsuitable material to be excavated and removed by contractor and a misrepresentation that the highway in question was a municipal as opposed to a state highway, thereby misleading bidders with respect to the scope of the work required to be performed); *see* Bruner & O'Connor, § 14:22.

30. *See generally* Guardian Construction Co. v. Tetra Tech Richardson, Inc., 583 A.2d 1378 (Del. Super. Ct. 1990) (holding, by adopting the parameters of §552 of the Restatement (Second) of Torts (1977), that contractor and subcontractor were entitled to pursue claim against design engineer for foreseeable economic losses, regardless of whether or not privity existed, when design engineer negligently miscalculated tidal heights and project benchmarks, which were used to develop project plans and specifications and which were known and intended to be for the guidance of those contractors); Gulf Contracting v. Bibb County, 795 F.2d 980 (11th Cir. 1986) (holding that contractor was entitled to pursue claim against architect and engineer for cost of removing alleged unanticipated debris on theory that architect and engineers were negligent in failing to disclose existence of subsurface debris in question in bid and contract documents and that the absence of a contractual or privity relationship between contractors and architect/engineer would not, as a matter of law, preclude recovery against architect/engineer). *See also* Appeal of

R. L. Coleman & Co., 1963 B.C.A. 3748, ASBCA No. 7334 (Apr. 30, 1963) (rejecting contractor's differing site conditions claim against government based on allegations that water table depicted on plans differed materially from condition actually encountered, but holding government liable for breach of warranty for faulty design); Appeal of Engineered Sys., Inc., 80-2 B.C.A. (CCH) §14,458 (Nov. 30, 1978) (contractor allowed to recover from government/owner on differing site conditions claim where drawings furnished by government/owner's engineer failed to accurately depict the location of dabbles on the project site).

31. *See* Fondedile, S. A. v. C. E. Maguire, 610 A.2d 87 (R.I. 1992) (contractor asserted negligence claim against design professional alleging that the design professional negligently failed to disclose movement of a sea wall in contract documents; court rejected contractor's claim finding that even if design professional withheld such information, contractor could not establish a causal link between its alleged damages and design professional's allegedly negligent conduct). *See generally* J. McBride and T. Touhie, *Government Contracts: Cyclopedic Guide to Law, Administration, Procedure,* § 29.70[4], Albany, NY: Matthew Bender, 1991. *See also* Richardson Electr. Co., Inc. v. Peter Francese & Son, Inc. 484 N.E.2d 108 (Mass. App. Ct. 1985). Although the *Richardson* decision did not directly involve a claim against a design professional (the owner's claim against the engineer was held in abeyance pending the outcome of the contractor's claim against the owner), that decision does recognize the right of a subcontractor to sue for differing site conditions under circumstances where (a) the owner and its engineer knew of the alleged differing site conditions prior to the construction of the project but did not disclose the information to bidders, and (b) the subcontractor was found to have exercised reasonable diligence in preparing its bid. Significantly, the court in *Richardson* observed that the relevant contract documents did not contain any disclaimer as to site information provided in the contract documents. *See also* Frederick Snare Corp. v. Maine-New Hampshire Interstate Bridge Auth., 41 F. Supp. 638 (D.N.H. 1941) (contractor allowed to recover on differing site conditions claim asserted against owner of project, despite the existence of contract provision requiring contractor to "investigate" and base his bid on his own opinion of the conditions, where engineers knew that no accurate soundings could be made to determine subsurface conditions in the four-day bidding period but withheld the information).

32. *See, e.g.,* Ohio Valley Contractors, Inc. v. Board of Educ. of Wetzel County, 391 S.E.2d 891 (W. Va. 1990) (holding that contractor stated valid claim against owner due to (a) ambiguities in the contract documents prepared by owner's architect concerning the authority of the architect who authorized additional excavation beyond that included in the contractor's bid and (b) the existence of factual issues as to whether the architect was authorized on behalf of the owner to direct the contractor to perform additional excavation).

33. *See, e.g.,* Bilotta Constr. Corp. v. Village of Mamaroneck, 199 A.D.2d 230 (N.Y. App. Div. 1993) (contractor asserted claim against owner and engineer on the basis of misrepresentation of information regarding estimates of elevations; court rejected contractor's claim, holding that, based on disclaimers in contract documents and provision requiring contractor to conduct its

own investigation prior to entering into the contract, any reliance by the contractor on such data was not justifiable and therefore could not support a misrepresentation claim against either the owner or the engineer); Zontelli & Sons, Inc. v. City of Nashwauk, 373 N.W.2d 744 (Minn. 1985) (contractor asserted claim against owner and consulting engineer for negligence and misrepresentation in preparation of estimates on which contractor bid, alleging that it encountered more concrete than estimated and that the amount of unsuitable material to be excavated was substantially understated and was of a differing quality than anticipated; court found engineer negligent because, among other things, engineer had "drastically underestimated" the quantity of concrete and unsuitable materials to be removed and had failed to indicate the unusual characteristics of those materials); APAC-Carolina, Inc. v. Greensboro-High Point Airport Auth., 431 S.E.2d 508 (N.C. Ct. App. 1993) (contractor asserted claim against owner and engineer due to substantial overruns in undercutting required; court refused to allow claim against engineer on the basis that the contractor had failed to adequately inspect available information, the contract clearly stated that any quantities mentioned in the contract were merely estimates, and, therefore, the contractor had failed to establish any justifiable reliance on information contained in the contract documents), *rev. denied*, 438 S.E.2d 197 (N.C. 1993); Raymond Int'l, Inc. v. Baltimore County, 412 A.2d 1296 (Md. Ct. Spec. App. 1980) (claim by contractor against owner and engineer arising out of allegations that quantities estimated in contract documents were inaccurate and grossly underestimated, resulting in the unit price representing an inadequate measure of compensation; court allowed recovery against engineer on the basis that the estimates were materially wrong and substantially inaccurate and engineer reasonably should have known information was inaccurate based upon engineer's prior involvement at the site), *cert. denied*, 449 U.S. 1013 (1980); L. Loyer Constr. Co. v. City of Novi, 446 N.W. 2d 364 (Mich. Ct. App. 1989) (contractor asserted claim against owner and engineer claiming that the work required to complete the project varied from estimates set forth in the contract documents on which the contractor based its bid and that the quantity variations necessitated the use of unplanned, less efficient methods of excavation and use of a different off-site dump than originally contemplated. Court rejected contractor's claim, holding that owner did not guarantee the representation as to soil conditions; that the risk that soil and water conditions might be different than expected was expressly assumed by contractor; that the quantities listed in the proposal were not guaranteed to be actual quantities; and that contractor had a duty to investigate the specific subsurface conditions as well as the site generally), *appeal denied*, 435 Mich. 871 (1990); Costanza Constr. Corp. v. City of Rochester, 147 A.D.2d 929 (N.Y. App. Div. 1989) (contractor asserted breach of contract, negligence, breach of warranty, and equitable adjustment claims against owner and engineer, alleging gross inaccuracies in estimates of cubic yards of rock to be excavated; court rejected contractor's claim because the contract documents clearly included a disclaimer by owner of any responsibility for accuracy of completeness of information on the drawings concerning existing conditions, including rock, and obligated contractor to satisfy itself as to site conditions; accordingly, as a matter of law, the contractor could not establish that it had justifiably relied on

information in the contract documents, thereby warranting dismissal of claims against owner and engineer), *appeal dismissed*, 541 N.E.2d 429 (N.Y. 1989).

34. *See, e.g.*, Northrup Contracting, Inc. v. Village of Bergen, 527 N.Y.S.2d 670 (Sup. Ct. 1986); W. H. Lyman Constr. Co. v. Village of Gurnee, 403 N.E.2d 1325 (Ill. App. Ct. 1980). In *Northrup*, a contractor sued an engineering firm and project owner, alleging that the engineering firm was negligent in (a) the preparation of test pits that failed to disclose high groundwater within the area of the contractor's work and (b) the administration of the construction contract — specifically, the engineer's delay in addressing and resolving the contractor's differing site conditions claim based on the alleged unanticipated high groundwater and in recommending termination of the contractor due to nonperformance (as a result of the unresolved nature of the contractor's claim). The court held that the contractor stated a valid legal claim against the engineering firm not only with respect to the claim of negligence in the preparation of contract documents, but also with respect to the claim that the engineer was negligent in the manner in which it administered the construction contract and addressed (or, more precisely, failed to timely address) the contractor's differing site conditions claim. Similarly, in the *Lyman* case, the court, while rejecting the contractor's differing site conditions claim on the rationale that the contractor had failed to undertake an adequate site investigation, did permit the contractor to proceed to trial against an engineering firm based on the contractor's allegations that the engineering firm had negligently administered the performance of the construction contract by withholding approval for many months of the contractor's method of sealing the manhole basis and otherwise failing to adequately address the contractor's differing site conditions claim.

In Brinderson Corp. v. Hampton Roads Sanitation District, 825 F.2d 41 (4th Cir. 1987), a contractor was allowed to pursue a differing site conditions claim against an owner despite the absence of the timely submission of the written notice required by the differing site conditions clause in light of the fact that "the owner's engineers were fully informed of all of the contractor's [information as it developed concerning the differing site condition claim]." The court held that the engineer's awareness of the contractor's differing site conditions claim would be imputed to the owner (given that the engineer was the owner's representative and agent during the construction phase of the project) and, accordingly, the contractor's failure to provide timely written notice to the owner as required by the contract documents did not defeat the contractor's claim. Although not clear from the court's decision in *Brinderson*, it appears that the engineer did not notify the owner of the engineer's awareness of the contractor's differing site conditions claims and, under such circumstances, the engineer could be found liable to the owner for the contractor's claim on the theory of indemnification. *See* Zontelli & Sons v. City of Nashwauk, 353 N.W. 2d 600 (Minn. Ct. App. 1984) (ruling that an owner may obtain indemnification from its project engineer for owner's payment of contractor's differing site condition claim based on finding that engineering firm breached its duty to owner to provide satisfactory plans and specifications), *judgment rev'd*, 373 N.W.2d. 744 (1985).

35. *See, e.g.*, Victor M. Solis Underground Util. & Paving Co. v. City of Laredo, 751 S.W.2d 532 (Tex.

App. 1988), *writ denied* (June 28, 1989). *Solis* involved the design and construction of a storm sewer system. The contractor in *Solis* brought an action for tortious interference with a contractual relationship against an engineering firm (and its project engineer) for recommending the contractor's termination. Under the terms of its contract with the city, the engineering firm was obligated to continuously inspect the contractor's work and report any failures in conforming to the project specifications. The contractor knew of this duty to inspect through his contract with the city. Evidence was presented at trial that the contractor was uncooperative and did not meet the plans and specifications. The court enumerated the elements of tortious contractual interference as: (1) the defendant maliciously interfered with a contractual relationship and (2) the defendant did so without legal justification or excuse. In applying these elements to the facts of the case, the court held that, since the contractor's work had not met the specifications, there was no evidence of maliciousness and the project engineer was justified in exercising his superior legitimate interest by recommending termination. Thus, neither element of the cause of action had been satisfied. In addition, the court discussed interference actions and distinguished between interference caused by third-party strangers and interference caused by a servant or agent. Concluding that the engineering firm was clearly the city's agent, the court stated that "[j]ust as an instructed verdict in favor of the City on the interference action would have been proper, because the cause of action must fail, so it was in the case of its agents." (751 S.W. 2d at 535) However, there was a strong dissent to this portion of the opinion. The dissent further argued that since the engineering firm was to serve as referee (with binding decisions) in all questions arising under the contract between the contractor and the city, it could not be the city's agent because it would be utterly inconsistent for a servant to act as an impartial referee for his master. *See also* Forte Bros., Inc. v. Nat'l Amusement, Inc., 525 A.2d 1301 (R.I. 1987) (holding that contractor can maintain cause of action for negligence against supervising architect/site engineer for failing to accurately measure removal of mass boulders by plaintiff, to report removal to the owner, and to authorize payment to plaintiff when contractor reasonably and directly relied on architect/engineer professionally rendering its contractual duty to do so); Fitzpatrick Constr. Corp. v. County of Suffolk, 138 A.D.2d 446 (N.Y. App. Div. 1988) (in an action by contractor against engineering firm alleging intentional interference with contractual relations, court held that contractor's vague reference to intentional course of conduct was insufficient to substantiate intentional interference claim against engineering firm), *appeal denied in part*, 534 N.E.2d 315 (1988); Costanza Constr. Corp. v. City of Rochester, 135 A.D.2d 1111 (N.Y. App. Div. 1987) (holding that interference that is negligent or incidental to a lawful purpose, but not intentional, is insufficient to maintain a claim against architect/engineering firm for tortious interference with a contractual relationship). In Pavers, Inc. v. Board of Regents of the University of Nebraska, 755 N.W.2d 400 (Neb. 2008), the Supreme Court of Nebraska held that a project owner was not able to obtain a downward equitable adjustment in unit price for quantity overruns due to the fact that the Owner's consulting engineer (a) was aware of the overruns and the Constructor's intention to be paid at the contract-stipulated unit price and (b) failed to timely

notify the Constructor of the project owner's intention to seek an equitable adjustment. These circumstances could easily lead to the assertion of a professional liability claims by the project owner against the consulting engineer.

36. However, the project owners do not always retain the consulting engineer to provide services relating to the investigation and evaluation of differing site condition claims. *See* §§ 4.0 and 6.1.

37. *See* Fontaine Bros., Inc. v. Springfield, 617 N.E.2d 1002 (Mass. App. Ct. 1993) (upholding determination by architect that contractor was not entitled to additional compensation for removal of below-grade debris where contract documents gave architect final review authority), *review denied*, 621 N.E.2d 685 (Mass. 1993).

38. Unreasonable delay in addressing and/or resolving such claims may subject the consulting engineer to liability.

39. *See* G. Smith, "Engineering Misfeasance in the Design of a 30-Ft Diameter TBM-Bored Tunnel—A Hypothetical Case/Claim Study," *Tunnel Business Magazine*, 7 (Apr. 2004). This article very effectively discusses a hypothetical involving a differing site condition claim that could materialize into a professional liability claim by the project owner against the consulting engineer and addresses how inadequate investigation or interpretation of available subsurface data by a consulting engineer and failure to take same into account in design may lead to a professional liability claim. The author states:

> The fact that a Contractor may be entitled to recover unanticipated additional costs from the Owner under a differing site conditions type of clause is usually—though not necessarily—the end of the story. Such a clause allocates the risk of unusual or unforeseen subsurface conditions to the Owner, but only as between the Owner and Contractor. What about the Engineer?

The article then discusses a hypothetical and based on the facts of that hypothetical states the following conclusion:

> Based on the available pre-bid geotechnical information, the Engineer knew or should have known of significant water ingress and rock support problems in major areas of the East Side Tunnel Corridor. That knowledge was not properly reflected in the Engineer's design for the East Side Project, and to that extent, the design was defective. The Engineer's design did not take into account conditions which the Engineer knew or should have known to expect, and to that extent, the design did not properly reflect the full scope of the work required for construction of the Project. This led to the situation where additional scope had to be added to the construction contract, which unfortunately was done under a differing site conditions declaration and paid for on a cost-plus basis, rather than being included within the competitive, lump-sum bid.

See also S. Stein and C. Popovsky, "Liability for Differing Site Conditions and the Risk-Sharing Philosophy," *The Construction Law.*, 20 (April 2000): 16–18, in which it is stated:

Public Works agencies and other participants in the construction industry have made great strides to improve the contracting environment for underground projects. The main focus of these efforts has properly been to develop new contract practices that more efficiently allocate the risk of unforeseen conditions between the Owner and the Contractor. But the project designer is hardly an uninvolved party in this process of risk allocation. The design professional often drafts the construction contract and wields considerable influence on the actual allocation of risk between the owner and contractor. The designer may be subject to liability if an owner or contractor claims damages arising from the design. If design professionals are unduly concerned with liability, their designs may be skewed in a conservative direction, thus frustrating the innovations or economies that are needed in modern underground construction. . . .

Although the purpose of "risk-sharing contracting practices" is to adjust the traditional balance of risk, the implementation of the philosophy significantly affects the design process, and therefore, must be included in the mix of factors considered in applying the design professional's standard of care. . . .

There is a fundamental tension in asking a design professional to set the baseline for anticipated underground conditions, thereby inviting the design professional to act conservatively out of concern for its own liability. Unnecessarily conservative designs defeat the purpose of the risk-sharing philosophy.

To implement proper risk sharing, the prediction of anticipated conditions and the design reflecting anticipated conditions must not be overly conservative. The goal of risk sharing is for the owner to receive bids based on likely conditions and pay for overcoming conditions worse than indicated. A system in which the designer assumes the worst-case scenario is no more efficient that the traditional system in which the contractor includes contingencies in its bid to cover potential underground conditions. The result either way will be bids with contingencies for conditions that are unlikely to occur. . . .

If designers are to set an unbiased contractual baseline against which actual underground conditions will be measured, they must have confidence that they will not be held liable for making reasonable, but ultimately incorrect, predictions. By properly applying the flexible doctrine of the design professional's standard of care, courts can do their part to alleviate this concern. Design professionals are to be judged according to their peers practicing under similar circumstances. In establishing that standard, it is important to consider whether the owner has adopted the risk-sharing contracting philosophy. If so, then it should be acknowledged that the design professional was never expected to preclude surprises during construction of their resulting change orders. When judging the reasonableness of the designer's geotechnical investigation and analyses on a risk-sharing project, the result, whether the prediction is accurate or not, becomes at best a secondary consideration. The focus must be on the reasonableness of the investigation and methodologies relied

upon in the analysis, given the many trade-offs that the design professional must consider in applying the professional standard of care.

The flexibility of the professional standard of care also can accommodate the fact that some owners more wholly embrace risk sharing than do others. For example, an owner may agree to utilize a DSC clause, include a geotechnical report in the contract documents, and remove disclaimers of the information provided. However, the same owner may also give specific instructions to the design professional, such as to err on the side of conservatism with regard to particular aspects of the design. Specific instructions from the owner simply become an additional factor in the mix of criteria that the design professional considers, and therefore one more circumstance to consider in applying the professional standard of care.

40. The economic loss doctrine and other issues related to a constructor's ability to recover on claims directly asserted against a consulting engineer are discussed in detail in chapters 15 and 17.

41. *See* § 7.0 of chapter 16 regarding the roles of project owner and consulting engineer in defending claims by the constructor.

42. Sweet and Schneier, *Legal Aspects of Architecture*, § 14.11C, pp. 299–300; § 25.07, p. 562.

43. As has been stated:

> Much has been written about the frustrations, limitations, and other perceived shortcomings and disadvantages that result from the inability in Design-Bid-Build to integrate and coordinate, in a timely manner, the respective roles of the geotechnical and design engineer(s) with those of the Constructor, especially in the specific context of projects with a significant subsurface construction component ("subsurface projects"). These perceived shortcomings and disadvantages include (a) the inability to timely and qualified input from the constructor during design development regarding constructability considerations and the scope and definition of pre-construction subsurface investigation, preparation of reports, and development of information, all of which would be beneficial to the constructor in the planning and prosecution of the work, including the Constructor's contemplations regarding the means, methods, techniques, sequences and procedures of construction (construction means and methods), and selection of equipment; and (b) the Engineer's lack of knowledge during design of the specific construction means and methods and equipment choices and decisions that will be made and implemented by the Constructor in the performance of the work, and the consequent inability of the Engineer to anticipate or predict whether those Constructor choices will influence or impact design assumptions and/or the behavior of site conditions during construction to a degree requiring reevaluation of design decisions.
>
> The ability to overcome these perceived shortcoming and disadvantages is especially challenging on publically procured projects in which, typically, construction contracts are awarded to the lowest bidder based upon "complete" design documents. In this context, the opportunity for direct and timely interaction and meaningful dialog between the con-

sulting engineer (or other Owner representative) and the successful bidder, prior to execution of a construction contract, for the purpose of revisiting design decisions in light of the Constructor's planned construction means and methods and/or equipment choices, are extremely limited and, in many jurisdictions, would violate public competitive bid laws. In addition, addressing these perceived shortcomings and disadvantages to a value-engineering process (under which the Constructor may propose changes to the design of permanent work) if the process is not carefully defined, and timely and appropriately implemented, result in unintended risk assumptions and ambiguity in risk allocation. Similarly, attempts to restrict and control the Constructor's construction means and methods and/or equipment choices through the submittal review process typically introduce ambiguity and uncertainty as to responsibility for construction means and methods and safety, resulting in ensuing conflict and disputes between project participants, as well as third parties.

In short, there has been no satisfactory resolution in the design-bid-build delivery method for the perceived shortcomings and disadvantages that result from the lack of timely and coordinated integration of the design and construction functions, especially in the context of subsurface projects. Given the intimate and direct correlation between design, construction methodology, equipment selections, and behavior of ground conditions during construction in subsurface projects, these perceived shortcomings and disadvantages have represented major challenges to the process of fairly allocating and managing risk in subsurface projects. Previously, many have recognized that reconciling this disfunctionality in achieving a comprehensive and collaborative effort to integrate the design and construction process in subsurface projects will have significant advantages to the overall project delivery approach, as well as to the fair allocation and effective management of risk.

Brierly and Hatem, *Design-Build Subsurface Projects* § 3.0, pp. 22–23.

44. B. Tehrani, "Construction Management Saves Time, Money and Improves Quality During Design and Construction," *North American Tunnel 2008 Proceedings*, 508.

45. *See* C. Clayton, *Managing Geotechnical Risk,* London: Thomas Telford, 2001, 24–26.

46. *See generally* R. Cushman and D. Tortorello, eds., *Differing Site Condition Claims*, Hoboken, NJ: Wiley, 1992, pp. 68–70; *see* C. A. Foster et al., eds. *Construction and Design Law*, § 12.2b.3. In major subsurface work, the relationship between adequacy of project design and engineering judgments regarding subsurface conditions is often interconnected, leading further to the assertion of combined design defect and differing site conditions claims. As Bruner & O'Connor have stated:

. . . With respect to the implied warranty of design adequacy, "design" is understood to include foundation design, which itself rests upon informed judgments about bearing capacity and other characteristics of subsurface soils. On most large projects, architects and engineers still prepare detailed design plans and specifications. With the growth of the design-build delivery method, however, under which the contractor furnishes both the detailed

design and construction to conform generally with stated owner performance requirements, the question of which party has a duty to explore subsurface conditions and assume
the risk of unanticipated conditions is a matter of careful contract negotiation. Because of
the inherent risks, even design-builders may seek to require the owner to provide the services of geotechnical consultants upon whose work product the design builder may rely in
preparation of the detailed design documents.

4A *Bruner & O'Connor*, §14.28.

47. Hatem, *Subsurface Conditions*, § 10.2.2.3., 313–40. The latter source contains detailed discussion
of a number of cases involving combined differing site condition and defective design claims by
constructors against project owners and/or engineering consultants.

48. *See, e.g.,* Kiewit Constr. Co. v. United States, 56 Fed. Cl. 414, 611–12 (2003). In *Kiewit*, a constructor asserted a combined differing site condition and defective design claim against the project owner. More specifically, the constructor contended that it was obligated to install and operate a dewatering system that exceeded the minimum required system guidelines specified in the
contract documents. The constructor claimed that it was unable to lower groundwater within the
required contract-specified limits and asserted a differing site condition claim alleging that the
problems were due to unexpected water encountered and that the dewatering specifications were
defective. Although the result in the case turned on a legal jurisdictional issue, the resolution of
that issue depended upon whether the differing site condition and defective design claims arose
out of the "same set of operative facts." The court drew a distinction between the two claims,
stating:

> Governing case law mandates that differing site condition claims and defective specifica-
> tion claims depend upon varying sets of operative facts. Operative facts are the essential
> facts that give rise to a cause of action. . . . The operative facts supporting a Type I differing
> site conditions claim filed pursuant to a standard Differing Site Conditions Clause include
> (1) whether conditions indicated in the contract at issue differed materially from conditions
> encountered by the Contractor during performance of the Contract; (2) whether conditions
> actually encountered by the Contractor were reasonably unforeseeable based upon all infor-
> mation available to the Contractor during the contract bidding; and (3) whether the Con-
> tractor reasonably relied upon its interpretation of the Contract, and was thus damaged
> from the material variation between expected and encountered conditions. . . . Thus, the
> operative facts necessary to maintain a differing site conditions claim in the instant case
> would focus on the Contract's description of the work site, particularly with respect to sub-
> surface conditions, and Kiewit's reliance on that description.
>
> On the other hand, a defective specifications claim . . . requires showing that a contrac-
> tor was misled by design specification errors presented within a government contract. . . .
> A defective specifications claim therefore focuses on the viability of design requirements
> that a Contractor is required to implement in a government contract. The operative facts

for a defective specifications claim in the instant case would concern the functioning of the Contract's dewatering system specifications. Thus, the Type I differing site conditions claim submitted to the Contracting Officer and the defective specifications claim made in Count I rely upon different operative facts.

Kiewit, 56 Fed. Cl. at 419–20.

In Interstate Contracting Corp. v. City of Dallas, 407 F.3d 708 (5th Cir. 2005), the constructor claimed that it was required to perform additional excavation work to construct a levee due to its inability to use available on-site excavated material and thus had the need to manufacture fill material for use in doing the work. The constructor asserted a claim for breach of implied warranty in differing site conditions. In essence, the constructor claimed that the project owner breached an implied warranty to provide accurate and suitable plans and specifications in light of the actual subsoil conditions encountered at the site. The court found that specific disclaimers included in the contract documents overrode both the differing site condition and defective design claims and thus negated any right of recovery of the constructor under either claim basis.

In Basin Paving Co. v. Mike M. Johnson, Inc., 27 P.3d 609 (Wash. Ct. App. 2001), the court ruled that the differing site condition provision was overridden by a specific risk allocation provision placing the burden of predicting rock formations on the constructor and specific disclaimers as to accuracy of boring data. Also, in S&M Constructors, Inc. v. Columbus, 70 Ohio St. 2d 69 (1982), the court ruled that specific disclaimers regarding site conditions overrode the *Spearin* implied warranty obligation of the project owner; *see also* Thomas & Marker Constr. Co. v. Wal-Mart Stores, Inc., No. 3:06-cv-406 2008 U.S. Dist. Lexis 79072 (Ohio Sept. 15, 2008).

Generally speaking, many courts have ruled that if a contract provides a specific remedy — i.e., a differing site condition clause — recovery will not be allowed on different theories such as breach of implied warranty or defective design unless specific independent facts are alleged or supported to justify the defective design claim. In Suffolk Construction Co., Inc. v. Division of Capital Asset Management, No. 05 Civ. 3631-BLS-2, (Mass. Sup. Ct., June 29, 2007), (Gants, J.), (unpublished),* 10–14, the court disallowed a constructor's implied warranty claim on the basis that the contract provided an adequate remedy in the differing site condition provision. In doing so, the court stated:

> Suffolk/NER alleges that DCAM breached what it contends was a warranty.... Suffolk/NER contends that this representation was false, since the plans and specifications in the RFP were incomplete and inaccurate, and that it is entitled to damages arising from this alleged breach of warranty....
>
> DCAM denies that [implied warranty] is controlling here, because it notes that its RFP provided that "[t]he plans and specifications contain all information and requirements of the project needed by prospective offerors to submit a proposal," not all information and requirements needed to complete the project....
>
> This Court need not decide now whether the nature of the representations . . . [is] suffi-

ciently different from those made in the RFP here as to render the [prior court precedent] inapplicable, because there are independent reasons why [prior court precedent] does not apply here and why the express warranty claim here must be dismissed. *Alpert* was decided in 1970, two years before the Legislature enacted G.L. c. 30, § 39N, which required all construction contracts with the Commonwealth to include a provision providing for an equitable adjustment in the contract price when the physical conditions on the site "differ substantially or materially from those shown on the plans or indicated in the contract documents or from those ordinarily encountered and generally recognized as inherent in work of the character provided for in the plans and contract documents and are of such a nature to cause an increase or decrease in the cost of performance of the work or a change in the construction methods required for the performance of the work which results in an increase or decrease in the cost of the work." . . . In *Alpert*, in contrast with the Contract in the instant case, there was no provision providing for an equitable adjustment of the contract price for unforeseen physical conditions on the site, and therefore no procedure within the terms of the contract equitably to adjust the contract price to take account of these materially different circumstances. In the absence of such a provision, the Court permitted a breach of warranty claim in order to award the contractor "adequate compensation" for the "extra work which was not contemplated by the parties." . . . Thus, it is plain from *Alpert* that the damages for breach of the warranty alleged are nothing more than the equitable adjustment now provided for under G.L. c. 30, §39N, which by statute must be incorporated in every construction contract with the Commonwealth.

Therefore, for all practical purposes, the enactment of G.L. c. 30, § 39N, with its provision for an equitable adjustment when there are unforeseen physical conditions on the site, has supplanted the need for a common law express warranty claim, and replaced it with a legal remedy under the statute. . . .

To allow Suffolk/NER to prosecute its breach of warranty claim here poses two unnecessary risks of confusion. First, it invites the misperception that Suffolk/NER is entitled to damages above and beyond (or different in kind from) the equitable adjustment it is entitled to by statute. Second, it diverts the factfinder to consider various issues that may be necessary to resolve a breach of warranty claim, when the factual issue the factfinder needs to resolve is whether the physical conditions on the site "differ substantially or materially from those shown on the plans or indicated in the contract documents or from those ordinarily encountered and generally recognized as inherent in work of the character provided for in the plans and contract documents and are of such a nature as to cause an increase or decrease in the cost of performance of the work or a change in the construction methods required for the performance of the work which results in an increase or decrease in the cost of the work." . . . In short, if the breach of warranty claim were allowed to survive, it would potentially encourage Suffolk/NER to believe that it may obtain damages above and beyond an equitable adjustment, which it may not obtain, or that it may obtain an equitable adjust-

ment without satisfying the statutory conditions set forth in G.L. c. 30, § 39N, which it may not. Therefore, the motion to dismiss the breach of warranty claim is allowed.

In Orlosky, Inc. v. United States, 64 Fed. Cl. 63, 69 (2005), the constructor asserted a combined differing site condition and defective design claim arising out of subsurface conditions. The court rejected the defective design claim on the basis that when alleged defective design concerns the same basis as the differing site condition claim, the breach of implied warranty/defective design claim collapses into the differing site condition claim and the constructor is allowed to pursue only its contractual remedy under the differing site condition clause. *See also* Comtrol, Inc. v. United States, 294 F.3d 1357 (Fed. Cir. 2002).

In M. A. DeAtley Construction, Inc. v. United States, 71 Fed. Cl. 370, 374–75 (2006), the court ruled that the differing site condition and defective design claim were to be considered independent, stating:

> In Count 2, Plaintiff sets forth a defective specifications claim . . . . Under this doctrine, where the "government uses specifications in a contract, there is an accompanying implied warranty that these specifications are free from errors." . . . Plaintiff argues that its defective specifications claim is sufficiently stated because the Government provided it with specifications, it followed those specifications, and it did not achieve a satisfactory result. . . .
>
> Defendant does not challenge the legal sufficiency of the defective specifications claim, but rather argues that "[although] differing site conditions and defective specifications claims are distinct in theory, they collapse into a single claim where [as here] the alleged defect in the specification is the failure of the Government-provided source to provide suitable rock from which the aggregate was crushed.". . . Defendant argues that since the two claims collapse into one, dismissal of Count 2 is appropriate.
>
> In its response, Plaintiff agrees that *Comtrol* represents the correct state of the law . . . However, Plaintiff asserts that its "claim for defective specifications is not based *solely* on differing site conditions.". . . In addition to that defect (the poor-quality rock), Plaintiff also asserts that the specifications were defective because they "did not allow any tolerance for the fine sieve.". . . Specifically, Plaintiff alleges that since the Government knew that it designated an aggregate source that was comprised of "highly weathered fractured material," the Government's gradation specifications should have "taken into account the material degradation of the rock.". . . Since the specifications did not allow for any degradation, when the designated rock presented with a higher than expected increase in fine material, it fell short of the contract specifications. Therefore, Plaintiff argues that since its defective specifications claim (Count 2) is distinct from its differing site conditions count (Count 3), Defendant's motion should be denied.
>
> Plaintiff's differing site conditions and defective specifications claims both arise from its encounter with the allegedly deficient aggregate source designated by the Government. . . . Although the claims are related, Plaintiff alleges a distinct basis for its defective specifica-

tions claim. . . . That is, Plaintiff alleges that the specifications were also defective because they did not allow any tolerance for the fine sieve. As a result, and due to the material degradation of the rock, the produced aggregate failed the relevant tests. . . .

See also Bruner & O'Connor, § 14.48, footnote 4, which states:

The differing site conditions clause is cumulative of other remedies and does not preclude claims brought under common-law principles for nondisclosure of material information, breach of implied warranty, misrepresentation, or mistake. . . .

However, footnote 4 of that same publication states that: "To the extent that a common-law claim is "merely a recharacterization of the claim which is redressable under the contract," federal precedent allows, only the claim redressable under the contract may be pursued. . . ."

In Universal Construction, Inc. v. United States, 71 Fed. Cl. 179, 182-83 (2006), the court rejected recovery on an independent breach of implied warranty basis stating:

In its briefs, plaintiff also asserts entitlement to recovery under a defective specification theory, but does not include the theory as a separate count in its complaint. Both the Type I differing site condition and defective specification theories are based on [the contractor's] alleged encounter with non-conforming soil materials in the borrow sources and will therefore be governed by the differing site conditions clause and the cases under that clause. [Comtrol, Inc. v. United States, 294 F.3d 1357, 1362 (Fed. Cir. 2002) (citing FAR 52.236-2(a)(1)(1994)] (holding that differing site condition claim and defective specification claim based upon contractor's encounter with quicksand at the work site collapse into a single claim).

The decision in *PCL Construction Services, Inc. v. United States*, 84 Fed. Cl. 408 (2008), *appeal dismissed*, 2009 WL 3489221 (Fed. Cir. Oct. 27, 2009), presented an interesting legal discussion relevant to the subject of combined defective design and differing site condition claims. In that case, PCL, a constructor, had filed a civil action against the government (the "first action") alleging, among other things, that the government breached its *Spearin* implied warranty obligation relative to the furnishing of defective and inaccurate project design and subsurface condition information. PCL did not prevail in the first action. 84 Fed. Cl. at 411. Subsequently, PCL commenced a second action against the government based on the same set of operative facts underlying the claims asserted in the first action, and alleging that PCL was entitled to recovery under the differing site condition clause contained in its contract with the government. *Id.* at 412. The Court of Federal Claims dismissed PCL's second action on the basis that the judgment in the first action — which essentially adjudicated the same claims and arose out of the same set of operative facts — precluded PCL from relitigating in the second action its claim based on the contractual differing site condition clause. *Id.* at 439.

49. Martin K. Eby Construction Co., Inc. v. Jacksonville Transportation Authority, 436 F. Supp. 2d 1276 (M.D. Fla. 2005), *aff'd*, 2006 Wl 1117952 (11th Cir. 2006).

50. Martin K. Eby Construction Co., Inc. v. Jacobs Civil, Inc., 2006 WL 1881359,*16 (M.D. Fla. 2006). More specifically, the court stated:

> Eby made the informed tactical decision in *Eby I* to sue the Owner of the . . . Project, the JTA, in contract, and, based on the provisions of that Contract, litigate its design and constructability claims before the Court. Eby, for its own reasons, chose not to "sue [Jacobs in the initial litigation]. The parties [in the initial litigation] presented evidence in detail pertaining to pre-bid design, specifications and drawings; the administration of the construction contract; and the problems encountered by Eby in constructing temporary access structures. Eby had a full and fair opportunity to litigate these issues. One month after losing on its contract claims, Eby brought the same design and constructability claims here against the engineers, designers, and consultants in tort, claiming breach of professional duty. The doctrines of *res judicata* and collateral estoppel [legal principles precluding repetitive litigation] guard against this type of tactical maneuvering, protecting adversaries from the expense and vexation of multiple lawsuits, conserving judicial resources, and minimizing the possibility of inconsistent decisions.

51. For a general discussion of the implied warranty doctrine, *see* S. Stein, *Construction Law* § 5.07[2] [b][i], Albany, NY: Matthew Bender, 1997 ; M. Branca, A. Silberman & J. Vento, Federal Government Construction Contracts, Second Edition (2010 American Bar Association), chapter 18, pp. 491–531. The rationale for allocating the risk of defective design to the project owner under the implied warranty doctrine is based on the principle that since the project owner (typically through a consulting engineer) undertakes to prepare and furnish the design to the constructor, the project owner should be responsible for the accuracy, completeness, and constructability of the design. As a consequence, the constructor generally is under no obligation to check and verify the adequacy or constructability of the design furnished by the project owner because the project owner assumed responsibility for the preparation and furnishing of that design. In other words, if the design furnished by the project owner is "defective," the project owner who furnished that design is responsible to the constructor based on the theory of breach of implied warranty of design adequacy.

   By way of distinction, and as discussed in chapter 16, above, the consulting engineer is obligated to perform its services, including preparation of design, in accordance with a degree of care ordinarily exercised by other members of its profession possessing similar skill and performing services under the same or similar circumstances (i.e., the professional standard of care). The distinction between the project owner's implied warranty obligation and the professional standard of care has been stated as follows:

   > Although the Owner — under its implied warranty obligation — bears the risk associated with design defects, it is critically important to emphasize that the Owner's implied warranty obligation risk is not necessarily or always the equivalent of the design professional's risk associated with the departure from the professional standard of care. Unlike the de-

sign professional's more limited negligence-based professional standard of care obligation, the Owner's implied warranty risk implies a warranty that the design is virtually perfect and adequate in all material respects. Specifically, an Owner may be liable to a Contractor for design defects, but may be unable to obtain indemnification, cost recovery, or other recourse against the design professional who prepared that design absent satisfactory proof (typically required in the form of expert testimony) that the design professional failed to adhere to the professional standard of care. . . .

Thus, while the project owner customarily relies on a design professional to prepare the Contract Documents that the Owner furnishes to the Contractor (and which form the basis of the Owner's implied warranty obligation), a design professional's professional standard of care liability risk to the Owner for defective plans and specifications is *not coterminous* with the design defect or implied warranty liability risk exposure of the owner to the contractor. The liability standard applicable to the owner for design defects/implied warranty is a no-fault, strict liability standard, whereas the liability of the design professional to the owner is measured under the negligence-based professional standard of care. Thus, the Owner may be liable to the contractor if the contract documents are unsuitable, inadequate, incomplete, or otherwise defective in any respect, but the design professional will not be liable to the owner for those defects unless the professional failed to prepare the design and contract documents in accordance with the professional standard of care.

D. Hatem, *Subsurface Conditions*, § 10.2.2.1(A), p. 286.

For example, in a situation in which the consulting engineer prepares the design and the contract documents in accordance with the professional standard of care and the constructor adheres to the requirements of the contract documents but there are design deficiencies (although the deficiencies are short of any departure from the professional standard of care), the project owner may be potentially liable to the constructor for the cost or time impacts resulting from those deficiencies but will have no recourse against the consulting engineer.

The case of Pittman Construction Co., Inc. v. City of New Orleans, 178 So. 2d 312 (La. Ct. App. 1965) demonstrates this point.

In *Pittman*, a contractor sued the city of New Orleans for the balance of a contract. The project involved the design and construction of a refuse incinerator on a site selected by the city (as owner of the project). The entire project was designed by the city's consulting engineer. The contract required the contractor to perform the work in strict accordance with detailed plans and specifications.

During the early stages of construction, the contractor encountered unexpected, unstable subsurface soil conditions. These conditions required the work to be suspended, and the engineer who had designed the project had to substantially redesign the piles for the foundation system. The contractor completed the remedial pile work but advised the city and the engineer (to no avail) that proceeding with a floating concrete slab design would result in considerable damage to the building due to the unstable soil conditions.

The engineer inspected the work for final acceptance, found it to be satisfactory, and certified to the city that the contractor had completed the project in accordance with plans and specifications. The city, however, noting the damage done by the sunken slabs, refused to accept the contractor's work as complete and withheld the contract balance. The contractor sued the city for monies owed on the basis that it had completed all work required under its contract and had strictly complied with the "defective" design furnished by the city. The city, in turn, asserted a third-party claim based on defective design against the engineer to recover costs for the remedial pile work, as well as the amounts of any award to the contractor against the city.

Relying on expert testimony proffered by the city and by the engineer that the design was normal and standard, and "in accordance with first-class engineering practice," the Louisiana Court of Appeals reversed an award in favor of the city against the engineer, stating:

> There is no charge here that the plans and specifications were such that the structure was either wholly or partially unfit for the purpose for which it was built. The only effect of the unknown soil conditions was to increase the cost of construction. The City selected the site; and in spite of [the contractor's] repeated entreaties and recommendations that changes be made in the plans and specifications, the City's representatives first refused but finally gave their consent to such changes but refused to pay the additional cost because of the limited budget the City had for the structure. The City's representatives dealt at arm's length with [the contractor] and the [engineer] and were kept fully informed at all times, during the preliminary preparations leading to the preparing of the plans and specifications and the contract, and all during the course of construction. When the City finally decided to have [the engineer] revise the plans and specifications, [the contractor] agreed to do the work with the understanding that the City was responsible for the extra cost. Since the only result from the unknown soil conditions was the additional cost of the construction, we cannot see how [the engineer] can be held liable on the ground of professional incompetency or negligence.
>
> In determining the liability of [the engineer], the same standard of care applied in the case of architects, physicians, attorneys, and others engaged in professional activities requiring the exercise of technical skill should be applied. The test is whether he performed his service in accordance with the skill usually exercised by others of his profession in the same general area; and the burden of providing he did not, is upon the party making the charge, in this case the City. . . . The City has not discharged this burden here because all expert testimony vindicates the professional skill and judgment exercised by [the engineer] in this case.

Pittman, 178 So. 2d at 320–21. *See also* Hamon Contractors, Inc. v. Carter & Burgess, Inc., 2009 WL 1152160 (Col. App. 2090) (affirming dismissal of a constructor's negligence claim against engineer on grounds that the constructor failed to demonstrate that its negligence claim against the engineer was based on any duty of the latter independent of the Owner's implied warranty obligation to the constructor).

In other words, even though the engineer's design was rendered inappropriate due to the

unstable soil conditions, the uncontroverted evidence established that the design (while, strictly speaking and in reality, "defective") was in conformance with the professional standard of care, leaving the owner with no legal recourse against the engineer and with liability to the contractor.

52.   *See* § 7.0 of chapter 16.

53.   *See, e.g.,* GLF Construction Corp. v. LAN/STV, 414 F.3d 553 (5th Cir. 2005) In *GLF*, a private sector design engineering firm was determined to be protected by state sovereign immunity law and therefore not liable to the constructor for claims based on defective design. More specifically, the court ruled that the *Spearin* implied warranty doctrine was not available to a constructor as against a private engineering firm, as the *Spearin* implied warranty obligation depended upon contractual privity which the constructor did not have with the private engineering firm. On appeal, the Fifth Circuit affirmed summary judgment in favor of the private engineering firm, stating:

> DART is a regional transportation authority . . . under Texas law where "an independent contractor of [a transportation] entity is performing a function of the entity or of a regional transportation authority . . . the Contractor is liable for damages only to the extent that the entity or authority would be liable if the entity or authority itself were performing the function." . . . GLF does not dispute that the engineering and supervisory services provided by LAN/STV fall within the ambit of DART's functions as a regional transportation authority. . . . Because LAN/STV was performing a function of DART, it is liable for damages to GLF "only to the extent" that DART would be liable if it had prepared the plans, drawings, and specifications and supervised the Project.
>
> The doctrine of sovereign immunity would bar tort claims of the sort alleged by GLF's if asserted against DART. GLF could, however, assert claims against DART for breach of contract. . . . GLF argues that, because it would have a cause of action against DART for breach of contract [and breach of implied warranty under the Spearin] article 6550d does not prohibit it from suing LAN/STV in tort. That is, GLF contends that, as long as the government entity could have been subjected to liability under some cause of action, the independent contractor performing a function that entity can be sued under any cause of action.
>
> We disagree. Texas law carves out certain exceptions to the general rule that DART, as a government entity, is immune from suit and liability. Through the Texas Tort Claims Act, it permits liability for certain tort claims . . . it permits liability for breach of contract through administrative remedies and, where the plaintiffs have exhausted those remedies, through suits for breach of contract . . . it also limits the maximum amount of liability for certain areas in which it has waived immunity from liability and suit. . . . Texas law thus limits DART's liability both in terms of the causes of action for which DART may be held liable and, for some claims, the maximum amount of recovery. Article 6550(d) effectively places LAN/STV, as an independent contractor performing DART's functions, in DART's shoes for purposes of liability. That is, as the language of the statute plainly states LAN/STV is liable "only to the extent" that the DART itself would be liable had it performed the same function. . . . Texas law would not permit DART to be held liable in tort on these facts. Ac-

cordingly, neither does Article 6550(d) permit LAN/STV, performing DART's functions to be held liable in tort. . . .

GLF also objects that the District Court's interpretation of Article 6550(d) creates immunity for independent contractors regardless of whether the Government would be liable, merely because of the fortuity that a different cause of action applies. GLF intimates that the District Court's interpretation of Article 6550(d) gives LAN/STV a windfall. We find this argument unpersuasive. As GLF acknowledges, it can pursue its claims directly against DART through DART's administrative procedures and, after exhausting that remedy, can file suit against DART for breach of contract. . . . Further, there is nothing to indicate that DART would be prevented from pursuing claims against LAN/STV for the alleged deficiencies in the company's performance. Thus, our reading of Article 6550(d) neither denies GLF a remedy nor immunizes LAN/STV from liability.

414 F.3d at 556–58.

In *Syvy v. Landmark Engineering, Inc.*, 2005 WL 791391 (Del. Super. Ct. 2005), Memorandum Op., an engineering firm sought derivative sovereign immunity protection from a civil suit and moved for summary judgment. The court denied summary judgment. The engineering firm's position was that it was entitled to immunity since it was simply fulfilling the State's predetermined specifications as set forth in the engineer's contract, and the state exercised an extraordinary degree of oversight over the performance of the engineer's services. In rejecting this argument and denying the engineer's motion for summary judgment, the court stated:

The Court also rejects the argument that DelDOT's control over the actions and decisions of Landmark provides a basis to find Landmark's conduct is immunized by the State Tort Claims Act. The interaction between DelDOT and Landmark is an important factor that the jury will be required to consider in deciding whether Landmark failed to meet the standard of care expected of engineering firms in the particular areas in which it contracted to perform. To what extent Landmark's discretion was limited by DelDOT; Landmark's advice was ignored by DelDOT; or DelDOT limited Landmark's responsibility only to particular aspects of the design and construction project, will all be critical factors for the jury's consideration in making its decision regarding Landmark's negligence. However, the Court cannot allow a company that has been contracted to perform engineering duties by the government to hide behind the alleged 'approval' of government employees. As a professional organization, Landmark had full knowledge of the engineering and safety standards applicable to its industry and may not violate those standards without being held accountable.

The Court is doubtful, however, that the standards are as black and white as the Plaintiffs allege. Therefore, reasonable professional discretion and choice of logical practical alternatives are appropriate so long as the general standard of care continues to be met. In addition, the Court is confident that the unique factual interplay between DelDOT and Landmark will be applicable to nearly every aspect of this contract and disparities regarding responsibility, obligations and decisions will simply be issues that the jury will need to decide. . . .

573

The other authority cited by the Defendant in support of its positions also are not applicable to the facts of this case. Those cases involve the immunization of private firms that are simply carrying out the orders and specifications of a governmental agency. If those were the facts here, it would make no sense for the State of Delaware to have hired Landmark in the first place since the type of consulting services provided would be irrelevant and of no value. If the facts presented at trial support the Defendant's theory that it provided no advice or guidance on the engineering of this project, but was merely fulfilling the ill conceived directions of a state agency, it is free to make a motion for a directed verdict at the close of Plaintiff's case. However, at the moment there is nothing to suggest or support such a conclusion. Again, this appears to be a case of the Defendant trying to fit the round peg of his contract into a square hole of governmental immunity and it does not fit. . . .

While the Court has found summary judgment is not warranted, it feels it is important, in order to avoid other problems at trial, to emphasize that the Plaintiffs will be required at trial to establish that recognized industry standards for this type of engineering work have been violated. General opinions, by an expert that he would have operated in a different matter or propounding general violations, will not be sufficient. Nor will the fact that alternatives were available but not considered be sufficient, unless the failure to consider such alternatives also violates recognized industry standards. In other words, the Plaintiffs must be prepared to establish to the jury what the industry standards are and how they have been violated. The Court recognizes that this was a tragic accident that caused harm to the Plaintiffs and it will be easy for counsel to look beyond the establishment of the negligence claim and concentrate their energy on the issue of damages. However, the issue of damages will never be reached unless the jury determines that Landmark is responsible for the harm based on its liability in failing to meet the requisite professional standards.

2005 WL 791391 at *2-3

In Martin K. Eby Construction Co., Inc. v. LAN/STV, 205 S.W.3d 16 (Tex. App. 2006), the court declined to apply derivative sovereign immunity in favor of a private engineering firm, stating:

Eby argues LAN/STV did not prove that DART would be immune from liability under the facts of this case and, as a result, LAN/STV did not conclusively establish its affirmative defense of immunity from liability. Eby argues the application of section 452.056(d) and article 6550d turns on whether DART would be immune from liability if it had performed the same function as LAN/STV (preparation of the construction plans), not whether DART would be immune from liability for the same type of claim as that asserted against LAN/STV (negligent misrepresentation). Eby also argues LAN/STV's interpretation of the statute would provide independent contractors a shield against liability that the legislature did not intend.

To support its argument that DART would not be immune from potential liability, Eby cites a Fifth Circuit case arising from the same facts. *See Martin K. Eby Constr. Co. v. Dallas Area*

Rapid Transit, 369 F. 3d 464, 471–72 (5th Cir. 2004). After Eby discovered the alleged misrepresentations in the plans prepared by LAN/STV, Eby initially sued DART in federal district court for breach of contact and for misrepresentation. DART moved to discuss on the grounds that Eby had not exhausted its administrative remedies and that Eby's misrepresentation was barred by governmental immunity. *Id.* at 467. The district court granted DART's motion on both grounds and dismissed Eby's claims. *Id.* Eby appealed the district court's order.

On appeal, the Fifth Circuit agreed, in part, with Eby. It looked at the substance of Eby's allegations, not at the characterization of the claim. *Id.* at 471–72. The court noted that Eby's misrepresentation claim "appears to be redundant to its first cause of action for breach of contract." *Id.* at 471. It noted that the "gravamen of both of Eby's claims is that DART's bid specifications contained material misrepresentations." *Id.* The court concluded that Eby's misrepresentation claim was "just a subset of its breach-of-contract claim" and, as presented, is a contractual claim, and should not have been dismissed as a tort claim barred by governmental immunity. *Id.* at 472.

Conversely, LAN/STV argues that Eby's focus on the word "function" ignores the phrase "only to the extent" in both statutory provisions. It argues "only to the extent" means that if DART is immune from tort liability, then LAN/STV is derivatively immune from tort liability. It argues the statutes cannot be interpreted to mean that if DART would not be immune from liability in contract, then LAN/STV is not immune from liability in tort.

LAN/STV cites *GLF Constr. Corp. v. LAN/STV*, 414 F. 3d 553 (5th Cir. 2005), a case with similar facts, to support its argument that it should be derivatively immune from liability. In *GLF Constr.*, DART awarded GLF a contract for construction of an extension of its light rail system. *Id.* at 555. GLF encountered problems with LAN/STV's plans and sued LAN/STV in tort for professional negligence and misrepresentation. As in this case, LAN/STV moved for summary judgment on the ground of derivative governmental immunity from liability pursuant to article 6550d. *Id.* Construing the term "only to the extent" in article 6550d, the court agreed with LAN/STV, concluding that "Texas law would not permit DART to be held liable in tort on these facts." *Id.* at 556-57. Although the court concluded that DART would be immune from liability in tort, it noted that GLF could pursue breach of contract claims against DART and that DART would not be immune from liability for those claims. *Id.* The court also noted that GLF did not argue that "its claims would be construed other than as tort claims if DART itself had performed the functions at issue" and limited its analysis to immunity from liability for tort claims. *Id.* at 556 n.3 (citing *Eby*, 369 F. 3d at 472). As a result, the court did not reach the issue raised here: whether LAN/STV has immunity from liability for claims that, if asserted against DART, would be construed as breach of contract claims, and for which DART would not have immunity from liability.

In essence, LAN/STV contends that it has immunity from liability, although it also contends that Eby is not without a remedy because DART is not immune from liability. But if DART is not immune from liability for performance of those functions, and LAN/STV

derives its immunity from DART, LAN/STV is not immune from liability for performance of those same functions. To conclude that LAN/STV has immunity from liability for performance of those functions would place it in a better, not a derivative, position compared to DART. And to do so we would have to ignore the significance of the legislature's emphasis on the function performed rather than on the characterization of the claim. Instead, we conclude that the determination of whether the independent contractor is entitled to derivative governmental immunity from liability depends on an analysis of the function performed, not simply the characterization of the claim. And we interpret the phrase "only to the extent" to mean that the damages available against an independent contractor are limited to those damages for which the government entity would be liable. *See Castro v. Cammerino*, 186 S.W. 3d 671, 678 (Tex. App. Dallas 2006, pet denied) (independent contractor of government entity entitled to protection of statutory tort damage cap pursuant to § 452 056(d) of transportation code); *see also Tooke v. City of Mexia*, 49 Tex. Sup. Ct. J. 819, 820, (Tex. June 30, 2006) (recovery barred despite waiver of immunity because consequential damages not allowed against government entity).

As a result, we conclude LAN/STV has not established that section 452 056(d) and article 6550d provide it immunity from liability as a matter of law for Eby's negligent misrepresentation claim against LAN/STV. We sustain Eby's first issue.

205 S.W. 32 at 19–21

54. *See* discussion in § 4.0 of chapter 15 and in § 6.2 of this chapter.

55. The baseline approach is defined and discussed in § 5.0, above.

56. R. Essex, *Geotechnical Baseline Reports for Construction*, § 1.3, p. 6; R. Essex, "Geotechnical Baseline Reports for Construction—Second edition," in *North American Tunnel 2008 Proceedings*, Reston, VA: ACSE, 640.

57. In a previously published paper, this author has explored some of the professional liability implications arising out of circumstances in which the baseline is established in a manner (more or less) at variance with a strict or rigorous interpretation of available geotechnical data. D. Hatem, "Geotechnical Baselines and Geotechnical Reality: One and the Same, Similar or Not Even Close — Professional Liability Implications," *The CA/T Professional Liability Reporter* 2 (1996): 1–8. In analyzing those professional liability implications, reference is made to case law precedent dealing with professional liability claims in the related context of quantity estimates developed by design and/or construction management professionals and furnished by the project owner to the constructor. Some of the principles derived from that case law are expected to have relevance in the context of professional liability claims involving use of the baseline approach. In several cases, constructors have asserted claims against both the project owner and the project owner's independently retained consulting engineer. As in the cases involving claims against *only* the project owner, the results in the cases against consulting engineers depend upon whether the estimated quantities were represented as only approximations and/or whether the

project owner disclosed relevant information (for example, data reports) upon which the estimates were based. *See, e.g.,* Bilotta Constr. Corp. v. Village of Mamaroneck, 199 A.D. 2d 230, 604 N.Y.S. 2d 966 (1993) (court rejected claim of contractor against owner and engineer on the basis of misrepresentation of information regarding elevations; in so holding, court held that the contract documents made clear that data concerning elevations was approximate only, with no guaranty of accuracy; that the existing grade elevations were approximations only and that the approximations were not to be relied upon by the contractor; and that the contractor was obligated to conduct its own investigation prior to entering into the contract; and, therefore, any reliance by the contractor upon such data was not reasonable and could not support a misrepresentation claim against either the owner or the engineer since the contractor did not establish justifiable reliance upon that data); Zontelli & Sons, Inc. v. City of Nashwauk, 373 N.W. 2d 744 (Minn. 1985) (claim against an owner and consulting engineer for negligence and misrepresentation in the preparation of estimates upon which contractor bid on a unit price basis; bid and contract documents contained no information regarding subsurface soil conditions; contractor asserted that it encountered more concrete than estimated and that the amount of unsuitable material to be excavated was substantially understated and, moreover, was a different quality than anticipated; contractor claimed that it had to pay more than four times the estimated unit price cost for performance of work and the city denied compensation for cost of work beyond unit prices bid; court refused to limit recovery to unite prices bid on theory that the facts presented an "extreme case" involving all "kinds of overruns and otherwise changed conditions, the extent and effect of which [were] so unusual as not to have been contemplated by the parties at the time of contracting"; the court also found the engineer negligent on the basis that the engineer had "drastically underestimated the quantity of concrete and unsuitable materials to be removed," had failed to indicate the unusual characteristics of those materials, and in other respects); APAC-Carolina, Inc. v. Greensboro-High Point Airport Auth., 431 S.E. 2d 508 (N.C. Ct. App. 1993) (contractor asserted claims against owner and engineer due to substantial overruns in undercutting required; court refused to allow claim against engineer on the basis that the contractor had failed to adequately inspect available information, the contract clearly stated that any quantities mentioned in the contract were merely estimates, and, therefore, the contractor had failed to establish any justifiable reliance on information contained in the contract documents); Raymond International, Inc. v. Baltimore County, 412 A.2d 1296 (Md. Ct. App. 1980) (claim by contractor against owner and engineer for fraud, negligent misrepresentation, and breach of warranty; contractor claimed that estimated quantities were inaccurate and grossly underestimated, resulting in the unit price representing an inadequate measure of compensation; court allowed recovery against the engineer finding that the estimates were materially wrong and substantially inaccurate and were based upon information that the engineer reasonably should have known was inaccurate in view of its prior involvement at the site); L. Loyer Construction Co. v. City of Novi, 446 N.W. 2d 364 (Mich. Ct. App. 1989) (contractor asserted claim against owner and engineer; contractor claimed that the work required to complete the project

varied from estimates set forth in the contract documents upon which the contractor based its bid; that the quantity variations necessitated the use of unplanned, less efficient methods of excavation and use of a different off-site dump than originally contemplated; that the specified unit prices did not adequately compensate the contractor for the additional quantities of work encountered; the court rejected the contractor's claim on the basis that the owner did not guaranty the representation as to soil and that water conditions might be different than expected was expressly assumed by the contractor; that the contractor had a duty to investigate the specific subsurface conditions, as well as the site generally; and the excavation and the disposal of the disputed work items were to be paid at the contractor unit price, not the contractor's actual cost); Costanza Construction Corp. v. City of Rochester, 147 A.D.2d 929, 537 N.Y.S.2d 394 (App. Div. 1989) (contractor asserted claim against owner and engineer due to alleged gross inaccuracies in estimates of cubic yards of rock to be excavated; contractor sought compensation beyond unit prices stipulated in contract; court rejected contractor's claim based on breach of contract, negligence, breach of warranty and equitable adjustment because the contract documents clearly included a disclaimer by the city of any responsibility for accuracy or completeness of information on the drawings concerning existing conditions, including rock, and obligated the contractor to satisfy itself as to site conditions; accordingly, as a matter of law, the contractor could not establish that it had justifiably relied upon information in the contract documents, thereby warranting dismissal of claims against owner and engineer).

58. R. Essex, *Geotechnical Baseline Reports for Construction: Suggested Guidelines*, § 1.3, p. 6.

59. S. Bartholomew et al., "Position Paper by the DRB Panel," in Opinion Papers on "Geotechnical Reports in Underground Construction," an unpublished collection of papers presented at the April 21, 1996, Underground Technology Research Council Forum in Washington, D.C., p. 2.

60. J. Cibinic and R. Nash, *Administration of Government Contracts*, 4th ed., Washington, DC: George Washington University, 2006, 499.

61. R. Essex, *Geotechnical Baseline Reports for Construction: Suggested Guidelines*, §§ 6.8, 10.0 (hereinafter, *Geotechnical Baseline Reports*); T. Freeman, S. Klein, G. Korbin, and W. Quirk, "Geotechnical Baseline Reports — A Review," *RETC Proceedings*, June 2009.

62. J. Monsees et al., "The Perspective of Engineering Firms: GDSRs Are Not Working as Envisioned," in Opinion Papers on "Geotechnical Reports in Underground Construction," an unpublished collection of papers presented at the April 21, 1996, Underground Technology Research Council Forum in Washington, D.C., p. 11. *See also* G. Korbin et al., "Consultants' Panel Report," in Opinion Papers on "Geotechnical Reports in Underground Construction," p. 1; R. Essex, *Geotechnical Baseline Reports*, n. 2, p. 9.

63. R. Essex, *Geotechnical Baseline Reports*, §§ 6.8, 9.2, 9.3, 10.0.

64. *See* D. J. Hatem, "Errors/Omissions Cost Recovery Claims," *The CA/T Professional Liability Reporter*, 1: 4 (June 1996).

65. Monsees, "The Perspective of Engineering Firms," n. 6, p. 7.

66. R. Essex, *Geotechnical Baseline Reports for Construction*, § 5.4, p. 20.

67. R. Essex, *Geotechnical Baseline Reports*, § 9.2. *See also* discussion in § 5.0, above.

68. R. Essex, *Geotechnical Baseline Reports*, § 10.0.

69. *See* note 39 above.

70. *See* J. Sweet, *On Construction Industry Contracts*, 3d ed., §§ 11.1, 11.6. Hoboken, NJ: Wiley, 1996.

71. *See* S. Bartholomew, "Position Paper by the DRB Panel," p. 7.

72. J. Monsees, "The Perspective of Engineering Firms," n. 6, p. 13; G. Korbin, "Consultants' Panel Report," n. 6, p. 4.

73. R. Essex, *Geotechnical Baseline Reports*, § 5.5.

74. *See* § 2.4, above; D. Hatem, "Professional Liability and Risk Allocation/Management Considerations for Design and Construction Management Professionals Involved in Subsurface Projects," in *Subsurface Conditions*; D. Hatem, "Differing Site Conditions: Liability Precautions for Design and Construction Management Professionals," *Def. Coun. J.*, (Oct. 1994: 555); D. Hatem, "Risk Allocation and Dispute Resolution on Construction Projects: Roles and Challenges for Legal Counsel," *The CA/T Professional Liability Reporter*, Vol. 2, No. 4 (June 1997), at 1, 4–6, and n. 4.

75. R. Smith, *Some Legal Perspectives on Geotechnical Reports: Predictable Uncertainty, Imperfect Justice and Other Concerns*, in Opinion Papers on "Geotechnical Reports in Underground Construction," an unpublished collection of papers presented at the April 21, 1996, Underground Technology Research Counsel Forum in Washington, D.C., pp. 17–19. For general discussion of the role of legal counsel in connection with risk allocation and dispute resolution on construction projects, *see* D. Hatem, "Risk Allocation and Dispute Resolution on Construction Projects: Roles and Challenges for Legal Counsel," *The CA/T Professional Liability Reporter*, Vol. 2, No. 4, at 1, 4–6, and n. 4 (Boston: June 1997).

76. G. Korbin, "Consultants' Panel Report," n. 6, p. 2. The significant interaction between project design, subsurface conditions (expected and encountered), the constructor's selected equipment (and operation and maintenance thereof), and other performance issues serves to underscore the advisability of not predicting in a baseline report constructor performance or construction conditions (e.g., expected dewatering requirements or water inflow during construction) that may be impacted by the constructor's means and methods or other performance factors within the constructor's discretion and ability to control. At a minimum, such predictions will lead to disputes over the interpretation and application of the baseline statements. *See* Kiewit-Atkinson-Kenny v. Massachusetts Water Resources Auth., Massachusetts Superior Court, No. 011920-BLS, Memorandum and Orders, dated March 5, 2002 and September 3, 2003; Sutton Corp. v. Metropolitan Distr. Comm'n, 38 Mass. App. Ct. 767, n.2 (1995), *rev'd in part*, 423 Mass. 200 (1996).

77. For example, Essex has noted that "[b]aseline statements regarding anticipated ground behavior should be presented in context with the means and methods selected by the contractor. The baseline statements should be clear that the ground can be expected to behave differently with alternate tools, methods, sequences and equipment." R. Essex, *Geotechnical Baseline Reports*, p. 25.

78. S. Bartholomew, "Position Paper by the DRB Panel," n. 3, p. 4.

79. Specifically, it has been recommended that the baseline definition exclude "[d]iscussion of the details of construction methods and equipment, rates of production, etc., that lie within the contractor's field of expertise, except those which are contractual requirements or are absolutely necessary for establishing the baselines and ensuring that the baselines are understandable." S. Bartholomew, "Position Paper by the DRB Panel," n. 3, p. 5. For additional discussion of the risk allocation implications associated with prescribing construction equipment on subsurface projects, *see* J. Reilly, "Owner Responsibilities in the Selection of Tunnel Boring Machines With Reference to Contractual Requirements and Construction Conditions," unpublished paper presented at the World Tunnel Conference/ International Tunneling Association 23d General Assembly, in Vienna, April 1977. Wolfgang Roth, in a position paper entitled "The Case Against Performance Specifications in Tunneling," presented at the North American Tunneling Conference in in Washington, D.C., in April, 1996, made some excellent points supporting the use of design or prescription-based specifications for construction means and methods and including equipment matters in connection with tunneling projects. Observing that "the choice of tunneling approach strongly depends on economic and investment decisions," Roth comments that "performance specifications allow such decisions to be made by the low-bid contractors willing to take the risk of 'getting by' with less on tunneling equipment and techniques, without having to pay the price for ground modification." As a solution, Roth proposes a "shift from performance — to prescription-based specifications." More specifically, Roth stated:

> Some may regard this approach to be in utter violation of conventional wisdom (i.e., "never tell a contractor how to do his work"). However, with today's rapidly advancing technologies, this traditional piece of advice may have outlived its usefulness. Particularly in the U.S., where contractors seem to be reluctant to apply new technologies on their own, the impetus for progress may well have to come from the owner's side. Prescription specifications are the only viable means of achieving this goal. With respect to site-specific knowledge and engineering expertise, owners and their consultants should have a distinct advantage over contractors. Hence, for the former to decide on the most appropriate means and methods of tunneling makes much more sense than relying on the contractor.
>
> Shifting construction risk to the owner is not only a question of fairness. Because contractors usually find ways to get reimbursed for many items through changed-conditions claims, assumption of some risk and liability by a knowledgeable and well-advised owner makes sound economic sense as well. Assuming a reasonable amount of known risk and liability cost, up front, would appear to much more desirable than gradually being forced to accept dispute settlements or court decisions on unexpected and costly changed-conditions claims — not to speak of risking construction mishaps. Finally, it should be pointed out that approval of contractor submittals under a performance-based contract puts the owners, designers and construction managers in the awkward position of having to take partial responsibility for tunneling equipment and techniques about which they had little input. In

contrast, approvals under a prescription-based contract merely make sure that the owner's prescription is followed. One would think that relying on one's own product is preferable to accepting the downside risk of somebody else's — particularly, if the latter is a low-bid contractor in search of changed conditions to make up for bid losses.

80. 192 F. 3d 711, 713 (7th Cir. 1999).

81. Quotations are from the record in the *CH2M Hill* case.

82. Although the baseline approach typically is employed in the preparation of geotechnical reports and/or portions of the contract documents issued *prior to* the award of the construction contract, there is no reason why that approach may not be utilized in connection with the preparation of a (post-award) contract modification, especially one relating to a differing site condition.

83. Prior to the proceedings before the Review Commission, an administrative law judge had found that CH2M Hill had not engaged in construction work within the meaning of the OSHA construction regulations. The judge found that the broad range of services *offered* in CH2M Hill's Master Agreement with the District were inapplicable and that the controlling agreement was Task Order 189 (which directly pertained to the C-T Tunnel Project). The administrative law judge found that Task Order 189 required CH2M Hill to render standard engineering services and that Hill's services were "primarily to act as a geotechnical consultant, to inspect the scheduled progress on CT-7, and to act as a go-between for Healy and the MMSD." The judge also found that drafting and interpreting a contract modification is not "construction work." He observed that drafting and interpreting a contract modification "does not . . . constitute safety supervision" and that they "are advisory, not supervisory activities."

    In this regard, it should be noted that the Master Agreement between the District and CH2M Hill identified a fairly broad range of services which CH2M Hill *could be requested to perform*, pursuant to specific task orders issued by the District in connection with the various projects that were included in the overall water pollution abatement program. These services included program management, planning, engineering, and construction management. Significantly, Task Order 189 relating to the CT-7 Tunnel set forth a more specific and limited description of services which may fairly be characterized as traditional engineering services and did *not* include program management, planning, or construction management services. In addition, CH2M Hill's role and performance in connection with the investigation and evaluation of the methane gas differing site condition and the preparation of the related contract modification on CT-8 and CT-7 tunnels likewise may be characterized as reasonably falling within the scope of *traditional* engineering services. Under these circumstances, it would appear that the broader scope of services offered and enabled in the Master Agreement with respect to project management, planning, and construction management services were irrelevant in the context of the specific and limited contractual service scope of Task Order 189 and the other circumstances at issue in the *CH2M Hill* case.

84. *See* discussion in § 5.1.4 of chapter 15, above.

85. For a general discussion of the interrelationship between civil liability and OSHA exposure for

design professionals, *see* D. Hatem, "Administrative, Regulatory and Registration Proceedings Involving Design Professionals," in S. Goldblatt, ed., *1991 Wiley Construction Law Update*, Hoboken, NJ: Wiley, 1991.

86. Commenting on the potential benefit to the public of megaproject public-private partnerships in terms of risk transfer to the private sector, the Government Accountability Office has recently stated:

> The public sector may also potentially benefit from transferring or sharing risks with the private sector. These risks include project construction and schedule risk. Various government officials told us because the private sector analyzes its costs, revenues, and risks throughout the life cycle of our project and adheres to scheduled toll increases, it is able to accept large amounts of risk at the outset of our project, although the private sector prices all project risks and then bases its final bid proposal, in part, on the level of risk involved.
>
> The transfer of construction costs and schedule risk to the private sector is especially important and valuable given the incidence of cost and schedule overruns on public projects. Between 1997 and 2003, we and others identified problems with major federally funded highway and bridge projects and with FHWA's oversight of them. We have reported that on many projects for which we could obtain information, costs had increased, sometime substantially, and that several factors accounted for the increases, including less than reliable initial cost estimates. We further reported that cost containment was not an explicit statutory or regulatory goal of FHWA's oversight and that the agency had done little to ensure that cost containment was an integral part of the states' project management. Since that time both Congress and DOT have taken action to improve the performance of major projects and federal oversights; however, indications of continuing problems remain. . . .

Government Accountability Office, *Highway Public-Private Partnerships: More Rigorous Up-Front Analysis Could Better Secure Potential Benefits and Protect The Public Interest*, GAO-08-44, pp. 21–22 (Feb. 2008). *See also Transportation Infrastructure Cost and Oversight Issues on Major Highway and Bridge Projects*, GAO-02-702-t (May 1, 2002); *Federal-Aid Highways: FHWA Needs A Comprehensive Approach to Approving Project Oversight*, GAO-05-173 (Jan. 2005); R. Hafer, "Design and Construction Risk Allocation and Management on Major PPP Transportation Projects, The Public Owner's Perspective," *Construction SuperConference 2007* (Dec. 13, 2007); D. Benjamin, "Designer's Perspective on PPP Risk Allocation," *Construction SuperConference 2007*; C. Kane, "Design and Construction Risks: Allocation and Management on Major PPP Transportation Projects," *Construction SuperConference 2007*; C. Covil, W. Grose, and G. Plumbridge, "Project Delivery Models, Risk Assessment and Allocation for Full Life-Cycle Tunnel Management," paper presented at the Rapid Excavation and Tunneling Conference, June 2005, Seattle; J. Buxbaum, and I. Ortiz, "Public Sector Decision Making for Public-Private Partnerships," NCHRP, Synthesis 391, Transportation Research Board, 2009, pp. 15–18; AECOM, *Case Studies of Transportation Public-Private Partnerships Around the World*, Final Report Work Order 05-002, prepared for Office of

Policy and Governmental Affairs, Federal Highway Administration, U.S. Department of Transportation, Washington, D.C., July 7, 2007; AECOM, *User Guidebook on Implementing Public-Private Partnerships for Transportation Infrastructure Projects in the United States*, Final Report Work Order 05-002, prepared for Office of Policy and Governmental Affairs, Federal Highway Administration, U.S. Department of Transportation, Washington, D.C., July 7, 2007; C. Checherita and J. Gifford, "Risk Sharing in Public Private Partnerships: General Considerations and an Evaluation of the U.S. Practice in Road Transportation," *Proceedings of the 87th Annual Meeting of the Transportation Research Board,* Washington, D.C., January 13–17, 2008; *Public-Private Partnerships: Accelerating Transportation Infrastructure Investment*, New York: McGraw-Hill Construction, SmartMarket Report, May 2009.

87. J. Reilly, "Alternative Contracting Methods," 2007 *RETC Proceedings.*

88. For an excellent general discussion of public-private partnerships, *see* J. Stainback, *Public/Private Finance and Development*, Hoboken, NJ: Wiley, 2000; *Innovation Wave: An Update on the Burgeoning Private Sector Role in United States Highway and Transit Infrastructure*, U.S. Department of Transportation, July 18, 2008; and E. Fishman, "Major Legal Issues for Highway Public-Private Partnerships," *Legal Res. Dig.* 51 (Jan. 2009).

89. *See* discussion in § 1.0 of this chapter.

90. The equitable sharing of risks in PPPs between the public owner and the concessionaire has been rationalized on the basis that

   • risks are apportioned on the basis of the party best able to manage them;
   • the extra costs that accrue to raising finance in the private sector are offset when the private consortium accepts the financial consequences of accepting the responsibility of certain risks.

   D. Cartlidge, *Public Private Partnerships in Construction*, New York: Taylor & Francis, 2006, p. 10.

91. As in more traditional project delivery approaches, risk registers should be prepared in the PPP approach that clearly identify risk and identify the project participant responsible for assuming (in whole or in part) or managing each identified risk. *See* D. Cartlidge, *Public Private Partnerships in Construction*, p. 179.

   To date there exists limited legal precedent or data regarding risk and liability issues associated with PPPs. In April 2007, Standard & Poor's issued a report entitled "The Anatomy of Construction Risk: Lessons from a Millennium of PPP Experience," based upon survey responses from lenders, constructors, public owners, technical (engineering) consultants, and financial advisors, owners, and concessionaires who have been involved in PPP projects. These responses revealed the following:

   • ". . . exposure to construction risk remains highly contingent on the specific characteristics of a project, its contractual provisions, and its associated transaction structuring. . . ." [p. 2]
   • ". . . by far the most frequently reported cause of distress affecting PPP construction

works relates to the inexperience, lack of commitment, lack of engagement, bureaucracy, and interference of public-sector project participants, and associated scope changes and enforced delays." [p. 2]

- Areas of concern for risk rank subsurface projects as relatively high.

Regarding "site conditions," the report stated:

> Unforeseen ground conditions are a key reason cited for construction delays. Some respondents pointed to circumstances under which preliminary subsurface investigations were rushed or incomplete, or where poor location of bore holes and trial pits resulted in deficient soil or rock sampling. Others highlighted the fact that, as geologic investigative techniques rely on sampling, the possibility for different ground conditions to be present between exploratory points always exists. In such cases—as with unexpected archeological or mining discoveries—respondents were keen to emphasize that these risks should remain entirely with the public sector or should, at least, be shared between the private and public-sector partners. [p. 8]

In substance, this report confirms that many of the "improved contracting practices" and other recommendations for fair risk allocation and dispute resolution on subsurface projects (*see* § 5.0 of this chapter) should be applied in the context of PPP subsurface projects.

92. *See* D. Hatem, ed., *Subsurface Conditions*; Brierly and Hatem, eds., *Design-Build Subsurface Projects*; D. Corkum and D. Hatem, "A Contracting Strategy for Managing Risk on Subsurface Projects Delivered Using Design-Build," *2003 RETC Proceedings*; G. Brierly and J. Smith, "Contracting Practices for Underground Projects," *Construction Law Update*, New York: Aspen, 2003; D. Hatem, "Public-Private Partnerships: Opportunities and Risks for Consulting Engineers Involved in Subsurface Projects," GeoHalifax, Sep. 23, 2009 (hereinafter cited as "Opportunities and Risks"); K. Kim, C. Kreider, and M. Valiquette, "North Carolina Department of Transportation's Practice and Experience with Design-Build Contracts: Geotechnical Perspective," *J. of the Transp. Res. Board, Soil Mechanics*, Vol. 2116 (2009): 47–52.

93. In some PPP arrangements—especially those in which the project owner assumes control over or use of the facility relatively proximate to construction completion, the project owner may seek to retain the right to assert direct claims against the design-build contractor or its consulting engineers engaged by the concessionaire. More specifically, the project owner may include provisions in its agreement with the concessionaire to the effect that the project owner is a third-party beneficiary of the concessionaire's agreement with its contractors and consulting engineers and that notwithstanding the lack of a direct contractual relationship (or privity) between the project owner and those contractors or consulting engineers, the project owner has the ability to assert claims against the latter based upon their failure to perform or adhere to obligations under their respective agreements with the concessionaire or others. In support of such contract provisions, the project owner typically advances the rationale that it has an interest in project completion consistent with the requirements of its agreement with the concessionaire, including satisfaction of budgetary, schedule, and quality expectations and, therefore,

should have the direct right to enforce obligations of, and assert claims against, all members of the concessionaire team who may compromise the achievement of those expectations.

The problem with this third-party beneficiary direct claim approach, at least from the perspective of the consulting engineer, is that it would subject the consulting engineer to risks associated with serving and satisfying at least three "masters" (i.e., the project owner, the concessionaire, and the design-build constructor) whose interests and expectations are likely to conflict. In addition, such an approach bypasses contractual privity and the economic loss doctrine as defenses that otherwise may well preclude such project owner claims. As such, the consulting engineer may be subjected to multiple and inconsistent claims and liabilities. The consulting engineer should resist such third-party beneficiary/direct claim approaches and allow for the enforcement and assertion of rights and obligations to be governed by and among those in direct contractual privity.

94. *See* D. Hatem, "Professional Liability Risk Exposure for Design Professionals: Design-Bid-Build v. Design-Build Projects: Professional Liability Insurance and Surety Considerations," *Underground Construction in Urban Environments*, ASCE, May 11, 2005.

95. For a discussion of Geotechnical Baseline Reports, *see* R. Essex, *Geotechnical Baseline Reports for Construction.*

96. *See* Altus Helyar Cost Consulting, "Infrastructure Ontario: Build Finance Risk Analysis and Risk Matrix," unpublished paper, Mar. 29, 2007; P. Megens, "Construction Risk and Project Finance: Risk Allocation As Viewed by Contractors and Financiers," *J. of Banking & Fin. L. & Pract.* 8 (Mar. 1997): 5–32; K. Brown, "Standardized Risk Allocation for PPPs: Will It Impact on Transition Costs and Efficiency?" *J. of Banking & Fin. L. & Pract* 17 (2006): 92; Partnerships Victoria, *Risk Allocation and Contractual Issues: A Guide,* Melbourne, Victoria: Dep't of Treasury & Finance (2001); A. Akintoye, M. Beck, and C. Hardcastle, *Public-Private Partnerships: Managing Risks and Opportunities,* United Kingdom: Blackwell Science, 2003.

For specific discussion of risk allocation for subsurface conditions in PPPs, *see* S. Cairney and K. Prior, "A Hypothetical Tunnel: Risk Allocation and Management on a NSW Infrastructure Project," *Australian Construction L. Bull.* 15 (Oct. 2003); P. Tobin, "The Allocation of Construction Risks on a Mega-BOT: The Taiwan High Speed Rail Project," *Int'l Construction L. Rev.* 24 (Oct. 2008): 484, 491, 505.

Some have raised serious doubts about whether given the unpredictability and uncertainties associated with subsurface conditions and the resultant cost in time contingency risk exposure associated therewith, a complex subsurface project may be procured and delivered using a PPP approach. Retrospectively considering this possibility in the specific context of Boston's CA/T Project, one commentator has stated:

> The project involved complex tunneling in an urban area, through 300-year-old sea walls whose precise location wa snot known, while finding, moving, and replacing 300 years of water, sewer, steam, electrical and telephone utility lines beneath the heart of the city. The project was to be completed while the elevated Central Artery remained in operation, and without disturbing ongoing MBTA service on the Blue and Red lines, which it

crossed, and without disrupting commercial establishments on either side of the project.

Should other delivery and financing strategies have been considered? The project might have been moved to design-build-operate-maintain (with full state and federal funding) if public officials had been willing to pay a "shadow toll" or an "availability payment" to a single contractor over a 25- to 35-year period sufficient to amortize the developer's cost for designing and building the project and for operating it over a similar concession period. But, this seems impractical given the extraordinary level of uncertainty where 300 years of utilities were located, and further, where a series of sea walls that previously divided the harbor from land were also located. How would such a procurement be structured to fairly compensate the contractor for the probable performance of a significant amount of changed underground work other than on a time and materials basis? The difficulty of asking the private sector to firmly (and fairly) price the construction work through downtown Boston would have likely precluded this approach.

The project might have been moved to design-build-finance-operate-maintain, a privately funded lifecycle delivery. But a privately financed version of the Big Dig would have required a tolling structure that repaid the initial delivery cost of the project, financing costs, and ongoing O&M costs. The privately funded version would face the same difficulty described above—how would a privately funded procurement be structured (where significant underground risk cannot be firmly and fairly priced) without the private sector including a substantial contingency in their proposal which would unfairly pass this contingency on to users through higher tolls?

Given the technical difficulty of the project, and the uncertainty over underground conditions, it is difficult to imagine a scenario in which the Big Dig project might have been positioned as a life cycle delivery procurement in either [design-build-operate-maintain or PPP], without paying a substantial premium for extensive changes in the scope of work caused by differing underground site conditions. The project might have been broken up into a smaller number of sections, which would have made the coordination efforts easier, but the decision to carve the project up as it was can be debated endlessly.

J. Miller, "Lessons Learned: An Assessment of Select Public-Private Partnerships in Massachusetts," Pioneer Institute White Paper No. 45, Dec. 2008, p. 24.

As discussed in the text of this chapter, these comments have substantial merit in circumstances in which (a) inadequate subsurface investigation has been conducted or made available to RFP respondents prior to procurement and/or (b) appropriate risk allocation provisions have not been included as part of the contractual regime. For a discussion of use of the PPP approach for megaprojects, *see* J. Koppenjan, "Public-Private Partnership and Mega-projects," in H. Priemus, B. Flyvbjerg, and B. van Wee, *Decision-Making on Mega-projects*, Cheltenhan, U.K.: Edward Elgar, 2008.

97. For a good discussion of risk allocation and management in the PPP model, *see* D. Grimsey and M. Lewis, *Public Private Partnerships*, Cheltenham, U.K.: Edward Elgar, 2004, Ch. 7. A problem related to unfair or inappropriate allocation of risk to the private sector participant(s) aris-

es in reverse when the latter are willing to voluntarily assume such risk. As has been stated:

> Some contractors may be too willing to accept inappropriate risk. Some authorities may have been tempted to transfer as much risk as possible to the private sector. But if the contractors accept inappropriate risk to win the competition, the subsequent realization of those risks within a very competitively priced contract may lead to problems for the contractor, and, therefore, for the authority.

G. Hodge and C. Greve, *The Challenge of Public-Private Partnerships*, Cheltenham, U.K.: Edward Elgar, 2005.

This problematic "reverse" risk allocation scenario has potentially adverse consequences not only for the public owner and concessionaire, but also for downstream project participants, such as the consulting engineer who is a subconsultant to the design-builder. More specifically, when prime PPP participants, such as the concessionaire or the design-builder, voluntarily and by contract accept inappropriate degrees of risk — for example, with respect to site conditions, design performance, or related warranties or guaranties — their opportunity to obtain an equitable adjustment "upstream" from the project owner when substantial risk materializes is precluded if the cost or time impacts were foreseeably within the degree of contractually-assumed risk. In such circumstances, those prime project participants may attempt to recover for those impacts by asserting professional liability claims against the consulting engineer. In other contexts, experience amply demonstrates that when risk is unfairly or inappropriately allocated, there is a substantially greater risk of professional liability claims against the consulting engineer by parties unable to obtain adequate contractual relief from their contracting parties. *See* § 2.4, above.

98. *See* D. J. Hatem, "Risk Allocation and Dispute Resolution on Construction Projects: Roles and Challenges for Legal Counsel," *The CA/T Professional Liability Reporter* (June 1997); Wern-Ping Chen, "Port of Miami Update — A View from Design Builder's Engineer," 2009 RETC, pp. 687, 698–99 (discussing financial, design, and construction risk allocation challenges in the context of a major subsurface PPP project); D. Hatem, "Opportunities and Risks." The two preceding sources discuss an innovative differing site condition risk allocation and contingency fund approach utilized on the Port of Miami PPP Tunnel Project.

99. *See* Munich Re Group, "Public-Private Partnership Projects, Insurance Cover as Part of the General Risk Management Strategy," ITA Conference Prague, May 8, 2007.

100. P. Varela, D. Follett, J. Debs, J. Onnembo, and C. J. Brasco, "Strange Bedfellows: How to Participate in a Public-Private Partnership Without Losing Your Shirt," *Construction SuperConference* (Session E-11, December 7, 2006) (hereinafter, "Strange Bedfellows").

101. The availability of project-specific insurance to cover the assumption or transfer of risk for cost overruns due to unanticipated subsurface conditions or defective design is quite restrictive in the present market. Moreover, the availability of such coverage is highly dependent upon project-specific risk assessments, evaluation of contractual risk allocation terms, and is subject to periodic monitoring of project developments measured relative to specified under-

writing assumptions. *See* D. Hatem, "Design-Build Risks and Professional Liability Insurance: A Disconnect," 2005 IRMI Construction Risk Conference; D. Hatem, "Project Alliancing, Integrated Project Delivery Approaches, and Public-Private Partnerships: Design Professional Roles, Responsibilities, Relationships and Risks—Professional Liability Insurance Issues and Challenges," Design Professional Roundtable, Apr. 2007; *see* D. Hatem, "Developing Risk Indicators for Evaluating Professional Liability Exposure on Major Public Projects: A Broader Dimensional Approach," *Design & Construction Mgmt. Prof. Rep.* (Donovan Hatem LLP, Feb.–Mar. 2004); D. Hatem, *Public Owner Programs for Design Professional Accountability and Project-Specific Professional Liability Insurance: Functional Alignment*, Transportation Research Board, Jan. 2008; *see* D. J. Hatem, "Insurance Practice Codes for Major Subsurface Projects: Help or Hindrance for Primary Projects Participants," Boston Society of Civil Engineers, Nov. 3, 2007; C. Wawrzyniak, W. Luig, and A. Dohmen, "Tunneling as PPP-Project: Risks From the Viewpoint of the Insurer on a Case Study of a Tunnel Collapse," *2010 North American Tunneling Conference Proceedings*; P. Gribbon, "Risk Management to Make Informed Contingency-Based CIP Decisions," *2010 North American Tunneling Conference Proceedings*; C. Laughton, "Cost and Schedule Contingency for Large Underground Projects: What the Owner Needs to Know," *2010 North American Tunneling Conference Proceedings*. For more detailed discussion, *see* §§ 1.0 and 2.0 of chapter 18.

102. A. Chew, G. Wood, & D. Storr, "PFI/PPP Project Agreements—Risk Allocation Issues to Consider in Flow-Down of Risks," *Int'l Construction L. Rev.* 22:1 (2005): 91–96.

103. *See* Corkum and Hatem, "A Contracting Strategy for Managing Risk on Subsurface Projects Delivered Using Design-Build," *RETC 2003 Proceedings*.

104. A. Chew, D. Storr, & G. Wood, "An Overview of Risk Allocation in Recent PPP Infrastructure Projects in Australia," *Int'l Construction L. Rev.* 22 (2005): 282, 289.

105. Chew, "An Overview of Risk Allocation in Recent PPP Infrastructure Projects in Australia," p. 294.

106. *See* § 4.0 of chapter 15, above. *See also* D. Hatem, "The Relevance and Potential Impact of Risk Allocation Provisions in Owner-Contractor Agreements on Professional Liability Experience of Design Professionals," *Design & Construction Mgmt. Prof. Rep.* (Oct. 2003).

107. Varela et al., "Strange Bedfellows."

108. *See* Corkum and Hatem, "A Contracting Strategy for Managing Risk on Subsurface Projects Delivered Using Design-Build."

109. *See* § 5.0 of this chapter.

110. *See* Corkum and Hatem, "A Contracting Strategy for Managing Risk on Subsurface Projects Delivered Using Design-Build."

111. *See* D. Hatem, "Design-Build Risks and Professional Liability Insurance: A Disconnect," 2005 IRMI Construction Risk Conference.

112. *See* Hatem, *Subsurface Conditions*, § 10.2.3.4(A).

113. *See* Hatem, *Subsurface Conditions*, § 10.1.2.2; Aliberti, LaRochelle & Hodson Eng'g Corp., Inc. v. FDIC, 844 F. Supp. 832 (D. Me. 1994).

114. Varela et al., "Strange Bedfellows."

CHAPTER 18

Professional Liability Insurance for Megaprojects

David J. Hatem, PC, Donovan Hatem LLP

This chapter examines the subject of professional liability insurance and the need for, and advisability of, project-specific professional liability insurance on megaprojects, in particular, subsurface megaprojects.[1] For the consulting engineer, involvement in a megaproject is an especially risky and claim-prone activity. That should be obvious from the preceding discussions in Part II of this book, which demonstrate that professional liability exposure for consulting engineers involved in megaprojects is, in significant respects, influenced by many factors beyond the ability of the consulting engineer to control so-called external risk factors.[2] Moreover, some consulting engineers are involved in more than one megaproject at once and often perform services on these projects in joint venture with other consulting engineers, resulting in the potential for joint and several liability among them. For the consulting engineer, project-specific professional liability insurance is the most effective, prudent, pragmatic, and realistic mechanism for the transfer and funding of these significant professional liability and joint and several exposures, and for the reasonable protection of firm assets.

1.0 Project-Specific Professional Liability Insurance on Megaprojects

Issue

What is so unique and challenging about the subject of underwriting project-specific professional liability insurance for megaprojects?

Analysis and Discussion

Megaprojects pose a substantial risk of professional liability exposure for consulting engineers, as amply demonstrated by the discussion in the preceding chapters. This substantial risk exposure exists both in quantifiable and characteristic terms. Conventional mechanisms for dealing with professional liability risk exposure—such as contractual

Aerial view of the Trans-Alaska Pipeline crossing a tributary of the Koyukuk River. The pipeline covers 800 miles from Prudhoe Bay on the Arctic Ocean to Valdez harbor on the southern coast of Alaska. It was built between 1974 and 1977, when the Alyeska Pipeline Service Company pumped the first crude oil through the system. As of 2009, 16 billion barrels of oil have been transported through the pipeline. The cost was estimated to be $900 million in 1969, but it grew to $8 billion by 1977 due to inflation, environmental costs, replacing of defective sections, and contingency estimates. Photograph by Steve Hillebrand, U.S. Fish and Wildlife Service, 2006.

risk allocation, limitation of liability and indemnification (to the extent attainable) in project owner and joint venture agreements, and risk transfer to practice or standard corporate insurance—may be neither available, adequate, nor effective to address and manage professional liability risk exposure for consulting engineers on megaprojects.[3] In many real and significant respects, a consulting engineer involved in a megaproject may in practical and legal effect be "betting the company."

Over the last few decades, these megaproject professional liability risks have existed, they have increasingly become known to and appreciated (and experienced) by some consulting engineers, and they have actually materialized in substantial claims against various consulting engineer firms. In the last decade, however, the reality and materialization of these megaproject professional liability risk exposures has significantly increased and has been manifested in the form of very substantial claims against consulting engineer firms.

Some contend that the real problem and solution rests with the project owner. The theory proceeds that if project owners are "educated" concerning principles of fair risk allocation and professional standard of care, and if they accept and plan for the contingency (if not the probable reality) that "mega" things can "go wrong" on megaprojects, then the risk of professional liability exposure for consulting engineers will significantly decrease. While this theory has a logical premise, the project owner community has demonstrated remarkably little interest in such "education" and, candidly, the engineering profession has given project owners little incentive to take more interest. More specifically, megaprojects are "magnets" for consulting engineers—they attract talent, opportunities for "once in a life time" design innovation and management acumen, unique project experience and reputational distinction (both for the firm and individually-employed engineers), significant opportunities for personal, professional, and reputational distinction, and substantial revenue and commercial benefits on a long-term planning (budgetary) basis. This magnet force provides a less than optimum context for consulting engineers to exert leverage over the megaproject owner community—itself a distinct and sporadic minority.

In addition, there are those who argue that professional liability insurance itself is the fuel that propels the substantial professional liability claims on megaprojects and that absent such insurance (especially project-specific insurance), no such (or fewer) claims would be asserted. This theory is a highly risky one for a consulting engineer to test, and one with potentially firm-threatening consequences.

The external and heightened risk factors discussed in §§ 4.0 and 5.0 of chapter 16 significantly account for the increased professional liability risk exposure for consulting engineers on megaprojects. These factors support the conclusion that professional liability risk exposure on megaprojects is, to a significant degree, beyond the control of

the consulting engineer. As such, conventional mechanisms for managing that risk exposure are significantly less effective.

Traditionally, project-specific professional liability insurance has been recognized as an important and effective mechanism for managing and transferring to an insurer some degree of professional liability risk exposure.[4] Project-specific professional liability insurance provides dedicated insurance coverage in defined limits for a specified duration to the benefit of the consulting engineer (including joint venture partners and subconsultants), coverage that is guaranteed (subject to continued availability of the coverage limits) typically for a period defined through substantial completion of the project, plus some extended reporting or discovery period.

Corporate or practice professional liability insurance is, in most instances, inadequate to address the degree of professional liability exposure for the consulting engineer involved on a megaproject. Dedicated or project-specific professional liability insurance is, in most cases, the most effective insurance or risk-transfer solution given the magnitude of that professional liability exposure. Moreover, project-specific insurance programs may be designed to align with project owner cost recovery and professional accountability programs, thereby facilitating the fair, efficient, and cost-effective resolution of professional liability claims against the consulting engineer.[5]

Project-specific professional liability insurance had been commercially available, more or less, for approximately 30 years. During that time, the underwriting and availability of such coverage has evolved, or more accurately, it has both progressed as well as periodically regressed. In part, these evolving underwriting practices have been influenced by both adverse claims experience under project-specific professional liability insurance, as well as market and competitive forces. All of these factors have, in turn, impacted the availability and cost of project-specific professional liability insurance.

In June 1977, the International Federation of Consulting Engineers (known by its initials in French, FIDIC) created a steering committee "to organize discussion on the dissatisfaction felt with the gaps in insurance coverage for large scale civil engineering projects and if possible to offer solutions." In June 1978, at a FIDIC project insurance seminar in London, the issue was stated as follows: "How can an insurance scheme be devised which will satisfy the interest of all or at least the very great majority?" The basic concern was not only about gaps in available coverage, but also about "duplications" and "triplications" in coverage procured by individual project participants. Questions asked included: "Must the various coverages be separately procured by the various project participants? Can gaps, duplications and triplications, and premium costs, be reduced by procurement of a single project-specific or wrap-up program embracing all required coverages on a project-specific basis?"

In December 1981, the FIDIC Project Insurance Steering Committee, in a program

entitled "Insurance on Large Civil Engineering Projects," stated perceived problems regarding design professional liability insurance as follows:

> § 4.2.2. Professional liability insurance is normally purchased by an Engineer under annual policies with a limit of indemnity "floating" over the whole spectrum of his activities. Insurers restrict indemnity in respect of any one occurrence and in the aggregate to all claims made under the policy during the policy year. Therefore, unless the indemnity is replenished following a claim, the indemnity available for claims from a specific project may be less than the policy limit due to the partial erosion of that limit by previously submitted claims, pending or settled on the same or another project.

An alternative approach was proposed:

> . . . [W]here Contracts are either very large, or complex, and contain an inherently high design risk, the traditional method whereby the Owner leaves the arranging of insurance to the Consulting Engineer and the Contractor can result in his not being as well protected as he might need or with to be. Moreover, he may not fully appreciate the risks that will remain to his account.
>
> In such circumstances, the [FIDIC] Steering Committee advocates the appointment by the Owner of a firm offering the requisite skills to provide comprehensive risk management advice. . . .
>
> In most circumstances involving the types of project under consideration, it could well be anticipated that the Advisor will recommend that an Owner-Controlled Comprehensive Project Insurance programme be adopted to eliminate some of the shortfalls that would make the traditional method inappropriate. . . .[6]

Due in substantial part to adverse claims experience on megaprojects, the professional liability insurance industry's willingness to provide provide-specific professional liability insurance has significantly diminished with market availability appreciably contracted. Today there are significantly fewer professional liability insurers in the project-specific market (even fewer on a primary basis) and fewer yet who possess the financial rating, capability, demonstrated claims management and resolution acumen, and sophistication and experience required for the underwriting of professional liability risk exposures on megaprojects.

Before discussing some of the professional liability risk exposure factors that have resulted in adverse claims on megaprojects, it is important to focus on the relevance of project owner–consulting engineer relationships to that exposure and experience. In § 3 of chapter 14, the IPO approach to the project owner–consulting engineer relationship on a megaproject was discussed. In the IPO approach — in which service scope and performance activities of the project owner and consulting engineer are merged or integrated — it may not be possible to segregate performance activities from responsibility

or to attribute them to either party. Moreover, as noted in chapter 14, the IPO approach may expose the consulting engineer to risk in areas that traditionally have been exclusively in the domain of the project owner.

Project-specific professional liability insurance covers the consulting engineer (and its subconsultants) and provides insurance coverage for professional liability claims arising out of the consulting engineer's performance of professional services traditionally performed by the engineering profession. Project owners are not covered under such insurance, nor are traditional project owner risk exposures. Thus, the IPO approach poses significant potential insurability issues under professional liability insurance available to the consulting engineer.

Although it is certainly fair to question the adequacy of service performance by the consulting engineer in accordance with an objective and fair process,[7] it is not appropriate to seek to hold such professionals responsible for project costs that result from the project owner's deliberate and strategic cost underestimation and other external risk factors (discussed in chapter 16) not attributable to the consulting engineer's failure to meet the professional standard of care. Given the industry's awareness of the probability of this scenario, and given the correlation between problems with external risk factors — such as cost underestimation — and professional liability exposure, those relatively few professional liability insurers interested in underwriting project-specific professional liability exposure on megaprojects do so on the underwriting assumption that project costs *will be* underestimated, which will lead first as a direct and inevitable result to the perception of a "cost overrun," and then to an increased likelihood (if not probability) of professional liability claims.

The claims experience of the project-specific professional liability insurance market, along with the increasing general awareness of the correlation between external risk factor problems and professional liability exposure, has resulted in that market significantly contracting. Those who remain in the market have responded by more selective underwriting of project insurance, including more discriminating project selection (e.g., some project types are excluded or disfavored, such as condominium, resorts, convention centers, casinos, and/or public projects generally), more restricted coverage terms, and higher premium costs. These are all fairly traditional responses of the insurance industry in this type of circumstance, in which high exposure is anticipated due to variables and factors not primarily or otherwise within the meaningful control of the consulting engineers insured under the policy.[8]

The claims experience of professional liability insurers supports the conclusion that there is a correlation between the perception (or reality) of "cost overrun" and the heightened risk of professional liability exposure for the consulting engineers. Significantly, this claims experience and correlation does not correspond to the traditional criteria utilized by the professional liability underwriters in evaluating risk expo-

sure for consulting engineers.[9] Traditionally, professional liability insurers have evaluated the potential exposure for their insured professional clients by putting themselves in the position of a prudent professional to determine the extent to which the professional will be exposed to risk due to factors such as design, technological and constructability challenges and complexities, contractual risk assumption, scope of responsibilities and role, and related obligations. This risk evaluation process involves examining identified project-specific risks and evaluating how those risks have been (or are planned to be) managed, allocated, or mitigated by contract, practice precautions, dispute resolution, and risk transfer mechanisms.

The heightened professional liability risks on megaprojects due to external risk factor problems are especially problematic for the insurers (as well as their consulting engineer insureds) in that most, if not all, of the external risk problems are primarily, if not exclusively, within the control of and/or caused by the project owner — i.e., not the consulting engineer insured under the professional liability policy. Moreover, as noted above, the project owner typically is not insured under the project-specific policy. As such, the insurer is exposed to risk largely attributable to and within the control of the project owner, as opposed to its consulting engineer insureds.

Professional liability insurers are prepared to respond according to policy coverage terms to project owner claims for "cost overruns" attributable to the alleged failure of the consulting engineer insureds to meet the professional standard of care. In fact, that is their business and that is the very purpose of the insurance. However, when cost overruns result (in whole or predominantly) from deliberate and strategic project owner cost underestimation — as distinct from cost overruns attributable to the consulting engineer's failure to meet the professional standard of care — professional liability insurers will quite correctly and appropriately take the position that they have no responsibility since the causes of the cost overrun were outside the control or responsibility of their consulting engineer insureds, i.e., not due to deficient performance. At root, the concern in such circumstances is that the variables that account for the heightened risk exposure are causally unrelated to deficient performance risk of the consulting engineer insureds that are underwritten by the insurers, yet those heightened risks expose the insurers and their professional insureds to professional liability risk exposure. The short answer to the professional liability insurers in these circumstances could be, "You are right, and you will not and should not be responsible in the final analysis in such circumstances. So why are you concerned about this issue of heightened risk due to cost overruns?"

Unfortunately, such an answer does not and will not satisfy the concerns of the professional liability insurance market, nor of their consulting engineer insureds, who will be drawn into claims and, for pragmatic reasons, may be required to pay on account of such claims of allegedly deficient performance that may have no foundation in fact or

reality. In effect, what is happening is that the "added" project cost, or "cost overrun," resulting from the project owner's strategic and deliberate cost underestimation leads project sponsors, external overseers, and the public at large to seek to hold someone accountable for the "cost overrun," with the consulting engineer becoming the prime target or "scapegoat." The project-specific insurance that provides risk transfer for professional liability exposure of the consulting engineer potentially "substitutes," in this scenario, for proper budget and contingency planning by the owner or the adequacy and stability of project funding.

Working with Lexington Insurance Company, the major professional liability project-specific professional liability insurer, this author assisted in formulating an approach designed to improve underwriting of professional liability risk on megaprojects so as to capture, evaluate, and periodically reevaluate professional liability risk exposures due to external risk factors. The approach is implemented through a due diligence and negotiation process centered on project-specific external risk factors and ultimately documented in a "Material Variations in Project-Specific Baseline Endorsement" to the project-specific policy. The intent of this process is to introduce more specificity and objectivity into the underwriting process and to provide greater confidence and comfort that all parties have mutual and documented expectations objectively defined in the endorsement as to the external risk factors that may influence and increase professional liability exposure. The purpose of this approach is not to prescribe or constrain project owner project planning and management approaches. Rather, it is to identify risk indicators emanating from certain external risk factors that may influence and heighten professional liability exposure of consulting engineers.

The baseline information regarding external risk factors comes directly from the project owner and the material variations are the product of a negotiation process between the project owner and the professional liability underwriter. External risk factors that are baselined typically include anticipated construction costs and professional fees; availability and stability of project funding; amount of project contingency; adequacy of the project owner's ability to manage and make timely decisions on project issues; risk allocation approach; dispute resolution processes; project procurement and delivery approach; status of relevant laws and regulations that may impact major project objectives and/or professional liability exposure; project owner cost recovery process;[10] and the legal status of the project owner's organization and governance. The intent is to define, articulate, and document (in the policy endorsement) these baselines as objectively and concisely as practicable so as to minimize the risk of subsequent coverage disputes.

Although some project owners may consider this approach to intrude into their project planning and management, the reality is that most professional liability underwriters are either headed in this direction or will price the premium (in the absence of such an endorsement) on a "worst case" underwriting set of assumptions. A significant

number of other professional liability insurers simply will decline to offer coverage on megaprojects. Once the project-specific policy is bound, the professional liability insurer will periodically monitor actual project events and developments relevant to the baseline factors and allowable variations as set forth in the endorsement. In this author's view, from the insured consulting engineer's perspective, this approach recognizes and reckons with the reality that professional liability exposure on a megaproject often derives from external risk factors beyond the control of, and not necessarily based upon, deficient performance of those professionals.

2.0 Project-Specific Professional Liability Insurance on Subsurface Megaprojects

Insurance practice codes—by which insurers on major subsurface projects define and mandate, as a condition of insurance coverage, practices that must be employed in the planning, design, and construction processes—are a relatively new and controversial development. This section will explore the background that accounts for that development and conclude that, in general, practice codes and related new insurance underwriting practices for major subsurface projects are appropriate and well-justified and represent a positive influence in risk management if reasonably and prudently conceived and implemented.

Subsurface projects—especially those involving a significant component of subsurface work ("subsurface megaprojects")—represent significant sources of potential risk and liability for all primary project participants, i.e., the project owner, the consulting engineer, and the constructor.[11] Insurance companies—especially those providing project-specific insurance underwritten for a particular subsurface megaproject—also face significant exposure in providing various types of insurance coverage for the primary project participants. These insurance coverages include builder's risk, commercial general liability, and professional liability. This section will focus more on project-specific professional liability insurance for subsurface megaprojects.

Traditionally, the processes involved in the evaluation of risk and liability exposure for primary project participants on subsurface megaprojects proceed somewhat independently of the insurance underwriting process. Specifically, project owners have (more or less) been encouraged to implement "improved contracting practices" designed to more fairly, realistically, and clearly allocate risk among the primary project participants and to facilitate the resolution of disputes. In contrast, insurance underwriters for primary project participants involved in subsurface megaprojects traditionally have focused mainly on the identification and assessment of risks associated with the technical design and constructability challenges and with the qualifications and experience

of the consulting engineer engaged to design the project. For the most part, insurance underwriters have not focused upon the client's planning, construction, and managerial decisions, choice of delivery method, delegation of design responsibility, use of performance versus design specifications, quality and quantity of subsurface investigation, and the qualifications or experience of the project owner to manage the performance of other primary project participants on subsurface megaprojects.

The loss experience of insurers providing project-specific insurance for subsurface megaprojects has not been positive, to say the least, by any definition or standard. In fact, most of those insurers—in all coverage lines, including professional liability insurance—have sustained significant losses, well beyond any underwriting expectation. This adverse loss experience has caused many insurers to exit the major subsurface project insurance market, and those remaining "in the arena" are searching for ways to significantly improve their underwriting approaches to the evaluation of project-specific risk on subsurface megaprojects. According to T. W. Mellors, insurers are of the opinion that tunneling requires reevaluation "in terms of fundamental principles under which coverage could be provided," and the "perception [is] that the tunneling industry [has] had an inconsistent approach to risk management in which the insurance industry had not previously quarried."[12]

The Joint Code of Practice

In October 2001, the Association of British Insurers (ABI), representing insurers and re-insurers in the London-based insurance market, expressed its increasing concerns to the British Tunneling Society (BTS) about losses on tunneling projects. The ABI advised the BTS that rather than withdraw entirely from providing insurance on tunneling projects or significantly restricting coverage scope—both of which are conventional options traditionally exercised by the insurance industry faced with similar concerns—it would work collaboratively with the tunneling industry to develop a "Joint Code of Practice" for the improved management of risk on tunneling projects. This initiative led to the September 2003 publication of *The Joint Code of Practice for Risk Management of Tunnel Works in the UK* (the "*Joint Code*"), the purpose of which is to promote the best practices for the minimization and management of risk associated with the design and construction of tunnels.[13] One of the recommendations of the *Joint Code* is that insurance should not be considered as a contingency fund for cost overruns or substitute for adequate risk management.

The *Joint Code* provides an excellent example of a well-conceived, comprehensive, and balanced attempt by the insurance industry—in collaboration with the engineering profession—to identify, manage, control, and mitigate risk exposure in the specific context of tunneling and underground projects.[14] It should be expected that proper implementation of the *Joint Code* will establish a positive precedent in not only minimizing and managing risk but also in maximizing the availability and scope of insurance coverage for such projects. The *Joint Code* defines practices for the identification of risks and their allocation between project participants and the management and control of those risks through all phases of project execution. Insurers providing coverage on the subject projects will require that project participants comply with the *Joint Code* if the construction value is £1 million or more (§ 2.2). However, if a project involves a construction value of less than £1 million but there is a potential for a significant risk to third parties, an insured should bring that risk to the attention of the insurance underwriters/providers during the negotiation/binder process for coverage. Non-compliance with the *Joint Code* by project participants could result in insurance suspension (until appropriate remedial action is undertaken) or cancellation. Compliance with the *Joint Code* is a precondition for parties to obtain insurance for the subject projects. The project owner is obligated to provide the project insurers and their representatives with right of access to the project and project information to confirm compliance with the *Joint Code*.

The *Joint Code* prescribes a number of prudent and important practices with respect to the identification, assessment, allocation, management, tracking, mitigation, and control of risk in projects involving tunnels and underground structures. The *Joint Code* contains discussion as to the roles and responsibilities and the requisite experience and qualifications of owners, designers, and construction contractors on such projects through all phases of project planning and execution. Regarding contracts, the *Joint Code* requires that risk be clearly allocated and responsibilities and duties of parties be "clearly and explicitly set out." The *Joint Code* emphasizes the critical importance of adequate pre-construction site and subsurface investigation and the project owner's obligation to provide information pertaining to the site and subsurface conditions to bidders. The project owner or its representative is obligated to prepare ground reference conditions or geotechnical baseline reports, which become part of the contract documents, and "shall provide the basis for comparison with ground conditions encountered in relation to those assumed and allowed for at the tender stage by the Contractor" (§ 7.2.8). Information about site and ground conditions must be fully disclosed. In the event that the project owner or its representative does not prepare a ground reference conditions or baseline conditions report, the tender or procurement documents shall require that each tenderer submit with the tender or bid "their own assessment" of anticipated ground conditions specified in a manner defined and fully described in the contract documents (§ 7.2.5). The contract documents are required to clearly identify key methods statements to be submitted with a tender that the project owner (or its representative) considers critical for construction of the project. In addition, tenderers are required to prepare their own project risk assessment for submission with a tender, as well as speci-

fied risk assessments appropriate for the particular means and methods of work performance allowed for (and/or described in the methods statements).[15]

The *Joint Code* mandates a constructor prequalification process. Evaluation and selection of a contractor is based upon criteria *beyond* lowest bid.

During construction, the constructor is required to submit methods statements which "clearly and unequivocally detail the methods and resources with which the constructor intends to construct the works and should cover all aspects of the works, including Specification, Design, Environment, Health and Safety, and Quality." Risk assessments are required to deal with specific risks "associated with construction methods and materials to be employed. The risk assessment shall demonstrate that the hazards and associated risks involved in the construction process have been fully identified and assessed and that the appropriate MS [methods statement] has included all mitigation necessary to reduce the impact of the risk to acceptable levels."

As for designers, the *Joint Code* requires (among other things) that the designer "ensure that adequate construction expertise is available at all times to undertake formal revisions of the design to assess and confirm the appropriateness of the design in terms of constructability" (§ 8.5.1). In addition, the *Joint Code* requires that the project owner provide for sufficient designer monitoring during construction "to ensure that the design being implemented is valid at all times" (§ 8.6.1).

The *Joint Code* requires that project insurers be notified immediately of any changes to the design and/or construction methods which result in greater risks to the project or third parties (§ 9.9.1). In addition, all value engineering proposals shall include a statement setting forth any technical benefits that would result from approval of the proposal, as well as any variation from previously established risk assessments (§ 9.9.2). Finally, as an important management of change requirement, the *Joint Code* mandates regular monitoring of ground conditions throughout construction and the assessment of any significant changes in ground conditions from those envisaged prior to the start of construction. The significance and potential impact of such changes in ground conditions must be evaluated in relation to methods statements, the design, and construction means and methods originally contemplated as part of project execution (§ 9.9.5).

While specifically prepared in relation to tunneling and other underground projects, most of the best practices prescribed and/or recommended in the *Joint Code* have application to all project types. In that respect, the substantial and salutary combined effort of the ABI and BTS in the preparation of the *Joint Code* will pave the way for broadened and other specifically tailored approaches to the assessment and management of risk on all project types.

In reality, what is happening with the promulgation of insurance practice codes is the alignment or convergence of the emphasis on "improved contracting practices" with new insurance underwriting approaches for major subsurface projects that focus on fac-

tors and considerations significantly beyond the purely technical design and construction issues and the qualifications and experiences of the engineering and construction firms.[16] At the center of both initiatives — improved contracting practices and new insurance underwriting approaches — is the project owner, and specifically its planning, contracting, and management decisions and qualifications.

In many respects, this development represents an important alignment of perspectives and initiatives. The alignment does not come without some degree of controversy and spirited debate. To the extent that insurers are attempting to influence how project owners plan, contract for, and manage their subsurface projects, some project owners may regard this as an unwarranted intrusion and an additional layer and burden of unnecessary oversight that will add unnecessary cost and/or time to the project and constrain their decision-making about available optional project planning, contracting, and management approaches. Similarly, some consulting engineers and constructors may regard insurance industry involvement in the promulgation, prescription, and mandating of practice codes and requirements for subsurface projects as beyond the appropriate province or expertise of that industry.

The availability of insurance for project participants involved in the design and construction of subsurface megaprojects is a critical factor that often influences, if not drives, a number of important decisions, such as whether the project may proceed at all, whether consulting engineers and constructors are willing to participate in the project and accept required degrees of risk or contractual risk allocation terms, and the effectiveness of contractual and other mechanisms for risk allocation and transfer and timely dispute resolution. Self-insurance or captive "insurance" does not provide an adequate substitute for project insurance, given the substantial degree of risk exposure, the amount of capitalization required, solvency requirements, and the duration of the exposure period (typically running contemporaneous with the entire design and construction process and some period thereafter for extended claims reporting).

In many important respects, there is the need for alignment between "improved contracting practices" and insurance underwriting on subsurface megaprojects. The salutary objectives of "improved contracting practices" for the timely, effective, and fair identification, assessment, and allocation of risk, and for the resolution of disputes, need to be understood in relation to the impact of those objectives on insurance coverage underwriting and availability and claim frequency and severity. Simply put, the very types of improved contracting practices that make risk acceptable and more palatable for direct project participants on subsurface megaprojects also serve to substantially and positively influence insurance companies in deciding whether to underwrite and provide coverage and, if so, on what terms.

Recognizing the correlation between "improved contracting practices" and insurance underwriting considerations, the alignment challenge becomes centered on how

to achieve the objectives of the improved contracting practices in a manner that maximizes the availability of insurance coverage. Accomplishing that challenge requires a recognition that many of the significant risks inherent in subsurface megaprojects are beyond (or certainly not entirely or predominantly within) the control of the consulting engineers and constructors and that their occurrence and the resultant impacts are substantially influenced by the project owner's decision-making on the various subjects encompassed within the scope of the "improved contracting practices," including fair risk allocation and timely dispute resolution.

Thus, as in the case of "improved contracting practices," the central focus is on the project owner as the participant with the most significant ability to influence timely, effective, and fair risk allocation and dispute resolution and, hence, the availability and terms of insurance coverage.

This should not be a terribly startling observation or revelation. Consulting engineers and constructors, and those who advise them, have recognized for decades the critically important decision-making role of the project owner in the planning, contracting for, and managing of subsurface projects. The prominent role of the project owner, how it chooses to exercise its decisions, and how those choices affect project risk materialization and the resolution of disputes has, until relatively recently, not been the focus of the insurance industry's underwriting attention. With this awareness promises to come a number of significant and prudent changes in the underwriting and availability of project insurance on subsurface projects. The *Joint Code* is but one approach that results from this awareness.

While one can legitimately debate whether and to what extent the insurance industry should prescribe or otherwise influence planning, management, design, or construction practices on subsurface megaprojects, what appears reasonably clear is that in the future, the industry will be more focused upon project owner planning, contracting, and management decisions and qualifications in underwriting and monitoring those projects.

Before overreacting to the approach of the *Joint Code*, one should initially acknowledge that it originated in part from substantial input from the engineering profession and proceeded to conscientiously compare the substantive provisions of that document with the corresponding "improved contracting practices." Putting aside the fact that the *Joint Code* employs some phraseology and recommended practices peculiar to the U.K., the number of similarities and consistencies between the substantive provisions of the *Joint Code* and the "improved contracting practices" is remarkable. In this more balanced context, the *Joint Code* may be viewed as more palatable (disregarding, for the moment, the fact that insurers participated in its preparation).

Project-specific insurance on subsurface megaprojects is an essential component of an effective risk management program for primary project participants. The availability,

terms, scope, and premium cost of such insurance are critical factors influencing, if not determining, a number of "go, no go" decisions on major subsurface projects, such as whether the project will proceed at all, whether consulting engineers and constructors will be willing to participate in the project, and, if so, the degrees of risk assumption/allocation they will accept. Withdrawal of insurers from underwriting and providing coverage for subsurface project risk is not acceptable.

Many of the influencing factors underlying insurance practice code promulgation also represent risk concerns for primary project participants involved in subsurface megaprojects. Primary project participants and the insurance industry have a substantial amount in common in their risk concerns associated with subsurface megaprojects.

The laudable objectives of the "improved contracting practices" designed to achieve the timely, effective, realistic, and fair identification, assessment, and allocation of risk need to be understood, translated, and effectively applied in the context of insurance industry underwriting and coverage for subsurface megaprojects.

The role of the insurance industry should be to promote and support these objectives, not to legislate, prescribe, or mandate them. While we can legitimately debate whether the insurance industry, by practice codes or otherwise, should prescribe or otherwise attempt to influence the planning, management, design, and construction of subsurface megaprojects, what is reasonably clear is that now and in the foreseeable future, the insurance industry will be more focused on this subject and how to address factors that influence risk on these projects.[17]

3.0 Recent Problematic Trends in Project-Specific Professional Liability Insurance

3.1. Introduction

For the last three decades project owners, consulting engineers, project grantors (federal and state), construction lenders, design-builders, and others have all recognized the benefits of a well-designed and structured project-specific professional liability insurance (P-S PLI) program, especially in connection with insuring, mitigating, and managing professional liability risk, and in (a) aligning professional accountability with adequate insurance coverage and (b) expediting the cost-effective resolution of professional liability claims, especially on projects involving substantial risk and construction values. (See chapter 11 for further discussion.)

Recently, however, some project owners as part of their owner-controlled insurance programs (OCIP) have developed or procured poorly designed P-S PLI programs that significantly undermine and erode virtually all of the salutary characteristics and ben-

efits of these programs and cost more (whether measured in insurance premium dollars, required self-insured funding obligations, or the cost of delays and inefficiencies in claims resolution). When these problematic P-S PLI programs are implemented on public sector projects — especially, when implemented on megaprojects — the public ends up paying significantly more for a relatively useless and dysfunctional insurance program and the interests of private sector participants insured under such programs are ill served. In addition, there are more subtle, but real and negative, consequences of such P-S PLI programs in the public sector context, including diminution in accountability of private sector participants to the public owner and potentially inappropriate use (either perceived or actual) of public dollars to fund self-insured retention (SIR) obligations (triggered by claims or findings of breach of professional duty of consulting engineers insured under the P-S PLI program).

3.2.   **Background**

P-S PLI programs are a mechanism to provide professional liability insurance coverage for consulting engineer breach of professional duty (e.g., negligence) in connection with services performed by those professionals on a specific project. The coverage is dedicated to, and designed for, the specific project and professional liability claims arising therefrom and is guaranteed for a specified duration (i.e., the policy period) and for an additional extended reporting (or so-called discovery) period. Project-specific policies have relatively substantial SIR obligations (somewhat like a deductible) that typically are funded by the various consulting engineers who are insured under the policy.[18] Many of these policies are underwritten with mandatory joint defense provisions under which the various consulting engineer insureds are obligated to jointly defend and settle claims asserted against one or more of them. This joint defense approach is reinforced by "insured versus insured" exclusions which preclude coverage for professional liability claims asserted by one consulting engineer insured against another. These programs are intended to maximize the availability of coverage for indemnity payments for claims by rendering more efficient, focused, and expedited resolution of professional liability claims against the consulting engineer insureds. Most project owners who purchase project-specific professional liability insurance as part of an OCIP recognize these benefits and often reference them as considerations motivating and underlying their decision to procure such programs. As such, when structured in the traditional manner outlined in this section, project-specific professional liability insurance programs provide an acknowledged benefit to project owners.

On public projects — especially megaprojects — P-S PLI programs provide a mechanism for facilitating consulting engineer accountability for deficient service perfor-

mance by aligning project owner "consultant performance evaluation" programs (also known as cost recovery programs) with the coverage terms and program functioning of the P-S PLI program.[19] Federal grantors (e.g., the Federal Transit Administration and the Federal Highway Administration) and oversight and regulatory agencies recognize and support the procurement of OCIP programs that include project-specific professional liability insurance programs. However, these federal agencies typically need and expect reasonable assurance (especially because the public owner pays the premium and will likely be reimbursed for a portion by federal grant funds) that consulting engineers (who are insured under the program) remain accountable for deficient performance (notwithstanding the procurement of a P-S PLI program) and have significant financial stake in the adequacy of their performance, i.e., they would be responsible for the funding and payment of the self-insured retention obligation(s). These considerations are also areas of concern to state auditors, inspectors general, and attorneys general, as well as other specific project overseers, regulators, and funding and appropriation sources. These are legitimate and warranted concerns that should be anticipated and addressed in the development and implementation of a well-conceived P-S PLI program.

3.3 Trends in the Development and Procurement of Project-Specific Professional Liability Insurance Programs

Recently, problematic trends appear to be emerging in connection with the development and procuring of project-specific professional liability insurance programs that undermine and eradicate most of the salutary characteristics and benefits of such programs.

Unreasonably High SIR Obligations

In part, this trend appears to be motivated by at least two independent and, in some instances, combined factors:

- A desire of project owners to reduce insurance premium cost by significantly increasing the SIR obligations (to amounts such as $5 million to $10 million on a per-claim basis).[20]

- The desire of some professional liability insurers to significantly reduce professional liability insured risk by providing coverage only above significantly and abnormally high SIR obligation(s) (again $5 million or more) on a per-claim basis.

These factors appear to be congruent and confluent; however, their combination is

neither in the best interest of project owners (especially public owners) nor consulting engineers (and potentially others) who will be insured under such programs.

In general, these insurance programs typically are procured with per-claim SIR levels of between $5 million and $10 million (and perhaps higher). While the coverage terms nominally include a joint defense provision and an insured-versus-insured exclusion, for reasons discussed below, in practice they are rendered ineffective and, in all probability, legally (and ethically) inoperative and unenforceable by virtue of the unusually high amounts of the per-claim SIR obligations.

Some project owners may attempt to mitigate the significant per-claim SIR funding obligations of the consulting engineer insureds by agreeing to pay all or a significant portion of the obligations. However, that act or offer of compromise will create an actual and perceived conflict of interest and legitimate accountability concerns for public owners, and these concerns, in all probability, will be raised by project overseers, regulators, and grantors at both the state and federal levels. Essentially, the issue will be that project owners should not, in effect, release or limit the liability of the consulting engineer by funding all or part of the SIR obligations in circumstances in which, by definition, the project owner has made or established a claim (or claims) against the consulting engineer based on the latter's deficient service performance that triggers the SIR obligations. In substance, the project owner would be absorbing or paying for the consulting engineer's negligence that resulted in the unnecessary expenditure of public funds. In addition, some project owners who contribute to the funding of the per-claim SIR obligations may assert that they are entitled—by virtue of that funding—to control the defense and settlement of claims that they make against the consulting engineer insureds. While this type of assertion logically makes no sense and poses ethical issues, that has not dissuaded some project owners from asserting such entitlement positions.

For the consulting engineer insured, how can such significant and multiple SIR obligations be funded? Corporate funds? For most projects, including megaprojects, this contingent (but very real and substantial) financial exposure can erode all profit for such firms, even when functioning as a joint venture and sharing risk with other firms.

Will corporate or practice professional liability insurance of consulting engineers fill the coverage gaps created by such abnormally and unreasonably high SIR levels? Probably not. Even were an insurer willing to fill the gaps, it would and should want to control the defense and resolution of claims against the consulting engineer insureds (within the gaps) and, most likely, the gaps would need to be filled by multiple practice professional liability insurers, each of which will rightfully insist on controlling the defense and resolution of claims against their respective consulting engineer insureds within the practice levels of coverage. In addition, in this scenario, each consulting engineer whose practice insurer will participate in providing coverage for the gaps will impose a separate deductible or self-insured retention obligation on the consulting engi-

neer. All of this practice insurer participation—even assuming hypothetically that such insurers would be willing to fill the gaps (which is a remote proposition, at best)—will render inoperative the joint defense and insured-versus-insured provisions of the project-specific professional liability insurance coverage. In addition, even were practice insurers willing to provide such coverage, typically any such commitment would be coterminous with the period of practice coverage—typically only one year. If the particular project were to gain a reputation as "problematic" or suffer a similar stigma (in the professional liability insurance underwriting world), practice insurers would probably decline in future years to provide coverage for the gaps, which is exactly what occurred on the Central Artery/Tunnel Project in Boston. However, the more likely scenario is that practice insurers, in the first instance (and independently of any adverse project claims experience), will decline any invitation or request to provide coverage for the gaps. This would be a sensible and understandable decision.

Regardless of whether consulting engineers or their practice insurance was responsible for funding the significant gap exposures created by abnormally high SIR obligations, consulting engineers should be allowed to assert claims against each other within such significant SIR obligations, and their practice insurers should be entitled to assert subrogation claims against other consulting engineers who are insured under the project-specific professional liability insurance program with respect to recovery of defense costs, indemnification, and other payments made within the practice insurer gaps layer.

In this context, given the substantial SIR exposures, joint defense and insured-versus-insured provisions under the P-S PLI program are likely to be legally unenforceable. However, if the insured violates the joint defense and insured-versus-insured requirements of the project policy, it will sacrifice coverage under the project-specific professional liability insurance policy, which is neither good for the consulting engineer insured nor for the project owner who paid the premium for that coverage.

The dysfunctionality of the claim defense and resolution process with such significantly high SIR layers will lead to lack of coordination in defense and settlement of claims, increased defense costs (legal and expert), delayed claim resolution, and reduced insurance limits (due to substantial erosion of available coverage by payment of defense and expert fees). For the project owner, this will mean less coverage available to pay claims and a more contentious, protracted, and expensive claims resolution process.

Because of all of these issues, reinsurance and excess participation in such ill-conceived P-S PLI program should and will be both problematic and expensive, even if available.

For the consulting engineer insured, these programs represent increased corporate dollar exposure and increased corporate insurance costs, as well as the potential for significant professional liability coverage gaps and non-insured professional liability exposure (if, as predicted, practice insurers prudently do not provide coverage for the SIR gaps).

Limited Coverage for Consulting Engineer Subconsultants on Design-Build Projects

Another problem with project-specific insurance can arise in the design-build project context and involves exclusion of coverage for claims by the design-builder against the consulting engineer subconsultants. The exclusion of that coverage renders any joint defense between the design-builder and its consulting engineer subconsultants inapplicable and requires the latter to attempt to obtain professional liability insurance coverage from their practice insurers.[21]

In this regard, the most significant professional liability claims (measured either in terms of frequency or severity) against consulting engineer subconsultants of the design-builder are those asserted by the latter against the former given the contractual privity between those parties. The exclusion of coverage for such claims under these P-S PLI programs, in conjunction with requests (or, worse yet, requirements) that the consulting engineer subconsultants contribute to the funding of the project-specific SIR obligations, makes absolutely no sense given the reality of the principal claim source exposure of the subconsultants (which will not be covered under the project-specific policy) and the fact that the subconsultant will derive minimal, if any, benefit from the project-specific policy.

Put another way, the principal source of professional liability risk exposures of the consulting engineer subconsultants — i.e., claims of the design-builder — will not be covered under such problematic P-S PLI programs, and the subconsultants may end up paying two SIR obligations — one under the substantial project-specific policy per-claim SIR obligations and a second under its own practice insurance policy (coverage under which could be triggered by claims of the design-builder against the subconsultant).

To further aggravate the situation, some professional liability insurers have exclusions under their practice policies for claims against the consulting engineer insured on projects in which project-policy (even if ill-conceived) is in effect.

Professional Protective Insurance Policies

Finally, another problematic trend involves the procurement by the project owner (OPPI) or constructor/design-builder (CPPI) of professional protective insurance policies. These policies represent a form of P-S PLI program, but with important distinctions and inherent problems and concerns for consulting engineers. Specifically, these policies provide coverage only to the procurer — i.e., either the project owner, constructor, or design-builder — and *not* to the consulting engineers. Although these policies generally are not an adequate substitute for a well-conceived P-S PLI program, they may have value in certain limited applications (e.g., in circumstances in which a particular

project does not require proactive risk management during construction or programmatic features for coordinated claims management and resolution). Although not excess in nature, coverage under these policies is triggered once the underlying practice coverage limits of the consulting engineers (or a defined sub-limit thereof) have been exhausted. The existence of these professional protective policies often is not disclosed to the consulting engineers. The OPPI or CPPI insurer also may reserve rights to subrogate against the consulting engineers.

The very existence of these protective policies typically leads to "downstream" pressure by the procurer or the protective insured (i.e., project owner, constructor, or design-builder) upon the consulting engineer (and its practice insurer) to pay out practice limits (whether justified or not by the reasonable claim value) in order to trigger the protective coverage. For these reasons, professional protective policies instigate and propel needless tension and conflict among the consulting engineers and other primary project participants (the latter of whom are covered under the protective policy), which can be extremely disruptive and undermine partnering and positive project relationships, especially when claims arise on an on-going construction project. These protective policies provide no meaningful opportunity for proactive risk management programs, such as those provided under certain well-designed P-S PLI programs, or for the joint and coordinated management, defense, and resolution of claims, because the practice or underlying insurers and the OPPI/CPPI insurer have no relationship and owe obligations to different insureds with conflicting interests. In the more "macro" perspective, these protective policies undermine the longer-term and larger-picture relationships among primary project participants and promote more adversarial relations among them during the progress of the project, complicate and protract the claim resolution process, and thereby jeopardize the important overall objectives of on-time and on-budget project completion.

3.4   Recommendations

These problematic trends should be arrested. Project owners should be aware of the serious insurability concerns, coverage depletion, and claims resolution disadvantages — especially on public projects — posed by these trends.

Consulting engineers (and other insureds) under proposed project-specific professional liability insurance policies containing these conditions should request their own firm's risk manager or corporate insurance broker to review the proposed program and how it would function relative to the corporate or practice coverage of the consulting engineer, with particular attention to the probability of coverage gaps and the creation of uninsured liability by such programs. The consulting engineer insured should recog-

nize that the project owner's OCIP broker does *not* represent the interests of the consulting engineers who are insured under the program.

Notes

1. Chapter 11 contains a detailed discussion of various types of insurance coverages required for effective risk management and risk transfer on a megaproject.

2. *See* §§ 4.0 and 5.0 of chapter 16, above.

3. For a discussion as to the advisability of aligning project risk assessment and management with project-specific insurance coverage programs, *see* P. Mead, "Current Trends in Risk Allocation in Construction Projects and Their Implications for Industry Participants," *Construction L. J.*, Vol. 23 (2007): 23, 42–44; P. Mead, "Evaluating the Role of the Insurance Industry in Determining Risk Allocation in Major Projects," *Australian Ins. L. Bull.* 21:9 (Aug. 2006); P. Tobin, "The Allocation of Construction Risks on a Mega-BOT: The Taiwan High Speed Rail Project," *Int'l Construction L. Rev.* 25:4 (Oct. 2008): 484, 494–95, 507–508.

4. B. LePatner and D. Pfeffer, *Professional Liability Insurance for Construction Projects: Now You See It, Now You Don't.* Retrieved on Feb. 15, 2009, from http://www.LePatner.com/prof-insur.htm. In that article, the authors identify concern with reliance upon practice professional liability insurance coverage on substantial projects and comment on the advisability of project-specific professional liability insurance, stating that:

   > For projects of substantial scope, Owners can avoid these disturbing experiences [i.e., limitations on availability of practice insurance] by putting into place a comprehensive project insurance program covering all design and construction team members before the commencement of construction. Often known as an Owners Controlled Insurance Program or "OCIP," such programs are designed to obviate the protracted nature and extensive risks of reliance on the basic professional liability insurance maintained by the project's design professionals. . . .
   >
   > As with OCIP coverage, a project professional liability policy provides liability coverage designated for a particular project will allow better control over the quality, quantity, and continuity of E&O insurance carried by design firms. A project professional policy protects the Owner's particular project while ensuring sufficient financial resources are available to correct problems and pay damages should problems arise out of their design professionals' negligence. A single stand-alone policy covering all design professionals on the project can be secured which will allow for more consistent coverage and better control over claims involving design professionals' error and omissions.

   See also R. Rogers and D. Hatem, "Project-Specific Professional Liability Insurance: Past, Present and Future," *Construction SuperConference 2006*; "Project Liability Insurance: An Update," *Guidelines for Improving Practice* 7, no. 5 (1982), Victor O. Schinnerer & Co., Inc.; P. Loots, "Worlds

Apart: EPC and EPCM Contracts: Risk Issues and Allocation," *Int'l Construction L. Rev.* 24 (July 2007): 252, 267; S. Wichern, "Protecting Design-Build Owners Through Design Liability Coverage, Independent Construction Managers, and Quality Control Procedures," *Transp. L. J.* 32, no. 1 (2004): 35–36. For a general discussion of project-specific liability insurance in the design-build context, see D. Hatem, "Design-Build Risks and Professional Liability Insurance: A Disconnect," International Risk Management Institute, Nov. 2005; C. Pavloff, "Project Specific Professional Liability Insurance," chapter 8 in A. Hickman, ed., *Design-Build Risk and Insurance*, 2d ed., Dallas: IRMI, 2006, 121–140; see D. J. Hatem, "Public Owner Programs for Design Professional Accountability and Project-Specific Professional Liability Insurance: Functional Alignment," Transportation Research Board (Jan. 2008); S. Kaplan et al., "OCIPs, CCIPs and Project Policies," *The Construction Law.* 23: 9, 11, 18.

5.　D. Hatem, "Public Owner Programs for Design Professional Accountability and Project-Specific Professional Liability Insurance: Functional Alignment," Transportation Research Board, Jan. 2008 (unpublished). Project-specific professional liability insurance is especially important in the design-build delivery context to protect the project owner from design deficiencies in completed project work, to protect the design-builder for its vicarious liability exposure for design errors of its consulting engineers, and to provide adequate and dedicated coverage for those consulting engineers. For these reasons, owners, design-builders, consulting engineers, and surety companies typically seek, procure, or require project-specific professional liability insurance on design-build projects, especially on subsurface megaprojects. *See* R. Duke, "Bonding Design-Build Projects," chapter 9 in A. Hickman, ed., *Design-Build Risk and Insurance,* 2d ed., Dallas: IRMI, 2002,141–48; *Bruner & O'Connor*, §12.95, p. 640–41; § 11:124, p. 387 (2002).

6.　FIDIC Project Insurance Steering Committee, "Insurance on Large Civil Engineering Projects," Dec. 1981. Retrieved on Feb. 15, 2009, from http://www1.fidic.org/resources/contracts/library_docs/consult_ins.asp.

7.　*See* D. Hatem, "Errors/Omissions Cost Recovery Claims Against Design and Construction Management Professionals," *The CA/T Prof. Liability Rep.* 1(4) (June 1996).

8.　Typically, and for sound reasons, the project owner is not an insured under such policies. D. Hatem, "The Owner as 'Additional Insured' under the Design Professional's Professional Liability Policy: Can It Be Done and, if So, How?" *The CA/T Prof. Liability Rep* 1(5) (1996).

9.　P. Loots, "Worlds Apart: EPC and EPCM Contracts: Risk Issues and Allocation," *Int'l Construction L. Rev.* 24 (July 2007): 252, 267; S. Wichern, "Protecting Design-Build Owners Through Design Liability Coverage, Independent Construction Managers, and Quality Control Procedures," *Transp. L. J.* 32 (2004): 35.

10.　The development and the effective and timely project owner implementation of a fair and objective consultant evaluation or cost recovery process to evaluate the adequacy of professional consultant performance is important on any publicly-funded project. The public, project overseers, and stakeholders reasonably are entitled to expect that the project owner has an effective and operational process to evaluate consultant performance and to hold consultants accountable for

deficient performance. *See* D. Hatem, "Errors/Omissions Cost Recovery Claims against Design and Construction Management Professionals," *CA/T Prof. Liability Rep.* 1(4) (1996); D. Hatem, "Public Owner Programs for Design Professional Accountability and Project-Specific Professional Liability Insurance: Functional Alignment," Transportation Research Board (Jan. 2008) (unpublished). When project owners fail to have such a process established or fail to promptly and effectively implement such a process, the risk of professional liability exposure substantially increases and escalates, often driven and fueled by the public perception that the professional consultants are "getting a free ride." This heightened professional liability risk exposure intensifies yet further in circumstances in which that public perception occurs in the midst of the public owner's untimely disclosure of significant "cost overruns." *See, e.g.*, "Analysis of Bechtel/Parsons Brinckerhoff's Reply to *The Boston Globe* Investigative News Series Concerning the Big Dig," Office of the Inspector General, Commonwealth of Massachusetts, Feb. 2003, pub. no. 18327-50-02/03-IGO. For these reasons, professional liability insurers have a keen and appropriate interest in inquiring as part of the project-specific insurance underwriting process as to the project owner's plans for developing and implementing a cost recovery or related consulting engineer evaluation process and in monitoring those processes throughout the project.

11. *See* detailed discussion in chapter 17; *see also* D. Hatem, "Professional Liability Risk and Project-Specific Professional Liability Insurance," Chartis Tunneling Projects Seminar, Donovan Hatem LLP, Boston/New York, Nov. 2009.

12. T. Mellors and D. Southcott, "A Code of Practice for Tunneling," Proceedings of the 30th ITA-AITES World Tunnel Congress, London: Elsevier, 2004; A. Adler, M. King, "The Delivery of Underground Construction Projects in the UK; A Review of Good Practice," *2009 RETC Proceedings.*

13. An international version of the *Joint Code* was published in January 2006 by the International Tunneling Insurance Group. For a good general discussion of insurance practice codes, *see* R. Goodfellow and T. Mellors, "Cracking the Code—Assessing Implementation in the U.S. of the Codes of Practice for Risk Management of Tunnel Works," *2007 RETC Proceedings.*

14. Notwithstanding this observation, the *Joint Code* has been the subject of much controversy and commentary in the underground design and construction community. *See, e.g.*, "Risk Management," ch. 4 in Edgerton, ed., *Recommended Contract Practices for Underground Construction*; H. W. Parker, "Risk Management Issues for Tunneling," George Fox Conference (Jan. 24, 2006); Munich Re Group, "The Code of Practice for Risk Management of Tunnel Works, Future Tunneling Insurance from the Insurers' Point of View," ITA Conference, Seoul (Apr. 25, 2006); Mellors and Southcott, *A Code of Practice for Tunneling*; "Roundtable Discussion: Issues Facing the Tunneling Industry," *Tunnel Business Magazine* (Aug. 2005); P. South, *Managing Risk in Construction*; Goodfellow and Mellors, "Cracking the Code"; R. Goodfellow, "Demystifying Risk Management," *Tunnels & Tunneling North America*, 9 (Sep. 2007); J. Tate, "Design/Build Agreement for the Niagara Tunnel Project," *2007 RETC Proceeding*; B. Edgerton, "Moving Toward a Standard of Best Practices," *Tunnel Business Magazine*, (Aug. 2007). On June 25, 2005, the American Underground Association unanimously adopted a resolution opposing the adoption or endorsement by the

International Tunneling Association of a proposed Code of Practice for Risk Management based on several factors, including:

- The "Code would act to negate the principal social philosophy of insurance, which is to spread the cost of extraordinary events, even if theoretically foreseeable, over a greater number of parties than the insured alone."
- By requiring a "robust," essentially fail-safe design, by placing the insurer in the final design approval role, and by requiring that the parties adhere to either regulation or the Code, whichever is more stringent, innovation would be stifled and the owner's and contractor's right to accept risks according to their own philosophy is usurped.
- Contrary to assertions of the supporters, the Code would add new layers of procedural and administrative costs and increase the time required to plan, design, and tender for projects.
- The United States plaintiff's bar could (and would) utilize the risk registered to the detriment of contractors, engineers, and owners in personal injury or tort litigation.
- Once a policy is issued, non-payment of premium is now, and should remain, the major reason for premature cancellation, but the Code would currently allow cancellation during the term of coverage for many highly subjective reasons.

At a Jardine Lloyd Thompson (JLT) Ltd. Tunneling Seminar held in London on July 17, 2008, Michael Spencer, Senior Construction Underwriter with Zurich Global Corporate UK, spoke on the subject of the *Joint Code*. JTL summarized Mr. Spencer's presentation as follows:

> The Joint Code of Practice for Risk Management of Tunnel Works in the UK was introduced in 2003 and was adapted for international use in 2006. Mr. Spencer said he felt that it has helped insurers: "I now have a tool which helps me explain to my clients some of the issues that we are interested in."

He said underwriters used to price a tunnel based on how long it was, how wide the tube was, how deep it was and the general ground conditions. But nowadays, insurers have moved on and want to see how a project is going to manage its risk.

The fundamental elements of the Code, according to Mr. Spencer, are:

- The creation and operation of a Risk Register.
- Monitoring, management, and mitigation of risks during the construction process. One of the vexatious areas concerns ground conditions, said Mr. Spencer. He explained that the Code suggests the use of ground baseline reports: if the ground encountered during the construction varies from the ground that was envisaged at the bid stage, there is the possibility to vary contract price. He said that this means the contractor is less likely to be put in a position where he might be tempted to cut corners.

Impact of the Code:

Mr. Spencer explained that it was difficult to measure the success of the Code as it has been

in place for less than five years — less than the lifecycle of design to completion of one tunnel. He said the Code helps to improve the insurability of tunnel projects and that this should bring more insurers into the tunnel insurance market, increase competition, and eventually lead to better terms and price for the buyer.

However, the reaction to the Code has been mixed. For contractors who already had sound risk management techniques in place, complying with the Code was easy, and it was then seen as a way to differentiate themselves from others. Some clients, on the other hand, because of the procurement process that the Code encourages, felt that it was interfering with the way in which they arrange their bid competitions.

The most disappointing part of the whole process, he said, is that it has been difficult to get the insurance industry involved in the process: "Most insurers are not in the slightest bit interested in insuring the construction of tunnels."

As for the future, Mr. Spencer said the ground conditions would remain a difficult area, as the construction industry hasn't solved how to allocate the risk of ground conditions. He said the sharing of technical data is something that has to be pushed for. He also pointed to the use of the risk register and said that his big worry is that they become bureaucratic and that it was important to make sure that they become effective tools to reduce risk.

But his main message to the audience was that it was vital to have the early involvement of insurers in the process, so that everyone is aware of what cover is available and what insurers will be looking for.

Jardine Lloyd Thompson Ltd., *Tunneling*, 2-4 (Aug. 2008).

15. The *Joint Code* contemplates the use and preparation of a risk register during the planning and design phase and encourages the continued use, updating, and revision of the risk register throughout construction. The issues of whether to disclose the risk register to construction bidders and, if so, for what purpose are the subject of discussion and debate in the design and construction community. *See* R. Goodfellow and P. Headland, "Transfer of a Project Risk Register from Design into Construction: Lessons Learned from the WSSC Bi-County Water Tunnel Project," *2009 RETC Proceedings*.

As a general matter, risk registers are intended to be "living" and dynamic documents, intrinsically dependent upon and subject to periodic updating and reassessment based upon new information, previously unanticipated design and construction considerations, or other unexpected conditions, project realities, or changes. In addition, risk registers, while to a degree based on available data, express opinions, evaluations, judgments, assessments, and recommendations, all of which are likely subject to differing opinions and perspectives and certainly not scientific in the sense of being empirically correct or not.

The evolutionary, dynamic, and evaluative nature of the risk register gives rise to the concern that bidders may rely upon it to develop pricing, schedule, and planning (including selection of construction means and methods and equipment) expectations based on the notion that the

risk register represented information or other objectively-based data upon which the bidder was to rely. This concern then leads to a further concern that such reliance could lead to post-award constructor claims for differing site conditions and for other equitable adjustments due to variations between what was represented in the risk register and conditions actually encountered by the constructor in the performance of the work.

How might such concerns be contractually anticipated and addressed? The following language in the bid documents may be considered:

> The risk register reflects the evaluative opinions and assessments of certain design and construction risks, and was prepared solely for use and reliance of the project owner and design engineer in the planning and design of the project. In reviewing the risk register, bidders are admonished to conduct their own independent review, identification and evaluation of all project risks, and to recognize that effective and realistic risk assessment for construction depends upon a continuous and iterative process. The evolutionary nature of risk identification, materialization, and assessment on a subsurface project, will be influenced, in part, by the constant and expected interaction of design, construction means and methods, and ground conditions. As such, any reliance on the risk register as a universal or static identification or assessment of project risk, including an identification and evaluation of appropriate risk mitigation measures would not be reasonable, especially given the limited purpose and reliance expectations inherent in the risk register preparation and the clear limitations on its accuracy and completeness.

> The risk register is not a contract document, nor does it constitute any express or implied indication of conditions, whether physical, site, or otherwise, to be encountered in the performance of the work. As such, any variance between any such conditions encountered in the performance of the work and the conditions explicitly or implicitly contemplated in the risk register shall not provide the basis for any claim or entitlement for equitable adjustment.

16. In many significant respects, the *Joint Code* approach is based on the same principles and objectives as the "Material Variations in Project-Specific Baseline Endorsement," discussed in § 1.0 of this chapter.

17. Recently, it has been reported that on a subsurface megaproject, a project-specific code of practice was developed and implemented as part of the owner-controlled insurance program. J. Tait, R. Delmar, H. Charalambu, and R. Everdell, "Design/Build Agreement for the Niagara Tunnel Project," 2007 *RETC Proceedings* (commenting positively on the development and implementation of a project-specific code of practice that was incorporated into an owner-controlled project-specific insurance policy). *See also* M. Feroz, E. Moonin, J. Grayson, "Lake Mead Intake No. 3, Las Vegas, NV: A Transparent Risk Management Approach Adopted by the Owner and the Design-Build Contractor and Accepted by the Insurer," 2010 *North American Tunneling Conference Proceedings* (discussing a project-specific risk management approach on a tunneling project developed for compliance with Code of Practice Standards).

18. For a detailed discussion of project-specific professional liability insurance programs, *see* R. Rogers and D. Hatem, "Project-Specific Professional Liability Insurance: Past, Present and Future," *Construction SuperConference* 2006; S. Kaplan et al., "OCIPs, CCIPs and Project Policies," *The Construction Law.*, American Bar Ass'n, Summer 2009, pp. 11, 18.

19. See D. Hatem, "Errors/Omissions Cost Recovery Claims against Design and Construction Management Professionals," *CA/T Prof. Liability Rep.* 1(4) (1996); D. Hatem, "Public Owner Programs for Consulting Engineer Accountability and Project-Specific Professional Liability Insurance: Functional Alignment," Transportation Research Board (Jan. 2008); D. Hatem, "Professional Liability Risk and Project-Specific Professional Liability Insurance," Chartis Tunneling Projects Seminar, Donovan Hatem LLP, Boston/New York, November 2009.

20. Typically, SIRs under P-S PLI programs have been set at between $250,000 to $1 million on a per-claim basis.

21. As to the importance of covering consulting engineer subconsultants of the design-builder under project-specific professional liability insurance programs, *see* R. Duk, "Bonding Design-Build Projects," ch. 9 in A. Hickman, ed., *Design-Build Risk and Insurance*, 2nd ed., Dallas: IRMI, 2002, pp. 141–48; *Bruner & O'Connor on Construction Law*, §12.95, p. 640-41; § 11:124, p. 387 (2002); D. Hatem, "Professional Liability Insurance: A Disconnect," Dallas: IRMI, November 2005; C. Pavloff, "Project-Specific Professional Liability Insurance," ch. 8 in A. Hickman, ed., *Design-Build Risk and Insurance*, 2nd ed., Dallas: IRMI, 2006, 121–40; D. Hatem, "Professional Liability Risk and Project-Specific Professional Liability Insurance," Chartis Tunneling Projects Seminar, Donovan Hatem LLP, Boston/New York, Nov. 2009.

Index

In page references, *n* after a page number indicates a note and *nn* indicates multiple notes. Page numbers in italics indicate photographs.

consulting engineer involvement during construction, 489–490, 552n
consulting engineer liability and owner–constructor agreements, 341, 408n
consulting engineer liability issues and, 494–538, 555–581nn
consulting engineer obligations to third parties, 464–469
contracting practices and, 490–494, 553–554n
cost and schedule considerations, 481–482, 488–489
owner defenses to subsurface condition claims, 507–508, 572–576n
owner project management, 48
public-private partnerships and, 542, 547–548
risk allocation and delivery methods, 377–378
risk allocation and public-private partnerships, 541–542, 547–548
risk allocation considerations, 485–488
risk identification considerations, 482–484
Digital Data Protocol (AIA), 264
discipline managers, work breakdown schedule and, 62
disclaimer provisions. *See* risk disclaimer provisions
dispute avoidance and resolution. *See also* claims; risk allocation; *specific cases and entities*
Boston Harbor Project, 43
claim resolution process overview, 209–214
constructability reviews and, 206–207
construction management and, 153, 194
consulting engineer liability and owner–constructor agreements, 337
consulting engineer scope of services and, 293
definitions, 214n
design delegation and, 365–366, 371–373
development of changes and, 195
Dispute Review Boards as tool, 210
earned value management use, 95
escrowing bid documents, 202
implementation considerations, 213–214
labor relations and, 138, 142, 143, 146
participant relationships as factor, 207–208
partnering as factor, 182–187, 207–209
problem-solving versus, 192
project delivery methods and, 263
project priorities and, 181
project risk profile use, 205
project-specific insurance overview, 600–601
real-time resolution, 224
risk allocation and, 205–206, 329

schedule control issues, 91
step elevation processes and, 183, 207, 208–209
subsurface condition risk allocation, 487
subsurface conditions disclosure and, 491
dispute resolution advisors, Caltrans use of, 211
dispute resolution step ladder
construction management and, 194
Dispute Review Boards and, 210
feedback loops and, 215
partnering and, 183, 207, 208–209
Dispute Review Boards, 210–212, 214, 216n
disqualification of engineers, accountability considerations, 461
documentation of projects. *See also* recordkeeping; reports and reporting; *specific aspects*
baseline approach and, 508–538, 576–581nn
change order process and, 197, 198–199, 202
consulting engineer scope of services and, 296–297
owner–constructor agreements and liability, 346–347
owner expectations and, 298–299
owner identity and, 292–293
project historians and, 113–114
project-specific insurance overview, 598, 612–614nn
quality considerations, 175–176
subsurface conditions disclosure and, 491–492
subsurface projects and public-private partnerships, 550
document storage and retrieval, design management and, 65–66
DOR. *See* designer of record
drafting, computer-aided. *See* building information modeling; computer-aided design and drafting
DRAs. *See* dispute resolution advisors
DRBs. *See* Dispute Review Boards
drilling logs, 455–456
drivers of projects, owner project planning and, 13, 16–17
drug testing, 47–48, 150
DSC clauses. *See* differing site condition clauses
Dugan & Meyers Construction Co., Inc. v. Ohio Department of Administrative Services, 466–469, 478–479n
Dukakis, Michael, 317n
duty of care, 343–344. *See also* professional standard of care
Dykes, A. R., 53

E

earned value management, description of, 94–95
East Side Tunnel Corridor, 560n
Eby cases. *See Martin K. Eby Construction Co., Inc. headings*

economic concerns. *See* cost *headings;* financing for projects
economic loss doctrine
consulting engineer liability and owner–constructor agreements, 335–346
consulting engineer liability and subsurface projects, 500, 562n
consulting engineer obligations to third parties, 463, 469
description of, 335, 344–346
negligent misrepresentation exception, 346–355, 408–409nn
public-private partnerships and subsurface projects, 584n
education. *See also* training programs; *specific aspects*
baseline approach and, 510–512
in building information modeling, 256–257
professional liability coverage and, 218
project-specific insurance overview, 590
EFTA. *See* European Free Trade Association
Egypt, Suez Canal construction, 5
EIS. *See* environmental impact statements
Eisenhower administration, 10, 272
EJCDC. *See* Engineers Joint Contracts Documents Committee
electric power supply, Boston Harbor Project, 45
Emanuel, Rahm, 271
eminent domain principle, 235
Empire State Building, 254
employment considerations. *See* labor considerations
employment discrimination, project labor agreements and, 147
energy consumption
fuel taxes and, 267–268
high-speed rail and, 270–272
MTA sustainability goals, 278
energy performance, LEED and, 253–255, 256, 275–278
engineering. *See also* consulting engineers; design *headings; specific issues*
Boston Harbor Project team, 39–42
budget development and, 78, 79
building information modeling and, 255–257
high-speed rail projects, 273–274
as inexact science, 53
professional judgments and false claims, 456–459
utility considerations, 123
engineering contracts. *See* contracts, engineering
Engineering News Record, construction cost index, 45
engineering reviews, dispute avoidance and resolution, 206–207
Engineering-Science, Inc., 522
engineer of record, risk allocation and delivery methods, 357, 359, 368, 369, 410–415nn. *See also* consulting engineers

project-specific insurance overview, 604

public-private partnerships and, 582*n*

standard of care and external risk factors, 444

federal law. *See* legal considerations

Federal Transit Administration
  approval process, 58–59
  federal funding application process, 20–22
  project-specific insurance overview, 604
  risk management, 24

federated models, description of, 257, 281*n*

Federico case. *See* D. Federico Co. v. New Bedford Redevelopment Authority

feedback loops, dispute and claim monitoring, 214

Feinman, Jay, 345–346

FEMA. *See* Federal Emergency Management Agency

FHWA. *See* Federal Highway Administration

FIDIC. *See* International Federation of Consulting Engineers

fiduciary duty claims. *See also* claims
  accountability considerations, 450–451
  integrated project organizations and, 311–312

field-level team, partnering and, 187–190

final design phase
  cost estimating and, 80–82
  design management and, 57–58
  risk allocation and delivery methods, 357–359, 395, 398
  subsurface project liability for consulting engineers, 501
  utility identification and, 127

financing for projects. *See also* cost *headings; specific aspects*
  Boston Harbor Project, 33–34, 42, 44
  Central Artery/Tunnel Project, 11–12, 586*n*
  change order process and, 193, 199
  corruption as issue, 234, 243–245
  federal funding application process, 20–22
  future of megaprojects, 248–249, 270–274
  insurance overview, 227, 231–232
  integrated project organizations and, 319–322*nn*
  international perspective, 237
  Interstate Highway System, 10–11
  labor relations and, 139, 144–146, 148
  logistics and, 103–104
  Manhattan Project, 9
  Marshall Plan, 10
  national assessments of infrastructure, 17
  non-traditional liability and other risk exposures, 451–461
  owner expectations and, 297–299
  Panama Canal construction, 5–6

project delivery methods and, 266–270

project-specific insurance overview, 595

project sponsor role, 15

standard of care and external risk factors, 440–446, 476*n*

subsurface projects and public-private partnerships, 539, 540, 543–551

sustainable design and, 276, 278–279

third-party considerations, 131–132

Transcontinental Railroad construction, 7–8

first named insured, responsibilities of, 226

fish, Grand Coulee Dam effects on, 9

Fitzpatrick Constr. Corp. v. County of Suffolk, 559*n*

flexibility of approach
  Boston Harbor Project planning, 34
  owner project planning and, 16
  risk allocation and delivery methods, 356

Fluor Corporation, 269

Flyvbjerg, Bent
  accountability considerations, 440–444, 474*n*, 475*n*, 477*nn*
  cost and schedule considerations, 11–12, 68–72, 247
  owner project planning, 24

follow-on claims, 225, 230. *See also* claims

Fondedile, S. A. v. C. E. Maguire, 406*n*, 556*n*

Fontaine Bros., Inc. v. Springfield, 560*n*

forecasting of costs. *See* cost estimating

Fore River Shipyard, 36

Forte Bros., Inc. v. Nat'l Amusement, Inc., 559*n*

Forth Rail Bridge, *290*

Forth Road Bridge, *289*

fragnets, performance measures and, 93

France
  international perspective, 237–238
  logistical considerations, 100–101
  Panama Canal construction, 5–6

Franklin Delano Roosevelt Lake, 9

fraudulent or false claims statutes. *See* false claims statutes

Frederick Snare Corp. v. Maine-New Hampshire Interstate Bridge Auth., 556*n*

free choice, consulting engineer liability and, 407*n*

French National Assembly, 101

Fruin-Colnon Corp. v. Niagara Frontier Transportation Authority, 377–380

FTA. *See* Federal Transit Administration

fuel taxes, 11, 267–268

functional compliance and acceptance, 17

funding for projects. *See* financing for projects

future of megaprojects
  American Recovery and Reinvestment Act and, 248, 270–274
  highway and road project applications, 255–257
  information deficit solutions, 249–255

liability considerations, 257–261

overview of, 247–249

project delivery methods and, 248, 261–266

public-private partnerships and, 266–270

sustainability and green design, 274–279

G

Gamond, Thomé de, 100–101

Gantt charts, 87, 98*n*

GAO. *See* Government Accountability Office

gas lines, utility identification, 124. *See also* utility considerations

gas taxes, 11, 267–268

GBR. *See* geotechnical baseline report

GDR. *See* geotechnical data report

GDSR. *See* geotechnical design summary report

General Building Constructors of New York State, Inc., 415*n*

general contractors, safety considerations, 164, 165, 168–170. *See also* contractor *headings*

General Services Administration, 251, 276

genesis stage, owner project planning and, 15–16

geologic investigations. *See* subsurface investigations

geotechnical baseline approach. *See also* baseline approach
  geotechnical data distinguished from, 512–517
  professional liability implications, 509–521, 578–582*nn*

geotechnical baseline report, 516–519, 548, 598

geotechnical data report, 512, 517, 518

geotechnical design summary report, 510

geotechnical engineers. *See also* consulting engineers; engineers; *specific issues*
  baseline approach responsibilities, 517–518
  owner–constructor agreements and liability, 338–339, 346
  scope of services, 295, 581*n*
  subsurface project liability issues, 496–497, 500, 514, 555*n*, 562*n*, 564*n*

geotechnical interpretive report, 512, 518

geotechnical investigations. *See* subsurface investigations

GLF Construction Corp. v. LAN/STV, 321*n*, 572–573*n*, 575*n*

Golden Spike, 7

Göltzsch Valley Bridge, *135–136*

good faith disagreements, false claims and, 456

Gorgas, William, 6

Gottfried, David, 275

Gotthard Base Tunnel, 233–234

Government Accountability Office, 268, 316*n*, 582*n*

governmental immunity, 309. *See also* sovereign immunity

dispute avoidance reviews and, 206
inspection and, 174–176
integrated project organizations and, 312
international perspective, 242–243
partnering and, 185, 186
responsibilities, 172–173
safety and, 165
standard of care overview, 424
testing and, 175–178
quality audits, 44–45, 178–179
quality, definition of, 171
quality managers, construction management and, 172–175, 177–178
quality-of-life needs, owner project planning and, 16–17
quality system work plans, elements of, 174
quantitative risk analysis, description of, 162–163. *See also* risk management and mitigation
quantity estimates, baseline approach and, 514–516, 576–578*n*
quantity surveys, design-builder responsibilities, 393–394
qui tam claimants, 452, 456

R

railway projects. *See also* transit projects; *specific projects*
future of megaprojects, 248, 270–274
history of megaprojects, 6–8
Shinkansen trains, *481–482*
range estimating, 72, 82. *See also* cost estimating
Raymond Int'l, Inc. v. Baltimore County, 557*n*, 577*n*
RE. *See* resident engineer
REA. *See* request for equitable adjustment
real estate acquisition. *See also* land acquisition; property acquisition
budget development and, 79
international perspective, 235, 238, 239
realism
cost overrun perception and, 439, 475*n*
history of megaprojects, 12
importance in scheduling, 22, 26, 86–88
real-time resolution, risk management and, 224
recordkeeping. *See also* documentation of projects; reports and reporting
change orders, logging of, 195
decisions, logging of, 63
drilling logs, 455–456
quality considerations, 174, 176
reference-class estimating, 71, 84–85. *See also* cost estimating
registers, risk. *See* risk registers
registration laws. *See also* legal considerations; licensing
design delegation and, 360–361, 410–411*nn*
integrated project organizations and, 311, 312, 314

registration requirements, design delegation and, 372
regulatory agencies. *See* federal agencies; public agencies; state and local government; *specific entities*
Reilly, John, 437, 444, 475*n*, 477*n*
relational contracts, integrated project delivery and, 264–265. *See also* contract *headings*
remediation. *See* contamination and remediation
reports and reporting. *See also* documentation of projects; *specific aspects*
baseline approach and, 508–538, 576–581*nn*
design management and, 63–64
earned value management and, 95
non-traditional liability and other risk exposures, 453–454
owner–constructor agreements and liability, 338–341, 346, 405–406*n*
quality considerations, 172, 175, 177, 178
risk and uncertainty as factors, 70
risk review and reporting, 158, 162
standard of care and external risk factors, 441–443, 446
reputational risks, 449, 461–462. *See also* public relations; risk *headings*
request for equitable adjustment, 456. *See also* equitable adjustment claims
requests for approval, change order process and, 195
requests for clarification, change order process and, 195
requests for information
building information modeling and, 252
change order process and, 194–195
design conflicts and, 250
project delivery methods and, 262
requests for proposal
change order process and, 195, 196, 202
insurance overview, 223
subsurface project liability issues, 565–566*n*
resident engineer. *See also* engineers
change order process and, 195–196
quality considerations, 172–175, 178–179
resolution ladder. *See* dispute resolution step ladder
resource-loaded schedules, performance measures and, 94
responsible control standard, 257–261
Restatement (Second) of Torts, Section 552, 347, 348
reward, balancing with risk, 314–315
RFAs. *See* requests for approval
RFCs. *See* requests for clarification
RFIs. *See* requests for information
RFPs. *See* requests for proposal
Rhode Island Supreme Court, consulting engineer liability, 406*n*
Richardson Electr. Co., Inc. v. Peter Francese & Son, Inc., 556*nn*

right-of-way takings, third-party considerations, 130
right to work states, project labor agreements and, 146–147
Rio Piedras campus, 24
risk. *See also* liability; *specific aspects*
categories of, 14, 159–160
external risk factors defined, 434
influence on cost and schedule, 70–72
insurance overview, 217, 219–223, 226, 231, 232
public-private partnerships and, 267
transferring cost of, 249
risk allocation. *See also* risk management and mitigation; *specific aspects*
baseline approach and, 508–512, 518–519, 525–526, 537
building information modeling and, 259
consulting engineer liability and owner–constructor agreements, 334–356, 353–355, 401–409*nn*, 561–562*n*
consulting engineer obligations to third parties, 469
consulting engineer scope of services and, 295–297
consulting engineer standard of care and, 332–334
cost estimating and, 81
delivery methods and, 328, 356–400, 409–422*nn*
design-bid-build and, 328, 357–392, 410–422*nn*
design-build and, 328, 392–400
dispute avoidance and, 205–206, 209
integrated project organizations and, 303, 308, 313, 320*n*
logistical considerations, 107
owner as decision-maker, 327–332, 341–342, 392, 400–401*n*, 485–488
principles of, 327–329, 336
project-specific insurance overview, 597–602
reverse risk allocation, 587*n*
standard of care and external risk factors, 433, 477*n*
standard of care overview, 426
subsurface project contracting practices, 492
subsurface project liability issues, 495, 500, 537, 540–551, 569*n*
subsurface project risk allocation, 485–489
subsurface projects and public-private partnerships, 538, 540–551, 583–588*nn*
risk-based estimates. *See also* cost estimating
description of, 74
probabilistic risk-based estimating, 82–84
risk disclaimer provisions. *See also specific types*
non-traditional liability and other risk exposures, 455–456